Fuzzy Intelligent Systems

Scrivener Publishing
100 Cummings Center, Suite 541J
Beverly, MA 01915-6106

Artificial Intelligence and Soft Computing for Industrial Transformation

Series Editor: Dr S. Balamurugan (sbnbala@gmail.com)

Scope: Artificial Intelligence and Soft Computing Techniques play an impeccable role in industrial transformation. The topics to be covered in this book series include Artificial Intelligence, Machine Learning, Deep Learning, Neural Networks, Fuzzy Logic, Genetic Algorithms, Particle Swarm Optimization, Evolutionary Algorithms, Nature Inspired Algorithms, Simulated Annealing, Metaheuristics, Cuckoo Search, Firefly Optimization, Bio-inspired Algorithms, Ant Colony Optimization, Heuristic Search Techniques, Reinforcement Learning, Inductive Learning, Statistical Learning, Supervised and Unsupervised Learning, Association Learning and Clustering, Reasoning, Support Vector Machine, Differential Evolution Algorithms, Expert Systems, Neuro Fuzzy Hybrid Systems, Genetic Neuro Hybrid Systems, Genetic Fuzzy Hybrid Systems and other Hybridized Soft Computing Techniques and their applications for Industrial Transformation. The book series is aimed to provide comprehensive handbooks and reference books for the benefit of scientists, research scholars, students and industry professional working towards next generation industrial transformation.

Publishers at Scrivener
Martin Scrivener (martin@scrivenerpublishing.com)
Phillip Carmical (pcarmical@scrivenerpublishing.com)

Fuzzy Intelligent Systems

Methodologies, Techniques, and Applications

Edited by
E. Chandrasekaran, R. Anandan, G. Suseendran, S. Balamurugan and Hanaa Hachimi

Scrivener Publishing

WILEY

This edition first published 2021 by John Wiley & Sons, Inc., 111 River Street, Hoboken, NJ 07030, USA and Scrivener Publishing LLC, 100 Cummings Center, Suite 541J, Beverly, MA 01915, USA

For more information about Scrivener publications please visit www.scrivenerpublishing.com.

Wiley Global Headquarters
111 River Street, Hoboken, NJ 07030, USA

For details of our global editorial offices, customer services, and more information about Wiley products visit us at www.wiley.com.

Library of Congress Cataloging-in-Publication Data

ISBN 978-1-119-76045-0

Cover image: Pixabay.Com
Cover design by Russell Richardson

Set in size of 11pt and Minion Pro by Manila Typesetting Company, Makati, Philippines

MIX
Paper from responsible sources
FSC
www.fsc.org
FSC® C013604

10 9 8 7 6 5 4 3 2 1

Contents

Preface

It is with immense pleasure that we introduce this book. Our objective in writing it is to foster advancements in the field and help disseminate results concerning recent applications and case studies in the areas of fuzzy logic, intelligent systems, and web-based applications among working professionals and those in education and research covering a broad cross section of technical disciplines.

The format of the book was designed to match the self-contained approach to fuzzy mathematics and fuzzy control systems theory that even students with no prior knowledge can easily understand. It enables both classroom and self-directed learners to create a strong foundation in fuzzy systems by being open and straightforward; following a brief introduction to the subject, the authors dive right into real-world applications of fuzzy logic revealing its practical flavor. The book is mainly intended to familiarize systems and control subjects for both senior undergraduate and first-year graduate students, with the fundamental mathematical theory and design methodology needed to understand and use fuzzy control systems. This self-contained textbook will provide a solid framework for designing and evaluating fuzzy control systems under unpredictable and irregular conditions. Students can gain a thorough understanding of fuzzy control systems theory by mastering its contents.

Engineers, both current and future, need systematic training in the analytic theory and rigorous design of fuzzy control systems to keep up with and advance the rapidly evolving field of applied control technologies. As a consequence, expert systems with fuzzy-logic capabilities make for a more versatile and innovative handling of problems. This book attempts to showcase the combination of fuzzy logic and neural networks known as a neuro-fuzzy system, which should result in a hybrid intelligent system by combining a human-like reasoning style of neural networks.

Listed below is a brief description of the subjects covered in each chapter of the book.

Chapter 1 explains the uncertain growth of cervical cancer. Cancer cells keep developing and apparently unpredictable behavior arises in a deterministic system because of great sensitivity to initial conditions. Images of cancer-based cell formation in the tissue are represented in this chapter and a fuzzy matrix method and sausage method are used along with the maximum modulus theorem to explain the complexity of these cancer cell (CC) images.

Chapter 2 deals with the use of a fuzzy convolutional neural network in a virtual classroom environment to detect students' emotions. Here, different feature extraction techniques are used for the face, eye and head (PCA for face, HAAR cascade for eye and LBP for head) and then emotion detection is carried out. The experimental results of the proposed method achieve an accuracy of 81.5%.

Chapter 3 presents a new labeling concept known as fuzzy quotient-3 cordial labeling, in which notations for some trees of diameter 5 are defined. The authors analyzed the existence of fuzzy quotient-3 cordial labeling of some trees of diameter 5 denoted by $\mathcal{T}_s^5$, $31 \le s \le 39$ and the existence of fuzzy quotient-3 cordial labeling was established and the work presented.

Chapter 4 introduces hybrid computational intelligence. After a brief review of optimization and meta-heuristic algorithms, the scope of swarm intelligence in overcoming the limitations of traditional methods is examined. Ant colony optimization and swarm optimization are also thoroughly covered. Next, multi-criteria decision problems and various tools for these problems, such as WSM, WPM, AHP, TOPSIS, ELECTRE and VIKOR, are covered along with their behavior and application.

Chapter 5 examines finite, simple, undirected graphs without loops or multiple edges. Graph labeling, which is an assignment of integers to the vertices or edges or both, has a well-developed broad range of applications. Graph labeling introduces the concept of fuzzy tri-magic and proves that some graphs are fuzzy tri-magic. In this chapter, we take the isomorphic caterpillar of diameter 5 and prove that it is fuzzy tri-magic. We also give the magic membership values, their corresponding edges and the number of magic membership values with various natures of m, n and a as tables.

Chapter 6 defines fuzzy tri-magic labeling and proves that the isomorphic caterpillar of diameter 5 graph $T^6_{2,3,5}$ admits fuzzy tri-magic by proving that the maximum difference between the number of K_i's and K_j's $(1 \le i \le 3)$ differs by at most 1 and $\left|K_i - K_j\right| \le \frac{2}{10^r}$ for $1 \le i, j \le 3$, $r \ge 2$.

Chapter 7 characterizes the three significant approaches of GFS hybridization: Michigan, Pittsburgh and CRL. This chapter clarifies each of these methodologies along with subcomponents, working style, points of interest and confinements. It likewise contrasts qualities of a conventional master framework and classifier system for genetic-fuzzy hybridization and subsequently presents the significance of structuring GFS. A similar assessment of every one of the mixture techniques prompts the CRL plan. The chapter also describes different points of interest of the ceaseless rule learning approach.

Chapter 8 discusses the design of a fuzzy technique-based system for a given task. In any given task, to make a decision by fuzzy logic, either a number is used with a combination of VMs or is created with a fresh VM based on current operational conditions such as task requirement, load and available resources, etc. In this era, service of the internet or implementation of cloud applications work by using virtual machines (VMs) in the cloud system.

Chapter 9 deals with the basic notation of fixed-point theory in fuzzy soft metric spaces. The common fixed-point result is proved for $(\alpha - \beta) - \psi -$ functions of the contractive type mappings. Another result is proved for fuzzy soft $\tilde{\alpha} - \tilde{\psi} -$ contractive type mappings and $\tilde{\alpha} - \textit{admissible}$ mappings in fuzzy soft metric space. The obtained results are very useful for uncertainty and decision-making problems.

Chapter 10 analyzes the asymptotic mean-square stability of an observer-based chaos synchronization with time-delay fuzzy stochastic systems. Utilizing the Lyapunov stability theory, a fuzzy-based stochastic system with time delay is designed, which is assumed to have asymptotic mean-square stability. Fuzzy-based chaotic synchronization has been the main focus of propagation delay and system uncertainties.

Chapter 11 discusses solving assignment problems using trapezoidal fuzzy numbers. Here, some arithmetic operations of TrFN are represented. Some assignment problems are fully solved by fuzzy numbers using the Hungarian method.

Chapter 12 discusses the connectedness of fuzzy graph with a real-life application on firefighting humanoid robots and resolving the matrix. The left resolving set and the right resolving set are defined for fuzzy digraph. Some theorems and corollaries are also proved in determining the set of the fuzzy digraph.

Chapter 13 proposes that some fuzzy graph families have a fuzzy edge-magic total labeling, which is discussed here with a brief example and extended with an application that finds a stronger friendship between two people using fuzzy edge-magic labeling.

Chapter 14 investigates the control of impulsive chaotic systems based on the Takagi-Sugeno (TS) fuzzy model. The asymptotic mean-square stability criterion is designed and a robust supervisory control is proposed.

When fuzzy-based impulsive chaotic systems are subjected to system uncertainties and external disturbance, the supervisory control can induce the designed system's convergence speed. The Genesio-Tesi chaotic model is utilized and the fuzzy logic toolbox in MATLAB is invoked, forgetting results.

Chapter 15 discusses ways to solve uncertainty problems, which are real-world problems that often turn out to be complex due to inserting an element of uncertainty either in parameters that define the problem or the situation in which the problem occurs. Because of various uncertainties arising in real-world situations, classical mathematics methods may not be successfully applied to solve them. However, fuzzy set theory (FST) and soft set theory (SST) can solve these uncertainty problems. As presented in this chapter, the application of mathematics is used to solve uncertainty. We prove some common fixed-points theorems in $\varphi - \psi$ weak contraction on soft fuzzy metric spaces by using control function or altering distance function. Here, we define mapping by using some proven results and obtain a result on the actuality of fixed points. To confirm the results, the basic concepts of soft sets and fuzzy sets are used.

The final chapter is devoted to On Soft $\alpha_{(\gamma,\beta)}$-Continuous Functions in Soft Topological Spaces.

Finally, we would like to thank all chapter authors for their valuable time and effort.

E. Chandrasekaran
R. Anandan
G. Suseendran
S. Balamurugan
Hanaa Hachimi
Editors
July 2021

1

Fuzzy Fractals in Cervical Cancer

T. Sudha and G. Jayalalitha*

Department of Mathematics, VISTAS, Chennai, India

Abstract

To describe complicated systems often requires a mathematical model because it is designed for precise description. To model dynamic processes in biology mathematics is used. Using mathematical and biological data to model the growth of cancer cell is a boom area of cancer disease.

Cancer cells keeps developing and apparently unpredictable behavior arising in a deterministic system because of great sensitivity to initial conditions. This chapter represents the images of cancer based on cell formation in the tissue. It explained the complexity of Cancer Cell (CC) images using Fuzzy matrix method, and Sausage method with Maximum Modulus theorem.

Matrices are used in representing the cancer cell images of different stage of Cancer patients. The value computed from a square matrix of numbers by a rule of combining products of the matrix entries And from Eigen Vectors shows the cancer cells extension by stretching or compressing and also Eigen values shows the factor of compressing. Eigen Vectors of Normal Cancer cells to Abnormal Cells a re-irregular. The method to find the dimension of irregular figures in Fractal Geometry is called Box-Counting method. Using Box Counting method the Area, perimeter and radius of the Cancer cells are used in Sausage method to find out the invasiveness of cancer cells and also the irregularity growth of cancer cells. Fuzzy Fractals is a noval mathematical combination. This approach is led to proper results which will improve the determination and the stage of the cancer.

Keywords: Fractals, fuzzy, fuzzy matrix, cervical cancer, sausage method

**Corresponding author*: g.jayalalithamaths.sbs@velsuniv.ac.in

E. Chandrasekaran, R. Anandan, G. Suseendran, S. Balamurugan and Hanaa Hachimi (eds.) Fuzzy Intelligent Systems: Methodologies, Techniques, and Applications, (1–26) © 2021 Scrivener Publishing LLC

1.1 Introduction

1.1.1 Fuzzy Mathematics

Fuzzy Mathematics is a branch of mathematics which contains Fuzzy Set theory and Fuzzy Logic. In 1965 Lotfi A. Zadeh introduced Fuzzy concepts.

1.1.1.1 Fuzzy Set

Fuzzy set is a generalization of a classical set and the membership function a generalization of the characteristic function [23]. Since we refer to a universal (crisp) set X, some elements of a fuzzy set may have the degree of membership zero [23]. Often it is appropriate to consider those elements of the universe that have a nonzero degree of membership in a fuzzy set [1, 23]. *Example: Is Ganesh is honest? Answer is; Extremely honest, very honest, slightly honest, sometime honest ......etc.*

For a fuzzy set, the characteristic function allows various degrees of membership for the elements of a given set [24]. If X is a collection of objects denoted generically by x, then fuzzy set Ã in X is a set of ordered pairs: $\tilde{A} = \{(x, \mu_{\tilde{A}(x)}) | x \in X\}$, $\mu_{\tilde{A}(X)}$ is called the membership function or grade of membership (also degree of compatibility or degree of truth) of x in A that maps X to the membership space M (When M contains only the two points 0 and 1, Ã is non fuzzy and $\mu_{\tilde{A}(X)}$ is identical to the characteristic function of a non fuzzy set) [24, 27].

The range of the membership function is a subset of the nonnegative real numbers whose superimum is finite [24]. Elements with a zero degree of membership are normally not listed [1, 24].

The application of Fuzzy set theory is a high-yielding and interesting area in the Medical field. For decision making problems Fuzzy set theory plays a very important role [7]. Fuzzy set theory has already been used in some medical expert systems [7]. Sanchez [8] formulated the diagnostic models involving fuzzy matrices representing the medical knowledge.

1.1.1.2 Fuzzy Logic

Fuzzy logic deals with reasoning with inexact or fuzzy concepts. Hence the well established isomorphism's between Boolean algebra, set theory and propositional logic can be extended in a natural way between fuzzy algebra, fuzzy set theory and fuzzy logic [2].

1.1.1.3 *Fuzzy Matrix*

Fuzzy matrices were introduced for the first time by Thomson [6] who discussed the convergence of powers of fuzzy matrix [2, 26, 28]. Fuzzy matrices play a vital role in scientific development. By a fuzzy matrix, we mean a matrix over a fuzzy algebra [26]. A Boolean matrix is a special case of a fuzzy matrix with entries from the set {0, 1} [28]. In practice, fuzzy matrices have proposed to represent fuzzy relations in a system based on fuzzy set theory [14, 15]. A fuzzy matrix can be interpreted as a binary fuzzy relation [2, 26].

Cagman *et al.* [13] defined fuzzy soft matrix theory and its application in decision making. A fuzzy associative matrix express fuzzy logic rules in matrix form this rules usually takes to variables as input, mapping clearly to a 2-dimensional matrix [10, 11], although theoretically a matrix of any number of dimensions is possible [12, 20].

1.1.2 Fractals

Mandelbrot defined Fractal as a special class of subsets of a complete metric space for which the Hausdorff–Besicovitch dimension strictly exceeds the topological dimension. In other words, a given set of randomized, hyperbolic, Iterated Function System (IFS) is able to generate a particular image as a fractal set [29]. Fractals are important because it CHANGE the most basic ways to analyze and understand experimental data. The term *Fractals* was coined by Benoit Mandelbrot in 1975. Fractals are kind of shapes that can be seen in nature. Lightning, Clouds are the examples of Fractals as shown in Figure 1.1. Cantor set, Sierpinski Triangle, Von Koch curve are also examples of fractals. One of the characteristic of Fractals is self-similarity. Three types of self-similarity found in fractals such as

- *Exact Self-Similarity* [17, 30]
  According to Perfect self-similarity each of the fractals is composed of smaller versions of itself.
- *Quasi-Self-Similarity* [17, 30]
  This is a loose form of self-similarity the fractal appears approximately (but not exactly) identical at different scales.
- *Statistical Self-Similarity* [17, 30]
  Random fractals are examples of fractals which are statistically self-similar, but neither exact nor quasi-self-similar.

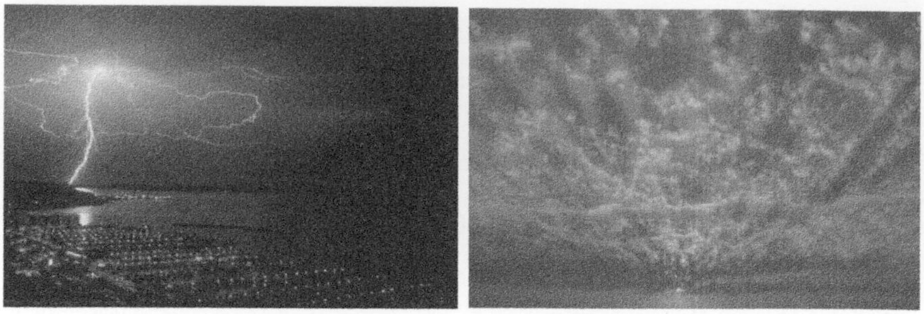

Figure 1.1 Examples of fractals.

1.1.2.1 *Fractal Geometry*

The shapes comes out from the Fractals geometry are rough and infinitely complex. However Fractals geometry is still about making shapes, measuring the shapes and defining the shapes [9].

Fractal geometry characterizes the complexity of the image analysis [9, 25]. It is helpful to qualifying the morphologies that are considered random or irregular. It also provides of pattern formation in diffusion and percolation [9]. It usually has a non-integer dimension and greater than topological dimension and less than Euclidean dimension [9].

The box-counting dimension is calculated as follows:

$$dim_B\, F = lim\ \delta \rightarrow 0-\ [log\ N_\delta(F)/log\ \delta] \tag{1.1}$$

where F is a non-empty bounded set in R^n, $N_\delta(F)$ is the minimum number of the sets covering F and their radii are no larger than δ [25]. Sample data can be obtained for $(-log\ \delta,\ log\ N_\delta(F))$ [25]. Slope of the line can be estimated of the box-counting dimension by the least-squares method [21, 22]. Images of cancer can be treated as 2D [25].

1.1.3 Fuzzy Fractals

In Fuzzy Fractals, the algorithm for a specific problem can be coined by incorporating the fuzzy set and fractals together and create a new dimension by considering the data as a time series problem. The Fuzzy Fractals are used to find the relationship between the crisp values and their properties for an investigation [29].

1.1.4 Cervical Cancer

Cancer is an abnormal growth of cells and is uncontrolled in a way that leads to metastasize shown in Figure 1.2 [5]. Cancer can be defined as a disease in which a group of abnormal cell grows uncontrollably by disregarding the normal rules of cell division [3]. Normal cells are constantly subject to signals that dictate whether the cell should divide, differentiate into another cell or die [3]. Cancer cells develop a degree of autonomy from these signals resulting in uncontrolled growth and proliferation. If this proliferation is allowed to continue and spreads, shown in Figure 1.7, it can be fatal [3, 5].

Initiation and progression of cancer depend on both external factors in the environment (tobacco, chemicals, radiation and infectious organisms) and factors within the cell (inherited mutations, hormones, immune conditions and mutations that occur from metabolism) [3]. Pap Smear Test shown in Figure 1.3 is a tool, to locate the cancer disease explains in the cervical part [4, 5]. Human Papilloma Virus [HPV] shown in Figure 1.7 infection is a necessary factor in the development of nearly all cases of Cervical Cancer [18, 19].

In this chapter, Section 1.2.1 explained Fuzzy method that gives uncertainty growth of Cancer cells and Section 1.2.2 shows the Sausage methods that shows the Invasiveness of the Cervix Cancer and also explained

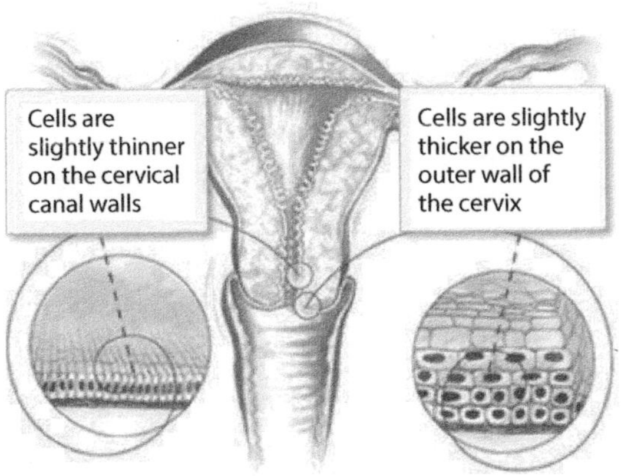

Cells are slightly thinner on the cervical canal walls
Cells are slightly thicker on the outer wall of the cervix

Figure 1.2 Cells of cervix.

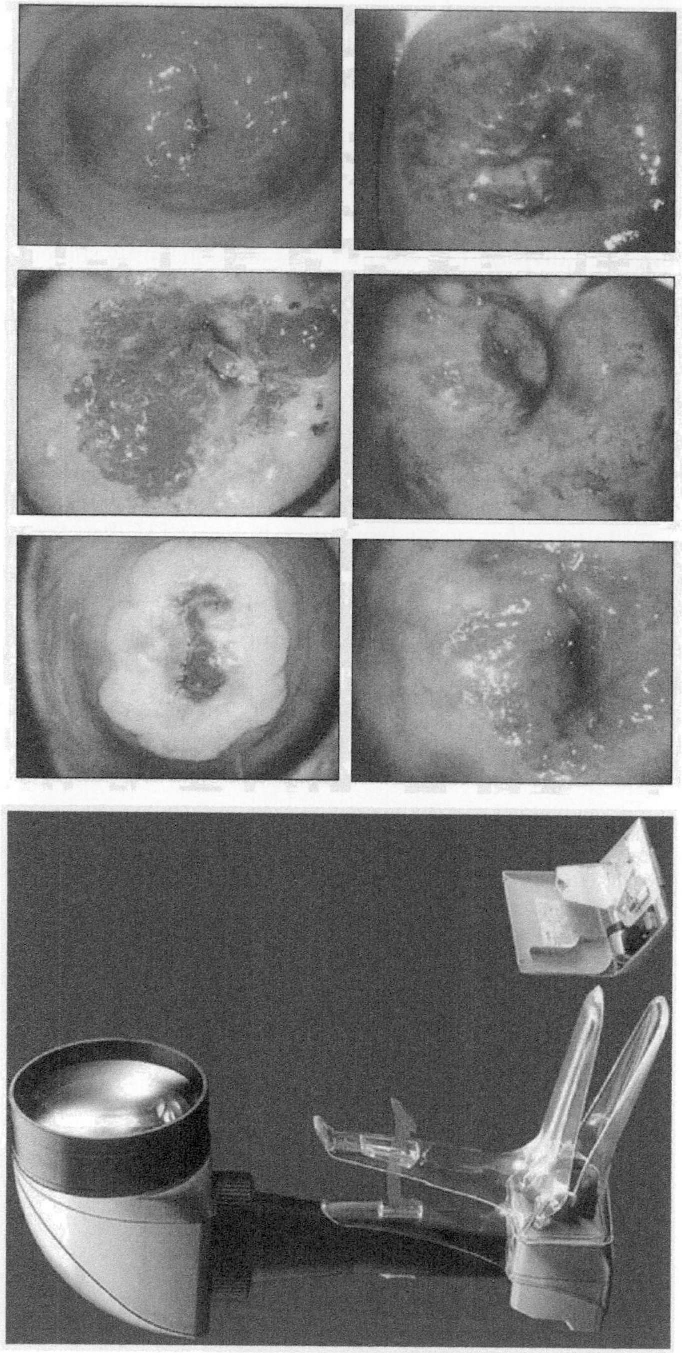

Figure 1.3 Pap smear test of the cervical cancer.

Maximum Modulus theorem in Section 1.4. In Section 1.5 Results are discussed.

1.2 Methods

1.2.1 Fuzzy Method

Here it explained uncertainty growth of cervix cells, for this many patients Cervix cancer cells images of different stages are taken. This is a 5-stage process.

- In first stage, the raw data (Normal, Abnormal) of the Cancer cells at hand is converted or transformed in to normal matrix.
- In the second stage, after obtaining Normal matrix next to find Determinant of the matrix to characterize the Matrices. The factors most often are products and product characteristics.
- In the third stage, calculate Eigen Values and Eigen Vectors of the matrices.
- In the fourth stage calculate the variation of Normal cells Eigen vectors and Abnormal cells Eigen Vectors, these values are not regular or vague.
- In fifth stage for different membership values of variation of Normal and Abnormal cells to construct Fuzzy Matrices, and calculate fuzzy Eigen values and Eigen Vectors.

Figures 1.4 and 1.5 show the images of Normal, Abnormal cells of Cervix cancer. Tables 1.1 and 1.2 explain the Data Analysis of Normal, Abnormal Cervix Cancer cells of scaling 2, 4, 6, 8, and 10 for Figures 1.4 and 1.5.

From Tables 1.1 and 1.2, a matrix of scaling 2, 4, 6, 8 and 10 is constructed to represent numerical data about two sets of factors in a matrix form and analyzes it to get numerical output in Table 1.3. Eigen Vectors are directions along which a Cancer cells transformation acts simply either by stretching or compressing. Eigen values are the factors by which the compression or stretch occurs.

So from the matrix obtained it is necessary to find Eigen values and eigenvectors to see in which direction the Cancer cells are stretching and

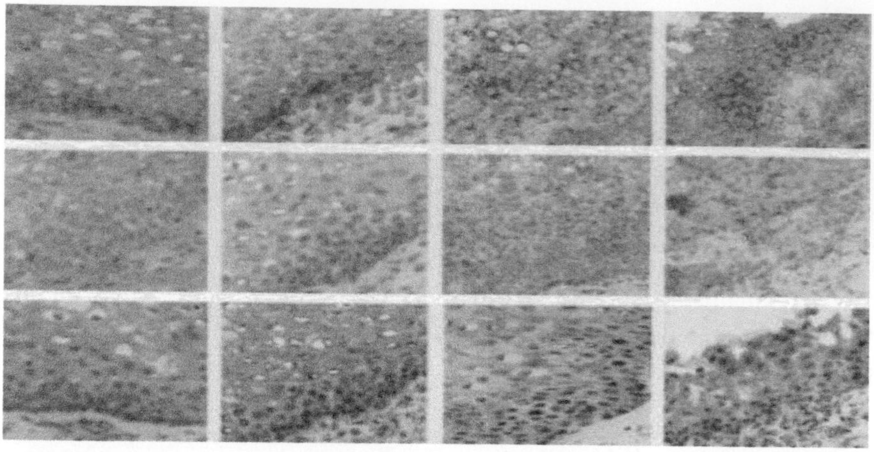

Figure 1.4 Normal cervix cell images.

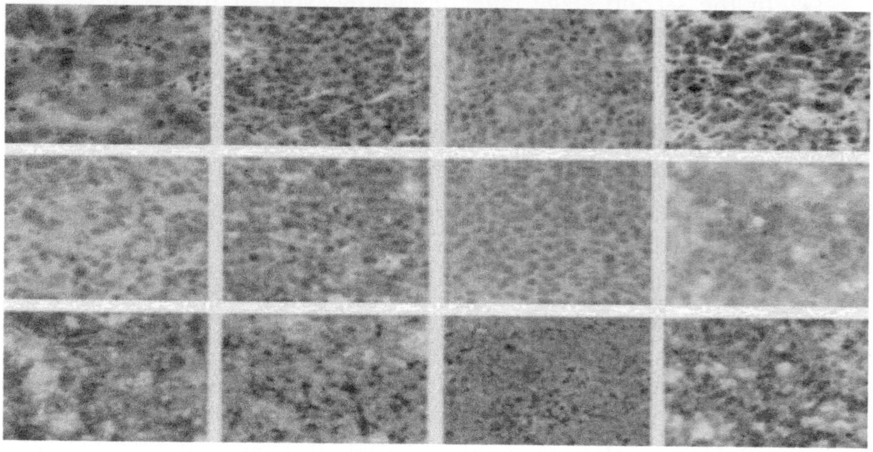

Figure 1.5 Abnormal cervix cell images.

the factors of stretching explained in Tables 1.4 and 1.5 for Normal and Abnormal Cancer cells.

- Find characteristic polynomial

$$|A - \lambda\, I| = 0 \tag{1.2}$$

- Find characteristic equation from the characteristic polynomial, where A is a Square matrix and is I is the Identity

Table 1.1 Analysis of normal cervical cancer.

Image	Scaling				
	2	**4**	**6**	**8**	**10**
1	139	82	61	44	34.8
2	202	104	69	49	35.5
3	271	164	107.667	89.5	68.7
4	307	169	115.8334	84.125	60.5
5	201	115.5	74	62.75	45
6	355	176.5	101.5	72.875	54.1
7	346	181.75	118	77.625	59.9
8	253	147.25	99.833	77.25	52.5

Table 1.2 Analysis of abnormal cervical cancer.

Image	Scaling				
	2	**4**	**6**	**8**	**10**
1	495	240	144	105.75	71.5
2	701	340	206	129	91.2
3	181	120	83	70	57
4	538	262	157	111.75	78.3
5	569	252	152	104	79.2
6	585	272	177	118	81.72
7	499	280	181	120	85.42
8	578	263.5	158.5	108.875	74.8
9	518	250	156	105	77.50
10	7,775	3,336.8	1,717.78	`00`	650.35
11	5,756	2,345	1,295.78	862	592.96
12	1,777	733	458.99	345	255.6

Table 1.3 Matrix of normal cervix cell and abnormal cervix cell.

Scaling	Normal cell of cervix matrix	Determinant value	Abnormal cell of cervix matrix	Determinant value
2	$\begin{bmatrix} 139 & 202 & 271 \\ 307 & 201 & 355 \\ 346 & 253 & 240 \end{bmatrix}$	6,351,250	$\begin{bmatrix} 495 & 701 & 181 \\ 538 & 569 & 585 \\ 499 & 578 & 374 \end{bmatrix}$	6,440,396
4	$\begin{bmatrix} 82 & 104 & 164 \\ 169 & 115 & 177 \\ 182 & 147 & 140 \end{bmatrix}$	717,990	$\begin{bmatrix} 240 & 340 & 120 \\ 262 & 252 & 272 \\ 280 & 264 & 250 \end{bmatrix}$	1,343,440
6	$\begin{bmatrix} 61 & 69 & 108 \\ 116 & 74 & 102 \\ 118 & 100 & 101 \end{bmatrix}$	165,538	$\begin{bmatrix} 144 & 206 & 83 \\ 157 & 152 & 177 \\ 181 & 159 & 156 \end{bmatrix}$	704,639
8	$\begin{bmatrix} 44 & 49 & 90 \\ 84 & 63 & 73 \\ 78 & 78 & 77 \end{bmatrix}$	72,402	$\begin{bmatrix} 44 & 49 & 90 \\ 84 & 63 & 73 \\ 78 & 78 & 77 \end{bmatrix}$	84,708
10	$\begin{bmatrix} 35 & 36 & 69 \\ 61 & 45 & 54 \\ 60 & 53 & 50 \end{bmatrix}$	22,197	$\begin{bmatrix} 72 & 91 & 57 \\ 78 & 79 & 82 \\ 85 & 75 & 78 \end{bmatrix}$	32,185

Table 1.4 Eigen values, Eigen vectors of normal cells of cervix.

	Normal cervix cells	
Scaling	**Eigen values**	**Eigen vectors**
2	(768, −118, −70)	V_1 (0.77, 1.04, 1), V_2 (−0.74, −0.40, 1) V_3 (0.35, −1.70, 1)
4	(426, −62, −27)	V_1 (0.77, 0.99, 1), V_2 (−1.33, 0.27, 1) V_3 (2.32, −4.01, 1)
6	(283, (−24 + 5.12i), (−24 − 5.12i))	V_1 (0.77, 0.91, 1) V_2 ((−1.43 − 3.4i), (0.45 + 4.06i), 1)) V_3 ((−1.43 + 3.4i), (0.44 − 4.06i), 1))
8	((213, (−14 + 11.43i), (−14 − 11.43i))	V_1 (0.80, 0.94, 1) V_2 ((−1.02 − 1.99i), (−0.15 + 2.14i), 1)) V_3 ((−1.02 + 1.99i), (−0.15 − 2.14i), 1))
10	(154, −14.4, −9.95)	V_1 (0.80, 0.98, 1), V_2 (−2.90, 2.07, 1) V_3 (−6.73, 6.5, 1)

matrix of identical dimension and λ is a scalar value called the Eigen values.

- Solve the characteristic equation and get the λ values
- Eigen vectors V for corresponding all λ values in equation

$$AV = \lambda V. \tag{1.3}$$

From Table 1.5 the variation between Normal Cervix cell to Abnormal Cervix cell is vague so based on the vague values a Fuzzy Matrix is constructed. From Fuzzy Matrix, Fuzzy Eigen Value and Eigen Vectors are calculated in Table 1.6 and shown in Figure 1.6.

1.2.2 Sausage Method

Sausage method is one of the methods in Fractals to find the dimension of irregular figures like Box Counting method [9, 25].

Table 1.5 Eigen values and Eigen vector of abnormal cell of cervix.

Scaling	Abnormal cells	
	Eigen values	**Eigen vectors**
2	((1,523, (−42.74 + 48.99i), (−42.74 − 48.99i))	V_1 (0.96, 1.16, 1) V_2 ((−2.73 + 2.86i), (1.64 − 2.39i), 1)) V_3 ((−2.73 − 2.86i), (1.64 + 2.39i), 1))
4	((759, (−8.42 + 41.24i), (−8.42 − 41.24i))	V_1 (0.88, 0.99, 1) V_2 ((−1.52 + 1.03i), (0.63 − 0.94i), 1)) V_3 ((−1.52 − 1.03i), (0.63 + 0.94i), 1))
6	((471, (−9.5 + 37.5i), (−9.5 − 37.5i))	V_1 (0.88, 0.99, 1) V_2 ((−1.11 + 1.11i), (0.22 − 1.03i), 1)) V_3 ((−1.11 − 1.11i), (0.22 + 1.03i), 1))
8	((324, (−4.48 + 15.54i), (−4.48 − 15.54i))	V_1 (0.94, 1.0, 1) V_2 ((−1.29 + 1.22i), (0.41 − 1.2i), 1)) V_3 ((−1.29 − 1.22i), (0.41 + 1.2i), 1))
10	((232, (−1.65 + 11.65i), (−1.65 − 11.65i))	V_1 (0.93, 1.0, 1) V_2 ((−0.99 + 0.88i), (0.07 − 0.84i), 1)) V_3 ((−0.99 − 0.87i), (0.07 + 0.84i), 1))

In this method including dimension we can find Invasiveness growth of the cell in Cervical Cancer, Skin Cancer, etc. The cancer cell dimension increases if the growth of the cancer cell increases [5, 16].

In this method the growth of Cancer cell invasiveness is explained. Using the invasiveness it can find the Cancer cell dimension, from the dimension, the grade of Cancer can be found [5]. Normal cervix cell images and abnormal cervix cell of scaling 2, 4, 6, 8, 10 and 3, 5, 7, 9 are separately taken for few images from Figures 1.4 and 1.5.

Perimeter is one of the measures to identify the cell growth. Interior shape of the cell can be identified by contour based features which ignore the interior of a shape, depends on finding the perimeter or boundary points of the cell.

The images were dilated with circles of increasing diameter in the pixels can be calculated and the [9] approximated Radius r in the pixels were calculated by

$$r = (A/\pi)^{1/2} \tag{1.4}$$

Table 1.6 Eigen values and Eigen vector of fuzzy matrix.

Scaling	Fuzzy matrix	Determinant value	Eigen values	Eigen vectors
2	$\begin{bmatrix} 0.3 & 0.2 & 1 \\ 0 & 0 & 1 \\ 0 & 0.5 & 1 \end{bmatrix}$	0.15	(−0.37, 1.37, 0.3)	V_1 (−0.68, −2.73, 1) V_2 (1.08, 0.73, 1) V_3 (1, 0, 0)
4	$\begin{bmatrix} 0.1 & 1 & 1 \\ 0 & 0 & 1 \\ 0 & 0.2 & 1 \end{bmatrix}$	0.02	(−0.17, 1.17, 0.1)	V_1 (17.92, −5.85, 1) V_2 (1.73, 0.85, 1) V_3 (1, 0, 0)
6	$\begin{bmatrix} 0.1 & 0.1 & 1 \\ 0 & 0.1 & 1 \\ 0 & 0 & 1 \end{bmatrix}$	0.01	(1, 0.1, 0.1)	V_1 (1, 0, 0) V_2 (1.23, 1.11, 1) V_3 (1.23, 1.11, 1)
8	$\begin{bmatrix} 0.2 & 0.1 & 1 \\ 0 & 0 & 1 \\ 0 & 0.1 & 1 \end{bmatrix}$	0.02	(−0.09, 1.09, 0.2)	V_1 (0.31, −10.91, 1) V_2 (1.22, 0.9, 1) V_3 (1, 0, 0)
10	$\begin{bmatrix} 0.1 & 1 & 1 \\ 0 & 0 & 1 \\ 0 & 0.1 & 1 \end{bmatrix}$	0.01	(−0.09, 1.09, 0.1)	V_1 (51.75, −10.91, 1) V_2 (1.93, 0.9, 1) V_3 (1, 0, 0)

where *A* denotes the area in pixel [9].

The slope Ks of the line can be calculated by regression method [9]

$$Ds = 2 - Ks \tag{1.5}$$

Where *Ds* denotes the estimated fractal capacity dimension [9].

The quantitative measure that can be found by the method of Sausage and it also calculated diameter of the cell [9].

$$Form\ Factor = \frac{4\pi Area}{(Perimeter)^2}\ [9] \tag{1.6}$$

$$Invaslog = -log\ (Form\ factor)\ [9] \tag{1.7}$$

The value of invaslog shows the invasiveness of the cervical cancer [9]. Using Equations (1.1), (1.4–1.7), the Area, Radius, Form factor and Invaslog of Normal and Abnormal Cancer cell images of few which are shown in Figures 1.4 and 1.5 are explained in Tables 1.7 and 1.8.

Regression lines are very useful to forecast the behaviours of a set of conditions will impact an outcome i.e. the dependent variable (y) by inputting different values for the independent variables (x).

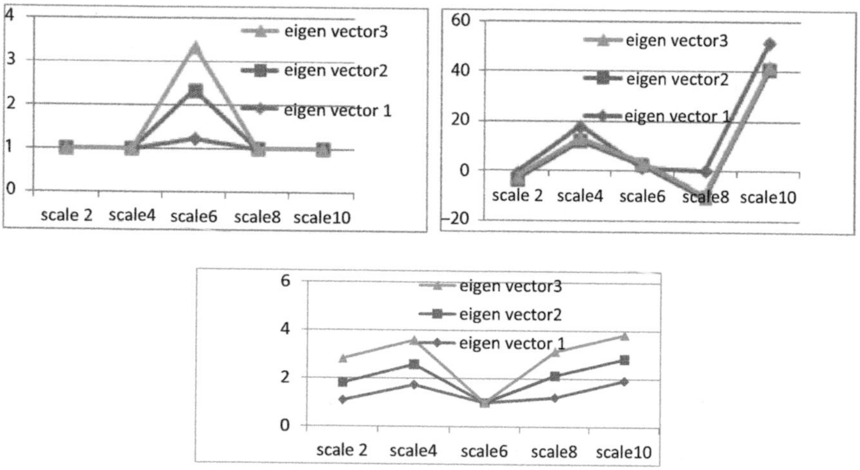

Figure 1.6 Graphical representation of fuzzy Eigen vectors.

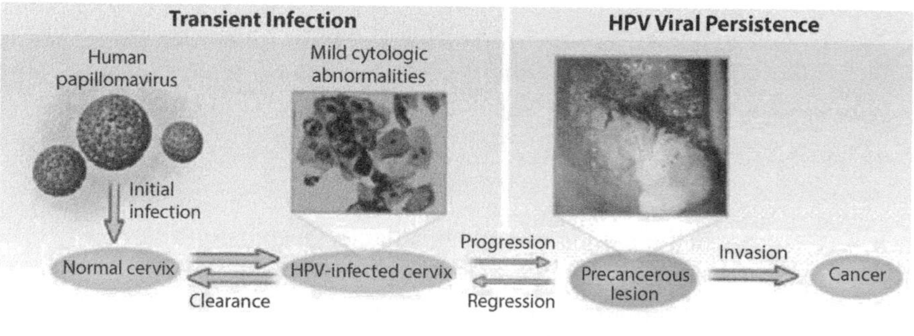

Figure 1.7 Human Papiloma Virus leads to cervical cancer [5].

Here to describe the interrelation of a Radius and Area of the Regression Lines are explained for few images of Normal, Abnormal Cervical cell in Table 1.9.

The Invasiveness growth of Cancer cells are also explained based on the graphical representations in Figures 1.8–1.11.

1.3 Maximum Modulus Theorem

Escape Set: The iteration produces value points are formed is unbounded and it is called Escape set. *Prisoner Set:* The iteration produces value points are bounded and it is called Prisoner set. *Boundary Set:* Points for which

Table 1.7 Normal cervix cell.

Images	Scaling	Area	Radius	Ks	Form factor	Invaslog
Image 1	2	2,740.5	29.5	0.0077	34.71	−1.54
	4	676.3	14.7		30.29	−1.48
	6	300	17.3		54.72	−1.74
	8	162	7.2		`15.94	−1.20
	10	109	5.9		342.43	−2.53
	3	1,224.7	19.7	0.0116	17.10	−1.23
	5	437	11.8		112.07	−2.05
	7	215.1	8.3		22.34	−1.35
	9	132	6.5		103.67	−2.02
Image 2	2	2,540	28.4	0.0087	4.52	−0.66
	4	607.4	24.6		3.18	−0.50
	6	256.5	9		2.63	−0.42
	8	136	6.6		2.18	−0.34
	10	83	5.1		2.15	−0.33
	3	1,109	18.8	0.0124	4.29	−0.63
	5	380.4	11		3.07	−0.49
	7	184	7.7		2.57	−0.41
	9	106	5.8		2.31	−0.37

(*Continued*)

Table 1.7 Normal cervix cell. (*Continued*)

Images	Scaling	Area	Radius	Ks	Form factor	Invaslog
Image 3	2	2,386	27.6	0.009	152.97	−2.18
	4	587	13.7		43.65	−1.64
	6	254	8.9		18.89	−1.28
	8	137	6.6		10.19	−1.01
	10	87	5.3		13.50	−1.13
	3	1053	18.3	0.0126	67.51	−1.83
	5	375	10.9		58.18	−1.76
	7	185	7.7		19.21	−1.28
	9	107	5.8		11.11	−1.05
Image 4	2	2,534.8	28.4	0.009	7.3	−0.86
	4	603.4	13.9		3.46	−0.54
	6	257	9		3.15	−0.50
	8	137.7	6.6		2.77	−0.44
	10	82.7	5.1		2.30	−0.36
	3	1,104.89	18.8	0.0125	5.34	−0.73
	5	378.5	10.9		3.36	−0.53
	7	182.6	7.6		2.55	−0.41
	9	105	5.8		2.50	−0.40

every neighbourhood contains both the escape and prisoner sets are called Boundary set.

Cervical Cancer cells are called the *Escaping set* of an entire Tissue which consists of all cells that tend to infinity under the repeated process. All other cells in the tissue stay bounded if it process are repeated and are said to be in the *Prisoner set*. These Cancer cells are called *Boundary set* because they are either escaping set or prisoner set. The growth of Cervical Cell is continuous. Cervical cancer cells are bounded and closed in the tissue based on the Maximum Modulus theorem [9, 25]. The Cervical cancer cells attain maximum boundary in tissue. It is never in its interior. It is easy to find the maximum boundary of Cancer cells of Cervix using Maximum Modulus theorem.

Table 1.8 Abnormal cervix cell.

	Scaling	Area	Radius	Ks	Form factor	Invaslog
Image 1	2	2,409	27.7	0.0091	179.13	−2.25
	4	598	13.8		117.42	−2.07
	6	263	9.1		91.80	−1.96
	8	146	6.8		50.96	−1.71
	10	90	5.4		70.69	−1.85
	3	1,071	18.5	0.0109	373.85	−2.57
	5	379	10.9		58.80	−1.77
	7	193	7.8		151.58	−2.18
	9	116	6		91.11	−1.96
Image 2	2	2,303	27	0.0094	28,940.35	−4.46
	4	576	7.6		7,238.23	−3.86
	6	256	9		3,216.99	−3.51
	8	144	6.8		1,809.56	−3.26
	10	92	5.4		1,156.11	−3.06
	3	1,024	18	0.0127	12,867.96	−4.11
	5	369	10.8		4,636.99	−3.66
	7	188	7.7		2,362.48	−3.37
	9	114	6		1,432.57	−3.16
Image 3	2	2,557	28.5	0.0085	265.56	−2.42
	4	634	25.1		124.49	−2.09
	6	279	9.4		71.55	−1.85
	8	156	7		78.41	−1.89
	10	98	5.6		49.26	−1.69
	3	1,131	18.9	0.0121	142.13	−2.15
	5	403	11.3		79.13	−1.89
	7	204	8		71.21	−1.85
	9	122	6.2		61.32	−1.79

(*Continued*)

Table 1.8 Abnormal cervix cell. (*Continued*)

	Scaling	Area	Radius	Ks	Form factor	Invaslog
Image 4	2	2395	27.6	0.0091	30,096.45	−4.48
	4	599	13.8		7,527.26	−3.87
	6	266	9.2		3,342.65	−3.52
	8	150	6.9		1,884.96	−3.28
	10	96	5.5		1,206.37	−3.08
	3	1,064	18.4	0.0125	13,370.62	−4.13
	5	383	11		4,812.92	−3.68
	6	195	7.9		2,540.44	−3.40
	9	118	6.1		1,482.83	−3.17

Table 1.9 Regression line for cancer cell image.

X	Y	$X-M_X$	$Y-M_Y$	$(X-M_X)^2 = SS_X$	$(X-M_X)(Y-M_Y) = S_P$
2,740.5	29.5	1,942.94	14.58	3,775,015.8436	2,8328.0652
676.3	14.7	−121.26	−0.22	14,703.9876	26.6772
300	17.3	−497.56	2.38	247,565.9536	−1,184.1928
162	7.2	−635.56	−7.72	403,936.5136	4,906.5232
109	5.9	−688.56	−9.02	474,114.8736	6,210.8112
M_X: 797.56	M_Y: 14.92				
3,987.8	74.6			4,915,337.172	38,287.884

X = Area, Y = Radius.

Regression Equation:

$y = bX + a$

$b = S_P/SS_X = 38{,}287.884/4{,}915{,}337.172 = 0.00779$

$a = M_Y - bM_X = 14.92 - (0.01 * 797.56) = 8.70743$

$y = 0.00779X + 8.70743$

1.4 Results

To identify the invasiveness growth, uncertainty of Cervical Cancer cells for the sample images of Normal and Abnormal cells from Figures 1.4 and 1.5, the fruitful results are obtained from the following methods.

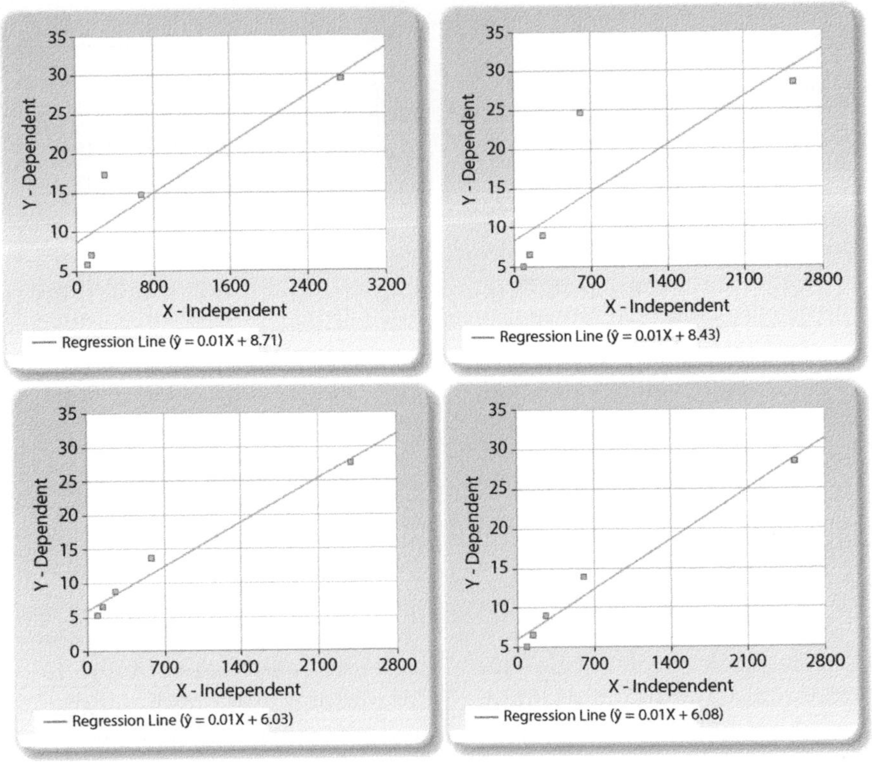

Figure 1.8 Linear regression lines of normal cervix cell (even scaling).

1.4.1 Fuzzy Method

This shows the data collection of Normal, Abnormal Cervical Cancer cell images of patients from various stages in Tables 1.1 and 1.2. Table 1.3 shows Cancer cells as model in the Data of Cervical Cancer cell images to perform perfectly calibrated computations which are obtained from matrix transformations. The Determinant value of all matrices obtained is non zero so rank of the matrices is same as the order of the matrices.

Tables 1.4 and 1.5 represent Eigen Vectors of Cervical Cancer cells that formed matrix which acts as transformation either by stretching or compressing reaching the maximum value 1 and Eigen values i.e. by the factors of compressing also reaching the maximum. Table 1.6 uses Fuzzy Eigen values and Eigen vectors based on the variation from Normal Cervix cells to Abnormal Cervix from Table 1.5 because the values are vague and is also shown in Figure 1.6 graphically. Eigen Vectors of Fuzzy matrix show the growth of Cancer cells stretching maximum and the uncertainty growth of

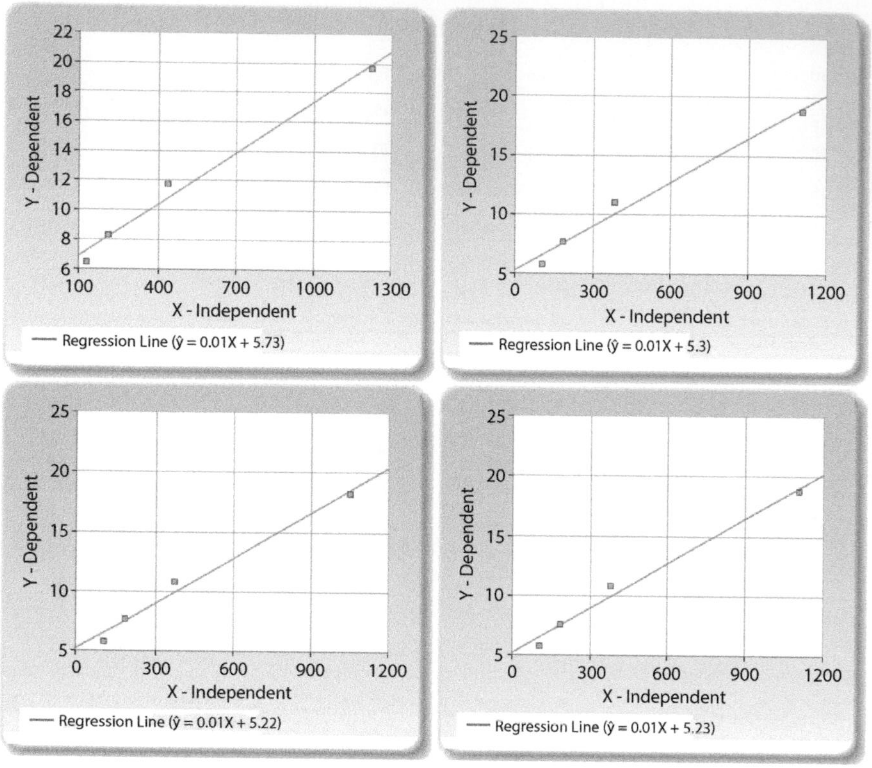

Figure 1.9 Linear regression lines of normal cervix cell (odd scaling).

Cancer cells and most of the growth of Normal cervix cell is going change to Abnormal cell.

1.4.2 Sausage Method

Box-counting method is an experimental method to find the dimension of the cells. Using Box-counting method and Equation (1.1), the Area and Perimeter of Cancer cells of Figures 1.4 and 1.5 of a few images of Normal, Abnormal Cancer cells are explained in Tables 1.7 and 1.8 of various scaling.

Using this Box-counting method Area, Perimeter and Equations (1.4–1.7) of Sausage method, Radius, Form factor and Invaslog are also explained in Tables 1.7 and 1.8. It shows that radius increases as the Form factors also increases and Ks values are also changing for each scaling. Form factor will increase then invasiveness also increases. It shows that invasiveness growth is uncertain. The dimension is increases due to invasiveness increase.

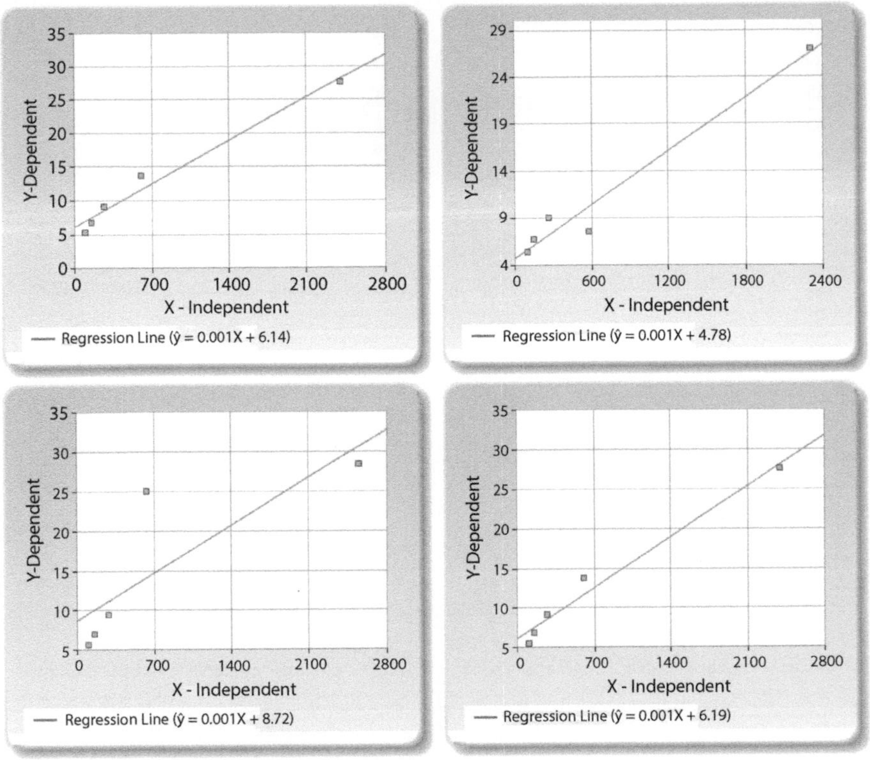

Figure 1.10 Linear regression lines of abnormal cervix cell (even scaling).

From the dimension of the cell it is easy to find grade of cancer. Using Equations (1.4–1.7), Table 1.9 shows the equation of Regression Lines of Normal and Abnormal Cervix cells of various scaling of few images are explained in Table 1.10. This method can analyze the invasiveness of the affected cells easily. This explained in Tables 1.11a and 1.11b.

The slope is changing for each scaling and also constant value. This shows that the growth of invasiveness is uncertainty i.e. it is Fuzzy.

1.5 Conclusion

Cervical Cancer is a preventable if effective spinning measures are in place. The cancer cells' growth is seen in Fuzzy method. Cancer cells are uncertainty and from the Sausage method explained invasiveness the cells of Cancer growth are uncertainty and these cells are bounded and Maximum

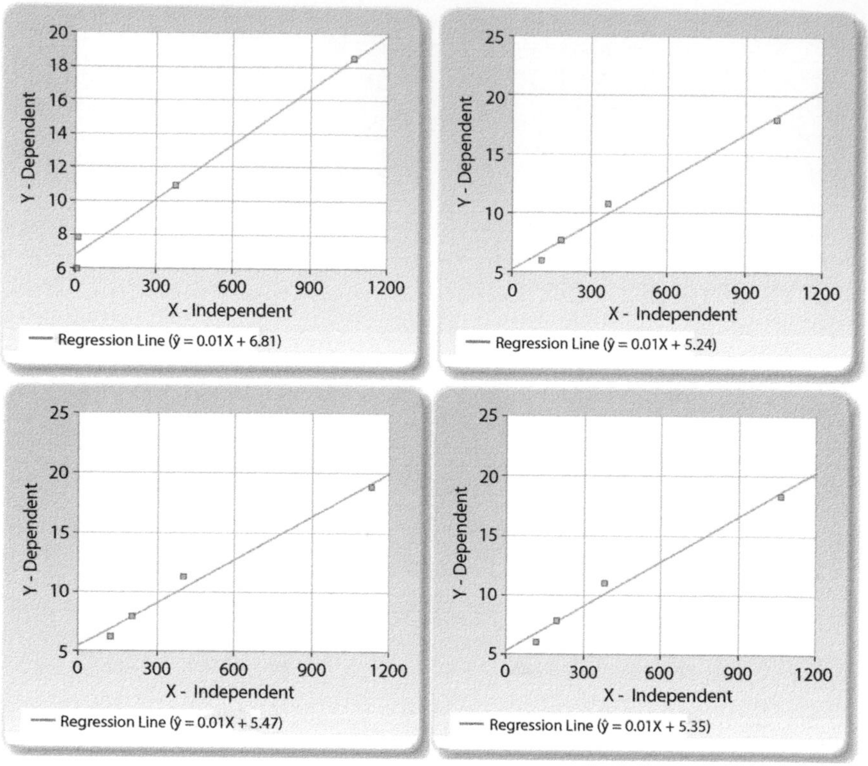

Figure 1.11 Linear regression lines of abnormal cervix cell (odd scaling).

Table 1.10 Regression lines for normal, abnormal cervical cells.

Scaling	Images	Normal cells of cervix	Abnormal cells of cervix
2 , 4, 6, 8, 10	Image 1	y = 0.0077x + 8.71	y = 0.0094x + 6.14
3, 5, 7, 9		y = 0.0116x + 5.73	y = 0.0109x + 6.81
2, 4, 6, 8, 10	Image 2	y = 0.0087x + 8.43	y = 0.0094x + 4.78
3, 5, 7, 9		y = 0.0124x + 5.3	Y = 0.0127x + 5.24
2, 4, 6, 8, 10	Image 3	y = 0.009x + 6.03	y = 0.0085x + 8.72,
3, 5, 7, 9		y = 0.0126x + 5.22	y = 0.0121x + 5.47
2, 4, 6, 8, 10	Image 4	y = 0.009x + 6.08	y = 0.0091x + 6.19
3, 5, 7, 9		y = 0.0125x + 5.23	y = 0.0125x + 5.35

Table 1.11a Maximum modulus theorem of normal cancer cells.

Image	Minimum	Maximum
1	−2.53	−1.23
2	−0.66	−0.33
3	−2.18	−1.01
4	−0.86	−0.36

Table 1.11b Maximum modulus theorem of abnormal cancer cells.

Image	Minimum	Maximum
1	−2.57	−1.71
2	−4.46	−3.06
3	−2.42	−1.69
4	−4.48	−3.08

Modulus theorem explained in the Cancer cells intensity tends to some value. Based on the dimension the invasiveness growth can be identified. The dimension of the cancer cell shows the complexity of a fractal like structure i.e. the Cancer cell growth. The growth of the Cervical Cancer cells are uncertainty therefore it form a Fuzzy Fractals. From these methods it is easy to find dimension of the Cancer cells through invasiveness. The higher the dimension shows the grade of cancer is high and the lower dimension shows the grade of cancer is lower. It is very helpful for the Pathologist to identify the grade of the Cancer and decide to start with appropriate treatment.

References

1. Zimmermann, H.-J., *Fuzzy Set Theory and its Applications*, Kluwer Academic Publishers, USA, 2001.
2. Meenakshi, A.R., *Fuzzy Matrix Theory and Applications*, KJP Publishers, India, 2008.

3. Hejmadi, M., *Introduction to Cancer Biology*, 2nd edition, ISBN978-87-7681-478-6, 2010. http://csbl.bmb.uga.edu/mirrors/JLU/DragonStar2017/download/introduction-to-cancer-biology.pdf
4. Ferlay, J. *et al.*, GLOBOCAN 2002: Cancer incidence, mortality and prevalence worldwide, in: *IARC Cancer Base*, vol. 5, IARC Press, Lyon, 2004.
5. Jayalalitha, G. and Uthayakumar, R., *Fractal Approach to Indentify the Grade of Cervical Cancer*, vol. 19, No. 1, pp. 125–139, World Scientific Publishing Company, 2011. https://www.worldscientific.com
6. Xin, L.J., Convergence of powers of controllable fuzzy matrices. *Fuzzy Sets Syst.*, 62, 83–88, 1994.
7. Sophia Porchelvi, R., Selvavathi, P., Vanitha, R., An Application of Fuzzy Matrices in Medical Diagnosis. *Int. J. Fuzzy Math. Archiv.*, 9, 2, 211–216, 2015.
8. Sanchez, E., Inverse of Fuzzy Relations, Application to Possibility distribution and Medical diagnosis. *Fuzzy Sets Syst.*, 2, 1, 75–86, 1979.
9. Uthayakumar, R. and Jayalalitha, G., Border Detection of Skin Cancer cells with Fractal Dimension. *Fractals*, 17, 2, 171–180, World Scientific Publishing Company, 2011.
10. Bellman, R.E. and Zadeh, L.A., Decision making in a Fuzzy environment. *Manage. Sci.*, 17B, 144B 164.2, 1970.
11. Beaula, T. and Mallika, Application of Fuzzy Matrices in Medical Diagnosis. *Int. J. Fuzzy Math. Archiv.*, 14, 1, 163–169, 2017.
12. Shimura, M., Fuzzy sets concept in rank ordering objects. *J. Math. Anal. Appl.*, 43, 717–733, 1973.
13. Cagman, N. and Enginoglu, S., Fuzzy soft matrix theory and its applications in Decision making. *Iran. J. Fuzzy Syst.*, 9, 1, 109–119, 2012.
14. Meenakshi, A.R. and Kaliraja, M., An Application of Interval valued fuzzy matrices in Medical Diagnosis. *Int. J. Math. Anal.*, 5, 36, 1791–1802, 2011.
15. Elizabeth, S. and Sujatha, L., Application of Fuzzy Membership Matrix in Medical Diagnosis and Decision Making. *Appl. Math. Sci.*, 7, 127, 6297–6307, 2013.
16. Pearse, E., An Introduction to Dimension Theory and Fractal Geometry, in: *Fractal Dimensions and Measures*, p. 2.
17. Falconer, K.J., *Fractal Geometry—Mathematical Foundations and Applications*, John Wiley, USA, 1997.
18. Kumar, V., Abbas, A.K., Nelson, F., Richard, M., *Robbins Basic Pathology*, 8th edition, pp. 718–721, Saunders Elsevier, USA, 2007.
19. Walboomers, J.M., Jacobs, M.V., Manos, M.M. *et al.*, Human Papillomavirus is a necessary cause of Invasive Cervical Cancer worldwide. *J. Pathol.*, 189, 1, 12–19, 1999.
20. Raich, V.V., Gawande, A., Triapath, R.K., Fuzzy Matrix Theory and its Application for Recognizing the Qualities of Effective Teacher. *Int. J. Fuzzy Math. Syst.*, 1, 1, 111–120, 2011.

21. Feng, Z. and Zhou, H., Computing method of Fractal dimension of image and its application. *J. Jiangsu Univ. Sci. Technol.*, 92–95, 6, 2001.
22. Hastings, H.M. and Sugihara, G., *Fractals, A User's Guide for the National Sciences*, Oxford University Press, Oxford, England, 1993.
23. Zimmermann, H.J., *Fuzzy Set Theory and its Applications*, Springer Science+ Business Media, LLC, USA, 1985.
24. Wei, Y., Building a type-2 fuzzy qualitative regression model, in: *Smart Innovation, Systems and Technologies*, pp. 527–532, 2012, DOI: 10.1007/978-3-642-29977-3_15.
25. Jayalalitha, G. and Uthayakumar, R., Estimating the Skin Cancer Using Fractals. *International Conference on Computational Intelligence and Multimedia Applications (ICCIMA 2007)*, 2007, DOI:10.1109/ICCIMA.186.
26. Dhar, M. and Baruah, H.K., Theory of Fuzzy Sets. *Int. J. Inf. Eng. Electron. Bus. (IJIEEB)*, 5, 3, 78–82, 2013.
27. *Intelligent Decision Technologies*, Springer Nature, 2012.
28. Dhar, M. and Baruah, H.K., The Complement of Normal Fuzzy Numbers, An Exposition. *Int. J. Intell. Syst. Appl.*, 08, 73–82, 2013.
29. Andres, J. and Rypka, M., Fuzzy Fractals and Hyper fractals. *Fuzzy Sets Syst.*, 300, 40–56, 2016.
30. Garg, A., A Review on Natural Phenomenon of Fractal Geometry. *Int. J. Comput. Appl.*, 86, 4, 43, 2014.

2

Emotion Detection in IoT-Based E-Learning Using Convolution Neural Network

Latha Parthiban[1]* and S. Selvakumara Samy[2]

[1]*Department of Computer Science, Pondicherry University CC, Pondicherry, India*
[2]*Department of Software Engineering, SRM Institute of Science and Tech., Kattankulathur Campus, Chennai, India*

Abstract

In this era of technological advancements, learning process has also taken a giant Leap which resulted in e-learning. Constraints in our learning system includes providing same content to all students with different skills that leads to lack of student motivation towards a subject, course etc. Adaptive learning strategy uses PCs as intelligent educating gadget providing learners with their requirement. In existing techniques, most instructors do not provide materials required for different level of learners. Innovations are quickly advancing today; training has likewise made support of innovation and offers advantageous approaches to build the information, instruction and proficiency status of people. With the growth of IoT, E-learning platforms provide ubiquity giving any place, any time access for learning. Dynamic student behaviour analysis is an important step towards improving IoT based e-learning for automated feedback and measuring student engagement. This research helps to identify e-learner's emotional state and change the learning content dynamically. Here, a combination of face-based emotion and learner pupil detection are used to understand the learner emotion towards the specific courses offered by the tutor. A hybrid architecture based on machine learning approach with Fuzzy Convolutional neural network (FCNN) is proposed for providing accurate results.

**Corresponding author*: lathaparthiban@yahoo.com

E. Chandrasekaran, R. Anandan, G. Suseendran, S. Balamurugan and Hanaa Hachimi (eds.)
Fuzzy Intelligent Systems: Methodologies, Techniques, and Applications, (27–44) © 2021 Scrivener Publishing LLC

Keywords: Principal component analysis (PCA), Haar cascade, local binary patterns, fuzzy convolutional neural network (FCNN), Internet of Things (IoT)

2.1 Introduction

E-learning has changed the class room with an educator to a PC/mobile-based framework that empowers us to study anywhere and on any occasion. E-learning offers the capability to visualize a wide variety of arrangements, as an instance, recordings, slideshows, word data and PDFs. Leading on-line publications (stay on line lessons) and talking with educators through visit and message discussions are additionally a preference that are reachable to customers as shown in Figure 2.1 which is an adaptive e-learning framework.

An individual who experiences constructive psychological well-being utilizes different resources and abilities to work effectively in everyday

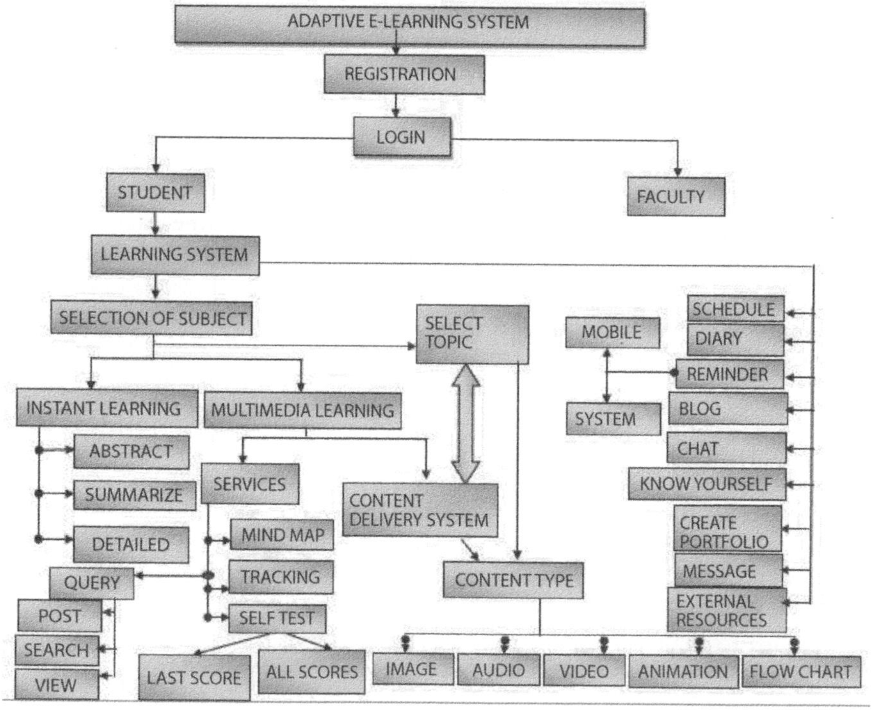

Figure 2.1 Adaptive E-Learning system.

life [1]. Emotions like feeling discouraged, tensed and furiousness may happen at various occasions and circumstances. If such emotions persist, it may end up in psychological wellness issues [2]. Proper feelings indicate positive emotional wellness. Uncooperative approach demonstrates emotional wellness issues. If the students are rationally sound, they will respond to a learning circumstance with a suitable emotion, irrespective of the occasion. If the students have issues, they may respond in an inverse path or in a tangled way. Passionate instruction, which is an important segment in quality training, is a basic way to create positive emotions in students [3].

E-learning is a creative way that provides a methodology to enhance the nature of education and learning. In e-learning frameworks, positive mindset is particularly important for ideal learning since it is essential for mental conditions that mirror a few human sentiments, behaviors, activity results, etc. [4]. In e-learning, it is necessary to make progressively sustainable association among students and material by motivating the students through animation.

E-learning has turned into a student focused, customized learning innovation. The vast majority of the past research has been on the physiological factor of the student, in light of the conventional classroom and personal learning [5]. Current training framework utilizes numerous strategies and devices, for example, electronic learning, versatile learning, issue-based learning, venture-based exercises, online dialog gatherings and talk discussions to encourage learning. Today, many advanced education organizations enable their students to learn providing them flexibility in time, area and their own pace. Senior students particularly want to have more comfortability in the learning stage [6].

One of the main issues in e-learning is the absence of strategies to perceive student conduct. In this work, student's behavior can be analyzed amid learning that is IoT enabled. E-learning applications like Udemy, Pluralsight, Khan Academy, Coursera, Udacity, edX, etc. do not analyze the learner's emotions and judge whether the website's content is understandable by all learners. Also the existing e-learning applications don't suggest the courses based on the learners attitude towards the specific course or tutor.

Research on emotion recognition is a challenging field with objective strategies to make powerful human PC collaboration. In this research, a combination of face-based emotion and pupil detection is used to understand the learner's emotions towards specific courses offered by the tutor. Analyzing the learner's mindset using machine learning techniques and changing the e-learning content would dynamically attract the learner making him involved [7].

Perceiving human emotions can have various applications in different fields, with the most encouraging one, the man–machine interaction. Using face-based emotion response framework, the IoT based e-learning platform can investigate the student's feeling towards a specific mentor, instructional content and delivery methodology. Based on student's reaction on whether they are happy or disturbed, the methodology can be adjusted to inspire the student [8]. Following the eye movements of the learner helps in improving the e-learning framework [9]. The proposed IoT-based e-learning model will address the issue of understanding and reacting to the student's emotions when they learn. This model will be useful to recognize the student's' learning abilities by estimating the face and eye-based emotion using machine learning systems.

2.2 Related Works

Internet instruction and e-learning philosophies have grown higher than ever after the bloom of data innovation age. Thus, the nature of instruction and number of online students has expanded significantly. The modernized method of IoT-based e-learning influences the learner's expectation to learn and adapt because of absence of any immediate supervision [10].

A teacher can give knowledge to the learner with his/her expertise [11]. Direct supervision encourages them to learn with the course objectives due to instant correspondence with the educator whenever required. Less correspondence results in learner's disappointment [12]. Information transfer through e-learning offers many advantages over the traditional training [13]. It was found that the data accumulated from eye signals demonstrate a person's level and point of convergence of thoughts [14], stress, basic reasoning, and exhaustion. Ismail and Mohamed [15] focused on the parts of courses that reflect learner's emotional thought, stress, basic reasoning, and fatigue.

Areej *et al.* assessed and recorded the eye gazes of individuals who were related with an e-learning module and their awareness and individual learning styles [16]. They got four scales from the critical collections of information: dynamic/intelligent, detecting/natural, visual/verbal, and consecutive/worldwide. Visual students showed regard for mixed media components, and higher verbal students displayed more consideration for printed material [17]. Mealha *et al.* analyzed data representation procedures for information in various settings (promoting, sites, TV news, and computer games) [18]. It reports an immediate connection of eyes, the eye-temples, and the mouth [19]. Pushpaja V. Saudagare and D.S Chaudhari analyzed a procedure to distinguish articulation from feelings through neural systems. It audits the different procedures of articulation identification utilizing MATLAB [20].

Muid Mufti and Assia Khanam analyzed a principle based on emotion in e-learning [21]. Outward appearances can give data on learner that can be used for evaluating a person's considerations and perspective [22]. Facial parts like forehead, eyes, nose, mouth, and so forth are the principal features used in frameworks [23]. Machine learning calculations have been utilized for facial acknowledgment to improve precision and identification [24, 25].

2.3 Proposed Methodology

2.3.1 Students Emotion Recognition Towards the Class

Figure 2.2 shows the proposed e-learning architecture. Facial image of the learner is captured and given as input from which three features are extracted. Principal Component Analysis (PCA) is utilized for facial emotion recognition.

Table 2.1 shows the accuracy of algorithms for different training set percentage of UMIST dataset for face recognition and Figure 2.3 shows its corresponding graph.

2.3.2 Eye Gaze-Based Student Engagement Recognition

The eye corners can be found effectively in the eye ROI. The vectors interfacing eye corners and iris focuses can be utilized to compute look position. In this work, a technique using a sliding window and Haar filter, is proposed. Haar cascade technique accomplishes high identification rate and lesser false rate as in Table 2.2 and Figure 2.4. The corresponding processing time of the algorithm is shown in Table 2.3 and Figure 2.5.

$$\text{Detection Rate} = \text{TP}/(\text{TP} + \text{TN}) * 100$$

$$\text{Accuracy} = (\text{TP} + \text{TN})/\text{Total data} * 100$$

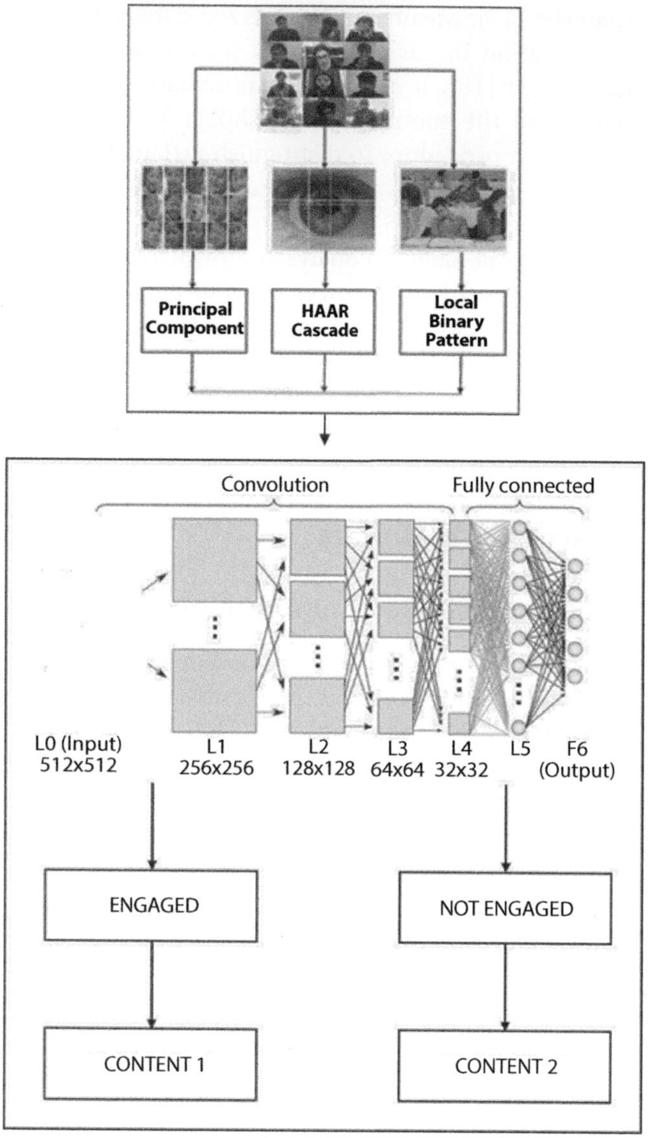

Figure 2.2 Proposed e-learning architecture.

Table 2.1 Accuracy of algorithms for face recognition.

Training set percentage (%)	Accuracy of algorithms			
	PCA (%)	**KPCA (%)**	**KFA (%)**	**LDA (%)**
30	57.19	28.06	58.89	60.83
40	50.36	22.67	65.33	63
50	48.75	18.46	65.38	63.69
60	54	20.45	70.91	69.09
70	54.29	15	79.38	71.88

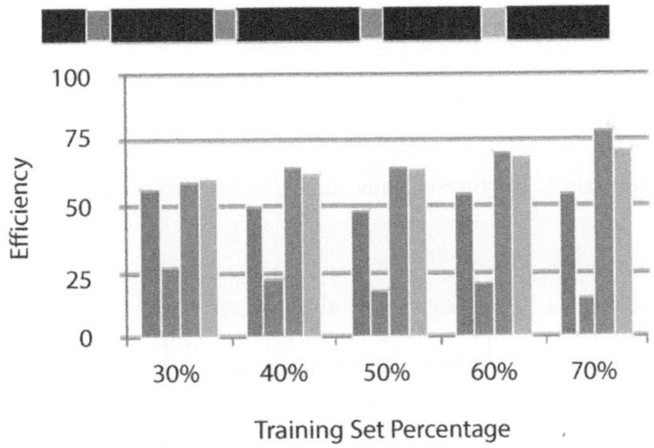

Figure 2.3 Face recognition results of UMIST dataset.

Table 2.2 Eye gaze detection algorithm accuracy.

Method	Detection rate	False positive rate
Pupil detection algorithm	55.69%	26.29%
Starburst algorithm	56.14%	23.18%
Haar Cascade	86.23%	11.1%

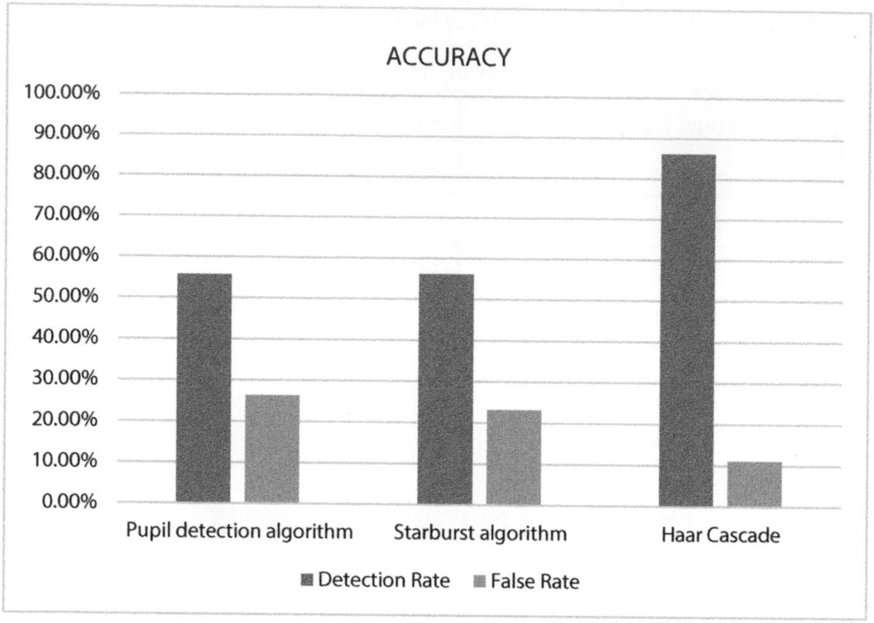

Figure 2.4 Pupil detection, Starburst, Haar cascade comparison chart.

Table 2.3 Processing time of eye gaze algorithm.

Method	Processing time/ms 5 frames	Processing time/ms 10 frames
Pupil detection algorithm	35	153
Starburst algorithm	24	124
Haar Cascade	13	35

2.3.3 Facial Head Movement-Based Student Engagement Recognition

Local Binary Patterns [26] is a standard spatio-transient surface descriptor. The LBP descriptor links the three symmetrical planes: XY, XT and YT of a video grouping. For the test assessment, LBP highlights were removed in two different ways:

(1) *Full video:* The total video is considered and LBP highlights are separated from it.

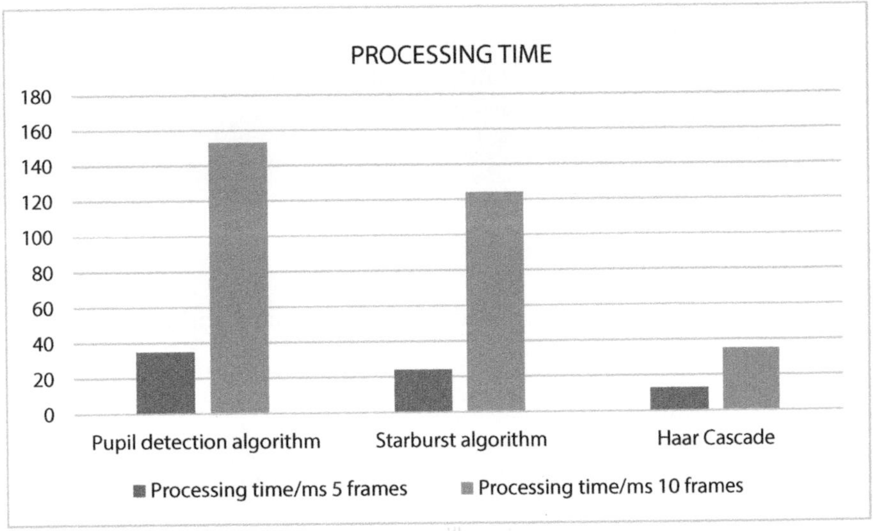

Figure 2.5 Pooling Techniques.

(2) *Shorter Segment:* A sliding window vf = [f1, f2, · , fk] of k outlines is taken at once and LBP highlights are separated.

2.4 Experimental Results

In this section, an overview of CNN is provided, after which experimental results are discussed in phases.

Convolutional Neural Network (CNN):
CNN [27, 28] is an important deep learning network with the following layers.

2.4.1 Convolutional Layer

The primary purpose of Convolution in case of a Convolutional Neural Network is to extract feature from Principal Component Analysis (PCA), Haar Cascade, Local Binary Pattern (LBP).

2.4.2 ReLU Layer

This layer provides the output $f_r = ReLU(x_i) = \max(0, x_i)$.

2.4.3 Pooling Layer

This layer helps in creating a compact feature map. Figure 2.6 shows the pooling techniques.

2.4.4 Fully Connected Layer

Here the 2D structure is transformed to 1D vector. The CNN structure is shown in Figure 2.7.

Experimental results were carried out in three phases for identifying the emotions of the e-learner.

1st Phase Experimental Results

1. Different types of input images like face emotions, iris and head position are extracted from Figures 2.8, 2.9 and 2.10.

   Figure 2.8 shows real time facial emotion recognition using PCA feature extraction algorithm. The learner emotions like

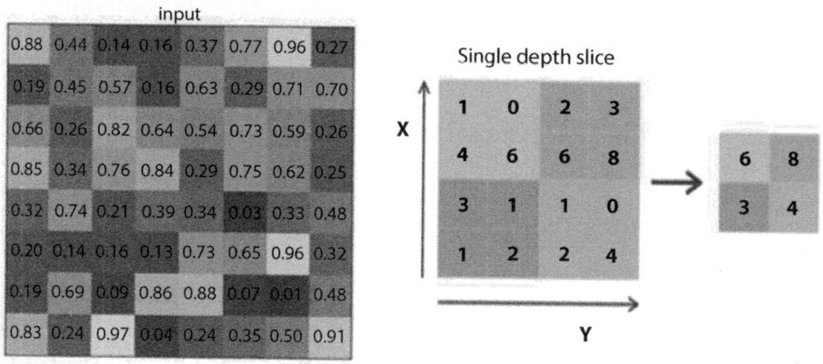

Figure 2.6 Pooling techniques.

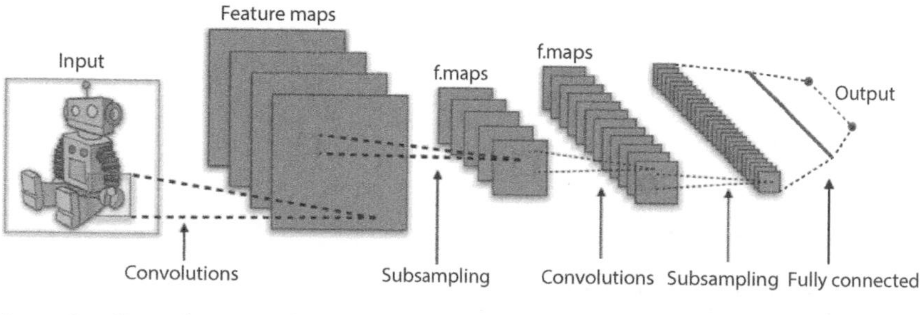

Figure 2.7 Typical CNN architecture.

Figure 2.8 Facial emotion recognition—surprise, neutral, happy, angry and sad.

Figure 2.9 Eye gaze movement detection—center, left, right, top and bottom.

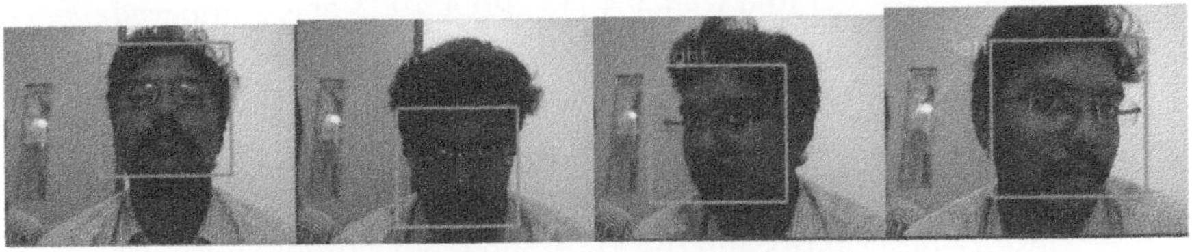

Figure 2.10 Face movement detection—up, down, right and left.

surprise, happy, neutral, angry and sad towards the e-learning content have been recognized by analyzing the real time input feature values.

Figure 2.9 explains eye gaze detection using Haar cascade technique. In this eye ROI and corners are analyzed dynamically, based on learner's attentiveness, drowsiness. The experimental results shows whether the learner finds the training content interesting, sleepy or boring.

Figure 2.10 explains facial movement detection using LBP. This experimental result shows whether the learners are distracted or focused towards the training content. The sequence of learner's head movements like center, up, down, left and right are recognized and based on it learner state has been detected. PyCharm tool is used for processing head movement identification.

2. 2nd phase experiment to compare the different feature extraction techniques. PCA, HAAR CASCADE, LBP and PCA + CNN

Table 2.4 shows the comparison of face recognition accuracy across feature descriptors. In this, the accuracy rate obtained

Table 2.4 Face recognition accuracy across feature descriptors.

Method	Recognition accuracy		
	FBET	SLE	eNTERFACE
PCA	80	78	76
PCA + QPSO	75	70	65
KFA	70	63	60
LDA	82.5	80	76
PCA + CNN	86.9	86.7	82.5

by PCA, PCA+QPSO, KFA, LDA, PCA + CNN is compared. From the accuracy rates it can be concluded that combination of PCA and CNN are able to give the better accuracy rates in all the three FBET, SLE and eNTERFACE.

Figure 2.11 exhibits the accuracy of face recognition across feature descriptors and the PCA and CNN combination was able to give compromising accuracy results in the three cases with accuracy levels of 86.9, 86.7 and 82.5% for FBET, SLE and eNTERFACE respectively.

Table 2.5 shows the comparison of iris recognition accuracy across feature descriptors. In this the accuracy rate

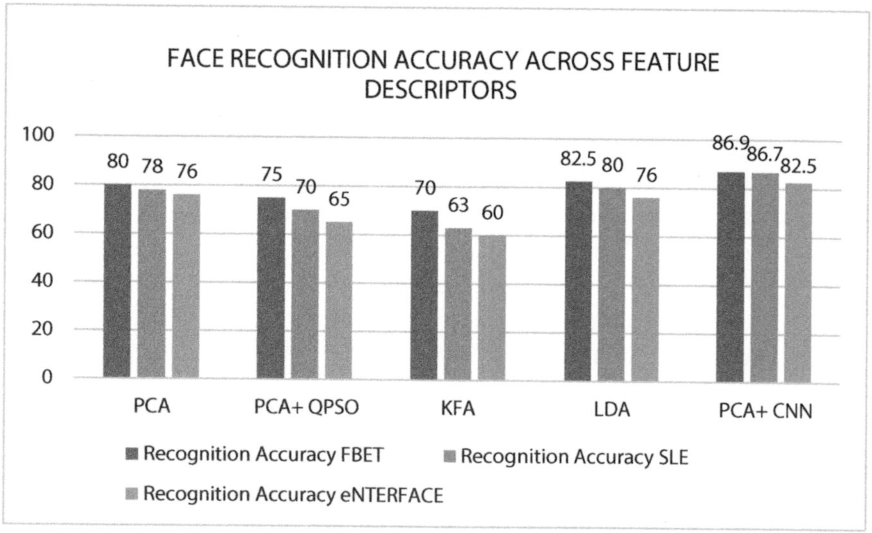

Figure 2.11 Face recognition accuracy across feature descriptors.

Table 2.5 Iris recognition accuracy across feature descriptors.

Method	Recognition accuracy		
	FBET	ICE 2005	ND-IRIS-0405
Pupil Detection Algorithm	77	76	77
Starburst Algorithm	72	73	75
Haar Cascade	81.5	80	78
Haar CascadE + CNN	84.6	84	82.5

obtained by Pupil detection algorithm, Starburst Algorithm, Haar cascade, Haarcascade + CNN are compared. From the accuracy rates, it could be identified from Figure 2.12, that a combination of Haar cascade and CNN are able to give the better accuracy rates in all the three FBET, ICE2005 and ND-IRIS-0405.

Table 2.6 shows the comparison of head movement accuracy across feature descriptors. In this the accuracy rate obtained by LDA, LBP and LBP+CNN are compared. From the accuracy rates in Figure 2.13, it can be identified that combination of LBP and CNN gives better accuracy rates for in both FBET and eNTERFACE.

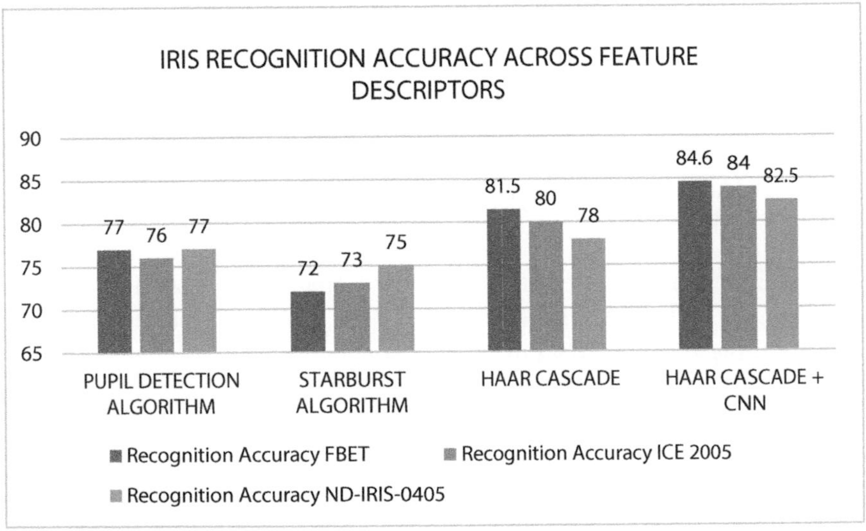

Figure 2.12 Iris recognition accuracy across feature descriptors.

Table 2.6 Comparison of head movement accuracy across feature descriptors.

Method	Recognition accuracy FBET	Recognition accuracy eNTERFACE
LDA	76	73
LBP	77	74
LBP + CNN	80	78

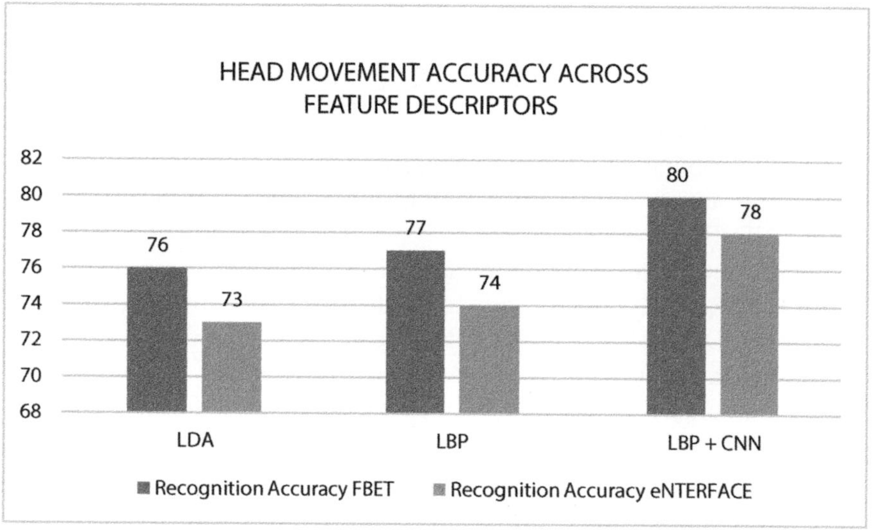

Figure 2.13 Comparison of head movement accuracy across feature descriptors.

3. PCA, HAAR CASCADE and LBP for the given input with SVM

   Experiments were carried out to compare PCA, HAAR and LBP with SVM and the accuracy for FBET is tabulated in Table 2.7 and shown in Figure 2.14.

4. PCA, Haar Cascade and LBP for the given input with CNN

   Final phase of experiments were carried out to compare the feature descriptors with CNN for FBET and the accuracy results were tabulated in Table 2.8 and shown in Figure 2.15.

Table 2.7 Comparison of FBET with SVM.

Feature	Model	FBET
PCA	SVM	75.5
Haar Cascade	SVM	73.5
LBP	SVM	70.6

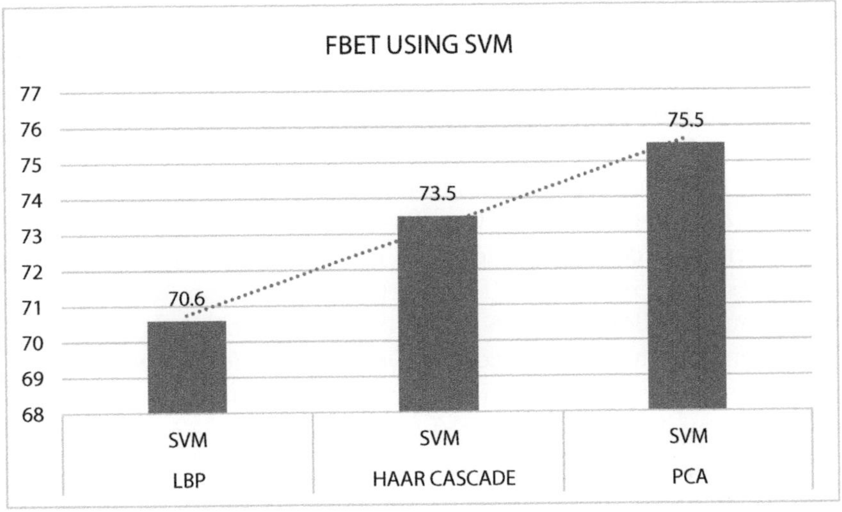

Figure 2.14 Comparison of FBET using SVM with accuracy of 73.

Table 2.8 Comparison of FBET model with CNN.

Feature	Model	FBET
PCA	CNN	82.5
Haar Cascade	CNN	81.5
LBP	CNN	80.6

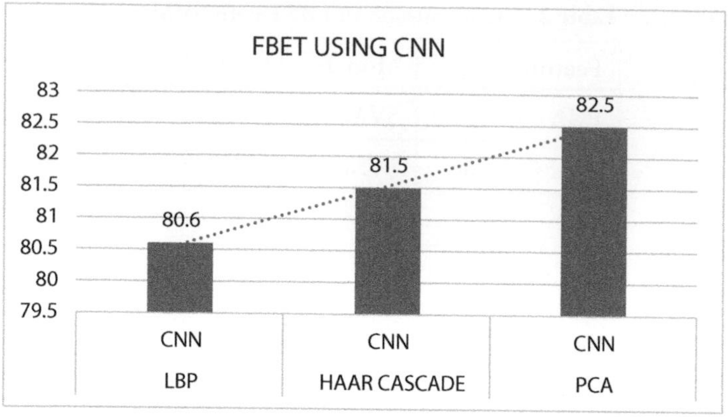

Figure 2.15 Comparison of FBET using SVM with accuracy of 81.5.

2.5 Conclusions

One of the major problems in conventional learning is the lack of methods to recognize learner behavior. Therefore, the current research addresses the problem of recognizing a learner's emotional state during learning. Finding less attentive students is important in classroom/e-learning systems because it allows teachers to understand the behavior of students and attentiveness towards the course. Designing an IoT-based e-learning hybrid system integrating facial emotion, eye gaze and face movements provided accurate and efficient results. Facial emotion recognition has been performed using PCA algorithm, student eye gaze based engagement prediction was performed using Haar Cascade algorithm and student head movement based engagement recognition has been analyzed using Local Binary Patterns. Experimental results provided by the feature descriptors with CNN provided high accuracy compared to SVM. Future work will be to improve the accuracy of emotion recognition using Fuzzy CNN.

References

1. Anastasia, S.K. and Marta, S.J., *Responding to the Mental Health Needs of Students*, pp. 12–15, Student Service, September, KSA, 2006.
2. Paola Pedrelli, Maren Nyer, Albert Yeung, Courtney Zulauf, Timothy Wilens., College Students: Mental Health Problems and Treatment Considerations, https://www.ncbi.nlm.nih.gov/entrez/eutils/elink.fcgi?dbfrom=pubmed&retmode=ref&cmd=prlinks&id=25142250 Acad Psychiatry. 39, 5, 503–511, 2015.

3. Zhao, H., Sun, B., Hu, X., Zhu, X., The Study of Emotional Education Based on Virtual Reality in E-Learning. *The 1st International Conference on Information Science and Engineering (ICISE2009)*, pp. 3540–3543, 2009.
4. Lanata, A., Armato, A., Valenza, G., Scilingo, E.P., Eye tracking and pupil size variation as response to affective stimuli: A preliminary study. *Pervasive Computing Technologies for Healthcare (PervasiveHealth), 5th International Conference*, May 23–26, 2012, Republic of Ireland, Dublin.
5. Sandanayake, T.C. and Madurapperuma, A.P., Emotional Reactions of Undergraduates in Digital Learning Environment. *International Conference on Information Technology*, e Asia, Sri Lanka, 2009.
6. Sandanayake, T.C. and Madurapperuma, A.P., Enhancing the Learning Environment by Identifying the Learner Behavior in an e-Learning System. *Int. Conference on Engineering Education and Research*, Korea, 2009.
7. Mehrabian, A., Communication without words. *Psychol. Today*, 53–56, 1968.
8. De, A., Saha, A., Dr. Palb, M.C., A Human Facial Expression Recognition Model based on Eigen Face Approach. *International Conference on Advanced Computing Technologies and Applications*, ICACTA, pp. 282–289, 2015.
9. Duchowski, A., *Eye Tracking Methodology: Theory and Practice*, Second editor, Springer, USA, 2007.
10. Fabri, M., Moore, D.J., Hobbs, D.J., Mediating the Expression of Emotion in Educational Collaborative Virtual Environments: An Experimental Study. *Int. J. Virtual Real.*, Springer Verlag, London, 2004.
11. Feidakis, M., Daradoumis, T., Caballé, S., Conesa, J., Measuring the Impact of Emotion Awareness on e-learning Situations. *2013 Seventh International Conference on Complex, Intelligent, and Software Intensive Systems*, Taichung, pp. 391–396, 2013.
12. Leghris, C. and Mrabet, R., Cost Comparison of E-Learning Solutions. *2006 7th International Conference on Information Technology Based Higher Education and Training*, NSW, Sydney, pp. 817–824, 2006.
13. Yu, J., An Infrastructure for Real-Time Interactive Distance E-Learning Environment. *2009 First International Conference on Information Science and Engineering*, Nanjing, pp. 3219–3222, 2009.
14. Al-Khalifa, H.S. and George, R.P., Eye Tracking and e-Learning: Seeing Through Your Students' Eyes. *eLearn Mag.*, 6, 8, 2010.
15. Haddioui, I.E. and Khaldi, M., Learner Behavior Analysis through Eye Tracking. *The 6th International Conference on Virtual Learning ICVL*, pp. 458–463, 2011.
16. Wabil, A.A., Gibreen, H.E., George, R.P., Dasary, B.A., Exploring the Validity of Learning Styles as Personalization Parameters in eLearning Environments: An Eyetracking Study. *2010 2nd International Conference on Computer Technology and Development (ICCTD 2010)*, pp. 174–178, 2010.
17. Porta, M., Ricotti, S., Perez, C.J., Emotional E-Learning through Eye Tracking. *Global Engineering Education Conference (EDUCON), 2012 IEEE*, pp. 1–6, 2012.

18. Mealha, O., Veloso, A., Almeida, S., Rodrigues, R., Roque, L., Marques, R., Manteigueiro, C., Eye Tracking Data Representation and Visualization: On Information and Communication studies at CETAC.MEDIA. *J. Eye Track., Visual Cognit. Emot.*, 2, 1, 65–75, 2012.
19. Ekman, P., Friesen, Constants across cultures in the face and emotion. *J. Pers. Soc. Psychol.*, 17, 2, 124–129, 1971.
20. Saudagare, P.V. and Chaudhari, D.S., Facial Expression Recognition using Neural Network—An Overview. *Int. J. Soft Comput. Eng. (IJSCE)*, ISSN: 2231-2307, 2, 1, March 2012.
21. Mufti, M. and Khanam, A., Fuzzy Rule Based Facial Expression Recognition. *International Conference on Computational Intelligence for Modelling Control and Automation,and International Conference on Intelligent Agents, Web Technologies and Internet Commerce (CIMCA-IAWTIC'06)*, IEEE, 2006, 0-7695-2731-0/06.
22. Mohamed Sathik, M. and Sofia, G., Identification of student comprehension using forehead wrinkles. *2011 International Conference on Computer, Communication and Electrical Technology (ICCCET)*, pp. 66–70, 2011.
23. Bailenson, J., Beall, A., Blascovich, J., Raimundo, M., Weishbush, M., Intelligent agents who wear your face: User's reactions to the virtual self, in: *Technical Report*, Center for the Virtual Environment and Behaviors Department of Psychology, University of California, Santa Barbara, 2000.
24. Brunelli, R. and Poggío, T., Facial Recognition: Features versus Templates. *IEEE Trans. Pattern Anal. Mach. Intell.*, 15, 10, 1042–1052, Oct. 1993.
25. Delac, K., Grgic, M., Grgic, S., Independent comparative study of PCA, ICA, and LDA on the FERET data set. *Int. J. Imaging Syst. Technol.*, 15, 5, 252–260, 2005, [Online]. Available: http://doi.wiley.com/10.1002/ima.2005.
26. Zhao, G. and Pietikainen, M., Dynamic texture recognition using local binary patterns with an application to facial expressions. *IEEE Trans. Pattern Anal. Mach. Intell.*, 29, 6, 915–928, 2007.
27. Deng, L. and Yu, D., Deep learning: Methods and applications. *Found. Trends Signal Process.*, 7, 3–4, 2014.
28. Christian, S., Toshev, A., Erhan, D., Deep neural networks for object detection, in: *Advances in Neural Information Processing Systems*, 2013.

3

Fuzzy Quotient-3 Cordial Labeling of Some Trees of Diameter 5—Part III

P. Sumathi[1] and J. Suresh Kumar[2*]

[1]*Department of Mathematics, C. Kandaswami Naidu College for Men, Anna Nagar, Chennai, India*
[2]*Department of Mathematics, St. Thomas College of Arts and Science, Koyambedu, Chennai, India*

Abstract

Let G be a simple, finite, undirected, plannar and connected graph of order p and size q. Let $|V|(G)$ and $E(G)$ be the vertex set and edge set of the graph. Let σ: $V(G) \rightarrow [0,1]$ be a function defined by $\sigma(\vartheta) = \frac{\gamma}{10}, \gamma \in Z_4 - \{0\}$. For each edge $\omega\vartheta$, define μ: $E(G) \rightarrow [0,1]$ by $\mu(\omega\vartheta) = \frac{1}{10}\left\lceil \frac{3\sigma(\omega)}{\sigma(\vartheta)} \right\rceil$ where $\sigma(\omega) \leq \sigma(\vartheta)$. Then σ is called fuzzy quotient-3 cordial labeling of G if for $i \neq j \in \left\{\frac{\gamma}{10}, \gamma \in Z_4 - \{0\}\right\}$, $v_\sigma(i)$ and $v_\sigma(j)$ differ by at most 1 and $e_\mu(i)$ and $e_\mu(j)$ differ by at most 1 where $v_\sigma(i)$ denotes the number of vertices mapped with the label i and $e_\mu(i)$ denotes the number of edges mapped with the label. If graph G admits fuzzy quotient-3 cordial labelling then G is called fuzzy quotient-3 cordial graph. In this paper, the existence of fuzzy quotient-3 cordial labeling on some trees of diameter 5 denoted by $\mathcal{T}_S^5$, $31 \leq s \leq 39$ is investigated and the works are presented in this paper.

Keywords: Tree, diameter of tree, fuzzy quotient-3 cordial graph

**Corresponding author*: jskumar.robo@gmail.com

E. Chandrasekaran, R. Anandan, G. Suseendran, S. Balamurugan and Hanaa Hachimi (eds.) Fuzzy Intelligent Systems: Methodologies, Techniques, and Applications, (45–72) © 2021 Scrivener Publishing LLC

3.1 Introduction

One of the important areas in graph theory is graph labeling. Graph labeling methods trace their origin to one introduced by Rosa [11] or one given by Graham & Sloane [12]. A graph labeling is an assignment of integers to the vertices or edges or both subject to certain conditions. The field of graph labeling has been creating a lot of interest and motivation among many researchers and this branch of mathematics has found several applications. Labeled graphs have its wide variety of applications in designing communication network addressing systems, determining ambiguities in X-ray crystallographic analysis, determining the radio astronomy and optimal circuit layouts. Besides their practical applications as indicated above their theoretical applications too are numerous not only in the theory of graphs but also in other areas of mathematics such as Combinatorial Number Theory, Linear Algebra and Group Theory. Owing to its wide applications in diverse fields of knowledge, an enormous body of literature has grown around the theme. More than two thousand research papers have been published so far in various graph labeling. The excellent dynamic survey on graph labeling by Gallian periodically gives an exhaustive survey on the results of graph labelings. Motivated by these labelings we introduced fuzzy quotient-3 cordial labeling and proved fuzzy quotient-3 cordial labeling for some families of graphs. In this paper, we proved that the trees of diameter 5 denoted by $\mathcal{T}_s^5$, $31 \leq s \leq 39$ are fuzzy quotient-3 Cordial.

3.2 Related Work

Excellent survey of graph labeling was given by Gallian [1]. The idea of cordial labeling was introduced by Cahit [2]. Sundaram, Ponraj and Somasundaram [3] introduced the product cordial labeling. In Ref. [3] they proved that trees, unicyclic graphs of odd order, triangular snakes, dragons and helm graphs are product cordial labelings. Sundaram and Somasundaram [4] also have introduced the notion of total product cordial labeling. In Refs. [4] and [5] Sundaram, Ponraj and Somasundaram proved the following graphs trees, all cycles except C_4, $K_{n,2n-1}$, C_n with some edges appended at each vertex, fans, double fans, wheel, helm are total product cordial. Ponraj, Sivakumar and Sundaram [6] introduced the notion k–Product cordial labeling of graphs. Jeyanthi and Maheshwari introduced the concept 3-product cordial labeling [7] and proved paths, stars, C_n if and only if $n \equiv 1,2(mod\ 3)$, $C_n \cup P_n$ are 3-product cordial. In [8] Ponraj *et al.* proved the path P_n iff $n \leq 11$, C_n iff $n = 5,6,7,8,9$ and 10, K_n iff $n \leq 2$, $P_n \cdot K_1$, $P_n \cdot 2K_1$, $K_{2,n}$ iff $n \equiv 0,3(mod\ 4)$, W_n iff $n = 5$ and $n = 9$, $\overline{K_n} + 2K_2$ iff $n \leq 2$ and the subdivision graph of $K_{1,n}$ are 4-product cordial. Sivakumar [9] proved the coronas $P_n \cdot K_1$, $P_n \cdot 2K_1$, $P_n \cdot K_1$, $S(P_n \cdot K_1)$, $S(P_n \cdot 2K_1)$, $S(C_n \cdot K_1)$ and $S(C_n \cdot 2K_1)$ are 4-total product cordial. Ponraj and Adaickalam in Ref. [10] proved that some star related graphs are quotient cordial.

3.3 Definition

Let σ: V(G) → [0,1] be a function defined by $\sigma(\vartheta) = \frac{\gamma}{10}$, $\gamma \in Z_4 - \{0\}$. For each edge $\omega\vartheta$, define μ: E(G) → [0,1] by $\mu(\omega\vartheta) = \frac{1}{10}\left[\frac{3\sigma(\omega)}{\sigma(\vartheta)}\right]$ where $\sigma(\omega) \leq \sigma(\vartheta)$. Then the function σ is called fuzzy quotient-3 cordial labeling of G, if the number of vertices having label i and the number of vertices having label j differ by at most 1, the number of edges having label i and the number of edges having label j differ by at most 1 where $i, j \in \left\{\frac{\gamma}{10}, r \in Z_4 - \{0\}\right\}, i \neq j$. The number of vertices having label i denotes $v_\sigma(i)$ and the number of edges having label i denotes $e_\mu(i)$ [8]. If graph G admits fuzzy quotient-3 cordial labelling then G is called fuzzy quotient-3 cordial graph.

3.4 Notations

The trees of diameter 5 denoted by $\mathcal{T}_s^5$, $31 \leq s \leq 39$, are defined as follows.

1. Let $\mathcal{T}_{31}^5$ be the tree obtained by attaching *m*, *n* path of length two to the first and second internal vertices of the path P_4.
2. Let $\mathcal{T}_{32}^5$ be the tree obtained by attaching *m* pendant edges through an edge to the first internal vertex and attaching *n* path of length two to the second internal vertex of the path P_4.
3. Let $\mathcal{T}_{33}^5$ be the tree obtained by attaching *m* path of length two to the first internal vertex attaching *n* pendant edges through an edge to the second internal vertex of the path P_4.
4. Let $\mathcal{T}_{34}^5$ be the tree obtained by attaching *m* path of length two to the first internal vertex and *n* path of length two to the second internal vertex of the path P_5.
5. Let $\mathcal{T}_{35}^5$ be the tree obtained by attaching *m* path of length two to the second internal vertex and *n* path of length two to the third internal vertex of the path P_5.

6. Let $\mathcal{T}_{36}{}^{5}$ be the tree obtained by attaching m pendant edges to the first internal vertex and attaching n pendant edges through a path P_3 to the second internal vertex of the path P_4.
7. Let $\mathcal{T}_{37}{}^{5}$ be the tree obtained by attaching m pendant edges through a path P_3 to the first internal vertex and attaching n pendant edges to the second internal vertex of the path P_4.
8. Let $\mathcal{T}_{38}{}^{5}$ be the tree obtained by attaching m pendant edges to the first internal vertex and attaching n path of length two through an edge to the second internal vertex of the path P_4.
9. Let $\mathcal{T}_{39}{}^{5}$ be the tree obtained by attaching m path of length two through an edge to the first internal vertex of the path P_4 and attaching n pendant edges to the second internal vertex of the path P_4.

Remarks:
By above notations $\mathcal{T}_{32}{}^{5} \cong \mathcal{T}_{33}{}^{5}$, $\mathcal{T}_{34}{}^{5} \cong \mathcal{T}_{35}{}^{5}$, $\mathcal{T}_{36}{}^{5} \cong \mathcal{T}_{37}{}^{5}$ and $\mathcal{T}_{38}{}^{5} \cong \mathcal{T}_{39}{}^{5}$.

3.5 Main Results

Theorem 1: The tree $\mathcal{T}_{31}{}^{5}$ is fuzzy quotient-3 cordial graph.

Proof:

Consider the tree $\mathcal{T}_{31}{}^{5}$.

Let t_4 be the path, $u_\theta^i (1 \le \theta \le m, 1 \le i \le 2)$ be the m path of length two attached to the first internal vertex t_2 of the path t_4 and $v_\kappa^i (1 \le \kappa \le n, 1 \le i \le 2)$ be the n path of length two attached to the second internal vertex t_3 of the path t_4.

Then the vertex set $V(\mathcal{T}_{31}{}^{5}) = \{t_h : 1 \le h \le 4\} \cup \{u_\theta{}^i : 1 \le \theta \le m, 1 \le i \le 2\}$
$\cup \{v_\kappa{}^i : 1 \le \kappa \le n, 1 \le i \le 2\}$

and the edge set $E(\mathcal{T}_{31}{}^{5}) = \{t_h t_{h+1} : 1 \le h \le 3\} \cup \{x_2 u_j{}^1 : 1 \le \theta \le m\}$
$\cup \{u_\theta{}^1 u_\theta{}^2 : 1 \le \theta \le m\}$
$\cup \{x_3 v_\kappa{}^1 : 1 \le \kappa \le n\} \cup v_\kappa{}^1 v_\kappa{}^2 : 1 \le \kappa \le n\}$.

$|V| = 2m + 2n + 4$ and $|E| = 2m + 2n + 3$.

We define $\sigma: V(\mathcal{T}_{31}{}^{5}) \rightarrow [0,1]$ by $\sigma(v) = \frac{\gamma}{10}, \gamma \in Z_4 - \{0\}$.

The vertices of the path t_h, $1 \le h \le 4$ are labeled as

$\sigma(t_1) = 0.2$
$\sigma(t_2) = 0.1$
$\sigma(t_3) = 0.1$
and $\sigma(t_4) = 0.1$

The labeling $\sigma(u_\theta^i), 1 \le \theta \le m, 1 \le i \le 2$ of m path of length two attached to the first internal vertex t_2 of the path t_4 are as follows.

$$\sigma(u_\theta^1) = 0.1 \quad if\ \theta \equiv 0,2\,(mod\,3) \quad for\ 1 \le \theta \le m$$

$$\sigma(u_\theta^1) = 0.3 \quad if\ \theta \equiv 1\,(mod\,3) \quad for\ 1 \le \theta \le m$$

$$\sigma(u_\theta^2) = 0.3 \quad if\ \theta \equiv 0\,(mod\,3) \quad for\ 1 \le \theta \le m$$

$$\sigma(u_\theta^2) = 0.2 \quad if\ \theta \equiv 1,2\,(mod\,3) \quad for\ 1 \le \theta \le m$$

The labeling $\sigma(v_\kappa^i), 1 \le \kappa \le n, 1 \le i \le 2$ of n path of length 2 attached to the second internal vertex t_3 of the path t_4 has following cases.

Case i: m ≡ 0 (mod 3)

$$\sigma(v_\kappa^1) = 0.1 \quad if\ \kappa \equiv 0,2\,(mod\,3) \quad for\ 1 \le \kappa \le n$$

$$\sigma(v_\kappa^1) = 0.3 \quad if\ \kappa \equiv 1\,(mod\,3) \quad for\ 1 \le \kappa \le n$$

$$\sigma(v_\kappa^2) = 0.2 \quad if\ \kappa \equiv 1,2\,(mod\,3) \quad for\ 1 \le \kappa \le n$$

$$\sigma(v_\kappa^2) = 0.3 \quad if\ \kappa \equiv 0\,(mod\,3) \quad for\ 1 \le \kappa \le n$$

Case ii: m ≡ 1 (mod 3)

$$\sigma(v_\kappa^1) = 0.1 \quad if\ \kappa \equiv 1,2\,(mod\,3) \quad for\ 1 \le \kappa \le n$$

$$\sigma(v_\kappa^1) = 0.3 \quad if\ \kappa \equiv 0\,(mod\,3) \quad for\ 1 \le \kappa \le n$$

$$\sigma(v_\kappa^2) = 0.2 \quad if\ \kappa \equiv 0,1\,(mod\,3) \quad for\ 1 \le \kappa \le n$$

$$\sigma(v_\kappa^2) = 0.3 \quad if\ \kappa \equiv 2\,(mod\,3) \quad for\ 1 \le \kappa \le n$$

Case iii: m ≡ 2 (mod 3)

$$\sigma(v_\kappa^1) = 0.1 \quad if\ \kappa \equiv 1,2\,(mod\,3) \quad for\ 1 \le \kappa \le n$$

$$\sigma(v_\kappa^1) = 0.3 \quad if\ \kappa \equiv 0\,(mod\,3) \quad for\ 1 \le \kappa \le n$$

$$\sigma\left(v_\kappa^2\right)=0.2 \quad \text{if } \kappa\equiv 0,1\,(mod\ 3) \quad \text{for } 1\le\kappa\le n$$

$$\sigma\left(v_\kappa^2\right)=0.3 \quad \text{if } \kappa\equiv 2\,(mod\ 3) \quad \text{for } 1\le\kappa\le n$$

For $i \in \left\{\frac{\gamma}{10}, \gamma \in Z_4 - \{0\}\right\}$, $v_\sigma(i)$ and $e_\mu(i)$ are tabulated below.

Table 3.1 $v_\sigma(i)$ and $e_\mu(i)$ for the tree $\mathcal{T}_{31}^5\left(\left\{i \in \frac{\gamma}{10}, \gamma \in Z_4 - \{0\}\right\}\right)$.

Nature of m and n	$v_\sigma(0.1)$	$v_\sigma(0.2)$	$v_\sigma(0.3)$	$e_\mu(0.1)$	$e_\mu(0.2)$	$e_\mu(0.3)$
$m\equiv 0(mod\ 3)$ $n\equiv 0(mod\ 3)$	$\frac{\lvert V\rvert-1}{3}+1$	$\frac{\lvert V\rvert-1}{3}$	$\frac{\lvert V\rvert-1}{3}$	$\frac{\lvert V\rvert-1}{3}$	$\frac{\lvert V\rvert-1}{3}$	$\frac{\lvert V\rvert-1}{3}$
$m\equiv 0(mod\ 3)$ $n\equiv 1(mod\ 3)$	$\frac{\lvert V\rvert}{3}$	$\frac{\lvert V\rvert}{3}$	$\frac{\lvert V\rvert}{3}$	$\frac{\lvert V\rvert}{3}$	$\frac{\lvert V\rvert}{3}$	$\frac{\lvert V\rvert}{3}-1$
$m\equiv 0(mod\ 3)$ $n\equiv 2(mod\ 3)$	$\frac{\lvert V\rvert+1}{3}$	$\frac{\lvert V\rvert+1}{3}$	$\frac{\lvert V\rvert+1}{3}-1$	$\frac{\lvert V\rvert+1}{3}-1$	$\frac{\lvert V\rvert+1}{3}$	$\frac{\lvert V\rvert+1}{3}-1$
$m\equiv 1(mod\ 3)$ $n\equiv 0(mod\ 3)$	$\frac{\lvert V\rvert}{3}$	$\frac{\lvert V\rvert}{3}$	$\frac{\lvert V\rvert}{3}$	$\frac{\lvert V\rvert}{3}$	$\frac{\lvert V\rvert}{3}$	$\frac{\lvert V\rvert}{3}-1$
$m\equiv 1(mod\ 3)$ $n\equiv 1(mod\ 3)$	$\frac{\lvert V\rvert+1}{3}$	$\frac{\lvert V\rvert+1}{3}$	$\frac{\lvert V\rvert+1}{3}-1$	$\frac{\lvert V\rvert+1}{3}-1$	$\frac{\lvert V\rvert+1}{3}$	$\frac{\lvert V\rvert+1}{3}-1$
$m\equiv 1(mod\ 3)$ $n\equiv 2(mod\ 3)$	$\frac{\lvert V\rvert-1}{3}+1$	$\frac{\lvert V\rvert-1}{3}$	$\frac{\lvert V\rvert-1}{3}$	$\frac{\lvert V\rvert-1}{3}$	$\frac{\lvert V\rvert-1}{3}$	$\frac{\lvert V\rvert-1}{3}$
$m\equiv 2(mod\ 3)$ $n\equiv 0(mod\ 3)$	$\frac{\lvert V\rvert+1}{3}$	$\frac{\lvert V\rvert+1}{3}$	$\frac{\lvert V\rvert+1}{3}-1$	$\frac{\lvert V\rvert+1}{3}-1$	$\frac{\lvert V\rvert+1}{3}$	$\frac{\lvert V\rvert+1}{3}-1$
$m\equiv 2(mod\ 3)$ $n\equiv 1(mod\ 3)$	$\frac{\lvert V\rvert-1}{3}+1$	$\frac{\lvert V\rvert-1}{3}$	$\frac{\lvert V\rvert-1}{3}$	$\frac{\lvert V\rvert-1}{3}$	$\frac{\lvert V\rvert-1}{3}$	$\frac{\lvert V\rvert-1}{3}$
$m\equiv 2(mod\ 3)$ $n\equiv 2(mod\ 3)$	$\frac{\lvert V\rvert}{3}$	$\frac{\lvert V\rvert}{3}$	$\frac{\lvert V\rvert}{3}$	$\frac{\lvert V\rvert}{3}$	$\frac{\lvert V\rvert}{3}$	$\frac{\lvert V\rvert}{3}-1$

It is clear from the above Table 3.1 that for $i \neq j \in \left\{\frac{\gamma}{10}, \gamma \in Z_4 - \{0\}\right\}$ $v_\sigma(i)$ and $v_\sigma(j)$ differ by at most 1 and $e_\mu(i)$ and $e_\mu(j)$ differ by at most 1. By the Definition 4.3, the tree $\mathcal{T}_{31}{}^5$ is admits fuzzy quotient-3 cordial labeling and hence the tree $\mathcal{T}_{31}{}^5$ is fuzzy quotient-3 cordial graph.

Theorem 2: The tree $\mathcal{T}_{32}{}^5$ is fuzzy quotient-3 cordial graph.
Proof:
Consider the tree $\mathcal{T}_{32}{}^5$.
Let t_4 be the path, u_θ $(1 \leq \theta \leq m)$ be the m pendant edges attached through an edge $u\,t_2$ to first internal vertex t_2 of the path t_4 and v_κ^i $(1 \leq \kappa \leq n, 1 \leq i \leq 2)$ be the n path of length two attached to the second internal vertex t_3 of the path t_4.

Then the vertex set $V(\mathcal{T}_{32}{}^5) = \{t_h : 1 \leq h \leq 4\} \cup \{u\} \cup \{u_\theta : 1 \leq \theta \leq m\}$
$\cup \{v_\kappa{}^i : 1 \leq \kappa \leq n, 1 \leq i \leq 2\}$
and the edge set $E(\mathcal{T}_{32}{}^5) = \{t_h t_{h+1} : 1 \leq h \leq 3\} \cup \{t_2 u\} \cup \{u u_\theta : 1 \leq \theta \leq m\}$
$\cup \{t_3 v_\kappa{}^1 : 1 \leq \kappa \leq n\} \cup \{v_\kappa{}^1 v_\kappa{}^2, 1 \leq \kappa \leq n\}$.

$|V| = m + 2n + 5$ and $|E| = m + 2n + 4$.

We define $\sigma : V(\mathcal{T}_{32}{}^5) \rightarrow [0,1]$ by $\sigma(v) = \frac{\gamma}{10}, \gamma \in Z_4 - \{0\}$.

$\sigma(u) = 0.1$

The vertices of the path t_h, $1 \leq h \leq 4$ are labeled as

$\sigma(t_1) = 0.2$
$\sigma(t_2) = 0.1$
$\sigma(t_3) = 0.3$
and $\sigma(t_4) = 0.3$

The labeling $\sigma(u_\theta)$, $1 \leq \theta \leq m$ of m pendant edges attached to the first internal vertex t_2 of the path t_4 are as follows.

$\sigma(u_\theta) = 0.3$ *if* $\theta \equiv 1 \ (mod\ 3)$ *for* $1 \leq \theta \leq m$
$\sigma(u_\theta) = 0.1$ *if* $\theta \equiv 2 \ (mod\ 3)$ *for* $1 \leq \theta \leq m$
$\sigma(u_\theta) = 0.2$ *if* $\theta \equiv 0 \ (mod\ 3)$ *for* $1 \leq \theta \leq m$

The labeling $\sigma(v_\kappa^i), 1 \leq \kappa \leq n, 1 \leq i \leq 2$ of n path of length two attached to the second internal vertex t_3 of the path t_4 has following cases.

Case i: m ≡ 0 (mod 3)

$\sigma(v_\kappa^1) = 0.1$ *if* $\kappa \equiv 0 \ (mod\ 3)$ *for* $1 \leq \kappa \leq n$

$\sigma(v_\kappa^1) = 0.3$ *if* $\kappa \equiv 1, 2 \ (mod\ 3)$ *for* $1 \leq \kappa \leq n$

$$\sigma(v_\kappa^2)=0.2 \quad if\ \kappa\equiv 0,2\,(mod\,3) \quad for\ 1\le\kappa\le n$$

$$\sigma(v_\kappa^2)=0.3 \quad if\ \kappa\equiv 1\,(mod\,3) \quad for\ 1\le\kappa\le n$$

Case ii: m ≡ 1 (mod 3)

$$\sigma(v_\kappa^1)=0.1 \quad if\ \kappa\equiv 0\,(mod\,3) \quad for\ 1\le\kappa\le n$$

$$\sigma(v_\kappa^1)=0.3 \quad if\ \kappa\equiv 1,2\,(mod\,3) \quad for\ 1\le\kappa\le n$$

$$\sigma(v_\kappa^2)=0.2 \quad if\ \kappa\equiv 0,2\,(mod\,3) \quad for\ 1\le\kappa\le n$$

$$\sigma(v_\kappa^2)=0.3 \quad if\ \kappa\equiv 1\,(mod\,3) \quad for\ 1\le\kappa\le n$$

Case iii: m ≡ 2 (mod 3)

$$\sigma(v_\kappa^1)=0.1 \quad if\ \kappa\equiv 0\,(mod\,3) \quad for\ 1\le\kappa\le n$$

$$\sigma(v_\kappa^1)=0.3 \quad if\ \kappa\equiv 1,2\,(mod\,3) \quad for\ 1\le\kappa\le n$$

$$\sigma(v_\kappa^2)=0.2 \quad if\ \kappa\equiv 0,1\,(mod\,3) \quad for\ 1\le\kappa\le n$$

$$\sigma(v_\kappa^2)=0.1 \quad if\ \kappa\equiv 2\,(mod\,3) \quad for\ 1\le\kappa\le n$$

For $i \in \left\{\frac{\gamma}{10}, \gamma \in Z_4 - \{0\}\right\}$, $v_\sigma(i)$ and $e_\mu(i)$ are tabulated below.

It is clear from the Table 3.2 that for $i \neq j \in \left\{\frac{\gamma}{10}, \gamma \in Z_4 - \{0\}\right\}$ $v_\sigma(i)$ and $v_\sigma(j)$ differ by at most 1 and $e_\mu(i)$ and $e_\mu(j)$ differ by at most 1. By the Definition 4.3, the tree $\mathcal{T}_{32}{}^5$ is admits fuzzy quotient-3 cordial labeling and hence the tree $\mathcal{T}_{32}{}^5$ is fuzzy quotient-3 cordial graph.

Theorem 3: The tree is fuzzy quotient-3 cordial graph.

Proof:

Consider the tree $\mathcal{T}_{33}{}^5$.

Let t_4 be the path, $v_\kappa^i\,(1\le\kappa\le m, 1\le i\le 2)$ be the m path of length two attached to the first internal vertex t_2 of the path t_4 and $u_\theta\ (1\le\theta\le n)$ be the

Table 3.2 $v_\sigma(i)$ and $e_\mu(i)$ for the tree $\mathcal{T}_{32}{}^5$ $\left(i \in \left\{\frac{\gamma}{10}, \gamma \in Z_4 - \{0\}\right\}\right)$.

Nature of *m* and *n*	$v_\sigma(0.1)$	$v_\sigma(0.2)$	$v_\sigma(0.3)$	$e_\mu(0.1)$	$e_\mu(0.2)$	$e_\mu(0.3)$
$m \equiv 0(mod\ 3)$ $n \equiv 0(mod\ 3)$	$\frac{\vert V\vert+1}{3}$	$\frac{\vert V\vert+1}{3}$	$\frac{\vert V\vert+1}{3}-1$	$\frac{\vert V\vert+1}{3}-1$	$\frac{\vert V\vert+1}{3}$	$\frac{\vert V\vert+1}{3}-1$
$m \equiv 0(mod\ 3)$ $n \equiv 1(mod\ 3)$	$\frac{\vert V\vert-1}{3}+1$	$\frac{\vert V\vert-1}{3}$	$\frac{\vert V\vert-1}{3}$	$\frac{\vert V\vert-1}{3}$	$\frac{\vert V\vert-1}{3}$	$\frac{\vert V\vert-1}{3}$
$m \equiv 0(mod\ 3)$ $n \equiv 2(mod\ 3)$	$\frac{\vert V\vert}{3}$	$\frac{\vert V\vert}{3}$	$\frac{\vert V\vert}{3}$	$\frac{\vert V\vert}{3}-1$	$\frac{\vert V\vert}{3}$	$\frac{\vert V\vert}{3}$
$m \equiv 1(mod\ 3)$ $n \equiv 0(mod\ 3)$	$\frac{\vert V\vert}{3}$	$\frac{\vert V\vert}{3}$	$\frac{\vert V\vert}{3}$	$\frac{\vert V\vert}{3}$	$\frac{\vert V\vert}{3}$	$\frac{\vert V\vert}{3}-1$
$m \equiv 1(mod\ 3)$ $n \equiv 1(mod\ 3)$	$\frac{\vert V\vert+1}{3}$	$\frac{\vert V\vert+1}{3}-1$	$\frac{\vert V\vert+1}{3}$	$\frac{\vert V\vert+1}{3}$	$\frac{\vert V\vert+1}{3}-1$	$\frac{\vert V\vert+1}{3}-1$
$m \equiv 1(mod\ 3)$ $n \equiv 2(mod\ 3)$	$\frac{\vert V\vert-1}{3}$	$\frac{\vert V\vert-1}{3}$	$\frac{\vert V\vert-1}{3}+1$	$\frac{\vert V\vert-1}{3}$	$\frac{\vert V\vert-1}{3}$	$\frac{\vert V\vert-1}{3}$
$m \equiv 2(mod\ 3)$ $n \equiv 0(mod\ 3)$	$\frac{\vert V\vert-1}{3}+1$	$\frac{\vert V\vert-1}{3}$	$\frac{\vert V\vert-1}{3}$	$\frac{\vert V\vert-1}{3}$	$\frac{\vert V\vert-1}{3}$	$\frac{\vert V\vert-1}{3}$
$m \equiv 2(mod\ 3)$ $n \equiv 1(mod\ 3)$	$\frac{\vert V\vert}{3}$	$\frac{\vert V\vert}{3}$	$\frac{\vert V\vert}{3}$	$\frac{\vert V\vert}{3}-1$	$\frac{\vert V\vert}{3}$	$\frac{\vert V\vert}{3}$
$m \equiv 2(mod\ 3)$ $n \equiv 2(mod\ 3)$	$\frac{\vert V\vert+1}{3}$	$\frac{\vert V\vert+1}{3}-1$	$\frac{\vert V\vert+1}{3}$	$\frac{\vert V\vert+1}{3}-1$	$\frac{\vert V\vert+1}{3}-1$	$\frac{\vert V\vert+1}{3}$

n pendant edges attached through an edge $u\,t_3$ to second internal vertex t_3 of the path t_4 and

Then the vertex set $V(\mathcal{T}_{33}{}^5) = \{t_h : 1 \le h \le 4\} \cup \{u\} \cup \{u_\theta : 1 \le \theta \le n\}$
$\cup \{v_\kappa{}^i : 1 \le \kappa \le m,\ 1 \le i \le 2\}$

and the edge set $E(\mathcal{T}_{33}{}^5) = \{t_h t_{h+1} : 1 \le h \le 3\} \cup \{t_3 u\} \cup \{u u_\theta : 1 \le \theta \le n\}$
$\cup \{t_2 v_\kappa{}^1 : 1 \le \kappa \le m\} \cup \{v_\kappa{}^1 v_\kappa{}^2, 1 \le \kappa \le m\}$.

$|V| = m + 2n + 5$ and $|E| = m + 2n + 4$.

We define $\sigma : V(\mathcal{T}_{33}{}^{5}) \rightarrow [0,1]$ by $\sigma(v) = \frac{\gamma}{10}, \gamma \in Z_4 - \{0\}$.

$\sigma(u) = 0.1$

The vertices of the path t_h, $1 \leq h \leq 4$ are labeled as

$\sigma(t_1) = 0.3$
$\sigma(t_2) = 0.3$
$\sigma(t_3) = 0.1$
and $\sigma(t_4) = 0.2$

The labeling $\sigma(u_\theta)$, $1 \leq \theta \leq n$ of n pendant edges attached to the second internal vertex t_3 of the path t_4 are as follows.

$\sigma(u_\theta) = 0.3$ $\quad$ *if* $\theta \equiv 1\ (mod\ 3)$ $\quad$ *for* $1 \leq \theta \leq n$
$\sigma(u_\theta) = 0.1$ $\quad$ *if* $\theta \equiv 2\ (mod\ 3)$ $\quad$ *for* $1 \leq \theta \leq n$
$\sigma(u_\theta) = 0.2$ $\quad$ *if* $\theta \equiv 0\ (mod\ 3)$ $\quad$ *for* $1 \leq \theta \leq n$

The labeling $\sigma(v_\kappa^i), 1 \leq \kappa \leq m, 1 \leq i \leq 2$ of m path of length two attached to the first internal vertex t_2 of the path t_4 has following cases.

Case i:* $n \equiv 0$ *(mod 3)

$$\sigma(v_\kappa^1) = 0.1 \quad if\ \kappa \equiv 0\ (mod\ 3) \quad for\ 1 \leq \kappa \leq m$$

$$\sigma(v_\kappa^1) = 0.3 \quad if\ \kappa \equiv 1,2\ (mod\ 3) \quad for\ 1 \leq \kappa \leq m$$

$$\sigma(v_\kappa^2) = 0.2 \quad if\ \kappa \equiv 0,2\ (mod\ 3) \quad for\ 1 \leq \kappa \leq m$$

$$\sigma(v_\kappa^2) = 0.3 \quad if\ \kappa \equiv 1\ (mod\ 3) \quad for\ 1 \leq \kappa \leq m$$

Case ii:* $n \equiv 1$ *(mod 3)

$$\sigma(v_\kappa^1) = 0.1 \quad if\ \kappa \equiv 0\ (mod\ 3) \quad for\ 1 \leq \kappa \leq m$$

$$\sigma(v_\kappa^1) = 0.3 \quad if\ \kappa \equiv 1,2\ (mod\ 3) \quad for\ 1 \leq \kappa \leq m$$

$$\sigma(v_\kappa^2) = 0.2 \quad if\ \kappa \equiv 0,2\ (mod\ 3) \quad for\ 1 \leq \kappa \leq m$$

$$\sigma(v_{\kappa}^{2})=0.3 \quad if\ \kappa\equiv 1(mod\ 3) \quad for\ 1\leq\kappa\leq m$$

Case iii: n ≡ 2 (mod 3)

$$\sigma(v_{\kappa}^{1})=0.1 \quad if\ \kappa\equiv 0(mod\ 3) \quad for\ 1\leq\kappa\leq m$$

$$\sigma(v_{\kappa}^{1})=0.3 \quad if\ \kappa\equiv 1,2(mod\ 3) \quad for\ 1\leq\kappa\leq m$$

$$\sigma(v_{\kappa}^{2})=0.2 \quad if\ \kappa\equiv 0,1(mod\ 3) \quad for\ 1\leq\kappa\leq m$$

$$\sigma(v_{\kappa}^{2})=0.1 \quad if\ \kappa\equiv 2(mod\ 3) \quad for\ 1\leq\kappa\leq m$$

For $i\in\left\{\frac{\gamma}{10},\gamma\in Z_4-\{0\}\right\}$, $v_{\sigma}(i)$ and $e_{\mu}(i)$ are tabulated below.

It is clear from the Table 3.3 that for $i\neq j\in\left\{\frac{\gamma}{10},\gamma\in Z_4-\{0\}\right\}$ $v_{\sigma}(i)$ and $v_{\sigma}(j)$ differ by at most 1 and $e_{\mu}(i)$ and $e_{\mu}(j)$ differ by at most 1. By Definition 4.3, the tree $\mathcal{T}_{33}{}^5$ is admits fuzzy quotient-3 cordial labeling and hence the tree $\mathcal{T}_{33}{}^5$ is fuzzy quotient-3 cordial graph.

Theorem 4: The tree $\mathcal{T}_{34}{}^5$ is fuzzy quotient-3 cordial graph.

Proof:

Consider the tree $\mathcal{T}_{34}{}^5$

Let t_5 be the path, $u_{\theta}^{i}(1\leq\theta\leq m,1\leq i\leq 2)$ be the m path of length two attached to the first internal vertex t_2 of the path t_5 and $v_{\kappa}^{i}(1\leq\kappa\leq n,1\leq i\leq 2)$ be the n path of length two attached to the second internal vertex t_3 of the path t_5 and

Then the vertex set $V(\mathcal{T}_{34}{}^5) = \{t_h : 1 \leq h \leq 5\} \cup \{u_{\theta}{}^{i} : 1 \leq \theta \leq m,\ 1 \leq i \leq 2\}$
$\cup \{v_{\kappa}{}^{i} : 1 \leq \kappa \leq n,\ 1 \leq i \leq 2\}$.

and the edge set $E(\mathcal{T}_{34}{}^5) = \{t_h t_{h+1} : 1 \leq h \leq 4\} \cup \{t_2 u_{\theta}{}^1 : 1 \leq \theta \leq m\}$
$\cup \{u_{\theta}{}^1 u_{\theta}{}^2 : 1 \leq \theta \leq m\} \cup \{t_3 v_{\kappa}{}^1 : 1 \leq \kappa \leq n\}$
$\cup \{v_{\kappa}{}^1 v_{\kappa}{}^2 : 1 \leq \kappa \leq n\}$.

$|V| = 2m + 2n + 5$ and $|E| = 2m + 2n + 4$.

We define $\sigma : V(\mathcal{T}_{34}{}^5) \rightarrow [0,1]$ by $\sigma(v)=\frac{\gamma}{10},\gamma\in Z_4-\{0\}$.

The vertices of the path t_h, $1 \leq h \leq 5$ are labeled as

$\sigma(t_1) = 0.2$
$\sigma(t_2) = 0.1$
$\sigma(t_3) = 0.1$

Table 3.3 $v_\sigma(i)$ and $e_\mu(i)$ for the tree $\mathcal{T}_{33}{}^5$ $\left(i \in \left\{\frac{\gamma}{10}, \gamma \in Z_4 - \{0\}\right\}\right)$.

Nature of m and n	$v_\sigma(0.1)$	$v_\sigma(0.2)$	$v_\sigma(0.3)$	$e_\mu(0.1)$	$e_\mu(0.2)$	$e_\mu(0.3)$
$n \equiv 0(mod\ 3)$ $m \equiv 0(mod\ 3)$	$\frac{\lvert V\rvert+1}{3}$	$\frac{\lvert V\rvert+1}{3}$	$\frac{\lvert V\rvert+1}{3}-1$	$\frac{\lvert V\rvert+1}{3}-1$	$\frac{\lvert V\rvert+1}{3}$	$\frac{\lvert V\rvert+1}{3}-1$
$n \equiv 0(mod\ 3)$ $m \equiv 1(mod\ 3)$	$\frac{\lvert V\rvert-1}{3}+1$	$\frac{\lvert V\rvert-1}{3}$	$\frac{\lvert V\rvert-1}{3}$	$\frac{\lvert V\rvert-1}{3}$	$\frac{\lvert V\rvert-1}{3}$	$\frac{\lvert V\rvert-1}{3}$
$n \equiv 0(mod\ 3)$ $m \equiv 2(mod\ 3)$	$\frac{\lvert V\rvert}{3}$	$\frac{\lvert V\rvert}{3}$	$\frac{\lvert V\rvert}{3}$	$\frac{\lvert V\rvert}{3}-1$	$\frac{\lvert V\rvert}{3}$	$\frac{\lvert V\rvert}{3}$
$n \equiv 1(mod\ 3)$ $m \equiv 0(mod\ 3)$	$\frac{\lvert V\rvert}{3}$	$\frac{\lvert V\rvert}{3}$	$\frac{\lvert V\rvert}{3}$	$\frac{\lvert V\rvert}{3}$	$\frac{\lvert V\rvert}{3}$	$\frac{\lvert V\rvert}{3}-1$
$n \equiv 1(mod\ 3)$ $m \equiv 1(mod\ 3)$	$\frac{\lvert V\rvert+1}{3}$	$\frac{\lvert V\rvert+1}{3}-1$	$\frac{\lvert V\rvert+1}{3}$	$\frac{\lvert V\rvert+1}{3}$	$\frac{\lvert V\rvert+1}{3}-1$	$\frac{\lvert V\rvert+1}{3}-1$
$n \equiv 1(mod\ 3)$ $m \equiv 2(mod\ 3)$	$\frac{\lvert V\rvert-1}{3}$	$\frac{\lvert V\rvert-1}{3}$	$\frac{\lvert V\rvert-1}{3}+1$	$\frac{\lvert V\rvert-1}{3}$	$\frac{\lvert V\rvert-1}{3}$	$\frac{\lvert V\rvert-1}{3}$
$n \equiv 2(mod\ 3)$ $m \equiv 0(mod\ 3)$	$\frac{\lvert V\rvert-1}{3}+1$	$\frac{\lvert V\rvert-1}{3}$	$\frac{\lvert V\rvert-1}{3}$	$\frac{\lvert V\rvert-1}{3}$	$\frac{\lvert V\rvert-1}{3}$	$\frac{\lvert V\rvert-1}{3}$
$n \equiv 2(mod\ 3)$ $m \equiv 1(mod\ 3)$	$\frac{\lvert V\rvert}{3}$	$\frac{\lvert V\rvert}{3}$	$\frac{\lvert V\rvert}{3}$	$\frac{\lvert V\rvert}{3}-1$	$\frac{\lvert V\rvert}{3}$	$\frac{\lvert V\rvert}{3}$
$n \equiv 2(mod\ 3)$ $m \equiv 2(mod\ 3)$	$\frac{\lvert V\rvert+1}{3}$	$\frac{\lvert V\rvert+1}{3}-1$	$\frac{\lvert V\rvert+1}{3}$	$\frac{\lvert V\rvert+1}{3}-1$	$\frac{\lvert V\rvert+1}{3}-1$	$\frac{\lvert V\rvert+1}{3}$

$\sigma(t_4) = 0.3$
and $\sigma(t_5) = 0.2$

The labeling $\sigma\left(u_\theta^i\right), 1 \le \theta \le m, 1 \le i \le 2$ of m path of length two attached to the first internal vertex t_2 of the path t_5 are as follows.

$$\sigma\left(u_\theta^1\right) = 0.3 \quad if\ \theta \equiv 2\,(mod\ 3) \quad for\ 1 \le \theta \le m$$

$$\sigma\left(u_\theta^1\right) = 0.1 \quad if\ \theta \equiv 0,1\,(mod\ 3) \quad for\ 1 \le \theta \le m$$

$$\sigma\left(u_\theta^2\right)=0.2 \quad \text{if } \theta \equiv 0,2\,(mod\,3) \quad for\ 1\leq\theta\leq m$$

$$\sigma\left(u_\theta^2\right)=0.3 \quad \text{if } \theta \equiv 1\,(mod\,3) \quad for\ 1\leq\theta\leq m$$

The labeling $\sigma\left(v_\kappa^i\right), 1\leq\kappa\leq n, 1\leq i\leq 2$ of n path of length two attached to the second internal vertex t_3 of the path t_5 has following cases.

Case i: m ≡ 0 (mod 3)

$$\sigma\left(v_\kappa^1\right)=0.1 \quad \text{if } \kappa \equiv 0,1\,(mod\,3) \quad for\ 1\leq\kappa\leq n$$

$$\sigma\left(v_\kappa^1\right)=0.3 \quad \text{if } \kappa \equiv 2\,(mod\,3) \quad for\ 1\leq\kappa\leq n$$

$$\sigma\left(v_\kappa^2\right)=0.2 \quad \text{if } \kappa \equiv 0,2\,(mod\,3) \quad for\ 1\leq\kappa\leq n$$

$$\sigma\left(v_\kappa^2\right)=0.3 \quad \text{if } \kappa \equiv 1\,(mod\,3) \quad for\ 1\leq\kappa\leq n$$

Case ii: m ≡ 1 (mod 3)

$$\sigma\left(v_\kappa^1\right)=0.1 \quad \text{if } \kappa \equiv 0,2\,(mod\,3) \quad for\ 1\leq\kappa\leq n$$

$$\sigma\left(v_\kappa^1\right)=0.3 \quad \text{if } \kappa \equiv 1\,(mod\,3) \quad for\ 1\leq\kappa\leq n$$

$$\sigma\left(v_\kappa^2\right)=0.2 \quad \text{if } \kappa \equiv 1,2\,(mod\,3) \quad for\ 1\leq\kappa\leq n$$

$$\sigma\left(v_\kappa^2\right)=0.3 \quad \text{if } \kappa \equiv 0\,(mod\,3) \quad for\ 1\leq\kappa\leq n$$

Case iii: m ≡ 2 (mod 3)

$$\sigma\left(v_\kappa^1\right)=0.1 \quad \text{if } \kappa \equiv 1,2\,(mod\,3) \quad for\ 1\leq\kappa\leq n$$

$$\sigma\left(v_\kappa^1\right)=0.3 \quad \text{if } \kappa \equiv 0\,(mod\,3) \quad for\ 1\leq\kappa\leq n$$

$$\sigma\left(v_\kappa^2\right)=0.2 \quad \text{if } \kappa \equiv 0,1\,(mod\,3) \quad for\ 1\leq\kappa\leq n$$

$$\sigma\left(v_\kappa^2\right)=0.3 \quad if\ \kappa \equiv 2\,(mod\ 3) \quad for\ 1 \leq \kappa \leq n$$

For $i \in \left\{\frac{\gamma}{10}, \gamma \in Z_4 - \{0\}\right\}$, $v_\sigma(i)$ and $e_\mu(i)$ are tabulated below.

It is clear from the Table 3.4 that for $i \neq j \in \left\{\frac{\gamma}{10}, \gamma \in Z_4 - \{0\}\right\}$ $v_\sigma(i)$ and $v_\sigma(j)$ differ by at most 1 and $e_\mu(i)$ and $e_\mu(j)$ differ by at most 1. By Definition 4.3, the tree $\mathcal{T}_{34}{}^5$ is admits fuzzy quotient-3 cordial labeling and hence the tree $\mathcal{T}_{34}{}^5$ is fuzzy quotient-3 cordial graph.

Table 3.4 $v_\sigma(i)$ and $e_\mu(i)$ for the tree $\mathcal{T}_{34}{}^5$ $\left(i \in \left\{\frac{\gamma}{10}, \gamma \in Z_4 - \{0\}\right\}\right)$.

Nature of *m* and *n*	$v_\sigma(0.1)$	$v_\sigma(0.2)$	$v_\sigma(0.3)$	$e_\mu(0.1)$	$e_\mu(0.2)$	$e_\mu(0.3)$
$m \equiv 0(mod\ 3)$ $n \equiv 0(mod\ 3)$	$\frac{\lvert V\rvert+1}{3}$	$\frac{\lvert V\rvert+1}{3}$	$\frac{\lvert V\rvert+1}{3}-1$	$\frac{\lvert V\rvert+1}{3}-1$	$\frac{\lvert V\rvert+1}{3}$	$\frac{\lvert V\rvert+1}{3}-1$
$m \equiv 0(mod\ 3)$ $n \equiv 1(mod\ 3)$	$\frac{\lvert V\rvert-1}{3}+1$	$\frac{\lvert V\rvert-1}{3}$	$\frac{\lvert V\rvert-1}{3}$	$\frac{\lvert V\rvert-1}{3}$	$\frac{\lvert V\rvert-1}{3}$	$\frac{\lvert V\rvert-1}{3}$
$m \equiv 0(mod\ 3)$ $n \equiv 2(mod\ 3)$	$\frac{\lvert V\rvert}{3}$	$\frac{\lvert V\rvert}{3}$	$\frac{\lvert V\rvert}{3}$	$\frac{\lvert V\rvert}{3}$	$\frac{\lvert V\rvert}{3}$	$\frac{\lvert V\rvert}{3}-1$
$m \equiv 1(mod\ 3)$ $n \equiv 0(mod\ 3)$	$\frac{\lvert V\rvert-1}{3}+1$	$\frac{\lvert V\rvert-1}{3}$	$\frac{\lvert V\rvert-1}{3}$	$\frac{\lvert V\rvert-1}{3}$	$\frac{\lvert V\rvert-1}{3}$	$\frac{\lvert V\rvert-1}{3}$
$m \equiv 1(mod\ 3)$ $n \equiv 1(mod\ 3)$	$\frac{\lvert V\rvert}{3}$	$\frac{\lvert V\rvert}{3}$	$\frac{\lvert V\rvert}{3}$	$\frac{\lvert V\rvert}{3}$	$\frac{\lvert V\rvert}{3}$	$\frac{\lvert V\rvert}{3}-1$
$m \equiv 1(mod\ 3)$ $n \equiv 2(mod\ 3)$	$\frac{\lvert V\rvert+1}{3}$	$\frac{\lvert V\rvert+1}{3}$	$\frac{\lvert V\rvert+1}{3}-1$	$\frac{\lvert V\rvert+1}{3}-1$	$\frac{\lvert V\rvert+1}{3}$	$\frac{\lvert V\rvert+1}{3}-1$
$m \equiv 2(mod\ 3)$ $n \equiv 0(mod\ 3)$	$\frac{\lvert V\rvert}{3}$	$\frac{\lvert V\rvert}{3}$	$\frac{\lvert V\rvert}{3}$	$\frac{\lvert V\rvert}{3}$	$\frac{\lvert V\rvert}{3}$	$\frac{\lvert V\rvert}{3}-1$
$m \equiv 2(mod\ 3)$ $n \equiv 1(mod\ 3)$	$\frac{\lvert V\rvert+1}{3}$	$\frac{\lvert V\rvert+1}{3}$	$\frac{\lvert V\rvert+1}{3}-1$	$\frac{\lvert V\rvert+1}{3}-1$	$\frac{\lvert V\rvert+1}{3}$	$\frac{\lvert V\rvert+1}{3}-1$
$m \equiv 2(mod\ 3)$ $n \equiv 2(mod\ 3)$	$\frac{\lvert V\rvert-1}{3}+1$	$\frac{\lvert V\rvert-1}{3}$	$\frac{\lvert V\rvert-1}{3}$	$\frac{\lvert V\rvert-1}{3}$	$\frac{\lvert V\rvert-1}{3}$	$\frac{\lvert V\rvert-1}{3}$

Theorem 5: The tree $\mathcal{T}_{35}{}^5$ is fuzzy quotient-3 cordial graph.
Proof:
Consider the tree $\mathcal{T}_{35}{}^5$
Let t_5 be the path, $u_\theta^i (1 \le \theta \le m, 1 \le i \le 2)$ be the m path of length two attached to the second internal vertex t_3 of the path t_5 and $v_\kappa^i (1 \le \kappa \le n, 1 \le i \le 2)$ be the n path of length two attached to the third internal vertex t_4 of the path t_5 and
Then the vertex set $V(\mathcal{T}_{35}{}^5) = \{t_h : 1 \le h \le 5\} \cup \{u_\theta{}^i : 1 \le \theta \le m, 1 \le i \le 2\}$
$\cup \{v_\kappa{}^i : 1 \le \kappa \le n, 1 \le i \le 2\}$.
and the edge set $E(\mathcal{T}_{35}{}^5) = \{t_h t_{h+1} : 1 \le h \le 4\} \cup \{t_3 u_\theta{}^1 : 1 \le \theta \le m\}$
$\cup \{u_\theta{}^1 u_\theta{}^2 : 1 \le \theta \le m\} \cup \{t_4 v_\kappa{}^1 : 1 \le \kappa \le n\}$
$\cup \{v_\kappa{}^1 v_\kappa{}^2 : 1 \le \kappa \le n\}$.
$|V| = 2m + 2n + 5$ and $|E| = 2m + 2n + 4$.
We define $\sigma : V(\mathcal{T}_{35}{}^5) \rightarrow [0,1]$ by $\sigma(v) = \frac{\gamma}{10}, \gamma \in Z_4 - \{0\}$.
The vertices of the path t_h, $1 \le h \le 5$ are labeled as

$\sigma(t_1) = 0.2$
$\sigma(t_2) = 0.3$
$\sigma(t_3) = 0.1$
$\sigma(t_4) = 0.1$
and $\sigma(t_5) = 0.2$

The labeling $\sigma(u_\theta^i), 1 \le \theta \le m, 1 \le i \le 2)$ of m path of length two attached to the second internal vertex t_3 of the path t_5 are as follows.

$$\sigma(u_\theta^1) = 0.3 \quad \text{if } \theta \equiv 2 \pmod 3 \quad \text{for } 1 \le \theta \le m$$

$$\sigma(u_\theta^1) = 0.1 \quad \text{if } \theta \equiv 0,1 \pmod 3 \quad \text{for } 1 \le \theta \le m$$

$$\sigma(u_\theta^2) = 0.2 \quad \text{if } \theta \equiv 0,2 \pmod 3 \quad \text{for } 1 \le \theta \le m$$

$$\sigma(u_\theta^2) = 0.3 \quad \text{if } \theta \equiv 1 \pmod 3 \quad \text{for } 1 \le \theta \le m$$

The labeling $\sigma(v_\kappa^i), 1 \le \kappa \le n, 1 \le i \le 2$ of n path of length two attached to the third internal vertex t_4 of the path t_5 has following cases.

Case i: m ≡ 0 (mod 3)

$$\sigma(v_\kappa^1) = 0.1 \quad \text{if } \kappa \equiv 0,1 \pmod 3 \quad \text{for } 1 \le \kappa \le n$$

$$\sigma(v_\kappa^1) = 0.3 \quad \text{if } \kappa \equiv 2 \pmod 3 \quad \text{for } 1 \le \kappa \le n$$

$$\sigma\left(v_\kappa^2\right)=0.2 \quad if\ \kappa\equiv 0,2\,(mod\ 3) \quad for\ 1\le\kappa\le n$$

$$\sigma\left(v_\kappa^2\right)=0.3 \quad if\ \kappa\equiv 1\,(mod\ 3) \quad for\ 1\le\kappa\le n$$

Case ii: m ≡ 1 (mod 3)

$$\sigma\left(v_\kappa^1\right)=0.1 \quad if\ \kappa\equiv 0,2\,(mod\ 3) \quad for\ 1\le\kappa\le n$$

$$\sigma\left(v_\kappa^1\right)=0.3 \quad if\ \kappa\equiv 1\,(mod\ 3) \quad for\ 1\le\kappa\le n$$

$$\sigma\left(v_\kappa^2\right)=0.2 \quad if\ \kappa\equiv 1,2\,(mod\ 3) \quad for\ 1\le\kappa\le n$$

$$\sigma\left(v_\kappa^2\right)=0.3 \quad if\ \kappa\equiv 0\,(mod\ 3) \quad for\ 1\le\kappa\le n$$

Case iii: m ≡ 2 (mod 3)

$$\sigma\left(v_\kappa^1\right)=0.1 \quad if\ \kappa\equiv 1,2\,(mod\ 3) \quad for\ 1\le\kappa\le n$$

$$\sigma\left(v_\kappa^1\right)=0.3 \quad if\ \kappa\equiv 0\,(mod\ 3) \quad for\ 1\le\kappa\le n$$

$$\sigma\left(v_\kappa^2\right)=0.2 \quad if\ \kappa\equiv 0,1\,(mod\ 3) \quad for\ 1\le\kappa\le n$$

$$\sigma\left(v_\kappa^2\right)=0.3 \quad if\ \kappa\equiv 2\,(mod\ 3) \quad for\ 1\le\kappa\le n$$

For $i \in \left\{\frac{\gamma}{10}, \gamma \in Z_4 - \{0\}\right\}$, $v_\sigma(i)$ and $e_\mu(i)$ are tabulated below.

It is clear from Table 3.5 that for $i \neq j \in \left\{\frac{\gamma}{10}, \gamma \in Z_4 - \{0\}\right\}$ $v_\sigma(i)$ and $v_\sigma(j)$ differ by at most 1 and $e_\mu(i)$ and $e_\mu(j)$ differ by at most 1. By Definition 4.3, the tree $\mathcal{T}_{35}{}^5$ is admits fuzzy quotient-3 cordial labeling and hence the tree $\mathcal{T}_{35}{}^5$ is fuzzy quotient-3 cordial graph.

Theorem 6: The tree $\mathcal{T}_{36}{}^5$ is fuzzy quotient-3 cordial graph.
Proof:
Consider the tree $\mathcal{T}_{36}{}^5$.

Table 3.5 $v_\sigma(i)$ and $e_\mu(i)$ for the tree $\mathcal{T}_{35}{}^5\left(i \in \left\{\frac{\gamma}{10}, \gamma \in Z_4 - \{0\}\right\}\right)$.

Nature of *m* and *n*	$v_\sigma(0.1)$	$v_\sigma(0.2)$	$v_\sigma(0.3)$	$e_\mu(0.1)$	$e_\mu(0.2)$	$e_\mu(0.3)$
$m \equiv 0(mod\,3)$ $n \equiv 0(mod\,3)$	$\frac{\lvert V\rvert+1}{3}$	$\frac{\lvert V\rvert+1}{3}$	$\frac{\lvert V\rvert+1}{3}-1$	$\frac{\lvert V\rvert+1}{3}-1$	$\frac{\lvert V\rvert+1}{3}$	$\frac{\lvert V\rvert+1}{3}-1$
$m \equiv 0(mod\,3)$ $n \equiv 1(mod\,3)$	$\frac{\lvert V\rvert-1}{3}+1$	$\frac{\lvert V\rvert-1}{3}$	$\frac{\lvert V\rvert-1}{3}$	$\frac{\lvert V\rvert-1}{3}$	$\frac{\lvert V\rvert-1}{3}$	$\frac{\lvert V\rvert-1}{3}$
$m \equiv 0(mod\,3)$ $n \equiv 2(mod\,3)$	$\frac{\lvert V\rvert}{3}$	$\frac{\lvert V\rvert}{3}$	$\frac{\lvert V\rvert}{3}$	$\frac{\lvert V\rvert}{3}$	$\frac{\lvert V\rvert}{3}$	$\frac{\lvert V\rvert}{3}-1$
$m \equiv 1(mod\,3)$ $n \equiv 0(mod\,3)$	$\frac{\lvert V\rvert-1}{3}+1$	$\frac{\lvert V\rvert-1}{3}$	$\frac{\lvert V\rvert-1}{3}$	$\frac{\lvert V\rvert-1}{3}$	$\frac{\lvert V\rvert-1}{3}$	$\frac{\lvert V\rvert-1}{3}$
$m \equiv 1(mod\,3)$ $n \equiv 1(mod\,3)$	$\frac{\lvert V\rvert}{3}$	$\frac{\lvert V\rvert}{3}$	$\frac{\lvert V\rvert}{3}$	$\frac{\lvert V\rvert}{3}$	$\frac{\lvert V\rvert}{3}$	$\frac{\lvert V\rvert}{3}-1$
$m \equiv 1(mod\,3)$ $n \equiv 2(mod\,3)$	$\frac{\lvert V\rvert+1}{3}$	$\frac{\lvert V\rvert+1}{3}$	$\frac{\lvert V\rvert+1}{3}-1$	$\frac{\lvert V\rvert+1}{3}-1$	$\frac{\lvert V\rvert+1}{3}$	$\frac{\lvert V\rvert+1}{3}-1$
$m \equiv 2(mod\,3)$ $n \equiv 0(mod\,3)$	$\frac{\lvert V\rvert}{3}$	$\frac{\lvert V\rvert}{3}$	$\frac{\lvert V\rvert}{3}$	$\frac{\lvert V\rvert}{3}$	$\frac{\lvert V\rvert}{3}$	$\frac{\lvert V\rvert}{3}-1$
$m \equiv 2(mod\,3)$ $n \equiv 1(mod\,3)$	$\frac{\lvert V\rvert+1}{3}$	$\frac{\lvert V\rvert+1}{3}$	$\frac{\lvert V\rvert+1}{3}-1$	$\frac{\lvert V\rvert+1}{3}-1$	$\frac{\lvert V\rvert+1}{3}$	$\frac{\lvert V\rvert+1}{3}-1$
$m \equiv 2(mod\,3)$ $n \equiv 2(mod\,3)$	$\frac{\lvert V\rvert-1}{3}+1$	$\frac{\lvert V\rvert-1}{3}$	$\frac{\lvert V\rvert-1}{3}$	$\frac{\lvert V\rvert-1}{3}$	$\frac{\lvert V\rvert-1}{3}$	$\frac{\lvert V\rvert-1}{3}$

Let t_4 be the path, u_θ $(1 \leq \theta \leq m)$ be the m pendant edges attached to the first internal vertex t_2 of the path t_4 and v_κ $(1 \leq \kappa \leq n)$ be the n pendant edges attached through a path of length two to the second internal vertex t_3 of the path t_4.

Then the vertex set $V(\mathcal{T}_{36}{}^5) = \{t_h : 1 \leq h \leq 4\} \cup \{u_\theta : 1 \leq \theta \leq m\}$

$$\cup \{v_\kappa : 1 \leq \kappa \leq n\} \cup \{u, v\}$$

and the edge set

$E(\mathcal{T}_{36}{}^5) = \{t_h t_{h+1} : 1 \le h \le 3\} \cup \{t_2 u_\theta : 1 \le \theta \le m\} \cup \{t_3 u, uv\}$
$\cup \{uv_\kappa : 1 \le \kappa \le n\}$.

$|V| = m + n + 6$ and $|E| = m + n + 5$.

We define $\sigma : V(\mathcal{T}_{36}{}^5) \to [0,1]$ by $\sigma(v) = \frac{\gamma}{10}, \gamma \in Z_4 - \{0\}$.

$\sigma(u) = 0.3$
$\sigma(v) = 0.1$

The vertices of the path t_h, $1 \le h \le 4$ are labeled as

$\sigma(t_1) = 0.2$
$\sigma(t_2) = 0.1$
$\sigma(t_3) = 0.3$
and $\sigma(t_4) = 0.2$

The labeling $\sigma(u_\theta)$, $1 \le \theta \le m$, of m pendant edges attached to the first internal vertex t_2 of the path t_4 are as follows.

$\sigma(u_\theta) = 0.1$ *if* $\theta \equiv 1 \ (mod\ 3)$ *for* $1 \le \theta \le m$
$\sigma(u_\theta) = 0.2$ *if* $\theta \equiv 2 \ (mod\ 3)$ *for* $1 \le \theta \le m$
$\sigma(u_\theta) = 0.3$ *if* $\theta \equiv 0 \ (mod\ 3)$ *for* $1 \le \theta \le m$

The labeling $\sigma(v_\kappa^i), 1 \le \kappa \le n, 1 \le i \le 2$ of n pendant edges attached through a path of length two to the second internal vertex t_3 of the path t_4 has following cases.

Case i: m ≡ 0 (mod 3)

$\sigma(v_\kappa) = 0.1$ *if* $\kappa \equiv 1 \ (mod\ 3)$ *for* $1 \le \kappa \le n$
$\sigma(v_\kappa) = 0.2$ *if* $\kappa \equiv 2 \ (mod\ 3)$ *for* $1 \le \kappa \le n$
$\sigma(v_\kappa) = 0.3$ *if* $\kappa \equiv 0 \ (mod\ 3)$ *for* $1 \le \kappa \le n$

Case ii: m ≡ 1 (mod 3)

$\sigma(v_\kappa) = 0.1$ *if* $\kappa \equiv 0 \ (mod\ 3)$ *for* $1 \le \kappa \le n$
$\sigma(v_\kappa) = 0.2$ *if* $\kappa \equiv 2 \ (mod\ 3)$ *for* $1 \le \kappa \le n$
$\sigma(v_\kappa) = 0.3$ *if* $\kappa \equiv 1 \ (mod\ 3)$ *for* $1 \le \kappa \le n$

Case iii: m ≡ 2 (mod 3)

$\sigma(v_\kappa) = 0.1$ *if* $\kappa \equiv 0 \ (mod\ 3)$ *for* $1 \le \kappa \le n$
$\sigma(v_\kappa) = 0.2$ *if* $\kappa \equiv 1 \ (mod\ 3)$ *for* $1 \le \kappa \le n$
$\sigma(v_\kappa) = 0.3$ *if* $\kappa \equiv 2 \ (mod\ 3)$ *for* $1 \le \kappa \le n$

For $i \in \left\{\frac{\gamma}{10}, \gamma \in Z_4 - \{0\}\right\}$, $v_\sigma(i)$ and $e_\mu(i)$ are tabulated below.

Table 3.6 $v_\sigma(i)$ and $e_\mu(i)$ for the tree $\mathcal{T}_{36}{}^5 \left(i \in \left\{\frac{\gamma}{10}, \gamma \in Z_4 - \{0\}\right\}\right)$.

Nature of *m* and *n*	$v_\sigma(0.1)$	$v_\sigma(0.2)$	$v_\sigma(0.3)$	$e_\mu(0.1)$	$e_\mu(0.2)$	$e_\mu(0.3)$
$m \equiv 0(mod\ 3)$ $n \equiv 0(mod\ 3)$	$\frac{\lvert V\rvert}{3}$	$\frac{\lvert V\rvert}{3}$	$\frac{\lvert V\rvert}{3}$	$\frac{\lvert V\rvert}{3}$	$\frac{\lvert V\rvert}{3}$	$\frac{\lvert V\rvert}{3}-1$
$m \equiv 0(mod\ 3)$ $n \equiv 1(mod\ 3)$	$\frac{\lvert V\rvert-1}{3}+1$	$\frac{\lvert V\rvert-1}{3}$	$\frac{\lvert V\rvert-1}{3}$	$\frac{\lvert V\rvert-1}{3}$	$\frac{\lvert V\rvert-1}{3}$	$\frac{\lvert V\rvert-1}{3}$
$m \equiv 0(mod\ 3)$ $n \equiv 2(mod\ 3)$	$\frac{\lvert V\rvert+1}{3}$	$\frac{\lvert V\rvert+1}{3}$	$\frac{\lvert V\rvert+1}{3}-1$	$\frac{\lvert V\rvert+1}{3}-1$	$\frac{\lvert V\rvert+1}{3}$	$\frac{\lvert V\rvert+1}{3}-1$
$m \equiv 1(mod\ 3)$ $n \equiv 0(mod\ 3)$	$\frac{\lvert V\rvert-1}{3}+1$	$\frac{\lvert V\rvert-1}{3}$	$\frac{\lvert V\rvert-1}{3}$	$\frac{\lvert V\rvert-1}{3}$	$\frac{\lvert V\rvert-1}{3}$	$\frac{\lvert V\rvert-1}{3}$
$m \equiv 1(mod\ 3)$ $n \equiv 1(mod\ 3)$	$\frac{\lvert V\rvert+1}{3}$	$\frac{\lvert V\rvert+1}{3}-1$	$\frac{\lvert V\rvert+1}{3}$	$\frac{\lvert V\rvert+1}{3}$	$\frac{\lvert V\rvert+1}{3}-1$	$\frac{\lvert V\rvert+1}{3}-1$
$m \equiv 1(mod\ 3)$ $n \equiv 2(mod\ 3)$	$\frac{\lvert V\rvert}{3}$	$\frac{\lvert V\rvert}{3}$	$\frac{\lvert V\rvert}{3}$	$\frac{\lvert V\rvert}{3}$	$\frac{\lvert V\rvert}{3}$	$\frac{\lvert V\rvert}{3}-1$
$m \equiv 2(mod\ 3)$ $n \equiv 0(mod\ 3)$	$\frac{\lvert V\rvert+1}{3}$	$\frac{\lvert V\rvert+1}{3}-1$	$\frac{\lvert V\rvert+1}{3}$	$\frac{\lvert V\rvert+1}{3}$	$\frac{\lvert V\rvert+1}{3}-1$	$\frac{\lvert V\rvert+1}{3}-1$
$m \equiv 2(mod\ 3)$ $n \equiv 1(mod\ 3)$	$\frac{\lvert V\rvert}{3}$	$\frac{\lvert V\rvert}{3}$	$\frac{\lvert V\rvert}{3}$	$\frac{\lvert V\rvert}{3}$	$\frac{\lvert V\rvert}{3}$	$\frac{\lvert V\rvert}{3}-1$
$m \equiv 2(mod\ 3)$ $n \equiv 2(mod\ 3)$	$\frac{\lvert V\rvert-1}{3}$	$\frac{\lvert V\rvert-1}{3}$	$\frac{\lvert V\rvert-1}{3}+1$	$\frac{\lvert V\rvert-1}{3}$	$\frac{\lvert V\rvert-1}{3}$	$\frac{\lvert V\rvert-1}{3}$

It is clear from Table 3.6 that for $i \neq j \in \left\{\frac{\gamma}{10}, \gamma \in Z_4 - \{0\}\right\}$ $v_\sigma(i)$ and $v_\sigma(j)$ differ by at most 1 and $e_\mu(i)$ and $e_\mu(j)$ differ by at most 1. By Definition 4.3, the tree $\mathcal{T}_{36}{}^5$ is admits fuzzy quotient-3 cordial labeling and hence the tree $\mathcal{T}_{36}{}^5$ is fuzzy quotient-3 cordial graph.

Theorem 7: The tree $\mathcal{T}_{37}{}^5$ is fuzzy quotient-3 cordial graph.
Proof:
Consider the tree $\mathcal{T}_{37}{}^5$.

Let t_4 be the path, $v_\kappa (1 \leq \kappa \leq m)$ be the m pendant edges attached through a path of length two to the first internal vertex t_2 of the path t_4 and u_θ $(1 \leq \theta \leq n)$ be the n pendant edges attached to the second internal vertex t_3 of the path t_4.

Then the vertex set $V(\mathcal{T}_{37}{}^5) = \{t_h : 1 \leq h \leq 4\} \cup \{u_\theta : 1 \leq \theta \leq n\}$
$\cup \{v_\kappa : 1 \leq \kappa \leq m\} \cup \{u, v\}$

and the edge set $E(\mathcal{T}_{37}{}^5) = \{t_h t_{h+1} : 1 \leq h \leq 3\} \cup \{t_3 u_\theta : 1 \leq \theta \leq m\} \cup \{t_2 u, uv\}$
$\cup \{uv_\kappa : 1 \leq \kappa \leq m\}$.

$|V| = m + n + 6$ and $|E| = m + n + 5$.

We define $\sigma : V(\mathcal{T}_{37}{}^5) \to [0,1]$ by $\sigma(v) = \frac{\gamma}{10}, \gamma \in Z_4 - \{0\}$.

$\sigma(u) = 0.3$
$\sigma(v) = 0.1$

The vertices of the path t_h, $1 \leq h \leq 4$ are labeled as

$\sigma(t_1) = 0.2$
$\sigma(t_2) = 0.3$
$\sigma(t_3) = 0.1$
and $\sigma(t_4) = 0.2$

The labeling $\sigma(u_\theta)$, $1 \leq \theta \leq n$, of n pendant edges attached to the second internal vertex t_3 of the path t_4 are as follows.

$\sigma(u_\theta) = 0.1$	*if* $\theta \equiv 1 \ (mod\ 3)$	*for* $1 \leq \theta \leq n$
$\sigma(u_\theta) = 0.2$	*if* $\theta \equiv 2 \ (mod\ 3)$	*for* $1 \leq \theta \leq n$
$\sigma(u_\theta) = 0.3$	*if* $\theta \equiv 0 \ (mod\ 3)$	*for* $1 \leq \theta \leq n$

The labeling $\sigma(v_\kappa^i), 1 \leq \kappa \leq m, 1 \leq i \leq 2$ of m path of length two attached to the first internal vertex t_2 of the path t_4 has following cases.

Case i: $n \equiv 0 \ (mod\ 3)$

$\sigma(v_\kappa) = 0.1$	*if* $\kappa \equiv 1 \ (mod\ 3)$	*for* $1 \leq \kappa \leq m$
$\sigma(v_\kappa) = 0.2$	*if* $\kappa \equiv 2 \ (mod\ 3)$	*for* $1 \leq \kappa \leq m$
$\sigma(v_\kappa) = 0.3$	*if* $\kappa \equiv 0 \ (mod\ 3)$	*for* $1 \leq \kappa \leq m$

Case ii: $n \equiv 1 \ (mod\ 3)$

$\sigma(v_\kappa) = 0.1$	*if* $\kappa \equiv 0 \ (mod\ 3)$	*for* $1 \leq \kappa \leq m$
$\sigma(v_\kappa) = 0.2$	*if* $\kappa \equiv 2 \ (mod\ 3)$	*for* $1 \leq \kappa \leq m$
$\sigma(v_\kappa) = 0.3$	*if* $\kappa \equiv 1 \ (mod\ 3)$	*for* $1 \leq \kappa \leq m$

Case iii: $n \equiv 2 \ (mod\ 3)$

$\sigma(v_\kappa) = 0.1$	*if* $\kappa \equiv 0 \ (mod\ 3)$	*for* $1 \leq \kappa \leq m$

$\sigma(v_\kappa) = 0.2$ $\quad$ *if* $\kappa \equiv 1\ (mod\ 3)$ $\quad$ *for* $1 \le \kappa \le m$
$\sigma(v_\kappa) = 0.3$ $\quad$ *if* $\kappa \equiv 2\ (mod\ 3)$ $\quad$ *for* $1 \le \kappa \le m$

For $i \in \left\{\frac{\gamma}{10}, \gamma \in Z_4 - \{0\}\right\}$, $v_\sigma(i)$ and $e_\mu(i)$ are tabulated below.

It is clear from Table 3.7 that for $i \neq j \in \left\{\frac{\gamma}{10}, \gamma \in Z_4 - \{0\}\right\}$ $v_\sigma(i)$ and $v_\sigma(j)$ differ by at most 1 and $e_\mu(i)$ and $e_\mu(j)$ differ by at most 1. By Definition 4.3, the tree $\mathcal{T}_{37^5}$ is admits fuzzy quotient-3 cordial labeling and hence the tree $\mathcal{T}_{37^5}$ is fuzzy quotient-3 cordial graph.

Table 3.7 $v_\sigma(i)$ and $e_\mu(i)$ for the tree $\mathcal{T}_{37^5}$ $\left(i \in \left\{\frac{\gamma}{10}, \gamma \in Z_4 - \{0\}\right\}\right)$.

Nature of *m* and *n*	$v_\sigma(0.1)$	$v_\sigma(0.2)$	$v_\sigma(0.3)$	$e_\mu(0.1)$	$e_\mu(0.2)$	$e_\mu(0.3)$
$n \equiv 0(mod\ 3)$ $m \equiv 0(mod\ 3)$	$\frac{\lvert V\rvert}{3}$	$\frac{\lvert V\rvert}{3}$	$\frac{\lvert V\rvert}{3}$	$\frac{\lvert V\rvert}{3}$	$\frac{\lvert V\rvert}{3}$	$\frac{\lvert V\rvert}{3}-1$
$n \equiv 0(mod\ 3)$ $m \equiv 1(mod\ 3)$	$\frac{\lvert V\rvert-1}{3}+1$	$\frac{\lvert V\rvert-1}{3}$	$\frac{\lvert V\rvert-1}{3}$	$\frac{\lvert V\rvert-1}{3}$	$\frac{\lvert V\rvert-1}{3}$	$\frac{\lvert V\rvert-1}{3}$
$n \equiv 0(mod\ 3)$ $m \equiv 2(mod\ 3)$	$\frac{\lvert V\rvert+1}{3}$	$\frac{\lvert V\rvert+1}{3}$	$\frac{\lvert V\rvert+1}{3}-1$	$\frac{\lvert V\rvert+1}{3}-1$	$\frac{\lvert V\rvert+1}{3}$	$\frac{\lvert V\rvert+1}{3}-1$
$n \equiv 1(mod\ 3)$ $m \equiv 0(mod\ 3)$	$\frac{\lvert V\rvert-1}{3}+1$	$\frac{\lvert V\rvert-1}{3}$	$\frac{\lvert V\rvert-1}{3}$	$\frac{\lvert V\rvert-1}{3}$	$\frac{\lvert V\rvert-1}{3}$	$\frac{\lvert V\rvert-1}{3}$
$n \equiv 1(mod\ 3)$ $m \equiv 1(mod\ 3)$	$\frac{\lvert V\rvert+1}{3}$	$\frac{\lvert V\rvert+1}{3}-1$	$\frac{\lvert V\rvert+1}{3}$	$\frac{\lvert V\rvert+1}{3}$	$\frac{\lvert V\rvert+1}{3}-1$	$\frac{\lvert V\rvert+1}{3}-1$
$n \equiv 1(mod\ 3)$ $m \equiv 2(mod\ 3)$	$\frac{\lvert V\rvert}{3}$	$\frac{\lvert V\rvert}{3}$	$\frac{\lvert V\rvert}{3}$	$\frac{\lvert V\rvert}{3}$	$\frac{\lvert V\rvert}{3}$	$\frac{\lvert V\rvert}{3}-1$
$n \equiv 2(mod\ 3)$ $m \equiv 0(mod\ 3)$	$\frac{\lvert V\rvert+1}{3}$	$\frac{\lvert V\rvert+1}{3}-1$	$\frac{\lvert V\rvert+1}{3}$	$\frac{\lvert V\rvert+1}{3}$	$\frac{\lvert V\rvert+1}{3}-1$	$\frac{\lvert V\rvert+1}{3}-1$
$n \equiv 2(mod\ 3)$ $m \equiv 1(mod\ 3)$	$\frac{\lvert V\rvert}{3}$	$\frac{\lvert V\rvert}{3}$	$\frac{\lvert V\rvert}{3}$	$\frac{\lvert V\rvert}{3}$	$\frac{\lvert V\rvert}{3}$	$\frac{\lvert V\rvert}{3}-1$
$n \equiv 2(mod\ 3)$ $m \equiv 2(mod\ 3)$	$\frac{\lvert V\rvert-1}{3}$	$\frac{\lvert V\rvert-1}{3}$	$\frac{\lvert V\rvert-1}{3}+1$	$\frac{\lvert V\rvert-1}{3}$	$\frac{\lvert V\rvert-1}{3}$	$\frac{\lvert V\rvert-1}{3}$

Theorem 8: The tree $\mathcal{T}_{38^5}$ is fuzzy quotient-3 cordial graph.
Proof:
Consider the tree $\mathcal{T}_{38^5}$.
Let t_4 be the path, u_θ $(1 \le \theta \le m)$ be the m pendant edges attached to the first internal vertex t_2 of the path t_4 and $v_\kappa^i (1 \le \kappa \le n, 1 \le i \le 2)$ be the n path of length two attached through an edge to the second internal vertex t_3 of the path t_4.
Then the vertex set $V(\mathcal{T}_{38^5}) = \{t_h : 1 \le h \le 4\} \cup \{u_\theta : 1 \le \theta \le m\} \cup \{v\}$

$\cup \{v_\kappa{}^i : 1 \le \kappa \le n, 1 \le i \le 2\}$

and the edge set $E(\mathcal{T}_{38^5}) = \{t_h t_{h+1} : 1 \le h \le 3\} \cup \{t_2 u_\theta : 1 \le \theta \le m\} \cup \{t_3 v\}$

$\cup \{u v_\kappa{}^1 : 1 \le \kappa \le n\} \cup \{v_\kappa{}^1 v_\kappa{}^2, 1 \le \kappa \le n\}$.

$|V| = m + 2n + 5$ and $|E| = m + 2n + 4$.
We define $\sigma : V(\mathcal{T}_{38^5}) \to [0,1]$ by $\sigma(v) = \frac{\gamma}{10}, \gamma \in Z_4 - \{0\}$.

$\sigma(v) = 0.3$

The vertices of the path t_h, $1 \le h \le 4$ are labeled as

$\sigma(t_1) = 0.2$
$\sigma(t_2) = 0.1$
$\sigma(t_3) = 0.3$
and $\sigma(t_4) = 0.2$

The labeling $\sigma(u_\theta)$, $1 \le \theta \le m$, of m pendant edges attached to the first internal vertex t_2 of the path t_4 are as follows.

$\sigma(u_\theta) = 0.1$	*if* $\theta \equiv 1 \ (mod\ 3)$	*for* $1 \le \theta \le m$
$\sigma(u_\theta) = 0.2$	*if* $\theta \equiv 0 \ (mod\ 3)$	*for* $1 \le \theta \le m$
$\sigma(u_\theta) = 0.3$	*if* $\theta \equiv 2 \ (mod\ 3)$	*for* $1 \le \theta \le m$

The labeling $\sigma(v_\kappa^i), 1 \le \kappa \le n, 1 \le i \le 2$ of n path of length two attached through an edge to the second internal vertex t_3 of the path t_4 has following cases.

Case i: m ≡ 0 (mod 3)

$$\sigma(v_\kappa^1) = 0.1 \quad if\ \kappa \equiv 2\ (mod\ 3) \quad for\ 1 \le \kappa \le n$$

$$\sigma(v_\kappa^1) = 0.3 \quad if\ \kappa \equiv 0,1\ (mod\ 3) \quad for\ 1 \le \kappa \le n$$

$$\sigma(v_\kappa^2) = 0.1 \quad if\ \kappa \equiv 1\ (mod\ 3) \quad for\ 1 \le \kappa \le n$$

$$\sigma(v_\kappa^2) = 0.2 \quad if\ \kappa \equiv 0,2\ (mod\ 3) \quad for\ 1 \leq \kappa \leq n$$

Case ii: m ≡ 1 (mod 3)

$$\sigma(v_\kappa^1) = 0.1 \quad if\ \kappa \equiv 2\ (mod\ 3) \quad for\ 1 \leq \kappa \leq n$$

$$\sigma(v_\kappa^1) = 0.3 \quad if\ \kappa \equiv 0,1\ (mod\ 3) \quad for\ 1 \leq \kappa \leq n$$

$$\sigma(v_\kappa^2) = 0.1 \quad if\ \kappa \equiv 1\ (mod\ 3) \quad for\ 1 \leq \kappa \leq n$$

$$\sigma(v_\kappa^2) = 0.2 \quad if\ \kappa \equiv 0,2\ (mod\ 3) \quad for\ 1 \leq \kappa \leq n$$

Case iii: m ≡ 2 (mod 3)

$$\sigma(v_\kappa^1) = 0.1 \quad if\ \kappa \equiv 1\ (mod\ 3) \quad for\ 1 \leq \kappa \leq n$$

$$\sigma(v_\kappa^1) = 0.3 \quad if\ \kappa \equiv 0,2\ (mod\ 3) \quad for\ 1 \leq \kappa \leq n$$

$$\sigma(v_\kappa^2) = 0.1 \quad if\ \kappa \equiv 2\ (mod\ 3) \quad for\ 1 \leq \kappa \leq n$$

$$\sigma(v_\kappa^2) = 0.2 \quad if\ \kappa \equiv 0,1\ (mod\ 3) \quad for\ 1 \leq \kappa \leq n$$

For $i \in \left\{\frac{\gamma}{10}, \gamma \in Z_4 - \{0\}\right\}$, $v_\sigma(i)$ and $e_\mu(i)$ are tabulated below.

It is clear from Table 3.8 that for $i \neq j \in \left\{\frac{\gamma}{10}, \gamma \in Z_4 - \{0\}\right\}$ $v_\sigma(i)$ and $v_\sigma(j)$ differ by at most 1 and $e_\mu(i)$ and $e_\mu(j)$ differ by at most 1. By Definition 4.3, the tree $\mathcal{T}_{38}{}^5$ is admits fuzzy quotient-3 cordial labeling and hence the tree $\mathcal{T}_{38}{}^5$ is fuzzy quotient-3 cordial graph.

Theorem 9: The tree $\mathcal{T}_{39}{}^5$ is fuzzy quotient-3 cordial graph.

Proof:

Consider the tree $\mathcal{T}_{39}{}^5$.

Let t_4 be the path, $v_\kappa^i (1 \leq \kappa \leq m, 1 \leq i \leq 2)$ be the m path of length two attached through an edge to the first internal vertex t_3 of the path t_4 and u_θ

Table 3.8 $v_\sigma(i)$ and $e_\mu(i)$ for the tree $\mathcal{T}_{38}{}^5\left(i \in \left\{\frac{\gamma}{10}, \gamma \in Z_4 - \{0\}\right\}\right)$.

Nature of *m* and *n*	$v_\sigma(0.1)$	$v_\sigma(0.2)$	$v_\sigma(0.3)$	$e_\mu(0.1)$	$e_\mu(0.2)$	$e_\mu(0.3)$
$m \equiv 0(mod\ 3)$ $n \equiv 0(mod\ 3)$	$\frac{\lvert V\rvert+1}{3}-1$	$\frac{\lvert V\rvert+1}{3}$	$\frac{\lvert V\rvert+1}{3}$	$\frac{\lvert V\rvert+1}{3}-1$	$\frac{\lvert V\rvert+1}{3}$	$\frac{\lvert V\rvert+1}{3}-1$
$m \equiv 0(mod\ 3)$ $n \equiv 1(mod\ 3)$	$\frac{\lvert V\rvert-1}{3}$	$\frac{\lvert V\rvert-1}{3}$	$\frac{\lvert V\rvert-1}{3}+1$	$\frac{\lvert V\rvert-1}{3}$	$\frac{\lvert V\rvert-1}{3}$	$\frac{\lvert V\rvert-1}{3}$
$m \equiv 0(mod\ 3)$ $n \equiv 2(mod\ 3)$	$\frac{\lvert V\rvert}{3}$	$\frac{\lvert V\rvert}{3}$	$\frac{\lvert V\rvert}{3}$	$\frac{\lvert V\rvert}{3}$	$\frac{\lvert V\rvert}{3}$	$\frac{\lvert V\rvert}{3}-1$
$m \equiv 1(mod\ 3)$ $n \equiv 0(mod\ 3)$	$\frac{\lvert V\rvert}{3}$	$\frac{\lvert V\rvert}{3}$	$\frac{\lvert V\rvert}{3}$	$\frac{\lvert V\rvert}{3}-1$	$\frac{\lvert V\rvert}{3}$	$\frac{\lvert V\rvert}{3}$
$m \equiv 1(mod\ 3)$ $n \equiv 1(mod\ 3)$	$\frac{\lvert V\rvert+1}{3}$	$\frac{\lvert V\rvert+1}{3}-1$	$\frac{\lvert V\rvert+1}{3}$	$\frac{\lvert V\rvert+1}{3}-1$	$\frac{\lvert V\rvert+1}{3}-1$	$\frac{\lvert V\rvert+1}{3}$
$m \equiv 1(mod\ 3)$ $n \equiv 2(mod\ 3)$	$\frac{\lvert V\rvert-1}{3}+1$	$\frac{\lvert V\rvert-1}{3}$	$\frac{\lvert V\rvert-1}{3}$	$\frac{\lvert V\rvert-1}{3}$	$\frac{\lvert V\rvert-1}{3}$	$\frac{\lvert V\rvert-1}{3}$
$m \equiv 2(mod\ 3)$ $n \equiv 0(mod\ 3)$	$\frac{\lvert V\rvert-1}{3}$	$\frac{\lvert V\rvert-1}{3}$	$\frac{\lvert V\rvert-1}{3}+1$	$\frac{\lvert V\rvert-1}{3}$	$\frac{\lvert V\rvert-1}{3}$	$\frac{\lvert V\rvert-1}{3}$
$m \equiv 2(mod\ 3)$ $n \equiv 1(mod\ 3)$	$\frac{\lvert V\rvert}{3}$	$\frac{\lvert V\rvert}{3}$	$\frac{\lvert V\rvert}{3}$	$\frac{\lvert V\rvert}{3}$	$\frac{\lvert V\rvert}{3}$	$\frac{\lvert V\rvert}{3}-1$
$m \equiv 2(mod\ 3)$ $n \equiv 2(mod\ 3)$	$\frac{\lvert V\rvert+1}{3}$	$\frac{\lvert V\rvert+1}{3}-1$	$\frac{\lvert V\rvert+1}{3}$	$\frac{\lvert V\rvert+1}{3}$	$\frac{\lvert V\rvert+1}{3}-1$	$\frac{\lvert V\rvert+1}{3}-1$

$(1 \le \theta \le n)$ be the n pendant edges attached to the second internal vertex t_2 of the path t_4.

Then the vertex set $V(\mathcal{T}_{39}{}^5) = \{t_h : 1 \le h \le 4\} \cup \{u_\theta : 1 \le \theta \le n\} \cup \{v\}$
$\cup \{v_\kappa{}^i : 1 \le \kappa \le m, 1 \le i \le 2\}$

and the edge set $E(\mathcal{T}_{39}{}^5) = \{t_h t_{h+1} : 1 \le h \le 3\} \cup \{t_3 u_\theta : 1 \le \theta \le n\} \cup \{t_2 v\}$
$\cup \{v v_\kappa{}^1 : 1 \le \kappa \le m\} \cup \{v_\kappa{}^1 v_\kappa{}^2, 1 \le \kappa \le m\}$.

$|V| = m + 2n + 5$ and $|E| = m + 2n + 4$.
We define $\sigma : V(\mathcal{T}_{39}{}^{5}) \rightarrow [0,1]$ by $\sigma(v) = \frac{\gamma}{10}, \gamma \in Z_4 - \{0\}$.

$\sigma(v) = 0.3$

The vertices of the path t_h, $1 \leq h \leq 4$ are labeled as

$\sigma(t_1) = 0.2$
$\sigma(t_2) = 0.3$
$\sigma(t_3) = 0.1$
and $\sigma(t_4) = 0.2$

The labeling $\sigma(u_\theta)$, $1 \leq \theta \leq n$, of n pendant edges attached to the second internal vertex t_3 of the path t_4 are as follows.

$\sigma(u_\theta) = 0.1 \quad \text{if } \theta \equiv 1 \ (mod\ 3) \quad \text{for } 1 \leq \theta \leq n$
$\sigma(u_\theta) = 0.2 \quad \text{if } \theta \equiv 0 \ (mod\ 3) \quad \text{for } 1 \leq \theta \leq n$
$\sigma(u_\theta) = 0.3 \quad \text{if } \theta \equiv 2 \ (mod\ 3) \quad \text{for } 1 \leq \theta \leq n$

The labeling $\sigma(v_\kappa^i), 1 \leq \kappa \leq m, 1 \leq i \leq 2$ of m path of length two attached through an edge to the first internal vertex t_2 of the path t_4 has following cases.

Case i: $n \equiv 0$ (mod 3)

$$\sigma(v_\kappa^1) = 0.1 \quad \text{if } \kappa \equiv 2 \ (mod\ 3) \quad \text{for } 1 \leq \kappa \leq m$$

$$\sigma(v_\kappa^1) = 0.3 \quad \text{if } \kappa \equiv 0,1 \ (mod\ 3) \quad \text{for } 1 \leq \kappa \leq m$$

$$\sigma(v_\kappa^2) = 0.1 \quad \text{if } \kappa \equiv 1 \ (mod\ 3) \quad \text{for } 1 \leq \kappa \leq m$$

$$\sigma(v_\kappa^2) = 0.2 \quad \text{if } \kappa \equiv 0,2 \ (mod\ 3) \quad \text{for } 1 \leq \kappa \leq m$$

Case ii: $n \equiv 1$ (mod 3)

$$\sigma(v_\kappa^1) = 0.1 \quad \text{if } \kappa \equiv 2 \ (mod\ 3) \quad \text{for } 1 \leq \kappa \leq m$$

$$\sigma(v_\kappa^1) = 0.3 \quad \text{if } \kappa \equiv 0,1 \ (mod\ 3) \quad \text{for } 1 \leq \kappa \leq m$$

$$\sigma(v_\kappa^2) = 0.1 \quad \text{if } \kappa \equiv 1 \ (mod\ 3) \quad \text{for } 1 \leq \kappa \leq m$$

$$\sigma(v_\kappa^2) = 0.2 \quad \text{if } \kappa \equiv 0,2 \ (mod\ 3) \quad \text{for } 1 \leq \kappa \leq m$$

Case iii: n ≡ 2 (mod 3)

$$\sigma\left(v_\kappa^1\right)=0.1 \quad if\ \kappa\equiv 1\,(mod\ 3) \quad for\ 1\le\kappa\le m$$

$$\sigma\left(v_\kappa^1\right)=0.3 \quad if\ \kappa\equiv 0,2\,(mod\ 3) \quad for\ 1\le\kappa\le m$$

$$\sigma\left(v_\kappa^2\right)=0.1 \quad if\ \kappa\equiv 2\,(mod\ 3) \quad for\ 1\le\kappa\le m$$

$$\sigma\left(v_\kappa^2\right)=0.2 \quad if\ \kappa\equiv 0,1\,(mod\ 3) \quad for\ 1\le\kappa\le m$$

For $i\in\left\{\frac{\gamma}{10},\gamma\in Z_4-\{0\}\right\}$, $v_\sigma(i)$ and $e_\mu(i)$ are tabulated below.

Table 3.9 $v_\sigma(i)$ and $e_\mu(i)$ for the tree $\mathcal{T}_{39^5}\left(i\in\left\{\frac{\gamma}{10},\gamma\in Z_4-\{0\}\right\}\right)$.

Nature of m and n	$v_\sigma(0.1)$	$v_\sigma(0.2)$	$v_\sigma(0.3)$	$e_\mu(0.1)$	$e_\mu(0.2)$	$e_\mu(0.3)$
$n\equiv 0(mod\ 3)$ $m\equiv 0(mod\ 3)$	$\frac{\lvert V\rvert+1}{3}-1$	$\frac{\lvert V\rvert+1}{3}$	$\frac{\lvert V\rvert+1}{3}$	$\frac{\lvert V\rvert+1}{3}-1$	$\frac{\lvert V\rvert+1}{3}$	$\frac{\lvert V\rvert+1}{3}-1$
$n\equiv 0(mod\ 3)$ $m\equiv 1(mod\ 3)$	$\frac{\lvert V\rvert-1}{3}$	$\frac{\lvert V\rvert-1}{3}$	$\frac{\lvert V\rvert-1}{3}+1$	$\frac{\lvert V\rvert-1}{3}$	$\frac{\lvert V\rvert-1}{3}$	$\frac{\lvert V\rvert-1}{3}$
$n\equiv 0(mod\ 3)$ $m\equiv 2(mod\ 3)$	$\frac{\lvert V\rvert}{3}$	$\frac{\lvert V\rvert}{3}$	$\frac{\lvert V\rvert}{3}$	$\frac{\lvert V\rvert}{3}$	$\frac{\lvert V\rvert}{3}$	$\frac{\lvert V\rvert}{3}-1$
$n\equiv 1(mod\ 3)$ $m\equiv 0(mod\ 3)$	$\frac{\lvert V\rvert}{3}$	$\frac{\lvert V\rvert}{3}$	$\frac{\lvert V\rvert}{3}$	$\frac{\lvert V\rvert}{3}-1$	$\frac{\lvert V\rvert}{3}$	$\frac{\lvert V\rvert}{3}$
$n\equiv 1(mod\ 3)$ $m\equiv 1(mod\ 3)$	$\frac{\lvert V\rvert+1}{3}$	$\frac{\lvert V\rvert+1}{3}-1$	$\frac{\lvert V\rvert+1}{3}$	$\frac{\lvert V\rvert+1}{3}-1$	$\frac{\lvert V\rvert+1}{3}-1$	$\frac{\lvert V\rvert+1}{3}$
$n\equiv 1(mod\ 3)$ $m\equiv 2(mod\ 3)$	$\frac{\lvert V\rvert-1}{3}+1$	$\frac{\lvert V\rvert-1}{3}$	$\frac{\lvert V\rvert-1}{3}$	$\frac{\lvert V\rvert-1}{3}$	$\frac{\lvert V\rvert-1}{3}$	$\frac{\lvert V\rvert-1}{3}$
$n\equiv 2(mod\ 3)$ $m\equiv 0(mod\ 3)$	$\frac{\lvert V\rvert-1}{3}$	$\frac{\lvert V\rvert-1}{3}$	$\frac{\lvert V\rvert-1}{3}+1$	$\frac{\lvert V\rvert-1}{3}$	$\frac{\lvert V\rvert-1}{3}$	$\frac{\lvert V\rvert-1}{3}$
$n\equiv 2(mod\ 3)$ $m\equiv 1(mod\ 3)$	$\frac{\lvert V\rvert}{3}$	$\frac{\lvert V\rvert}{3}$	$\frac{\lvert V\rvert}{3}$	$\frac{\lvert V\rvert}{3}$	$\frac{\lvert V\rvert}{3}$	$\frac{\lvert V\rvert}{3}-1$
$n\equiv 2(mod\ 3)$ $m\equiv 2(mod\ 3)$	$\frac{\lvert V\rvert+1}{3}$	$\frac{\lvert V\rvert+1}{3}-1$	$\frac{\lvert V\rvert+1}{3}$	$\frac{\lvert V\rvert+1}{3}$	$\frac{\lvert V\rvert+1}{3}-1$	$\frac{\lvert V\rvert+1}{3}-1$

It is clear from Table 3.9 that for $i \neq j \in \left\{\frac{\gamma}{10}, \gamma \in Z_4 - \{0\}\right\}$ $v_\sigma(i)$ and $v_\sigma(j)$ differ by at most 1 and $e_\mu(i)$ and $e_\mu(j)$ differ by at most 1. By Definition 4.3, the tree $\mathcal{T}_{39}{}^5$ is admits fuzzy quotient-3 cordial labeling and hence the fuzzy quotient-3 cordial graph.

3.6 Conclusion

Fuzzy graph theory is finding an increasing number of application in modeling real time systems. Many authors discussed various types of labeling and its applications. We have introduced the new concept called fuzzy quotient-3 cordial labeling and proved some families of graphs are fuzzy quotient-3 cordial labeling. As every graph does not admit fuzzy quotient-3 cordial labeling it is very interesting to investigate graphs or graph families which admit fuzzy quotient-3 cordial labeling. The fuzzy quotient-3 cordial labeling for some more family of graphs and application of fuzzy quotient-3 cordial on certain class of graphs shall be our future work.

References

1. Gallian, J.A., A dynamic survey of graph labeling. *Electron. J. Comb., 17*, 60–62, 2014.
2. Cahit, I., Cordial graphs-a weaker version of graceful and harmonious graphs. *Arscombinatoria, 23*, 201–207, 1987.
3. Sundaram, M., Ponraj, R., Somasundaram, S., Product cordial labeling of graphs. *Bull. Pure Appl. Sci.(Math. Stat.) E, 23*, 155–163, 2004.
4. Sundaram, M., Ponraj, R., Somasundram, S., Total product cordial labeling of graphs. *Bull. Pure Appl. Sci. Sect. E Math. Stat., 25*, 199–203, 2006.
5. Sundaram, M., Ponraj, R., Somasundram, S., Some results on total product cordial labeling of graphs. *J. Indian Acad. Math., 28*, 309–320, 2006.
6. Ponraj, R., Sivakumar, M., Sundaram, M., k-Product cordial labeling of graphs. *Int. J. Contemp. Math. Sci., 7*, 15, 733–742, 2012.
7. Jeyanthi, P. and Maheswari, A., 3-Product cordial labelling. *SUT J. Math.*, 48, 12, 231–240, 2012.
8. Ponraj, R., Sivakumar, M., Sundaram, M., On 4-product cordial graphs, Inter. *J. Math. Arch., 7*, 2809–2814, 2012.
9. Sivakumar, M., On 4-total product cordiality of some corona graphs. *Internat. J. Math. Combin., 3*, 99–106, 2016.
10. Ponraj, R. and Adaickalam, M.M., Quotient cordial labeling of some star related graphs. *J. Indian Acad. Math., 37*, 2, 313–324, 2015.

11. Rosa, A., On certain valuations of the vertices of a graph. Theory of Graphs (Internat. Symposium), Rome, 1967.
12. Graham, R.L., James, N., Sloane, A., On additive bases and harmonious graphs. *SIAM J. Alg. Discr. Meth.*, 1.4, 382–404, 1980.

4

Classifying Fuzzy Multi-Criterion Decision Making and Evolutionary Algorithm

Kirti Seth[1]* and Ashish Seth[2]

[1]*School of Computer and Information Engineering, INHA University, Tashkent, Uzbekistan*
[2]*School of Global Convergence Studies, INHA University, Incheon, South Korea*

Abstract
During last two decades, hybrid computational intelligence is inspired by nature intelligence and multi-criteria decision making. Nature intelligence is global optimization framework as a collection of algorithms for dominating robotic swarm due to superb potency of the natural swarm systems. These techniques work in a manner that mimics the behavior of swarms. Swarms are basically large numbers of homogenized and easy agents, that interacts among themselves and their environment locally with none central management. The other important aspect for hybrid computational intelligence is multi-criterion decision problem. Decision making is the process of selecting the best alternative where precision of data plays a major role. In the problem of decision making, sometimes, several criteria are considering at a time. Experts are needed to find quantitative and qualitative decision for finding the performance of every possible alternative with regards to every criterion. This chapter provides an introduction to hybrid computational intelligence. It covers a brief review of optimization, and meta-heuristic. It also examines the scope of swarm intelligence in overcoming the limitations of traditional methods. It thoroughly covers Ant Colony Optimization and Swarm Optimization. The chapter then briefly introduces Multi criteria decision problem and various tools for these problems such as WSM, WPM, AHP, TOPSIS, ELECTRE, and VIKOR. This chapter discusses on the behavior and application of these tools.

Keywords: Ant colony optimization, fuzzy logic, fuzzy set, MCDM, TOPSIS, analytical hierarchical process, decision making, evolutionary algorithm

**Corresponding author*: k.seth@inha.uz

E. Chandrasekaran, R. Anandan, G. Suseendran, S. Balamurugan and Hanaa Hachimi (eds.)
Fuzzy Intelligent Systems: Methodologies, Techniques, and Applications, (73–92) © 2021
Scrivener Publishing LLC

4.1 Introduction

Optimization is a technique that provides us the most effective findings with the smallest amount of resources. In other words, it is a way of finding an associate action that ensures to maximize or rather minimize the worth of an objective function. Basically, optimization aims at finding the criteria that find the behavior of system which increases productivity and reduce waste.

Figure 4.1 shows the hierarchy of optimization methods.

Optimization techniques were mainly invented because the traditional methods like mathematics and logics were facing difficulties in solving the optimization problems. These techniques are divided into following two broad categories:

- Classical Optimization Techniques, and
- Bio-Inspired Optimization Techniques.

4.1.1 Classical Optimization Techniques

These techniques are not robust. A mere change in the definition of the problem demands a completely different method. These techniques are basically classified into two parts:

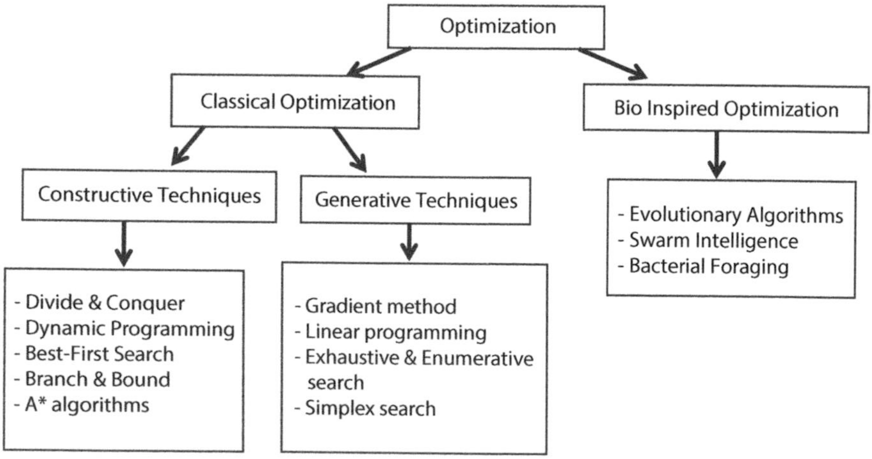

Figure 4.1 Classification of optimization techniques.

Table 4.1 Comparison between classical constructive and generative techniques.

Classical constructive techniques	Classical generative techniques
1. Initially work with the partial solutions and as it increments the full solution is constructed.	1. Works with the complete solutions and generate them as a whole. This can be interrupted anytime.
2. (a) It requires discrete search space (b) Based on decomposition method in which it arranges the search space is presented in the form of a tree	2. Most of the time this technique has solution but that solution is neither global nor local optimal.
3. Divide & Conquer, Dynamic Programming, Best-First Search, Branch & Bound and A & A* algorithms.	3. Gradient method, Linear programming, Exhaustive & Enumerative search, Rosenrock's optimization algorithm and Nelder–Mead Simplex search.

- Constructive Optimization Techniques,
- Generative Optimization Techniques.

Comparison of above two techniques is shown in Table 4.1.

The classical methods of optimization are not always applicable for every problem; moreover they are too costly in terms of both time and resources. Today, these classical methods of optimization come up with hefty complexities and also they have the problem of getting stuck in local optimum. In order to trounce these complexities and problems there is the need of moving towards some new techniques. The present scenario has really ensured to mark the shift from all these intense classical techniques to even undertaking a completely new species that is linked with the optimization techniques which are best referred as the bio-inspired optimization techniques.

4.1.2 The Bio-Inspired Techniques Centered on Optimization

This is the category of the optimization methods that rely on techniques inspired naturally, like social interactions, human brain, or Darwinian evolution. These methods try and simulate the behaviors of all the species that are found in nature, such as bees, ants and many more in order to extract data that is used for the development of just simple and other robust strategies of optimization.

Figure 4.2 shows the hierarchy of Nature-Inspired Algorithms.

Bio-inspired techniques are powerful strategies for planning distributed control and optimization algorithms that are being applied with success to a spread of scientific and engineering issues. These techniques achieve good performance on a large spectrum of static issues and also exhibit a high degree of flexibility and robustness during a dynamic surroundings. It has got some strength like:

1. Bio-inspired techniques are easy to implement,
2. They are straightforward to apply,
3. They do not rely upon the function for optimization.

Figure 4.3 shows components of Bio-Inspired Computing.

Bio-inspired optimization techniques study the models and analyze extremely the complex phenomenon for which there is just no known analytic and affordable solution available. It consists particularly of the intense evolutionary algorithms, increasing swarm intelligence, established artificial neural networks alongside the fuzzy systems, applied mathematics, possibility theory, and the intense Bayesian networks. These techniques

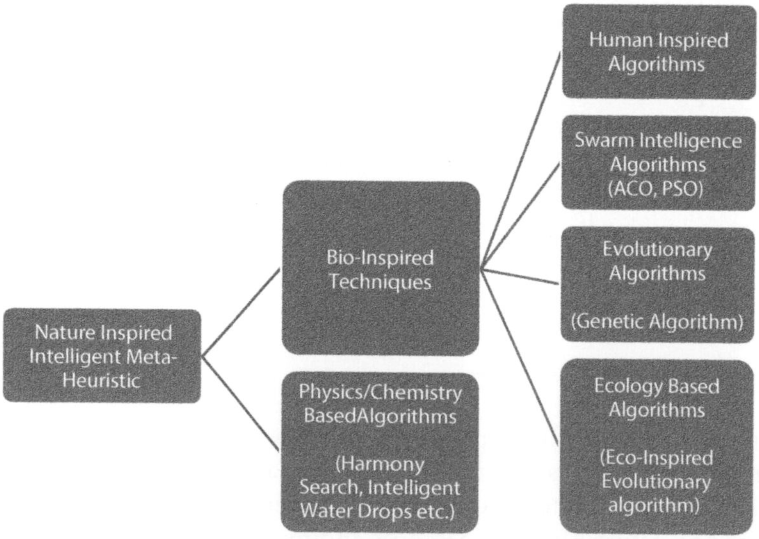

Figure 4.2 Hierarchy of nature-inspired algorithms.

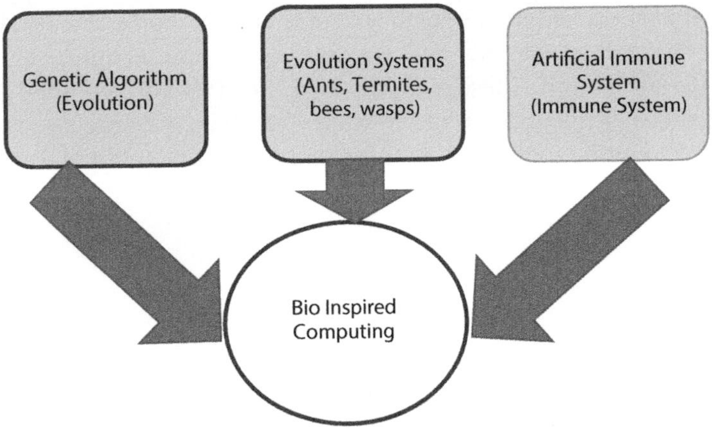

Figure 4.3 Components of bio-inspired computing.

have more tolerance centered on imprecision with an inclusion of the partial truth, the uncertainty and noise. Bio-inspired optimization is evident as an umbrella term that seeks to cover a good sort of various optimization approaches that are supported by the principles of various increasingly biological systems. The classifications of bio-inspired techniques are as given below:

- Evolutionary Algorithms,
- Swarm Intelligence,
- Bacterial Foraging.

4.1.2.1 Swarm Intelligence

During last decade the optimization techniques that are intensely inspired by the swarm intelligence have become very popular because of the amazing efficiency of the natural swarm systems. Swarm intelligence is very crucial as it was essentially brought in the limelight by both Beni and Wang [1] with in the world optimization more so as a framework and as a group of algorithms for dominant robotic system. These techniques work in a manner that mimics the behavior of swarms. Swarms are basically large numbers of same and straightforward agents, which interact among themselves and their surroundings locally without any central control. On the other side, swarm intelligence was outlined by Bonabeau *et al.* [2] as "the emerging collective intelligence of set of easy agents". In other words, it can also be defined as the branch of the artificial intelligence denoted as (AI) that is a highly accustomed seek to ensure that they model the behavior of all the swarms in nature such as bees, ants, wasps and termites, further as from different natural. These natural swarm individuals have very limited capability of their own. So, in order to survive, these individuals cooperate and interact among themselves with certain behavioral pattern. This interaction among the swarm individuals maybe of two sorts as given by Belal *et al.* [3]:

- The Direct, and
- The Indirect

Evidently, direct interaction can be evident through the audio–visual contact of one person to another. Indirect interaction is bound to take place when an individual ensured to best respond to the changes done to setting by the opposite individual, just like pheromone trails of the ants. This form of indirect interaction is also known as stigmergy, implying that; communication is facilitated through environment as given by Dorigo *et al.* [4].

Apparently, the Swarm-based algorithms are basically ranked to being a great family of these nature-inspired algorithms as accorded by Panigrahi *et al.* [5]. Robustness and flexibility is the main advantage of these algorithms over the traditional techniques. It makes this technique successful for dealing complex problems. During the chapter we target on some most productive as well as the optimization techniques that are inspired by swarm intelligence.

4.1.2.2 The Optimization on Ant Colony

The Ant Colony Optimization denoted as (ACO) is deemed as a relatively new random heuristic approach for solving optimization problems as given by Dorigo *et al.* [6]. It is attained from the approach of the real ants seeking to optimize their tracks. Within the early nineties Colorni *et al.* [7] proposed the first ACO working algorithm, called the Ant System (AS). Ant system is the initial member of ACO class algorithms. The main underlying plan behind this is the active parallel search over the many as well as constructive and computational threads that are supported by localized data issue and a dynamic issue as well that contains. ACO is the paradigm for coming up with the increasing meta-heuristic algorithms that are evident for combinatorial optimization issues. It is the main application of the ACO algorithm. The collective behavior of various search threads of ant system has made it effective for finding solution for combinatorial on various optimization problems.

Consequently, the combinatorial optimization problem is outlined as the group of the intense basic components. On the same note, a subset of components represents an answer to all the problems. The objective is to ensure that one finds a minimum cost that is feasible solution.

Evidently, the Meta-heuristic algorithms are the immense kind of algorithms that, so as to free from all the local optima, in seeking to drive some basic heuristic. Heuristic can be either the articulated as being the constructive heuristic or even the local search heuristic. Constructive heuristic emanates from the null solution and seeks to add several elements seeking to ensure that they build an honest as well as a complete solution and local search heuristic starts from a whole solution and iteratively modify some parts so as to realize a much better solution.

ACO basically have some following concepts:

1. *Ants:* are basic working entities for ACO. Following are important properties of Ants:
   a) Move from one node to another.
   b) Path is selected by the ants according to the pheromone strength.
   c) Selected path represents candidate solution.
   d) As soon as ant finds solution it laid down pheromone on the path, amount of pheromone depends on the solution quality.
2. *Pheromone Trails:*
   a) Individual ants are centred on laying a chemical substance named the great pheromone trails while moving from one node to another in both directions.
   b) This pheromone evaporates over time gradually.
   c) Because multiple ants are using path pheromone trail collects on the path.
3. *ACO Concept:*
   a) Ants move from one node to another this movement helps ants to find shortest path.
   b) Movement of ant is random.
   c) Each ant deposit pheromone on the travelled path.
   d) The path that to follow is detected
   e) Number of pheromone on the path is directly seen to be much proportional to the probability of following path.

Ant colony optimization algorithm solves the optimization problem by repeating the following two steps:

1. Pheromone model is used to find candidate solution,
2. Pheromone value is changed with the help of candidate solution.

Actually the ant colony optimization algorithm uses the artificial ants which imitates the behavior of real ants and co-operates the solution of a given problem by seeking to exchange the information via various pheromones.

- State Transition

$$p_{ij}^{k}(t)\begin{cases} \dfrac{(\tau_{pq}(t))^{\alpha}(\eta_{ij}(t))^{\beta}}{\sum k\,\varepsilon\, allowed_k(\tau_{ik}(t))^{\alpha}(\eta_{ik}(t))^{\beta}} ; if\ j\,\varepsilon\, allowed_k \\ 0 \qquad ; otherwise \end{cases} \tag{4.1}$$

Here,

$T_{pq}(t)$ = intensity of the pheromone trail between node (p, q) at time t,

D_{pq} = distance between (p, q),

η = 1/d (visibility of node (p, q)), allowed is the set of all the denoted nodes that tend to immensely remain to highly be frequently visited by the ant k positioned at node p

and α, β = parameters that determines the entire relative importance linked with the working pheromone trail versus visibility.

This equation gives the identified probability that which the ant k at node p chooses to move ensure that it moves to node q. Initially the algorithm determines the positions of ant at increasingly different nodes and the initial value identified, of τ_{pq}.

- Pheromone Trail Updating

Pheromone trail of ants is updated in order to improve the solutions in future. Rules for global updation:

$$\tau_{pq}(t+1) = \rho\tau_{pq}(t) + \sum_{k=1}^{m} \Delta\tau_{pq}^{k} \tag{4.2}$$

Where,

$$\Delta\tau_{pq}^{k} = \begin{cases} \dfrac{Q}{L_k} & ;\textit{if } (p,q) \textit{ is visited by the } k^{th} \textit{ ant in the current cycle} \\ 0 & ; \textit{otherwise} \end{cases} \tag{4.3}$$

$$\Delta\tau_{pq} = \sum_{k=1}^{m} \Delta\tau_{pq}^{k} \tag{4.4}$$

Here,

ρ = trail persistence, (value of ρ mostly lies between letter 0 and 1)
L_k = tour length for kth ant
Q = trail quality constant.
Figure 4.4 shows the applications of Ant Colony Optimization.

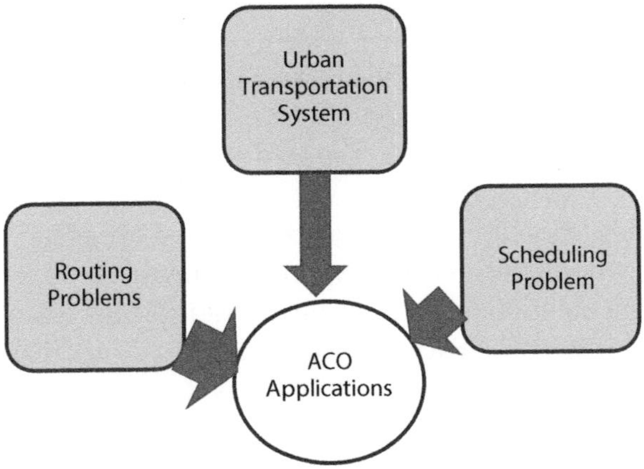

Figure 4.4 Applications of (ACO).

4.1.2.3 *Particle Swarm Optimization (PSO)*

Apparently, the population based search algorithms are good alternatives especially; when the search space mostly prove being too large to provide the search. However, these algorithms do not guarantee the optimal solution. The (PSO) is one of the increasingly population which is referred as the based optimization technique. It was first brought to the light in the year 1995. They described it as being an algorithm that is very adaptive, which is mostly and intensely based on the entire evident social-psychological metaphors. In this, it is clear that the increasing population of various individuals tend to adapt to the situation by seeking to return stochastically towards all the previously regions that have been successful as given by Kennedy and Eberhart [8]. PSO uses swarming behavior of both the flocks as well as birds, various schools of fish and even the most increasing human social behavior that contributes to the emergency of intelligent matters.

PSO is deemed as being a general-purpose metaheuristic algorithm that may be easily applicable to many kinds of the increasing optimization problems. It is intensely and increasingly based on the identified observations of all the coordinated movements that is linked with some social animal groups, mostly the bird flocks. The fundamental issue in the development of the PSO algorithm is:

- To share social information and
- To utilize information gained by individuals.

The basic idea that is linked with PSO was attained from the research on the behavior that is evident on bird swarms that are looking for food. This can easily be understood with the following scenario: Notably, a group of birds is seeking to randomly search for food mostly in an identified area. Food may be search by following the bird that is nearer to the source of food.

PSO is highly learned from such a scenario and even later used for the purpose of solving all the identified optimization problems. In the entire of PSO, each single solution has to be a "bird" that is identified as "particle" in the entire of search space. Each particle has fitness values that seem much and frequently evaluated by the entire of fitness functions that are yet to be optimized. Again, they have the velocity that helps in directing the flying of all the particles. The first is the personal best known as pbest that is the best value known to be so far.

- *Update velocity and position:* Under the Equation (4.5) is used for the purpose of updating the entire velocity and Equation (4.6) is used for updating the position.

$$\overrightarrow{v_i(t)} = \underbrace{w\overrightarrow{v_i(t-1)}}_{inertia} + \underbrace{c_1 r_1\left(\overrightarrow{x_i^{\#}(t-1)} - \overrightarrow{x_i(t-1)}\right)}_{personal\ influence} + \underbrace{c_2 r_2\left(\overrightarrow{x^*(t-1)} - \overrightarrow{x_i(t-1)}\right)}_{social\ influence} \tag{4.5}$$

$$\overrightarrow{x_i(t)} = \overrightarrow{x_i(t-1)} + \overrightarrow{v_i(t)} \tag{4.6}$$

Here, $\overrightarrow{x_i(t)}$ is the position vector in iteration t of particle i, $\overrightarrow{v_i(t)}$ is the velocity vector in iteration t of particle i, $x_i^{\#}(t)$ is the best position so far of particle i in iteration t, c_1 is the positive constant that is referred as the coefficient of the increasing self-recognition component, c_2 is regarded as the positive constant that is w is the variable called inertia factor whose value is nearly setup to vary between 1 and nearly 0.

4.1.2.4 *Summary of PSO*

1. First Introduced by a person referred as Kennedy and Eberhart in the year 1995.
2. This algorithm is highly determined by the behavior of birds and fishes.
3. This is a swarm intelligence based algorithm.
4. It is non-deterministic optimization algorithm.
5. It is based on population.
6. Its performance may be compared with genetic algorithms.

4.2 Multiple Criteria That is Used for Decision Making (MCDM)

Decision making is the method where accuracy of data plays a significant role to ensure that one selects the best alternative. It gives the procedure to seek the best alternative that is attained from a group of available possible alternatives. In some cases, the problem of decision making considers many criteria at a time. Various experts are needed to ensure that they provide qualitative as well as quantitative decision that can be used for the sake of performance determination. Evidently, multi criteria decision making problem refers to screening, prioritizing, ranking, or choosing a group of alternatives. These problems sometimes ends in unsure, imprecise, indefinite knowledge that makes the entire of decision-making methods appear more complex and even more challenging. Therefore, the introduction of the fuzzy set theory to multi-criteria evaluation methods is now viewed as being an effective approach.

This discipline began in the 1960s and over time has developed into a replacement kind of issues arose and square measure to be solved. MCDA is a deletion that read as Multiple Criteria call Analysis/Aiding, and it's conjointly referred as MCDM. MCDM is that the "best" priorities derivation technique [9, 14]. It's a sub branch of operational analysis. Operational analysis is usually deemed to be a subfield of mathematics; here we tend to use advanced analytical ways to urge best or nearly best solutions (approximate) in advanced decision-making issues. This operational analysis is concentrated on real world issues in producing, marketing, data technology (IT), transportation and lots of different fields. For that reason, operational analysis overlaps with different disciplines, preponderantly branch of knowledge and operations management. MCDA could be a sub branch of operational analysis which solely handles call issues that uses multiple criteria to seek out the most effective potential answer.

Decision making is that method of choosing the most effective various wherever exactness of knowledge plays a serious role. Within the drawback of higher cognitive process typically many criteria area unit are considered at a time. Multiple attributes/criteria are normally centered on forming a hierarchy.

Zeleny [10] proposed, almost every alternative, example an emerging action plan, an organization, or a product that appears as being of any type, may be able to evaluate on the basis of all highlighted attributes. An attribute is deemed being a quality. Sub-attributes can be obtained by breaking down the attributes further into even intense lower levels of attributes as shown in figure and seeking to evaluate an alternative. Due to this one to one parallelism occurs between attribute and criterion, for a while attribute are also suggested as criteria and are used in an interchangeably manner in MCDM context.

The set of alternatives are considering as Ai (i = 1, 2, 3...n) and number of criteria also taken as Cj (j = 1, 2, 3,... m).

Using both of these sets we can find the performance of each alternative Ai with regards to every alternative Cj.

Apparently, this multi criteria decision making problem is well known with the help of a better example: Let's say there is a group of two persons (X and Y), who intend to ensure that he determines which car he/she has to buy based on certain factors. First, we seek to let the evaluation factors be 2006 [11].

Therefore, many steps are used for this multi criteria decision making problems such as ranking, prioritizing, screening, and selecting an alternative set. These problems typically result in imprecise, indefinite, uncertain data that formulate the entire process of decision-making more complex and much challenging. So, the set theory of fuzzy is introduced with the multi-criteria evaluation methods that are centered to establishing an effective approach as proposed by Deng in 1999 [12] and Seetha Lakshmi in 2013 [13].

For handling advanced issues in deciding their square measure many strategies have been projected. Specifically, these strategies square measure considering the matter of selecting the most effective different from a finite set of alternatives with relevancy criteria. The strategies square measures include WSM, WPM, AHP, VIKOR, PROMETHEE, TOPSIS, ELECTRE, evidentiary Reasoning, SMAA, RSA and DRSA. During this chapter we

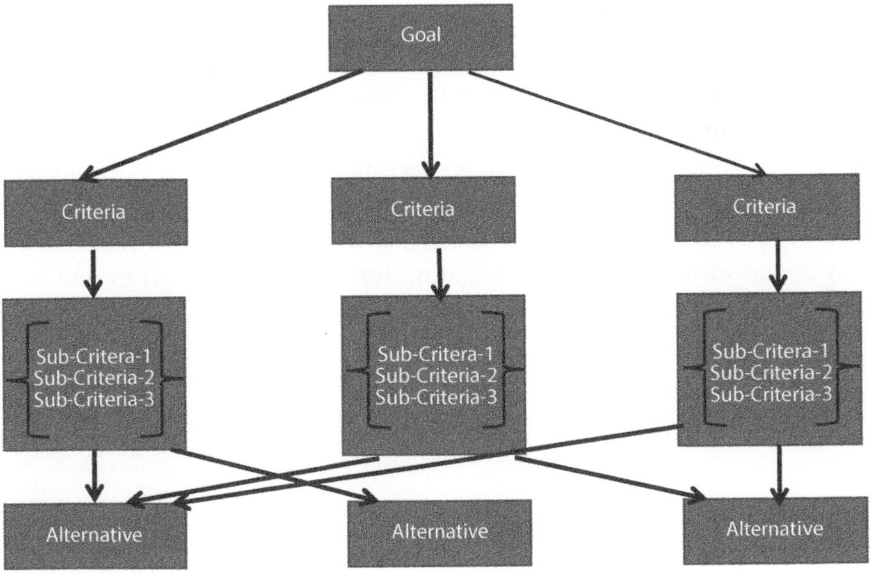

Figure 4.5 Hierarchical structure of MCDM.

have a tendency to specialize in fuzzy multi-criteria analysis and a few similarity primarily based approaches like TOPSIS.

Hierarchical structure of Multi-Criteria Decision Making is given in Figure 4.5.

4.2.1 WSM Method

The most commonly used approach is Weighted Sum Model (WSM). This is also known as a single dimensional problem as given by Triantaphyllou *et al.* in 1998 [14]. The best alternative is calculated by using the following expression.

$$A_{WSM} = max_i \sum_{j=1}^{n} a_{ij} w_{ij} \tag{4.7}$$

where, A_{WSM} = WSM score of the best alternative,

n = number of all the identified decision criteria,

aij = is the seemingly actual value of the *i-th* alternative in terms of the *j-th* criterion,

and *Wj* = is articulated as the weight of importance of the *j*-th criterion.

4.2.2 WPM Method

WPM stands for the reputable (Weighted Product Model) that seem much in likeness to the WSM. Or we may say that this method is a modification of the WSM method. This method is suggested with the aim of overcoming some weaknesses of the WSM method as given by Triantaphyllou *et al.* in 1998 [14]. A lot happens in this method whereby; there is the multiplication of the various ratios each standing for a different criterion. On the same note, the alternatives AK and AL are calculated by using the following product.

$$R(AK/AL) = \prod_{j=1}^{n} (AK/AL)^{w_j}$$

where n = the criteria numbers used

aij = actual value of the *i-th* alternative in terms of the *jth* criterion,

and *Wj* = the weight of the entire *j-th* criterion.

If the value of $R(AK / AL)$ is more or seemingly will appear in a situation being greater than one then it implies that the alternative K will now be more suitable than other alternative considered AL.

Under such a situation, the alternative is better than or even equal to all. Therefore, the dimensionless analysis as there is reduction in regard to units of access from the provided structure. This method can also use the relative value instead of actual values as advantage view.

4.2.3 Analytic Hierarchy Process (AHP)

In MCDM, one method that is most popular is known as Analytic Hierarchy Process (AHP) proposed by Mikhailov and Tsvetinov in 2004 [15]. That is a mathematical method. The decision making problems of any type of subject can be solved by using this method. Saaty proposed an underlying semantically scale that ranging from 1 to 9 as shown in Table 4.2 that is used in hierarchy between two elements for finding the relative preferences in matrix.

In AHP, the main objective is ranking the criteria on decision as proposed by Seetha Lakshmi in 2013 [13]. In this method, pair-wise comparisons are used for establishing preferences between criteria and alternatives. The best rank is always a most suitable alternative for Decision Makers (DM).

In AHP there are two kinds of unit input further as output. The particular measurement inputs include weight, worth and height or use

Table 4.2 Pairwise Comparison Scales (presented by Saaty, 1980 [19]).

Preference of alternative (numeric value)	Preference of alternative (linguistic meaning)
1	The Equal Importance
3	The Moderate Importance
5	Implicated Importance that is strong
7	The implicated Very Strong Importance
9	Increased Extreme Importance
2,4,6,8	Intermediate values that lies between the adjacent scale values.

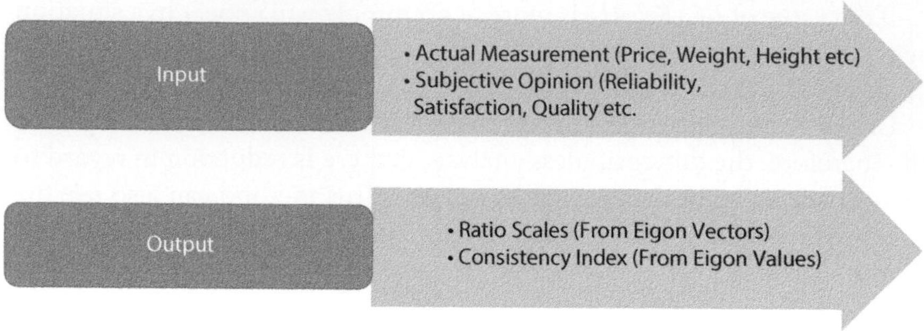

Figure 4.6 Input/output measures of AHP.

subjective opinions inputs like satisfaction, quality and responsibility as shown in Figure 4.6. Among the few of the AHP outputs one is magnitude relation scale that describes DMs preferences in scrutiny 2 parts in deciding process exploitation vividness of importance. Eigen vectors that area unit accustomed derive the priorities among compared parts area unit used for getting magnitude relation scale. Consistency index (CI) is another output taken from the Eigen values that area unit accustomed acquires priority vectors.

In decision making process for checking the consistency of comparing two elements the consistency ration is proposed by Saaty. In order to obtain consistency ratio (CR), (RI) is given below.

AHP has the following steps:

Algorithm:

1. Outline the goal of the decision problem.
2. Find groups of criteria, sub-criteria, alternatives etc.
3. Create a pair-wise comparison matrix of elements in each group using the Saaty scale.
4. Normalizing matrix weights (dividing every row weight by the total of all weights in every column).
5. Priority Vector (out coming result of relative weights) is derived, (by the sum of each row of normalized weights).
6. Maximum Eigen value vector is computed (product value of pair wise matrix and the priority vector).

7. Computing the consistency index.
   a) Adding all maximum Eigen value vector
   b) deducted by the quantity that represents the dimensions of the comparison matrix (e.g. if their square measures three alternatives then the dimension is adequate to 3) and (c.) Divided by the dimensions of the comparison matrix minus one.
8. Computing the consistency ratio.
   The consistency ratio is computed by dividing the consistency index (CI) by the random consistency index. A consistency check is complete to see if the ratio is less than 0.1. (If consistency ratio ≤ 0.1 then inconsistency is acceptable or if consistency ratio >0.1 then subjective judgment is need to revise).
9. Appraise the criteria and alternatives with regard to the weight.
10. Find ranking.

4.2.4 TOPSIS

It provides the ideal technique similar for ideal solutions.

It is a method of multiple-criteria decision analysis brought in lime light in 1981 by Yoon. It uses the finite numbers of criteria for ranking the alternatives [16].

TOPSIS has been applied in many fields as proposed by Chen *et al.* in 2006 [17] and Bottani *et al.* [18] like supply chain management, business, logistics, marketing management, energy management, chemical engineering, etc. and is not limited to a specific field.

In TOPSIS, the best alternative is chosen among all on the bases of distant measure, which is alternative distance. On the other side the benefit criteria is minimize and cost criteria is maximizes by using negative ideal solution. Here, all the bad values are consisting by negative solution and all best values are consisting by positive solution.

TOPSIS has following ten steps.

1. To select linguistic rating for each criterion and alternative.
2. To assign weight for each criterion with the help of decision maker.
3. To evaluate alternatives based on the weightage of each criterion.
4. To calculate aggregate fuzzy rating for all alternatives with each criterion.
5. (i) Normalize fuzzy rating for elimination of anomalies.

   (ii) Calculate Normalize fuzzy decision matrix.

6. To calculate weighted normalized fuzzy decision matrix.
7. To compute fuzzy positive ideal solution (FPIS) and fuzzy negative ideal solution (FNIS) for all alternatives.
8. To measure distance of each weighted alternative with the help of FPIS and FNIS.
9. (i) Calculate closeness coefficient for each alternative.
10. Rank all alternatives according to closeness co-efficient.

Alternative with higher the rank is better the solution. TOPSIS method is simple to use and implement it supports quantitative values. This method is commonly used in various real-life problems. For supporting this method there are also many tools.

The limitation of this methodology is that it does not support uncertain values. Due to this limitation this method may suffer from rank reversal problem.

4.2.5 VIKOR

VIKOR is one of the methods that is used in MCDA, developed by Serafim Opricovic in 1998 as given by Triantaphyllou *et al.* in 1998 [14]. Many fields used by VIKOR are given in the following.

MCDM problems under

1. Intuitionist Environment,
2. Neural Network,
3. Suppliers Selection, etc.

Primary goal of this technique is to find various possible alternatives according to various clashing criteria and fix rank for all alternatives.

The alternative which has the highest rank known is most suited alternative for decision matrix.

VIKOR has the same positive and negative ideal solutions as define in the TOPSIS. Similarly, as TOPSIS the FPIS is an alternative which defines highest ranked value for benefit and lowest ranked value for cost and FNIS is an alternative which defines lowest ranked value for benefit and highest ranked value for cost.

The VIKOR differs from TOPSIS in terms of aggregation function and normalization method. In TOPSIS, the alternative which is too far from negative solution and nearest to positive solution is selected as best alternative. This may like to have a decision which not only makes as much profit as possible but it is most suitable to avoid the risk as much as possible. Besides, computing is the best alternative in the VIKOR base on extracting closeness measure to PIS.

4.3 Conclusion

This chapter classifies Multi-Criteria Decision Making and evolutionary algorithm. Evolutionary algorithms are also known as Bio-Inspired algorithms. Some important evolutionary algorithms are explained in this chapter e.g. Ant Colony Optimization, Swarm Intelligence, etc. There are lots of other evolutionary algorithms like cuckoo search, harmonic optimization, etc. Further, we discuss about MCDM problems.

References

1. Beni, and Wang, Swarm intelligence in cellular robotic systems, in: *NATO Advanced Workshop on Robots and Biological Systems*, Il Ciocco, Tuscany, Italy, 1989.
2. Bourque, *et al.*, The guide to the software engineering body of knowledge 2004 version. *IEEE Software*, 16, 6, 35–44, 1999.
3. Belal, *et al.*, Swarm Intelligence, in: *Handbook of Bioinspired Algorithms and Applications*, Series: CRC Computer & Information Science, Vol. 7, Chapman & Hall, (Ed.), 2006.
4. Dorigo, *et al.*, Ant algorithms and stigmergy. *Future Gener. Comput. Syst.*, 16, 8, 851–871, 2000.
5. Panigrahi, *et al.*, *Handbook of Swarm Intelligence. Series: Adaptation, Learning, and Optimization*, vol. 7, Springer, Verlag Berlin Heidelberg, 2011.
6. Dorigo, M., and Di Caro, G., *The Ant Colony Optimization:* a new metaheuristic. In Proceeding of 1999 Congress on Evolutionary Computational (CEC99), pages 1470–1477. IEEE, 1999.

7. Colorni, *et al.*, Distributed optimization by ant colonies. *Proceedings of ECAL'91, European Conference on Artificial Life*, Elsevier Publishing, Amsterdam, 1991.
8. Kennedy, and Eberhart, *Swarm Intelligence*, Morgan Kaufmann Publishers, Inc., San Francisco, CA, 2001.
9. Brestovac, G. and Grgurina, R., *Applying Multi-Criteria Decision Analysis Methods in Embedded Systems Design*, Master thesis in School of Innovation, Design and Engineering, Malardalen University Sweden, 2013.
10. Zeleny, M., Multiple criteria decision making: Eight concepts of optimality. *Hum. Syst. Manage.*, 17, 2, 97–107, 1998.
11. Abramowicz, W., Kaczmarek, M., Zyskowski, D., Duality in Web Service Reliability. *Proceedings of the Advanced International Conference on Telecommunications and International Conference on Internet and Web Applications and Services (AICT/ICIW 2006)*, IEEE Computer Society, 0-7695-2522-9/06, 2006.
12. Deng, H., Multicriteria analysis with fuzzy pairwise comparisons. *Int. J. Approximate Reasoning*, 21, 3, 215–231, 1999.
13. Seetha Lakshmi, V., Decision Making in Academic Institutions—A Fuzzy Ahp Approach. *Int. J. Eng. Sci. Technol. (IJEST)*, 5, 02, 11–23, 2013.
14. Triantaphyllou, E., Shu, B., Nieto Sanchez, S., Ray, T., Multi-Criteria Decision Making: An Operations Research Approach, in: *Encyclopedia of Electrical and Electronics Engineering*, vol. 15, J.G. Webster (Ed.), pp. 175–186, John Wiley & Sons, New York, NY, 1998.
15. Mikhailov, P. and Tsvetinov, Evaluation of Services using a Fuzzy Analytic Hierarchy Process. *Appl. Soft Comput.*, Elsevier, 5, 1, 23–33, 2004, logistics services.
16. Chen, C.T., Extensions of the TOPSIS for group decision-making under fuzzy environment. *Fuzzy Sets*, 114, 1, 1–9, 2000.
17. Chen, C.T., Lin, C.T., Huang, S.F., A fuzzy approach for supplier evaluation and selection in supply chain management. *Int. J. Prod. Econ.*, 102, 2, 289–3.01.95 and systems 114.1: 1–9, 2006.
18. Bottani, E. and Rizzi, A., A fuzzy TOPSIS methodology to support outsourcing of logistics services. *Supply Chain Manag.: An Int. J.*, 11, 4, 294–308, 2006.
19. Saaty, T.L., *The analytic hierarchy process: planning, priority setting, resource allocation*, McGraw-Hill International Book Co., New York, London, 1980.

5

Fuzzy Tri-Magic Labeling of Isomorphic Caterpillar Graph $\mathcal{T}^{6}_{2,3,4}$ of Diameter 5

P. Sumathi[1] and C. Monigeetha[2*]

[1]*Department of Mathematics, C. Kandaswami Naidu College for Men, Anna Nagar, Chennai, India*
[2]*Department of Mathematics, Sri Muthukumaran Arts and Science College, Chikkarayapuram, Chennai, India*

Abstract

Let G be a finite, simple, undirected and non-trivial graph. A fuzzy graph is said to admit tri-magic labeling if the number of magic membership values K_i's ($1 \leq i \leq 3$) differs by at most 1 and $|K_i - K_j| \leq \frac{2}{10^r}$ for $1 \leq i, j \leq 3$, $r \geq 2$. The fuzzy graph which admits a tri-magic labeling is called a fuzzy tri-magic labeling graph. The fuzzy tri-magic labeling graphs are denoted by $\tilde{T}m_0G$. A caterpillar is defined as a tree in which all the vertices are within distance one of a central path. In this paper we have taken the isomorphic caterpillar of diameter 5 and proved that it is fuzzy tri-magic and we also gave the magic membership values, their corresponding edges and the number of magic membership values as tables.

Keywords: Fuzzy labeling, magic membership value, fuzzy tri-magic labeling, diameter of a graph, caterpillar graph

5.1 Introduction

The graphs considered here are finite, simple, undirected and non-trivial [1]. Graph theory has a good development in graph labeling and has a broad range of applications [2]. Fuzzy is a newly emerging mathematical

**Corresponding author*: monimagendra@gmail.com

E. Chandrasekaran, R. Anandan, G. Suseendran, S. Balamurugan and Hanaa Hachimi (eds.) Fuzzy Intelligent Systems: Methodologies, Techniques, and Applications, (93–154) © 2021 Scrivener Publishing LLC

framework to exhibit the phenomenon of uncertainty in real-life tribulations. A fuzzy set is defined mathematically by assigning a value to each possible individual in the universe of discourse, representing its grade or membership which corresponds to the degree to which that individual is similar or compatible with the concept represented the fuzzy set. In this paper it is proved that isomorphic caterpillar of diameter 5 is Fuzzy tri-magic.

Definition 1. Fuzzy Graph
A fuzzy graph G: (σ, μ) is a pair of functions $\sigma : V \to [0, 1]$ and $\mu : V \times V \to [0, 1]$, where for all $u, v \in V$, we have $\mu(u, v) \leq \sigma(u) \bigwedge \sigma(v)$.

Definition 2. Fuzzy Labeling
Let $G = (V,E)$ be a graph, the fuzzy graph G: (σ, μ) is said to have a fuzzy labeling, if $\sigma : V \to [0, 1]$ and $\mu : V \times V \to [0, 1]$ is bijective such that the membership value of edges and vertices is distinct and $\mu(uv) \leq \sigma(u) \bigwedge \sigma(v)$ for all $u, v \in V$.

Definition 3. Magic Membership Value (MMV)
Let G: (σ, μ) be a fuzzy graph; the induced map $g{:}E(G) \to [0, 1]$ defined by $g(uv) = \sigma(u) + \mu(uv) + \sigma(v)$ is said to be a magic membership value. It is denoted by MMV.

Definition 4. Fuzzy Tri-Magic Labeling
A fuzzy graph is said to admit tri-magic labeling if the magic membership values K_i's, $1 \leq i \leq 3$ are constants where number of K_i's and K_j's differ by at most 1 and $|K_i - K_j| \leq \frac{2}{10^r}$ for $1 \leq i, j \leq 3, r \geq 2$.

Definition 5. Fuzzy Tri-Magic Labeling Graph
A fuzzy labeling graph which admits a tri-magic labeling is called a fuzzy tri-magic labeling graph. The fuzzy tri-magic labeling graphs are denoted by $\tilde{T}m_0G$.

Definition 6. Diameter of a Graph
The maximum distance between two vertices of a graph is called the diameter of a graph.

Definition 7. Caterpillar Graph
A caterpillar graph G, is a tree having a chordless path P_t on t vertices, called central path, which contains at least one end point of every edge. Vertices connecting the leaves with the central path are called support vertices.

Notation 1

Let $\mathcal{T}^{s_1}_{t_1, t_2, t_3}$ is a tree obtained by attaching m pendant edges, n pendant edges and a pendant edges to the path P_s at the vertices v_{t_1+1}, v_{t_2+1} and v_{t_3+1} respectively.

5.2 Main Result

Theorem 1: The caterpillar graph $\mathcal{T}^{6}_{2,3,4}$ of diameter 5 admits fuzzy tri-magic labeling for $m, n \geq 3$.

Proof:

Let G be a caterpillar graph $\mathcal{T}^{6}_{2,3,4}$ of diameter 5. Let m, n and a be the pendant edges attaching to the path P_6 at the vertices v_2, v_3 and v_4, respectively. Let the vertex set and edge set of $\mathcal{T}^{6}_{2,3,4}$ be

$$V(G) = \{v_j: 1 \leq j \leq 6\} \cup \{x_j: 1 \leq j \leq m\} \cup \{y_j: 1 \leq j \leq n\} \cup \{z_j: 1 \leq j \leq a\} \text{ and}$$

$$E(G) = \{v_j v_{j+1}: 1 \leq j \leq 5\} \cup \{v_2 x_j: 1 \leq j \leq m\} \cup \{v_3 y_j: 1 \leq j \leq n\} \cup \{v_4 z_j: 1 \leq j \leq a\}$$

$$|V(G)| = \mathrm{m} + \mathrm{n} + \mathrm{a} + 6 \text{ and } |E(G)| = \mathrm{m} + \mathrm{n} + \mathrm{a} + 5$$

Let $r \geq 2$ be any positive integer.

Define $\sigma : V \to [0, 1]$ such that

$$\sigma(v_j) = (2m + 2n + 2a + 27 - j)\frac{1}{10^r} \quad 1 \leq j \leq 6$$

Define $\mu : V \times V \to [0, 1]$ by

$$\mu(v_2 x_j) = (7 + j)\frac{1}{10^r} \qquad \text{for } 1 \leq j \leq m$$

$$\mu(v_3 y_j) = (m + 10 + j)\frac{1}{10^r} \qquad \text{for } 1 \leq j \leq n$$

$$\mu(v_5 z_j) = (m + n + 13 + j)\frac{1}{10^r} \qquad \text{for } 1 \leq j \leq a$$

$$\mu(v_1 v_2) = \frac{1}{10^r}, \mu(v_2 v_3) = \frac{3}{10^r}, \mu(v_3 v_4) = \frac{4}{10^r}, \mu(v_4 v_5) = \frac{6}{10^r}$$

$$\text{and } \mu(v_5 v_6) = \frac{7}{10^r}$$

Case (i) If $m \equiv 0(mod\ 3)$
Subcase (i) If $n \equiv 0(mod\ 3)$

$$\sigma(x_j) = (2m+2n+2a+20-j)\frac{1}{10^r} \quad \text{for } 1 \le j \le \frac{m}{3}$$

$$\sigma(x_j) = (2m+2n+2a+19-j)\frac{1}{10^r} \quad \text{for } \frac{m}{3}+1 \le j \le \frac{2}{m}$$

$$\sigma(x_j) = (2m+2n+2a+18-j)\frac{1}{10^r} \quad \text{for } \frac{2m}{3}+1 \le j \le m$$

$$\sigma(y_j) = (m+2n+2a+18-j)\frac{1}{10^r} \quad \text{for } 1 \le j \le \frac{n}{3}$$

$$\sigma(y_j) = (m+2n+2a+17-j)\frac{1}{10^r} \quad \text{for } \frac{n}{3}+1 \le j \le \frac{2n}{3}$$

$$\sigma(y_j) = (m+2n+2a+16-j)\frac{1}{10^r} \quad \text{for } \frac{2n}{3}+1 \le j \le n.$$

Subcase (i)a If $a \equiv 0(mod\ 3)$

$$\sigma(z_j) = (m+n+2a+16-j)\frac{1}{10^r} \quad \text{for } 1 \le j \le \frac{a}{3}$$

$$\sigma(z_j) = (m+n+2a+15-j)\frac{1}{10^r} \quad \text{for } \frac{a}{3}+1 \le \frac{2a}{3}$$

$$\sigma(z_j) = (m+n+2a+14-j)\frac{1}{10^r} \quad \text{for } \frac{2a}{3}+1 \le j \le a.$$

Subcase (i)b If $a \equiv 1(mod\ 3)$

$$\sigma(z_j) = (m+n+2a+16-j)\frac{1}{10^r} \quad \text{for } 1 \le j \le \frac{a-1}{3}$$

$$\sigma(z_j) = (m+n+2a+15-j)\frac{1}{10^r} \quad \text{for } \frac{a-1}{3}+1 \le i \le \frac{2(a-1)}{3}$$

$$\sigma(z_j) = (m+n+2a+14-j)\frac{1}{10^r} \quad \text{for } \frac{2(a-1)}{3}+1 \le j \le a.$$

Subcase (i)c If $a \equiv 2(mod\ 3)$

$$\sigma(z_j)=(m+n+2a+16-j)\frac{1}{10^r} \quad \text{for } 1 \le j \le \frac{a+1}{3}$$

$$\sigma(z_j)=(m+n+2a+15-j)\frac{1}{10^r} \quad \text{for} \left(\frac{a+1}{3}\right)+1 \le j \le \frac{2a-1}{3}$$

$$\sigma(z_j)=(m+n+2a+14-j)\frac{1}{10^r} \quad \text{for} \left(\frac{2a-1}{3}\right)+1 \le j \le a.$$

From different nature of *m*, *n*, MMVs K_i's, their corresponding edges and number of K_i's ($1 \le i \le 3$) are given in Table 5.1.

Subcase (ii) If $n \equiv 1(mod\ 3)$

$$\sigma(x_j)=(2m+2n+2a+20-j)\frac{1}{10^r} \quad \text{for } 1 \le j \le \frac{m}{3}$$

$$\sigma(x_j)=(2m+2n+2a+19-j)\frac{1}{10^r} \quad \text{for } \frac{m}{3}+1 \le j \le \frac{2m}{3}$$

$$\sigma(x_j)=(2m+2n+2a+18-j)\frac{1}{10^r} \quad \text{for } \frac{2m}{3}+1 \le j \le m$$

$$\sigma(y_j)=(m+2n+2a+18-j)\frac{1}{10^r} \quad \text{for } 1 \le j \le \frac{n-1}{3}$$

$$\sigma(y_j)=(m+2n+2a+17-j)\frac{1}{10^r} \quad \text{for } \frac{n-1}{3}+1 \le j \le \frac{2(n-1)}{3}$$

$$\sigma(y_j)=(m+2n+2a+16-j)\frac{1}{10^r} \quad \text{for } \frac{2(n-1)}{3}+1 \le j \le n.$$

Subcase (ii)a If $a \equiv 0(mod\ 3)$

$$\sigma(z_j)=(m+n+2a+16-j)\frac{1}{10^r} \quad \text{for } 1 \le j \le \frac{a}{3}$$

$$\sigma(z_j)=(m+n+2a+15-j)\frac{1}{10^r} \quad \text{for } \frac{a}{3}+1 \le j \le \frac{2a}{3}$$

$$\sigma(z_j)=(m+n+2a+14-j)\frac{1}{10^r} \quad \text{for } \frac{2a}{3}+1 \le j \le a.$$

Table 5.1 MMVs K_i's, their corresponding edges and the number of K_i's $(1 \leq i \leq 3)$.

Nature of m, n	Nature of a	Edges	MMV K_i's, $1 \leq i \leq 3$	Number of K_i's, $1 \leq i \leq 3$
$m \equiv 0(mod\ 3), n \equiv 0(mod\ 3)$	$a \equiv 0(mod\ 3)$	$g(v_2 x_j)$ if $1 \leq j \leq \frac{m}{3}$ $g(v_1 v_2), g(v_2 v_3)$ $g(v_3 y_j)$ if $1 \leq j \leq \frac{n}{3}$ $g(v_4 z_j)$ if $1 \leq j \leq \frac{a}{3}$	$(4m+4n+4a+52)\frac{1}{10^r}$ for i = 1	$\frac{m+n+a+6}{3}$ for i = 1
		$g(v_2 x_j)$ if $\frac{m}{3}+1 \leq j \leq \frac{2m}{3}$ $g(v_3 v_4), g(v_4 v_5)$ $g(v_3 y_j)$ if $\frac{n}{3}+1 \leq j \leq \frac{2n}{3}$ $g(v_4 z_j)$ if $\frac{a}{3}+1 \leq j \leq \frac{2a}{3}$	$(4m+4n+4a+51)\frac{1}{10^r}$ for i = 2	$\frac{m+n+a+6}{3}$ for i = 2

(*Continued*)

Table 5.1 MMVs K_i's, their corresponding edges and the number of K_i's ($1 \le i \le 3$). (*Continued*)

Nature of m, n	Nature of a	Edges	MMV K_i's, $1 \le i \le 3$	Number of K_i's, $1 \le i \le 3$
		$g(v_2x_j)$ if $\frac{2m}{3}+1 \le j \le m$ $g(v_5v_6)$ $g(v_3y_j)$ if $\frac{2n}{3}+1 \le j \le n$ $g(v_4z_j)$ if $\frac{2a}{3}+1 \le j \le a$	$(4m+4n+4a+50)\frac{1}{10^r}$ for i = 3	$\frac{m+n+a+3}{3}$ for i = 3
	$a \equiv 1(mod\ 3)$	$g(v_2x_j)$ if $1 \le j \le \frac{m}{3}$ $g(v_1v_2), g(v_2v_3)$ $g(v_3y_j)$ if $1 \le j \le \frac{n}{3}$ $g(v_4z_j)$ if $1 \le j \le \frac{a-1}{3}$	$(4m+4n+4a+52)\frac{1}{10^r}$ for i = 1	$\frac{m+n+a+5}{3}$ for i = 1

(*Continued*)

Table 5.1 MMVs K_i's, their corresponding edges and the number of K_i's ($1 \le i \le 3$). (*Continued*)

Nature of m, n	Nature of a	Edges	MMV K_i's, $1 \le i \le 3$	Number of K_i's, $1 \le i \le 3$
		$g(v_2x_j)$ if $\frac{m}{3}+1 \le j \le \frac{2m}{3}$ $g(v_3v_4), g(v_4v_5)$ $g(v_3y_j)$ if $\frac{n}{3}+1 \le j \le \frac{2n}{3}$ $g(v_4z_j)$ if $\frac{a-1}{3}+1 \le j \le \frac{2(a-1)}{3}$	$(4m+4n+4a+51)\frac{1}{10^r}$ for i = 2	$\frac{m+n+a+5}{3}$ for i = 2
		$g(v_2x_j)$ if $\frac{2m}{3}+1 \le j \le m$ $g(v_5v_6)$ $g(v_3y_j)$ if $\frac{2n}{3}+1 \le j \le n$ $g(v_4z_j)$ if $\frac{2(a-1)}{3}+1 \le j \le a$	$(4m+4n+4a+50)\frac{1}{10^r}$ for i = 3	$\frac{m+n+a+5}{3}$ for i = 3

(*Continued*)

Table 5.1 MMVs K_i's, their corresponding edges and the number of K_i's $(1 \le i \le 3)$. (*Continued*)

Nature of m, n	Nature of a	Edges		MMV K_i's, $1 \le i \le 3$	Number of K_i's, $1 \le i \le 3$
	$a \equiv 2(mod\ 3)$	$g(v_2x_j)$	if $1 \le j \le \frac{m}{3}$	$(4m+4n+4a+52)\frac{1}{10^r}$ for i = 1	$\frac{m+n+a+7}{3}$ for i = 1
		$g(v_1v_2), g(v_2v_3)$			
		$g(v_3y_j)$	if $1 \le j \le \frac{n}{3}$		
		$g(v_4z_j)$	if $1 \le j \le \frac{a+1}{3}$		
		$g(v_2x_j)$	if $\frac{m}{3}+1 \le j \le \frac{2m}{3}$	$(4m+4n+4a+51)\frac{1}{10^r}$ for i = 2	$\frac{m+n+a+4}{3}$ for i = 2
		$g(v_3v_4), g(v_4v_5)$			
		$g(v_3y_j)$	if $\frac{n}{3}+1 \le j \le \frac{2n}{3}$		
		$g(v_4z_j)$	if $\frac{a+1}{3}+1 \le j \le \frac{2a-1}{3}$		

(*Continued*)

Table 5.1 MMVs K_i's, their corresponding edges and the number of K_i's ($1 \le i \le 3$). (*Continued*)

Nature of m, n	Nature of a	Edges	MMV K_i's, $1 \le i \le 3$	Number of K_i's, $1 \le i \le 3$
		$g(v_2x_j)$ if $\frac{2m}{3}+1 \le j \le m$ $g(v_5v_6)$ $g(v_3y_j)$ if $\frac{2n}{3}+1 \le j \le n$ $g(v_4z_j)$ if $\frac{2a-1}{3}+1 \le i \le a$	$(4m+4n+4a+50)\frac{1}{10^r}$ for i = 3	$\frac{m+n+a+4}{3}$ for i = 3

Subcase (ii)b If $a \equiv 1(mod\,3)$

$$\sigma(z_j) = (m+n+2a+16-j)\frac{1}{10^r} \quad \text{for } 1 \leq j \leq \frac{a+2}{3}$$

$$\sigma(z_j) = (m+n+2a+15-j)\frac{1}{10^r} \quad \text{for} \left(\frac{a+2}{3}\right)+1 \leq j \leq \frac{2a+1}{3}$$

$$\sigma(z_j) = (m+n+2a+14-j)\frac{1}{10^r} \quad \text{for} \left(\frac{2a+1}{3}\right)+1 \leq j \leq a.$$

Subcase (ii)c If $a \equiv 2(mod\,3)$

$$\sigma(z_j) = (m+n+2a+16-j)\frac{1}{10^r} \quad \text{for } 1 \leq j \leq \frac{a+1}{3}$$

$$\sigma(z_j) = (m+n+2a+15-j)\frac{1}{10^r} \quad \text{for} \left(\frac{a+1}{3}\right)+1 \leq j \leq \frac{2(a+1)}{3}$$

$$\sigma(z_j) = (m+n+2a+14-j)\frac{1}{10^r} \quad \text{for } \frac{2(a+1)}{3}+1 \leq j \leq a.$$

From different nature of *m*, *n*, MMVs K_i's, their corresponding edges and number of K_i's ($1 \leq i \leq 3$) are given in Table 5.2.

Table 5.2 MMVs K_i's, their corresponding edges and the number of K_i's ($1 \le i \le 3$).

Nature of m, n	Nature of a	Edges	MMV K_i's, $1 \le i \le 3$	Number of K_i's, $1 \le i \le 3$
$m \equiv 0(mod\ 3),\ n \equiv 1(mod\ 3)$	$a \equiv 0(mod\ 3)$	$g(v_2x_j)$ if $1 \le j \le \frac{m}{3}$ $g(v_1v_2), g(v_2v_3)$ $g(v_3y_j)$ if $1 \le j \le \frac{n-1}{3}$ $g(v_4z_j)$ if $1 \le j \le \frac{a}{3}$	$(4m+4n+4a+52)\frac{1}{10^r}$ for i = 1	$\frac{m+n+a+5}{3}$ for i = 1
		$g(v_2x_j)$ if $\frac{m}{3}+1 \le j \le \frac{2m}{3}$ $g(v_3v_4), g(v_4v_5)$ $g(v_3y_j)$ if $\frac{n-1}{3}+1 \le j \le \frac{2(n-1)}{3}$ $g(v_4z_j)$ if $\frac{a}{3}+1 \le j \le \frac{2a}{3}$	$(4m+4n+4a+51)\frac{1}{10^r}$ for i = 2	$\frac{m+n+a+5}{3}$ for i = 2

(*Continued*)

Table 5.2 MMVs K_i's, their corresponding edges and the number of K_i's ($1 \le i \le 3$). (*Continued*)

Nature of m, n	Nature of a	Edges	MMV K_i's, $1 \le i \le 3$	Number of K_i's, $1 \le i \le 3$
		$g(v_2x_j)$ if $\frac{2m}{3}+1 \le j \le m$ $g(v_5v_6)$ $g(v_3y_j)$ if $\frac{2(n-1)}{3}+1 \le j \le n$ $g(v_4z_j)$ if $\frac{2a}{3}+1 \le j \le a$	$(4m+4n+4a+50)\frac{1}{10^r}$ for $i=3$	$\frac{m+n+a+5}{3}$ for $i=3$
	$a \equiv 1 (mod\ 3)$	$g(v_2x_j)$ if $1 \le j \le \frac{m}{3}$ $g(v_1v_2), g(v_2v_3)$ $g(v_3y_j)$ if $1 \le j \le \frac{n-1}{3}$ $g(v_4z_j)$ if $1 \le j \le \frac{a+2}{3}$	$(4m+4n+4a+52)\frac{1}{10^r}$ for $i=1$	$\frac{m+n+a+7}{3}$ for $i=1$

(*Continued*)

Table 5.2 MMVs K_i's, their corresponding edges and the number of K_i's ($1 \leq i \leq 3$). (*Continued*)

Nature of m, n	Nature of a	Edges	MMV K_i's, $1 \leq i \leq 3$	Number of K_i's, $1 \leq i \leq 3$
		$g(v_2 x_j)$ if $\frac{m}{3}+1 \leq j \leq \frac{2m}{3}$ $g(v_3 v_4), g(v_4 v_5)$ $g(v_3 y_j)$ if $\frac{n-1}{3}+1 \leq j \leq \frac{2(n-1)}{3}$ $g(v_4 z_j)$ if $\frac{a+2}{3}+1 \leq j \leq \frac{2a+1}{3}$	$(4m+4n+4a+51)\frac{1}{10^r}$ for i = 2	$\frac{m+n+a+4}{3}$ for i = 2
		$g(v_2 x_j)$ if $\frac{2m}{3}+1 \leq j \leq m$ $g(v_5 v_6)$ $g(v_3 y_j)$ if $\frac{2(n-1)}{3}+1 \leq j \leq n$ $g(v_4 z_j)$ if $\frac{2a+1}{3}+1 \leq j \leq a$	$(4m+4n+4a+50)\frac{1}{10^r}$ for i = 3	$\frac{m+n+a+4}{3}$ for i = 3

(*Continued*)

Table 5.2 MMVs K_i's, their corresponding edges and the number of K_i's $(1 \le i \le 3)$. (*Continued*)

Nature of m, n	Nature of a	Edges	MMV K_i's, $1 \le i \le 3$	Number of K_i's, $1 \le i \le 3$
	$a \equiv 2(mod\ 3)$	$g(v_2x_j)$ if $1 \le j \le \frac{m}{3}$ $g(v_1v_2), g(v_2v_3)$ $g(v_3y_j)$ if $1 \le j \le \frac{n-1}{3}$ $g(v_4z_j)$ if $1 \le j \le \frac{a+1}{3}$	$(4m+4n+4a+52)\frac{1}{10^r}$ for i = 1	$\frac{m+n+a+6}{3}$ for i = 1
		$g(v_2x_j)$ if $\frac{m}{3}+1 \le j \le \frac{2m}{3}$ $g(v_3v_4), g(v_4v_5)$ $g(v_3y_j)$ if $\frac{n-1}{3}+1 \le j \le \frac{2(n-1)}{3}$ $g(v_4z_j)$ if $\frac{a+1}{3}+1 \le j \le \frac{2(a+1)}{3}$	$(4m+4n+4a+51)\frac{1}{10^r}$ for i = 2	$\frac{m+n+a+6}{3}$ for i = 2

(*Continued*)

Table 5.2 MMVs K_i's, their corresponding edges and the number of K_i's ($1 \leq i \leq 3$). (*Continued*)

Nature of *m*, *n*	Nature of *a*	Edges	MMV K_i's, $1 \leq i \leq 3$	Number of K_i's, $1 \leq i \leq 3$
		$g(v_2 x_j)$ if $\frac{2m}{3}+1 \leq j \leq m$ $g(v_5 v_6)$ $g(v_3 y_j)$ if $\frac{2(n-1)}{3}+1 \leq j \leq n$ $g(v_4 z_j)$ if $\frac{2(a+1)}{3}+1 \leq j \leq a$	$(4m+4n+4a+50)\frac{1}{10^r}$ for i = 3	$\frac{m+n+a+3}{3}$ for i = 3

Subcase (iii) If $n \equiv 2(mod\ 3)$

$$\sigma(x_j)=(2m+2n+2a+20-j)\frac{1}{10^r} \quad \text{for } 1 \le j \le \frac{m}{3}$$

$$\sigma(x_j)=(2m+2n+2a+19-j)\frac{1}{10^r} \quad \text{for } \frac{m}{3}+1 \le j \le \frac{2m}{3}$$

$$\sigma(x_j)=(2m+2n+2a+18-j)\frac{1}{10^r} \quad \text{for } \frac{2m}{3}+1 \le j \le m$$

$$\sigma(y_j)=(m+2n+2a+18-j)\frac{1}{10^r} \quad \text{for } 1 \le j \le \frac{n+1}{3}$$

$$\sigma(y_j)=(m+2n+2a+17-j)\frac{1}{10^r} \quad \text{for } \left(\frac{n+1}{3}\right)+1 \le j \le \frac{2n-1}{3}$$

$$\sigma(y_j)=(m+2n+2a+16-j)\frac{1}{10^r} \quad \text{for } \left(\frac{2n-1}{3}\right)+1 \le j \le n.$$

Subcase (iii)a If $a \equiv 0(mod\ 3)$

$$\sigma(z_j)=(m+n+2a+16-j)\frac{1}{10^r} \quad \text{for } 1 \le j \le \frac{a}{3}$$

$$\sigma(z_j)=(m+n+2a+15-j)\frac{1}{10^r} \quad \text{for } \frac{a}{3}+1 \le j \le \frac{2a}{3}$$

$$\sigma(z_j)=(m+n+2a+14-j)\frac{1}{10^r} \quad \text{for } \frac{2a}{3}+1 \le j \le a.$$

Subcase (iii)b If $a \equiv 1(mod\ 3)$

$$\sigma(z_j)=(m+n+2a+16-j)\frac{1}{10^r} \quad \text{for } 1 \le j \le \frac{a-1}{3}$$

$$\sigma(z_j)=(m+n+2a+15-j)\frac{1}{10^r} \quad \text{for } \left(\frac{a-1}{3}\right)+1 \le j \le \frac{2a+1}{3}$$

$$\sigma(z_j)=(m+n+2a+14-j)\frac{1}{10^r} \quad \text{for } \left(\frac{2a+1}{3}\right)+1 \le j \le a.$$

Subcase (iii)c If $a \equiv 2(mod\, 3)$

$$\sigma(z_j)=(m+n+2a+16-j)\frac{1}{10^r} \quad \text{for } 1\le j\le \frac{a-1}{3}$$

$$\sigma(z_j)=(m+n+2a+15-j)\frac{1}{10^r} \quad \text{for } \left(\frac{a-1}{3}\right)+1\le j\le \frac{2a-1}{3}$$

$$\sigma(z_j)=(m+n+2a+14-j)\frac{1}{10^r} \quad \text{for } \left(\frac{2a-1}{3}\right)+1\le j\le a.$$

From different nature of *m*, *n*, MMVs K_i's, their corresponding edges and number of K_i's ($1 \le i \le 3$) are given in Table 5.3.

Case (ii) If $m \equiv 1(mod\, 3)$
Subcase (i) If $n \equiv 0(mod\, 3)$

$$\sigma(x_j)=(2m+2n+2a+20-j)\frac{1}{10^r} \quad \text{for } 1\le j\le \frac{m-1}{3}$$

$$\sigma(x_j)=(2m+2n+2a+19-j)\frac{1}{10^r} \quad \text{for } \frac{m-1}{3}+1\le j\le \frac{2(m-1)}{3}$$

$$\sigma(x_j)=(2m+2n+2a+18-j)\frac{1}{10^r} \quad \text{for } \frac{2(m-1)}{3}+1\le j\le m$$

$$\sigma(y_j)=(m+2n+2a+18-j)\frac{1}{10^r} \quad \text{for } 1\le j\le \frac{n}{3}$$

$$\sigma(y_j)=(m+2n+2a+17-j)\frac{1}{10^r} \quad \text{for } \frac{n}{3}+1\le j\le \frac{2n}{3}$$

$$\sigma(y_j)=(m+2n+2a+16-j)\frac{1}{10^r} \quad \text{for } \frac{2n}{3}+1\le j\le n.$$

Subcase (i)a If $a \equiv 0(mod\, 3)$

$$\sigma(z_j)=(m+n+2a+16-j)\frac{1}{10^r} \quad \text{for } 1\le j\le \frac{a}{3}$$

$$\sigma(z_j)=(m+n+2a+15-j)\frac{1}{10^r} \quad \text{for } \frac{a}{3}+1\le j\le \frac{2a}{3}$$

$$\sigma(z_j)=(m+n+2a+14-j)\frac{1}{10^r} \quad \text{for } \frac{2a}{3}+1\le j\le a$$

Table 5.3 MMVs K_i's, their corresponding edges and the number of K_i's ($1 \le i \le 3$).

Nature of m, n	Nature of a	Edges	MMV K_i's, $1 \le i \le 3$	Number of K_i's, $1 \le i \le 3$
$m \equiv 0(mod\ 3), n \equiv 2(mod\ 3)$	$a \equiv 0(mod\ 3)$	$g(v_2x_j)$ if $1 \le j \le \frac{m}{3}$ $g(v_1v_2), g(v_2v_3)$ $g(v_3y_j)$ if $1 \le j \le \frac{n+1}{3}$ $g(v_4z_j)$ if $1 \le j \le \frac{a}{3}$	$(4m+4n+4a+52)\frac{1}{10^r}$ for i = 1	$\frac{m+n+a+5}{3}$ for i = 1
		$g(v_2x_j)$ if $\frac{m}{3}+1 \le j \le \frac{2m}{3}$ $g(v_3v_4), g(v_4v_5)$ $g(v_3y_j)$ if $\frac{n+1}{3}+1 \le j \le \frac{2n-1}{3}$ $g(v_4z_j)$ if $\frac{a}{3}+1 \le j \le \frac{2a}{3}$	$(4m+4n+4a+51)\frac{1}{10^r}$ for i = 2	$\frac{m+n+a+5}{3}$ for i = 2

(Continued)

Table 5.3 MMVs K_i's, their corresponding edges and the number of K_i's ($1 \le i \le 3$). (*Continued*)

Nature of m, n	Nature of a	Edges	MMV K_i's, $1 \le i \le 3$	Number of K_i's, $1 \le i \le 3$
		$g(v_2x_j)$ if $\frac{2m}{3}+1 \le j \le m$ $g(v_5v_6)$ $g(v_3y_j)$ if $\frac{2n-1}{3}+1 \le j \le n$ $g(v_4z_j)$ if $\frac{2a}{3}+1 \le j \le a$	$(4m+4n+4a+50)\frac{1}{10^r}$ for i = 3	$\frac{m+n+a+5}{3}$ for i = 3
	$a \equiv 1(mod\ 3)$	$g(v_2x_j)$ if $1 \le j \le \frac{m}{3}$ $g(v_1v_2), g(v_2v_3)$ $g(v_3y_j)$ if $1 \le j \le \frac{n+1}{3}$ $g(v_4z_j)$ if $1 \le j \le \frac{a-1}{3}$	$(4m+4n+4a+52)\frac{1}{10^r}$ for i = 1	$\frac{m+n+a+7}{3}$ for i = 1

(*Continued*)

Table 5.3 MMVs K_i's, their corresponding edges and the number of K_i's ($1 \le i \le 3$). (*Continued*)

Nature of m, n	Nature of a	Edges	MMV K_i's, $1 \le i \le 3$	Number of K_i's, $1 \le i \le 3$
		$g(v_2x_j)$ if $\frac{m}{3}+1 \le j \le \frac{2m}{3}$ $g(v_3v_4), g(v_4v_5)$ $g(v_3y_j)$ if $\frac{n+1}{3}+1 \le j \le \frac{2n-1}{3}$ $g(v_4z_j)$ if $\frac{a-1}{3}+1 \le j \le \frac{2a+1}{3}$	$(4m+4n+4a+51)\frac{1}{10^r}$ for i = 2	$\frac{m+n+a+4}{3}$ for i = 2
		$g(v_2x_j)$ if $\frac{2m}{3}+1 \le j \le m$ $g(v_5v_6)$ $g(v_3y_j)$ if $\frac{2n-1}{3}+1 \le j \le n$ $g(v_4z_j)$ if $\frac{2a+1}{3}+1 \le j \le a$	$(4m+4n+4a+50)\frac{1}{10^r}$ for i = 3	$\frac{m+n+a+4}{3}$ for i = 3

(*Continued*)

Table 5.3 MMVs K_i's, their corresponding edges and the number of K_i's ($1 \le i \le 3$). (*Continued*)

Nature of m, n	Nature of a	Edges	MMV K_i's, $1 \le i \le 3$	Number of K_i's, $1 \le i \le 3$
	$a \equiv 2(mod\ 3)$	$g(v_2x_j)$ if $1 \le j \le \frac{m}{3}$ $g(v_1v_2), g(v_2v_3)$ $g(v_3y_j)$ if $1 \le j \le \frac{n+1}{3}$ $g(v_4z_j)$ if $1 \le j \le \frac{a-1}{3}$	$(4m+4n+4a+52)\frac{1}{10^r}$ for i = 1	$\frac{m+n+a+6}{3}$ for i = 1
		$g(v_2x_j)$ if $\frac{m}{3}+1 \le j \le \frac{2m}{3}$ $g(v_3v_4), g(v_4v_5)$ $g(v_3y_j)$ if $\frac{n+1}{3}+1 \le j \le \frac{2n-1}{3}$ $g(v_4z_j)$ if $\frac{a-1}{3}+1 \le j \le \frac{2a-1}{3}$	$(4m+4n+4a+51)\frac{1}{10^r}$ for i = 2	$\frac{m+n+a+6}{3}$ for i = 2

(*Continued*)

Table 5.3 MMVs K_i's, their corresponding edges and the number of K_i's ($1 \le i \le 3$). (*Continued*)

Nature of m, n	**Nature of** a	**Edges**	**MMV** K_i**'s,** $1 \le i \le 3$	**Number of** K_i**'s,** $1 \le i \le 3$
		$g(v_2x_j)$ if $\frac{2m}{3}+1 \le j \le m$ $g(v_5v_6)$ $g(v_3y_j)$ if $\frac{2n-1}{3}+1 \le j \le n$ $g(v_4z_j)$ if $\frac{2a-1}{3}+1 \le j \le a$	$(4m+4n+4a+50)\frac{1}{10^r}$ for i = 3	$\frac{m+n+a+3}{3}$ for i = 3

Subcase (i)b If $a \equiv 1(mod\,3)$

$$\sigma(z_j) = (m+n+2a+16-j)\frac{1}{10^r} \quad \text{for } 1 \le j \le \frac{a+2}{3}$$

$$\sigma(z_j) = (m+n+2a+15-j)\frac{1}{10^r} \quad \text{for } \left(\frac{a+2}{3}\right)+1 \le j \le \frac{2a+1}{3}$$

$$\sigma(z_j) = (m+n+2a+14-j)\frac{1}{10^r} \quad \text{for } \left(\frac{2a+1}{3}\right)+1 \le j \le a.$$

Subcase (i)c If $a \equiv 2(mod\,3)$

$$\sigma(z_j) = (m+n+2a+16-j)\frac{1}{10^r} \quad \text{for } 1 \le j \le \frac{a+1}{3}$$

$$\sigma(z_j) = (m+n+2a+15-j)\frac{1}{10^r} \quad \text{for } \left(\frac{a+1}{3}\right)+1 \le j \le \frac{2(a+1)}{3}$$

$$\sigma(z_j) = (m+n+2a+14-j)\frac{1}{10^r} \quad \text{for } \frac{2(a+1)}{3}+1 \le j \le a.$$

From different nature of *m*, *n*, MMVs K_i's, their corresponding edges and number of K_i's ($1 \le i \le 3$) are given in Table 5.4.

Subcase (ii) If $n \equiv 1(mod\,3)$

$$\sigma(x_j) = (2m+2n+2a+20-j)\frac{1}{10^r} \quad \text{for } 1 \le j \le \frac{m-1}{3}$$

$$\sigma(x_j) = (2m+2n+2a+19-j)\frac{1}{10^r} \quad \text{for } \frac{m-1}{3}+1 \le j \le \frac{2(m-1)}{3}$$

$$\sigma(x_j) = (2m+2n+2a+18-j)\frac{1}{10^r} \quad \text{for } \frac{2(m-1)}{3}+1 \le j \le m$$

$$\sigma(y_j) = (m+2n+2a+18-j)\frac{1}{10^r} \quad \text{for } 1 \le j \le \frac{n+2}{3}$$

$$\sigma(y_j) = (m+2n+2a+17-j)\frac{1}{10^r} \quad \text{for } \left(\frac{n+2}{3}\right)+1 \le j \le \frac{2n+1}{3}$$

$$\sigma(y_j) = (m+2n+2a+16-j)\frac{1}{10^r} \quad \text{for } \left(\frac{2n+1}{3}\right)+1 \le j \le n.$$

Table 5.4 MMVs K_i's, their corresponding edges and the number of K_i's $(1 \le i \le 3)$.

Nature of m, n	Nature of a	Edges	MMV K_i's, $1 \le i \le 3$	Number of K_i's, $1 \le i \le 3$
$m \equiv 1(mod\ 3),\ n \equiv 0(mod\ 3)$	$a \equiv 0(mod\ 3)$	$g(v_2x_j)$ if $1 \le j \le \frac{m-1}{3}$ $g(v_1v_2), g(v_2v_3)$ $g(v_3y_j)$ if $1 \le j \le \frac{n}{3}$ $g(v_4z_j)$ if $1 \le j \le \frac{a}{3}$	$(4m+4n+4a+52)\frac{1}{10^r}$ for i = 1	$\frac{m+n+a+5}{3}$ for i = 1
		$g(v_2x_j)$ if $\frac{m-1}{3}+1 \le j \le \frac{2(m-1)}{3}$ $g(v_3v_4), g(v_4v_5)$ $g(v_3y_j)$ if $\frac{n}{3}+1 \le j \le \frac{2n}{3}$ $g(v_4z_j)$ if $\frac{a}{3}+1 \le j \le \frac{2a}{3}$	$(4m+4n+4a+51)\frac{1}{10^r}$ for i = 2	$\frac{m+n+a+5}{3}$ for i = 2

(Continued)

Table 5.4 MMVs K_i's, their corresponding edges and the number of K_i's ($1 \le i \le 3$). *(Continued)*

Nature of m, n	Nature of a	Edges	MMV K_i's, $1 \le i \le 3$	Number of K_i's, $1 \le i \le 3$
		$g(v_2x_j)$ if $\frac{2(m-1)}{3}+1 \le j \le m$ $g(v_5v_6)$ $g(v_3y_j)$ if $\frac{2n}{3}+1 \le j \le n$ $g(v_4z_j)$ if $\frac{2a}{3}+1 \le j \le a$	$(4m+4n+4a+50)\frac{1}{10^r}$ for i = 3	$\frac{m+n+a+5}{3}$ for i = 3
	$a \equiv 1(mod\ 3)$	$g(v_2x_j)$ if $1 \le j \le \frac{m-1}{3}$ $g(v_1v_2), g(v_2v_3)$ $g(v_3y_j)$ if $1 \le j \le \frac{n}{3}$ $g(v_4z_j)$ if $1 \le j \le \frac{a+2}{3}$	$(4m+4n+4a+52)\frac{1}{10^r}$ for i = 1	$\frac{m+n+a+7}{3}$ for i = 1

(Continued)

Table 5.4 MMVs K_i's, their corresponding edges and the number of K_i's $(1 \le i \le 3)$. *(Continued)*

Nature of ***m, n***	**Nature of** ***a***	**Edges**	**MMV** K_i**'s,** $1 \le i \le 3$	**Number of** K_i**'s,** $1 \le i \le 3$
		$g(v_2x_j)$ if $\frac{m-1}{3}+1 \le j \le \frac{2(m-1)}{3}$ $g(v_3v_4), g(v_4v_5)$ $g(v_3y_j)$ if $\frac{n}{3}+1 \le j \le \frac{2n}{3}$ $g(v_4z_j)$ if $\frac{2a+1}{3}+1 \le j \le \frac{2a+1}{3}$	$(4m+4n+4a+51)\frac{1}{10^r}$ for i = 2	$\frac{m+n+a+4}{3}$ for i = 2
		$g(v_2x_j)$ if $\frac{2(m-1)}{3}+1 \le j \le m$ $g(v_5v_6)$ $g(v_3y_j)$ if $\frac{2n}{3}+1 \le j \le n$ $g(v_4z_j)$ if $\frac{2a+1}{3}+1 \le j \le a$	$(4m+4n+4a+50)\frac{1}{10^r}$ for i = 3	$\frac{m+n+a+4}{3}$ for i = 3

(Continued)

Table 5.4 MMVs K_i's, their corresponding edges and the number of K_i's ($1 \le i \le 3$). (Continued)

Nature of m, n	Nature of a	Edges	MMV K_i's, $1 \le i \le 3$	Number of K_i's, $1 \le i \le 3$
	$a \equiv 2(mod\ 3)$	$g(v_2 x_j)$ if $1 \le j \le \dfrac{m-1}{3}$ $g(v_1 v_2), g(v_2 v_3)$ $g(v_3 y_j)$ if $1 \le j \le \dfrac{n}{3}$ $g(v_4 z_j)$ if $1 \le j \le \dfrac{a+1}{3}$	$(4m+4n+4a+52)\dfrac{1}{10^r}$ for $i = 1$	$\dfrac{m+n+a+6}{3}$ for $i = 1$
		$g(v_2 x_j)$ if $\dfrac{m-1}{3}+1 \le j \le \dfrac{2(m-1)}{3}$ $g(v_3 v_4), g(v_4 v_5)$ $g(v_3 y_j)$ if $\dfrac{n}{3}+1 \le j \le \dfrac{2n}{3}$ $g(v_4 z_j)$ if $\dfrac{a+1}{3}+1 \le j \le \dfrac{2(a+1)}{3}$	$(4m+4n+4a+51)\dfrac{1}{10^r}$ for $i = 2$	$\dfrac{m+n+a+6}{3}$ for $i = 2$

(Continued)

Table 5.4 MMVs K_i's, their corresponding edges and the number of K_i's $(1 \le i \le 3)$. (*Continued*)

Nature of m, n	Nature of a	Edges	MMV K_i's, $1 \le i \le 3$	Number of K_i's, $1 \le i \le 3$
		$g(v_2x_j)$ if $\frac{2(m-1)}{3}+1 \le j \le m$ $g(v_5v_6)$ $g(v_3y_j)$ if $\frac{2n}{3}+1 \le j \le n$ $g(v_4z_j)$ if $\frac{2(a+1)}{3}+1 \le j \le a$	$(4m+4n+4a+50)\frac{1}{10^r}$ for i = 3	$\frac{m+n+a+3}{3}$ for i = 3

Subcase (ii)a If $a \equiv 0(mod\ 3)$

$$\sigma(z_j)=(m+n+2a+16-j)\frac{1}{10^r} \quad \text{for } 1 \le j \le \frac{a}{3}$$

$$\sigma(z_j)=(m+n+2a+15-j)\frac{1}{10^r} \quad \text{for } \frac{a}{3}+1 \le j \le \frac{2a}{3}$$

$$\sigma(z_j)=(m+n+2a+14-j)\frac{1}{10^r} \quad \text{for } \frac{2a}{3}+1 \le j \le a.$$

Subcase (ii)b If $a \equiv 1(mod\ 3)$

$$\sigma(z_j)=(m+n+2a+16-j)\frac{1}{10^r} \quad \text{for } 1 \le j \le \frac{a-1}{3}$$

$$\sigma(z_j)=(m+n+2a+15-j)\frac{1}{10^r} \quad \text{for } \left(\frac{a-1}{3}\right)+1 \le j \le \frac{2a+1}{3}$$

$$\sigma(z_j)=(m+n+2a+14-j)\frac{1}{10^r} \quad \text{for } \left(\frac{2a+1}{3}\right)+1 \le j \le a.$$

Subcase (ii)c If $a \equiv 2(mod\ 3)$

$$\sigma(z_j)=(m+n+2a+16-j)\frac{1}{10^r} \quad \text{for } 1 \le j \le \frac{a-1}{3}$$

$$\sigma(z_j)=(m+n+2a+15-j)\frac{1}{10^r} \quad \text{for } \left(\frac{a-1}{3}\right)+1 \le j \le \frac{2a-1}{3}$$

$$\sigma(z_j)=(m+n+2a+14-j)\frac{1}{10^r} \quad \text{for } \left(\frac{2a-1}{3}\right)+1 \le j \le a.$$

From different nature of m, n, MMVs K_i's, their corresponding edges and number of K_i's ($1 \le i \le 3$) are given in Table 5.5.

Table 5.5 MMVs K_i's, their corresponding edges and the number of K_i's ($1 \le i \le 3$).

Nature of m, n	Nature of a	Edges	MMV K_i's, $1 \le i \le 3$	Number of K_i's, $1 \le i \le 3$
$m \equiv 1 (mod\ 3), n \equiv 1 (mod\ 3)$	$a \equiv 0 (mod\ 3)$	$g(v_2 x_j)$ if $1 \le j \le \frac{m-1}{3}$ $g(v_1 v_2), g(v_2 v_3)$ $g(v_3 y_j)$ if $1 \le j \le \frac{n+2}{3}$ $g(v_4 z_j)$ if $1 \le j \le \frac{a}{3}$	$(4m+4n+4a+52)\frac{1}{10^r}$ for i = 1	$\frac{m+n+a+7}{3}$ for i = 1
		$g(v_2 x_j)$ if $\frac{m-1}{3}+1 \le j \le \frac{2(m-1)}{3}$ $g(v_3 v_4), g(v_4 v_5)$ $g(v_3 y_j)$ if $\frac{n+2}{3}+1 \le j \le \frac{2n+1}{3}$ $g(v_4 z_j)$ if $\frac{a}{3}+1 \le j \le \frac{2a}{3}$	$(4m+4n+4a+51)\frac{1}{10^r}$ for i = 2	$\frac{m+n+a+4}{3}$ for i = 2

(*Continued*)

Table 5.5 MMVs K_i's, their corresponding edges and the number of K_i's ($1 \le i \le 3$). (*Continued*)

Nature of m, n	Nature of a	Edges	MMV K_i's, $1 \le i \le 3$	Number of K_i's, $1 \le i \le 3$
		$g(v_2x_j)$ if $\frac{2(m-1)}{3}+1 \le j \le m$ $g(v_5v_6)$ $g(v_3y_j)$ if $\frac{2n+1}{3}+1 \le j \le n$ $g(v_4z_j)$ if $\frac{2a}{3}+1 \le j \le a$	$(4m+4n+4a+50)\frac{1}{10^r}$ for $i=3$	$\frac{m+n+a+4}{3}$ for $i=3$
	$a \equiv 1(mod\ 3)$	$g(v_2x_j)$ if $1 \le j \le \frac{m-1}{3}$ $g(v_1v_2), g(v_2v_3)$ $g(v_3y_j)$ if $1 \le j \le \frac{n+2}{3}$ $g(v_4z_j)$ if $1 \le j \le \frac{a-1}{3}$	$(4m+4n+4a+52)\frac{1}{10^r}$ for $i=1$	$\frac{m+n+a+6}{3}$ for $i=1$

(*Continued*)

Table 5.5 MMVs K_i's, their corresponding edges and the number of K_i's $(1 \le i \le 3)$. *(Continued)*

Nature of m, n	**Nature of a**	**Edges**	**MMV K_i's, $1 \le i \le 3$**	**Number of K_i's, $1 \le i \le 3$**
		$g(v_2x_j)$ if $\frac{m-1}{3}+1 \le j \le \frac{2(m-1)}{3}$ $g(v_3v_4), g(v_4v_5)$ $g(v_3y_j)$ if $\frac{n+2}{3}+1 \le j \le \frac{2n+1}{3}$ $g(v_4z_j)$ if $\frac{a-1}{3}+1 \le j \le \frac{2a+1}{3}$	$(4m+4n+4a+51)\frac{1}{10^r}$ for i = 2	$\frac{m+n+a+6}{3}$ for i = 2
		$g(v_2x_j)$ if $\frac{2(m-1)}{3}+1 \le j \le m$ $g(v_5v_6)$ $g(v_3y_j)$ if $\frac{2n+1}{3}+1 \le j \le n$ $g(v_4z_j)$ if $\frac{2a+1}{3}+1 \le j \le a$	$(4m+4n+4a+50)\frac{1}{10^r}$ for i = 3	$\frac{m+n+a+3}{3}$ for i = 3

(Continued)

Table 5.5 MMVs K_i's, their corresponding edges and the number of K_i's ($1 \le i \le 3$). (*Continued*)

Nature of m, n	Nature of a	Edges		MMV K_i's, $1 \le i \le 3$	Number of K_i's, $1 \le i \le 3$
	$a \equiv 2 (mod\ 3)$	$g(v_2 x_j)$ $g(v_1 v_2), g(v_2 v_3)$ $g(v_3 y_j)$ $g(v_4 z_j)$	if $1 \le j \le \frac{m-1}{3}$ if $1 \le j \le \frac{n+2}{3}$ if $1 \le j \le \frac{a-1}{3}$	$(4m+4n+4a+52)\frac{1}{10^r}$ for i = 1	$\frac{m+n+a+5}{3}$ for i = 1
		$g(v_2 x_j)$ $g(v_3 v_4), g(v_4 v_5)$ $g(v_3 y_j)$ $g(v_4 z_j)$	if $\frac{m-1}{3}+1 \le j \le \frac{2(m-1)}{3}$ if $\frac{n+2}{3}+1 \le j \le \frac{2n+1}{3}$ if $\frac{a-1}{3}+1 \le j \le \frac{2a-1}{3}$	$(4m+4n+4a+51)\frac{1}{10^r}$ for i = 2	$\frac{m+n+a+5}{3}$ for i = 2

(*Continued*)

Table 5.5 MMVs K_i's, their corresponding edges and the number of K_i's ($1 \le i \le 3$). (*Continued*)

Nature of m, n	**Nature of a**	**Edges**	**MMV K_i's, $1 \le i \le 3$**	**Number of K_i's, $1 \le i \le 3$**
		$g(v_2x_j)$ if $\frac{2(m-1)}{3}+1 \le j \le m$ $g(v_5v_6)$ $g(v_3y_j)$ if $\frac{2n+1}{3}+1 \le j \le n$ $g(v_4z_j)$ if $\frac{2a-1}{3}+1 \le j \le a$	$(4m+4n+4a+50)\frac{1}{10^r}$ for i = 3	$\frac{m+n+a+5}{3}$ for i = 3

Subcase (iii) If $n \equiv 2(mod\ 3)$

$$\sigma(x_j)=(2m+2n+2a+20-j)\frac{1}{10^r} \quad \text{for } 1\le j\le \frac{m-1}{3}$$

$$\sigma(x_j)=(2m+2n+2a+19-j)\frac{1}{10^r} \quad \text{for } \frac{m-1}{3}+1\le j\le \frac{2(m-1)}{3}$$

$$\sigma(x_j)=(2m+2n+2a+18-j)\frac{1}{10^r} \quad \text{for } \frac{2(m-1)}{3}+1\le j\le m$$

$$\sigma(y_j)=(m+2n+2a+18-j)\frac{1}{10^r} \quad \text{for } 1\le j\le \frac{n+1}{3}$$

$$\sigma(y_j)=(m+2n+2a+17-j)\frac{1}{10^r} \quad \text{for } \left(\frac{n+1}{3}\right)+1\le j\le \frac{2n-1}{3}$$

$$\sigma(y_j)=(m+2n+2a+16-j)\frac{1}{10^r} \quad \text{for } \left(\frac{2n-1}{3}\right)+1\le j\le n.$$

Subcase (iii)a If $a \equiv 0(mod\ 3)$

$$\sigma(z_j)=(m+n+2a+16-j)\frac{1}{10^r} \quad \text{for } 1\le j\le \frac{a}{3}$$

$$\sigma(z_j)=(m+n+2a+15-j)\frac{1}{10^r} \quad \text{for } \frac{a}{3}+1\le j\le \frac{2a}{3}$$

$$\sigma(z_j)=(m+n+2a+14-j)\frac{1}{10^r} \quad \text{for } \frac{2a}{3}+1\le j\le a.$$

Subcase (iii)b If $a \equiv 1(mod\ 3)$

$$\sigma(z_j)=(m+n+2a+16-j)\frac{1}{10^r} \quad \text{for } 1\le j\le \frac{a+2}{3}$$

$$\sigma(z_j)=(m+n+2a+15-j)\frac{1}{10^r} \quad \text{for } \left(\frac{a+2}{3}\right)+1\le j\le \frac{2a+1}{3}$$

$$\sigma(z_j)=(m+n+2a+14-j)\frac{1}{10^r} \quad \text{for } \left(\frac{2a+1}{3}\right)+1\le j\le a.$$

Subcase (iii)c If $a \equiv 2(mod\,3)$

$$\sigma(z_j) = (m+n+2a+16-j)\frac{1}{10^r} \quad \text{for } 1 \le j \le \frac{a+1}{3}$$

$$\sigma(z_j) = (m+n+2a+15-j)\frac{1}{10^r} \quad \text{for } \left(\frac{a+1}{3}\right)+1 \le j \le \frac{2(a+1)}{3}$$

$$\sigma(z_j) = (m+n+2a+14-j)\frac{1}{10^r} \quad \text{for } \frac{2(a+1)}{3}+1 \le j \le a.$$

From different nature of m, n, MMVs K_i's, their corresponding edges and number of K_i's ($1 \le i \le 3$) are given in Table 5.6.

Case (iii) If $m \equiv 2(mod\,3)$
Subcase (i) If $n \equiv 0(mod\,3)$

$$\sigma(x_j) = (2m+2n+2a+20-j)\frac{1}{10^r} \quad \text{for } 1 \le j \le \frac{m+1}{3}$$

$$\sigma(x_j) = (2m+2n+2a+19-j)\frac{1}{10^r} \quad \text{for } \left(\frac{m+1}{3}\right)+1 \le j \le \frac{2m-1}{3}$$

$$\sigma(x_j) = (2m+2n+2a+18-j)\frac{1}{10^r} \quad \text{for } \left(\frac{2m-1}{3}\right)+1 \le j \le m$$

$$\sigma(y_j) = (m+2n+2a+18-j)\frac{1}{10^r} \quad \text{for } 1 \le j \le \frac{n}{3}$$

$$\sigma(y_j) = (m+2n+2a+17-j)\frac{1}{10^r} \quad \text{for } \frac{n}{3}+1 \le j \le \frac{2n}{3}$$

$$\sigma(y_j) = (m+2n+2a+16-j)\frac{1}{10^r} \quad \text{for } \frac{2n}{3}+1 \le j \le n.$$

Table 5.6 MMVs K_i's, their corresponding edges and the number of K_i's $(1 \le i \le 3)$.

Nature of m, n	Nature of a	Edges		MMV K_i's, $1 \le i \le 3$	Number of K_i's, $1 \le i \le 3$
$m \equiv 1(mod\ 3), n \equiv 2(mod\ 3)$	$a \equiv 0(mod\ 3)$	$g(v_2x_j)$	if $1 \le j \le \frac{m-1}{3}$	$(4m+4n+4a+52)\frac{1}{10^r}$ for i = 1	$\frac{m+n+a+6}{3}$ for i = 1
		$g(v_1v_2), g(v_2v_3)$			
		$g(v_3y_j)$	if $1 \le j \le \frac{n+1}{3}$		
		$g(v_4z_j)$	if $1 \le j \le \frac{a}{3}$		
		$g(v_2x_j)$	if $\frac{m-1}{3}+1 \le j \le \frac{2(m-1)}{3}$	$(4m+4n+4a+51)\frac{1}{10^r}$ for i = 2	$\frac{m+n+a+6}{3}$ for i = 2
		$g(v_3v_4), g(v_4v_5)$			
		$g(v_3y_j)$	if $\frac{n+1}{3}+1 \le j \le \frac{2n-1}{3}$		
		$g(v_4z_j)$	if $\frac{a}{3}+1 \le j \le \frac{2a}{3}$		

(*Continued*)

Table 5.6 MMVs K_i's, their corresponding edges and the number of K_i's ($1 \le i \le 3$). (*Continued*)

Nature of *m, n*	Nature of *a*	Edges	MMV K_i's, $1 \le i \le 3$	Number of K_i's, $1 \le i \le 3$
		$g(v_2x_j)$ if $\frac{2(m-1)}{3}+1 \le j \le m$ $g(v_5v_6)$ $g(v_3y_j)$ if $\frac{2n-1}{3}+1 \le j \le n$ $g(v_4z_j)$ if $\frac{2a}{3}+1 \le j \le a$	$(4m+4n+4a+50)\frac{1}{10^r}$ for i = 3	$\frac{m+n+a+3}{3}$ for i = 3
	$a \equiv 1(mod\ 3)$	$g(v_2x_j)$ if $1 \le j \le \frac{m-1}{3}$ $g(v_1v_2), g(v_2v_3)$ $g(v_3y_j)$ if $1 \le j \le \frac{n+1}{3}$ $g(v_4z_j)$ if $1 \le j \le \frac{a+2}{3}$	$(4m+4n+4a+52)\frac{1}{10^r}$ for i = 1	$\frac{m+n+a+5}{3}$ for i = 1

(*Continued*)

Table 5.6 MMVs K_i's, their corresponding edges and the number of K_i's ($1 \le i \le 3$). *(Continued)*

Nature of m, n	Nature of a	Edges	MMV K_i's, $1 \le i \le 3$	Number of K_i's, $1 \le i \le 3$
		$g(v_2x_j)$ if $\frac{m-1}{3}+1 \le j \le \frac{2(m-1)}{3}$ $g(v_3v_4), g(v_4v_5)$ $g(v_3y_j)$ if $\frac{n+1}{3}+1 \le j \le \frac{2n-1}{3}$ $g(v_4z_j)$ if $\frac{a+2}{3}+1 \le j \le \frac{2a+1}{3}$	$(4m+4n+4a+51)\frac{1}{10^r}$ for i = 2	$\frac{m+n+a+5}{3}$ for i = 2
		$g(v_2x_j)$ if $\frac{2(m-1)}{3}+1 \le j \le m$ $g(v_5v_6)$ $g(v_3y_j)$ if $\frac{2n-1}{3}+1 \le j \le n$ $g(v_4z_j)$ if $\frac{2a+1}{3}+1 \le j \le a$	$(4m+4n+4a+50)\frac{1}{10^r}$ for i = 3	$\frac{m+n+a+5}{3}$ for i = 3

(Continued)

Table 5.6 MMVs K_i's, their corresponding edges and the number of K_i's ($1 \le i \le 3$). (*Continued*)

Nature of m, n	Nature of a	Edges		MMV K_i's, $1 \le i \le 3$	Number of K_i's, $1 \le i \le 3$
	$a \equiv 2 (mod\ 3)$	$g(v_2x_j)$ $g(v_1v_2), g(v_2v_3)$ $g(v_3y_j)$ $g(v_4z_j)$	if $1 \le j \le \frac{m-1}{3}$ if $1 \le j \le \frac{n+1}{3}$ if $1 \le j \le \frac{a+1}{3}$	$(4m+4n+4a+52)\frac{1}{10^r}$ for i = 1	$\frac{m+n+a+7}{3}$ for i = 1
		$g(v_2x_j)$ $g(v_3v_4), g(v_4v_5)$ $g(v_3y_j)$ $g(v_4z_j)$	if $\frac{m-1}{3}+1 \le j \le \frac{2(m-1)}{3}$ if $\frac{n+1}{3}+1 \le j \le \frac{2n-1}{3}$ if $\frac{a+1}{3}+1 \le j \le \frac{2(a+1)}{3}$	$(4m+4n+4a+51)\frac{1}{10^r}$ for i = 2	$\frac{m+n+a+4}{3}$ for i = 2

(*Continued*)

Table 5.6 MMVs K_i's, their corresponding edges and the number of K_i's ($1 \le i \le 3$). (*Continued*)

Nature of m, n	Nature of a	Edges	MMV K_i's, $1 \le i \le 3$	Number of K_i's, $1 \le i \le 3$
		$g(v_2x_j)$ if $\frac{2(m-1)}{3}+1 \le j \le m$ $g(v_5v_6)$ $g(v_3y_j)$ if $\frac{2n-1}{3}+1 \le j \le n$ $g(v_4z_j)$ if $\frac{2(a+1)}{3}+1 \le j \le a$	$(4m+4n+4a+50)\frac{1}{10^r}$ for i = 3	$\frac{m+n+a+4}{3}$ for i = 3

Subcase (i)a If $a \equiv 0(mod\ 3)$

$$\sigma(z_j)=(m+n+2a+16-j)\frac{1}{10^r} \quad \text{for } 1\le j\le \frac{a}{3}$$

$$\sigma(z_j)=(m+n+2a+15-j)\frac{1}{10^r} \quad \text{for } \frac{a}{3}+1\le j\le \frac{2a}{3}$$

$$\sigma(z_j)=(m+n+2a+14-j)\frac{1}{10^r} \quad \text{for } \frac{2a}{3}+1\le j\le a.$$

Subcase (i)b If $a \equiv 1(mod\ 3)$

$$\sigma(z_j)=(m+n+2a+16-j)\frac{1}{10^r} \quad \text{for } 1\le j\le \frac{a-1}{3}$$

$$\sigma(z_j)=(m+n+2a+15-j)\frac{1}{10^r} \quad \text{for } \left(\frac{a-1}{3}\right)+1\le j\le \frac{2a+1}{3}$$

$$\sigma(z_j)=(m+n+2a+14-j)\frac{1}{10^r} \quad \text{for } \left(\frac{2a+1}{3}\right)+1\le j\le a.$$

Subcase (i)c If $a \equiv 2(mod\ 3)$

$$\sigma(z_j)=(m+n+2a+16-j)\frac{1}{10^r} \quad \text{for } 1\le j\le \frac{a-1}{3}$$

$$\sigma(z_j)=(m+n+2a+15-j)\frac{1}{10^r} \quad \text{for } \left(\frac{a-1}{3}\right)+1\le j\le \frac{2a-1}{3}$$

$$\sigma(z_j)=(m+n+2a+14-j)\frac{1}{10^r} \quad \text{for } \left(\frac{2a-1}{3}\right)+1\le j\le a.$$

From different nature of *m*, *n*, MMVs K_i's, their corresponding edges and number of K_i's ($1 \le i \le 3$) are given in Table 5.7.

Table 5.7 MMVs K_i's, their corresponding edges and the number of K_i's $(1 \leq i \leq 3)$.

Nature of m, n	Nature of a	Edges	MMV K_i's, $1 \leq i \leq 3$	Number of K_i's, $1 \leq i \leq 3$
$m \equiv 2(mod\ 3), n \equiv 0(mod\ 3)$	$a \equiv 0(mod\ 3)$	$g(v_2x_j)$ if $1 \leq j \leq \frac{m+1}{3}$ $g(v_1v_2), g(v_2v_3)$ $g(v_3y_j)$ if $1 \leq j \leq \frac{n}{3}$ $g(v_4z_j)$ if $1 \leq j \leq \frac{a}{3}$	$(4m+4n+4a+52)\frac{1}{10^r}$ for i = 1	$\frac{m+n+a+7}{3}$ for i = 1
		$g(v_2x_j)$ if $\frac{m+1}{3}+1 \leq j \leq \frac{2m-1}{3}$ $g(v_3v_4), g(v_4v_5)$ $g(v_3y_j)$ if $\frac{n}{3}+1 \leq j \leq \frac{2n}{3}$ $g(v_4z_j)$ if $\frac{a}{3}+1 \leq j \leq \frac{2a}{3}$	$(4m+4n+4a+51)\frac{1}{10^r}$ for i = 2	$\frac{m+n+a+4}{3}$ for i = 2

(Continued)

Table 5.7 MMVs K_i's, their corresponding edges and the number of K_i's ($1 \le i \le 3$). (*Continued*)

Nature of *m*, *n*	Nature of *a*	Edges	MMV K_i's, $1 \le i \le 3$	Number of K_i's, $1 \le i \le 3$
		$g(v_2x_j)$ if $\frac{2m-1}{3}+1 \le j \le m$ $g(v_5v_6)$ $g(v_3y_j)$ if $\frac{2n}{3}+1 \le j \le n$ $g(v_4z_j)$ if $\frac{2a}{3}+1 \le j \le a$	$(4m+4n+4a+50)\frac{1}{10^r}$ for i = 3	$\frac{m+n+a+4}{3}$ for i = 3
	$a \equiv 1(mod\ 3)$	$g(v_2x_j)$ if $1 \le j \le \frac{m+1}{3}$ $g(v_1v_2), g(v_2v_3)$ $g(v_3y_j)$ if $1 \le j \le \frac{n}{3}$ $g(v_4z_j)$ if $1 \le j \le \frac{a-1}{3}$	$(4m+4n+4a+52)\frac{1}{10^r}$ for i = 1	$\frac{m+n+a+6}{3}$ for i = 1

(*Continued*)

Table 5.7 MMVs K_i's, their corresponding edges and the number of K_i's $(1 \le i \le 3)$. (*Continued*)

Nature of m, n	Nature of a	Edges	MMV K_i's, $1 \le i \le 3$	Number of K_i's, $1 \le i \le 3$
		$g(v_2x_j)$ if $\frac{m+1}{3}+1 \le j \le \frac{2m-1}{3}$ $g(v_3v_4), g(v_4v_5)$ $g(v_3y_j)$ if $\frac{n}{3}+1 \le j \le \frac{2n}{3}$ $g(v_4z_j)$ if $\frac{a-1}{3}+1 \le j \le \frac{2a+1}{3}$	$(4m+4n+4a+51)\frac{1}{10^r}$ for i = 2	$\frac{m+n+a+6}{3}$ for i = 2
		$g(v_2x_j)$ if $\frac{2m-1}{3}+1 \le j \le m$ $g(v_5v_6)$ $g(v_3y_j)$ if $\frac{2n}{3}+1 \le j \le n$ $g(v_4z_j)$ if $\frac{2a+1}{3}+1 \le j \le a$	$(4m+4n+4a+50)\frac{1}{10^r}$ for i = 3	$\frac{m+n+a+3}{3}$ for i = 3

(*Continued*)

Table 5.7 MMVs K_i's, their corresponding edges and the number of K_i's ($1 \le i \le 3$). (*Continued*)

Nature of m, n	Nature of a	Edges	MMV K_i's, $1 \le i \le 3$	Number of K_i's, $1 \le i \le 3$
	$a \equiv 2(mod\ 3)$	$g(v_2x_j)$ if $1 \le j \le \frac{m+1}{3}$ $g(v_1v_2), g(v_2v_3)$ $g(v_3y_j)$ if $1 \le j \le \frac{n}{3}$ $g(v_4z_j)$ if $1 \le j \le \frac{a-1}{3}$	$(4m+4n+4a+52)\frac{1}{10^r}$ for i = 1	$\frac{m+n+a+5}{3}$ for i = 1
		$g(v_2x_j)$ if $\frac{m+1}{3}+1 \le j \le \frac{2m-1}{3}$ $g(v_3v_4), g(v_4v_5)$ $g(v_3y_j)$ if $\frac{n}{3}+1 \le j \le \frac{2n}{3}$ $g(v_4z_j)$ if $\frac{a-1}{3}+1 \le j \le \frac{2a-1}{3}$	$(4m+4n+4a+51)\frac{1}{10^r}$ for i = 2	$\frac{m+n+a+5}{3}$ for i = 2

(*Continued*)

Table 5.7 MMVs K_i's, their corresponding edges and the number of K_i's ($1 \le i \le 3$). (*Continued*)

Nature of m, n	Nature of a	Edges	MMV K_i's, $1 \le i \le 3$	Number of K_i's, $1 \le i \le 3$
		$g(v_2 x_j)$ if $\frac{2m-1}{3}+1 \le j \le m$ $g(v_5 v_6)$ $g(v_3 y_j)$ if $\frac{2n}{3}+1 \le j \le n$ $g(v_4 z_j)$ if $\frac{2a-1}{3}+1 \le j \le a$	$(4m+4n+4a+50)\frac{1}{10^r}$ for i = 3	$\frac{m+n+a+5}{3}$ for i = 3

Subcase (ii) If $n \equiv 1(mod\ 3)$

$$\sigma(x_j)=(2m+2n+2a+20-j)\frac{1}{10^r} \quad \text{for } 1\le j\le \frac{m+1}{3}$$

$$\sigma(x_j)=(2m+2n+2a+19-j)\frac{1}{10^r} \quad \text{for } \left(\frac{m+1}{3}\right)+1\le j\le \frac{2m-1}{3}$$

$$\sigma(x_j)=(2m+2n+2a+18-j)\frac{1}{10^r} \quad \text{for } \left(\frac{2m-1}{3}\right)+1\le j\le m$$

$$\sigma(y_j)=(m+2n+2a+18-j)\frac{1}{10^r} \quad \text{for } 1\le j\le \frac{n-1}{3}$$

$$\sigma(y_j)=(m+2n+2a+17-j)\frac{1}{10^r} \quad \text{for } \left(\frac{n-1}{3}\right)+1\le j\le \frac{2n+1}{3}$$

$$\sigma(y_j)=(m+2n+2a+16-j)\frac{1}{10^r} \quad \text{for } \left(\frac{2n+1}{3}\right)+1\le j\le n.$$

Subcase (ii)a If $a \equiv 0(mod\ 3)$

$$\sigma(z_j)=(m+n+2a+16-j)\frac{1}{10^r} \quad \text{for } 1\le j\le \frac{a}{3}$$

$$\sigma(z_j)=(m+n+2a+15-j)\frac{1}{10^r} \quad \text{for } \frac{a}{3}+1\le j\le \frac{2a}{3}$$

$$\sigma(z_j)=(m+n+2a+14-j)\frac{1}{10^r} \quad \text{for } \frac{2a}{3}+1\le j\le a.$$

Subcase (ii)b If $a \equiv 1(mod\ 3)$

$$\sigma(z_j)=(m+n+2a+16-j)\frac{1}{10^r} \quad \text{for } 1\le j\le \frac{a+2}{3}$$

$$\sigma(z_j)=(m+n+2a+15-j)\frac{1}{10^r} \quad \text{for } \left(\frac{a+2}{3}\right)+1\le j\le \frac{2a+1}{3}$$

$$\sigma(z_j)=(m+n+2a+14-j)\frac{1}{10^r} \quad \text{for } \left(\frac{2a+1}{3}\right)+1\le j\le a.$$

Subcase (ii)c If $a \equiv 2(mod\ 3)$

$$\sigma(z_j)=(m+n+2a+16-j)\frac{1}{10^r} \quad \text{for } 1\leq j\leq \frac{a+1}{3}$$

$$\sigma(z_j)=(m+n+2a+15-j)\frac{1}{10^r} \quad \text{for} \left(\frac{a+1}{3}\right)+1\leq j\leq \frac{2a-1}{3}$$

$$\sigma(z_j)=(m+n+2a+14-j)\frac{1}{10^r} \quad \text{for} \left(\frac{2a-1}{3}\right)+1\leq j\leq a.$$

From different nature of *m*, *n*, MMVs K_i's, their corresponding edges and number of K_i's $(1 \leq i \leq 3)$ are given in Table 5.8.

Subcase (iii) If $n \equiv 2(mod\ 3)$

$$\sigma(x_j)=(2m+2n+2a+20-j)\frac{1}{10^r} \quad \text{for } 1\leq j\leq \frac{m+1}{3}$$

$$\sigma(x_j)=(2m+2n+2a+19-j)\frac{1}{10^r} \quad \text{for} \left(\frac{m+1}{3}\right)+1\leq j\leq \frac{2m-1}{3}$$

$$\sigma(x_j)=(2m+2n+2a+18-j)\frac{1}{10^r} \quad \text{for} \left(\frac{2m-1}{3}\right)+1\leq j\leq m$$

$$\sigma(y_j)=(m+2n+2a+18-j)\frac{1}{10^r} \quad \text{for } 1\leq j\leq \frac{n-1}{3}$$

$$\sigma(y_j)=(m+2n+2a+17-j)\frac{1}{10^r} \quad \text{for} \left(\frac{n-1}{3}\right)+1\leq j\leq \frac{2n-1}{3}$$

$$\sigma(y_j)=(m+2n+2a+16-j)\frac{1}{10^r} \quad \text{for} \left(\frac{2n-1}{3}\right)+1\leq j\leq n.$$

Table 5.8 MMVs K_i's, their corresponding edges and the number of K_i's ($1 \le i \le 3$).

Nature of m, n	Nature of a	Edges		MMV K_i's, $1 \le i \le 3$	Number of K_i's, $1 \le i \le 3$
$m \equiv 2(mod\ 3), n \equiv 1(mod\ 3)$	$a \equiv 0(mod\ 3)$	$g(v_2x_j)$	if $1 \le j \le \frac{m+1}{3}$	$(4m+4n+4a+52)\frac{1}{10^r}$ for i = 1	$\frac{m+n+a+6}{3}$ for i = 1
		$g(v_1v_2), g(v_2v_3)$			
		$g(v_3y_j)$	if $1 \le j \le \frac{n-1}{3}$		
		$g(v_4z_j)$	if $1 \le j \le \frac{a}{3}$		
		$g(v_2x_j)$	if $\frac{m+1}{3}+1 \le j \le \frac{2m-1}{3}$	$(4m+4n+4a+51)\frac{1}{10^r}$ for i = 2	$\frac{m+n+a+6}{3}$ for i = 2
		$g(v_3v_4), g(v_4v_5)$			
		$g(v_3y_j)$	if $\frac{n-1}{3}+1 \le j \le \frac{2n+1}{3}$		
		$g(v_4z_j)$	if $\frac{a}{3}+1 \le j \le \frac{2a}{3}$		

(Continued)

Table 5.8 MMVs K_i's, their corresponding edges and the number of K_i's $(1 \le i \le 3)$. (*Continued*)

Nature of m, n	Nature of a	Edges	MMV K_i's, $1 \le i \le 3$	Number of K_i's, $1 \le i \le 3$
		$g(v_2x_j)$ if $\frac{2m-1}{3}+1 \le j \le m$ $g(v_5v_6)$ $g(v_3y_j)$ if $\frac{2n+1}{3}+1 \le j \le n$ $g(v_4z_j)$ if $\frac{2a}{3}+1 \le j \le a$	$(4m+4n+4a+50)\frac{1}{10^r}$ for i = 3	$\frac{m+n+a+3}{3}$ for i = 3
	$a \equiv 1(mod\ 3)$	$g(v_2x_j)$ if $1 \le j \le \frac{m+1}{3}$ $g(v_1v_2), g(v_2v_3)$ $g(v_3y_j)$ if $1 \le j \le \frac{n-1}{3}$ $g(v_4z_j)$ if $1 \le j \le \frac{a+2}{3}$	$(4m+4n+4a+52)\frac{1}{10^r}$ for i = 1	$\frac{m+n+a+5}{3}$ for i = 1

(*Continued*)

Table 5.8 MMVs K_i's, their corresponding edges and the number of K_i's ($1 \le i \le 3$). (*Continued*)

Nature of *m*, *n*	Nature of *a*	Edges	MMV K_i's, $1 \le i \le 3$	Number of K_i's, $1 \le i \le 3$
		$g(v_2x_j)$ if $\frac{m+1}{3}+1 \le j \le \frac{2m-1}{3}$ $g(v_3v_4), g(v_4v_5)$ $g(v_3y_j)$ if $\frac{n-1}{3}+1 \le j \le \frac{2n+1}{3}$ $g(v_4z_j)$ if $\frac{a+2}{3}+1 \le j \le \frac{2a+1}{3}$	$(4m+4n+4a+51)\frac{1}{10^r}$ for i = 2	$\frac{m+n+a+5}{3}$ for i = 2
		$g(v_2x_j)$ if $\frac{2m-1}{3}+1 \le j \le m$ $g(v_5v_6)$ $g(v_3y_j)$ if $\frac{2n+1}{3}+1 \le j \le n$ $g(v_4z_j)$ if $\frac{2a+1}{3}+1 \le j \le a$	$(4m+4n+4a+50)\frac{1}{10^r}$ for i = 3	$\frac{m+n+a+5}{3}$ for i = 3

(*Continued*)

Table 5.8 MMVs K_i's, their corresponding edges and the number of K_i's ($1 \le i \le 3$). (*Continued*)

Nature of m, n	Nature of a	Edges	MMV K_i's, $1 \le i \le 3$	Number of K_i's, $1 \le i \le 3$
	$a \equiv 2(mod\ 3)$	$g(v_2x_j)$ if $1 \le j \le \frac{m+1}{3}$ $g(v_1v_2), g(v_2v_3)$ $g(v_3y_j)$ if $1 \le j \le \frac{n-1}{3}$ $g(v_4z_j)$ if $1 \le j \le \frac{a+1}{3}$	$(4m+4n+4a+52)\frac{1}{10^r}$ for i = 1	$\frac{m+n+a+7}{3}$ for i = 1
		$g(v_2x_j)$ if $\frac{m+1}{3}+1 \le j \le \frac{2m-1}{3}$ $g(v_3v_4), g(v_4v_5)$ $g(v_3y_j)$ if $\frac{n-1}{3}+1 \le j \le \frac{2n+1}{3}$ $g(v_4z_j)$ if $\frac{a+1}{3}+1 \le j \le \frac{2a-1}{3}$	$(4m+4n+4a+51)\frac{1}{10^r}$ for i = 2	$\frac{m+n+a+4}{3}$ for i = 2

(*Continued*)

Table 5.8 MMVs K_i's, their corresponding edges and the number of K_i's $(1 \le i \le 3)$. *(Continued)*

Nature of m, n	**Nature of a**	**Edges**	**MMV K_i's, $1 \le i \le 3$**	**Number of K_i's, $1 \le i \le 3$**
		$g(v_2x_j)$ if $\frac{2m-1}{3}+1 \le j \le m$ $g(v_5v_6)$ $g(v_3y_j)$ if $\frac{2n+1}{3}+1 \le j \le n$ $g(v_4z_j)$ if $\frac{2a-1}{3}+1 \le j \le a$	$(4m+4n+4a+50)\frac{1}{10^r}$ for i = 3	$\frac{m+n+a+4}{3}$ for i = 3

Subcase (iii)a If $a \equiv 0(mod\ 3)$

$$\sigma(z_j)=(m+n+2a+16-j)\frac{1}{10^r} \quad \text{for } 1 \le j \le \frac{a}{3}$$

$$\sigma(z_j)=(m+n+2a+15-j)\frac{1}{10^r} \quad \text{for } \frac{a}{3}+1 \le j \le \frac{2a}{3}$$

$$\sigma(z_j)=(m+n+2a+14-j)\frac{1}{10^r} \quad \text{for } \frac{a}{3}+1 \le j \le a.$$

Subcase (iii)b If $a \equiv 1(mod\ 3)$

$$\sigma(z_j)=(m+n+2a+16-j)\frac{1}{10^r} \quad \text{for } 1 \le j \le \frac{a+2}{3}$$

$$\sigma(z_j)=(m+n+2a+15-j)\frac{1}{10^r} \quad \text{for } \left(\frac{a+2}{3}\right)+1 \le j \le \frac{2a+1}{3}$$

$$\sigma(z_j)=(m+n+2a+14-j)\frac{1}{10^r} \quad \text{for } \left(\frac{2a+1}{3}\right)+1 \le j \le a.$$

Subcase (iii)c If $a \equiv 2(mod\ 3)$

$$\sigma(z_j)=(m+n+2a+16-j)\frac{1}{10^r} \quad \text{for } 1 \le j \le \frac{a+1}{3}$$

$$\sigma(z_j)=(m+n+2a+15-j)\frac{1}{10^r} \quad \text{for } \left(\frac{a+1}{3}\right)+1 \le j \le \frac{2(a+1)}{3}$$

$$\sigma(z_j)=(m+n+2a+14-j)\frac{1}{10^r} \quad \text{for } \frac{2(a+1)}{3}+1 \le j \le a.$$

From different nature of *m, n*, MMVs K_i's, their corresponding edges and number of K_i's $(1 \le i \le 3)$ are given in Table 5.9.

Hence the maximum difference between the number of K_i's is 1 and $|K_i - K_j| \le \frac{2}{10^r}$ for $1 \le i, j \le 3$. Hence the caterpillar graph $\mathcal{T}^{6}_{2,3,4}$ of diameter 5 admits fuzzy tri-magic labeling for $m, n \ge 3$.

Table 5.9 MMVs K_i's, their corresponding edges and the number of K_i's ($1 \le i \le 3$).

Nature of m, n	Nature of a	Edges	MMV K_i's, $1 \le i \le 3$	Number of K_i's, $1 \le i \le 3$
$m \equiv 2(mod\ 3), n \equiv 2(mod\ 3)$	$a \equiv 0(mod\ 3)$	$g(v_2x_j)$ if $1 \le j \le \frac{m+1}{3}$ $g(v_1v_2), g(v_2v_3)$ $g(v_3y_j)$ if $1 \le j \le \frac{n-1}{3}$ $g(v_4z_j)$ if $1 \le j \le \frac{a}{3}$	$(4m+4n+4a+52)\frac{1}{10^r}$ for i = 1	$\frac{m+n+a+5}{3}$ for i = 1
		$g(v_2x_j)$ if $\frac{m+1}{3}+1 \le j \le \frac{2m-1}{3}$ $g(v_3v_4), g(v_4v_5)$ $g(v_3y_j)$ if $\frac{n-1}{3}+1 \le j \le \frac{2n-1}{3}$ $g(v_4z_j)$ if $\frac{a}{3}+1 \le j \le \frac{2a}{3}$	$(4m+4n+4a+51)\frac{1}{10^r}$ for i = 2	$\frac{m+n+a+5}{3}$ for i = 2

(Continued)

Table 5.9 MMVs K_i's, their corresponding edges and the number of K_i's ($1 \le i \le 3$). (*Continued*)

Nature of m, n	Nature of a	Edges	MMV K_i's, $1 \le i \le 3$	Number of K_i's, $1 \le i \le 3$
		$g(v_2 x_j)$ if $\frac{2m-1}{3}+1 \le j \le m$ $g(v_5 v_6)$ $g(v_3 y_j)$ if $\frac{2n-1}{3}+1 \le j \le n$ $g(v_4 z_j)$ if $\frac{2a}{3}+1 \le j \le a$	$(4m+4n+4a+50)\frac{1}{10^r}$ for i = 3	$\frac{m+n+a+5}{3}$ for i = 3
	$a \equiv 1 (mod\ 3)$	$g(v_2 x_j)$ if $1 \le j \le \frac{m+1}{3}$ $g(v_1 v_2), g(v_2 v_3)$ $g(v_3 y_j)$ if $1 \le j \le \frac{n-1}{3}$ $g(v_4 z_j)$ if $1 \le j \le \frac{a+2}{3}$	$(4m+4n+4a+52)\frac{1}{10^r}$ for i = 1	$\frac{m+n+a+7}{3}$ for i = 1

(*Continued*)

Table 5.9 MMVs K_i's, their corresponding edges and the number of K_i's ($1 \le i \le 3$). (*Continued*)

Nature of m, n	Nature of a	Edges	MMV K_i's, $1 \le i \le 3$	Number of K_i's, $1 \le i \le 3$
		$g(v_2x_j)$ if $\frac{m+1}{3}+1 \le j \le \frac{2m-1}{3}$ $g(v_3v_4), g(v_4v_5)$ $g(v_3y_j)$ if $\frac{n-1}{3}+1 \le j \le \frac{2n-1}{3}$ $g(v_4z_j)$ if $\frac{a+2}{3}+1 \le j \le \frac{2a+1}{3}$	$(4m+4n+4a+51)\frac{1}{10^r}$ for i = 2	$\frac{m+n+a+4}{3}$ for i = 2
		$g(v_2x_j)$ if $\frac{2m-1}{3}+1 \le j \le m$ $g(v_5v_6)$ $g(v_3y_j)$ if $\frac{2n-1}{3}+1 \le j \le n$ $g(v_4z_j)$ if $\frac{2a+1}{3}+1 \le j \le a$	$(4m+4n+4a+50)\frac{1}{10^r}$ for i = 3	$\frac{m+n+a+4}{3}$ for i = 3

(*Continued*)

Table 5.9 MMVs K_i's, their corresponding edges and the number of K_i's ($1 \le i \le 3$). (*Continued*)

Nature of *m, n*	Nature of *a*	Edges		MMV K_i's, $1 \le i \le 3$	Number of K_i's, $1 \le i \le 3$
	$a \equiv 2(mod\ 3)$	$g(v_2x_j)$	if $1 \le j \le \frac{m+1}{3}$	$(4m+4n+4a+52)\frac{1}{10^r}$ for i = 1	$\frac{m+n+a+6}{3}$ for i = 1
		$g(v_1v_2), g(v_2v_3)$			
		$g(v_3y_j)$	if $1 \le j \le \frac{n-1}{3}$		
		$g(v_4z_j)$	if $1 \le j \le \frac{a+1}{3}$		
		$g(v_2x_j)$	if $\frac{m+1}{3}+1 \le j \le \frac{2m-1}{3}$	$(4m+4n+4a+51)\frac{1}{10^r}$ for i = 2	$\frac{m+n+a+6}{3}$ for i = 2
		$g(v_3v_4), g(v_4v_5)$			
		$g(v_3y_j)$	if $\frac{n-1}{3}+1 \le j \le \frac{2n-1}{3}$		
		$g(v_4z_j)$	if $\frac{a+1}{3}+1 \le j \le \frac{2(a+1)}{3}$		

(*Continued*)

Table 5.9 MMVs K_i's, their corresponding edges and the number of K_i's ($1 \le i \le 3$). *(Continued)*

Nature of m, n	Nature of a	Edges	MMV K_i's, $1 \le i \le 3$	Number of K_i's, $1 \le i \le 3$
		$g(v_2x_j)$ if $\frac{2m-1}{3}+1 \le j \le m$ $g(v_5v_6)$ $g(v_3y_j)$ if $\frac{2n-1}{3}+1 \le j \le n$ $g(v_4z_j)$ if $\frac{2(a+1)}{3}+1 \le j \le a$	$(4m+4n+4a+50)\frac{1}{10^r}$ for i = 3	$\frac{m+n+a+3}{3}$ for i = 3

5.3 Conclusion

In this chapter, we have taken isomorphic caterpillar of diameter 5 graph $\mathcal{T}^{6}_{2,3,4}$ and shown that the graph admits fuzzy tri-magic by proving the maximum difference between the number of K_i's $(1 \le i \le 3)$ is 1 and $|K_i - K_j| \le \frac{2}{10^r}$ for $1 \le i,j \le 3$, $r \ge 2$; we also tabulated MMVs K_i's, their corresponding edges and the number of K_i's $(1 \le i \le 3)$. All the remaining cases of caterpillar of diameter 5 are also done by us and they will be published in the upcoming papers.

References

1. Gallian, J.A., A dynamic survey of graph labeling. *Electron. J. Comb.*, 17, DS6, 2017.
2. Harary, F., *Graph theory*, Narosa Publishing House Pvt. Ltd, New Delhi, reprint 2013.
3. Sumathi, P. and Monigeetha, C., Fuzzy tri-magic labeling of some star related graphs. *J. Emerg. Technol. Innov. Res. (JETIR)*, 6, 1, 661–667, 2019.
4. Sumathi, P. and Esther Felicia, R., Enresdowedness of some caterpillar graphs. *Int. J. Pure Appl. Math.*, 118, 10, 73–86, 2018.
5. Felix, J. and Cappelle, M., *1-Identifying Codes on Caterpillar Graphs*, Instituto de Informatica INF UFG, Goiânia, 7 November 2016.
6. Sumathi, P. and Monigeetha, C., Fuzzy tri-magic labeling of isomorphic caterpillar of diameter 5—Paper 1. *J. Eng. Comput. Archit.*, 10, 3, 182–189, 2020.
7. Sumathi, P. and Monigeetha, C., Fuzzy tri-magic labeling of isomorphic caterpillar of diameter 5—Paper 2. *J. Inf. Comput. Sci.*, 10, 3, 1463–1481, 2020.

6

Fuzzy Tri-Magic Labeling of Isomorphic Caterpillar Graph $\mathcal{J}^{6}_{2,3,5}$ of Diameter 5

P. Sumathi[1] and C. Monigeetha[2]*

[1]*Department of Mathematics, C. Kandaswami Naidu College for Men, Anna Nagar, Chennai, India*
[2]*Department of Mathematics, Sri Muthukumaran Arts and Science College, Chikkarayapuram, Chennai, India*

Abstract
Let G be a finite, simple, undirected graph without loops or multiple edges. A fuzzy graph is said to admit tri-magic labeling if the number of magic membership values K_i's ($1 \leq i \leq 3$) differ by at most 1 and $|K_i - K_j| \leq \frac{2}{10^r}$ for $1 \leq i, j \leq 3$, $r \geq 2$. The fuzzy graph which admits a tri-magic labeling is called a fuzzy tri-magic labeling graph. The fuzzy tri-magic labeling graphs are denoted by $\tilde{T}m_0G$. A caterpillar is defined as a tree in which all the vertices are within distance one of a central path. In this paper it is proved that isomorphic caterpillar of diameter 5 is fuzzy tri-magic.

***Keywords*:** Fuzzy labeling, magic membership value, fuzzy tri-magic labeling, diameter of a graph, caterpillar graph

6.1 Introduction

The graphs considered here are finite, simple, undirected and non-trivial [1]. Graph theory has a good development in the graph labeling and has a broad range of applications [2]. Fuzzy is a newly emerging mathematical framework to exhibit the phenomenon of uncertainty in real life

**Corresponding author*: monimagendra@gmail.com

E. Chandrasekaran, R. Anandan, G. Suseendran, S. Balamurugan and Hanaa Hachimi (eds.) Fuzzy Intelligent Systems: Methodologies, Techniques, and Applications, (155–216) © 2021 Scrivener Publishing LLC

tribulations. A fuzzy set is defined mathematically by assigning a value to each possible individual in the universe of discourse, representing its grade or membership which corresponds to the degree to which that individual is similar or compatible with the concept represented the fuzzy set. In this paper it is proved that isomorphic caterpillar of diameter 5 is fuzzy tri-magic.

Definition 1. Fuzzy Graph
A fuzzy graph G: (σ,μ) is a pair of functions $\sigma : V \to [0, 1]$ and $\mu : V \times V \to [0, 1]$, where for all $u, v \in V$, we have $\mu(u, v) \leq \sigma(u) \bigwedge \sigma(v)$.

Definition 2. Fuzzy Labeling
Let $G = (V,E)$ be a graph, the fuzzy graph G: (σ, μ) is said to have a fuzzy labeling, if $\sigma : V \to [0, 1]$ and $\mu : V \times V \to [0, 1]$ is bijective such that the membership value of edges and vertices is distinct and $\mu(uv) \leq \sigma(u) \bigwedge \sigma(v)$ for all $u, v \in V$.

Definition 3. Magic Membership Value (MMV) [3]
Let G: (σ,μ) be a fuzzy graph; the induced map $g{:}E(G) \to [0,1]$ defined by $g(uv) = \sigma(u) + \mu(uv) + \sigma(v)$ is said to be a magic membership value. It is denoted by MMV.

Definition 4. Fuzzy Tri-Magic Labeling
A fuzzy graph is said to admit tri-magic labeling if the magic membership values K_i's, $1 \leq i \leq 3$ are constants where number of K_i's and K_j's differ by at most 1 and $|K_i - K_j| \leq \frac{2}{10^r}$ for $1 \leq i, j \leq 3$, $r \geq 2$.

Definition 5. Fuzzy Tri-Magic Labeling Graph
A fuzzy labeling graph which admits a tri-magic labeling is called a fuzzy tri-magic labeling graph. The fuzzy tri-magic labeling graphs are denoted by $\tilde{T}m_0G$.

Definition 6. Diameter of a Graph
The maximum distance between two vertices of a graph is called the diameter of a graph.

Definition 7. Caterpillar Graph [4, 5]
A caterpillar graph G, is a tree having a chordless path P_t on t vertices, called central path, which contains at least one end point of every edge. Vertices connecting the leaves with the central path are called support vertices.

Notation 1 [6, 7]
Let $\mathcal{T}^{s_1}_{t_1, t_2, t_3}$ is a tree obtained by attaching m pendant edges, n pendant edges and a pendant edges to the path P_s at the vertices v_{t_1+1}, v_{t_2+1} and v_{t_3+1} respectively.

6.2 Main Result

Theorem 1: The caterpillar graph $\mathcal{T}^{6}_{2,3,5}$ of diameter 5 admits fuzzy tri-magic labeling for $m, n \geq 3$.

Proof:
Let G be a caterpillar graph $\mathcal{T}^{6}_{2,3,5}$ of diameter 5. Let m, n and a be the pendant edges attaching to the path P_6 at the vertices v_2, v_3 and v_5, respectively. Let the vertex set and edge set of $\mathcal{T}^{6}_{2,3,5}$ be

$V(G) = \{v_j: 1 \leq j \leq 6\} \cup \{x_j: 1 \leq j \leq m\} \cup \{y_j: 1 \leq j \leq n\} \cup \{z_j: 1 \leq j \leq a\}$ and

$E(G) = \{v_j v_{j+1}: 1 \leq j \leq 5\} \cup \{v_2 x_j: 1 \leq j \leq m\} \cup \{v_3 y_j: 1 \leq j \leq n\} \cup \{v_5 z_j: 1 \leq j \leq a\}$

$$|V(G)| = m + n + a + 6 \text{ and } |E(G)| = m + n + a + 5$$

Let $r \geq 2$ be any positive integer.
Define $\sigma\ V \rightarrow [0, 1]$ such that

$$\sigma(v_j) = (2m + 2n + 2a + 28 - j)\frac{1}{10^r} \quad 1 \leq j \leq 6$$

Define $\mu\ V \times V \rightarrow [0, 1]$ by

$$\mu(v_2 x_j) = (7 + j)\frac{1}{10^r} \qquad \text{for } 1 \leq j \leq m$$

$$\mu(v_3 y_j) = (m + 10 + j)\frac{1}{10^r} \qquad \text{for } 1 \leq j \leq n$$

$$\mu(v_5 z_j) = (m + n + 14 + j)\frac{1}{10^r} \qquad \text{for } 1 \leq j \leq a$$

$$\mu(v_1 v_2) = \frac{1}{10^r}, \mu(v_2 v_3) = \frac{3}{10^r}, \mu(v_3 v_4) = \frac{4}{10^r}, \mu(v_4 v_5) = \frac{6}{10^r} \text{ and } \mu(v_5 v_6) = \frac{7}{10^r}$$

Case (i) If $m \equiv 0(mod\ 3)$
Subcase (i) If $n \equiv 0(mod\ 3)$

$$\sigma(x_j) = (2m + 2n + 2a + 21 - j)\frac{1}{10^r} \quad \text{for } 1 \le j \le \frac{m}{3}$$

$$\sigma(x_j) = (2m + 2n + 2a + 20 - j)\frac{1}{10^r} \quad \text{for } \frac{m}{3} + 1 \le j \le \frac{2m}{m}$$

$$\sigma(x_j) = (2m + 2n + 2a + 19 - j)\frac{1}{10^r} \quad \text{for } \frac{2m}{3} + 1 \le j \le m$$

$$\sigma(y_j) = (m + 2n + 2a + 19 - j)\frac{1}{10^r} \quad \text{for } 1 \le j \le \frac{n}{3}$$

$$\sigma(y_j) = (m + 2n + 2a + 18 - j)\frac{1}{10^r} \quad \text{for } \frac{n}{3} + 1 \le j \le \frac{2n}{3}$$

$$\sigma(y_j) = (m + 2n + 2a + 17 - j)\frac{1}{10^r} \quad \text{for } \frac{2n}{3} + 1 \le j \le n.$$

Subcase (i)a If $a \equiv 0(mod\ 3)$

$$\sigma(z_j) = (m + n + 2a + 17 - j)\frac{1}{10^r} \quad \text{for } 1 \le j \le \frac{a}{3}$$

$$\sigma(z_j) = (m + n + 2a + 16 - j)\frac{1}{10^r} \quad \text{for } \frac{a}{3} + 1 \le j \le \frac{2a}{3}$$

$$\sigma(z_j) = (m + n + 2a + 15 - j)\frac{1}{10^r} \quad \text{for } \frac{2a}{3} + 1 \le j \le a.$$

Subcase (i)b If $a \equiv 1(mod\ 3)$

$$\sigma(z_j) = (m + n + 2a + 17 - j)\frac{1}{10^r} \quad \text{for } 1 \le j \le \frac{a-1}{3}$$

$$\sigma(z_j) = (m + n + 2a + 16 - j)\frac{1}{10^r} \quad \text{for } \frac{a-1}{3} + 1 \le i \le \frac{2(a-1)}{3}$$

$$\sigma(z_j) = (m + n + 2a + 14 - j)\frac{1}{10^r} \quad \text{for } \frac{2(a-1)}{3} + 1 \le j \le a.$$

Subcase (i)c If $a \equiv 2(mod\ 3)$

$$\sigma(z_j)=(m+n+2a+17-j)\frac{1}{10^r} \quad \text{for } 1\leq j\leq \frac{a+1}{3}$$

$$\sigma(z_j)=(m+n+2a+16-j)\frac{1}{10^r} \quad \text{for } \left(\frac{a+1}{3}\right)+1\leq j\leq \frac{2a-1}{3}$$

$$\sigma(z_j)=(m+n+2a+15-j)\frac{1}{10^r} \quad \text{for } \left(\frac{2a-1}{3}\right)+1\leq j\leq a.$$

From different nature of *m*, *n*, MMVs K_i's, their corresponding edges and number of K_i's ($1 \leq i \leq 3$) are given in Table 6.1.

Subcase (ii) If $n \equiv 1(mod\ 3)$

$$\sigma(x_j)=(2m+2n+2a+21-j)\frac{1}{10^r} \quad \text{for } 1\leq j\leq \frac{m}{3}$$

$$\sigma(x_j)=(2m+2n+2a+20-j)\frac{1}{10^r} \quad \text{for } \frac{m}{3}+1\leq j\leq \frac{2m}{3}$$

$$\sigma(x_j)=(2m+2n+2a+19-j)\frac{1}{10^r} \quad \text{for } \frac{2m}{3}+1\leq j\leq m$$

$$\sigma(y_j)=(m+2n+2a+19-j)\frac{1}{10^r} \quad \text{for } 1\leq j\leq \frac{n-1}{3}$$

$$\sigma(y_j)=(m+2n+2a+18-j)\frac{1}{10^r} \quad \text{for } \frac{n-1}{3}+1\leq j\leq \frac{2(n-1)}{3}$$

$$\sigma(y_j)=(m+2n+2a+17-j)\frac{1}{10^r} \quad \text{for } \frac{2(n-1)}{3}+1\leq j\leq n.$$

Subcase (ii)a If $a \equiv 0(mod\ 3)$

$$\sigma(z_j)=(m+n+2a+17-j)\frac{1}{10^r} \quad \text{for } 1\leq j\leq \frac{a}{3}$$

$$\sigma(z_j)=(m+n+2a+16-j)\frac{1}{10^r} \quad \text{for } \frac{a}{3}+1\leq j\leq \frac{2a}{3}$$

$$\sigma(z_j)=(m+n+2a+15-j)\frac{1}{10^r} \quad \text{for } \frac{2a}{3}+1\leq j\leq a.$$

Table 6.1 MMVs K_i's, their corresponding edges and the number of K_i's ($1 \le i \le 3$).

Nature of m, n	Nature of a	Edges	MMV K_i's, $1 \le i \le 3$	Number of K_i's, $1 \le i \le 3$
$m \equiv 0(mod\ 3), n \equiv 0(mod\ 3)$	$a \equiv 0(mod\ 3)$	$g(v_2x_j)$ if $1 \le j \le \frac{m}{3}$ $g(v_1v_2), g(v_2v_3)$ $g(v_3y_j)$ if $1 \le j \le \frac{n}{3}$ $g(v_5z_j)$ if $1 \le j \le \frac{a}{3}$	$(4m+4n+4a+54)\frac{1}{10^r}$ for $i=1$	$\frac{m+n+a+6}{3}$ for $i=1$
		$g(v_2x_j)$ if $\frac{m}{3}+1 \le j \le \frac{2m}{3}$ $g(v_3v_4), g(v_4v_5)$ $g(v_3y_j)$ if $\frac{n}{3}+1 \le j \le \frac{2n}{3}$ $g(v_5z_j)$ if $\frac{a}{3}+1 \le j \le \frac{2a}{3}$	$(4m+4n+4a+53)\frac{1}{10^r}$ for $i=2$	$\frac{m+n+a+6}{3}$ for $i=2$

(Continued)

Table 6.1 MMVs K_i's, their corresponding edges and the number of K_i's $(1 \le i \le 3)$. *(Continued)*

Nature of *m, n*	Nature of *a*	Edges	MMV K_i's, $1 \le i \le 3$	Number of K_i's, $1 \le i \le 3$
		$g(v_2x_j)$ if $\frac{2m}{3}+1 \le j \le m$ $g(v_5v_6)$ $g(v_3y_j)$ if $\frac{2n}{3}+1 \le j \le n$ $g(v_5z_j)$ if $\frac{2a}{3}+1 \le j \le a$	$(4m+4n+4a+52)\frac{1}{10^r}$ for i = 3	$\frac{m+n+a+3}{3}$ for i = 3
	$a \equiv 1(mod\ 3)$	$g(v_2x_j)$ if $1 \le j \le \frac{m}{3}$ $g(v_1v_2), g(v_2v_3)$ $g(v_3y_j)$ if $1 \le j \le \frac{n}{3}$ $g(v_5z_j)$ if $1 \le j \le \frac{a-1}{3}$	$(4m+4n+4a+54)\frac{1}{10^r}$ for i = 1	$\frac{m+n+a+5}{3}$ for i = 1

(Continued)

Table 6.1 MMVs K_i's, their corresponding edges and the number of K_i's ($1 \le i \le 3$). (*Continued*)

Nature of m, n	Nature of a	Edges	MMV K_i's, $1 \le i \le 3$	Number of K_i's, $1 \le i \le 3$
		$g(v_2x_j)$ if $\frac{m}{3}+1 \le j \le \frac{2m}{3}$ $g(v_3v_4), g(v_4v_5)$ $g(v_3y_j)$ if $\frac{n}{3}+1 \le j \le \frac{2n}{3}$ $g(v_5z_j)$ if $\frac{a-1}{3}+1 \le j \le \frac{2(a-1)}{3}$	$(4m+4n+4a+53)\frac{1}{10^r}$ for $i=2$	$\frac{m+n+a+5}{3}$ for $i=2$
		$g(v_2x_j)$ if $\frac{2m}{3}+1 \le j \le m$ $g(v_5v_6)$ $g(v_3y_j)$ if $\frac{2n}{3}+1 \le j \le n$ $g(v_5z_j)$ if $\frac{2(a-1)}{3}+1 \le j \le a$	$(4m+4n+4a+52)\frac{1}{10^r}$ for $i=3$	$\frac{m+n+a+5}{3}$ for $i=3$

(*Continued*)

Table 6.1 MMVs K_i's, their corresponding edges and the number of K_i's ($1 \le i \le 3$). (*Continued*)

Nature of m, n	Nature of a	Edges	MMV K_i's, $1 \le i \le 3$	Number of K_i's, $1 \le i \le 3$
	$a \equiv 2 (mod\ 3)$	$g(v_2x_j)$ if $1 \le j \le \frac{m}{3}$ $g(v_1v_2), g(v_2v_3)$ $g(v_3y_j)$ if $1 \le j \le \frac{n}{3}$ $g(v_5z_j)$ if $1 \le j \le \frac{a+1}{3}$	$(4m+4n+4a+54)\frac{1}{10^r}$ for i = 1	$\frac{m+n+a+7}{3}$ for i = 1
		$g(v_2x_j)$ if $\frac{m}{3}+1 \le j \le \frac{2m}{3}$ $g(v_3v_4), g(v_4v_5)$ $g(v_3y_j)$ if $\frac{n}{3}+1 \le j \le \frac{2n}{3}$ $g(v_5z_j)$ if $\frac{a+1}{3}+1 \le j \le \frac{2a-1}{3}$	$(4m+4n+4a+53)\frac{1}{10^r}$ for i = 2	$\frac{m+n+a+4}{3}$ for i = 2

(*Continued*)

Table 6.1 MMVs K_i's, their corresponding edges and the number of K_i's $(1 \le i \le 3)$. *(Continued)*

Nature of m, n	Nature of a	Edges	MMV K_i's, $1 \le i \le 3$	Number of K_i's, $1 \le i \le 3$
		$g(v_2x_j)$ if $\frac{2m}{3}+1 \le j \le m$ $g(v_5v_6)$ $g(v_3y_j)$ if $\frac{2n}{3}+1 \le j \le n$ $g(v_5z_j)$ if $\frac{2a-1}{3}+1 \le j \le a$	$(4m+4n+4a+52)\frac{1}{10^r}$ for i = 3	$\frac{m+n+a+4}{3}$ for i = 3

Subcase (ii)b If $a \equiv 1(mod\ 3)$

$$\sigma(z_j)=(m+n+2a+17-j)\frac{1}{10^r} \quad \text{for } 1 \le j \le \frac{a+2}{3}$$

$$\sigma(z_j)=(m+n+2a+16-j)\frac{1}{10^r} \quad \text{for } \left(\frac{a+2}{3}\right)+1 \le j \le \frac{2a+1}{3}$$

$$\sigma(z_j)=(m+n+2a+15-j)\frac{1}{10^r} \quad \text{for } \left(\frac{2a+1}{3}\right)+1 \le j \le a.$$

Subcase (ii)c If $a \equiv 2(mod\ 3)$

$$\sigma(z_j)=(m+n+2a+17-j)\frac{1}{10^r} \quad \text{for } 1 \le j \le \frac{a+1}{3}$$

$$\sigma(z_j)=(m+n+2a+16-j)\frac{1}{10^r} \quad \text{for } \left(\frac{a+1}{3}\right)+1 \le j \le \frac{2(a+1)}{3}$$

$$\sigma(z_j)=(m+n+2a+15-j)\frac{1}{10^r} \quad \text{for } \frac{2(a+1)}{3}+1 \le j \le a.$$

From different nature of *m*, *n*, MMVs K_i's, their corresponding edges and number of K_i's ($1 \le i \le 3$) are given in Table 6.2.

Subcase (iii) If $n \equiv 2(mod\ 3)$

$$\sigma(x_j)=(2m+2n+2a+21-j)\frac{1}{10^r} \quad \text{for } 1 \le j \le \frac{m}{3}$$

$$\sigma(x_j)=(2m+2n+2a+20-j)\frac{1}{10^r} \quad \text{for } \frac{m}{3}+1 \le j \le \frac{2m}{3}$$

$$\sigma(x_j)=(2m+2n+2a+19-j)\frac{1}{10^r} \quad \text{for } \frac{2m}{3}+1 \le j \le m$$

$$\sigma(y_j)=(m+2n+2a+19-j)\frac{1}{10^r} \quad \text{for } 1 \le j \le \frac{n+1}{3}.$$

$$\sigma(y_j)=(m+2n+2a+18-j)\frac{1}{10^r} \quad \text{for } \left(\frac{n+1}{3}\right)+1 \le j \le \frac{2n-1}{3}$$

$$\sigma(y_j)=(m+2n+2a+17-j)\frac{1}{10^r} \quad \text{for } \left(\frac{2n-1}{3}\right)+1 \le j \le n.$$

Table 6.2 MMVs K_i's, their corresponding edges and the number of K_i's ($1 \le i \le 3$).

Nature of m, n	Nature of a	Edges	MMV K_i's, $1 \le i \le 3$	Number of K_i's, $1 \le i \le 3$
$m \equiv 0(mod\ 3),\ n \equiv 1(mod\ 3)$	$a \equiv 0(mod\ 3)$	$g(v_2x_j)$ if $1 \le j \le \frac{m}{3}$ $g(v_1v_2), g(v_2v_3)$ $g(v_3y_j)$ if $1 \le j \le \frac{n-1}{3}$ $g(v_5z_j)$ if $1 \le j \le \frac{a}{3}$	$(4m+4n+4a+54)\frac{1}{10^r}$ for i = 1	$\frac{m+n+a+5}{3}$ for i = 1
		$g(v_2x_j)$ if $\frac{m}{3}+1 \le j \le \frac{2m}{3}$ $g(v_3v_4), g(v_4v_5)$ $g(v_3y_j)$ if $\frac{n-1}{3}+1 \le j \le \frac{2(n-1)}{3}$ $g(v_5z_j)$ if $\frac{a}{3}+1 \le j \le \frac{2a}{3}$	$(4m+4n+4a+53)\frac{1}{10^r}$ for i = 2	$\frac{m+n+a+5}{3}$ for i = 2

(*Continued*)

Table 6.2 MMVs K_i's, their corresponding edges and the number of K_i's ($1 \le i \le 3$). (*Continued*)

Nature of m, n	**Nature of** a	**Edges**	**MMV** K_i**'s,** $1 \le i \le 3$	**Number of** K_i**'s,** $1 \le i \le 3$
		$g(v_2x_j)$ if $\frac{2m}{3}+1 \le j \le m$ $g(v_5v_6)$ $g(v_3y_j)$ if $\frac{2(n-1)}{3}+1 \le j \le n$ $g(v_5z_j)$ if $\frac{2a}{3}+1 \le j \le a$	$(4m+4n+4a+52)\frac{1}{10^r}$ for i = 3	$\frac{m+n+a+5}{3}$ for i = 3
	$a \equiv 1 (mod\ 3)$	$g(v_2x_j)$ if $1 \le j \le \frac{m}{3}$ $g(v_1v_2), g(v_2v_3)$ $g(v_3y_j)$ if $1 \le j \le \frac{n-1}{3}$ $g(v_5z_j)$ if $1 \le j \le \frac{a+2}{3}$	$(4m+4n+4a+54)\frac{1}{10^r}$ for i = 1	$\frac{m+n+a+7}{3}$ for i = 1

(*Continued*)

Table 6.2 MMVs K_i's, their corresponding edges and the number of K_i's ($1 \le i \le 3$). (*Continued*)

Nature of m, n	Nature of a	Edges	MMV K_i's, $1 \le i \le 3$	Number of K_i's, $1 \le i \le 3$
		$g(v_2x_j)$ if $\frac{m}{3}+1 \le j \le \frac{2m}{3}$ $g(v_3v_4), g(v_4v_5)$ $g(v_3y_j)$ if $\frac{n-1}{3}+1 \le j \le \frac{2(n-1)}{3}$ $g(v_5z_j)$ if $\frac{a+2}{3}+1 \le j \le \frac{2a+1}{3}$	$(4m+4n+4a+53)\frac{1}{10^r}$ for $i=2$	$\frac{m+n+a+4}{3}$ for $i=2$
		$g(v_2x_j)$ if $\frac{2m}{3}+1 \le j \le m$ $g(v_5v_6)$ $g(v_3y_j)$ if $\frac{2(n-1)}{3}+1 \le j \le n$ $g(v_5z_j)$ if $\frac{2a+1}{3}+1 \le j \le a$	$(4m+4n+4a+52)\frac{1}{10^r}$ for $i=3$	$\frac{m+n+a+4}{3}$ for $i=3$

(*Continued*)

Table 6.2 MMVs K_i's, their corresponding edges and the number of K_i's ($1 \leq i \leq 3$). (*Continued*)

Nature of m, n	Nature of a	Edges	MMV K_i's, $1 \leq i \leq 3$	Number of K_i's, $1 \leq i \leq 3$
	$a \equiv 2(mod\ 3)$	$g(v_2x_j)$ if $1 \leq j \leq \frac{m}{3}$ $g(v_1v_2), g(v_2v_3)$ $g(v_3y_j)$ if $1 \leq j \leq \frac{n-1}{3}$ $g(v_5z_j)$ if $1 \leq j \leq \frac{a+1}{3}$	$(4m+4n+4a+54)\frac{1}{10^r}$ for i = 1	$\frac{m+n+a+6}{3}$ for i = 1
		$g(v_2x_j)$ if $\frac{m}{3}+1 \leq j \leq \frac{2m}{3}$ $g(v_3v_4), g(v_4v_5)$ $g(v_3y_j)$ if $\frac{n-1}{3}+1 \leq j \leq \frac{2(n-1)}{3}$ $g(v_5z_j)$ if $\frac{a+1}{3}+1 \leq j \leq \frac{2(a+1)}{3}$	$(4m+4n+4a+53)\frac{1}{10^r}$ for i = 2	$\frac{m+n+a+6}{3}$ for i = 2

(*Continued*)

Table 6.2 MMVs K_i's, their corresponding edges and the number of K_i's ($1 \le i \le 3$). (*Continued*)

Nature of m, n	Nature of a	Edges	MMV K_i's, $1 \le i \le 3$	Number of K_i's, $1 \le i \le 3$
		$g(v_2x_j)$ if $\frac{2m}{3}+1 \le j \le m$ $g(v_5v_6)$ $g(v_3y_j)$ if $\frac{2(n-1)}{3}+1 \le j \le n$ $g(v_5z_j)$ if $\frac{2(a+1)}{3}+1 \le j \le a$	$(4m+4n+4a+52)\frac{1}{10^r}$ for i = 3	$\frac{m+n+a+3}{3}$ for i = 3

Subcase (iii)a If $a \equiv 0(mod\ 3)$

$$\sigma(z_j) = (m+n+2a+17-j)\frac{1}{10^r} \quad \text{for } 1 \le j \le \frac{a}{3}$$

$$\sigma(z_j) = (m+n+2a+16-j)\frac{1}{10^r} \quad \text{for } \frac{a}{3}+1 \le j \le \frac{2a}{3}$$

$$\sigma(z_j) = (m+n+2a+15-j)\frac{1}{10^r} \quad \text{for } \frac{2a}{3}+1 \le j \le a.$$

Subcase (iii)b If $a \equiv 1(mod\ 3)$

$$\sigma(z_j) = (m+n+2a+17-j)\frac{1}{10^r} \quad \text{for } 1 \le j \le \frac{a-1}{3}$$

$$\sigma(z_j) = (m+n+2a+16-j)\frac{1}{10^r} \quad \text{for } \left(\frac{a-1}{3}\right)+1 \le j \le \frac{2a+1}{3}$$

$$\sigma(z_j) = (m+n+2a+15-j)\frac{1}{10^r} \quad \text{for } \left(\frac{2a+1}{3}\right)+1 \le j \le a.$$

Subcase (iii)c If $a \equiv 2(mod\ 3)$

$$\sigma(z_j) = (m+n+2a+17-j)\frac{1}{10^r} \quad \text{for } 1 \le j \le \frac{a-1}{3}$$

$$\sigma(z_j) = (m+n+2a+16-j)\frac{1}{10^r} \quad \text{for } \left(\frac{a-1}{3}\right)+1 \le j \le \frac{2a-1}{3}$$

$$\sigma(z_j) = (m+n+2a+15-j)\frac{1}{10^r} \quad \text{for } \left(\frac{2a-1}{3}\right)+1 \le j \le a.$$

From different nature of m, n, MMVs K_i's, their corresponding edges and number of K_i's ($1 \le i \le 3$) are given in Table 6.3.

Table 6.3 MMVs K_i's, their corresponding edges and the number of K_i's ($1 \le i \le 3$).

Nature of m, n	Nature of a	Edges	MMV K_i's, $1 \le i \le 3$	Number of K_i's, $1 \le i \le 3$
$m \equiv 0(mod\ 3), n \equiv 2(mod\ 3)$	$a \equiv 0(mod\ 3)$	$g(v_2x_j)$ if $1 \le j \le \frac{m}{3}$ $g(v_1v_2), g(v_2v_3)$ $g(v_3y_j)$ if $1 \le j \le \frac{n+1}{3}$ $g(v_5z_j)$ if $1 \le j \le \frac{a}{3}$	$(4m+4n+4a+54)\frac{1}{10^r}$ for i = 1	$\frac{m+n+a+5}{3}$ for i = 1
		$g(v_2x_j)$ if $\frac{m}{3}+1 \le j \le \frac{2m}{3}$ $g(v_3v_4), g(v_4v_5)$ $g(v_3y_j)$ if $\frac{n+1}{3}+1 \le j \le \frac{2n-1}{3}$ $g(v_5z_j)$ if $\frac{a}{3}+1 \le j \le \frac{2a}{3}$	$(4m+4n+4a+53)\frac{1}{10^r}$ for i = 2	$\frac{m+n+a+5}{3}$ for i = 2

(*Continued*)

Table 6.3 MMVs K_i's, their corresponding edges and the number of K_i's ($1 \le i \le 3$). (*Continued*)

Nature of m, n	Nature of a	Edges	MMV K_i's, $1 \le i \le 3$	Number of K_i's, $1 \le i \le 3$
		$g(v_2x_j)$ if $\frac{2m}{3}+1 \le j \le m$ $g(v_5v_6)$ $g(v_3y_j)$ if $\frac{2n-1}{3}+1 \le j \le n$ $g(v_5z_j)$ if $\frac{2a}{3}+1 \le j \le a$	$(4m+4n+4a+52)\frac{1}{10^r}$ for i = 3	$\frac{m+n+a+5}{3}$ for i = 3
	$a \equiv 1(mod\ 3)$	$g(v_2x_j)$ if $1 \le j \le \frac{m}{3}$ $g(v_1v_2), g(v_2v_3)$ $g(v_3y_j)$ if $1 \le j \le \frac{n+1}{3}$ $g(v_5z_j)$ if $1 \le j \le \frac{a-1}{3}$	$(4m+4n+4a+54)\frac{1}{10^r}$ for i = 1	$\frac{m+n+a+7}{3}$ for i = 1

(*Continued*)

Table 6.3 MMVs K_i's, their corresponding edges and the number of K_i's $(1 \le i \le 3)$. (*Continued*)

Nature of m, n	Nature of a	Edges	MMV K_i's, $1 \le i \le 3$	Number of K_i's, $1 \le i \le 3$
		$g(v_2x_j)$ if $\frac{m}{3}+1 \le j \le \frac{2m}{3}$ $g(v_3v_4), g(v_4v_5)$ $g(v_3y_j)$ if $\frac{n+1}{3}+1 \le j \le \frac{2n-1}{3}$ $g(v_5z_j)$ if $\frac{a-1}{3}+1 \le j \le \frac{2a+1}{3}$	$(4m+4n+4a+53)\frac{1}{10^r}$ for i = 2	$\frac{m+n+a+4}{3}$ for i = 2
		$g(v_2x_j)$ if $\frac{2m}{3}+1 \le j \le m$ $g(v_5v_6)$ $g(v_3y_j)$ if $\frac{2n-1}{3}+1 \le j \le n$ $g(v_5z_j)$ if $\frac{2a+1}{3}+1 \le j \le a$	$(4m+4n+4a+52)\frac{1}{10^r}$ for i = 3	$\frac{m+n+a+4}{3}$ for i = 3

(*Continued*)

Table 6.3 MMVs K_i's, their corresponding edges and the number of K_i's ($1 \le i \le 3$). (*Continued*)

Nature of m, n	Nature of a	Edges		MMV K_i's, $1 \le i \le 3$	Number of K_i's, $1 \le i \le 3$
	$a \equiv 2 (mod\ 3)$	$g(v_2x_j)$	if $1 \le j \le \frac{m}{3}$	$(4m+4n+4a+54)\frac{1}{10^r}$ for i = 1	$\frac{m+n+a+6}{3}$ for i = 1
		$g(v_1v_2), g(v_2v_3)$			
		$g(v_3y_j)$	if $1 \le j \le \frac{n+1}{3}$		
		$g(v_5z_j)$	if $1 \le j \le \frac{a-1}{3}$		
		$g(v_2x_j)$	if $\frac{m}{3}+1 \le j \le \frac{2m}{3}$	$(4m+4n+4a+53)\frac{1}{10^r}$ for i = 2	$\frac{m+n+a+6}{3}$ for i = 2
		$g(v_3v_4), g(v_4v_5)$			
		$g(v_3y_j)$	if $\frac{n+1}{3}+1 \le j \le \frac{2n-1}{3}$		
		$g(v_5z_j)$	if $\frac{a-1}{3}+1 \le j \le \frac{2a-1}{3}$		

(*Continued*)

Table 6.3 MMVs K_i's, their corresponding edges and the number of K_i's ($1 \le i \le 3$). (*Continued*)

Nature of m, n	Nature of a	Edges	MMV K_i's, $1 \le i \le 3$	Number of K_i's, $1 \le i \le 3$
		$g(v_2x_j)$ if $\frac{2m}{3}+1 \le j \le m$ $g(v_5v_6)$ $g(v_3y_j)$ if $\frac{2n-1}{3}+1 \le j \le n$ $g(v_5z_j)$ if $\frac{2a-1}{3}+1 \le j \le a$	$(4m+4n+4a+52)\frac{1}{10^r}$ for $i=3$	$\frac{m+n+a+3}{3}$ for $i=3$

Case (ii) If $m \equiv 1(mod\,3)$
Subcase (i) If $n \equiv 0(mod\,3)$

$$\sigma(x_j)=(2m+2n+2a+21-j)\frac{1}{10^r} \quad \text{for } 1 \le j \le \frac{m-1}{3}$$

$$\sigma(x_j)=(2m+2n+2a+20-j)\frac{1}{10^r} \quad \text{for } \frac{m-1}{3}+1 \le j \le \frac{2(m-1)}{3}$$

$$\sigma(x_j)=(2m+2n+2a+19-j)\frac{1}{10^r} \quad \text{for } \frac{2(m-1)}{3}+1 \le j \le m$$

$$\sigma(y_j)=(m+2n+2a+19-j)\frac{1}{10^r} \quad \text{for } 1 \le j \le \frac{n}{3}$$

$$\sigma(y_j)=(m+2n+2a+18-j)\frac{1}{10^r} \quad \text{for } \frac{n}{3}+1 \le j \le \frac{2n}{3}$$

$$\sigma(y_j)=(m+2n+2a+17-j)\frac{1}{10^r} \quad \text{for } \frac{2n}{3}+1 \le j \le n.$$

Subcase (i)a If $a \equiv 0(mod\,3)$

$$\sigma(z_j)=(m+n+2a+17-j)\frac{1}{10^r} \quad \text{for } 1 \le j \le \frac{a}{3}$$

$$\sigma(z_j)=(m+n+2a+16-j)\frac{1}{10^r} \quad \text{for } \frac{a}{3}+1 \le j \le \frac{2a}{3}$$

$$\sigma(z_j)=(m+n+2a+15-j)\frac{1}{10^r} \quad \text{for } \frac{2a}{3}+1 \le j \le a.$$

Subcase (i)b If $a \equiv 1(mod\,3)$

$$\sigma(z_j)=(m+n+2a+17-j)\frac{1}{10^r} \quad \text{for } 1 \le j \le \frac{a+2}{3}$$

$$\sigma(z_j)=(m+n+2a+16-j)\frac{1}{10^r} \quad \text{for } \left(\frac{a+2}{3}\right)+1 \le j \le \frac{2a+1}{3}$$

$$\sigma(z_j)=(m+n+2a+15-j)\frac{1}{10^r} \quad \text{for } \left(\frac{2a+1}{3}\right)+1 \le j \le a$$

Subcase (i)c If $a \equiv 2(mod\ 3)$

$$\sigma(z_j) = (m+n+2a+17-j)\frac{1}{10^r} \quad \text{for } 1 \leq j \leq \frac{a+1}{3}$$

$$\sigma(z_j) = (m+n+2a+16-j)\frac{1}{10^r} \quad \text{for } \left(\frac{a+1}{3}\right)+1 \leq j \leq \frac{2(a+1)}{3}$$

$$\sigma(z_j) = (m+n+2a+15-j)\frac{1}{10^r} \quad \text{for } \frac{2(a+1)}{3}+1 \leq j \leq a.$$

From different nature of *m*, *n*, MMVs K_i's, their corresponding edges and number of K_i's ($1 \leq i \leq 3$) are given in Table 6.4.

Subcase (ii) If $n \equiv 1(mod\ 3)$

$$\sigma(x_j) = (2m+2n+2a+21-j)\frac{1}{10^r} \quad \text{for } 1 \leq j \leq \frac{m-1}{3}$$

$$\sigma(x_j) = (2m+2n+2a+20-j)\frac{1}{10^r} \quad \text{for } \frac{m-1}{3}+1 \leq j \leq \frac{2(m-1)}{3}$$

$$\sigma(x_j) = (2m+2n+2a+19-j)\frac{1}{10^r} \quad \text{for } \frac{2(m-1)}{3}+1 \leq j \leq m$$

$$\sigma(y_j) = (m+2n+2a+19-j)\frac{1}{10^r} \quad \text{for } 1 \leq j \leq \frac{n+2}{3}$$

$$\sigma(y_j) = (m+2n+2a+18-j)\frac{1}{10^r} \quad \text{for } \left(\frac{n+2}{3}\right)+1 \leq j \leq \frac{2n+1}{3}$$

$$\sigma(y_j) = (m+2n+2a+17-j)\frac{1}{10^r} \quad \text{for } \left(\frac{2n+1}{3}\right)+1 \leq j \leq n.$$

Subcase (ii)a If $a \equiv 0(mod\ 3)$

$$\sigma(z_j) = (m+n+2a+17-j)\frac{1}{10^r} \quad \text{for } 1 \leq j \leq \frac{a}{3}$$

$$\sigma(z_j) = (m+n+2a+16-j)\frac{1}{10^r} \quad \text{for } \frac{a}{3}+1 \leq j \leq \frac{2a}{3}$$

$$\sigma(z_j) = (m+n+2a+15-j)\frac{1}{10^r} \quad \text{for } \frac{2a}{3}+1 \leq j \leq a.$$

Table 6.4 MMVs K_i's, their corresponding edges and the number of K_i's $(1 \le i \le 3)$.

Nature of m, n	Nature of a	Edges	MMV K_i's, $1 \le i \le 3$	Number of K_i's, $1 \le i \le 3$
$m \equiv 1(mod\ 3), n \equiv 0(mod\ 3)$	$a \equiv 0(mod\ 3)$	$g(v_2x_j)$ if $1 \le j \le \frac{m-1}{3}$ $g(v_1v_2), g(v_2v_3)$ $g(v_3y_j)$ if $1 \le j \le \frac{n}{3}$ $g(v_5z_j)$ if $1 \le j \le \frac{a}{3}$	$(4m+4n+4a+54)\frac{1}{10^r}$ for i = 1	$\frac{m+n+a+5}{3}$ for i = 1
		$g(v_2x_j)$ if $\frac{m-1}{3}+1 \le j \le \frac{2(m-1)}{3}$ $g(v_3v_4), g(v_4v_5)$ $g(v_3y_j)$ if $\frac{n}{3}+1 \le j \le \frac{2n}{3}$ $g(v_5z_j)$ if $\frac{a}{3}+1 \le j \le \frac{2a}{3}$	$(4m+4n+4a+53)\frac{1}{10^r}$ for i = 2	$\frac{m+n+a+5}{3}$ for i = 2

(Continued)

Table 6.4 MMVs K_i's, their corresponding edges and the number of K_i's ($1 \le i \le 3$). (*Continued*)

Nature of m, n	Nature of a	Edges	MMV K_i's, $1 \le i \le 3$	Number of K_i's, $1 \le i \le 3$
		$g(v_2x_j)$ if $\frac{2(m-1)}{3}+1 \le j \le m$ $g(v_5v_6)$ $g(v_3y_j)$ if $\frac{2n}{3}+1 \le j \le n$ $g(v_5z_j)$ if $\frac{2a}{3}+1 \le j \le a$	$(4m+4n+4a+52)\frac{1}{10^r}$ for $i=3$	$\frac{m+n+a+5}{3}$ for $i=3$
	$a \equiv 1 (mod\ 3)$	$g(v_2x_j)$ if $1 \le j \le \frac{m-1}{3}$ $g(v_1v_2), g(v_2v_3)$ $g(v_3y_j)$ if $1 \le j \le \frac{n}{3}$ $g(v_5z_j)$ if $1 \le j \le \frac{a+2}{3}$	$(4m+4n+4a+54)\frac{1}{10^r}$ for $i=1$	$\frac{m+n+a+7}{3}$ for $i=1$

(*Continued*)

Table 6.4 MMVs K_i's, their corresponding edges and the number of K_i's ($1 \le i \le 3$). (*Continued*)

Nature of m, n	**Nature of** a	**Edges**	**MMV** K_i**'s,** $1 \le i \le 3$	**Number of** K_i**'s,** $1 \le i \le 3$
		$g(v_2x_j)$ if $\frac{m-1}{3}+1 \le j \le \frac{2(m-1)}{3}$ $g(v_3v_4), g(v_4v_5)$ $g(v_3y_j)$ if $\frac{n}{3}+1 \le j \le \frac{2n}{3}$ $g(v_5z_j)$ if $\frac{a+2}{3}+1 \le j \le \frac{2a+1}{3}$	$(4m+4n+4a+53)\frac{1}{10^r}$ for i = 2	$\frac{m+n+a+4}{3}$ for i = 2
		$g(v_2x_j)$ if $\frac{2(m-1)}{3}+1 \le j \le m$ $g(v_5v_6)$ $g(v_3y_j)$ if $\frac{2n}{3}+1 \le j \le n$ $g(v_5z_j)$ if $\frac{2a+1}{3}+1 \le j \le a$	$(4m+4n+4a+52)\frac{1}{10^r}$ for i = 3	$\frac{m+n+a+4}{3}$ for i = 3

(*Continued*)

Table 6.4 MMVs K_i's, their corresponding edges and the number of K_i's ($1 \le i \le 3$). (*Continued*)

Nature of m, n	Nature of a	Edges	MMV K_i's, $1 \le i \le 3$	Number of K_i's, $1 \le i \le 3$
	$a \equiv 2(mod\ 3)$	$g(v_2x_j)$ if $1 \le j \le \frac{m-1}{3}$ $g(v_1v_2), g(v_2v_3)$ $g(v_3y_j)$ if $1 \le j \le \frac{n}{3}$ $g(v_5z_j)$ if $1 \le j \le \frac{a+1}{3}$	$(4m+4n+4a+54)\frac{1}{10^r}$ for i = 1	$\frac{m+n+a+6}{3}$ for i = 1
		$g(v_2x_j)$ if $\frac{m-1}{3}+1 \le j \le \frac{2(m-1)}{3}$ $g(v_3v_4), g(v_4v_5)$ $g(v_3y_j)$ if $\frac{n}{3}+1 \le j \le \frac{2n}{3}$ $g(v_5z_j)$ if $\frac{a+1}{3}+1 \le j \le \frac{2(a+1)}{3}$	$(4m+4n+4a+53)\frac{1}{10^r}$ for i = 2	$\frac{m+n+a+6}{3}$ for i = 2

(*Continued*)

Table 6.4 MMVs K_i's, their corresponding edges and the number of K_i's ($1 \le i \le 3$). *(Continued)*

Nature of m, n	Nature of a	Edges	MMV K_i's, $1 \le i \le 3$	Number of K_i's, $1 \le i \le 3$
		$g(v_2 x_j)$ if $\frac{2(m-1)}{3}+1 \le j \le m$ $g(v_5 v_6)$ $g(v_3 y_j)$ if $\frac{2n}{3}+1 \le j \le n$ $g(v_5 z_j)$ if $\frac{2(a+1)}{3}+1 \le j \le a$	$(4m+4n+4a+52)\frac{1}{10^r}$ for i = 3	$\frac{m+n+a+3}{3}$ for i = 3

Subcase (ii)b If $a \equiv 1(mod\ 3)$

$$\sigma(z_j)=(m+n+2a+17-j)\frac{1}{10^r} \quad \text{for } 1 \le j \le \frac{a-1}{3}$$

$$\sigma(z_j)=(m+n+2a+16-j)\frac{1}{10^r} \quad \text{for } \left(\frac{a-1}{3}\right)+1 \le j \le \frac{2a+1}{3}$$

$$\sigma(z_j)=(m+n+2a+15-j)\frac{1}{10^r} \quad \text{for } \left(\frac{2a+1}{3}\right)+1 \le j \le a.$$

Subcase (ii)c If $a \equiv 2(mod\ 3)$

$$\sigma(z_j)=(m+n+2a+17-j)\frac{1}{10^r} \quad \text{for } 1 \le j \le \frac{a-1}{3}$$

$$\sigma(z_j)=(m+n+2a+16-j)\frac{1}{10^r} \quad \text{for } \left(\frac{a-1}{3}\right)+1 \le j \le \frac{2a-1}{3}$$

$$\sigma(z_j)=(m+n+2a+15-j)\frac{1}{10^r} \quad \text{for } \left(\frac{2a-1}{3}\right)+1 \le j \le a.$$

From different nature of m, n, MMVs K_i's, their corresponding edges and number of K_i's ($1 \le i \le 3$) are given in Table 6.5.

Subcase (iii) If $n \equiv 2(mod\ 3)$

$$\sigma(x_j)=(2m+2n+2a+21-j)\frac{1}{10^r} \quad \text{for } 1 \le j \le \frac{m-1}{3}$$

$$\sigma(x_j)=(2m+2n+2a+20-j)\frac{1}{10^r} \quad \text{for } \frac{m-1}{3}+1 \le j \le \frac{2(m-1)}{3}$$

$$\sigma(x_j)=(2m+2n+2a+19-j)\frac{1}{10^r} \quad \text{for } \frac{2(m-1)}{3}+1 \le j \le m$$

$$\sigma(y_j)=(m+2n+2a+19-j)\frac{1}{10^r} \quad \text{for } 1 \le j \le \frac{n+1}{3}$$

$$\sigma(y_j)=(m+2n+2a+18-j)\frac{1}{10^r} \quad \text{for } \left(\frac{n+1}{3}\right)+1 \le j \le \frac{2n-1}{3}$$

$$\sigma(y_j)=(m+2n+2a+17-j)\frac{1}{10^r} \quad \text{for } \left(\frac{2n-1}{3}\right)+1 \le j \le n.$$

Table 6.5 MMVs K_i's, their corresponding edges and the number of K_i's $(1 \le i \le 3)$.

Nature of m, n	Nature of a	Edges		MMV K_i's, $1 \le i \le 3$	Number of K_i's, $1 \le i \le 3$
$m \equiv 1(mod\ 3), n \equiv 1(mod\ 3)$	$a \equiv 0(mod\ 3)$	$g(v_2x_j)$	if $1 \le j \le \frac{m-1}{3}$	$(4m+4n+4a+54)\frac{1}{10^r}$ for i = 1	$\frac{m+n+a+7}{3}$ for i = 1
		$g(v_1v_2), g(v_2v_3)$			
		$g(v_3y_j)$	if $1 \le j \le \frac{n+2}{3}$		
		$g(v_5z_j)$	if $1 \le j \le \frac{a}{3}$		
		$g(v_2x_j)$	if $\frac{m-1}{3}+1 \le j \le \frac{2(m-1)}{3}$	$(4m+4n+4a+53)\frac{1}{10^r}$ for i = 2	$\frac{m+n+a+4}{3}$ for i = 2
		$g(v_3v_4), g(v_4v_5)$			
		$g(v_3y_j)$	if $\frac{n+2}{3}+1 \le j \le \frac{2n+1}{3}$		
		$g(v_5z_j)$	if $\frac{a}{3}+1 \le j \le \frac{2a}{3}$		

(Continued)

Table 6.5 MMVs K_i's, their corresponding edges and the number of K_i's ($1 \le i \le 3$). (*Continued*)

Nature of m, n	Nature of a	Edges	MMV K_i's, $1 \le i \le 3$	Number of K_i's, $1 \le i \le 3$
		$g(v_2x_j)$ if $\frac{2(m-1)}{3}+1 \le j \le m$ $g(v_5v_6)$ $g(v_3y_j)$ if $\frac{2n+1}{3}+1 \le j \le n$ $g(v_5z_j)$ if $\frac{2a}{3}+1 \le j \le a$	$(4m+4n+4a+52)\frac{1}{10^r}$ for $i=3$	$\frac{m+n+a+4}{3}$ for $i=3$
	$a \equiv 1(mod\ 3)$	$g(v_2x_j)$ if $1 \le j \le \frac{m-1}{3}$ $g(v_1v_2), g(v_2v_3)$ $g(v_3y_j)$ if $1 \le j \le \frac{n+2}{3}$ $g(v_5z_j)$ if $1 \le j \le \frac{a-1}{3}$	$(4m+4n+4a+54)\frac{1}{10^r}$ for $i=1$	$\frac{m+n+a+6}{3}$ for $i=1$

(*Continued*)

Table 6.5 MMVs K_i's, their corresponding edges and the number of K_i's ($1 \le i \le 3$). *(Continued)*

Nature of m, n	Nature of a	Edges	MMV K_i's, $1 \le i \le 3$	Number of K_i's, $1 \le i \le 3$
		$g(v_2x_j)$ if $\frac{m-1}{3}+1 \le j \le \frac{2(m-1)}{3}$ $g(v_3v_4), g(v_4v_5)$ $g(v_3y_j)$ if $\frac{n+2}{3}+1 \le j \le \frac{2n+1}{3}$ $g(v_5z_j)$ if $\frac{a-1}{3}+1 \le j \le \frac{2a+1}{3}$	$(4m+4n+4a+53)\frac{1}{10^r}$ for i = 2	$\frac{m+n+a+6}{3}$ for i = 2
		$g(v_2x_j)$ if $\frac{2(m-1)}{3}+1 \le j \le m$ $g(v_5v_6)$ $g(v_3y_j)$ if $\frac{2n+1}{3}+1 \le j \le n$ $g(v_5z_j)$ if $\frac{2a+1}{3}+1 \le j \le a$	$(4m+4n+4a+52)\frac{1}{10^r}$ for i = 3	$\frac{m+n+a+3}{3}$ for i = 3

(Continued)

Table 6.5 MMVs K_i's, their corresponding edges and the number of K_i's $(1 \le i \le 3)$. (*Continued*)

Nature of m, n	Nature of a	Edges	MMV K_i's, $1 \le i \le 3$	Number of K_i's, $1 \le i \le 3$
	$a \equiv 2 (mod\ 3)$	$g(v_2 x_j)$ if $1 \le j \le \frac{m-1}{3}$ $g(v_1 v_2), g(v_2 v_3)$ $g(v_3 y_j)$ if $1 \le j \le \frac{n+2}{3}$ $g(v_5 z_j)$ if $1 \le j \le \frac{a-1}{3}$	$(4m+4n+4a+54)\frac{1}{10^r}$ for i = 1	$\frac{m+n+a+5}{3}$ for i = 1
		$g(v_2 x_j)$ if $\frac{m-1}{3}+1 \le j \le \frac{2(m-1)}{3}$ $g(v_3 v_4), g(v_4 v_5)$ $g(v_3 y_j)$ if $\frac{n+2}{3}+1 \le j \le \frac{2n+1}{3}$ $g(v_5 z_j)$ if $\frac{a-1}{3}+1 \le j \le \frac{2a-1}{3}$	$(4m+4n+4a+53)\frac{1}{10^r}$ for i = 2	$\frac{m+n+a+5}{3}$ for i = 2

(*Continued*)

Table 6.5 MMVs K_i's, their corresponding edges and the number of K_i's ($1 \le i \le 3$). (*Continued*)

Nature of m, n	Nature of a	Edges	MMV K_i's, $1 \le i \le 3$	Number of K_i's, $1 \le i \le 3$
		$g(v_2x_j)$ if $\frac{2(m-1)}{3}+1 \le j \le m$ $g(v_5v_6)$ $g(v_3y_j)$ if $\frac{2n+1}{3}+1 \le j \le n$ $g(v_5z_j)$ if $\frac{2a-1}{3}+1 \le j \le a$	$(4m+4n+4a+52)\frac{1}{10^r}$ for i = 3	$\frac{m+n+a+5}{3}$ for i = 3

Subcase (iii)a If $a \equiv 0(mod\ 3)$

$$\sigma(z_j)=(m+n+2a+17-j)\frac{1}{10^r} \quad \text{for } 1 \leq j \leq \frac{a}{3}$$

$$\sigma(z_j)=(m+n+2a+16-j)\frac{1}{10^r} \quad \text{for } \frac{a}{3}+1 \leq j \leq \frac{2a}{3}$$

$$\sigma(z_j)=(m+n+2a+15-j)\frac{1}{10^r} \quad \text{for } \frac{2a}{3}+1 \leq j \leq a.$$

Subcase (iii)b If $a \equiv 1(mod\ 3)$

$$\sigma(z_j)=(m+n+2a+17-j)\frac{1}{10^r} \quad \text{for } 1 \leq j \leq \frac{a+2}{3}$$

$$\sigma(z_j)=(m+n+2a+16-j)\frac{1}{10^r} \quad \text{for } \left(\frac{a+2}{3}\right)+1 \leq j \leq \frac{2a+1}{3}$$

$$\sigma(z_j)=(m+n+2a+15-j)\frac{1}{10^r} \quad \text{for } \left(\frac{2a+1}{3}\right)+1 \leq j \leq a.$$

Subcase (iii)c If $a \equiv 2(mod\ 3)$

$$\sigma(z_j)=(m+n+2a+17-j)\frac{1}{10^r} \quad \text{for } 1 \leq j \leq \frac{a+1}{3}$$

$$\sigma(z_j)=(m+n+2a+16-j)\frac{1}{10^r} \quad \text{for } \left(\frac{a+1}{3}\right)+1 \leq j \leq \frac{2(a+1)}{3}$$

$$\sigma(z_j)=(m+n+2a+15-j)\frac{1}{10^r} \quad \text{for } \frac{2(a+1)}{3}+1 \leq j \leq a.$$

From different nature of m, n, MMVs K_i's, their corresponding edges and number of K_i's ($1 \leq i \leq 3$) are given in Table 6.6.

Table 6.6 MMVs K_i's, their corresponding edges and the number of K_i's ($1 \le i \le 3$).

Nature of m, n	Nature of a	Edges	MMV K_i's, $1 \le i \le 3$	Number of K_i's, $1 \le i \le 3$
$m \equiv 1(mod\ 3), n \equiv 2(mod\ 3)$	$a \equiv 0(mod\ 3)$	$g(v_2x_j)$ if $1 \le j \le \frac{m-1}{3}$ $g(v_1v_2), g(v_2v_3)$ $g(v_3y_j)$ if $1 \le j \le \frac{n+1}{3}$ $g(v_5z_j)$ if $1 \le j \le \frac{a}{3}$	$(4m+4n+4a+54)\frac{1}{10^r}$ for i = 1	$\frac{m+n+a+6}{3}$ for i = 1
		$g(v_2x_j)$ if $\frac{m-1}{3}+1 \le j \le \frac{2(m-1)}{3}$ $g(v_3v_4), g(v_4v_5)$ $g(v_3y_j)$ if $\frac{n+1}{3}+1 \le j \le \frac{2n-1}{3}$ $g(v_5z_j)$ if $\frac{a}{3}+1 \le j \le \frac{2a}{3}$	$(4m+4n+4a+53)\frac{1}{10^r}$ for i = 2	$\frac{m+n+a+6}{3}$ for i = 2

(Continued)

Table 6.6 MMVs K_i's, their corresponding edges and the number of K_i's ($1 \le i \le 3$). (*Continued*)

Nature of m, n	Nature of a	Edges	MMV K_i's, $1 \le i \le 3$	Number of K_i's, $1 \le i \le 3$
		$g(v_2x_j)$ if $\frac{2(m-1)}{3}+1 \le j \le m$ $g(v_5v_6)$ $g(v_3y_j)$ if $\frac{2n-1}{3}+1 \le j \le n$ $g(v_5z_j)$ if $\frac{2a}{3}+1 \le j \le a$	$(4m+4n+4a+52)\frac{1}{10^r}$ for i = 3	$\frac{m+n+a+3}{3}$ for i = 3
	$a \equiv 1(mod\ 3)$	$g(v_2x_j)$ if $1 \le j \le \frac{m-1}{3}$ $g(v_1v_2), g(v_2v_3)$ $g(v_3y_j)$ if $1 \le j \le \frac{n+1}{3}$ $g(v_5z_j)$ if $1 \le j \le \frac{a+2}{3}$	$(4m+4n+4a+54)\frac{1}{10^r}$ for i = 1	$\frac{m+n+a+5}{3}$ for i = 1

(*Continued*)

Table 6.6 MMVs K_i's, their corresponding edges and the number of K_i's ($1 \le i \le 3$). (*Continued*)

Nature of m, n	Nature of a	Edges	MMV K_i's, $1 \le i \le 3$	Number of K_i's, $1 \le i \le 3$
		$g(v_2x_j)$ if $\frac{m-1}{3}+1 \le j \le \frac{2(m-1)}{3}$ $g(v_3v_4), g(v_4v_5)$ $g(v_3y_j)$ if $\frac{n+1}{3}+1 \le j \le \frac{2n-1}{3}$ $g(v_5z_j)$ if $\frac{a+2}{3}+1 \le j \le \frac{2a+1}{3}$	$(4m+4n+4a+53)\frac{1}{10^r}$ for i = 2	$\frac{m+n+a+5}{3}$ for i = 2
		$g(v_2x_j)$ if $\frac{2(m-1)}{3}+1 \le j \le m$ $g(v_5v_6)$ $g(v_3y_j)$ if $\frac{2n-1}{3}+1 \le j \le n$ $g(v_5z_j)$ if $\frac{2a+1}{3}+1 \le j \le a$	$(4m+4n+4a+52)\frac{1}{10^r}$ for i = 3	$\frac{m+n+a+5}{3}$ for i = 3

(*Continued*)

Table 6.6 MMVs K_i's, their corresponding edges and the number of K_i's ($1 \le i \le 3$). (*Continued*)

Nature of m, n	Nature of a	Edges		MMV K_i's, $1 \le i \le 3$	Number of K_i's, $1 \le i \le 3$
	$a \equiv 2(mod\ 3)$	$g(v_2x_j)$	if $1 \le j \le \frac{m-1}{3}$	$(4m+4n+4a+54)\frac{1}{10^r}$ for i = 1	$\frac{m+n+a+7}{3}$ for i = 1
		$g(v_1v_2), g(v_2v_3)$			
		$g(v_3y_j)$	if $1 \le j \le \frac{n+1}{3}$		
		$g(v_5z_j)$	if $1 \le j \le \frac{a+1}{3}$		
		$g(v_2x_j)$	if $\frac{m-1}{3}+1 \le j \le \frac{2(m-1)}{3}$	$(4m+4n+4a+53)\frac{1}{10^r}$ for i = 2	$\frac{m+n+a+4}{3}$ for i = 2
		$g(v_3v_4), g(v_4v_5)$			
		$g(v_3y_j)$	if $\frac{n+1}{3}+1 \le j \le \frac{2n-1}{3}$		
		$g(v_5z_j)$	if $\frac{a+1}{3}+1 \le j \le \frac{2(a+1)}{3}$		

(*Continued*)

Table 6.6 MMVs K_i's, their corresponding edges and the number of K_i's ($1 \le i \le 3$). (*Continued*)

Nature of m, n	Nature of a	Edges	MMV K_i's, $1 \le i \le 3$	Number of K_i's, $1 \le i \le 3$
		$g(v_2x_j)$ if $\frac{2(m-1)}{3}+1 \le j \le m$ $g(v_5v_6)$ $g(v_3y_j)$ if $\frac{2n-1}{3}+1 \le j \le n$ $g(v_5z_j)$ if $\frac{2(a+1)}{3}+1 \le j \le a$	$(4m+4n+4a+52)\frac{1}{10^r}$ for $i=3$	$\frac{m+n+a+4}{3}$ for $i=3$

Case (iii) If $m \equiv 2(mod\ 3)$
Subcase (i) If $n \equiv 0(mod\ 3)$

$$\sigma(x_j)=(2m+2n+2a+21-j)\frac{1}{10^r} \quad \text{for } 1\le j\le \frac{m+1}{3}$$

$$\sigma(x_j)=(2m+2n+2a+20-j)\frac{1}{10^r} \quad \text{for } \left(\frac{m+1}{3}\right)+1\le j\le \frac{2m-1}{3}$$

$$\sigma(x_j)=(2m+2n+2a+19-j)\frac{1}{10^r} \quad \text{for } \left(\frac{2m-1}{3}\right)+1\le j\le m$$

$$\sigma(y_j)=(m+2n+2a+19-j)\frac{1}{10^r} \quad \text{for } 1\le j\le \frac{n}{3}$$

$$\sigma(y_j)=(m+2n+2a+18-j)\frac{1}{10^r} \quad \text{for } \frac{n}{3}+1\le j\le \frac{2n}{3}$$

$$\sigma(y_j)=(m+2n+2a+17-j)\frac{1}{10^r} \quad \text{for } \frac{2n}{3}+1\le j\le n.$$

Subcase (i)a If $a \equiv 0(mod\ 3)$

$$\sigma(z_j)=(m+n+2a+17-j)\frac{1}{10^r} \quad \text{for } 1\le j\le \frac{a}{3}$$

$$\sigma(z_j)=(m+n+2a+16-j)\frac{1}{10^r} \quad \text{for } \frac{a}{3}+1\le j\le \frac{2a}{3}$$

$$\sigma(z_j)=(m+n+2a+15-j)\frac{1}{10^r} \quad \text{for } \frac{2a}{3}+1\le j\le a.$$

Subcase (i)b If $a \equiv 1(mod\ 3)$

$$\sigma(z_j)=(m+n+2a+17-j)\frac{1}{10^r} \quad \text{for } 1\le j\le \frac{a-1}{3}$$

$$\sigma(z_j)=(m+n+2a+16-j)\frac{1}{10^r} \quad \text{for } \left(\frac{a-1}{3}\right)+1\le j\le \frac{2a+1}{3}$$

$$\sigma(z_j)=(m+n+2a+15-j)\frac{1}{10^r} \quad \text{for } \left(\frac{2a+1}{3}\right)+1\le j\le a.$$

Subcase (i)c If $a \equiv 2(mod\,3)$

$$\sigma(z_j)=(m+n+2a+17-j)\frac{1}{10^r} \quad \text{for } 1\le j\le \frac{a-1}{3}$$

$$\sigma(z_j)=(m+n+2a+16-j)\frac{1}{10^r} \quad \text{for } \left(\frac{a-1}{3}\right)+1\le j\le \frac{2a-1}{3}$$

$$\sigma(z_j)=(m+n+2a+15-j)\frac{1}{10^r} \quad \text{for } \left(\frac{2a-1}{3}\right)+1\le j\le a.$$

From different nature of m, n, MMVs K_i's, their corresponding edges and number of K_i's ($1 \le i \le 3$) are given in Table 6.7.

Subcase (ii) If $n \equiv 1(mod\,3)$

$$\sigma(x_j)=(2m+2n+2a+21-j)\frac{1}{10^r} \quad \text{for } 1\le j\le \frac{m+1}{3}$$

$$\sigma(x_j)=(2m+2n+2a+20-j)\frac{1}{10^r} \quad \text{for } \left(\frac{m+1}{3}\right)+1\le j\le \frac{2m-1}{3}$$

$$\sigma(x_j)=(2m+2n+2a+19-j)\frac{1}{10^r} \quad \text{for } \left(\frac{2m-1}{3}\right)+1\le j\le m$$

$$\sigma(y_j)=(m+2n+2a+19-j)\frac{1}{10^r} \quad \text{for } 1\le j\le \frac{n-1}{3}$$

$$\sigma(y_j)=(m+2n+2a+18-j)\frac{1}{10^r} \quad \text{for } \left(\frac{n-1}{3}\right)+1\le j\le \frac{2n+1}{3}$$

$$\sigma(y_j)=(m+2n+2a+17-j)\frac{1}{10^r} \quad \text{for } \left(\frac{2n+1}{3}\right)+1\le j\le n.$$

Subcase (ii)a If $a \equiv 0(mod\,3)$

$$\sigma(z_j)=(m+n+2a+17-j)\frac{1}{10^r} \quad \text{for } 1\le j\le \frac{a}{3}$$

$$\sigma(z_j)=(m+n+2a+16-j)\frac{1}{10^r} \quad \text{for } \frac{a}{3}+1\le j\le \frac{2a}{3}$$

$$\sigma(z_j)=(m+n+2a+15-j)\frac{1}{10^r} \quad \text{for } \frac{2a}{3}+1\le j\le a.$$

Table 6.7 MMVs K_i's, their corresponding edges and the number of K_i's $(1 \le i \le 3)$.

Nature of m, n	Nature of a	Edges		MMV K_i's, $1 \le i \le 3$	Number of K_i's, $1 \le i \le 3$
$m \equiv 2(mod\ 3), n \equiv 0(mod\ 3)$	$a \equiv 0(mod\ 3)$	$g(v_2x_j)$	if $1 \le j \le \frac{m+1}{3}$	$(4m+4n+4a+54)\frac{1}{10^r}$ for i = 1	$\frac{m+n+a+7}{3}$ for i = 1
		$g(v_1v_2), g(v_2v_3)$			
		$g(v_3y_j)$	if $1 \le j \le \frac{n}{3}$		
		$g(v_5z_j)$	if $1 \le j \le \frac{a}{3}$		
		$g(v_2x_j)$	if $\frac{m+1}{3}+1 \le j \le \frac{2m-1}{3}$	$(4m+4n+4a+53)\frac{1}{10^r}$ for i = 2	$\frac{m+n+a+4}{3}$ for i = 2
		$g(v_3v_4), g(v_4v_5)$			
		$g(v_3y_j)$	if $\frac{n}{3}+1 \le j \le \frac{2n}{3}$		
		$g(v_5z_j)$	if $\frac{a}{3}+1 \le j \le \frac{2a}{3}$		

(*Continued*)

Table 6.7 MMVs K_i's, their corresponding edges and the number of K_i's ($1 \le i \le 3$). *(Continued)*

Nature of m, n	**Nature of** a	**Edges**	**MMV** K_i**'s,** $1 \le i \le 3$	**Number of** K_i**'s,** $1 \le i \le 3$
		$g(v_2x_j)$ if $\frac{2m-1}{3}+1 \le j \le m$ $g(v_5v_6)$ $g(v_3y_j)$ if $\frac{2n}{3}+1 \le j \le n$ $g(v_5z_j)$ if $\frac{2a}{3}+1 \le j \le a$	$(4m+4n+4a+52)\frac{1}{10^r}$ for i = 3	$\frac{m+n+a+4}{3}$ for i = 3
	$a \equiv 1(mod\ 3)$	$g(v_2x_j)$ if $1 \le j \le \frac{m+1}{3}$ $g(v_1v_2), g(v_2v_3)$ $g(v_3y_j)$ if $1 \le j \le \frac{n}{3}$ $g(v_5z_j)$ if $1 \le j \le \frac{a-1}{3}$	$(4m+4n+4a+54)\frac{1}{10^r}$ for i = 1	$\frac{m+n+a+6}{3}$ for i = 1

(Continued)

Table 6.7 MMVs K_i's, their corresponding edges and the number of K_i's ($1 \le i \le 3$). (*Continued*)

Nature of m, n	Nature of a	Edges	MMV K_i's, $1 \le i \le 3$	Number of K_i's, $1 \le i \le 3$
		$g(v_2x_j)$ if $\frac{m+1}{3}+1 \le j \le \frac{2m-1}{3}$ $g(v_3v_4), g(v_4v_5)$ $g(v_3y_j)$ if $\frac{n}{3}+1 \le j \le \frac{2n}{3}$ $g(v_5z_j)$ if $\frac{a-1}{3}+1 \le j \le \frac{2a+1}{3}$	$(4m+4n+4a+53)\frac{1}{10^r}$ for i = 2	$\frac{m+n+a+6}{3}$ for i = 2
		$g(v_2x_j)$ if $\frac{2m-1}{3}+1 \le j \le m$ $g(v_5v_6)$ $g(v_3y_j)$ if $\frac{2n}{3}+1 \le j \le n$ $g(v_5z_j)$ if $\frac{2a+1}{3}+1 \le j \le a$	$(4m+4n+4a+52)\frac{1}{10^r}$ for i = 3	$\frac{m+n+a+3}{3}$ for i = 3

(*Continued*)

Table 6.7 MMVs K_i's, their corresponding edges and the number of K_i's ($1 \le i \le 3$). (*Continued*)

Nature of *m, n*	**Nature of *a***	**Edges**	**MMV K_i's, $1 \le i \le 3$**	**Number of K_i's, $1 \le i \le 3$**
	$a \equiv 2(mod\ 3)$	$g(v_2x_j)$ if $1 \le j \le \frac{m+1}{3}$ $g(v_1v_2), g(v_2v_3)$ $g(v_3y_j)$ if $1 \le j \le \frac{n}{3}$ $g(v_5z_j)$ if $1 \le j \le \frac{a-1}{3}$	$(4m+4n+4a+54)\frac{1}{10^r}$ for i = 1	$\frac{m+n+a+5}{3}$ for i = 1
		$g(v_2x_j)$ if $\frac{m+1}{3}+1 \le j \le \frac{2m-1}{3}$ $g(v_3v_4), g(v_4v_5)$ $g(v_3y_j)$ if $\frac{n}{3}+1 \le j \le \frac{2n}{3}$ $g(v_5z_j)$ if $\frac{a-1}{3}+1 \le j \le \frac{2a-1}{3}$	$(4m+4n+4a+53)\frac{1}{10^r}$ for i = 2	$\frac{m+n+a+5}{3}$ for i = 2

(*Continued*)

Table 6.7 MMVs K_i's, their corresponding edges and the number of K_i's ($1 \le i \le 3$). (*Continued*)

Nature of m, n	Nature of a	Edges	MMV K_i's, $1 \le i \le 3$	Number of K_i's, $1 \le i \le 3$
		$g(v_2 x_j)$ if $\frac{2m-1}{3}+1 \le j \le m$ $g(v_5 v_6)$ $g(v_3 y_j)$ if $\frac{2n}{3}+1 \le j \le n$ $g(v_5 z_j)$ if $\frac{2a-1}{3}+1 \le j \le a$	$(4m+4n+4a+52)\frac{1}{10^r}$ for $i=3$	$\frac{m+n+a+5}{3}$ for $i=3$

Subcase (ii)b If $a \equiv 1(mod\ 3)$

$$\sigma(z_j) = (m+n+2a+17-j)\frac{1}{10^r} \quad \text{for } 1 \le j \le \frac{a+2}{3}$$

$$\sigma(z_j) = (m+n+2a+16-j)\frac{1}{10^r} \quad \text{for } \left(\frac{a+2}{3}\right)+1 \le j \le \frac{2a+1}{3}$$

$$\sigma(z_j) = (m+n+2a+15-j)\frac{1}{10^r} \quad \text{for } \left(\frac{2a+1}{3}\right)+1 \le j \le a.$$

Subcase (ii)c If $a \equiv 2(mod\ 3)$

$$\sigma(z_j) = (m+n+2a+17-j)\frac{1}{10^r} \quad \text{for } 1 \le j \le \frac{a+1}{3}$$

$$\sigma(z_j) = (m+n+2a+16-j)\frac{1}{10^r} \quad \text{for } \left(\frac{a+1}{3}\right)+1 \le j \le \frac{2a-1}{3}$$

$$\sigma(z_j) = (m+n+2a+15-j)\frac{1}{10^r} \quad \text{for } \left(\frac{2a-1}{3}\right)+1 \le j \le a.$$

From different nature of *m*, *n*, MMVs K_i's, their corresponding edges and number of K_i's ($1 \le i \le 3$) are given in Table 6.8.

Subcase (iii) If $n \equiv 2(mod\ 3)$

$$\sigma(x_j) = (2m+2n+2a+21-j)\frac{1}{10^r} \quad \text{for } 1 \le j \le \frac{m+1}{3}$$

$$\sigma(x_j) = (2m+2n+2a+20-j)\frac{1}{10^r} \quad \text{for } \left(\frac{m+1}{3}\right)+1 \le j \le \frac{2m-1}{3}$$

$$\sigma(x_j) = (2m+2n+2a+19-j)\frac{1}{10^r} \quad \text{for } \left(\frac{2m-1}{3}\right)+1 \le j \le m$$

$$\sigma(y_j) = (m+2n+2a+19-j)\frac{1}{10^r} \quad \text{for } 1 \le j \le \frac{n-1}{3}$$

$$\sigma(y_j) = (m+2n+2a+18-j)\frac{1}{10^r} \quad \text{for } \left(\frac{n-1}{3}\right)+1 \le j \le \frac{2n-1}{3}$$

$$\sigma(y_j) = (m+2n+2a+17-j)\frac{1}{10^r} \quad \text{for } \left(\frac{2n-1}{3}\right)+1 \le j \le n.$$

Table 6.8 MMVs K_i's, their corresponding edges and the number of K_i's $(1 \le i \le 3)$.

Nature of m,n	Nature of a	Edges		MMV K_i's, $1 \le i \le 3$	Number of K_i's, $1 \le i \le 3$
$m \equiv 2 (mod\ 3), n \equiv 1 (mod\ 3)$	$a \equiv 0 (mod\ 3)$	$g(v_2 x_j)$	if $1 \le j \le \frac{m+1}{3}$	$(4m+4n+4a+54)\frac{1}{10^r}$ for i = 1	$\frac{m+n+a+6}{3}$ for i = 1
		$g(v_1 v_2), g(v_2 v_3)$			
		$g(v_3 y_j)$	if $1 \le j \le \frac{n-1}{3}$		
		$g(v_5 z_j)$	if $1 \le j \le \frac{a}{3}$		
		$g(v_2 x_j)$	if $\frac{m+1}{3}+1 \le j \le \frac{2m-1}{3}$	$(4m+4n+4a+53)\frac{1}{10^r}$ for i = 2	$\frac{m+n+a+6}{3}$ for i = 2
		$g(v_3 v_4), g(v_4 v_5)$			
		$g(v_3 y_j)$	if $\frac{n-1}{3}+1 \le j \le \frac{2n+1}{3}$		
		$g(v_5 z_j)$	if $\frac{a}{3}+1 \le j \le \frac{2a}{3}$		

(Continued)

Table 6.8 MMVs K_i's, their corresponding edges and the number of K_i's ($1 \le i \le 3$). (*Continued*)

Nature of m,n	Nature of a	Edges	MMV K_i's, $1 \le i \le 3$	Number of K_i's, $1 \le i \le 3$
		$g(v_2x_j)$ if $\frac{2m-1}{3}+1 \le j \le m$ $g(v_5v_6)$ $g(v_3y_j)$ if $\frac{2n+1}{3}+1 \le j \le n$ $g(v_5z_j)$ if $\frac{2a}{3}+1 \le j \le a$	$(4m+4n+4a+52)\frac{1}{10^r}$ for i = 3	$\frac{m+n+a+3}{3}$ for i = 3
	$a \equiv 1(mod\ 3)$	$g(v_2x_j)$ if $1 \le j \le \frac{m+1}{3}$ $g(v_1v_2), g(v_2v_3)$ $g(v_3y_j)$ if $1 \le j \le \frac{n-1}{3}$ $g(v_5z_j)$ if $1 \le j \le \frac{a+2}{3}$	$(4m+4n+4a+54)\frac{1}{10^r}$ for i = 1	$\frac{m+n+a+5}{3}$ for i = 1

(*Continued*)

Table 6.8 MMVs K_i's, their corresponding edges and the number of K_i's ($1 \le i \le 3$). (*Continued*)

Nature of m,n	Nature of a	Edges	MMV K_i's, $1 \le i \le 3$	Number of K_i's, $1 \le i \le 3$
		$g(v_2x_j)$ if $\frac{m+1}{3}+1 \le j \le \frac{2m-1}{3}$ $g(v_3v_4), g(v_4v_5)$ $g(v_3y_j)$ if $\frac{n-1}{3}+1 \le j \le \frac{2n+1}{3}$ $g(v_5z_j)$ if $\frac{a+2}{3}+1 \le j \le \frac{2a+1}{3}$	$(4m+4n+4a+53)\frac{1}{10^r}$ for i = 2	$\frac{m+n+a+5}{3}$ for i = 2
		$g(v_2x_j)$ if $\frac{2m-1}{3}+1 \le j \le m$ $g(v_5v_6)$ $g(v_3y_j)$ if $\frac{2n+1}{3}+1 \le j \le n$ $g(v_5z_j)$ if $\frac{2a+1}{3}+1 \le j \le a$	$(4m+4n+4a+52)\frac{1}{10^r}$ for i = 3	$\frac{m+n+a+5}{3}$ for i = 3

(*Continued*)

Table 6.8 MMVs K_i's, their corresponding edges and the number of K_i's ($1 \le i \le 3$). (*Continued*)

Nature of m,n	Nature of a	Edges		MMV K_i's, $1 \le i \le 3$	Number of K_i's, $1 \le i \le 3$
	$a \equiv 2(mod\ 3)$	$g(v_2x_j)$	if $1 \le j \le \frac{m+1}{3}$	$(4m+4n+4a+54)\frac{1}{10^r}$ for i = 1	$\frac{m+n+a+7}{3}$ for i = 1
		$g(v_1v_2), g(v_2v_3)$			
		$g(v_3y_j)$	if $1 \le j \le \frac{n-1}{3}$		
		$g(v_5z_j)$	if $1 \le j \le \frac{a+1}{3}$		
		$g(v_2x_j)$	if $\frac{m+1}{3}+1 \le j \le \frac{2m-1}{3}$	$(4m+4n+4a+53)\frac{1}{10^r}$ for i = 2	$\frac{m+n+a+4}{3}$ for i = 2
		$g(v_3v_4), g(v_4v_5)$			
		$g(v_3y_j)$	if $\frac{n-1}{3}+1 \le j \le \frac{2n+1}{3}$		
		$g(v_5z_j)$	if $\frac{a+1}{3}+1 \le j \le \frac{2a-1}{3}$		

(*Continued*)

Table 6.8 MMVs K_i's, their corresponding edges and the number of K_i's ($1 \le i \le 3$). (*Continued*)

Nature of m,n	Nature of a	Edges	MMV K_i's, $1 \le i \le 3$	Number of K_i's, $1 \le i \le 3$
		$g(v_2x_j)$ if $\frac{2m-1}{3}+1 \le j \le m$ $g(v_5v_6)$ $g(v_3y_j)$ if $\frac{2n+1}{3}+1 \le j \le n$ $g(v_5z_j)$ if $\frac{2a-1}{3}+1 \le j \le a$	$(4m+4n+4a+52)\frac{1}{10^r}$ for $i=3$	$\frac{m+n+a+4}{3}$ for $i=3$

Subcase (iii)a If $a \equiv 0 (mod\ 3)$

$$\sigma(z_j) = (m+n+2a+17-j)\frac{1}{10^r} \quad \text{for } 1 \leq j \leq \frac{a}{3}$$

$$\sigma(z_j) = (m+n+2a+16-j)\frac{1}{10^r} \quad \text{for } \frac{a}{3}+1 \leq j \leq \frac{2a}{3}$$

$$\sigma(z_j) = (m+n+2a+15-j)\frac{1}{10^r} \quad \text{for } \frac{2a}{3}+1 \leq j \leq a.$$

Subcase (iii)b If $a \equiv 1 (mod\ 3)$

$$\sigma(z_j) = (m+n+2a+17-j)\frac{1}{10^r} \quad \text{for } 1 \leq j \leq \frac{a+2}{3}$$

$$\sigma(z_j) = (m+n+2a+16-j)\frac{1}{10^r} \quad \text{for } \left(\frac{a+2}{3}\right)+1 \leq j \leq \frac{2a+1}{3}$$

$$\sigma(z_j) = (m+n+2a+15-j)\frac{1}{10^r} \quad \text{for } \left(\frac{2a+1}{3}\right)+1 \leq j \leq a.$$

Subcase (iii)c If $a \equiv 2 (mod\ 3)$

$$\sigma(z_j) = (m+n+2a+17-j)\frac{1}{10^r} \quad \text{for } 1 \leq j \leq \frac{a+1}{3}$$

$$\sigma(z_j) = (m+n+2a+16-j)\frac{1}{10^r} \quad \text{for } \left(\frac{a+1}{3}\right)+1 \leq j \leq \frac{2(a+1)}{3}$$

$$\sigma(z_j) = (m+n+2a+15-j)\frac{1}{10^r} \quad \text{for } \frac{2(a+1)}{3}+1 \leq j \leq a.$$

From different nature of m, n, MMVs K_i's, their corresponding edges and number of K_i's ($1 \leq i \leq 3$) are given in Table 6.9.

Hence the maximum difference between the number of K_i's is 1 and $|K_i - K_j| \leq \frac{2}{10^r}$ for $1 \leq i, j \leq 3$. Hence the caterpillar graph $\mathcal{T}^{6}_{2,3,5}$ of diameter 5 admits fuzzy tri-magic labeling for $m, n \geq 3$.

Table 6.9 MMVs K_i's, their corresponding edges and the number of K_i's $(1 \le i \le 3)$.

Nature of m, n	Nature of a	Edges		MMV K_i's, $1 \le i \le 3$	Number of K_i's, $1 \le i \le 3$
$m \equiv 2(\text{mod } 3), n \equiv 2(\text{mod } 3)$	$a \equiv 0(\text{mod } 3)$	$g(v_2 x_j)$	if $1 \le j \le \frac{m+1}{3}$	$(4m+4n+4a+54)\frac{1}{10^r}$ for i = 1	$\frac{m+n+a+5}{3}$ for i = 1
		$g(v_1 v_2), g(v_2 v_3)$			
		$g(v_3 y_j)$	if $1 \le j \le \frac{n-1}{3}$		
		$g(v_5 z_j)$	if $1 \le j \le \frac{a}{3}$		
		$g(v_2 x_j)$	if $\frac{m+1}{3}+1 \le j \le \frac{2m-1}{3}$	$(4m+4n+4a+53)\frac{1}{10^r}$ for i = 2	$\frac{m+n+a+5}{3}$ for i = 2
		$g(v_3 v_4), g(v_4 v_5)$			
		$g(v_3 y_j)$	if $\frac{n-1}{3}+1 \le j \le \frac{2n-1}{3}$		
		$g(v_5 z_j)$	if $\frac{a}{3}+1 \le j \le \frac{2a}{3}$		

(Continued)

Table 6.9 MMVs K_i's, their corresponding edges and the number of K_i's ($1 \le i \le 3$). (*Continued*)

Nature of m, n	Nature of a	Edges	MMV K_i's, $1 \le i \le 3$	Number of K_i's, $1 \le i \le 3$
		$g(v_2x_j)$ if $\frac{2m-1}{3}+1 \le j \le m$ $g(v_5v_6)$ $g(v_3y_j)$ if $\frac{2n-1}{3}+1 \le j \le n$ $g(v_5z_j)$ if $\frac{2(a+1)}{3}+1 \le j \le a$	$(4m+4n+4a+52)\frac{1}{10^r}$ for i = 3	$\frac{m+n+a+3}{3}$ for i = 3

Table 6.9 MMVs K_i's, their corresponding edges and the number of K_i's ($1 \le i \le 3$). (*Continued*)

Nature of m, n	Nature of a	Edges	MMV K_i's, $1 \le i \le 3$	Number of K_i's, $1 \le i \le 3$
		$g(v_2x_j)$ if $\frac{2m-1}{3}+1 \le j \le m$ $g(v_5v_6)$ $g(v_3y_j)$ if $\frac{2n-1}{3}+1 \le j \le n$ $g(v_5z_j)$ if $\frac{2a}{3}+1 \le j \le a$	$(4m+4n+4a+52)\frac{1}{10^r}$ for i = 3	$\frac{m+n+a+5}{3}$ for i = 3
	$a \equiv 1(mod\ 3)$	$g(v_2x_j)$ if $1 \le j \le \frac{m+1}{3}$ $g(v_1v_2), g(v_2v_3)$ $g(v_3y_j)$ if $1 \le j \le \frac{n-1}{3}$ $g(v_5z_j)$ if $1 \le j \le \frac{a+2}{3}$	$(4m+4n+4a+54)\frac{1}{10^r}$ for i = 1	$\frac{m+n+a+7}{3}$ for i = 1

(*Continued*)

Table 6.9 MMVs K_i's, their corresponding edges and the number of K_i's ($1 \le i \le 3$). *(Continued)*

Nature of m, n	Nature of a	Edges	MMV K_i's, $1 \le i \le 3$	Number of K_i's, $1 \le i \le 3$
		$g(v_2x_j)$ if $\frac{m+1}{3}+1 \le j \le \frac{2m-1}{3}$ $g(v_3v_4), g(v_4v_5)$ $g(v_3y_j)$ if $\frac{n-1}{3}+1 \le j \le \frac{2n-1}{3}$ $g(v_5z_j)$ if $\frac{a+2}{3}+1 \le j \le \frac{2a+1}{3}$	$(4m+4n+4a+53)\frac{1}{10^r}$ for i = 2	$\frac{m+n+a+4}{3}$ for i = 2
		$g(v_2x_j)$ if $\frac{2m-1}{3}+1 \le j \le m$ $g(v_5v_6)$ $g(v_3y_j)$ if $\frac{2n-1}{3}+1 \le j \le n$ $g(v_5z_j)$ if $\frac{2a+1}{3}+1 \le j \le a$	$(4m+4n+4a+52)\frac{1}{10^r}$ for i = 3	$\frac{m+n+a+4}{3}$ for i = 3

(Continued)

Table 6.9 MMVs K_i's, their corresponding edges and the number of K_i's ($1 \le i \le 3$). *(Continued)*

Nature of m, n	Nature of a	Edges	MMV K_i's, $1 \le i \le 3$	Number of K_i's, $1 \le i \le 3$
	$a \equiv 2(mod\ 3)$	$g(v_2x_j)$ if $1 \le j \le \frac{m+1}{3}$ $g(v_1v_2), g(v_2v_3)$ $g(v_3y_j)$ if $1 \le j \le \frac{n-1}{3}$ $g(v_5z_j)$ if $1 \le j \le \frac{a+1}{3}$	$(4m+4n+4a+54)\frac{1}{10^r}$ for i = 1	$\frac{m+n+a+6}{3}$ for i = 1
		$g(v_2x_j)$ if $\frac{m+1}{3}+1 \le j \le \frac{2m-1}{3}$ $g(v_3v_4), g(v_4v_5)$ $g(v_3y_j)$ if $\frac{n-1}{3}+1 \le j \le \frac{2n-1}{3}$ $g(v_5z_j)$ if $\frac{a+1}{3}+1 \le j \le \frac{2(a+1)}{3}$	$(4m+4n+4a+53)\frac{1}{10^r}$ for i = 2	$\frac{m+n+a+6}{3}$ for i = 2

(Continued)

6.3 Conclusion

A graph labeling is an assignment of integers to the vertices or edges, or both, subject to certain conditions [1]. The fuzzy graph $G: (\sigma, \mu)$ is said to have a fuzzy labeling, if $\sigma : V \rightarrow [0, 1]$ and $\mu : V \times V \rightarrow [0, 1]$ are bijective such that the membership value of edges and vertices is distinct and $\mu(u, v) \leq \sigma(u) \wedge \sigma(v)$ for all $u, v \in V$ [5]. In the previous papers, we have introduced the concept of fuzzy tri-magic labeling and proved some star related graphs are fuzzy tri-magic. In addition, we have proved that some ladder graphs and generalized Jahangir graph are fuzzy tri-magic. Then we extended our work and proved that some trees of diameter less than 5 and isomorphic caterpillar of diameter 5 are fuzzy tri-magic [6, 7]. In this paper, we have taken isomorphic caterpillar of diameter 5 graph $\mathfrak{I}^{6}_{2,3,5}$ and shown that the graph admit fuzzy tri-magic by proving the maximum difference between the number of K_i's $(1 \leq i \leq 3)$ is 1 and $|K_i - K_j| \leq \frac{2}{10^r}$ for $1 \leq i,j \leq 3, r \geq 2$; we also tabulated MMVs K_i's, their corresponding edges and the number of K_i's $(1 \leq i \leq 3)$. All the remaining cases of caterpillar of diameter 5 are also done by us and they will be published in the upcoming papers.

References

1. Gallian, J.A., A dynamic survey of graph labeling. *Electron. J. Comb.*, 17, DS6, 2017.
2. Harary, F., *Graph theory*, Narosa Publishing House Pvt. Ltd, New Delhi, reprint 2013.
3. Sumathi, P. and Monigeetha, C., Fuzzy tri-magic labeling of some star related graphs. *J. Emerg. Technol. Innov. Res. (JETIR)*, 6, 1, 661–667, ISSN 2349-5162, 2019.
4. Sumathi, P. and Esther Felicia, R., Enresdowedness of some caterpillar graphs. *Int. J. Pure Appl. Math.*, 118, 10, 73–86, 2018.
5. Felix, J. and Cappelle, M., *1-Identifying Codes on Caterpillar Graphs*, Instituto de Informatica INF UFG, Instituto de Informatica INF UFG, 7 November Goiânia, 2016.
6. Sumathi, P. and Monigeetha, C., Fuzzy tri-magic labeling of isomorphic caterpillar of diameter 5—Paper 1. *J. Eng. Comput. Archit.*, 10, 3, 182–189, 2020.
7. Sumathi, P. and Monigeetha, C., Fuzzy tri-magic labeling of isomorphic caterpillar of diameter 5—Paper 2. *J. Inf. Comput. Sci.*, 10, 3, 1463–1481, 2020.

7

Ceaseless Rule-Based Learning Methodology for Genetic Fuzzy Rule-Based Systems

B. Siva Kumar Reddy[1*], R. Balakrishna[2] and R. Anandan[2]

[1]Department of Computer Science and Engineering, Navodaya Institute of Technology, c/o, Navodaya Education Trust, Bijangera Road, Raichur, Karnataka, India

[2]Vels Institute of Science Technology and Advanced Studies (VISTAS), Chennai, Tamil Nadu, India

Abstract

Genetic learning forms supporting the ceaseless rule learning (CRL) approach are described by taking care of the preparation issue in a few stages. As a result, they comprises of minimum, two stages: an age procedure, that builds up an essential arrangement of fluffy principles speaking to the information existing inside the informational collection, and a post-preparing process, with the capacity of refining the past standard set in order to dispose of the excess guidelines that developed during the age stage and to pick those fluffy principles that collaborate in an ideal way.

Genetic Fuzzy Rule-Based Systems (GFRBSs) fortifying the CRL approach are normally called multi-stage Genetic Fuzzy Rule-Based Systems. The multi-stage structure might be an immediate result of the path during which GFRBSs bolstered the CRL approach settle the Chance Constrained Programming (CCP). These kind of frameworks endeavor to comprehend the CCP through a way that blends the advantages of the Pittusburg and Michigan approach [14]. The objective of the CRL approach is proportional back the component of the pursuit space by encoding singular standards in chromosome like in Michigan approach, however the assessment conspire take the participation of rules viable like in Pitt approach.

**Corresponding author*: sivakumar.reddy@navodaya.edu.in

E. Chandrasekaran, R. Anandan, G. Suseendran, S. Balamurugan and Hanaa Hachimi (eds.) Fuzzy Intelligent Systems: Methodologies, Techniques, and Applications, (217–242) © 2021 Scrivener Publishing LLC

The generation process forces competition between fuzzy rules, as in genetic learning processes grounded on the Michigan approach, to get a fuzzy rule set composed of the simplest possible fuzzy rules. To do so, a fuzzy rule generating method is run several times by an ceaseless covering method that wraps it and analyses the covering that the consecutively rules learnt cause within the training data set. Hence, the cooperation among the fuzzy rules generated within the different runs is merely briefly addressed by means of a rule penalty criterion. The later post-processing stage forces cooperation between the fuzzy rules generated in generation process by refining or eliminating the previously generated redundant or excessive fuzzy rules so as to get a final fuzzy rule set that demonstrates an efficient performance.

Keywords: Fuzzy logic, fuzzy rules, genetic algorithms, chromosomes, ceaseless rule, rule-based systems, machine learning

7.1 Introduction

This chapter affords vast design sights of genetic learning. In order to achieve hybridization of Fuzzy Reasoning (Fuzzy Logic) with Genetic algorithms (GL), several techniques had been taken into consideration. This gives an in-depth discussion on quite simply to be had designs for Genetic-Fuzzy hybridization as well as applications set up based totally upon existing strategies. The complete evaluation on the Genetic policy gaining knowledge is provided as a part of transformative fuzzy modeling. The transformative doubtful modeling concentrates on 4 major methods of Genetic-Fuzzy layout, i.e. The Michigan, the Pittsburg, the Ceaseless Rule Understanding (CRL) and Genetic Cooperative-Competitive Learning (GCCL). The traits of some of these methods have definitely been mentioned.

This chapter accommodates a conversation on the underneath additives of most important hybrid methods alongside with their regulations and contrasts among each other. In the area of clever choice support system, major application domain names are taking advantages of system mastering procedures, in particular Genetic-Fuzzy hybridization [1]. A survey at some stage in studies within the region of diverse created applications is documented. This investigation covers a number of important packages domain names wherein the maker understanding is known as for to be built. The actual international packages of assorted domain names including class, remedy, manage structures, robotics, journey sector, stock and additionally percentage, networking, and many others use hybrid structures of GFS on the way to obtain optimized policy discovering. Based on the decision made, the segment justifies the variety of the studies study executed and mentioned on this thesis. As an end result of enormous examination assessment on Genetic-Fuzzy hybridization, it has in reality been observed that no generalized structure making use of transformative fuzzy strategy has been evolved in the discipline of schooling to resolve the issues which lack mathematical formulation.

7.1.1 Integration of Evolutionary Algorithms and Fuzzy Logic

Current years have contributed to a wonderful deal of new crossbreed evolutionary structures. There are numerous methods to intermix a traditional evolutionary set of rules for fixing optimization problems. Transformative computing is based on Evolutionary Algorithms (EA). Genetic Algorithms being one of the popular types of EA have not in particular evolved as system studying methods like other strategies together with neural networks [6] but have been successfully put on several search, combinatorial as well as optimization problems. However, it is popular that an understanding assignment can be designed as an optimization issue, and also for this reason may be fixed through development that's efficaciously provided by means of EA. Fuzzy Logic elements a mathematical way to stand for and also manage. Fuzzy Logic gives a mathematical technique to face for as well as manage ambiguity of day by day existence [2]. FL is no longer supplied as a manage technique, however as a method of refining facts with the aid of permitting partial set subscription instead of a crisp collection subscription or non-club. With the help of Fuzzy Reasoning primarily based system, the expertise representation has clearly been viable in a human affordable way utilizing linguistic guidelines to speak about choice approaches; however at the same time, fuzzy structures are experiencing failure of self-gaining knowledge as well as desires documentation of knowledge which needs an additional persistent maintenance. At the alternative cease, Genetic Formulas offer robust seek abilities both global and also neighborhood in complex regions whereas Fuzzy Equipment existing bendy reasoning techniques allow you to cope with inaccuracy and uncertainty. The linguistic illustration of information enables a human to engage with an FS in a pleasant, seamless way. Therefore, hybridization of FL with GA comes to be critical to acquire blessings of both the abovementioned strategies. In this aspect of hybridization of GA and also FL, two primary hybrid techniques are assessed that are told as beneath.

7.1.2 Fuzzy Logic Aided Evolutionary Algorithm

This approach is likewise known as Genetic Algorithms managed with the aid of Fuzzy Logic. In this method GA uses FL in a good way to trade its parameters or drivers to improve its efficiency. Intrinsic specs of GA inclusive of physical fitness characteristic and quitting popular are fuzzified. For this reason, computational sources can be maximized from overusage [3]. This strategy is extra categorized into preferred in addition to effective subtypes that are advised as under.

7.1.3 Adaptive Genetic Algorithm That Adapt Manage Criteria

In this approach, FLCs are used to dynamically calculate best values for the GA Parameters. The objective is to regulate GA optimization procedure. The instance of this approach is clarified as beneath. The manage parameters of GA consist of anomaly in addition to crossover prices, populace length and many others can be dynamically calculated through Fuzzy Reasoning controller (FLC). E.g. Xu and Yukovich have categorized the scale of populaces as little, medium and massive [7].

7.1.4 Genetic Algorithm With Fuzzified Genetic Operators

In this method, specific fuzzified variations of Genetic operators have simply been proposed which includes fuzzy connective crossover for actual-coded Genetic Algorithms and smooth operators.

7.1.5 Genetic Fuzzy Systems

In this sort of technique, GA is used to improve the efficiency of FLC. As GA is computationally high-priced, GA-based total tuning is typically performed off-line yet if assimilation of FLC is achieved with optimization, it possible to be controlled online. In order to hybridize GA with FS, it's needed to incorporate fuzzy knowledge in GA. The studies focus on genetic policy discovering for fuzzified knowledge presentation. The available Genetic Fuzzy structures are talked about very well in the coming sections [8].

A GFS is basically a fuzzy device improved by way of a learning process based totally upon evolutionary computation, that includes any approach of EC family along with Genetic Formulas, genetic indicates, and also evolutionary methods. One of the maximum considerable kinds of GFS is the Genetic Fuzzy Guideline Based System (GFRBS), where GA is used to discover or music (enhancing criterion) distinct components of an Unclear

Guideline Based System (FRBS). In the layout of GFS, a GA is used to seek out the overall performance of Fuzzy Reasoning controller (FLC) but the performance of FLC relies upon its Knowledgebase (KB) being composed Database (DB) as well as Rule base (RB). In order to achieve design of FRBS, responsibilities along with growing reasoning system along with era of fuzzy policy set (KB or FRB) are needed to be satisfied. FRBSs are unable to research themselves, but require the KB to be originated from expert expertise in order to dispose of such constraint transformatively. Getting to know process becomes crucial to use to automate FRBS format. By the usage of this sort of discovering system, FRBS may be certain routinely. The noted form of design can be considered as an optimization or seek issue. In order to repair optimization troubles, GAs are selected due to huge skills including:

- Being a worldwide seek approach, GAs can check out large search space.
- Able to discover close to ideal treatments in complex search areas.
- Able to provide prevalent code framework and additionally fair performance.

As a result of the above discussed abilities, it's far viable to encompass a priori. Information in GA might be in types of linguistic variable, fuzzy membership, parameters of Function, fuzzy rules and so forth. Lastly, GFS can be created. As displayed in Figure 7.1.

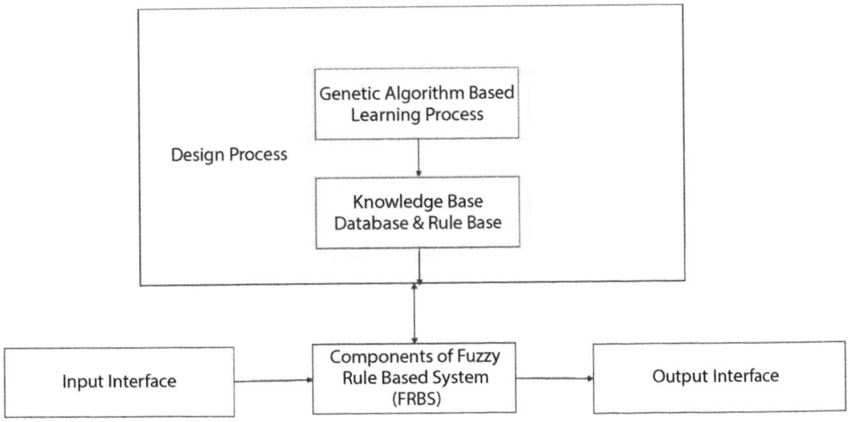

Figure 7.1 Fundamental Structure of Genetic Fuzzy Rule Based (GFRB) System.

Figure 7.1 illustrates the fundamental structure of Genetic Fuzzy Rule Based System. The Fashion of GFRBS is made up the usage of 3 layers which might be discussed as under Reference [13].

Interface Layer

The bottom layer of the Genetic-Fuzzy Rule Based System is known as interface layer. It is made up of three principal components: Environment, FRBS and Output User interface. This layer is basically established using input user interface, contrast with fuzzy system and refined outcome of FRBS.

Right here, the input interface defines the members of an application domain as well as engage with FL layer that is chargeable for developing and also implementing the fuzzy based system. The FL layer is simplified as beneath.

FL Layer

The intermediate layer of the GFRB system is called as FL layer. It connects with the interface layer to have input variables. This layer consists of several components along with Fuzzification User Interface, Reasoning Mechanism and Defuzzification User Interface. This layer is at risk of make the approaches which might be related to fuzzy device execution. The enter consumer interface makes a choice the contributors or the variables of the application area name for you to produce fuzzification. The inference device is made the usage of the members which can be selected inside the input interface in addition to will sincerely be associated with the technique of manufacturing the FRBS [5]. The end result user interface is answerable for defuzzification of enter variables. It substances the results created with the aid of Fuzzy System (FS).

Repository Layer

The top maximum layer of the Genetic Fuzzy Rule Based System is referred to as database layer. This Repository layer plays key role in of making of GFRBS. In order to layout, GFRBS, transformative strategies are needed to be included that allows you to obtain automatic generation or alteration of complete part of the Knowledge Base (KB). KB is an Aggregate of data Base (DB) and Rule Base (RB). The standards of Knowledge Base include fuzzy regulations in addition to club features [12]. Both the components have interaction with inference device of the middle layer. In order to obtain optimization, it's essential to find appropriate knowledge base (KB).

7.1.6 Genetic Learning Process

In the element that stood in Figure 7.1, designing GFS calls for to include Genetic mastering system for creating or optimizing the knowledgebase. GFRBS is a layout approach for FRBSs which incorporates evolutionary strategies to accomplish the computerized generation or adjustment of the whole or part of the knowledgebase. In order to enhance guidelines, GA wishes to browse the genotype region together with it, moreover desires a few devices creating new variations from the present current prospect solutions. The goal of the hunt technique is to make the maximum of or minimize a health characteristic that explains the desired efficiency of the machine. In summary, the genetic technique is the final result of the communication is among the evaluation alternative in addition to creation of genetically inscribed candidate alternatives, which represents the contents of the KB of an FRBS [10].

7.2 Existing Technology and its Review

7.2.1 Techniques for Rule-Based Understanding with Genetic Algorithm

Generating system which uses discovering techniques is sufficiently capable of changing their hidden framework with the intention of enhancing their overall performance or first-rate of their knowledge consistent with certain standards. With connection with Genetic rule, getting to know the use of GA so that it will optimize FLC, essential methods are decided as follows.

7.2.2 Strategy A: GA Primarily Based Optimization for Computerized Built FLC

The "A" technique is often appropriate for fixing complicated obligations. For a complicated job, it is very hard to design KB manually due to the fact that in such conditions performance of GFS cannot be carried out in step with assumptions. Automatic layout of FLC via GA gives solution for critical tasks finally ends up being carrier for intricate jobs. GA makes use of data of DB, RB in addition to consequent part of each guideline of the FLC. The predefined schooling set is utilized by GA strings to beautify FLC. Because of this, most reliable FLC can be advanced with versions to make system based on such approach is an important undertaking [4].

7.2.3 Strategy B: GA Based Optimization of Manually Created FLC

The functioning characteristic of the "B" method is based on developer's knowledge of the system to be controlled. In order for technique etymological know-how representation, styles of variables are determined and specific etymological terms are designed based on wishes of the problem. The wide variety of input mixes for the style of FLC depends upon the number of input variables and their etymological terms. In order to propose the DB of the FLC manually, it's far required to have distribution of subscription capabilities and additionally variables through developer and suitable design of RB is made possible later. This sort of layout of FLC may be adaptable but it is not superior additionally in this method, where a GA is used to track the DB and/or RB of the FLC with the Assistance of training situations [10]. After the GA-primarily based tuning more than the FLC may have the ability to decide the final results for a set of inputs inside a reasonably accuracy hassle.

Figure 7.2 represents strategies especially "A" and additionally "B" at the side of their characteristics for establishing Genetic-Fuzzy Systems.

Strategy A: GA primarily based optimization for computerized built FLC	**Strategy B: GA based enhancement for physically built FLC**
• Handles complex process	• Handles simple process
• Utilizes information of experts of GA	• Utilizes designer knowledge
• Complex	• Complexity is less
• Must produce an ideal FLC	• May not produce an ideal FLC
• More tedious procedure from execution of GA point of view	• Less tedious procedure from execution of GA point of view

Figure 7.2 Strategies for GA based FLC optimization.

7.2.4 Methods of Hybridization for GFS

Even though GA developed it is not particularly designed for learning as they're utilized as a global search formulation. Besides the surfing activity, they do offer a group of advantages for ML. Several methods for ML are based at the search of an exquisite version and additionally they're extremely adaptable due to the fact that the very identical GA can be used with diverse depictions as shown in Figure 7.4. In a Rule Based (RB) system, to accomplish a task of studying rules, there are 2 main styles quite simply to be had to encode guidelines within populations of people of GA as obtained Number 3.

Style 1: The "Chromosome = Rule" Method
In the design 1, each chromosome coded with a single rule, and also the complete policy collection are furnished by using integrating numerous chromosome in a populace referred to as coverage cooperation or via diverse evolutionary runs is known as rule competition. As an example, the Michigan technique as well as the Ceaseless Rule Learning (CRL) approach is a depictive technique of Style 1.

Style 2: The "Chromosome = set of rules" Method
In style 2, every chromosome represents a set of rules famously called the "Chromosome = Set of rules" [11]. In this example, a chromosome advances a full RB and also they compete among them collectively with the evolutionary system. E.g. The Pittsburgh approach is the consultant technique of style 2.

In order to give RBL process with distinct stages of complexities, evolutionary algorithms (EA) give three methods for evolving rule based systems like, the Pittsburgh Method, the Ceaseless rule learning (CRL) method and Michigan method as displayed in Figure 7.3.

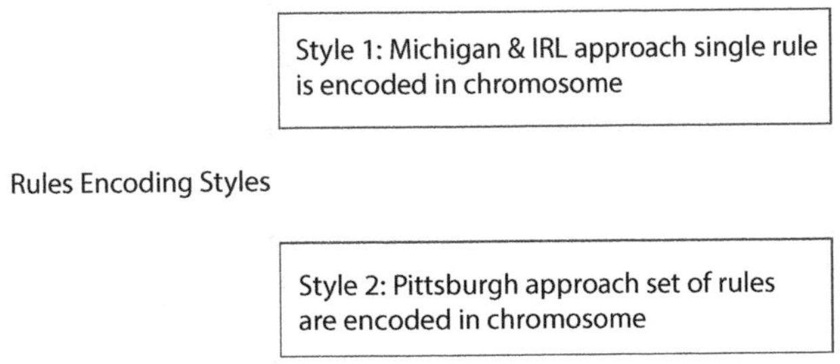

Style 1: Michigan & IRL approach single rule is encoded in chromosome
Rules Encoding Styles
Style 2: Pittsburgh approach set of rules are encoded in chromosome

Figure 7.3 Rule encoding styles in genetic fuzzy hybrid systems.

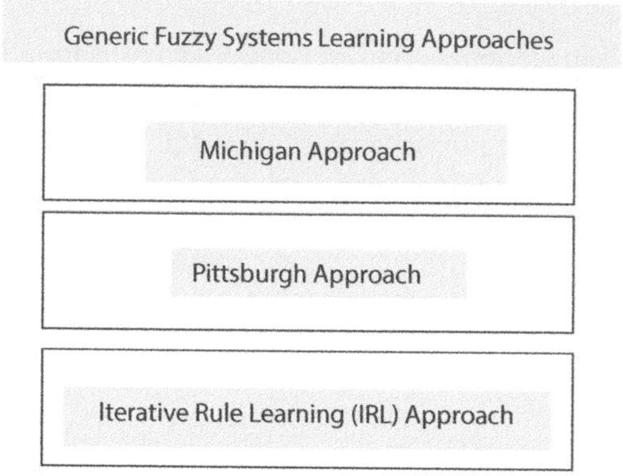

Figure 7.4 Methods for Genetic Fuzzy System.

7.2.4.1 The Michigan Strategy—Classifier System

Learning Classifier System (LCS) is a ML intelligence technique which incorporates reinforced learning, transformative computing and also various other heuristics to adaptive systems. This method represents "Chromosome= rule" method as found in Figure 7.1. In order to create populaces of rules immediately, Classifier System (CSs) or production rule systems are created. Learning Classifier Systems are a sort of rule based system (RBL) with normal mechanisms for processing the policies in parallel, for flexible era of recent recommendations, and for trying out the performance of current guidelines. These structures permit performance and also getting to know without the "fragile" features of one of the most expert systems in AI. CSs are particularly equal, message passing away, policy based systems that study through credit assignment and rule exploration [9]. CSs typically operate in environments that showcase numerous of the subsequent features:

- Big amount of unimportant or noisy records may be included;
- Undisturbed actual time wished for activity; and
- Implicit or vague goals.

Figure 7.5 indicates assessment of standard expert system in addition to classifier system alongside with attributes of each of them. These attributes are narrated as beneath.

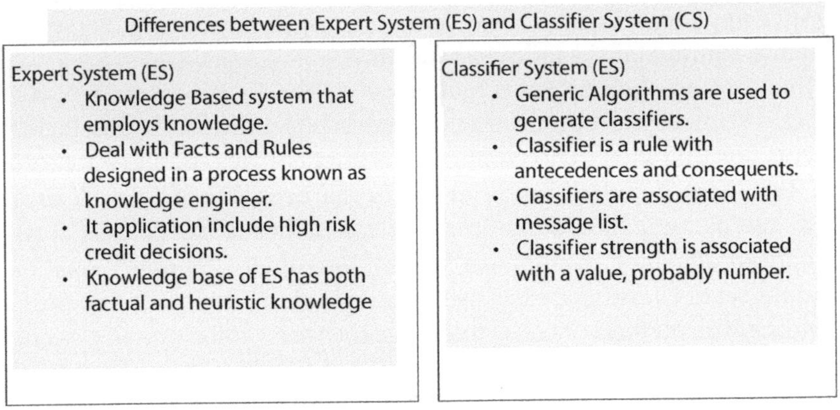

Figure 7.5 ES and CS differences.

CSs are exceptional than traditional expert systems (ES) by using several advantages such as guidelines are required to design knowledge engineer. In expert system at the same time as in Classifier System (CS), classifier rules are produced via a GA. In the ES, regulations are stored as well as processed in a straightforward means. Further to no added specification for rule system are available to calculate strength of rule in addition to development which can't be attained. Each classifier has to go through performance assessment system and also have a strength criterion; a variety of it is targeted to every classifier, after that. Figure 7.5 differentiates attributes of expert system in addition to classifier system.

The prototype representation of Classifier Equipment (CS) as shown in Figure 7.6 is composed of three subsystems in the system which are listed below:

1. A rule based production system which processes arriving messages from the environment and sends output messages to the environment.
2. A credit assignment system which receives pay-off from the environment and identifies which rules are held responsible for the feedback.
3. A classifier discovery system with Genetic Algorithm which clubs existing rules with new rules introduced [9].

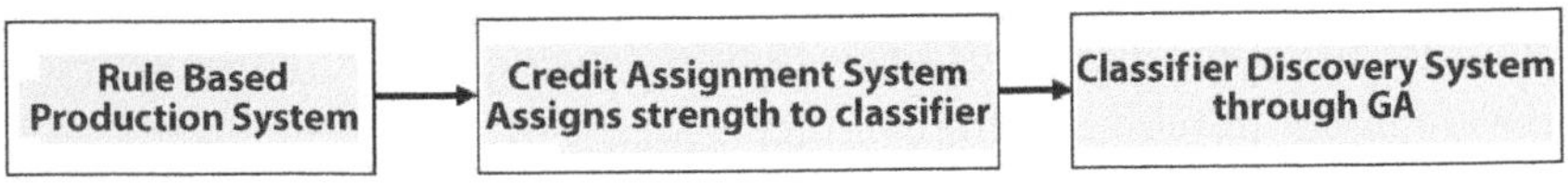

Figure 7.6 Classifier System (CS) subsystems.

After implementing the above sub-systems, the operating of classifier system is summed up as indexed beneath:

The working of classifiers is reinforced via the Credit assessment (CA) System. Primarily, a GA chooses excessive physical health classifiers as parents creating kids by Recombining elements from the parent classifiers. Right here, popular health and fitness characteristic of GA isn't always used; alternatively the bodily fitness of a classifier is installed by way of toughness calculated with the CA system. In regular CS implementations, from the set of Classifiers, excessive sturdiness classifiers constitute the GA populace. The method of GA is to change the worst collection of classifiers by these days produced robust classifiers. As a result of this technique, the high overall performance of the classifier can be attained.

The complying with strategies are the fundamental techniques based on transformative Fuzzy modeling utilizing the Michigan strategy. Transformative fuzzy modeling has certainly due to the fact been carried out to an ever-growing style of domains, branching right into areas as diverse as chemistry, medicine, telecommunications, biology, as well as geophysics. Some applications are narrated below.

A Genetic Algorithm based totally learning process has been proposed to set up the most beneficial data base of a Fuzzy Logic controller preserving its rule base that's formerly defined [15].

In 1999, Ishibushi *et al.* have provided fuzzy classifier structures for excessive dimensional sample type issues and also in 2000, Juang *et al.* have absolutely furnished genetic information for fuzzy controller design. In 1999, Shi *et al.* long passed over GA based totally technique to evolve fuzzy professional machine for huge complex issues. This system can progress the rule of thumb set at the side of perfect variety of guidelines inside it, track the subscription capabilities and additionally evolve the membership function.

Valenzuela-Rendon has advocated linguistic RB expertise the usage of Michigan Approach. This suggestion presents the very first GFS primarily based upon the Michigan approach for finding out RBs with DNF fuzzy rules. This method includes a reward Distribution scheme that requires knowledge of the right action, and thus, have to be considered as a supervised learning algorithm.

In GFS, the inference system is represented via the whole populace having numerous rules collaborating. In order to advocate the simplest action, these guidelines remain in consistent competition in addition to coordinate to develop a powerful fuzzy system. Recognition of specific rules answerable for notable system conduct is a very difficult task.

In 1978, the LCS based totally upon Michigan technique was made by Holland & Reitman. In 1988, De Jong has sincerely tested 2 special techniques for learning the rule of thumb collection of production system. In 1991, the considerable studies service the classifier Systems has truly been proposed via Valenzuela-Rendon.

Limitations of The Michigan Technique

- Michigan method is in particular concerned about approximately non-stop learning in non-inductive problems. Among the major regulations is the hazard entailed due to random modification completed with the aid of GA for applications in particular made to accomplish safety. The reason in the back of this restriction is mentioned below.
- The online rule learning process is accomplished in which each and every single rule is manipulated as well as for this reason requires an intense evaluation of the overall performance of each and every rule. Such a machine can adapt to differing ecological situations routinely. In this example, the regulation is changed each single time.
- The diverse different restriction notified is: the Michigan method based system may also fail if collaborating with complex environment.
- Further, this method stands for the knowledge of a solitary entity that learns out through communique with the environment in addition to afterward being adapted to it as an alternative to evolution of feasible options.

7.2.4.2 The Pittsburgh Method

As shown in Figure 7.7, in the Pittsburgh rule learning approach, the idea is to impart intelligence via development. In this technique, an evolution may be generated among individuals and adaptions through competition in environment. This approach is especially tailored for schooling in both inductive in addition to non-inductive issues. In the Pittsburgh method, each individual stands for a total entity of understanding and additionally due to this kind of framework, individuals are not required to connect with each other for the assessment of the knowledge. For this motive, the requirement of credit assignment, in addition to, consequently the definition of complicated algorithms with that goal aren't needed. The individuals are accountable in getting specific performance as they are assigned with performance measure.

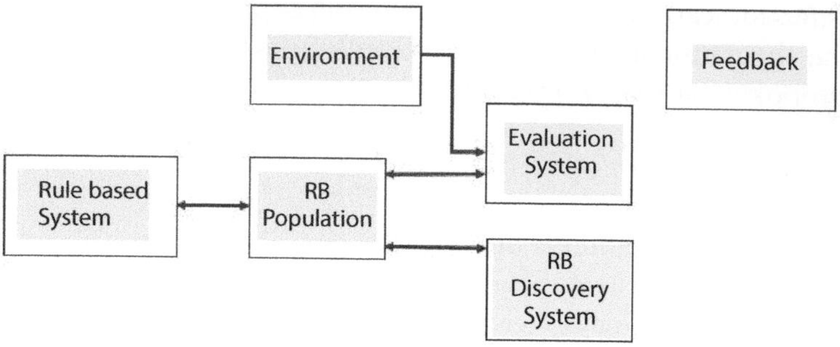

Figure 7.7 Pittsburgh rule learning approach.

Figure 7.7 stands for the block diagram of subsystems of Pittsburgh technique.

Rule Base and the Population of RBs

To produce the learning procedure, it is required to create a populace of potential answers for the issue. The number of inhabitants in potential arrangements is planned from RBs through a typical preparing structure to take care of a particular issue. Each RB in the populace is assessed by applying it to tackle the issue. Feedback is produced from the environment. Every RB is assessed autonomously and no cooperation between individuals of the populace happens during the assessment. To start the learning procedure, an underlying populace of RB is required. At times, it is acquired from accessible information, while in different cases; it is arbitrarily created.

The Evaluation System

As expressed in the Pittsburgh framework, every RB is to be assessed. This assessment of RB is in view of the impact of the association of the standard based framework, applying the relating RB, with nature. Because of this association, the condition produces a criticism that is utilized by the assessment framework to create the assessment of the RB. The assessment is very unique relying upon the application and the environment. The assessment framework frequently becomes the most tedious component of the procedure. Relatively, this methodology offers greater straightforwardness contrasted with the Michigan approach by delivering autonomous assessment of populace. Here, bigger computational endeavors for free assessments are required; consequently this methodology is liberated from clashes, created because of interaction.

The Rule Base Discovery System

When the procedure of assessment of populace of RB is finished, new RBs are to be looked, and, RB disclosure framework is to be presented. This framework produces another populace alongside set of hereditary administrator to the past generation. The standard base disclosure framework for the Pittsburgh approach is not quite the same as the Michigan approach by the accompanying qualities:

The Level of Replacement

In the Michigan approach, the quantity of replaced individuals at every generation has to be sufficiently low to save the performance of the system, as it is the after effect of the communication between the individuals though in Pittsburgh approach the exhibition of the best individual is accomplished and subsequently because of that exhibition, there can stay consistent as long as the best individual is kept up.

The Timing of Evaluation and Discovery

In the Michigan approach, revelation is applied with a lower recurrence than credit task. In this methodology, constant learning is made conceivable to arrive at a consistent state circumstance before making another generation while the Pittsburg approach actualizes predefined preparing cycle which must be applied for every individual in the populace. Thus, the disclosure stage happens after a total preparing cycle for every individual.

The Pittsburgh approach encourages to remember extra advancement measures for the wellness work, along these lines bears the usage of multi-target streamlining. In 1991, Thrift has introduced a pioneer take a shot at the Pittsburgh approach for learning Rule Base. This technique works by utilizing a total choice table that speaks to an extraordinary instance of fresh connection characterized over the assortments of fuzzy sets relating to the info and yield factors. At long last, the GA utilizes a number coding.

Summing up the previously mentioned attributes of the Michigan and the Pittsburgh approaches, Figure 7.8 is built which shows recognizable attributes of the Michigan approach and the Pittsburgh approach.

Various types of Rule based frameworks have been structured and advanced utilizing this approach among them critical models are introduced as follows:

- Concept learning can be developed by GABIL framework which comprises of RBs with Boolean guidelines. This framework persistently learns and refines idea order rules structure its communication with condition.

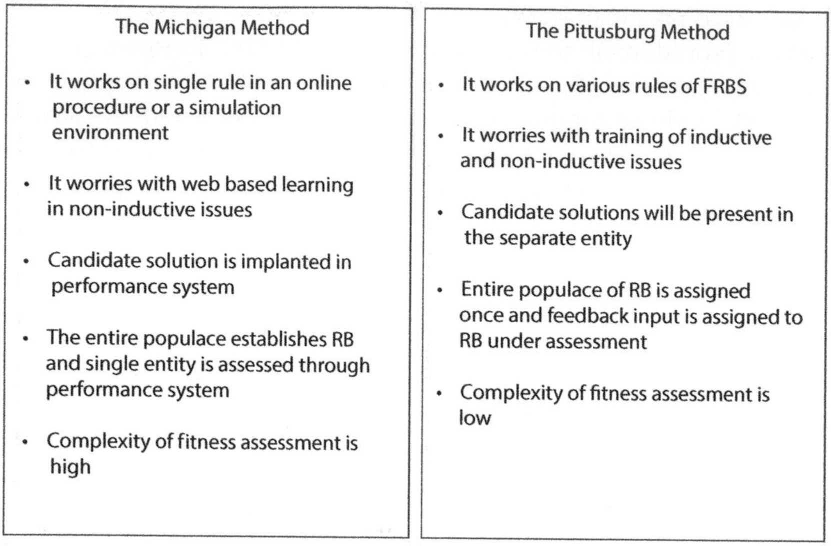
The Michigan Method
It works on single rule in an online procedure or a simulation environment
It worries with web based learning in non-inductive issues
Candidate solution is implanted in performance system
The entire populace establishes RB and single entity is assessed through performance system
Complexity of fitness assessment is high
The Pittusburg Method
It works on various rules of FRBS
It worries with training of inductive and non-inductive issues
Candidate solutions will be present in the separate entity
Entire populace of RB is assigned once and feedback input is assigned to RB under assessment
Complexity of fitness assessment is low

Figure 7.8 Michigan approach versus Pittsburg approach.

- Genetic Based Inductive Learning (GIL) frameworks structured by C.Z. Janikow, use coding of RBs utilizing sensible portrayal for learning idea depictions.
- Classification with genuine esteemed portrayal for ceaseless factors that uses RBs utilizing Genetic Algorithm is accomplished.
- Evolutionary learning of fuzzy guidelines (ELF) technique is proposed and applied to the issue of managing a self-sufficient robot by Bonarini in 1993. The key issue of ELF is to locate a little guideline base which just contains significant principles.

Impediments of the Pittsburg Approach

The Pittsburg approach assesses the number of inhabitants in the whole fuzzy framework for each age. It assesses readiness for every RB of the populace and rehashes the equivalent process for the whole RB, in this manner requesting progressively computational assets. Henceforth, the computational expense of this methodology is high, which is the significant impediment of the Pittsburg approach.

Various forms of rule based structures have honestly been developed and progressed using this technique. Among them sizable examples exist adhering to:

Idea mastering may be advanced by using GABIL device which incorporates RBs with boolean rules. This system continually discovers in addition to exceptional-tunes concept category policies broaden its interaction with setting. Genetic Based Inductive Understanding (GIL) systems created by way of C.Z. Janikow, use coding of RBs utilizing sensible representation for getting to know precept summaries. Category with actual valued illustration for chronic variables that uses RBs utilizing Genetic Formula is attained. Evolutionary learning of fuzzy rules (FAIRY) technique is proposed and associated with the problem of leading an impartial robot through Bonarini in 1993. The trick difficulty of FAIRY is to find a touch guiding principle base which simply consists of crucial tips.

Limitations of the Pittsburg Method

The Pittsburg approach examines the populace of the complete fuzzy system for each generation technology. It reviews fitness and health for every RB of the population as well as repeats the precise same system for the entire RB, as a result requiring more computational resources. Hence, the computational price of this approach is high, that is the main constraint of the Pittsburg approach.

7.3 Research Design

7.3.1 The Ceaseless Rule Learning Approach (CRL)

The significant downside of the Michigan approach and the Pittsburg approach is the utilization of enormous measure of PC memory for looking through various fuzzy rules. To defeat the above expressed issue, a ceaseless guideline learning approach (CRL) is structured. The CRL (Ceaseless Rule Learning) approach depends on the approach of "Chromosome is rule". The prime motivation to build up this methodology is to coordinate the best highlights of the Michigan and the Pittsburg approaches. In this approach, another standard is added to the standard set, in a ceaseless design, for each run of GA. The Ceaseless Rule Learning (CRL) approach was first proposed by Supervised Inductive Algorithm (SIA) planned by Venturini in 1993 and it has been broadly created in the field of GFRBs. This methodology works by consolidating the styles of the Michigan and the Pittsburgh approaches. Like the Michigan approach, every chromosome in the populace speaks to a solitary standard, yet like the Pittsburg approach, simply the best person is considered to frame some portion of the last arrangement. Because of this sort of calculation, the created RB eventually disposes of the rest of the chromosomes in the populace. Along these lines, in the ceaseless model, the GA gives a fractional answer for the issue of learning, and, it is rehashed on numerous occasions to get the total arrangement of rules.

7.3.2 Multistage Processes of Ceaseless Rule Learning

The learning procedure using Ceaseless Rule Learning (CRL) is made out of two significant stages. This kind of GFRBS is dependent on CRL approach is prominently known as multi-stage GFRBSs. Figure 7.9 speaks to two pioneer stages required to create CRL.

So as to create a RB, which establishes a genuine answer for the learning issue, the GA is inserted into a ceaseless plan like the accompanying:

Stage 1: Use a GA to get a standard for the framework.
Stage 2: Incorporate this standard into the last arrangement of rules.
Stage 3: Penalize this standard.
Stage 4: If the arrangement of rules created till now is satisfactory to take care of the issue, wind up returning it as the arrangement. Something else, come back to stage 1.

A transformative calculation is utilized to locate a solitary standard, in this way giving a halfway arrangement. The transformative calculation is then utilized ceaselessly for the disclosure of new rules, until a suitable guideline base is fabricated. A punishment procedure is applied each time another standard is included. As an impact of this procedure, repetitive

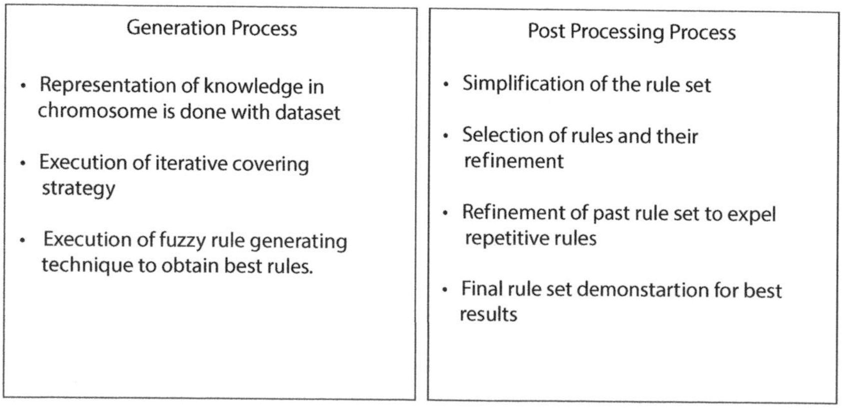

Generation Process
• Representation of knowledge in chromosome is done with dataset
• Execution of iterative covering strategy
• Execution of fuzzy rule generating technique to obtain best rules.
Post Processing Process
• Simplification of the rule set
• Selection of rules and their refinement
• Refinement of past rule set to expel repetitive rules
• Final rule set demonstartion for best results

Figure 7.9 CRL stages.

guidelines are maintained a strategic distance from. Chromosomes contend with each GA run, picking the best guideline per run. The worldwide arrangement is shaped by these best guidelines. Learning calculations that utilize the CRL approach don't envision any connection between them during the time spent acquiring rules. Along these lines, the last arrangement of rules as a rule needs an a posteriori procedure which will alter or potentially fit the said set.

So as to actualize a learning calculation dependent on GAs utilizing the CRL approach, following sub parts are required.

Figure 7.10 speaks to sub parts of CRL which are talked about as follows.

1. A model for choosing the best guideline in every emphasis
   This part is utilized to decide the great principles. The choice models about the rule quality are additionally introduced which incorporates number of models secured, standards of consistency of the standard or measures of effortlessness.
2. A Penalty Criterion
   This part of rule is frequently related, despite the fact that it isn't important, with the disposal of the models secured by the past principles.
3. A Determination Criterion
   This segment is utilized to decide the affirmation about the fulfilment of the set of rules. It begins working when enough principles are accessible to speak to the models in the preparation set. The principle usefulness of this part is to check whether all the models in the preparation set are adequately secured or not.

Points of Interest Offered by CRL Approach

- The huge favorable position of CRL is that it diminishes the inquiry space, on the grounds that in each arrangement of emphasis, the learning technique just looks for a solitary best rule rather than the entire RB.

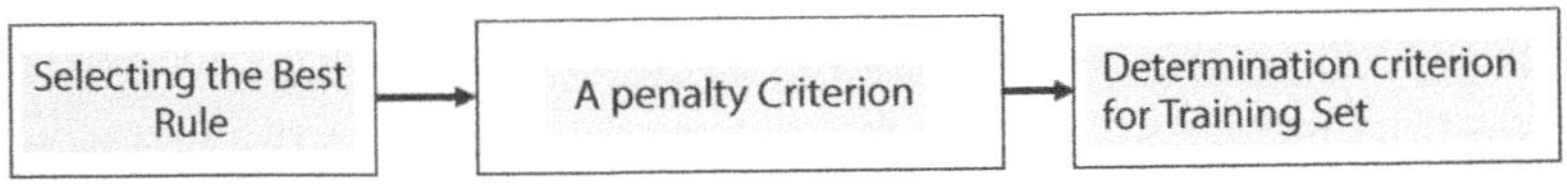

Figure 7.10 CRL Sub Components.

- This methodology joins the speed of the Michigan approach with the straightforwardness of the wellness assessment of the Pittsburgh approach.
- The Michigan approach gives web-based figuring out how to non-inductive learning issues though CRL approach encourages disconnected inductive learning issues.

There are various instances of CRL approach for Genetic principle learning in the writing; the major among them are introduced beneath.

Directed Inductive Algorithm (SIA) utilizes a solitary GA that continues identifying the controls and disposing of the models secured by the last mentioned. SIA can just work with fresh information. Investor (Methodology to acquire GFRBSs under the CRL approach) has been proposed for structuring various kinds of FRBS for assortment of the issue spaces i.e. fuzzy displaying, fuzzy control and fuzzy grouping. In requests to work with MOGUL, a client needs to characterize developmental procedure in each of the GFRBS learning stages. Head honcho works with various fuzzy models for example graphic Mamdani type and surmised Mamdani type just as TSK FRBSs.

SLAVE (Structural Learning Algorithm in Vague Environment) is a Genetic learning process dependent on CRL way to deal with plan DNF Mamdani type FRBSs that was proposed by Gonza'lez in 1993 and later refined in different research papers of Gonza'lez and Perez. SLAVE dispatches another GA to locate another rule subsequent to having dispensed with the models secured by the last principle got. SLAVE was intended to work with or without semantic data. The Genetic age process runs a GA for getting the best standard as indicated by various highlights, doles out a relative covering an incentive to each model, and evacuates the models with a covering esteem more noteworthy than a steady.

7.3.3 Other Approaches of Genetic Rule Learning

Another significant methodology is recognized as Genetic Cooperative–Competitive Learning (GCCL) to give Genetic standard learning. In this methodology, the standard base can be encoded with the assistance of a total populace or a subset of populace. In this model the chromosomes contend and coordinate all the while with one another.

COGIN (Coverage-based Genetic Induction) proposed by Greene and Smith in 1993, REGAL and LOGENPRO are the fruitful instances of GCCL sort of learning approach.

7.4 Findings or Result Discussion so for in the Area of GFS Hybridization

It has been seen that there are numerous true applications effectively structured to help the need of canny choice help and to accomplish improvement utilizing Genetic Fuzzy hybridization. The significant applications were acquired because of the above mentioned referenced methodologies and are clarified as follows:

Example Recognition establishes a significant utilization of FRBS as FRBSs give a reasonable intent to characterize fragmented and loose information. As referenced before, SLAVE has been applied to tackle characterization issue of myocardial localized necrosis. The arrangement of the phonetic principles produced by SLAVE is increasingly justifiable and progressively valuable to the clinical specialists. SLAVE has likewise been applied to analyze threat. So as to analyze bosom malignancy in females, Wisconsin Breast Cancer Diagnosis (WBCD) database is structured utilizing the nine qualities with 683 examples speaking to the arrangement of dangerous qualities. The symptomatic precise classifier framework utilizing transformative fuzzy guidelines has been created by Pena-Reyes and Sipper.

Wang *et al.* proposed a few GA-based information mix systems to naturally coordinate numerous standard sets in a disseminated information condition. Additionally, a self-coordinating information based cerebrum tumor symptomatic framework dependent on these techniques was effectively evolved. Here, Genetic Algorithm produces an ideal or about ideal guideline set from these underlying information inputs. Besides, a rule-refinement plot is proposed to refine deduction rules through communication with the condition.

The Genetic-Fuzzy principle base framework (GFRBS) utilizing the Pittsburg approach has been intended too for grouping in bosom malignancy determination. Here, KB comprises of participation capacity and its parameters. Afterward, it recognizes the best single guideline for arrangement. GFS demonstrating has been utilized to gauge human dental age from tooth ejection status what's more, tolerant ordered ages. Here, a FRBS is contrasted and the master information and is naturally produced from a lot of information gathered by the analyst. GFRBS dependent on the Pittsburg Approach has been planned.

GFRBS for etymological and fuzzy displaying has been accomplished in various applications for assortment of areas, which are quickly described as follows.

There are two diverse Genetic learning forms comprised of two phases that are planned for semantic FRBS dependent on first creating RB.

These two RB learning forms considered for the main stage are: WM adhoc information driven strategy and Thrift's GFRBS. An adjustment of the Genetic learning process is planned which creates numerous RBs from various fuzzy segments and going along with them in a worldwide RB and applying a Genetic choice procedure to acquire the best sub set of rules. In 1994, the emotional capability of rice tastes utilizing tangible test is planned by Ishibushi *et al.* This test has been performed to recognize nature of rice utilizing Genetic fuzzy arrangement.

In the field of conduct based apply autonomy, GA based framework has been intended for automated framework so as to explore, design and work in reality with shrewd conduct. Programmed age of structure of apply autonomy framework is conceivable through developmental methodologies. So as to accomplish programmed age of structure, the target work is planned such a way, that it is skilled to watch the automated conduct advanced by the methods for the EA.

A learning classifier framework dependent on Michigan-style Learning Fuzzy-Classifier Framework (LCS) has been intended for the administered learning errands. Here, the issue of interpretability in LCSs, and plan of Fuzzy-UCS—an online exactness-based LFCS design has been tended to.

So as to improve social guideline arrangements, the choice emotionally supportive network is structured by Abraham *et al.*, which is famously known as EvoPOL. EvoPOL is a fuzzy induction based choice emotionally supportive network that utilizes a transformative calculation (EA) to enhance the on and the off chances that rule its parameters for social guideline policies. A computational knowledge system has been intended to adapt to the issue of controlling the dynamical model for an illness so as to give a few understanding identified with the clinical treatment. A Genetic fuzzy framework way to deal with control a nonlinear powerful model of the HIV disease is introduced.

The electronic choice emotionally supportive network prevalently known as WBISC-DSS is a confirmation process which is planned utilizing transformative fuzzy figuring for a college of Berkeley, California. This framework has been created to permit programmed changing of the user inclinations. These inclinations can be viewed as the parameters of the Fuzzy Logic model as degrees of significance of the pre-owned factors. Lee and Takagi have proposed the structure technique for fuzzy framework which employs Genetic Algorithm. Here, GA incorporates three plan stages: enrolment capacities, the quantity of fuzzy guidelines, and the standard subsequent parameters to acquire ideal fuzzy framework. A choice model for exchanging framework has been structured that joins Fuzzy Logic furthermore, specialized investigation to discover examples and patterns in the budgetary files. The fuzzy model is streamlined by using a Genetic Algorithm and the verifiable information.

The characterization of rules in dermatology informational collections and bosom malignant growth informational index for medication has been found by GA. In this work, skin illnesses like psoriasis, seborrheic dermatitis, lichen planus, pityriasis rosea, constant dermatitis and pityriasis rubra pilaris are found by actualizing a few in the event that rules utilize GA. This framework has additionally been embedded so as to decide the patients experiencing bosom disease. The objective of this exploration work is to discover the patients to whom the disease may re-happen. The bilingual inquiry order through Genetic Algorithm with machine learning strategies has been planned with an Integrated Genetic Algorithm (GA) and AI (ML) approach for the inquiry order in cross-language question noting.

A developmental framework is intended for finding fuzzy grouping rules. All together to perform order task, three techniques were utilized to remove fuzzy arrangement rules utilizing EA. These three strategies are Genetic determination of fuzzy principles from a huge number of fuzzy applicant rules, Genetic decrease of Genetic space, and Genetic learning of fuzzy arrangement rules. So as to anticipate, IPO under evaluating, a forecast framework has been planned utilizing the Genetic Algorithm. The Michigan approach has been used for producing the Transformative Rule-Based System for IPO under-estimating.

A Genetic-Fuzzy hybridization approach has been executed in movement decision conduct models to give understanding into the movement decision conduct that is required in structure and arranging of transport frameworks of the urban open vehicle systems. A way to deal with a traditional system improvement issue or the transportation issue has been intended to improve the appropriation organize for recognizing most limited course for the appropriation of vehicles. So as to accomplish improvement, Genetic Algorithm is planned while fuzzy sets have been utilized to speak to the loose data identified with temporary data, for example, costs, requests and different factors.

7.5 Conclusion

The section presents the essentialness of hybridization of delicate processing strategies in request to plan answer for genuine applications with wanted qualities. Being two prime constituents, GA and FS give focal points to AI, search and furthermore, improvement. Here, the need of hybridization of GA with FS is clarified. In request to accomplish such joining, two significant

GA-Fuzzy mixture approaches have been broke down: Fuzzy Logic helped developmental calculation and Genetic-Fuzzy Systems. The section clarifies GFS in wide scopes of approaches for Genetic standard learning. The general structure of GFS has been introduced alongside two significant methodologies for enhanced guideline getting the hang of utilizing GA for programmed produced FLC just as physically planned FLC. The procedures of Genetic-Fuzzy hybridization are organized utilizing two well-known styles of encoding: "Chromosome is rule" approach and "Chromosome is set of rule" approach. Genetic Fuzzy hybridization approaches are planned utilizing both of the two above expressed styles. GFS hybridization is characterized into three significant approaches: the Michigan, the Pittsburgh and the CRL. The part clarifies each of these methodologies alongside subcomponents, working style, points of interest and confinements.

It likewise contrasts qualities of conventional master framework and Classifier System for Genetic-Fuzzy hybridization and subsequently presents the significance of structuring GFS. Similar assessment of every one of the mixture technique prompts the plan of CRL. The part likewise describes different points of interest of the Ceaseless Rule Learning approach. Broad writing overview of GFS on the changed areas, for example, order, medication, AI, the executives, and so on has been introduced. In outline, it may very well be expressed that hybridization of Genetic-Fuzzy methodologies is effective so as to accomplish rule learning in an enhanced manner and consequently can be one of the most reasonable strategies for the AI. So as to plan a framework, in light of Genetic standard gaining from fuzzified input, Genetic-Fuzzy System is required. The methodology like CRL is required to accomplish the Genetic principle learning utilizing FLC. It has been seen from the writing audit on GFS, that reality issues which depend on numerical equation can be effectively planned and executed utilizing GA with FLC. The noteworthy perception likewise says that there is no conventional system yet produced for issue lacking numerical detailing utilizing Genetic fuzzy half and half methodology request to accomplish enhancement for rule learning. The examination work is a stage towards the equivalent.

References

1. Russo, M., FuGeNSys: A genetic neural system for fuzzy modeling. *IEEE Trans. Fuzzy Syst.*, 6, 373–388, June 1998.
2. Sanchez, E., Genetic algorithms neural networks and fuzzy logic systems. *Proc. 2nd Int. Conf. Fuzzy Logic Neural Networks*, pp. 17–19, 1992.

3. Ishigami, H., Fukuda, T., Shibata, T., Arai, F., Structure optimization of fuzzy neural network by genetic algorithm. *Fuzzy Sets Syst.*, 71, 257–264, 1995.
4. Karr, C.L. and Gentry, E.J., Fuzzy control of pH using genetic algorithms. *IEEE Trans. Fuzzy Syst.*, 1, 46–53, Apr. 1993.
5. Kim, D. and Kim, C., Forecasting time series with genetic fuzzy predictor ensemble. *IEEE Trans. Fuzzy Syst.*, 5, 523–535, Oct. 1997.
6. Korning, P.G., Training neural networks by means of genetic algorithms working on very long chromosomes. *Int. J. Neural Syst.*, 6, 3, 299–316, 1995.
7. Koza, J.R., Jr, *Genetic Programming*, The MIT Press, MA, Cambridge, 1992.
8. Kwon, O.-K., Chang, W., Joo, Y.-H., Park, J.-B., GA-based fuzzy neural network modeling. *Proc. Engineering Intelligent Systems EIS'98*, 1998-Feb.-9.
9. Setnes, M. and Roubos, H., GA-fuzzy modeling and classification: Complexity and performance. *IEEE Trans. Fuzzy Syst.*, 8, 509–522, Oct. 2000.
10. Setnes, M., Supervised fuzzy clustering for rule extraction. *IEEE Trans. Fuzzy Syst.*, 8, 416–424, Aug. 2000.
11. Spears, W.M., Crossover or mutation? *Proc. Foundations Genetic Algorithms Workshop*, pp. 221–237, 1992.
12. *Evolutionary Computations I*, Institute of Physics Publishing, CT, Bristol, 2000.
13. Bengio, S., Bengio, Y., Cloutier, J., Use of genetic programming for the search of a learning rule for neural networks. *Proc. 1st Conf. Evolutionary Computation IEEE World Congr. Computational Intelligence*, pp. 324–327, 1994.
14. Cordón, Genetic Fuzzy Rule-Based Systems Based on the Iterative Rule Learning Approach, in: *Advances in Fuzzy Systems—Applications and Theory*, 2001.
15. Cordon, O. and Herrera, F., A three stage evolutionary process for learning descriptive and approximative fuzzy logic controller knowledge bases from examples. *Int. J. Approx. Reason.*, 17, 4, 369–407, 1997.

8

Using Fuzzy Technique Management of Configuration and Status of VM for Task Distribution in Cloud System

Yogesh Shukla[1*], Pankaj Kumar Mishra[2] and Ramakant Bhardwaj[3]

[1]VIT Bhopal University, Bhopal, India
[2]School of Applied Physics, Amity University, Madhya Pradesh, Gwalior, India
[3]Department of Mathematics, Amity University Kolkata, Kolkata, India

Abstract
In any serving system server management and distribution of task work is a key feature. This chapter is designed for fuzzy technique-based system for the above-given task. In any given task to make decisions by fuzzy logic either a number used with the combination of VM or make a fresh VM on the basis of current operational conditions for example task requirement,load and available resources etc. The technique generates in this chapter help to provide better Qos, saving of power and help to reduce the requirement of physical resources. This proposed technique is effective and validated by comparing of many existing systems. The result of the simulation verified that this fuzzy system technique is standard technique of resource management, power saving and QoS.

In implementation of cloud applications are work by the using virtual machines called VMs in cloud system. The VMs worked using the many software configurations in place of direct connections in physical manner. Management of configuration and allocation of physical connections also manage by using virtual platform. In present business environment increment of cost is not acceptable. So we have only solution to utilize the available resources with full efficiently without any extra investment and get the SLO.

Keywords: QoS, VM management, Vmin, cloud computing, fuzzy logic

**Corresponding author*: yogeshparashar4jan@gmail.com

E. Chandrasekaran, R. Anandan, G. Suseendran, S. Balamurugan and Hanaa Hachimi (eds.) Fuzzy Intelligent Systems: Methodologies, Techniques, and Applications, (243–268) © 2021 Scrivener Publishing LLC

8.1 Introduction

Today's world is full of Virtual Machines (VMs). Virtual machines support to run the applications implemented in cloud or the internet services inside the cloud system. By virtual allocation, VMs are generated. Here, it practically means to operate the machine by the software configurations in place of physical connections and manage the configuration of physical infrastructure. These service providers for cloud also maintain the minimum level of quality which is called Quality of Service (QoS). Quality of Service is also known as Service Level Objective (SLO). Service Level Objective should be achieved by increasing the infrastructure. But these approaches need huge investment on infrastructure and also increase the running cost and maintenance in the cloud. In the present environment of competitive business, increment in cost is not acceptable. So an efficient utilization of available resources is the only way to achieve the Service Level Objective. In this way, SLO can also be achieved without extra investment.

Task distribution, VM configuration and VM status of adaptive management are required by the cloud manager to utilize the available resources efficiently. This management of cloud depends on the current task queue length, current work load, power saving policies, etc. These things are dynamically configuring and connect to each other and balance among the above state things should be managed by a system which is based on Fuzzy logic.

In the age of computation, cloud computing generates a real world to satisfy many customers. For doing the management of cloud computing, there are many factors responsible like resource utilization, availability, reliability, etc. [21].

Here this chapter depends on a Fuzzy logic-based system and organizes this chapter in following manner. A brief literature review is provided in Section 8.2. An overview of fuzzy logic controller is given in Section 8.3. Simulation configurations in the architecture system are explained in Section 8.4. Section 8.5 explains the simulation results. Finally 8.6 explains the conclusion and gives some suggestions for future possible work [22].

8.2 Literature Review

Task distribution is a procedure which is used to distribute the implementation of tasks in the environment of cloud on resources distribution

[6]. Most common method to do task distribution is done by using the optimization techniques to find out optimal task to VM pair for given object function and constraints. Refs. [3], [4], [5], [8], [15], [16] and [17] explained the number of techniques that work for given objective function and constrains to give the optimal task to VM pair.

All these techniques have the same common optimization algorithm. Utilization of these algorithms has many common differences in the terms of use of algorithm which can also be seen here. To achieve the tasks balancing over available VMs in Ref. [3] apply the optimization technique which is based on Honey Bee Behavior. This algorithm manages the task implementation priorities. Ref. [5] worked for cut-off date unnatural task arrangement using self-adaptive learning and this technique is called particle swarm optimization. Although Ref. [15] also used PSO (particle swarm optimization) technique they worked for compelled task execution time and information move cost.

Genetic algorithm for multi-objective was used in Ref. [8], whereby this technique we able to get more than one optimal objective simultaneously. Task execution cost, minimizing assignment transfer time, assignment queue length and power consumption are four different tasks achieved by using this technique. When the task set span is minimum, the load of entire system depends and balances by using ant colony optimization [16]. IDEA (Improved differential evolution algorithm) is the method which was developed by using the Taguchi method and a differential evolution algorithm (DEA) together for the purpose present in Ref. [17]. Any system of multi-objective optimization always approaches in two types of objectives. In first objective they have to optimize the processing and receiving cost and in second object optimized receiving time, waiting time and processing time. Other than optimization, fuzzy logic approach was also used. The fuzzy logic is also another technique for task scheduling. When the decision of any problem is complex and degree of overlapping is shown by the some variables, then fuzzy logic technique is used for solving same. Many machines are designed and controlled by the system of fuzzy logic. Many applications of fuzzy logic can be seen in refrigerators, TV, washing machine and other household products. Technology of fuzzy logic is also used in virtual machine to predict the upcoming job assignment of virtual machines, allowing for the desires of memory, bandwidth and space of disk are vague [12]. The model for the task scheduling is worked with uncertain workload for virtual data centers and presented uncertain nodes availability [9]. This reference arrangement was found as a two-target enhancement which is a bargain as a compromise between the normal reaction time and accessibility of Virtual Data Center. To do the advancement, it requires the accessibility of VDC and remaining task at hand qualities. By utilizing a development sort of types I and II of the fluffy-based indicator is proposed for Load Balance and virtual information-based accessibility. Refs. [1, 14] worked on genetic algorithm and fuzzy logic which belong to the hybrid job scheduling algorithm. For reducing the number of iterations, here we required the fuzzy logic by hereditary calculation to communicate.

8.3 Logic System for Fuzzy

In fluffy rationale, there is a variable which is at the same time is having a place with more than one class with a restricted degree. The enrolment work has characterized the level of participation. If we told in natural language then fuzzy logic is near to decision making. In modeling of system fuzzy logic is principally useful. Here information cannot be defined accurately, but some important concepts can be clear. In scientific and industrial area, application of fuzzy logic technology has achieved many applications, just because of effectiveness and simplicity of fuzzy logic.

Figure 8.1 represents an emblematic system of Fuzzy Logic Controller. This system is developed with four different principles i.e. a Fuzzy rule base, a de Fuzzifier, a fuzzifier and inference engine. The fuzzification is a method, where crisp values changed in the form of degree of sponsorship with dissimilar classes. Calculation of membership degree is done by function of sponsorship. By using the fuzzification, association of variables is enabled with linguistic term.

L, H and M show the temperature of crisp value in Figure 8.2. In this figure, L, M and H are three categories which represent the membership of

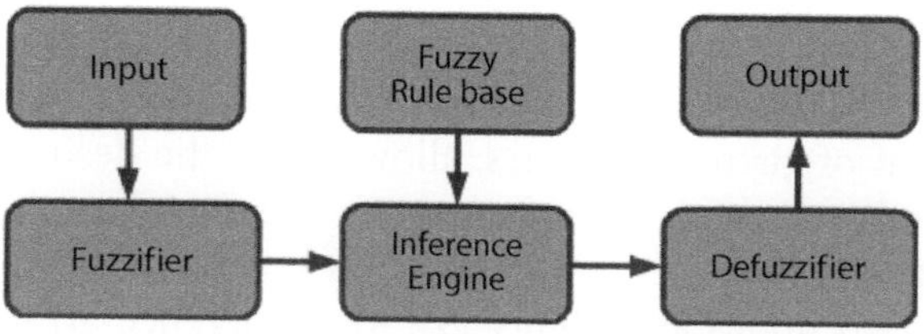

Figure 8.1 Fuzzy Logic Controller (FLC) system representation [2].

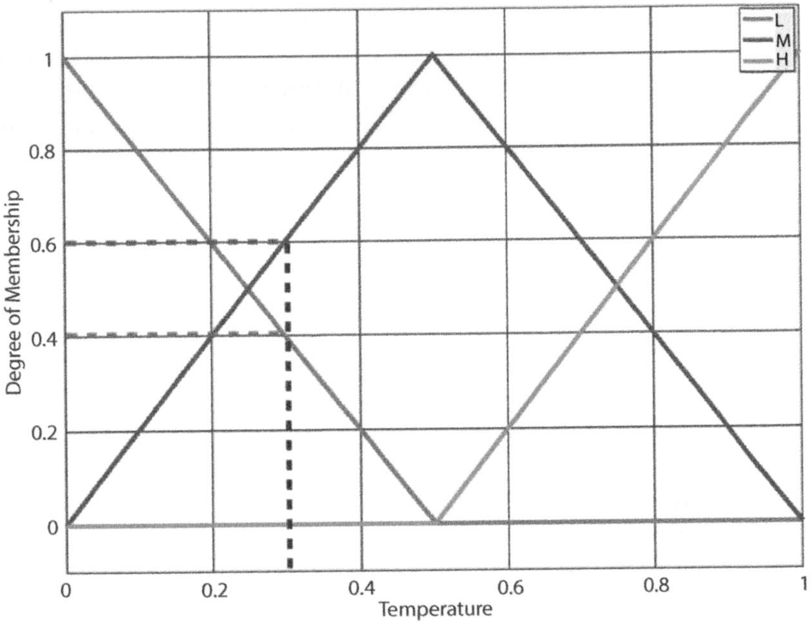

Figure 8.2 In triangular membership function process of fuzzification [13].

0.4, 0.6 and 0 respectively and show that 0.3 task is on priority. Here black dashed line represents 0.3, red dashed line represents 0.4, and blue dashed line 0.6. There are many shapes of membership functions like bell shaped, trapezoidal, sigmoid, Gaussian, where Figure 8.2 has a membership function of triangular shape. The figure type of membership function exactly depends on the actual applications.

The rule related to fuzzy input and output is known as Fuzzy Rule Base. It is a series which belongs to s sequence of IF and THEN. If we take any example like system is cooling then it can be written as:

In the event that temperature appeared in framework is L, THEN intensity of cooler is set to H.

On the off chance that temperature appeared in framework is M, THEN intensity of cooler is set to M.

In the event that temperature appeared in framework is H, THEN intensity of cooler is set to L.

These types of rules have required the much proficiency in the application field.

Now another definition of Inference Engine is that all the rules of fuzzy present in the rule based on fuzzy are executed by the inference Engine. By this Engine we are able to get one output for one rule.

One more important term is De-Fuzzification; we get the output from the inference engine in fuzzy form. This fuzzy form of output can be used by the non-fuzzy system, but before using it must be converted into crisp value. The transformation of fuzzy value into crisp value is performed by the De-Fuzzification. The process of De-Fuzzification is done by different ways like Max Membership, Mean Max Membership and weighted Average, etc.

8.4 Proposed Algorithm

8.4.1 Architecture of System

Figure 8.3 represents the architecture of proposed system. In this system, there are 4 blocks known as fuzzy logic decision making block, five blocks for information extraction and two blocks for VM controlling.

Each block works in following manner:

- ➢ The squares which are utilized to separate important data from VMs and the line of assignment, are known as Information extraction blocks.
- ➢ Current Task length in MIPS is known as Task Length.
- ➢ Priority of execution of current task is known as task priority.
- ➢ Resources of VM are known as resource used by VM.

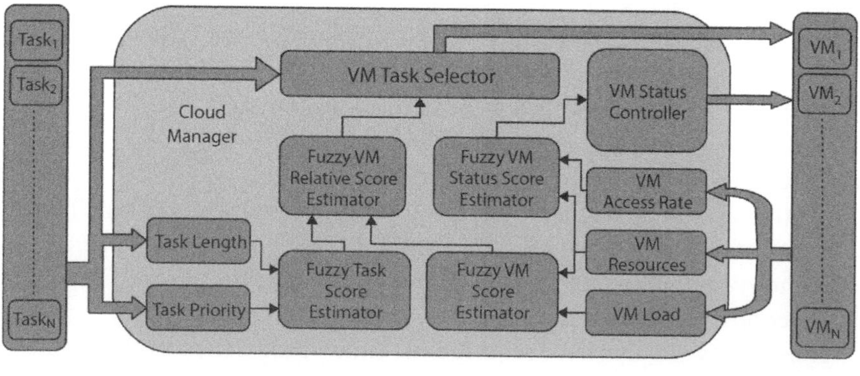

Figure 8.3 Representation of blocks of different functions and their internal connection [7].

- Current load of VM known as VM Load.
- The blocks are used to make specific decisions are called Fuzzy Logic Decision Making Blocks. These decisions basically depend on inputs providing by fuzzy logic.
- To get the specific decision, the need to handle the task depends on the basis of VM configuration and load. This block estimator is known as Fuzzy VM score Estimator.
- Estimate fitness between requirements of task and VM capability is called fuzzy VM relative score estimator.
- To decide the functioning status of VM, which ids depend on VM access rate and VM resource utilization is known as VM status score estimator.
- The blocks which are used to select the best VM from the present assignment is known as VM task selector. In this process task selector takes the inputs from estimator of fuzzy relative score and selects highest relative score of VM.
- Based on VM status score, VM task selector maintains the states of all VM. There are two different threshold values i.e. t_s and t_d, where $0< t_s < t_d< 1$ which are defined VM status against the VM score .VM status keeps running if VM score $<t_s$,VM status is shutdown only if $t_s \geq$ VM score $>t_d$ and VM status is dissolve otherwise VM score $\geq t_d$.

In any fuzzy system selection of function for membership is very important and the most tricky task. These selected functions for membership support to explain fuzziness. In this system variable of way changes their membership to altered classes. The performance of fuzzy system degraded drastically by the improper selection of fuzzy membership function. Figure 8.4(a) shows the proposed triangular membership functions, which is utilized for the VM Load, VM assets and Task length. These three parameters are responsible for the direct transformation in level of participation starting with one then onto the next class. This consideration of variable is the region to select the triangular membership function.

Figure 8.4(b) shows the rate of access by the two-sided Gaussian membership functions. It is necessary to increase the importance speedily then rate of linear. Two-sided Gaussian function of membership rapidly transects from current class to higher class and huskily leaves the present class. In this function continuous symmetric transition is considered as a task priority. In Figure 8.4(c) shows the variable which is used for task priority.

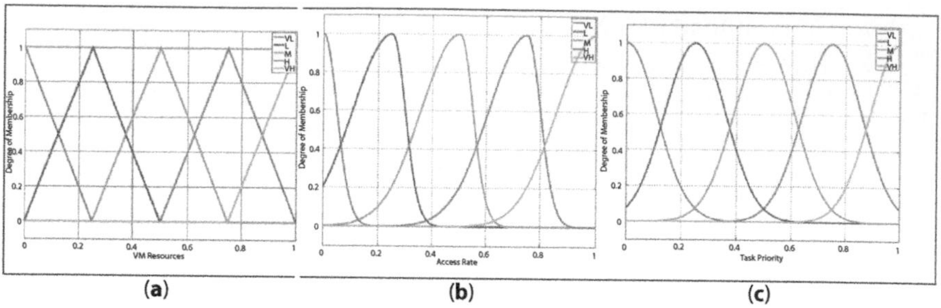

Figure 8.4 Fuzzy estimators based membership function shown in graphs. Graph (a) is based on triangular function, (b) is based on two-sided Gaussian Function and (c) is based on Gaussian [23].

8.4.2 Terminology of Model

The terminologies used in algorithm, firstly explained, then proceed to its descriptions are shown in Table 8.1.

Table 8.1 Terminology of models.

Symbol to represent	Abbreviation	Explanation
TL	Task length	The ith task length = TL_i
VM(*C*)	VM Capacity of implementation	The ith VM rate of task execution = $VM(C^i_{VM})$
VM(*L*)	Current consignment on VM	The ith VM rate of current implementation of task = $VM(L^i_{VM})$
VM(*R*)	Access Rate of VM	The *i*th VM per unit time assigned task number = $VM(R^i)$
T_w	Waiting Time of assignment (Task)	Explained the time then the ith VM can start implementation of the requested assignment (Task) $T^i_w = L^i_c / C^i_{VM}$
$T_{e,j}$	Execution Time of assignment (Task)	The time mandatory by the ith VM to accomplish the jth assignment (Task) $T^i_{e,j} = TL_j / C^i_{VM}$

(Continued)

Table 8.1 Terminology of models. (*Continued*)

Symbol to represent	Abbreviation	Explanation
$T_{t,j}$	Total time of assignment (Task) Completion	Addition of Assignment Waiting Time and Task Execution Time $T^i_{t,j} = T^i_w / T^i_{e,j}$
TP	Priority assignment (Task)	The backwards of required greatest Total Task Completion Time for the ith task = TP_i
F_{TS}	Score Estimator of Fuzzy Task	$F_{TS}(TL_i, TP_i)$
S_{TS}	Score of Fuzzy Task	Task achieve of ith assignment calculated by Fuzzy Task Score Estimator $F_{TS}(S^i_{TS})$
F_{VM}	Fuzzy VM Score Estimator	$F_{VM}(L^i_c, C^i_{VM})$
S_{VM}	Fuzzy VM Score	VM score of ith VM calculated by score of Fuzzy VM Estimator $F_{VM}(S^i_{VM})$
F_{VMR}	Fuzzy VM Score of virtual Estimator	$F_{VMR}(S^i_{TS}, S^i_{VM})$
S_j	Comparative Score of Fuzzy VM	Relative VM score of ith VM for jth task calculated by Fuzzy VM Relative Score Estimator $F_{VMR} = S^i_j$
F_{SS}	Fuzzy VM Status Score Estimator	$F_{SS}(R^i_c, C^i_{VM})$
S_{SS}	Fuzzy VM Status Score	VM status score of ith VM calculated by Fuzzy VM Status Score Estimator F_{VM}

8.4.3 Algorithm Proposed

Let TL_{new} is the task length and TP_{new} priority of newly arrived task respectively

---

N = total numbers of VMs currently running in VM.Start Main Routine
for i = 1 to N

$$T_w^i = \frac{TL_{new}}{C_{VM}^i}$$

$$T_{e,j}^i = \frac{TL_j}{C_{VM}^i}$$

$$T_{t,j}^i = T_w^i + T_{e,j}^i$$

endfor
$VM_{available} = 0$
for i = 1 to N

$$\text{if}\left(T_{t,j}^i > \frac{1}{TP_{new}}\right)$$

$VM_{available} = 1$
break;
endif
endfor
if ($VM_{available}$ == 0)
CreateNewVM();
else
AssignTask();
endif
End Main Routine

Start Sub – Routine CreateNewVM

$$C_{VM}^{new} = TL_{new} \times TP_{new};$$

create new VM_{new} with configuration C_{VM}^{new};
assign Task to VM_{new}.
End Sub – Routine CreateNewVM

Start Sub – Routine AssignTask
$S_p = 0;$
VMselected = 0;
for i = 1 to N

$S_{VM}^{i} = F_{VM}\left(L_c^i, C_{VM}^i\right);$

$S_{TS}^{i} = F_{TS}(TL_i, TP_i);$

$S_c^i = F_{VMR}\left(S_{TS}^i, S_{VM}^i\right);$

$\text{if}\left(S_c^i > S_p\right)$

$S_p = S_c^i;$

$VM_{selected} = i;$
endif
endfor
assign Task to VMselected.
End Sub – Routine AssignTask

Start Sub – Routine VMStausControl
for i = 1 to N
if(isIdle(VM_i))

$S_{SS}^{i} = F_{SS}\left(R_c^i, C_{VM}^i\right);$

if $\left(S_{SS}^{i} > TH_{dissolve}\right)$

Dissolve the VM_i;

elseif $\left(S_{SS}^{i} > TH_{sleep}\right)$

Set VM to Sleep
else
do nothing
endif
endif

endfor
End Sub – Routine VMStatus Control

8.4.4 Explanations of Proposed Algorithm

Figure 8.5 describes the proposed algorithm about the task completion. In this system the manager of cloud waits for the arrival of new task, when the new task is received it is available in task queue as soon as it received. This undertaking removes the errand related boundaries like task priority and assignment (task) length. As above algorithm once the cloud manager found the relative values, then checks all the VMs for $T_{t,j}^{i} > \frac{1}{TP_{new}}$. But if the cloud manger did not stumble on any VM then it moves to generate fresh task that is shown in algorithm that called the sub routine assign task.

In this algorithm VM score calculates the relative VMs using fuzzy rules as shown in Table 8.2. Figure 8.3 is used as fuzzy task score estimator which

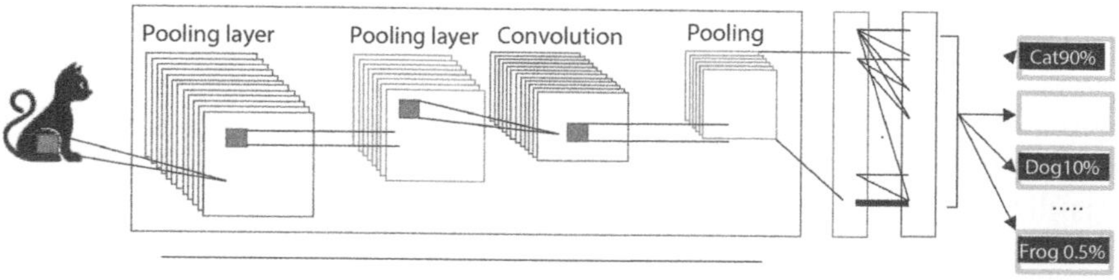

Figure 8.5 Structure of convolution neural network [10].

Table 8.2 Fuzzy controllers for the fuzzy rules and surf plots.

		Amalgamation of safety measures						
		IaaS coating	**PaaS layer**				**SaaS coating**	
Class mechanisms	**TC**	**ID**	**DCP**	**SSH**	**IDE**	**vTPM**	**SSL**	**DC**
Towering protection	T	T	T	T	T	T	T	T
Common protection	T	F	T	T	F	T	T	F
some-how secure	F	F	T	T	T	F	T	F
low protection	F	F	T	T	F	F	T	F

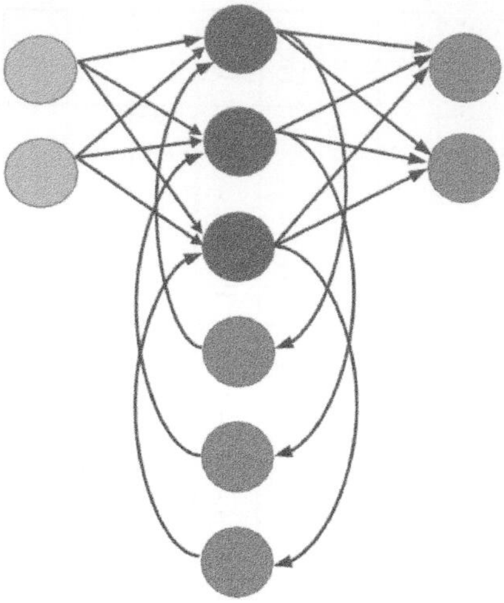

Figure 8.6 Structure of recurrent neural network [13].

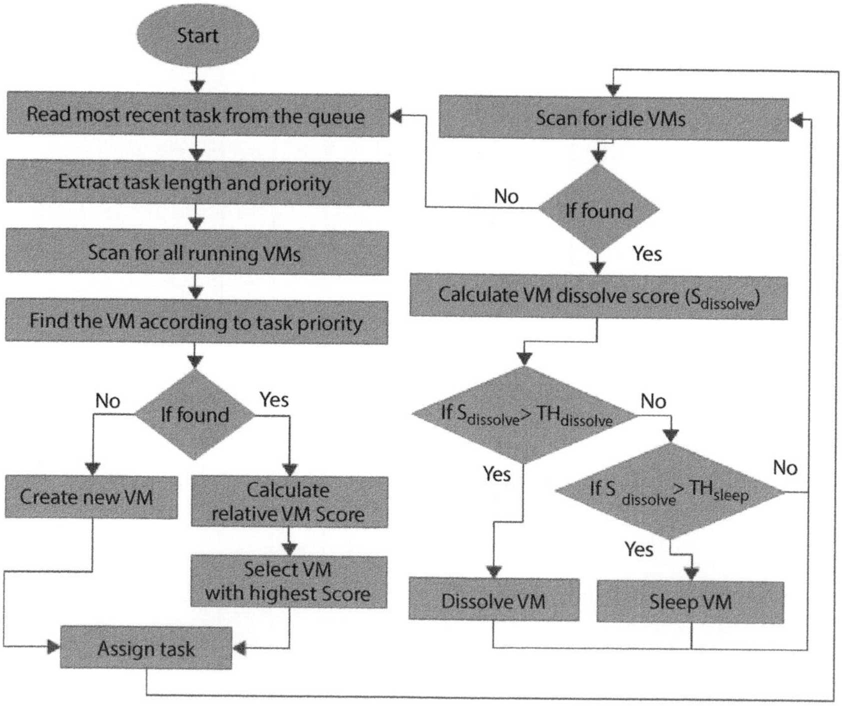

Figure 8.7 The proposed algorithm flow chart [11].

received task length and priority values for estimate VM relative score. The neural network design in two types such as convolution neural network shown in Figure 8.5 and recurrent neural network shown in Figure 8.6. Rules and the values of fuzzy estimator, defined in Table 8.2 are responsible to calculate the score. The fuzzy task score basically worked on two types of inputs. One contribution is for fluffy relative score and second info chooses for the execution limit and current burden for the cloud supervisor filters all the running VMs. Figure 8.7 shows the flow chart of proposed algorithm for calculating the assign task.

Table 8.4 explained the rule by which estimator block estimate VM score. VM relative estimator need VM score work as second input. All running VMs same procedure is repeated again and again and output score which is relative are stored. Out of these scores the highest score is worked as input task.

The status of VMs is managed by the cloud manager, for this cloud manger scans rate of accessing and execution capacity of each VM. For generating Table 8.6 rate of accessing and execution capacity of VMs values are used by fuzzy rule to estimate their status score.

Now we compared this calculated status score with $TH_{dissolve}$. If the VM score greater than $TH_{dissolve}$ then dissolved the VM and again claim for its resources. If this does not happen then recheck the score in opposition to TH_{sleep}. The score can deposit into sleep state or should be kept running.

8.5 Results of Simulation

8.5.1 Cloud System Numerical Model

When we developed numerical method, we consider compulsory the following rules:

1. Firstly we assume that the configuration understands by memory, processing capacity, etc. which are known as load balancer of each virtual machine in the cloud.
2. After this immediately the load balancer can catch the running state for each VM.
3. There is no postponement to choosing and allotting the undertakings to VMs by the heap balancer.
4. There is no time required for booting by the VM, so VM starts executing assigned task promptly.
5. Million instructions units are required to consider the incoming task size.

6. Million instructions per second units are used to consider VMs capacities.

OCTAVE/MATLAB computing software are used to calculate numerically for performing the evaluation of the proposed algorithm. Arrival rate is represented by λ, which is in Poisson process form during the simulation task. During the simulation maximum task length and minimum task length of the random length task are generated. Generation of random task length depends on uniform discrete distribution. For age of undertaking needs and characterizing the VM execution limits same way used by random length task [18–20].

8.5.2 Evaluation Terms Definition

For evaluating the performance of the algorithm following measures are used:

1. The cloud serving failure task within given time period is known as SLA Failure.
2. The length of the SLA Failure task is known as SLA Failure task length.
3. The booting of VMs from sleep mode is known VM Reboots. VMs cannot serve the current task then this operation booting of VMs is required.
4. The formation of new VM from the available unused resources is known as VM Reforms. This VM reforms worked only at the point when the current undertaking can't be taken care of by the previously dozing VMs.
5. The efficiency which is responsible for the cloud resources utilized to serve task is known as Resource Utilization Efficiency and it is calculated as following:

$$\text{Resource Utilization Efficiency} = \frac{\sum_{i=1}^{N} TL_i}{\sum_{i=1}^{N}\left(\sum_{j=1}^{A_i} C_{VM}^{j}\right)} \times \text{M1o}$$

Here

The cloud load at th time = TL_i

VMs active number and running ith time = A_i

Execution capability of the VM = C^{j}_{VM}
Simulation complete time or task arrival discreet event = L_i

8.5.3 Environment Configurations Simulation

The algorithm simulation appropriately a few significant parameters would be essential to configure in Table 8.3. These parameters also contained in Table 8.3 and their values also listed in same table.

8.5.4 Outcomes of Simulation

Graphical presentation of the outcomes of simulation is presented here. The arranged calculation results are additionally contrasted and two standard assignment planning calculations are named as Random Selection and Round Robin.

Above table concludes that the proposed algorithm provides similar result for both Min–Max and Min–Min. The increment and achievement of this algorithm is 15% better than that of the resource utilization compared to other algorithm. For the mean value and for the best value, it increases efficiency 21%. For completion of SLO time line, this proposed algorithm reduces the rate of failure of SLO to 50% as compared to other algorithms present in Table 8.5. The given algorithm span outperforms other algorithm for all given values and achieve the maximum improvement of 29%. If we compare our algorithm in terms of the power expenditure, it has less expenditure of power. It reduces the average load condition with 9% near to and higher load consumption 21% and full load of consumption of about 16%.

Table 8.3 The parameters of simulation and their values.

A. Parameter of Configuration	*B*. Parameter Value
C. Capacity of Total implementation presented	*D*. 101 MIPS
E. Task Length Minimum	*F*. 101 MI
G. Minimum Task implementation Time	*H*. 1 s
I. Maximum Task Execution Time	*J*. 10 s
K. Sleep of Threshold	*L*. 0.5
M. Dissolve Threshold	*N*. 0.7
O. Time of Total Simulation	*P*. 100 s

8.6 Conclusion

This chapter concludes that, we have implemented the VM Status based on the fuzzy logic and task assignment scheme for the Cloud systems. It is being observed from the result that the proposed technique has conveyed the ensured SLA by a factor of 2.5 by decreasing the task number and cloud failure (Figure 8.8). Furthermore, the guaranteed SLA will be reduced by a factor by 8.0 if the total task length failed (Figure 8.9) which is very more than the 2.5. It can be evident from the results that the proposed method is managing the cloud by minimizing the loss due to SLA disagreement.

The amount of reboots of VMS are managed by the proposed method which in turn causes a delay within the response by an element of 4.99 as shown in Figure 8.10 and so Figure 8.11 shows the reduction in the number of VM reforms is with the factor of 2.98. Reboot number displays the organization intelligibility of the VMs states to ensure that the primary widespread VM organization is held in reserve for operation. While the decrease inside the amount of VM changes shows that the VMs are designed such that most of the time the cloud can get the dynamic VMs for the assignments SLA necessity it additionally lessens the span.

In Figure 8.12, it is clear that the efficiency of algorithm shows the proposed algorithm which maintains a relative margin fifty. This margin is

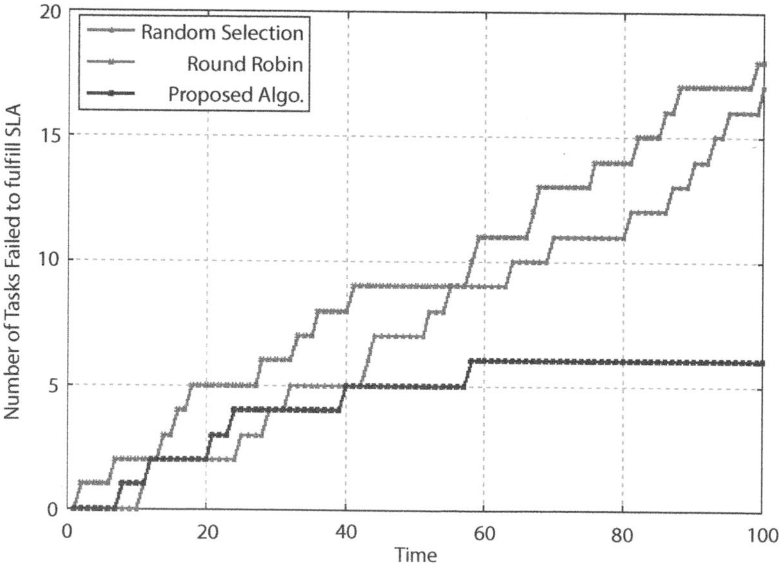

Figure 8.8 Graph for failed requested of SLA by cloud with respect to simulation time due to shortage of resources.

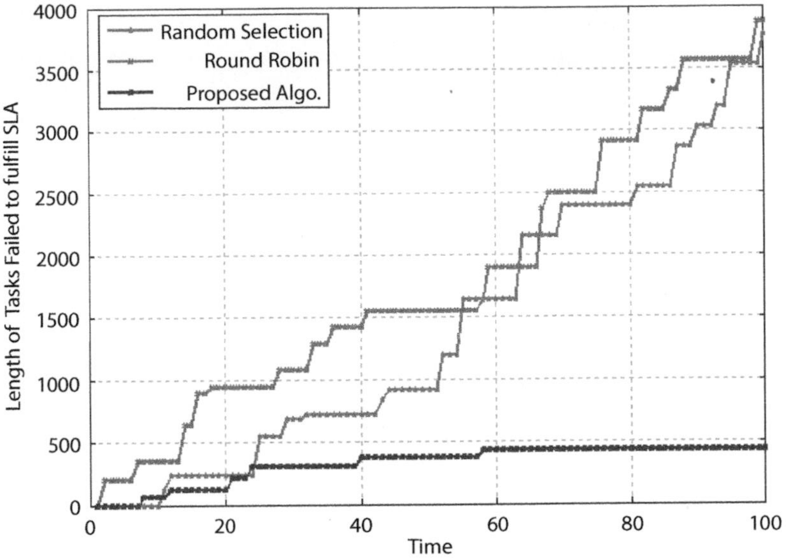

Figure 8.9 Graph for total span of the tasks which abortive to accept the requested SLA with respect to simulation time by cloud due shortage of resources.

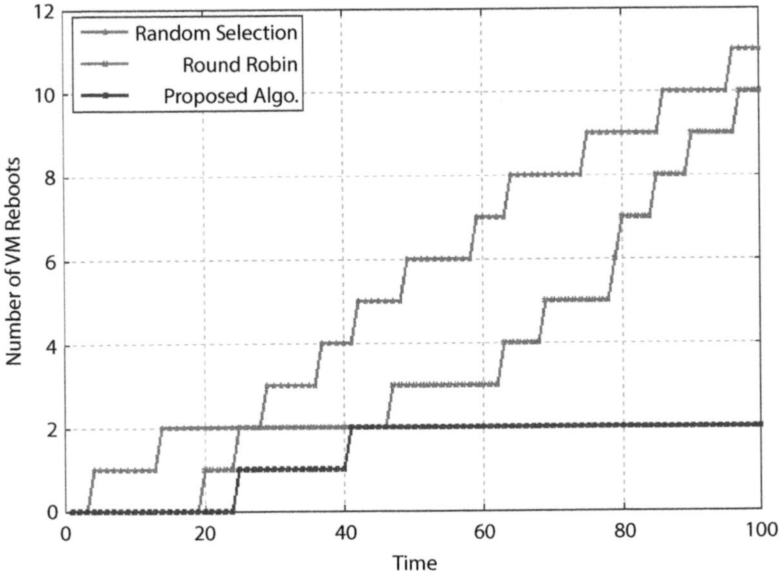

Figure 8.10 Graph for VM is rebooted counting for task assignment sleep mode with respect to simulation.

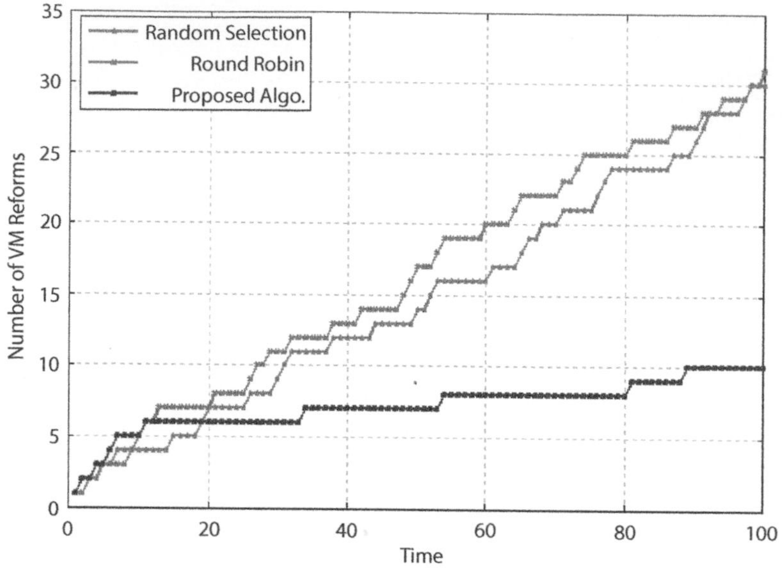

Figure 8.11 Graph for number of times VM is reformed with respect to simulation time from the offered assets for handing over of assignment.

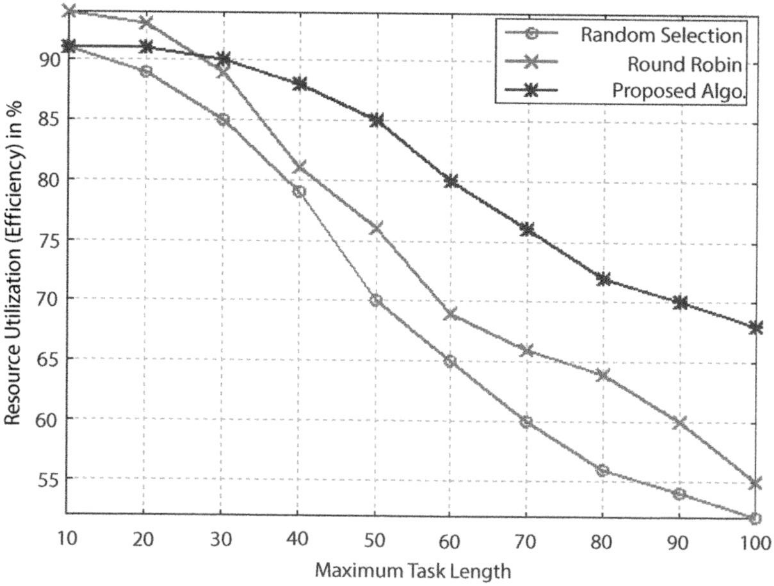

Figure 8.12 Graph for the difference of the cloud source consumption effectiveness with due to maximum length of task.

Table 8.4 Different work load conditions in comparison to resource utilization efficiency (%).

Average task length	Proposed			Max-Min			Min-Min			Round robin		
	Mean	**Std.**	**Best**	**Mean**	**Std.**	**Best**	**Mean**	**Std.**	**Best**	**Mean**	**Std.**	**Best**
25	72.77	2.68	75.24	71.26	2.61	74.38	68.33	2.33	71.64	60.63	2.63	65.27
50	82.91	4.46	85.10	74.71	4.59	79.22	73.28	4.68	76.47	65.95	5.95	68.92
75	92.18	10.23	95.66	68.09	9.54	73.18	69.28	9.72	74.89	59.22	9.82	66.81
100	75.16	15.25	85.52	65.15	15.83	69.53	60.55	15.05	67.51	62.74	16.74	72.40

Table 8.5 With different work load comparison of SLO failure or SLO deadline violation (%).

Average task length	Proposed			Max-Min			Min-Min			Round robin		
	Mean	**Std.**	**Best**	**Mean**	**Std.**	**Best**	**Mean**	**Std.**	**Best**	**Mean**	**Std.**	**Best**
25	1.41	2.08	1.26	3.61	2.44	3.36	3.45	2.58	3.25	6.31	4.12	5.11
50	2.26	3.94	2.12	5.34	4.15	5.03	6.02	4.36	5.67	8.53	7.57	7.62
75	4.19	6.32	3.97	8.86	6.24	7.75	7.76	6.12	6.77	10.22	9.24	8.49
100	4.45	9.02	4.17	10.53	10.38	9.29	9.87	9.15	8.83	14.45	11.81	11.72

Table 8.6 With different average task length comparison of power consumption in percentage of 100% resource utilization.

Average task length	Proposed			Max-Min			Min-Min			Round robin		
	Mean	Std.	Best	Mean	Std.	Best	Mean	Std.	Best	Mean	Std.	Best
25	346.5	6.39	339.6	354.2	8.46	344.1	356.3	8.55	344.42	397.6	14.34	367.3
50	567.2	24.6	553.4	661.0	28.2	626.4	673.3	28.4	634.3	732.7	56.8	662.1
75	776.5	47.4	744.9	1,067.9	69.2	981.6	1,015.4	69.0	956.3	1,148.5	96.2	1051.9
100	1260.1	112.3	1,204.8	1,360.5	149.6	1,259.0	1,560.3	153.6	1,419.9	1,663.7	186.8	1464.8

increased with the increment of load and this attainment reflects that this algorithm manages the cloud with efficiency. After keen analysis of the result and outcomes the present algorithm has a capacity to unutilized efficiency resources in following manner:

- Mostly complete the task according SLA required.
- Reduction of cloud reaction time.
- Increment of resources utilization efficiency.

In this chapter we compare the result of proposed algorithm with the conventional algorithm and absorb that the result of proposed algorithm provides better results. This algorithm also has scope for improvement by find the membership function of tuning and rule base.

This modification has to be done in future work.

References

1. Shojafar, M., Javanmardi, S., Abolfazli, S., Cordeschi, N., Erratum to: FUGE: A joint meta-heuristic approach to cloud job scheduling algorithm using fuzzy theory and a genetic method. *Cluster Comput.*, 18, 2, 845–845, 2015.
2. Chen, H., Wang, F., Helian, N., Akanmu, G., User-priority guided Min-Min scheduling algorithm for load balancing in cloud computing. *2013 National Conference on Parallel Computing Technologies (PARCOMPTECH)*, 2013.
3. D.B.L.d. and Krishna, P.V., Honey bee behavior inspired load balancing of tasks in cloud computing environments. *Appl. Soft Comput.*, 13, 5, 2292–2303, 2013.
4. Tsai, C.-W. and Rodrigues, J.J.P.C., Metaheuristic Scheduling for Cloud: A Survey. *IEEE Syst. J.*, 8, 1, 279–291, 2014.
5. Zuo, X., Zhang, G., Tan, W., Self-Adaptive Learning PSO-Based Deadline Constrained Task Scheduling for Hybrid IaaS Cloud. *IEEE Trans. Autom. Sci. Eng.*, 11, 2, 564–573, 2014.
6. Adabi, S., Movaghar, A., Rahmani, A.M., Bi-level fuzzy based advanced reservation of Cloud workflow applications on distributed Grid resources. *J. Supercomput.*, 67, 1, 175–218, 2013.
7. Poola, D., Garg, S.K., Buyya, R., Yang, Y., Ramamohanarao, K., Robust Scheduling of Scientific Workflows with Deadline and Budget Constraints in Clouds. *2014 IEEE 28th International Conference on Advanced Information Networking and Applications*, 2014.

8. Ramezani, F., Lu, J., Taheri, J., Hussain, F.K., Evolutionary algorithm-based multi-objective task scheduling optimization model in cloud environments. *World Wide Web*, 18, 6, 1737–1757, Oct. 2015.
9. Kong, X., Lin, C., Jiang, Y., Yan, W., Chu, X., Efficient dynamic task scheduling in virtualized data centers with fuzzy prediction. *J. Netw. Comput. Appl.*, 34, 4, 1068–1077, 2011.
10. Lin, W., Liang, C., Wang, J.Z., Buyya, R., Bandwidth-aware divisible task scheduling for cloud computing. *Softw.: Pract. Exp.*, 44, 2, 163–174, 2012.
11. Garg, S.K., Toosi, A.N., Gopalaiyengar, S.K., Buyya, R., SLA-based virtual machine management for heterogeneous workloads in a cloud datacenter. *J. Netw. Comput. Appl.*, 45, 108–120, 2014.
12. Nine, M.S.Q.Z., Azad, M.A.K., Abdullah, S., Rahman, R.M., Fuzzy logic based dynamic load balancing in virtualized data centers. *2013 IEEE International Conference on Fuzzy Systems (FUZZ-IEEE)*, 2013.
13. Toosi, A.N. and Buyya, R., A Fuzzy Logic-Based Controller for Cost and Energy Efficient Load Balancing in Geo-distributed Data Centers. *2015 IEEE/ACM 8th International Conference on Utility and Cloud Computing (UCC)*, Limassol, pp. 186–194, 2015.
14. Javanmardi, S., Shojafar, M., Amendola, D., Cordeschi, N., Liu, H., Abraham, A., Hybrid Job Scheduling Algorithm for Cloud Computing Environment. IBICA, in: *Advances in Intelligent Systems and Computing*, vol. 303, Springer, Cham, 2014.
15. Pandey, S., Wu, L., Guru, S.M., Buyya, R., A Particle Swarm Optimization-Based Heuristic for Scheduling Workflow Applications in Cloud Computing Environments. *2010 24th IEEE International Conference on Advanced Information Networking and Applications*, 2010.
16. Li, K., Xu, G., Zhao, G., Dong, Y., Wang, D., Cloud Task Scheduling Based on Load Balancing Ant Colony Optimization. *2011 Sixth Annual Chinagrid Conference*, 2011.
17. Tsai, J.-T., Fang, J.-C., Chou, J.-H., Optimized task scheduling and resource allocation on cloud computing environment using improved differential evolution algorithm. *Comput. Oper. Res.*, 40, 12, 3045–3055, 2013.
18. Hayat, B., Kim, K.H., Kim, K., A study on fuzzy logic based cloud computing. *Cluster Comput.*, 21, 589–603, 2018, https://doi.org/10.1007/s10586-017-0953-x.
19. Masdari, M., Salehi, F., Jalali, M., Bidaki, M., A survey of PSO-based scheduling algorithms in cloud computing. *J. Netw. Syst. Manage.*, 25, 1, 122–158, 2017.
20. Wang, B. and Li, J., Load balancing task scheduling based on Multi-Population Genetic Algorithm in cloud computing, in: *2016 35th Chinese Control Conference (CCC)*, IEEE, pp. 5261–5266, 2016.
21. Agrawal, M., Bansal, R., Choudhary, A., Agrawal, A.P., Hetrogenous Computing Task Scheduling Using Improved Harmony Search Optimization,

in: *2018 International Conference on Advances in Computing, Communication Control and Networking (ICACCCN)*, IEEE, pp. 11–15, 2018.
22. Agarwal, M. and Srivastava, G.M.S., A cuckoo search algorithm-based task scheduling in cloud computing, in: *Advances in Computer and Computational Sciences*, pp. 293–299, Springer, Singapore, 2018.
23. Sheikholeslami, F. and Navimipour, N.J., Service allocation in the cloud environments using multi-objective particle swarm optimization algorithm based on crowding distance. *Swarm Evol. Comput.*, 35, 53–64, 2017.

9

Theorems on Fuzzy Soft Metric Spaces

Qazi Aftab Kabir[1], Ramakant Bhardwaj[2,3]* and Ritu Shrivastava[4]

[1]*Department of Mathematics, Govt. Degree College Surankote, Jammu & Kashmir, India*
[2]*Department of Mathematics, Amity University Kolkata, West Bangal, India*
[3]*Department of Mathematics, APS University, Rewa, India*
[4]*School of Foundation, Bahrain Polytechnic, Isa Town, Kingdom of Bahrain*

Abstract

In 1965 Zadeh presented the idea of fuzzy sets as another approach to speak to ambiguity in our regular day to day existence. In the following decade Kramosil and Michalek presented the idea of fuzzy metric space in 1975. In this chapter, we provide four kinds of mappings satisfying fuzzy soft metric space. First we prove a common fixed point results for fuzzy soft $(\alpha - \beta) - \psi -$ functions of the contractive type and second we prove fuzzy soft $\tilde{\alpha} - \tilde{\psi}$ – contractive type mappings and $\tilde{\alpha}$ – *admissible* mappings in fuzzy soft metric space. We also study fuzzy soft sets and systems for satisfy fuzzy $\Psi - \Phi$ contractive mappings in fuzzy soft metric spaces. The obtained results in this chapter will generalize well known results. One example is also proved for support of these established results.

Keywords: Fixed point (FP), soft set (SS), fuzzy soft set (FSS), fuzzy metric space (FMS), fuzzy soft metric (FSMS), $(\alpha - \beta) - \psi -$ contractive maps (CM), $\tilde{\alpha}$ – *admissible* mappings

9.1 Introduction

In 1965 Zadeh presented the idea of fuzzy sets as another approach to deal with address lack of clarity in customary everyday presence. The hypothesis of softs sets began by Molodstov [23] which assists with tackling issues in all

**Corresponding author*: rkbhardwaj100@gmail.com

E. Chandrasekaran, R. Anandan, G. Suseendran, S. Balamurugan and Hanaa Hachimi (eds.) Fuzzy Intelligent Systems: Methodologies, Techniques, and Applications, (269–284) © 2021 Scrivener Publishing LLC

areas. After at that point, the properties and applications on this hypothesis have been concentrated by numerous creators [6, 8–11, 15–19, 21, 22]. Maji *et al.* [17] started a few tasks in SS and has likewise instituted FSS. Many fascinating uses of delicate set hypothesis have been extended by implanting the thoughts of fuzzy sets [1, 2, 5–7, 13, 15, 16, 19–22]. Beaula *et al.* [3] presented a meaning of the fuzzy soft measurement space and furthermore give the idea of FS-open balls and FS-closed ball.

The basic result on fixed point theory is "Banach contraction principle" which has been generalized with many ways in metric spaces. In 2002, Ref. [14] proved a fuzzy version of fuzzy systems. Also in 2018, Ref. [24] showed the concept of $\alpha - \psi -$ CM and established some FP theorems in metric spaces.

In this chapter, we introduce a concept of FS $(\alpha - \beta) - \psi -$ CM and FS $\tilde{\alpha} - \tilde{\psi} -$ CM with $\tilde{\alpha}$ – *admissible* mappings in FSMS and proved FP theorems for this type of mappings in complete FSM space.

9.2 Preliminaries

Definition 1. [12] If $(X, M, *)$ is a FMS

1. A seq. $\{x_n\}$ in X is said to be a Cauchy sequence iff

$$\lim_{n\to\infty} M(x_{n+p}, x_n, t) = 1 \ \forall p > 0, t > 0.$$

2. A seq. $\{x_n\}$ in X is converging to x in X iff

$$\lim_{n\to\infty} M(x_n, x, t) = 1. \text{ A FMS } (X, M, *) \text{ is called complete, iff every Cauchy sequence} \dashrightarrow x \ \forall x \ in \ X$$

Definition 2. [13] If $(X, M, *)$ is a FMS. Then, a mapping M is called continuous on $X \times X \times (0, \infty)$ if

$$\lim_{n\to\infty} M(x_{n+p,} y_n, t) = M(x, y, t)$$

When $\{(x_n, y_n, t_n)\}$ is the seq. in $X \times X \times (0, \infty)$ which conv. to $(x, y, t) \in X \times X \times (0, \infty)$, *i.e.*,

$$lim_{n\to\infty} M(x_{n+p}, x_n, t) = \lim_{n\to\infty} M(y_{n+p}, y_n, t) = 1 \text{ and}$$
$$\lim_{n\to\infty} M(x, y, t_n) = M(x, y, t).$$

Definition 3. [16] Let $\mathcal{CB}(X)$ is taken as the set of all nonempty closed bounded subsets of X. Then $\forall\ C,B,A \in \mathcal{CB}(X)$ and $t > 0$,

$$M_{\bar{\vee}}(A,B,t) = \min\{\min_{a\in A} M^{\bar{\vee}}(a,B,t), \min_{b\in B} M^{\bar{\vee}}(A,b,t)\}$$

Where $M^{\bar{\vee}}(C,y,t) = \max\{M(z,y,t\} : z \in C\}$.

9.3 FSMS

.If $\tilde{X}$ is an absolute SS,
$SP(\tilde{X})$ = collection of all soft points collections in $\tilde{X}$.
$\mathbb{R}(E^*)$ = set of all non-negative soft real numbers.
$[0,1](E)$ = soft real number in closed interval 0 and 1
$(0, \infty)(E)$ = soft real no $\in (0, \infty)$

Definition 4. A SFS, $S \in \tilde{X}$ is a set of ordered pairs:

$$S = \left\{\left(\widetilde{x_e}, \mu_s(\widetilde{x_e})\right) : \widetilde{x_e} \in \tilde{X}, e \in E\right\},$$

Where
$\mu_s : \tilde{X} \rightarrow [0,1](E)$ = soft membership function
$\mu_s(\widetilde{x_e})$ = grade of soft membership of $(\widetilde{x_e}) \in$ S.

Definition 5. [17]
$\tilde{*} : [0,1](E) \times [0,1](E) \rightarrow [0,1](E). \tilde{*}$ is said to be continuous soft t-norm if:

(i). $\tilde{*}$ is commutative and associativite;
(ii). $\tilde{*}$ is continuous;
(iii). $\tilde{a} \tilde{*} \tilde{1} = \tilde{a}, \forall \tilde{a} \tilde{\in} [0,1](E)$.
(iv). $\tilde{a} \tilde{*} \tilde{b} \tilde{\leq} \tilde{c} \tilde{*} \tilde{d}$, if $\tilde{a} \leq \tilde{c}, \tilde{b} \tilde{\leq} \tilde{d}$ *and* $\tilde{a}, \tilde{b}, \tilde{c}, \tilde{d} \tilde{\in}$ $[0,1](E)$.

Definition 6. [3] A mapping d: $FSC(\widetilde{F_G}) \times FSC(\widetilde{F_G}) \rightarrow \mathbb{R}(A)^*$ is said to be a FSM on FE:

$$(FSM_1)\, d\left(\widetilde{F_{g^1}}, \widetilde{F_{g^2}}\right) \geq 0 \forall \widetilde{F_{g^1}}, \widetilde{F_{g^2}} \in FSM(\widetilde{F_G}).$$

$$(FSM_2)\, d\left(\widetilde{F_{g^1}}, \widetilde{F_{g^2}}\right) = 0 \; if \; and \; only \; if \; \widetilde{F_{g^1}} = \widetilde{F_{g^2}}$$

$$(FSM_3)\, d\left(\widetilde{F_{g^1}},\widetilde{F_{g^2}}\right)=d(\widetilde{F_{g^1}},\widetilde{F_{g^2}})\forall \widetilde{F_{g^1}},\widetilde{F_{g^2}} \in FSM(\widetilde{F_G})$$

$$(FSM_4)\, d\left(\widetilde{F_{g^1}},\widetilde{F_{g^2}}\right)=d(\widetilde{F_{g^1}},\widetilde{F_{g^2}})+d(\widetilde{F_{g^2}},\widetilde{F_{g^3}})\forall \widetilde{F_{g^1}},\widetilde{F_{g^2}},\widetilde{F_{g^3}} \in FSM(\widetilde{F_G})$$

Definition 7. [3]

$$(\widetilde{F_G},d,\tilde{*})=\text{FSMS}$$

$\widetilde{H_G}$, = fuzzy soft subspace of $\widetilde{F_G}$,
$d\left(\tilde{F}_g,\widetilde{H_G}\right)=\sup\left\{\frac{d\left(\widetilde{Fg},\widetilde{H_G}\right)}{for} every\ fuzzy\ soft\ point\ \tilde{F}_g\ in\ \widetilde{H_G}\right\}$ = distance between $\tilde{F}_g$ *and* $\widetilde{H_G}$,

Definition 8. [4] A FSMS $(\widetilde{F_G},d,\tilde{*})$ is known to be complete, if every Cauchy seq ⇢ some FS point of $\widetilde{F_G}$

Definition 9 [3] If $(\tilde{E},\tilde{d})$, $(\widetilde{E'},\tilde{\rho})$ are two FSMS.
The mappings $\varphi_\psi=(\varphi,\psi:(\tilde{E},\tilde{d})\rightarrow(\widetilde{E'},\tilde{\rho})$ is called a fuzzy soft mapping, if $\varphi:\tilde{E}\rightarrow\widetilde{E'}$ and $\psi: E\rightarrow\widetilde{E'}$ are two mappings.

Definition 9. [1] If $A \subseteq E$. (F, A) is said to be a SS over (X, E), if F is a mapping $F: A \rightarrow P(X)$.

Example 1. Let $\mathcal{U}$ be a non-empty finite subset of parameters and $(\widetilde{F_G},d,\tilde{*})$ be a fuzzy soft metric space. The mapping $T: \widetilde{F_G}\rightarrow G(\widetilde{F_G})\times\tilde{\mathbb{R}}\rightarrow\tilde{I}$

$$T(\tilde{u},\tilde{v},t)=minM_e(\tilde{u}(e),\tilde{v}(e),\tilde{t}(e))$$

will be fuzzy metric on $G(\widetilde{F_G})$.

Example 2. Let $X=\{3,9,\ldots\ldots\ldots 3^n\}\cup M(x_1,x_2,t)=|x_1-x_2|$, for $x_1,x_2\in X$; then X will be called complete FSMS. We say a $(\alpha-\beta)-\psi-$ contractive mapping $(T,\varphi):\widetilde{F_G}\rightarrow G(\widetilde{F_G})$ as

$$T(x_1)=\begin{cases}\{3^n,1\}, & x=3^n, n=0,1,2,3\ldots \\ \{0,3\}, & x=0.\end{cases}$$

Hence T is continuous.

9.4 Main Results

If $(\widetilde{F_G},d,\tilde{*})$ is a complete FSMS, if $T\colon \widetilde{F_G}\to G(\widetilde{F_G})$ is a $(\alpha-\beta)-\psi-$CM, we define a mapping $h\colon \widetilde{F_G}\to 2^{\widetilde{F_G}}\setminus\{0\}$ as $h(\widetilde{F_G})=(\alpha-\beta)-\psi-(\widetilde{F_G},T(\widetilde{F_G}))$ for $b\in(0,1]$. We define a set

$$(\alpha-\beta)-\psi-J_b^{\widetilde{F_G}}\in\widetilde{F_G}$$

As

$$(\alpha-\beta)-\psi-J_b^{\widetilde{F_G}}=\Big\{\widetilde{F^{g'}}\in T(\widetilde{F_G}):b\big[d(\alpha-\beta)-\psi-\big(\widetilde{F_G},\widetilde{F^{g'}}\big)$$
$$+d\big(T(\widetilde{F_G}),T(\widetilde{F^{g'}})\big)\le d\big(\widetilde{F^{g'}},T\big(\widetilde{F^{g''}}\big)\big)\Big\}.$$

Definition 10. Let $T:FSMS(\tilde{E})\to FSMS(\tilde{E})$ *and* $(\alpha-\beta)-\psi$: $FSMS(\tilde{E})\to FSMS(\tilde{E})\to\mathcal{R}(E)$. Then T will be FS $(\alpha-\beta)-\psi$-admissible,

When $\widetilde{F^{g'}},\widetilde{F^{g''}}\,\tilde{\in}\,FSMS(\tilde{E})$

$$(\alpha-\beta)-\psi-\big(\widetilde{F^{g'}},\widetilde{F^{g''}}\big)\le\tilde{1}\Rightarrow(\alpha-\beta)-\psi-(T\widetilde{F^{g'}},\widetilde{F^{g''}})\,\tilde{\le}\,\tilde{1}$$

Definition 11. If $(\widetilde{F_G},d,\tilde{*})$ is a complete FSMS and $(T,\varphi):\widetilde{F_G}\to G(\widetilde{F_G})$ is a given FS mapping. Then (T,φ) is FS $(\alpha-\beta)-\psi-$CM, if $\exists$ two FS functions $((\alpha-\beta),\varnothing):FSMS(\tilde{E})\to FSMS(\tilde{E})\to\mathcal{R}(E),\psi\,\tilde{\in}\,\Psi$:

$$((\alpha-\beta),\varnothing\big(\widetilde{F^{g'}},\widetilde{F^{g''}}\big)\tilde{d}\big((T,\varphi)\widetilde{F^{g'}},(T,\varphi)\widetilde{F^{g''}}\big)\,\tilde{\le}\,\psi\big(\tilde{d}\big(\widetilde{F^{g'}},\widetilde{F^{g''}}\big)\big),\forall\widetilde{F^{g'}},\widetilde{F^{g''}}\in FSMS(\tilde{E}).$$

Theorem 1. If $(\widetilde{F_G},d,\tilde{*})$ is a complete FSMS, $T:\widetilde{F_G}\to G(\widetilde{F_G})$ is a $(\alpha-\beta)-\psi-$CM. If $\exists\, k\in(0,1)$:

For any $\widetilde{F_G} \in \widetilde{F_G}$ $\exists$ $\widetilde{F^{g'}} \in J_b^{\widetilde{F_G}}$ satisfying

$$d\left(\widetilde{F^{g'}},T\left(\widetilde{F^{g'}}\right)\right) \leq k(\alpha-\beta)-\psi - \left[\begin{array}{c} d(\alpha-\psi)\left(\widetilde{F_G},\widetilde{F^{g'}}\right)+d(\alpha-\psi)\left(T\left(\widetilde{F_G}\right),T\left(\widetilde{F^{g'}}\right)\right) \\ +d(\alpha-\psi)\left(T\left(\widetilde{F^{g'}}\right),T\left(\widetilde{F_G}\right)\right) \end{array}\right], \quad (9.1)$$

Where $J_b^{\widetilde{F_G}} =$

$$\{\widetilde{F^{g'}} \in T(\widetilde{F_G}): b\left\{\begin{array}{c} d(\alpha-\psi)\left(\widetilde{F_G},\widetilde{F^{g'}}\right)+d(\alpha-\psi)\left(T\left(\widetilde{F^{g'}}\right),T(\widetilde{F_G})\right] \\ \leq d(\alpha-\psi)\left(\widetilde{F^{g'}},T\left(\widetilde{F^{g'}}\right)\right)+d(\alpha-\psi)\left(T\left(\widetilde{F^{g'}}\right),\widetilde{F^{g'}}\right) \end{array}\right\}.$$

Then This is a FP in $\widetilde{F_G}$.

Theorem 2. If $(\widetilde{F_G},d,\tilde{*})$ is a complete FSMS and let $T:\widetilde{F_G}\rightarrow G(\widetilde{F_G})$ be a $(\alpha-\beta)-\psi$ –CM. If $\exists$ $k \in (0,1)$:

For any $\widetilde{F_G} \in \widetilde{F_G}$ $\exists$ $\widetilde{F^{g'}} \in J_b^{\widetilde{F_G}}$ satisfying

$$d\left(\widetilde{F^{g'}},T\left(\widetilde{F^{g'}}\right)\right) \leq k(\alpha-\beta)-\psi - \left[\begin{array}{c} d\left(\widetilde{F_G},\widetilde{F^{g'}}\right)+d\left(T\left(\widetilde{F_G}\right),T\left(\widetilde{F^{g'}}\right)\right) \\ +d\left(T\left(\widetilde{F^{g'}}\right),T\left(\widetilde{F_G}\right)\right) \end{array}\right], \quad (9.2)$$

Where $J_b^{\widetilde{F_G}} =$

$$\{\widetilde{F^{g'}} \in T(\widetilde{F_G}): b\left\{\begin{array}{c} d\left(\widetilde{F_G},\widetilde{F^{g'}}\right)+d\left(T\left(\widetilde{F^{g'}}\right),T(\widetilde{F_G})\right] \\ \leq d\left(\widetilde{F^{g'}},T\left(\widetilde{F^{g'}}\right)\right)+d\left(T\left(\widetilde{F^{g'}}\right),\widetilde{F^{g'}}\right) \end{array}\right\}.$$

Then This is a fixed point in $\widetilde{F_G}$.

Proof: For $\widetilde{F_G} \in \widetilde{F_G}$, $T(\widetilde{F_G}) \in G(\widetilde{F_G})$. For any constant $b \in (0,1) J_b^{\widetilde{F_G}}$ is nonempty.

For $\widetilde{F_1^g} \in \widetilde{F_G}, \exists\, \widetilde{F_1^g} \in J_b^{\widetilde{F_0^g}}$ such that

$$d\left(\widetilde{F_1^g}, T\left(\widetilde{F_1^g}\right)\right) \leq k(\alpha-\beta) - \psi - d\left[\begin{array}{c}\left(\widetilde{F_0^g}, \widetilde{F_1^g}\right) + d\left(\widetilde{F_0^g}, T\left(\widetilde{F_1^g}\right)\right) \\ +d\left(T\left(\widetilde{F_0^g}\right), \widetilde{F_1^g}\right) + d(\widetilde{F_1^g}, T\left(\widetilde{F_0^g}\right)\end{array}\right],$$

For $\widetilde{F_1^g} \in \widetilde{F_G}, \exists\, \widetilde{F_2^g} \in J_b^{\widetilde{F_1^g}}$, satisfying

$$d\left(\widetilde{F_2^g}, T\left(\widetilde{F_2^g}\right)\right) \leq k(\alpha-\beta) - \psi - \{d\left(\widetilde{F_1^g}, \widetilde{F_2^g}\right) + d\left[\begin{array}{c}\widetilde{F_1^g}, T\left(\widetilde{F_2^g}\right) \\ +d\left(T\left(\widetilde{F_1^g}\right), \widetilde{F_2^g}\right) + d\left(\widetilde{F_2^g}, T\left(\widetilde{F_1^g}\right)\right)\end{array}\right]$$

taking this process, a sequence $\left\{\widetilde{F_n^g}\right\} \subset \widetilde{F_G}$ will be obtained:

$$\widetilde{F_{n+1}^g} \in J_b^{\widetilde{F_n^g}}$$

And

$$d\left(\widetilde{F_{n+1}^g}, T\left(\widetilde{F_{n+1}^g}\right)\right) \leq k(\alpha-\beta) - \psi - \left[d\left(\widetilde{F_n^g}, \widetilde{F_{n+1}^g}\right) + d\left(\begin{array}{c}\widetilde{F_n^g}, T\left(\widetilde{F_{n+1}^g}\right)\right) \\ +d(T\left(\widetilde{F_n^g}\right), \widetilde{F_{n+1}^g}\end{array}\right)\right],$$

$$n = 0, 1, 2, 3, 4, \ldots\ldots\ldots\ldots$$

Now we will show $\left\{\widetilde{F_n^g}\right\}$ Cauchy sequence in $\widetilde{F_G}$.

On the one hand,

$$d\left(\widetilde{F_{n+1}^{g}},T\left(\widetilde{F_{n+1}^{g}}\right)\right)\leq k(\alpha-\beta)-\psi-\left[\begin{array}{c}d\left(\widetilde{F_{n}^{g}},\widetilde{F_{n+1}^{g}}\right)+d\left(\widetilde{F_{n}^{g}},T\left(\widetilde{F_{n+1}^{g}}\right)\right)\\ +d(\alpha-\beta)\left(T\left(\widetilde{F_{n}^{g}}\right),\widetilde{F_{n+1}^{g}}\right)+d\left(\widetilde{F_{n+1}^{g}},T\left(\widetilde{F_{n}^{g}}\right)\right)\end{array}\right],$$
$$n=0,1,2,3,4,\ldots\ldots\ldots\ldots$$

And from the other hand

$$\widetilde{F_{n+1}^{g}}\in J_{b}^{\widetilde{F_{n}^{g}}}\Rightarrow b(\alpha-\beta)-\psi-\left[\begin{array}{c}d\left(\widetilde{F_{n}^{g}},\widetilde{F_{n+1}^{g}}\right)\\ +d(\alpha-\beta)\left(T\left(\widetilde{F_{n}^{g}}\right),T\left(\widetilde{F_{n+1}^{g}}\right)\right)\end{array}\right]$$
$$\leq d(\alpha-\beta)\left(\widetilde{F_{n+1}^{g}},T\left(\widetilde{F_{n+1}^{g}}\right)\right),$$
$$n=0,1,2,3,4,\ldots\ldots\ldots\ldots$$

By the above inequalities we have

$$d(\alpha-\beta)\left(\widetilde{F_{n+1}^{g}},\widetilde{F_{n+2}^{g}}\right)+d(\alpha-\beta)\left(T\left(\widetilde{F_{n+1}^{g}}\right),T\left(\widetilde{F_{n+2}^{g}}\right)\right)$$
$$\leq\frac{k}{b}\left[d(\alpha-\beta)-\psi-\left(\widetilde{F_{n}^{g}},\widetilde{F_{n+1}^{g}}\right)\right],\qquad n=0,1,2,3,4,\ldots\ldots\ldots\ldots$$
$$d(\alpha-\beta)-\psi-\left(\widetilde{F_{n+1}^{g}},T\left(\widetilde{F_{n+1}^{g}}\right)\right)$$
$$\leq\frac{k}{b}\left[(\alpha-\beta)-\psi-\left(\widetilde{F_{n}^{g}},T\left(\widetilde{F_{n+1}^{g}}\right)\right)\right],\qquad n=0,1,2,3,4,\ldots\ldots\ldots\ldots$$

Hence, easy to prove,

$$d(\alpha-\beta)-\psi-\left(\widetilde{F_{n}^{g}},\widetilde{F_{n+1}^{g}}\right)+d(\alpha-\beta)\left(T\left(\widetilde{F_{n}^{g}}\right),T\left(\widetilde{F_{n+1}^{g}}\right)\right)$$
$$\leq C^{n}\left[d(\alpha-\beta)\left(\widetilde{F_{0}^{g}},\widetilde{F_{1}^{g}}\right)\right],$$
$$n=0,1,2,3,4,\ldots\ldots\ldots\ldots$$
$$d(\alpha-\beta)-\psi-\left(\widetilde{F_{n}^{g}},T(\widetilde{F_{n}^{g}})\right)\leq C^{n}d(\alpha-\beta)(\widetilde{F_{0}^{g}},\widetilde{F_{1}^{g}}),\qquad n=0,1,2,3,4,\ldots\ldots\ldots\ldots$$

Where C is k/b

$\forall$ *m and n are elements of* G and m is greater than n

$$d(\alpha-\beta)-\psi-\left(\widetilde{F_n^g},\widetilde{F_m^g}\right)$$
$$\leq d(\alpha-\beta)\left(\widetilde{F_n^g},\widetilde{F_{n+1}^g}\right)+d(\alpha-\beta)\left(\widetilde{F_{n+1}^g},\widetilde{F_{n+2}^g}\right)+\ldots\ldots\ldots\ldots$$
$$+d(\alpha-\beta)\left(\widetilde{F_{m-1}^g},\widetilde{F_m^g}\right)$$
$$\leq(C^n+C^{n+1}+\ldots\ldots\ldots\ldots+C^{u-1})d(\alpha-\beta)-\psi-(\widetilde{F_0^g},\widetilde{F_1^g})$$
$$\leq\frac{C^n}{1-C}d(\alpha-\beta)-\psi-(\widetilde{F_0^g},\widetilde{F_1^g})$$

Where $C=\frac{k}{b}$, since $k<b\Rightarrow C^n\rightarrow 0\,as\,n\rightarrow\infty\Rightarrow\left\{\widetilde{F_n^g}\right\}$ is a Cauchy sequence, taken by the completeness of $\widetilde{F_G},\exists\,\widetilde{F_G}\in\widetilde{F_G}$ such that $lim_{n\rightarrow\infty}\widetilde{F_n^g}=\widetilde{F_G}$.

Now we will show that $\widetilde{F_G}$ is a fixed point of T, i.e. $\widetilde{F_G}\in T(\widetilde{F_G})$. Since $\left\{\widetilde{F_n^g}\right\}$ is a Cauchy sequence converging to $\widetilde{F_G}$ and $\left\{h\left(\widetilde{F_n^g}\right)\right\}=\left\{d\left(\widetilde{F_n^g},T(\widetilde{F_n^g}\right)\right\}$ is decreasing, therefore, converges to 0. h Being lower semi-continuous, therefore, we have $0\leq h(\widetilde{F_G})\leq\frac{lim}{v\rightarrow\infty}h\left(\widetilde{F_n^g}\right)=0\Rightarrow h(\widetilde{F_G})=0$. Also by closeness of $T(\widetilde{F_G})\Rightarrow\widetilde{F_G}\in T(\widetilde{F_G})$

Hence the result.

Corollary 1. If $(\widetilde{F_G},d,*)$ is a complete FSMS space, $T:\widetilde{F_G}\mapsto k(\widetilde{F_G})$ be a $(\alpha-\beta)-\psi$ –CM. If $k\in(0,1)$:

For any $\widetilde{F_G}\in\widetilde{F_G},\widetilde{F^{g'}}\in J_b^{\widetilde{F_G}}$,

$$d(\alpha-\beta)-\psi\left(\widetilde{F^{g'}},T\left(\widetilde{F^{g'}}\right)\right)\leq k(\alpha-\beta)-\psi-\left[d\left(\widetilde{F_G},\widetilde{F^{g'}}\right)\right],$$

Then T has a fixed point in $\widetilde{F_G}$.

9.5 Fuzzy Soft $\tilde{\alpha}-\tilde{\psi}$–Contractive Type Mappings and $\tilde{\alpha}$ – Admissible Mappings

Now we prove FS $\tilde{\alpha}-\tilde{\psi}$ –CM type mappings and $\tilde{\alpha}-$*admissible* mappings in FSMS

Let $\tilde{\psi}:[0,\infty)\to[0,1]$:

$$\sum_{n=1}^{\infty}\tilde{\psi}^{n}(t)=1\forall t>0,$$

where $\tilde{\psi}^{n}$ = nth iteration of $\tilde{\psi}$.

Lemma 1. $\tilde{\psi}:[0,\infty)\to[0,1]$:
Let $\tilde{\psi}$ be decreasing, $\Rightarrow\forall\tilde{t}>0, \lim_{n\to\infty}\psi^{n}(\tilde{t})=1\Rightarrow\psi(\tilde{t})>1$.

Definition 12. Let (X, d) be a metric space If $T:X\to X$ is a function, where (X,d) is metric space.

T is an $\alpha-\psi$ –CM if $\exists$ two functions α: $X\times X\to[0,+\infty)$, $\psi\in\Psi$:

$$\alpha(x, y)d(Tx, Ty)\leq\psi(d(x, y))$$

$$\forall\, x, y\in X.$$

Definition 13. If $(\tilde{X},\tilde{F}_g,\tilde{*})$ is FSMS and $\tilde{T}:\tilde{X}\to\tilde{X}$. Then $\tilde{T}$ is an $\tilde{\alpha}-\tilde{\psi}$ –CM if $\exists$ functions $\tilde{\alpha}$: $\tilde{X}\times\tilde{X}\to[0,+\infty)$ and $\psi\in\Psi$:

$$\tilde{\alpha}(\tilde{x},\tilde{y})\tilde{F}_g(\widetilde{Tx},\widetilde{Ty},\tilde{t})\tilde{\geq}\tilde{\psi}\left(\tilde{F}_g(\tilde{x},\tilde{y},\tilde{t}\right)$$

For all $\tilde{x},\tilde{y}$ *are in* $\tilde{X}$.

Definition 14. If $\tilde{T}:\tilde{X}\to\tilde{X}$, $\tilde{\alpha}$: $\tilde{X}\times\tilde{X}\times[0,\infty)\to[0,1]$.
Then $\tilde{T}$ is $\tilde{\alpha}$ –admissible if $\tilde{x},\tilde{y}\in\tilde{X},\tilde{\alpha}(\tilde{x},\tilde{y},\tilde{t})\leq1\Rightarrow\alpha(\widetilde{Tx},\widetilde{Ty},\tilde{t})\leq1$.

Example 3. Taking b $\tilde{X}=[0,1]$.

$\tilde{T}:\tilde{X}\to\tilde{X},\tilde{\alpha}:\tilde{X}\times\tilde{X}\times[0,\infty)\to[0,1]$ by

$$\widetilde{Tx} = \begin{cases} \tilde{x}^{1/3}, & \textit{if } \tilde{X} \textit{ is in closed interbal } 0 \textit{ and } 1 \\ \textit{zero} & \textit{otherwise} \end{cases}$$

And

$$\tilde{\alpha}(\tilde{x},\tilde{y},\tilde{t}) = \begin{cases} 1 \textit{ if } \tilde{x},\tilde{y} \textit{ are in closed interbal } 0 \textit{ and } 1 \\ \textit{zero} \qquad \textit{otherwise} \end{cases}$$

$\tilde{T}$ will be $\tilde{\alpha}$ –admissible.

Theorem 3. Suppose $(\tilde{X},\tilde{F}_g,\tilde{*})$ is a complete FSMS and $\tilde{T}:\tilde{X}\rightarrow\tilde{X}$ is a $\tilde{\alpha}-\tilde{\psi}-$ CM:

(i) $\tilde{T}$ will be soft $\tilde{\alpha}$ –admissible;
(ii) $\exists\,\tilde{x}_0 \in \tilde{X} \Rightarrow \alpha(\widetilde{X_0},\widetilde{TX_0},\tilde{t})\tilde{\leq}\tilde{1}$
(iii) $\tilde{T}$ is taken to be soft Continuous.

$\tilde{T}$ will contain unique FP, $\Rightarrow x^{*}\tilde{\in}X:\widetilde{TX^{*}}=X^{*}$.

Proof. Let $\tilde{x}_0 \in \tilde{X}:\alpha(\widetilde{X_0},\widetilde{TX_0},\tilde{t})\tilde{\leq}\tilde{1}$.
Taking seq. $\{\tilde{x}_n\}\in\tilde{X}:\tilde{x}_{n+1}=\widetilde{TX}_n\ \forall\, n\in N$

If $\tilde{x}_n=\tilde{x}_{n+1}$ for some $n \in N$, then $\tilde{x}^{*}=\widetilde{X_n}$ is a fixed point for $\tilde{T}$. Assume that $\tilde{x}^{*}\neq\widetilde{X_n}$ for all $n \in N$. since $\tilde{T}$ is a soft $\tilde{\alpha}$ –admissible, we have

$$\tilde{\alpha}(\widetilde{X_0},\widetilde{X_1},\tilde{t})=\tilde{\alpha}(\widetilde{X_0},\widetilde{TX_0},\tilde{t})\tilde{\leq}\tilde{1}$$
$$\Rightarrow\tilde{\alpha}(\widetilde{TX_0},\widetilde{TX_1},\tilde{t})=\tilde{\alpha}(\widetilde{X_1},\widetilde{X_2},\tilde{t})\tilde{\leq}\tilde{1}$$

By Mathematical-induction, we get

$$\tilde{\alpha}\left(\widetilde{X_n},\widetilde{X_{n+1}},\tilde{t}\right)\tilde{\leq}\tilde{1}n\in N$$

Using Equation (9.1) with $X=\tilde{x}_{n-1}$, $\tilde{y}=\tilde{x}_n$ and using Equation (9.2) we obtain

$$\tilde{F}_g\left(\widetilde{X_n},\widetilde{X_{n+1}},\tilde{t}\right)=\tilde{F}_g\left(\widetilde{TX_{n-1}},\widetilde{TX_n},\tilde{t}\right)\tilde{\geq}\tilde{\alpha}\left(\widetilde{X_{n-1}},\widetilde{X_n},\tilde{t}\right)\tilde{F}_g\left(\widetilde{TX_{n-1}},\widetilde{TX_n},\tilde{t}\right)$$
$$\tilde{\geq}\psi\left(\tilde{F}_g\widetilde{X_{n-1}},\widetilde{X_n},\tilde{t}\right)$$

By induction, we get

$$\tilde{F}_g\left(\widetilde{X_n},\widetilde{X_{n+1}},\tilde{t}\right)\tilde{\geq}\psi^n\tilde{F}_g\left(\widetilde{X_0},\widetilde{X_1},\tilde{t}\right)\forall n\in N$$

Let $n \in N$ and $\tilde{t}\,\tilde{\geq}\, 0$. For any p the positive integer

$$\tilde{F}_g\left(\widetilde{X_n},\widetilde{X_{n+p}},\tilde{t}\right)\tilde{\geq}\tilde{F}_g\left(\widetilde{X_n},\widetilde{X_{n+1}},\frac{\tilde{t}}{p}\right)*\tilde{F}_g\left(\widetilde{X_{n+1}},\widetilde{X_{n+2}},\frac{\tilde{t}}{p}\right)*\ldots*\tilde{F}_g\left(\widetilde{X_{n+p-1}},\widetilde{X_{n+p}},\frac{\tilde{t}}{p}\right)$$

$$\lim_{n\to\infty}\tilde{F}_g\left(\widetilde{X_n},\widetilde{X_{n+p}},\tilde{t}\right)\tilde{\geq}\tilde{1}*\ldots*\tilde{1}$$

Therefore $\{\tilde{x}_n\}$ is a Cauchy sequence in FSMS $(\tilde{X},\tilde{F}_g,\tilde{*})$, so convergent.
While $(\tilde{X},\tilde{F}_g,\tilde{*})$ is complete, $\exists\,\widetilde{x^*}\in\tilde{X}\Rightarrow\widetilde{X_n}\to\widetilde{x^*}$ as $n\to\infty$.

$$\tilde{X}_{n+1}=\tilde{T}\tilde{X}_n\to\widetilde{TX}^*\ as\ n\to\infty\ (because\ of\ continuity)$$

$\Rightarrow X^*=\widetilde{TX^*}$, i.e. $\widetilde{x^*}$ is a unique FP of $\tilde{T}$.

Theorem 4. If $(\tilde{X},\tilde{F}_g,\tilde{*})$ is a complete FSMS and $\tilde{T}:\tilde{X}\to\tilde{X}$ is a $\tilde{\alpha}-\tilde{\psi}$ –CM:

i. $\tilde{T}$ taken to be soft $\tilde{\alpha}$ –admissible;
ii. $\exists\,\tilde{x}_0\in\tilde{X}\Rightarrow\tilde{\alpha}(\widetilde{X_0},\widetilde{TX_0},\tilde{t})\tilde{\leq}\tilde{1}$
iii. If $\{\tilde{x}_n\}$ is a sequence in X: $\tilde{\alpha}\left(\widetilde{X_n},\widetilde{X_{n+1}},\tilde{t}\right)\tilde{\leq}\tilde{1}$ *for all n and* $\widetilde{X_n}\to\tilde{X}\in\tilde{X}$ as $n\to\infty$, then $\tilde{\alpha}\left(\widetilde{X_n},\tilde{X},\tilde{t}\right)\tilde{\leq}\tilde{1}$ *for all n.*

Then $\tilde{T}$ has a unique FP.

Proof. As the proof of *Theorem 3*, and $\{\tilde{x}_n\}$ being a Cauchy sequence in complete FSMS $(\tilde{X},\tilde{F}_g,\tilde{*})$. Then, $\exists\,\widetilde{x^*}\in\tilde{X}:\widetilde{X_n}\to\widetilde{X^*}$ *as* $n\to\infty$. And other side, form (2) & the hypothesis (iii) we have $\alpha\left(\widetilde{X_n},\widetilde{X^*},\tilde{t}\right)\tilde{\leq}\tilde{1}$ *for all n.*

From Equations (9.1), (9.3) we get and applying triangular axiom

$$\tilde{F}_g(\widetilde{TX^*},\widetilde{X^*},\tilde{t})\tilde{\geq}\tilde{F}_g\left(\widetilde{TX^*},\widetilde{TX_n},\frac{\tilde{t}}{2}\right)*\tilde{F}_g\left(\widetilde{TX_n},\widetilde{TX^*},\frac{\tilde{t}}{2}\right)\tilde{\geq}\tilde{\alpha}\left(\widetilde{X_n},\widetilde{X^*},\frac{\tilde{t}}{2}\right)$$

$$*\tilde{F}_g\left(\widetilde{TX_n},\widetilde{TX^*},\frac{\tilde{t}}{2}\right)\tilde{\geq}\psi\left(\tilde{F}_g\left(\widetilde{X_n},\widetilde{X^*},\frac{\tilde{t}}{2}\right)*\tilde{F}_g\left(\widetilde{TX_{n+1}},\widetilde{X^*},\frac{\tilde{t}}{2}\right)\right)$$

Taking $n \to \infty$, at $t = 1 \Rightarrow \tilde{F}_g(\widetilde{TX^*}, \widetilde{X^*}, \tilde{t}) = 1$

$$\Rightarrow \widetilde{TX^*} = \widetilde{X^*}.$$

Example 4. If $\tilde{X}$ *is taken as colsed interbal* 0 *and* 1 with the standard FSM, define $\tilde{u} * \tilde{v} = \tilde{u}\tilde{v} \, \forall \, \tilde{u}, \tilde{v} \in [0,1]$,

$$\tilde{F}_g(\widetilde{x^*}, \widetilde{y^*}, \tilde{t}) = \frac{\tilde{t}}{\forall \tilde{t} + |\widetilde{x^*} - \widetilde{y^*}|}, \ \forall \widetilde{x^*}, \widetilde{y^*} \in \tilde{X}$$

$$\forall \tilde{t} > 0, \tilde{T} : \tilde{X} \to \tilde{X} \text{ by}$$

$$\widetilde{Tx} = \begin{cases} \widetilde{x/2}, & \text{if } 0 \precsim \tilde{x} \precsim 1' \\ 0, & \text{if } \tilde{x} < zero. \end{cases}$$

It is clear that FS contraction theory will be true in this condition

$$\tilde{F}_g(\widetilde{T.5}, \widetilde{T1}, \tilde{t}) \gtrsim \tilde{F}_g(.5, 1, \tilde{t}) = .5 < 1.$$

Defining $\tilde{\alpha} : \tilde{X} \times \tilde{X} \times [0, \infty) \to [0,1]$:

$$\tilde{\alpha}(\tilde{x}, \tilde{y}, \tilde{t}) = \begin{cases} 1 & \text{if } \tilde{x}, \tilde{y} \text{ are in closed interbal } 0 \text{ and } 1 \\ & zero, \quad otherwise. \end{cases}$$

Clearly $\tilde{T}$ is a $\tilde{\alpha} - \tilde{\psi}$ –contractive mapping with $\psi(\tilde{t}) = \frac{\tilde{t}}{2}$ *for all* $\tilde{t} \geq 0$.

Clearly T is continuous. To complete the proof we will prove that $\tilde{T}$ is soft $\tilde{\alpha}$ –admissible.

Now $\tilde{x}, \tilde{y}$ are taken two arbitrary elements of X:

$\tilde{\alpha}(\tilde{x}, \tilde{y}, \tilde{t}) \precsim \tilde{1} \Rightarrow \tilde{x}, \tilde{y}$ will be in closed interval 0 and 1

we have

$$\widetilde{Tx} = \frac{\tilde{x}}{2} \in [0,1], \ \widetilde{Ty} = \frac{\tilde{y}}{2} \in [0,1] \, and \, \tilde{\alpha}(\widetilde{Tx}, T\tilde{y}, \tilde{t}) = 1.$$

Then $\tilde{T}$ is soft $\tilde{\alpha}$ –admissible.

References

1. Ahmad, B. and Kharal, A., On Fuzzy Soft Sets. *Adv. Fuzzy Syst.*, 2009, Article ID 586507, 6 pages, 2009.
2. Ayglu, A. and Aygn, H., Introduction to fuzzy soft groups. *Comput. Math. Appl.*, 58, 1279–1286, 2009.
3. Beaulaa, T. and Gunaseeli, C., On fuzzy soft metric spaces. *Malaya J. Mat.*, 2, 3, 197–202, 2014.
4. Beaulaa, T. and Raja, R., Completeness in Fuzzy Soft Metric Space. *Malaya J. Mat. S*, 2, 438–442, 2015.
5. Chang, C.L., Fuzzy topological spaces. *J. Math. Anal. Appl.*, 24, 191–201, 1968.
6. Cagman, N., Citak, F., Enginoglu, S., Fuzzy parameterized fuzzy soft set theory and its applications. *Turk. J. Fuzzy Syst.*, 1, 21–35, 2010.
7. Cagman, N., Citak, F., Enginoglu, S., FP-soft set theory and its applications. *Ann. Fuzzy Math. Inform.*, 2, 2, 219–226, 2011.
8. Das, S. and Samanta, S.K., Soft real sets, soft real numbers and their properties. *J. Fuzzy Math.*, 20, 3, 551–576, 2012.
9. Das, S. and Samanta, S.K., on soft metric spaces. *J. Fuzzy Math.*, 21, 707–734, 2013.
10. Feng, F., Jun, Y.B., Liu, X., Li, L., An adjustable approach to fuzzy soft set based decision making. *J. Comput. Appl. Math.*, 234, 10–20, 2010.
11. Feng, F., Liu, X.Y., Leoreanu-Fotea, V., Jun, Y.B., Soft sets and soft rough sets. *Inf. Sci.*, 181, 1125–1137, 2011.
12. Gopal, V. and Vetro, C., Some new fixed point theorems in fuzzy metric spaces. *Iran. J. Fuzzy Syst.*, 11, 95–107, 2014.
13. Grabiec, M., Fixed points in fuzzy metric spaces. *Fuzzy Sets Syst.*, 27, 385–389, 1988.
14. Gregori, V. and Sapena, A., On fixed point theorems in fuzzy metric spaces. *Fuzzy Sets Syst.*, 125, 245–252, 2002.
15. Hong, S., Fixed points for modified fuzzy contractive set-valued mappings in fuzzy metric spaces. *Fixed Point Theory Appl.*, 1, 1–12, 2014.
16. Kabir, Q.A., Verma, R., Jamal, R., fixed point theorem for contractive mapping in fuzzy soft metric spaces. *Int. J. Emerging Technol.*, 10, 2b, 114–118, 2019.
17. Maji, P.K., Biswas, R., Roy, A.R., Fuzzy soft sets. *J. Fuzzy Math.*, 9, 3, 589–602, 2001.
18. Maji, P.K., Roy, A.R., Biswas, R., An application of soft sets in a decision making problem. *Comput. Math. Appl.*, 44, 8–9, 1077–1083, 2002.
19. Maji, P.K., Biswas, R., Roy, A.R., Soft set theory. *Comput. Math. Appl.*, 45, 555–562, 2003.
20. Majumdar, P. and Samanta, S.K., Generalised fuzzy soft sets. *Comput. Math. Appl.*, 59, 1425–1432, 2010.

21. Mihet, D., A Banach contraction theorem in fuzzy metric spaces. *Fuzzy Sets Syst.*, 144, 431–439, 2004.
22. Mihet, D., On fuzzy contractive mappings in fuzzy metric spaces. *Fuzzy Sets Syst.*, 158, 915–921, 2007.
23. Molodtsov, D., Soft set theory first results. *Comput. Math. Appl.*, 37, 19–31, 1999.
24. Sayed, A.F. and Alahmari, A., Fuzzy soft α ψcontractive type mappings and some fixed point theorems in fuzzy soft metric spaces. *Ann. Fuzzy Math. Inform.*, 15, 1, 73–87, 2018.

10

Synchronization of Time-Delay Chaotic System with Uncertainties in Terms of Takagi–Sugeno Fuzzy System

Sathish Kumar Kumaravel*, **Suresh Rasappan**† and **Kala Raja Mohan**‡

Department of Mathematics, Vel Tech Dr. Rangarajan Dr. Sagunthala R & D Institute of Science and Technology, Avadi, Tamil Nadu, Chennai, India

Abstract

In this paper, the asymptotic mean square stability of an observer-based chaos synchronization to time delay fuzzy stochastic system is analyzed. Utilizing the Lyapunov stability theory, fuzzy-based stochastic system with time delay is designed, which is assumed to have asymptotic mean square stability. Fuzzy-based chaotic synchronization has been the main attention in propagation delay and system uncertainties.

Keywords: Chaos, synchronization, fuzzy, Takagi-Sugeno system, uncertainties, mean square stable, delay, Lyapunov stability

10.1 Introduction

Nowadays, the observer designs the chaotic systems which is an interesting research area. Fault detection, control engineering, state estimation, etc., are some potential applications for the observer-based control design. Fuzzy-based control is a powerful tool for controlling non-linear systems with uncertainties.

**Corresponding author*: k.sathi89@gmail.com

†*Corresponding author*: mrpsuresh83@gmail.com

‡*Corresponding author*: kalamohan24@yahoo.co.in

E. Chandrasekaran, R. Anandan, G. Suseendran, S. Balamurugan and Hanaa Hachimi (eds.) Fuzzy Intelligent Systems: Methodologies, Techniques, and Applications, (285–314) © 2021 Scrivener Publishing LLC

This paper investigates the observer-based synchronization of a time delay fuzzy chaotic system with uncertainties [1, 2]. An asymptotically mean square stability criteria is designed [4, 5]. The problem of state estimation for fuzzy-based chaotic time-delay with uncertainties in system is analyzed. A robust supervisory observer is proposed.

When the fuzzy time-delay chaotic systems are subjected to system uncertainties and external disturbances, a robust supervisory control can accelerate the convergence speed of the synchronization error between two designed systems [3, 6, 7]. For numerical simulations, MATLAB fuzzy logic tool box is utilized.

10.2 Statement of the Problem and Notions

The stochastic time-delay chaotic systems in terms of T–S fuzzy based model is described as follows:

$$\begin{aligned} &R^l : \text{If } Z_1(t_s) \text{ is } M_1^l \; and \ldots Z_j(t_s) \text{ is } M_j^l \text{ then} \\ &dx_c(t_s) = [(A_{1l}(t_s) + \Delta A_{1l}(t_s))x_c(t_s) \\ &\quad +(A_{2l}(t_s) + \Delta A_{2l}(t_s))x_c(t_s - \tau)]dt_s \\ &\quad +[(A_{3l}(t_s) + \Delta A_{3l}(t_s))x_c(t_s) \\ &\quad +(A_{4l}(t_s) + \Delta A_{4l}(t_s))x_c(t_s - \tau)]dw(t_s) \\ &y(t_s) = Cx_c(t_s), l = 1,2,3,\ldots,r. \end{aligned} \tag{10.1}$$

in which $x_c(t_s) \in \mathbb{R}^n$ represents the state space vector of the dynamics, $y(t_s) \in \mathbb{R}^m$ denotes the output of the given dynamics, $x_c(t_s - \tau)$ takes representation as delay state vector, A_{1l}, A_{2l}, A_{3l}, A_{4l} *and* C are system matrices, ΔA_{1l}, ΔA_{2l}, ΔA_{3l}, ΔA_{4l} *and* C are corresponding uncertainties. τ is considered as constant time delay, M_j^l is the fuzzy set, r is the number of fuzzy rule and $z(t_s) = [z_1(t_s), z_2(t_s), \ldots z_j(t_s)]^T$ are premise variables associated with system states.

The center of gravity defuzzification method is utilized to get the output of fuzzy time delay chaotic system which is described by

$$dx_c(t_s) = \frac{\begin{bmatrix} \sum_{l=1}^{r} W_l(z)[(A_{1l} + \Delta A_{1l}(t_s))x_c(t_s) \\ +(A_{2l} + \Delta A_{2l}(t_s))x_c(t_s - \tau)]dt_s \\ +[(A_{3l} + \Delta A_{3l}(t_s))x_c(t_s) \\ +(A_{4l} + \Delta A_{4l}(t_s))x_c(t_s - \tau)]dw(t_s) \end{bmatrix}}{\sum_{l=1}^{r} W_l(z)} \tag{10.2}$$

$$y(t_s) = Cx_c(t_s)$$

where

$$W_l(z)=\prod_{i=1}^{j} M_i^l(z_j)$$

and $M_i^l(z_j)$ is the grade membership function of M_i^l corresponding to $z_i(t_s)$ provided as

$$\mu_l(z)=\frac{w_l(z)}{\sum_{l=1}^{r} w_l(z)}$$

Therefore the state of the fuzzy system Equations (10.1) and (10.2) is given as

$$\begin{aligned}
dx_c(t_s)=&\sum_{l=1}^{r}\mu_l(z)[(A_{1l}(t_s)+\Delta A_{1l}(t_s))x_c(t_s)\\
&+(A_{2l}(t_s)+\Delta A_{2l}(t_s))x_c(t_s-\tau)]dt_s\\
&+[(A_{3l}(t_s)+\Delta A_{3l}(t_s))x_c(t_s)\\
&+(A_{4l}(t_s)+\Delta A_{4l}(t_s))x_c(t_s-\tau)]dw(t_s)\\
y(t_s)=&\,Cx_c(t_s)
\end{aligned} \tag{10.3}$$

Considering the assumptions

$$\Delta A(t_s)=\sum_{l=1}^{r}\mu_l(z)\Delta A_{1l}(t_s)$$

$$\Delta A_{d1}(t_s)=\sum_{l=1}^{r}\mu_l(z)\Delta A_{2l}(t_s)$$

$$\Delta A_{d3}(t_s)=\sum_{l=1}^{r}\mu_l(z)\Delta A_{4l}(t_s)$$

Hence, the state of the system Equation (10.3) is modified as

$$\begin{aligned} dx_c(t_s) = & \Big[\sum_{l=1}^{r} \mu_l(z)(A_{1l}(x_c(t_s)) + A_{2l}x_c(t_s - \tau)) \\ & + \Delta A(t_s)x_c(t_s) + \Delta A_{d_1} x_c(t_s - \tau)\Big]dt_s \\ & + \Big[\sum_{l=1}^{r} \mu_l(z)(A_{3l}(x_c(t_s)) + A_{4l}x_c(t_s - \tau)) \\ & + \Delta A_{d_2}(t_s)x_c(t_s) + \Delta A_{d_3}(t_s)x_c(t_s - \tau)]dw(t_s) \\ y(t_s) = & \ Cx_c(t_s) \end{aligned} \tag{10.4}$$

Consider the uncertainties forced upon the matching condition, $E_A(t_s)$ and $E_d(t_s)$ exist such that

$\Delta A(t_s) = BE_A(t_s)$, $\Delta A_d(t_s) = BE_d(t_s)$, $B \in \mathbb{R}^{n\times p}$ are known matrices.

The uncertainties in Equation (10.4) are represented as

$$\begin{aligned} \Delta A(t_s)x_c(t_s) &= B\zeta_1(x_c(t_s),t_s) \\ \Delta A_{d_1}(t_s)x_c(t_s - \tau) &= B\zeta_2(x_c(t_s - \tau),t_s) \\ \Delta A_{d_2}(t_s)x_c(t_s) &= B\zeta_3(x_c(t_s),t_s) \\ \Delta A_{d_3}(t_s)x_c(t_s - \tau) &= B\zeta_4(x_c(t_s - \tau),t_s) \end{aligned}$$

where ζ_1, ζ_2, ζ_3, ζ_4 are uncertainties, which are unknown parameters. The fuzzy observer design is under the estimation of these uncertainties.

Therefore Equation (10.4) becomes

$$\begin{aligned} dx_c(t_s) = & \Big[\sum_{l=1}^{r} \mu_l(z)(A_{1l}(x_c(t_s)) + A_{2l}x_c(t_s - \tau)) \\ & + B\zeta_1(x_c(t_s),t_s) + B\zeta_2(x_c(t_s - \tau),t_s)]dt_s \\ & + \Big[\sum_{l=1}^{r} \mu_l(z)(A_{3l}(x_c(t_s)) + A_{4l}x_c(t_s - \tau)) \\ & + B\zeta_3(x_c(t_s),t_s) + B\zeta_4(x_c(t_s - \tau),t_s)]dw(t_s) \\ y(t_s) = & \ Cx_c(t_s). \end{aligned} \tag{10.5}$$

Consider the ith order of uncertainties $\zeta_1(x_c(t_s), t_s)$, ζ_{li} as the Equation (10.5), that intended by Mamdani fuzzy inference system. Hence ζ_{1i} takes the form as

$$R^j : \text{If } x_{c1}(t_s) \text{ is } \tilde{M}_1^j \text{ and} \ldots x_n(t_s) \text{ is } \tilde{M}_n^j, \text{ then } \hat{\zeta}_{1i} \text{ is } \tilde{D}_{ij}, j = 1,2,3,4\ldots, q.$$

The output of the system Equation (10.5) is defined by

$$\hat{\zeta}_{1i}(x_c/\theta_i) = \frac{\sum_{j=1}^{q} \theta_{ij}\left(\prod_{h=1}^{n} \mu_{\tilde{M}_h^j}(x_h)\right)}{\sum_{j=1}^{q} \prod_{h=1}^{n} \mu_{\tilde{M}_h^j}(x_h)} \tag{10.6}$$

$$\hat{\zeta}_{1i}(x_c/\theta_i) = \theta_i^T \omega(x_c).$$

where $\theta_i = (\theta_{i1}, \theta_{i2}, \ldots, \theta_{iq})^T$ is a self tuning parameter, θ_{ij} represents the center of $\tilde{D}_{ij}$ for $i = 1, 2, 3, \ldots, p$; j = 1, 2, 3, …, q, and $\omega(x_c)$ that denotes the basic fuzzy function.

The estimator of ζ_1 takes the form as $\hat{\zeta}_{1i}(x_c/\theta) = \theta_i^T \omega(x_c), \theta \in \mathbb{R}^{p\times q}$.

The optimal parameter θ_* is defined by

$$\theta_* = arg\ min_{\theta\in\Omega_\theta}(sup\|\hat{\zeta}_1(x_c/\theta) - \hat{\zeta}_1(x_c(t_s),t_s)\|)$$

which satisfies

$$\|\hat{\zeta}_1(x_c/\theta^*) - \hat{\zeta}_1(x_c,t_s)\| \le \zeta_1)$$

where

$$\Omega_\theta = \left(\theta / trace(\theta^T\theta) < M_\theta^2\right),$$

The trace value of the matrix, M_θ is designed constant, ζ_1 is an unknown parameter and treated as upper bound, which satisfies the inequality

$$\|\zeta_2(x_c(t_s - \tau)), t_s\| \le \zeta_2,$$

and $\omega(x_c)$ is uniformly continuous then the existes an Lipschitz Constant

$$||\omega(x_c)-\hat{\omega}(x_c)||\leq\gamma||x-\hat{x}||.$$

Hence, the fuzzy based observer for the stochastic time-delay chaotic dynamic Equation (10.1) is defined as

R^l: If $Z_1(t_s)$ is M_1^l and ... and $Z_j(t_s)$ is M_1^l, then

$$\begin{aligned} d\hat{x}_c(t_s) &= [A_{1l}\hat{x}_c(t_s)+A_{2l}\hat{x}_c(t_s-\tau)+L_l(y(t_s)-\hat{y}(t_s)) \\ &\quad +B(\hat{\zeta}_1(\hat{x}_c)/\theta)+u_1(t_s)+u_2(t_s)]dt_s \\ &\quad +[A_{3l}\hat{x}_c(t_s)+A_{4l}\hat{x}_c(t_s-\tau)+L_l(y(t_s)-\hat{y}(t_s)) \\ &\quad +B(\hat{\zeta}_1(\hat{x}_c/\theta)+u_1(t_s)+u_2(t_s)]dw(t_s), \\ \hat{y}(t_s) &= C\hat{x}_c(t_s), l=1,2,3,\ldots,r. \end{aligned} \tag{10.7}$$

where L_l is designed feedback gain matrices, u_1 and u_2 are supervisory control.

Therefore the output of the fuzzy systems Equation (10.6) is

$$\begin{aligned} d\hat{x}_c(t_s) &= \Big[\sum_{l=1}^{r}\mu_l(z)\big[A_{1l}\hat{x}_c(t_s)+A_{2l}\hat{x}_c(t_s-\tau)+L_l(y(t_s)-\hat{y}(t_s)) \\ &\quad +B(\hat{\zeta}_1(\hat{x}_c/\theta)+u_1(t_s)+u_2(t_s)\big]\Big]dt_s \\ &\quad +\Big[\sum_{l=1}^{r}\mu_l(z)[A_{3l}\hat{x}_c(t_s)+A_{4l}\hat{x}_c(t_s-\tau) \\ &\quad +L_l(y(t_s)-\hat{y}(t_s))+B(\hat{\zeta}_1(\hat{x}_c/\theta)+u_1(t_s)+u_2(t_s)]\Big]dw(t_s), \\ \hat{y}(t_s) &= C\hat{x}_c(t_s), l=1,2,3,\ldots,r. \end{aligned}$$

The error dynamics of fuzzy observer system is defined as

$$de(t_s)=dx_c(t_s)-d\hat{x}_c(t_s).$$

This implies that error dynamic is

$$\begin{aligned} de(t_s) &= \left[\sum_{l=1}^{r} \mu_l(z)[(A_{1l}(t_s) - L_l C)e(t_s) + A_{2l}e(t_s - \tau)]\right. \\ &\quad + B(\zeta_1(x_c(t_s), t_s) - \hat{\zeta}_1(\hat{x}_c/\theta) - u_1(t_s)) \\ &\quad \left. + B(\zeta_1(x_c(t_s - \tau), t_s) - u_2(t_s))\right]dt_s \\ &\quad + \left[\sum_{l=1}^{r} \mu_l(z)[(A_{3l}(t_s) - L_l C)e(t_s) + A_{4l}e(t_s - \tau)\right] \\ &\quad - B(\hat{\zeta}_1(\hat{x}_c/\theta) + u_1(t_s)) - B(u_2(t_s))]dw(t_s). \end{aligned} \tag{10.8}$$

10.3 Main Result

Define the two state variables for stochastic time-delay chaotic system Equation (10.4) as

$$\begin{aligned} f(t_s) &= \sum_{l=1}^{r} \mu_l(z)(A_{1l}x_c(t_s) + A_{2l}x_c(t_s - \tau)) \\ &\quad + B\zeta_1(x_c(t_s), t_s) + B\zeta_1(x_c(t_s - \tau), t_s) \\ g(t_s) &= \sum_{l=1}^{r} \mu_l(z)(A_{3l}x_c(t_s) + A_{4l}x_c(t_s - \tau)) \\ &\quad + B\zeta_3(x_c(t_s), t_s) + B\zeta_4(x_c(t_s - \tau), t_s). \end{aligned}$$

Then the stochastic time delay chaotic system is

$$x_c(t_s) - x_c(t_s - \tau) = \int_{t_s - \tau}^{t_s} dx_c(s) = \int_{t_s - \tau}^{t_s} f(s)ds + \int_{t_s - \tau}^{t} g(s)dw(s).$$

Theorem 1

Suppose the positive definite matrices are P, Q, S, R, D_0, D_1 and the feedback gain is L_i, $i = 1, 2, 3, 4, \ldots, r$, therefore existed $PB = C^T$ and together with the inequalities

$$\begin{aligned} \left[(A_{1i} - L_i C)^T P + P(A_{1i} - L_i C) + R + D_0 + D_1 + PA_{2i}R^{-1}A_{2i}^T\right] &\leq -Q_i, \\ \lambda_{min}(Q_i) &\geq 2\gamma M_\theta \|C\|. \end{aligned}$$

where λ_{min} represents the least eigen value of a matrix. Then the stochastic time delay error dynamics is asymptotically mean square stable. The supervisory control is given as

$$u_1 = \hat{\zeta}_1 \frac{B^T Pe}{||B^T Pe||}, u_2 = \hat{\zeta}_2 \frac{B^T Pe}{||B^T Pe||}$$

where $\hat{\zeta}_1$ and $\hat{\zeta}_2$ stand for the estimators of ζ_1 and ζ_2. The error dynamic is asymptotically stable in the mean square by applying

$$\begin{aligned}
\dot{\theta} &= 2\eta\omega(\hat{x})B^T Pe, \\
\dot{\hat{\zeta}}_1 &= 2\eta_1 e^T PB, \\
\dot{\hat{\zeta}}_2 &= 2\eta_2 e^T PB.
\end{aligned}$$

where η, η_1, η_2 represent positive adaption constants.

Proof:
Consider the Lyapunov–Krasovskii function:

$$V(t_s) = e^T Pe + \frac{1}{2\eta} tr(\tilde{\theta}^T \tilde{\theta}) + \frac{1}{2\eta_1} \tilde{\zeta}_1^2 + \frac{1}{2\eta_2} \tilde{\zeta}_2^2 + \int_{t_s-\tau}^{t_s} e^T(\sigma) Se(\sigma) d\sigma,$$

where

$$\begin{aligned}
&\tilde{\theta} = \theta^* - \theta, \\
&\tilde{\zeta}_1 = \zeta_1 - \hat{\zeta}_1, \\
&\tilde{\zeta}_2 = \zeta_2 - \hat{\zeta}_2,
\end{aligned}$$

Then the derivatives can be arrived by *Itö* formula that

$$\begin{aligned}
dv(t_s) &= \mathbb{L}V(t_s)dt + 2e^T Pg(t_s)dw(t_s) \\
\mathbb{L}V(t_s) &= V_{t_s}(t_s) + V_e(t_s) f(t_s) + \frac{1}{2} trace(g^T V_{ee} g)
\end{aligned}$$

Therefore

$$\begin{aligned}\mathbb{L}V(t_s) &= 2e^T P\Big(\Big[\sum_{i=1}^{r}\mu_i(z)[(A_{1i}(t_s)-L_iC)e(t_s)+A_{2i}e(t_s-\tau)]\\
&+B(\zeta_1(x_c(t_s),t_s)-\hat{\zeta}_1(\hat{x}_c/\theta)-u_1(t_s))\\
&+B(\zeta_2(x_c(t_s-\tau),t_s)-u_2(t_s))\Big]\Big)+e^TSe+g^TPg\\
&-\frac{1}{\eta}tr(\tilde{\theta}^T\dot{\hat{\theta}})-\frac{1}{\eta_1}\tilde{\zeta}_1\dot{\hat{\zeta}}_1-\frac{1}{\eta_2}\tilde{\zeta}_2\dot{\hat{\zeta}}_2-e^T(t_s-\tau)Se(t_s-\tau).\end{aligned} \tag{10.9}$$

Now consider the relation

$$g^TPg \le e^TD_0e + e^T(t_s-\tau)D_1e(t_s-\tau).$$

Then

$$\begin{aligned}\mathbb{L}V(t_s) &= 2e^T P\Big(\Big[\sum_{i=1}^{r}\mu_i(z)[(A_{1i}(t_s)-L_iC)e(t_s)\\
&+A_{2i}e(t_s-\tau)]+B(\zeta_1(x_c(t_s),t_s)-\hat{\zeta}_1(\hat{x}_c/\theta)-u_1(t_s))\\
&+B(\zeta_2(x_c(t_s-\tau),t_s)-u_2(t_s))\Big]\Big)+e^TSe+e^TD_0e\\
&+e^T(t_s-\tau)D_1e(t_s-\tau)-\frac{1}{\eta}tr(\tilde{\theta}^T\dot{\hat{\theta}})-\frac{1}{\eta_1}\tilde{\zeta}_1\dot{\hat{\zeta}}_1\\
&-\frac{1}{\eta_2}\tilde{\zeta}_2\dot{\hat{\zeta}}_2-e^T(t_s-\tau)Se(t_s-\tau)\\
&\le \sum_{i=1}^{r}\mu_i[e^TP(A_{1i}-L_iC)^Te+e^T(A_{1i}-L_iC)Pe\\
&+2e^TPA_{2i}e(t_s-\tau)]+2e^TPB(\zeta_1(x_c(t_s),t_s)-\hat{\zeta}_1(\hat{x}_c/\theta))\\
&-2e^TPB(u_1)+2e^TPB(\zeta_2(x_c(t_s-\tau))-u_2)+e^TSe\\
&+e^TD_0e+e^T(t_s-\tau)D_1e(t_s-\tau)-\frac{1}{\eta}tr(\tilde{\theta}^T\dot{\theta})\\
&-\frac{1}{\eta_1}\tilde{\zeta}_1\dot{\hat{\zeta}}_1-\frac{1}{\eta_2}\tilde{\zeta}_2\dot{\hat{\zeta}}_2-e^T(t_s-\tau)Se(t_s-\tau).\end{aligned}$$

Now consider the relation

$$2e^T PA_{2i}e(t_s-\tau)\le e^T PA_{2i}R^{-1}A_{2i}^T Pe+e^T(t_s-\tau)Re(t_s-\tau).$$

Therefore Equation (10.8) becomes

$$\begin{aligned}
\mathbb{L}V(t_s) \le & \sum_{i=1}^{r}\mu_i e^T[P(A_{1i}-L_iC)^T+(A_{1i}-L_iC)P+PA_{2i}R^{-1}A_{2i}^T P+S]e \\
& +e^T(t_s-\tau)Re(t_s-\tau)+2e^T PB(\zeta_1(x_c(t_s),t_s)-\hat{\zeta}_1(\hat{x}_c/\theta)) \\
& -2e^T PB(u_1)+2e^T PB(\zeta_2(x_c(t_s-\tau))-u_2)+e^T D_0 e \\
& +e^T(t_s-\tau)D_1 e(t_s-\tau)-\frac{1}{\eta}tr(\tilde{\theta}^T\dot{\theta})-\frac{1}{\eta_1}\tilde{\zeta}_1\dot{\hat{\zeta}}_1-\frac{1}{\eta_2}\tilde{\zeta}_2\dot{\hat{\zeta}}_2 \\
& -e^T(t_s-\tau)Se(t_s-\tau). \\
\le & \sum_{i=1}^{r}\mu_i e^T[P(A_{1i}-L_iC)^T+(A_{1i}-L_iC)P+R+D_0+D_1 \\
& +PA_{2i}R^{-1}A_{2i}^T P\big]e++2e^T PB(\zeta_1(x_c(t_s),t_s)-\hat{\zeta}_1(\hat{x}_c/\theta)) \\
& -2e^T PB(u_1)+2e^T PB(\zeta_2(x_c(t_s-\tau),t_s)) \\
& -2e^T PBu_2-\frac{1}{\eta}tr(\tilde{\theta}^T\dot{\theta})-\frac{1}{\eta_1}\tilde{\zeta}_1\dot{\hat{\zeta}}_1-\frac{1}{\eta_2}\tilde{\zeta}_2\dot{\hat{\zeta}}_2.
\end{aligned} \tag{10.10}$$

Again consider the relation as

$$\begin{aligned}
\zeta_1(x_c(t_s),t_s)-\hat{\zeta}_1(\hat{x}_c/\theta) = & \zeta_1(x_c(t_s),t_s)-\hat{\zeta}_1(\hat{x}_c/\theta)+\hat{\zeta}_1(\hat{x}_c/\theta^*) \\
& -\hat{\zeta}_1(\hat{x}_c/\theta^*)+\hat{\zeta}_1(x/\theta^*)-\hat{\zeta}_1(x/\theta^*) \\
= & (\zeta_1-\hat{\zeta}_1(\hat{x}_c/\theta^*))+\hat{\zeta}_1((\hat{x}_c/\theta^*) \\
& -(\hat{x}_c/\theta))+\hat{\zeta}_1((x/\theta^*)-(\hat{x}_c/\theta^*)) \\
& (\zeta_1-\hat{\zeta}_1(\hat{x}_c/\theta^*))+\tilde{\theta}^T\omega(\hat{x}) \\
& +\theta^{*T}(\omega(x_c)-\omega(\hat{x})),
\end{aligned} \tag{10.11}$$

and

$$P(A_{1i}-L_iC)^T+(A_{1i}-L_iC)P+R+D_0+D_1+PA_{2i}R^{-1}A_{2i}^T P\le -Q_i.$$

Now, Equation (10.10) becomes

$$
\begin{aligned}
\mathbb{L}V(t_s) \le & \sum\nolimits_{i=1}^{r} \mu_i e^T(-Q_i)e + 2e^T PB(\zeta_1(x_c(t_s),t_s) - \hat{\zeta}_1(\hat{x}_c/\theta) \\
& + \hat{\zeta}_1(\hat{x}_c/\theta^*) - \hat{\zeta}_1(\hat{x}_c/\theta^*) + \hat{\zeta}_1(x/\theta^*) - \hat{\zeta}_1(x/\theta^*)) \\
& - 2e^T PB(u_1) + 2e^T PB(\zeta_2(x_c(t_s-\tau),t_s)) - 2e^T PBu_2 \\
& - \frac{1}{\eta} tr(\tilde{\theta}^T \dot{\theta}) - \frac{1}{\eta_1}\tilde{\zeta}_1 \dot{\hat{\zeta}}_1 - \frac{1}{\eta_2}\tilde{\zeta}_2 \dot{\hat{\zeta}}_2 \\
\le & \sum\nolimits_{i=1}^{r} \mu_i e^T(-Q_i)e + 2e^T PB(\zeta_1 - \hat{\zeta}_1(\hat{x}_c/\theta^*)) \\
& + 2e^T PB(\tilde{\theta}^T \omega(\hat{x})) + 2e^T PB(\theta^{*T}(\omega(x_c) - \omega(\hat{x}))) \\
& - 2e^T PB(u_1) + 2e^T PB(\zeta_2(x_c(t_s-\tau),t_s)) - 2e^T PBu_2 \\
& - \frac{1}{\eta} tr(\tilde{\theta}^T \dot{\theta}) - \frac{1}{\eta_1}\tilde{\zeta}_1 \dot{\hat{\zeta}}_1 - \frac{1}{\eta_2}\tilde{\zeta}_2 \dot{\hat{\zeta}}_2 \\
\le & \sum\nolimits_{i=1}^{r} \mu_i e^T(-Q_i)e + 2e^T PB\left\|\zeta_1 - \hat{\zeta}_1(\hat{x}_c/\theta^*)\right\| \\
& + 2e^T PB\tilde{\theta}^T \omega(\hat{x}) + 2e^T PB(\theta^{*T}\gamma) \| x - \hat{x} \| \\
& - 2e^T PB(u_1) + 2e^T PB\zeta_2 - 2e^T PBu_2 \\
& - \frac{1}{\eta} tr(\tilde{\theta}^T \dot{\theta}) - \frac{1}{\eta_1}\tilde{\zeta}_1 \dot{\hat{\zeta}}_1 - \frac{1}{\eta_2}\tilde{\zeta}_2 \dot{\hat{\zeta}}_2 \\
\le & \sum\nolimits_{i=1}^{r} \mu_i e^T(-Q_i)e + 2\gamma \|e\|^2 \|C\| M_\theta \\
& + \frac{1}{\eta} tr[\tilde{\theta}^T(2\eta\omega\hat{x}e^T PB - \dot{\theta})] - 2e^T PB(u_1) + 2e^T PB\zeta_2 \\
& - 2e^T PBu_2 + 2e^T PB\zeta_1 - \frac{1}{\eta_1}\tilde{\zeta}_1 \dot{\hat{\zeta}}_1 - \frac{1}{\eta_2}\tilde{\zeta}_2 \dot{\hat{\zeta}}_2 \\
\le & \sum\nolimits_{i=1}^{r} \mu_i e^T(-Q_i)e + 2\gamma \| e \|^2 \|C\| M_\theta \\
& + \frac{1}{\eta} tr[\tilde{\theta}^T(2\eta\omega\hat{x}e^T PB - \dot{\theta})] \\
& + 2e^T PB(\hat{\zeta}_1 - u_1) + 2e^T PB(\hat{\zeta}_2 - u_2) \\
& + \frac{1}{\eta_1}(2\eta_1 e^T PB - \dot{\hat{\zeta}}_1) + \frac{1}{\eta_2}(2\eta_2 e^T PB - \dot{\hat{\zeta}}_2)\tilde{\zeta}_2
\end{aligned}
\tag{10.12}
$$

Now assuming the adoptive law into Equation (10.11) and invoking the inequality it is led to the result in Equation (10.12)

$$\mathbb{L}V(t_s) \leq -e^T \beta e, \beta > 0$$

Consequently

$$dV(t_s) = -e^T \beta e + 2e^T Pg(t_s) dw(t_s)$$

Taking expectation, it follows that

$$\mathbb{E}\left[dV(t_s)\right] = \mathbb{E}\left[-e^T \beta e\right] + \mathbb{E}\left[2e^T Pg(t_s)\ dw(t_s)\right].$$

As a result,

$$dv(t_s) \leq -e^T \beta e. \tag{10.12A}$$

By this $V \in L_\infty$, from which it follows that

$$e, \tilde{\theta}, \tilde{\zeta}_1, \tilde{\zeta}_2, u_1, u_2 \in L_\infty.$$

Integrating Equation (10.12A) from 0 to ∞ results in

$$\beta \int_0^\infty ee^T\, dt_s < V(0) - V(\infty) < \infty.$$

This implies that $e \in L_2$, the Lipschitz condition is applied to this estimation lead to $\dot{e} \in L_\infty$. Using the Barbalat lemma, it is seen that $e \to 0$ as $t_s \to \infty$, Therefore the system is asymptotically stable in mean square.

The output feedback control procedure is applied to stochastic time delay for obtaining fuzzy observer. The stochastic chaotic time delay output feedback system is defined by

$$\begin{aligned} dx_c(t_s) &= \left[\sum_{i=1}^{r} \mu_i(z)(A_{1i} + \Delta A_{1i})x_c(t_s) + (A_{2i} + \Delta A_{2i})(x_c(t_s - \tau)) + Bu(t_s)\right] dt_s \\ &\quad + \left[\sum_{i=1}^{r} \mu_i(z)(A_{3i} + \Delta A_{3i})x_c(t_s) + (A_{4i} + \Delta A_{4i})(x_c(t_s - \tau)) + Bu(t_s)\right] dw(t_s) \\ y(t_s) &= Cx_c(t_s) \end{aligned}$$

and the corresponding observer is

$$\begin{aligned} d\hat{x}_c(t_s) &= \Big[\sum_{i=1}^{r} \mu_i(z)(A_{1i}\hat{x}_c(t_s) + A_{2i}(t_s))x_c(t_s - \tau) \\ &\quad + L_i(y(t_s) - \hat{y}(t_s)) - BK_i\hat{x}_c(t_s)\Big]dt_s \\ &\quad + \Big[\sum_{i=1}^{r} \mu_i(z)(A_{3i}\hat{x}_c(t_s) + A_{3i}(t_s))x_c(t_s - \tau) \\ &\quad + L_i(y(t_s) - \hat{y}(t_s)) - BK_i\hat{x}_c(t_s)\Big]dw(t_s) \\ \hat{y}(t_s) &= C\hat{x}_c(t_s). \end{aligned}$$

Now the system can be represented as

$$\begin{aligned} dx_c(t_s) &= \sum_{i=1}^{r} \mu_i(z)[A_{1i}x_c(t_s) + A_{2i}x_c(t_s - \tau) + B\zeta_1(x_c(t_s), t_s) \\ &\quad + B\zeta_2(x_c(t_s - \tau), t_s) + Bu(t_s)]dt_s \\ &\quad + \sum_{i=1}^{r} \mu_i(z)[A_{3i}x_c(t_s) + A_{4i}x_c(t_s - \tau) + B\zeta_1(x_c(t_s), t_s) \\ &\quad + B\zeta_2(x_c(t_s - \tau), t_s) + Bu(t_s)]dw(t_s) \\ y(t_s) &= Cx_c(t_s). \end{aligned}$$

Theorem 2

Suppose a fuzzy controller for the system Equation (10.11) is defined as

$$u(t_s) = \sum_{l=1}^{r} \mu_i[-K_i - L_i M]\hat{x}_c - \hat{\zeta}_1(\hat{x}_c/\theta) - u_1 - u_2,$$

If the supervisory controller $\hat{\zeta}_1(\hat{x}_c/\theta), u_1, u_2$, and Theorem 3 follows LMI criterion

$$(A_{1i} - BK_i)^T M + M(A_{1i} - BK_i) + U + V_0 + V_1 + MA_{2i}U^{-1}A_{2i}^T M^T \leq -N_i V_i$$

then the observer-based fuzzy stochastic chaotic time delay system is asymptotically stable in the mean square.

Proof: The Lyapunov–Krasovskii integro-differential equation is defined as follows:

$$
\begin{aligned}
V(ts) &= \hat{x}^T M\hat{x} + e^T Pe + \frac{1}{2\eta} tr(\tilde{\theta}^T\tilde{\theta}) + \frac{1}{2\eta}\tilde{\zeta}_1^2 + \frac{1}{2\eta}\tilde{\zeta}_2^2 \\
&+ \int_{t_s-\tau}^{t_s} e^T(\sigma)Se(\sigma)d\sigma + \int_{t_s-\tau}^{t_s} \hat{x}^T(\sigma)S\hat{x}_c(\sigma)d\sigma, \\
\mathbb{L}V(t_s) &= \left[\sum_{i=1}^{r} \mu_i(2\hat{x}^T(A_{1i} - BK_i)\hat{x}_c(t_s) + 2\hat{x}^T A_{2i}\hat{x}_c(t_s - \tau)) \right. \\
&\left. + 2\hat{x}^T ML_iCe \right] \\
&\left[\sum_{i=1}^{r} \mu_i[2e^T P(A_{1i} - L_iC)e(t_s) + 2e^T PA_{2i}e(t_s - \tau)]\right] \\
&+ 2e^T PB\zeta_1 + 2e^T PB\zeta_2 + 2e^T PBu(t_s) + 2e^T PBK_i\hat{x} \\
&- \frac{1}{\eta} tr(\tilde{\theta}^T\dot{\theta}) - \frac{1}{\eta_1}\tilde{\zeta}_1\dot{\hat{\zeta}}_1 - \frac{1}{\eta_2}\tilde{\zeta}_2\dot{\hat{\zeta}}_2 \\
&- e^T(t_s)Se(t_s) - e^T(t_s - \tau)Se(t_s - \tau) + \hat{x}^T W\hat{x} \\
&- \hat{x}_c(t_s - \tau)^T W\hat{x}_c(t_s - \tau) + g^T(t_s)Wg(t_s) + g^T(t_s)Pg(t_s)
\end{aligned}
$$

Now consider the relation

$$
\begin{aligned}
g^T(t_s)Wg(t_s) &\leq \hat{x}^T V_0\hat{x} + \hat{x}^T(t_s - \tau)V_1\hat{x}_c(t_s - \tau) \\
g^T(t_s)Pg(t_s) &\leq e^T D_0 e + e^T(t_s - \tau)D_1 e(t_s - \tau)
\end{aligned}
$$

$$
\begin{aligned}
\mathbb{L}V(t_s) &\leq \sum_{i=1}^{r} \mu_i e(t_s)^T \left[(A_{1i} - L_iC)^T P + P(A_{1i} - L_iC) + R + D_0 + D_1 \right. \\
&\left. + PA_{2i}R^{-1}A_{2i}^T P\right] e(t_s) + 2e^T PB\zeta_1 + 2e^T PB\zeta_2 + 2e^T PBu(t_s) \\
&- \frac{1}{\eta} tr(\tilde{\theta}^T\dot{\theta}) - \frac{1}{\eta_1}\tilde{\zeta}_1\dot{\hat{\zeta}}_1 - \frac{1}{\eta_2}\tilde{\zeta}_2\dot{\hat{\zeta}}_2 \\
&+ \sum_{i=1}^{r} \mu_i 2\hat{x}^T ML_iCe + \sum_{i=1}^{r} \mu_i\hat{x}^T \left[(A_{1i} - BK_i)^T M \right. \\
&\left. + M(A_{1i} - BK_i) + MA_{2i}U^{-1}A_{2i}^T M + U + V_0 + V_1\right]\hat{x}_c(t_s)
\end{aligned}
$$

Upon substituting

$$u(t_s)=\sum_{l=1}^{r}\mu_i[-K_i-L_iM]\hat{x}_c-\hat{\zeta}_1(\hat{x}_c/\theta)-u_1-u_2,$$

One is led to the inequality

$$\begin{aligned}
\mathbb{L}V(t_s)\leq&\sum_{i=1}^{r}\mu_i e(t_s)^T\left[(A_{1i}-L_iC)^T P+P(A_{1i}-L_iC)+R+D_0+D_1\right.\\
&\left.+PA_{2i}R^{-1}A_{2i}^T P\right]e(t_s)\\
&+2e^T PB(\zeta_1-\hat{\zeta}_1(\hat{x}_c/\theta)-u_1)2e^T PB\left(\zeta_2-u_2-\frac{1}{\eta}tr(\tilde{\theta}^T\dot{\theta})\right.\\
&-\frac{1}{\eta_1}\tilde{\zeta}_1\dot{\hat{\zeta}}_1-\frac{1}{\eta_2}\tilde{\zeta}_2\dot{\hat{\zeta}}_2\\
&+\sum_{i=1}^{r}\mu_i\hat{x}^T[(A_{1i}-BK_i)^T M+M(A_{1i}-BK_i)\\
&+MA_{2i}U^{-1}A_{2i}^T M+U+V_0+V_1\big]\hat{x}_c(t_s)
\end{aligned}$$

Adopting the results from Theorem 3 yields

$$\begin{aligned}
\leq&-\beta e^T e+\sum_{i=1}^{r}\mu_i\hat{x}^T[(A_{1i}-BK_i)^T M+M(A_{1i}-BK_i)\\
&+MA_{2i}U^{-1}A_{2i}^T M+U+V_0+V_1]\hat{x}_c(t_s)
\end{aligned}$$

Given the stability conditions, it follows that

$$\begin{aligned}
\mathbb{L}V(t_s)\ &\leq\ -\beta e^T e-\sum_{i=1}^{r}\mu_i\lambda_{min}(N_i)\|\hat{x}\|^2,\\
&\leq\ \beta e^T e-\alpha\hat{x}^T\hat{x},\alpha>0
\end{aligned}$$

Therefore

$$dV(t_s)=-e^T\beta e-\alpha\hat{x}^T\hat{x}+2e^T Pg(t_s)dw(t_s)$$

Taking expectation, it follows that

$$\begin{aligned} \mathbb{E}[dV(t_s)] &= \mathbb{E}[-e^T \beta e - \alpha \hat{x}^T \hat{x})] + \mathbb{E}[2e^T Pg(t_s)\, dw(t_s)] \\ dv(t_s) &\leq -e^T \beta e - \alpha \hat{x}^T \hat{x} \end{aligned}$$

Hence by Barbalat stability theorem, e and $\hat{x}$ are simultaneously approached. Hence it is synchronized.

The stochastic delayed chaotic system is designed as tracking reference model. The fuzzy based reference model for stochastic time-delay chaotic system is

$$\begin{aligned} dx_{cm}(t_s) &= \left[\sum_{i=1}^{r} \mu_i(\overline{A}_{1i}x_m(t_s) + \overline{A}_{2i}x_m(t_s-\tau) + \overline{B}_i r(t_s))\right]dt_s \\ &\quad + \left[\sum_{i=1}^{r} \mu_i(\overline{A}_{3i}x_m(t_s) + \overline{A}_{4i}x_m(t_s-\tau) + \overline{B}_i r(t_s))\right]dw(t_s), \\ y_m(t_s) &= Cx_m(t_s) \end{aligned}$$

where $\overline{A}_{1i} = A_{1i} - BK_i, \overline{A}_{2i} = A_{2i}\, \overline{A}_{3i} = A_{3i} - BK_i, \overline{A}_{4i} = A_{4i}$, $\overline{B}_i = BK_{mi}, K_{mi}$ is a known real matrix and $r(t_s)$ is reference input.

The observer for tracking control is

$$\begin{aligned} d\hat{x}_c(t_s) = &\sum_{i=1}^{r} [(A_{1i} - BK_i)\hat{x}_c(t_s) + A_{2i}\hat{x}_c(t_s - \tau) \\ &+ L_i(y(t_s) - \hat{y}(t_s)) + BK_{mi} r(t_s)]dt_s \\ &+ \sum_{i=1}^{r} [(A_{3i} - BK_i)\hat{x}_c(t_s) + A_{4i}\hat{x}_c(t_s - \tau) \\ &+ L_i(y(t_s) - \hat{y}(t_s)) + BK_{mi} r(t_s)]dw(t_s) \\ \hat{y}(t_s) = &\ C\hat{x}_c(t_s). \end{aligned}$$

Therefore the fuzzy reference model can be written as

$$dx_{cm}(t_s)=\sum_{i=1}^{r}\mu_i[(A_{1i}-BK_i)x_m(t_s)+A_{2i}x_m(t_s-\tau)+BK_{mi}r(t_s)]dt_s$$
$$+\sum_{i=1}^{r}\mu_i[(A_{3i}-BK_i)x_m(t_s)+A_{4i}x_m(t_s-\tau)$$
$$+BK_{mi}r(t_s)]dw(t_s)$$
$$y_m(t_s)=Cx_m(t_s).$$

The error vector is defined as

$$\begin{aligned} e(t_s) &= x_c(t_s)-\hat{x}_m(t_s), \\ \bar{x}_c(t_s) &= x_m(t_s)-\hat{x}_c(t_s) \end{aligned}$$

which implies that the error dynamics provided by $e(t_s)$ and $\bar{x}_c$ is

$$\begin{aligned} de(t_s) &= \sum_{i=1}^{r}\mu_i[(A_{1i}-L_iC)e(t_s)+A_{2i}e(t_s-\tau) \\ &+B\zeta_2-BK_{mi}r(t_s)+Bu(t_s)]dt_s \\ &\sum_{i=1}^{r}\mu_i[(A_{3i}-L_iC)e(t_s)+A_{4i}e(t_s-\tau) \\ &+B\zeta_2-BK_{mi}r(t_s)+Bu(t_s)]dw(t_s) \\ \text{and } d\bar{x}_c &= \sum_{i=1}^{r}\mu_i[(A_{1i}-BK_i)\bar{x}_c(t_s)+A_{2i}\bar{x}_c(t_s-\tau)-L_iC\bar{x}_c(t_s)]dt_s \\ &+\sum_{i=1}^{r}\mu_i[(A_{3i}-BK_i)\bar{x}_c(t_s)+A_{4i}\bar{x}_c(t_s-\tau)-L_iC\bar{x}_c(t_s)]dw(t_s) \end{aligned} \tag{10.13}$$

Theorem 3
If the stability conditions from Theorem 1 and 2 hold the fuzzy controller then it is defined as

$$u(t_s)=\sum_{i=1}^{r}\mu_i(-K_i\hat{x}_c-L_iM\hat{x}+K_{mi}r(t_s))-\hat{\zeta}_1(\hat{x}_c/\theta)-u_1-u_2,$$

then the closed loop system Equation (10.13) is guaranteed by asymptotic mean square stability.

Proof:
The Lyapunov–Krasovskii functional candidate is chosen as

$$V(t_s)=\bar{x}_c^T M\bar{x}_c+e^T Pe+\frac{1}{2\eta}tr(\tilde{\theta}^T\tilde{\theta})+\frac{1}{2\eta}\tilde{\zeta}_1^2+\frac{1}{2\eta}\tilde{\zeta}_2^2$$

$$+\int_{t_s-\tau}^{t_s} e^T(\sigma)Se(\sigma)d\sigma+\int_{t_s-\tau}^{t_s}\bar{x}_c^T(\sigma)S\bar{x}_c(\sigma)d\sigma$$

and the asymptotic stability is derived.

10.4 Numerical Illustration

For the numerical simulation, the MATLAB dde23 solver and Fuzzy logic tool box are utilized.

In this investigation, the Sportt chaotic Jerk system is utilized. The state space representation of the Sportt chaotic Jerk system is defined by

$$\begin{aligned}\dot{x}_1&=x_2\\ \dot{x}_2&=x_3\\ \dot{x}_3&=|x_1|-1-ax_3-bx_2\end{aligned}$$

where a and b are positive parameters. For the values of a = 0.6 and b = 1, the above equation is sketched as chaotic nature.

The Sprott chaotic Jerk system involving uncertainty is represented by

$$\begin{aligned}\dot{x}_1&=x_2+0.01x_1\\ \dot{x}_2&=x_3+0.02x_2\\ \dot{x}_3&=|x_1|-1-ax_3-bx_2+0.01|x_1|\end{aligned}\tag{10.14}$$

The matrix representation of the system Equation (10.14) is defined as

$$\dot{X}=XA$$

Here, the vector X represents

$$X = \begin{bmatrix} x_1 & x_2 & x_3 \end{bmatrix}^T$$

$$A = \begin{bmatrix} 0 & 1 & 0 \\ 0 & 0 & 1 \\ 1 & -b & -a \end{bmatrix}$$

$$B = \begin{bmatrix} 0 \\ 0 \\ -1 \end{bmatrix}$$

and the uncertainty

$$\Delta A = \begin{bmatrix} 0.01 & 0 & 0 \\ 0 & 0.02 & 0 \\ 0.01 & 0 & 0 \end{bmatrix}$$

Figures 10.1 to 10.4 show the time delay Sprott chaotic Jerk system with uncertainties.

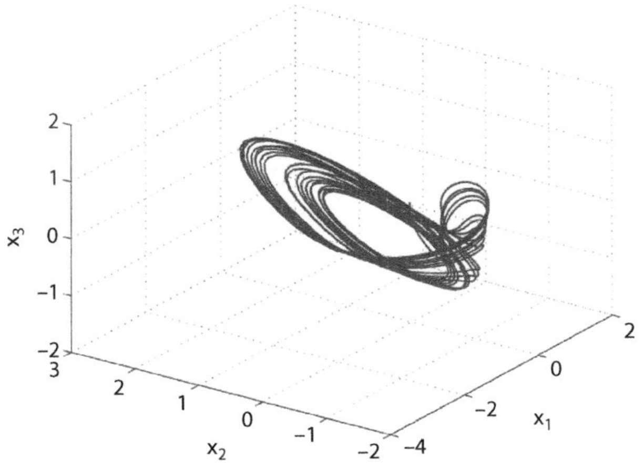

Figure 10.1 The chaotic nature of Jerk system with uncertainties.

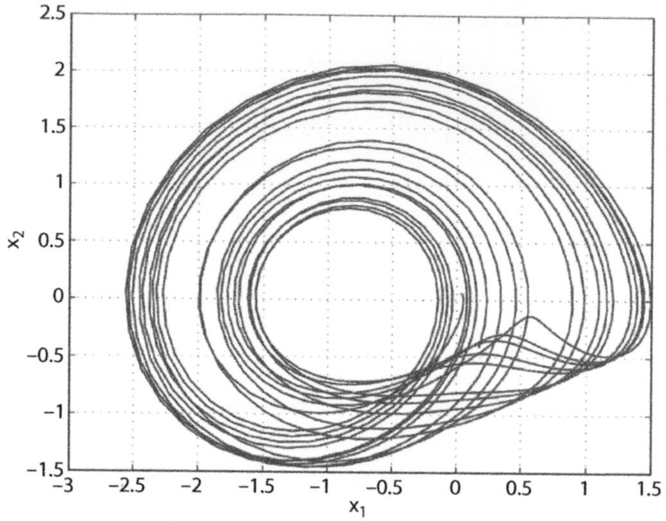

Figure 10.2 The chaotic nature of Jerk system with uncertainties between x_1 and x_2.

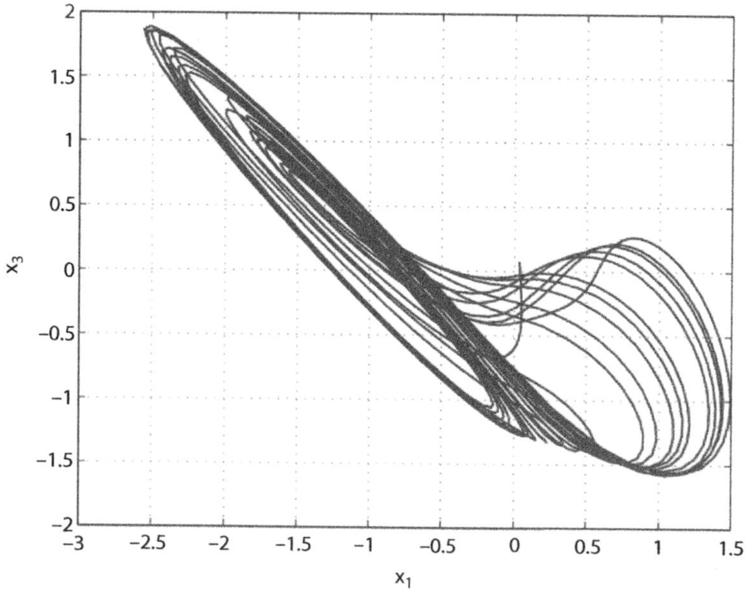

Figure 10.3 The chaotic nature of Jerk system with uncertainties between x_1 and x_3.

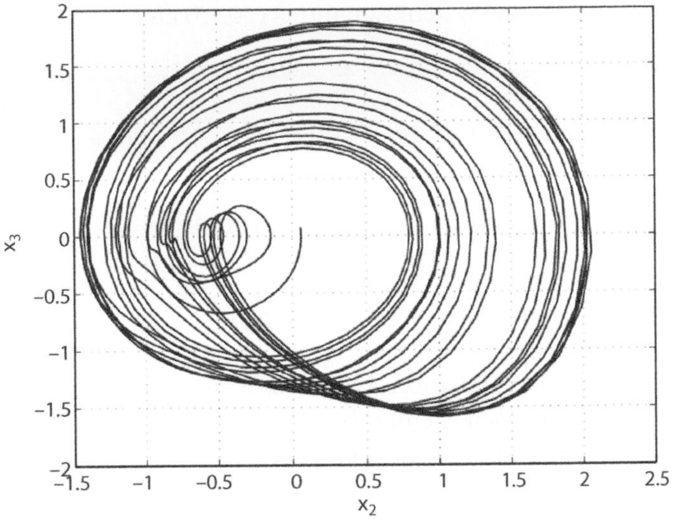

Figure 10.4 The chaotic nature of Jerk system with uncertainties between x_2 and x_3.

The reference model is defined by the Sprott Chaotic Jerk system. It takes the following form:

$$\begin{aligned} \dot{x}_1 &= x_2 + 0.01x_1 \\ \dot{x}_2 &= x_3 + 0.02x_2 \\ \dot{x}_3 &= |x_1| - 1 - ax_3 - bx_2 + 0.01x_1 \end{aligned} \tag{10.15}$$

The observer system is defined by Sprott chaotic Jerk system, which tracks the control input

$$\begin{aligned} \dot{\hat{x}}_1 &= \hat{x}_2 + 0.01\hat{x}_1 + u_1 \\ \dot{\hat{x}}_2 &= \hat{x}_3 + 0.02\hat{x}_2 + u_2 \\ \dot{\hat{x}}_3 &= |\hat{x}_1| - 1 - a\hat{x}_3 - b\hat{x}_2 + 0.01\hat{x}_1 + u_3 \end{aligned} \tag{10.16}$$

The error vector is defined by

$$\dot{e}_i = \dot{x}_i - \dot{\hat{x}}_i$$

Hence the error of the system Equations (10.15) and (10.16) is described as

$$\begin{aligned} \dot{e}_1 &= e_2 + 0.01e_1 - u_1 \\ \dot{e}_2 &= e_3 + 0.02e_2 - u_2 \\ \dot{e}_3 &= |x_1| - |\hat{x}_1| - ae_3 - be_2 + 0.01e_2 - u_3 \end{aligned} \tag{10.17}$$

The objective is to design the control law u_i, $i = 1, 2, 3$, for stabilizing error variables of the system at the origin.

For the derivation of updation law for adjusting the parameter value, the Lyapunov-based approach is employed.

Consider the Lyapunov–Krasovskii function

$$V(e) = \frac{1}{2}e_1^2 + \frac{1}{2}e_2^2 + \frac{1}{2}e_3^2 + \frac{1}{2}\phi_a^2 + \frac{1}{2}\phi_b^2 \tag{10.18}$$

The unknown parameters are estimated under

$$\begin{aligned} \phi_a &= a - \hat{a} \\ \phi_b &= b - \hat{b} \end{aligned}$$

The continuous first partial derivative of Equation (10.18) is obtained as

$$\begin{aligned} \dot{V}(\dot{e}) &= e_1\dot{e}_1 + e_2\dot{e}_2 + e_3\dot{e}_3 + \phi_a(-\dot{\hat{a}}) + \phi_b(-\dot{\hat{b}}) \\ &= e_1(e_2 + 0.01e_1 - u_1)_1 + e_2(e_3 + 0.02e_2 - u_2) \\ &\quad + e_3(|x_1| - |\hat{x}_1| - ae_3 - be_2 + 0.01e_2 - u_3) \end{aligned} \tag{10.19}$$

Now define the adaptive control functions

$$\begin{aligned} u_1 &= e_2 + 0.01e_1 - e_1 \\ u_2 &= e_3 + 0.02e_2 - e_2 \\ u_3 &= |x_1| - |\hat{x}_1| - be_2 + 0.01e_2 \end{aligned} \tag{10.20}$$

The supervisory control is updated by

$$\dot{\hat{a}} = \phi_a$$

$$\dot{\hat{b}} = \phi_b$$

Substituting the error dynamics Equations (10.17) and (10.20) into Equation (10.19), which gives

$$\dot{V} = -e_1^2 - e_2^2 - e_3^2 - \phi_a^2 - \phi_b^2$$

The condition satisfy for a negative definite function. Therefore, the system Equation (10.17) is globally asymptotic stable. Figures 10.5, 10.6 and 10.7 depict the synchronization of the states x_1, x_2 and x_3, respectively.

Figure 10.8 depicts the convergence curve of the dynamics Equation (10.17).

The output of the system Equation (10.15) is imported into MATLAB Fuzzy FIS. In input, the input variables are defined by x_1, x_2 and x_3.

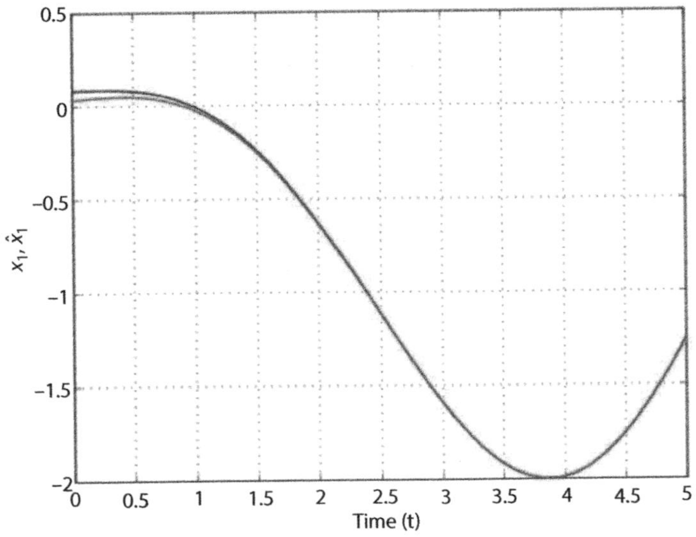

Figure 10.5 Synchronization between x_1 and $\hat{x}_1$.

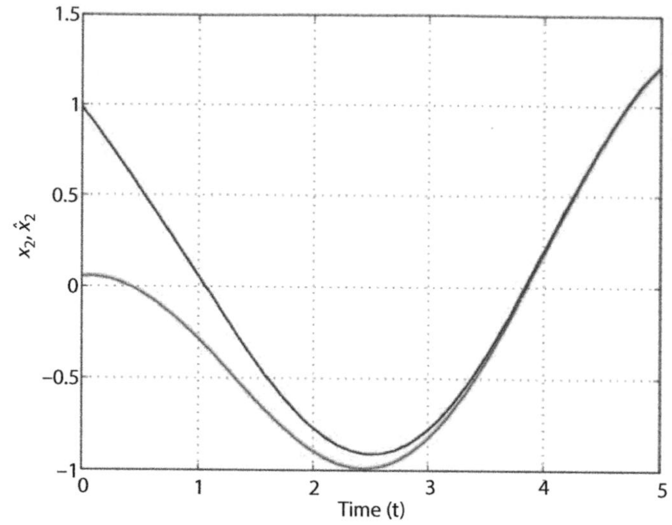

Figure 10.6 Synchronization between x_2 and $\hat{x}_2$.

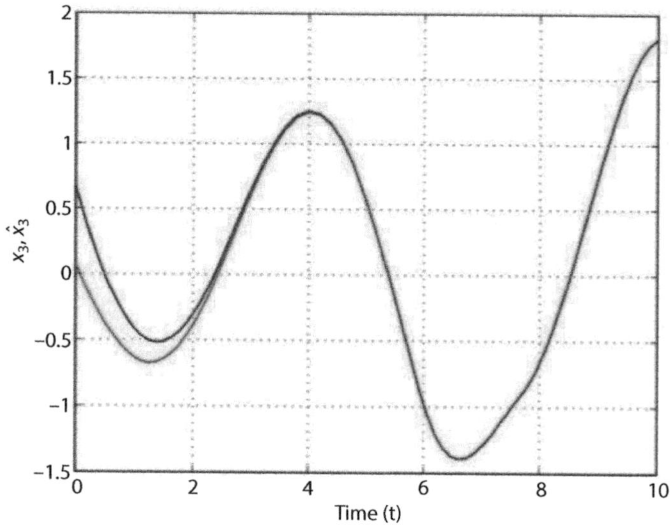

Figure 10.7 Synchronization between x_3 and $\hat{x}_3$.

The Gaussian membership is chosen as input membership function. Figure 10.9 explains the input membership function of Sprott chaotic Jerk system.

The output membership function is also chosen as "Gaussian" membership function.

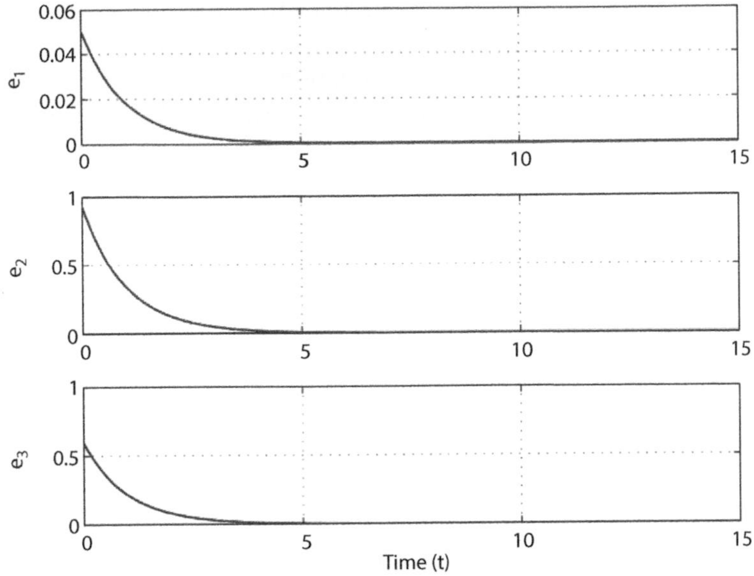

Figure 10.8 Error dynamics of chaotic Jerk system.

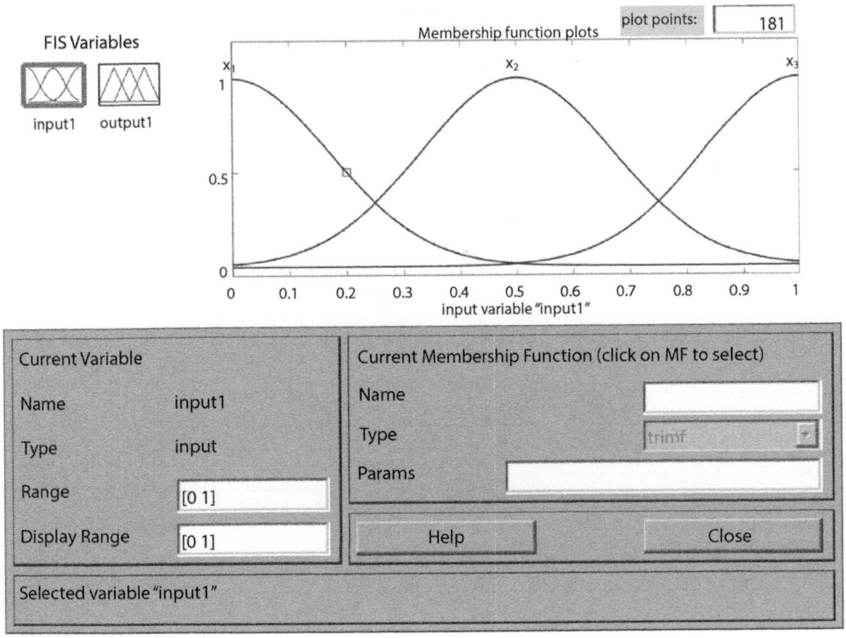

Figure 10.9 Input membership function Sprott time-delay chaotic Jerk systems with uncertainties.

Figure 10.10 shows the output membership function of the Sprott Chaotic Jerk system.

The fuzzy rule is framed as the combination of x_1, x_2 and x_3.

The following 9 rules are framed for time delayed chaotic Sprott Jerk system are shown Figure 10.9.

1. If (input in x_1), then (output in x_1).
2. If (input in x_1), then (output in x_2).
3. If (input in x_1), then (output in x_3).
4. If (input in x_2), then (output in x_1).
5. If (input in x_2), then (output in x_2).
6. If (input in x_2), then (output in x_3).
7. If (input in x_3), then (output in x_1).
8. If (input in x_3), then (output in x_2).
9. If (input in x_3), then (output in x_3).

Figure 10.12 depicts surface area for the output of the fuzzy rules. Figure 10.13 depicts surface area of the fuzzy rules.

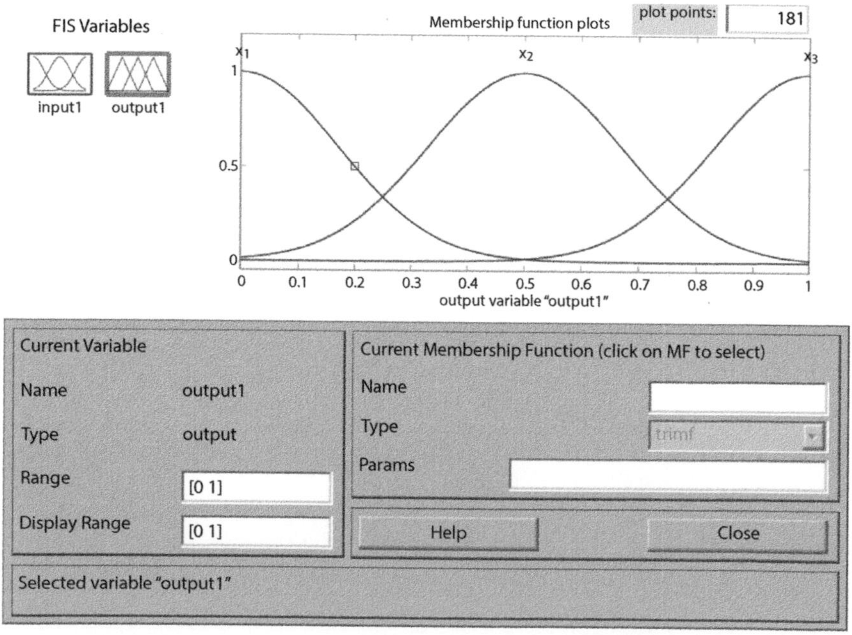

Figure 10.10 Output membership function Sprott time-delay chaotic Jerk systems with uncertainties.

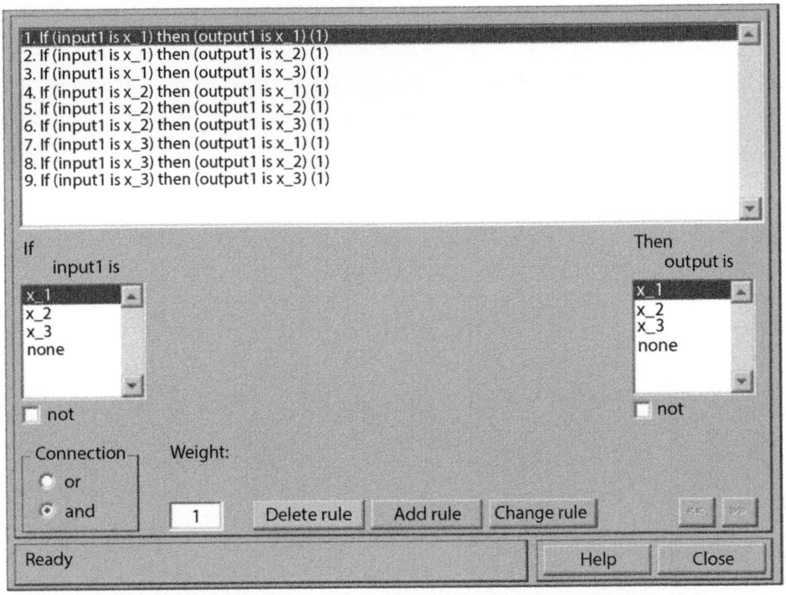

Figure 10.11 Fuzzy rules for the synchronization of chaotic Jerk system with uncertainties.

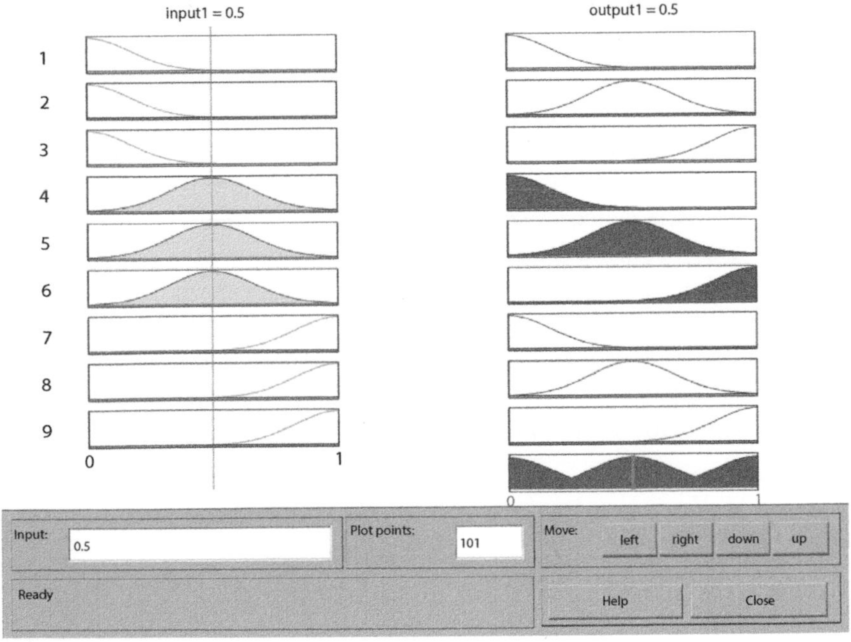

Figure 10.12 Output for fuzzy rules.

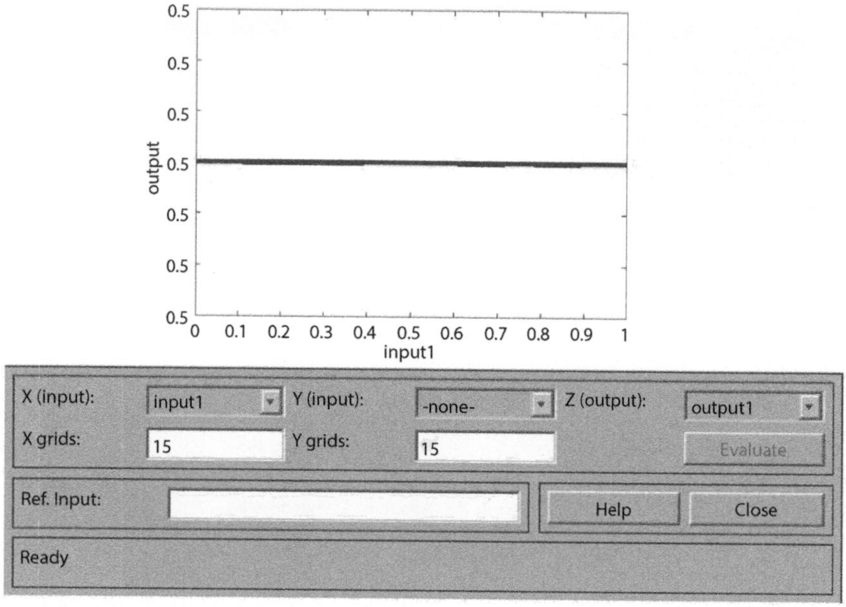

Figure 10.13 Surface of the fuzzy rules.

10.5 Conclusion

In this chapter, the observer-based fuzzy time delay chaotic synchronization involved with uncertainties has been investigated. Takagi–Sugeno fuzzy inference system is utilized to frame the fuzzy membership functions. The center of gravity method is applied for getting defuzzification of the system. The synchronization of the systems depends on LMI and the supervisory control. Based on the Schur compliment law, the LMI is designed. For the numerical simulation part, the Sprott Jerk chaotic system is implemented. By invoking MATLAB fuzzy logic tool box, the Sprott chaotic systems membership functions rules are framed. Gaussion membership function is used for the numerical calculation. It is seen that numerical calculation supports the derived results.

References

1. Takagi, T. and Sugeno, M., Fuzzy identification of systems and its applications to modeling and control. *IEEE Trans. Syst. Man Cybern. B Cybern.*, 15, 1, 116–132, 1985.

2. Sugeno, M. and Kang, G.T., Structure identification of fuzzy model. *Fuzzy Sets Syst.*, 28, 15–33, 1988.
3. Tanaka, K., Ikeda, T., Wang, H.O., A unified approach to controlling chaos via an LMI-based fuzzy control system design. *IEEE Trans. Circuits Syst. I Fundam. Theory Appl.*, 45, 10, 1021–1040, 1998.
4. Lian, K.Y., Chiu, C.S., Chiang, T.S., Liu, P., LMI-based fuzzy chaotic synchronization and communications. *IEEE Trans. Fuzzy Syst.*, 9, 4, 539–553, 2001.
5. Lain, K.Y., Liu, P., Wu, T.C., Lin, W.C., Chaotic control using fuzzy model-based methods. *Int. J. Bifurcat. Chaos*, 12, 8, 1827–1841, 2002.
6. Wang, Y.W., Guan, Z.H., Wang, H.O., LMI-based fuzzy stability and synchronization of Chen's system. *Phys. Lett. A*, 320, 154–159, 2003.
7. Jiang, W., Dong, Q., Bin, D., Observer-based robust adaptive variable universe fuzzy control for chaotic system. *Chaos Solitons Fractals*, 23, 1013–1032, 2002.

11

Trapezoidal Fuzzy Numbers (TrFN) and its Application in Solving Assignment Problems by Hungarian Method: A New Approach

Rahul Kar[1]*, A.K. Shaw[2] and J. Mishra[3]

[1]*Department of Mathematics, Springdale High School, Kalyani, India*
[2]*Department of Mathematics, Regent Education and Research Foundation, Kolkata, India*
[3]*Gyan Ganga Institute of Technology and Sciences, Jabalpur, India*

Abstract
Nowadays, uncertainty is a common thing in science and technology. It is also undesirable. Based on alternative view, it should be avoided by all possible means. Based on modern view uncertainty is considered essential to science and technology, as it is not only the unavoidable plague but it has also impacted a great utility. Fuzzy set theory mainly developed based on inexactness, vagueness, relativity etc. Fuzzy set may be used in mathematical modelling in every scientific discipline. It can also be used for improving the generality of analytical solution. It has many uses in various streams like operation research, control theory differential equations, fuzzy system reliability, optimization and management sciences, etc. In this paper we first describe Trapezoidal Fuzzy Number (TrFN) with arithmetic operations and solve an assignment problem using Hungarian method for Trapezoidal Fuzzy Number (TrFN).

Keywords: Fuzzy set, trapezoidal fuzzy number (TrFN), Hungarian method, assignment algorithm

**Corresponding author*: rkar997@gmail.com

E. Chandrasekaran, R. Anandan, G. Suseendran, S. Balamurugan and Hanaa Hachimi (eds.) Fuzzy Intelligent Systems: Methodologies, Techniques, and Applications, (315–334) © 2021 Scrivener Publishing LLC

11.1 Introduction

In practical field we are sometimes faced with a type of problem which consists in assigning men to offices, jobs to machines, classes in a school to rooms, drivers to trucks, delivery trucks to different routes or problems to different research teams, etc in which the assignees possess varying degrees of efficiency, called cost or effectiveness. The basic assumption of this type of problem is that one person can perform one job at a time. An assignment plan is optimal if it minimizes the total cost or effectiveness or maximizes the profit of performing all the jobs. Assignment problem is a special type of transportation problem in which the objectives is to optimize the effect of allocating a number of jobs to an equal number of facilities. It is appropriate to investigate the assignment problem by using fuzzy optimization methodologies. The applicable theoretical methods can be referred to as fuzzy set theory and triangular fuzzy number. Fuzzy set theory was first invented by Zadeh [26]. The most generalized steam of fuzzy sets theory is this intuitionistic fuzzy set (IFS). Atanassov first introduced IFS. We frequently deal with indistinct or unclear information in our daily life moments. Statistical data available is sometimes indistinct, sometimes unclear or sometimes inexact. Intuitionistic fuzzy sets (IFS) mainly used to deal with inexact and unclear data, except all the other several fuzzy sets of higher order. If in any statistical data based case where available information is full of vagueness to define the impreciseness by the conventional fuzzy set, in that type circumstances the only appropriate or alternative approach is IFS. In fuzzy sets we only considered the degree of acceptance whereas the characterizing of IFS is made by a membership function and a non-membership function. For this the sum of membership function and a non-membership function values is less than one. First investigated and introduced the concept of fuzzy numbers and its arithmetic operations. The notion of a fuzzy number as a fuzzy subset of the real line was introduced by Dubois and Prade [6]. After that definition of intuitionistic fuzzy number proposed. In our daily life a big problem is that, the data which we collect for our mathematical or statistical use are full of vagueness or sometimes incomplete or insufficient, and the probabilistic approach to the conventional reliability analysis is inadequate to account for such built-in uncertainties in data. On the basis of this uncertainty concept of fuzzy introduced the fuzzy reliability. It has been introduced and formulated either in the context of the possibility measure or as a transition from fuzzy success state to fuzzy failure state. Then system reliability was evaluated by Mahapatra and Roy. They considered reliability of components as triangular intuitionistic fuzzy number. Recently, there are a number of studies involving IFNs and its application some of them are Chen *et al.* (2016), Dubey and

Mehra (2011), Guha and Chakraborty (2010), Liu (2013), Mahapatra and Roy [15], Wei (2014), Zhao (2015) and with its reliability to deal with indistinctness, an abundance of studies have been conducted to further develop and enrich IFS theory by Chang (2006), Garg (2012), Rani and Garg (2013), Lei and Xu (2015), Wan and Dong (2015), Wu and Chiclana (2014). In this paper, we have presented the definition and some operations of Trapezoidal fuzzy number (TrFN) and then try to utilize those properties to solve an optimization problem.

11.2 Preliminary

11.2.1 Definition

A GTrFN $\tilde{A}=(a_1,b_1,c_1,d_1;w)$ is a fuzzy set of the real line R whose membership function $\mu_{\tilde{A}}(x): R \to [0,w]$ is defined as

$$\mu_{\tilde{A}}^{w} = \begin{cases} \mu_{\tilde{L}A}^{w}(x) = w\left(\dfrac{x-a_1}{b_1-a_1}\right) & For\ a_1 \le x \le b_1, \\ w & For\ b_1 \le x \le c_1, \\ \mu_{\tilde{R}A}^{w}(x) = w\left(\dfrac{d_1-x}{d_1-c_1}\right) & For\ c_1 \le x \le d_1, \\ & otherwise \\ 0 & \end{cases}$$

Where $a_1 < b_1 < c_1 < d_1$ and $w \in (0,1]$.

Now if $w = 1$ the generalized trapezoidal fuzzy number $\tilde{A}$ is called Trapezoidal Fuzzy Number (TrFN) and is denoted as $\tilde{A}=(a_1,b_1,c_1,d_1)$

$$\mu_{\tilde{A}}(x) = \begin{cases} \mu_{\tilde{L}A}(x) = w\left(\dfrac{x-a_1}{b_1-a_1}\right) & For\ a_1 \le x \le b_1, \\ 1 & For\ b_1 \le x \le c_1, \\ \mu_{\tilde{R}A}(x) = \left(\dfrac{d_1-x}{d_1-c_1}\right) & For\ c_1 \le x \le d_1, \\ & otherwise \\ 0 & \end{cases}$$

11.2.2 Some Arithmetic Operations of Trapezoidal Fuzzy Number

❖ **Properties 1**

- If TrFN $\overset{\sim i}{A}{}^{\psi}_{TrFN} = \left(a^{\psi}{}_1, b^{\psi}{}_1, c^{\psi}{}_1, d^{\psi}{}_1\right)$ and $\hat{y} = ka^{\psi}\,(k > 0)$, then $\overset{\sim i}{Y}_{TrFN} = k\overset{\sim i}{A}{}^{\psi}_{TrFN}$ is a TrFN $\left(ka^{\psi}{}_1, kb^{\psi}{}_1, kc^{\psi}{}_1, kd^{\psi}{}_1\right)$.
- If $\hat{y} = ka^{\psi}\,(k < 0)$, then $\overset{\sim i}{Y}_{TrFN} = k\overset{\sim i}{A}{}^{\psi}_{TrFN}$ is a TrFN $\left(kd^{\psi}{}_1, kc^{\psi}{}_1, kb^{\psi}{}_1, ka^{\psi}{}_1\right)$.

❖ **Properties 2**

If $\overset{\sim i}{A}{}^{\psi}_{TrFN} = \left(a^{\psi}{}_1, b^{\psi}{}_1, c^{\psi}{}_1, d^{\psi}{}_1\right)$ and $\overset{\sim i}{B}{}^{\psi}_{TrFN} = \left(a^{\psi}{}_2, b^{\psi}{}_2, c^{\psi}{}_2, d^{\psi}{}_2\right)$ are two TrFN then $\overset{\sim i}{C}{}^{\psi}_{TrFN} = \overset{\sim i}{A}{}^{\psi}_{TrFN} \oplus \overset{\sim i}{B}{}^{\psi}_{TrFN}$ is also TrFN.

$$\overset{\sim i}{A}{}^{\psi}_{TrFN} \oplus \overset{\sim i}{B}{}^{\psi}_{TrFN} = \left(a^{\psi}{}_1 + a^{\psi}{}_2, b^{\psi}{}_1 + b^{\psi}{}_2, c^{\psi}{}_1 + c^{\psi}{}_2, d^{\psi}{}_1 + d^{\psi}{}_2\right)$$

❖ **Properties 3**

If $\overset{\sim i}{A}{}^{\psi}_{TrFN} = \left(a^{\psi}{}_1, b^{\psi}{}_1, c^{\psi}{}_1, d^{\psi}{}_1\right)$ and $\overset{\sim i}{B}{}^{\psi}_{TrFN} = \left(a^{\psi}{}_2, b^{\psi}{}_2, c^{\psi}{}_2, d^{\psi}{}_2\right)$ are two TrFN then $\overset{\sim i}{C}{}^{\psi}_{TrFN} = \overset{\sim i}{A}{}^{\psi}_{TrFN} \Theta \overset{\sim i}{B}{}^{\psi}_{TrFN}$ is also TrFN.

$$\overset{\sim i}{A}{}^{\psi}_{TrFN} \Theta \overset{\sim i}{B}{}^{\psi}_{TrFN} = \left(a^{\psi}{}_1 - a^{\psi}{}_2, b^{\psi}{}_1 - b^{\psi}{}_2, c^{\psi}{}_1 - c^{\psi}{}_2, d^{\psi}{}_1 - d^{\psi}{}_2\right)$$

❖ **Properties 4**

If $\overset{\sim i}{A}{}^{\psi}_{TrFN} = \left(a^{\psi}{}_1, b^{\psi}{}_1, c^{\psi}{}_1, d^{\psi}{}_1\right)$ and $\overset{\sim i}{B}{}^{\psi}_{TrFN} = \left(a^{\psi}{}_2, b^{\psi}{}_2, c^{\psi}{}_2, d^{\psi}{}_2\right)$ are two TrFN then $\overset{\sim i}{P}{}^{\psi}_{TrFN} = \overset{\sim i}{A}{}^{\psi}_{TrFN} \odot \overset{\sim i}{B}{}^{\psi}_{TrFN}$ is an approximated TrFN.

$$\overset{\sim i}{A}{}^{\psi}_{TrFN} \odot \overset{\sim i}{B}{}^{\psi}_{TrFN} = \left(a^{\psi}{}_1 a^{\psi}{}_2, b^{\psi}{}_1 b^{\psi}{}_2, c^{\psi}{}_1 c^{\psi}{}_2, d^{\psi}{}_1 d^{\psi}{}_2\right)$$

❖ **Properties 5**

If $\overset{\sim i}{A}{}^{\psi}_{TrFN} = \left(a^{\psi}{}_1, b^{\psi}{}_1, c^{\psi}{}_1, d^{\psi}{}_1\right)$ and $\overset{\sim i}{B}{}^{\psi}_{TrFN} = \left(a^{\psi}{}_2, b^{\psi}{}_2, c^{\psi}{}_2, d^{\psi}{}_2\right)$ are two TrFN then $\overset{\sim i}{P}{}^{\psi}_{TrFN} = \overset{\sim i}{A}{}^{\psi}_{TrFN} \div \overset{\sim i}{B}{}^{\psi}_{TrFN}$ is an approximated TrFN.

$$\overset{\sim i}{A}{}^{\psi}_{TrFN} \div \overset{\sim i}{B}{}^{\psi}_{TrFN} = \left(a^{\psi}{}_1 / a^{\psi}{}_2, b^{\psi}{}_1 / b^{\psi}{}_2, c^{\psi}{}_1 / c^{\psi}{}_2, d^{\psi}{}_1 / d^{\psi}{}_2\right)$$

11.3 Theoretical Part

11.3.1 Mathematical Formulation of an Assignment Problem

Consider a situation of assignment 'm' jobs (or workers) to 'n' machines. Also let C_{ij} be the cost of assigning *i*th job (i = 1,2,……..m) to *j*th machine (j = 1,2,……n). The objective is to assign the jobs to the machines (one job per machine) at the least total cost or the maximum total profit.

In the assignment problem, job represents 'source' and machines represent 'destinations'. The supply at each source is one, i.e. $a_i = 1$, for all I and demand at each destination is one, i.e. $b_j = 1$, for all j.

The assignment problem can be represented in the form of n × n cost matrix or effectiveness matrix (C_{ij}) as given in the following table:

Machine

job	1		...	j	...	n	supply (a_i)
1	C_{11}	C_{12}	...	C_{1j}	...	C_{1n}	1
2	C_{21}	C_{22}	...	C_{2j}	...	C_{2n}	1
⋮							⋮
i	C_{i1}	C_{i2}	...	C_{ij}	...	C_{in}	1
⋮	⋮						⋮
n	C_{n1}	C_{n2}	...	C_{nj}	...	C_{nn}	1
Demand (b_1)	1	1	...	1	...	1	

Let x_{ij} denote the assignment of the *i*th job the *j*th machine, since the assignment must be made on a one-to-one basis, we have

$$x_{ij} = \begin{cases} 1, & \textit{if } i-th \textit{ job is assigned to the } j-th \textit{ machine} \\ 0, & \textit{otherwise} \end{cases}$$

Then the mathematical model of the assignment problem can be posed as follows:

$$\text{Optimize } z = \sum_{i=1}^{n} \sum_{j=1}^{n} c_{ij} x_{ij}$$

Subject to the constraints

$$\sum_{j=1}^{n} x_{ij} = 1, j = 1,2,3,\ldots\ldots\ldots\ldots\ldots, n$$ [∵ only one job will be assigned to one machine]

$$\sum_{i=1}^{n} x_{ij} = 1, j = 1,2,3,\ldots\ldots\ldots\ldots\ldots, n$$ [∵ Only one machine should be assigned to one job] and $x_{ij} = 0 or 1 \forall i, j$

From the above discussion, some characteristic of the assignment model can be over served as given below:

(i) Here total cost matrix is a square matrix i.e., m = n in the assignment model. If m ≠ n it is necessary to make m = n by adding fictitious jobs or machines;
(ii) As the assignment model requires a one-to-one assignment, the number of solution variables in an n × n problem is exactly n. This means that the assignment model is inherently degenerate;
(iii) The total number of possible solutions for n × n assignment problem is always n!

11.3.2 Method for Solving an Assignment Problem

Among various methods for solving an assignment problem, some of them are cited below.

11.3.2.1 Enumeration Method

In enumeration method all possible assignments among the given resource are listed (e.g. man, machine, etc.) and activities (e.g. job, work center, etc.) is encountered. Then that assignment is selected as an optimal solution which gives the minimum cost, time, distance, etc. or gives the maximum profit. If two or more assignments give the same minimum cost for maximum profit, the problem has an alternative optimal solution.

For 4 × 4 assignment problem, we have to evaluate a total 4! i.e. 24 assignments for finding the optimal solution. Thus for solving an assignment problem by this method, a huge work are needed. So this method is not suitable for manual calculations.

11.3.2.2 Regular Simplex Method

All the assignment problem can be solved by regular simplex method. But in general, n × n i.e. 2n constraints. In particular, for 4 × 4 assignment problem, there are 16 decision variable and 8 constraints which are much laborious what solving the problem by simplex method. Thus simplex method is also not suitable in in solving assignment problem manually.

11.3.2.3 Transportation Method

Since an assignment problem is a special type of transportation problem, we can solve it by transportation method as discuss in this section. Now, for non-degenerate solution in transportation problem, we have m + n – 1 basic feasible solutions. So in an assignment problem, we should have n + n – 1, that is 2n – 1 basic feasible solutions. But as is seen from the constraints that every basic feasible solution consists of n basic variables each being equal to 1 and (n – 1) basic variables each of which is equal to 0. Thus if we apply the transportation algorithm to solve the assignment problem we shall have to perform a large number of iterations for the resolution of degeneracy until the optimal solution is obtained. So transportation method in assignment problem involves a huge job. Thus the method is also not suitable for practical handling.

11.3.2.4 Hungarian Method

The Hungarian mathematician D. Konig developed an efficient method for finding an optimal solution without making direct comparison of every solution due to the special structure of assignment model. Known as the Hungarian method the method is based on the following theorems:

Theorem 1. The optimal solution of the assignment model remains the same if a constant is added or subtracted to/from all the elements of the row or column of the assignment cost matrix.

Proof. Let the cost matrix of an assignment problem be $(C_{ij})_{n\times n}$ and suppose u_i and v_j are added or subtracted to/from all the elements of the *i*th row and *j*th column of the cost matrix. Then the new cost elements are

$$C_{ij}^{/} = C_{ij} \pm u_i \pm v_j$$

This yields the new objective function as

$$z^{/} = \sum_{i=1}^{n}\sum_{j=1}^{n} c_{ij}^{/} x_{ij}$$

$$= \sum_{i=1}^{n}\sum_{j=1}^{n} (C_{ij} \pm u_i \pm v_j) x_{ij}$$

$$= \sum_{i=1}^{n}\sum_{j=1}^{n} (C_{ij} x_{ij}) \pm \sum_{i=1}^{n}\sum_{j=1}^{n} (u_i x_{ij}) \pm \sum_{i=1}^{n}\sum_{j=1}^{n} (v_j x_{ij})$$

$$= z \pm \sum_{i=1}^{n} u_i \sum_{j=1}^{n} x_{ij} \pm \sum_{i=1}^{n} v_j \sum_{j=1}^{n} x_{ij}$$

$$= z \pm \sum_{i=1}^{n} u_i \pm \sum_{j=1}^{n} v_j$$

Since

$$\sum_{i=1}^{n} x_{ij} \; and \sum_{j=1}^{n} x_{ij} = 1$$

Where z is the value of the objective function all the original assignment problem.

$$\therefore z' = z \pm \text{constant},$$

Where the constant is independent of x_{ij}. Hence an assignment x_{ij} which minimizes z will also minimize z'. Thus the optimal assignment of the original problem must be the optimal assignment of the new problem.

Note. In general, it is possible to scale up the cost matrix by adding or subtracting a constant number to/from every element without affecting the interrelationship of the elements.

Also we can divide or multiply every element of the cost matrix by a positive constant.

Although search scaling operations effect the value of the objective function, but they do not affect the final allocation in assignment problems. Using this operations, negative cost elements can be made non-negative.

Theorem 2. If for an assignment problem (minimization problem), all $c_{ij} \geq 0$ and we can find a set $x_{ij} = x_{ij}^{l}$ such that

$$\sum_{i=1}^{n}\sum_{j=1}^{n} c_{ij}x_{ij}^{l} = 0$$

Then this solution is optimal,

Proof. Since we have $c_{ij} \geq 0$ and also $x_{ij} \geq 0$, so $z = \sum_{i=1}^{n}\sum_{j=1}^{n} c_{ij}x_{ij}^{l}$ is non-negative. Hence its minimum value is zero which is obtained for. Therefore, the present solution is an optimal solution.

Note. These theorems can be used in two different way to solve the assignment problem. By Theorem 1 we can introduce a number of zeros to the cost matrix, that is, the assignment matrix. Then the assignment can be made in sense of Theorem 2. Then the assignment is made in the cells with the derived zero cost.

11.3.3 Computational Processor of Hungarian Method (For Minimization Problem)

To obtain an optimal solution following are the steps in Figure 11.1:

Step 1. At first a cost matrix has to prepare, sometimes it may not be a square matrix, then add a dummy row or dummy column with zero cost elements.

Step 2. Now first reduced cost matrix must find out by subtract the minimum element in each row from all the elements of the respective rows. By subtracting from the new matrix, there will be at least one zero in each row.

Step 3. In first reduced cost matrix all column and row does not get the zero then again smallest cost element in each column from all elements

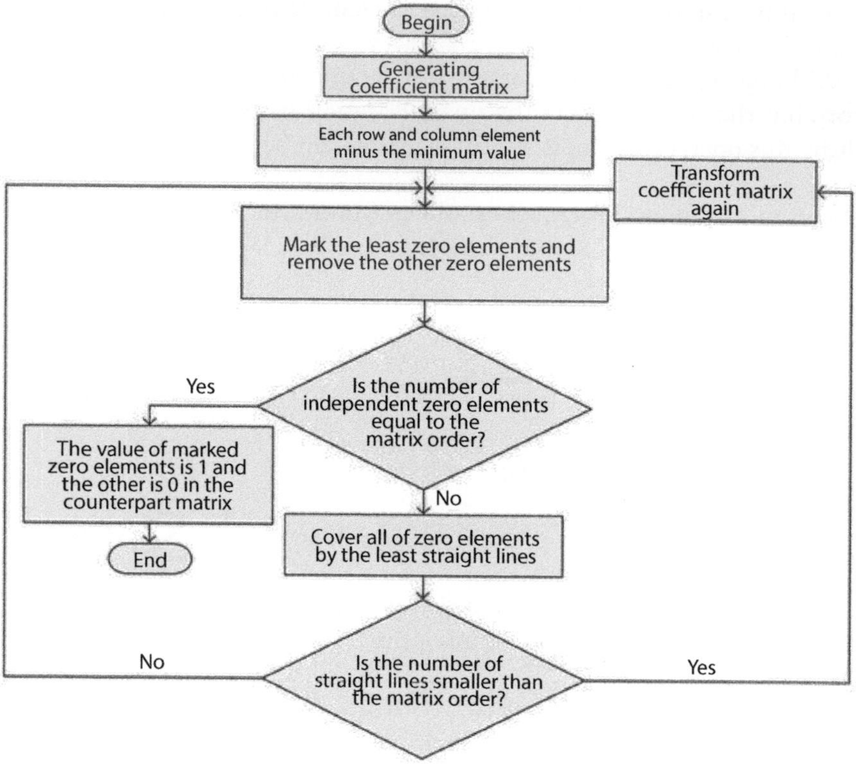

Figure 11.1 Flow chart of Hungarian method.

of the respective columns has to subtracted. As a result, there would be at least one zero in each row and column of second reduced cost matrix.

Step 4

(i) Starting with first row of second reduced matrix, examine all the rows of this matrix which contains only one zero in it. Mark this zero within the circle and cross out the columns containing these assigned zeros. Continue checking all the rows in this manner.

(ii) Start from the first column and examine all the uncovered columns to find the columns containing exactly one remaining zero. Mark this zero within the circle as an assignment will be made there. Cross out the rows containing these assigned zeros.

Continue steps 1 and 2 to cross out all zeros.

Step 5. If the order of the cost matrix is equal to number of covering lines, then the assignment made in step 4 is the optimal solution, otherwise go to the next step.

Step 6. Find the smallest element among the uncrossed elements and select it. After that subtract the smallest element from all the uncrossed elements and add the same at the point of intersection of two crossed out lines whereas the other elements crossed by the lines remain unchanged.

Step 7. Repeat the procedure from step 4 till an optimum solution is attained.

11.4 Application With Discussion

Problem 1:
To describe the method using fuzzy number one assignment problem is represented using cost matrix. Here all the elements reflect the times a computer takes to complete the respective jobs in hours. In this complexity time is reduced.

Now locate the minimum elements of every row in Figure 11.2. The minimum elements A, B, C, D are all respectively (8, 9, 10, 11), (4, 5, 6, 7), (15, 16, 17, 18) and (10, 11, 12, 13). Now subtract these minimum elements from all the other elements of the respective row. Here it is noted that except column II every row and as well as every column have at least

	I	II	III	IV
A	(8,9,10,11)	(26,27,28,29)	(17,18,19,20)	(11,12,13,14)
B	(13,14,15,16)	(28,29,30,31)	(4,5,6,7)	(26,27,28,29)
C	(38,39,40,41)	(19,20,21,22)	(18,19,20,21)	(15,16,17,18)
D	(19,20,21,22)	(26,27,28,29)	(24,25,26,27)	(10,11,12,13)

Figure 11.2 Matrix 1.

one zero. Repeat the procedure of subtraction of the minimum element for column II. Then the second matrix is obtained in Figure 11.3.

We have zeros in the cells (1,1), (2,3), (3,2), (3,4) and (4,4) in Figure 11.4. Write down the required number of horizontal and vertical lines to cover all the zeros. If the cost matrix order is four, then it needs at least four lines.

Then assignment made in the cells (1,1), (2,3) and (4,4), each for the first, second and fourth rows contains just one zero. Etiquet the individual cells with an omnipresent stage. Since there are two zeros in third row, no assignment is made in third row. Now the allocated cells draw those vertical lines. The second column of the cell (3,2) contains a zero and this column is also untouched. Marked that particular by □. No unmarked zero left so the optimal assignment is $A \rightarrow I, B \rightarrow III, C \rightarrow II, D \rightarrow IV$ shown in Figure 11.5.

The minimum cost time is calculated in Figure 11.5. Minimum cost (time) = sum of cost of cells (1,1), (2,3), (4,4) and (3,2) = (8, 9, 10, 11) + (4, 5, 6, 7) + (19, 20, 21, 22) + (10, 11, 12, 13) = (41, 45, 49, 53).

	I	II	III	IV
A	(0,0,0,0)	(18,18,18,18)	(9,9,9,9)	(3,3,3,3)
B	(9,9,9,9)	(24,24,24,24)	(0,0,0,0)	(22,22,22,22)
C	(23,23,23,23)	(4,4,4,4)	(3,3,3,3)	(0,0,0,0)
D	(9,9,9,9)	(16,16,16,16)	(14,14,14,14)	(0,0,0,0)

Figure 11.3 Matrix 2.

	I	II	III	IV
A	(0,0,0,0)	(14,14,14,14)	(9,9,9,9)	(3,3,3,3)
B	(9,9,9,9)	(20,20,20,20)	(0,0,0,0)	(22,22,22,22)
C	(23,23,23,23)	(0,0,0,0)	(3,3,3,3)	(0,0,0,0)
D	(9,9,9,9)	(12,12,12,12)	(14,14,14,14)	(0,0,0,0)

Figure 11.4 Matrix 3.

	I	II	III	IV
A	(0,0,0,0)	(14,14,14,14)	(9,9,9,9)	(3,3,3,3)
B	(9,9,9,9)	(20,20,20,20)	(0,0,0,0)	(22,22,22,22)
C	(23,23,23,23)	(0,0,0,0)	(3,3,3,3)	(0,0,0,0)
D	(9,9,9,9)	(12,12,12,12)	(14,14,14,14)	(0,0,0,0)

Figure 11.5 Matrix 4.

Problem 2:
Let us consider the assignment problem represented by the cost matrix as shown in Figure 11.6.

Now locate the minimum elements of every row. All the minimum elements of A, B, C, D are respectively (10, 11, 12, 13), (5, 6, 7, 8), (12, 13, 14, 15) and (17, 18, 19, 20). Now subtract these minimum elements from all the other elements of the respective row. Here it is noted that except for columns II and IV, every row and as well as every column has at least one zero. Repeat the procedure of subtraction of the minimum element for columns II and IV. Then the second matrix is obtained in Figure 11.7.

We have zeros in the cells (1,1), (2,3), (3,2), (3,3), (4,1), (4,2) and (4,4) in Figure 11.8. To cover all the zeros, draw the minimum number of

	I	II	III	IV
A	(10,11,12,13)	(25,26,27,28)	(15,16,17,18)	(20,21,22,23)
B	(15,16,17,18)	(30,31,32,33)	(5,6,7,8)	(15,16,17,18)
C	(35,36,37,38)	(20,21,22,23)	(12,13,14,15)	(24,25,26,27)
D	(17,18,19,20)	(25,26,27,28)	(24,25,26,27)	(20,21,22,23)

Figure 11.6 Matrix 1.

	I	II	III	IV
A	(0,0,0,0)	(15,15,15)	(5,5,5,5)	(10,10,10,10)
B	(10,10,10,10)	(25,25,25,25)	(0,0,0,0)	(10,10,10,10)
C	(23,23,23,23)	(8,8,8,8)	(0,0,0,0)	(12,12,12,12)
D	(0,0,0,0)	(8,8,8,8)	(7,7,7,7)	(3,3,3,3)

Figure 11.7 Matrix 2.

	I	II	III	IV
A	(0,0,0,0)	(7,7,7,7)	(5,5,5)	(7,7,7,7)
B	(10,10,10,10)	(17,17,17,17)	(0,0,0,0)	(7,7,7,7)
C	(23,23,23,23)	(0,0,0,0)	(0,0,0,0)	(9,9,9,9)
D	(0,0,0,0)	(0,0,0,0)	(7,7,7,7)	(0,0,0,0)

Figure 11.8 Matrix 3.

horizontal and vertical lines. As the order of the cost matrix is four, then at least four lines are required.

In the cells, then assignment (1,1), (2,3), (3,2) and (4,4), for the 1st, 2nd, 3rd and 4th rows each contain a single zero. Marked that particular cells with □. No unmarked zero is left so the optimal assignment is $A \rightarrow I$, $B \rightarrow III$, $C \rightarrow II$, $D \rightarrow IV$ shown in Figure 11.9.

	I	II	III	IV
A	(0,0,0,0)	(7,7,7,7)	(5,5,5)	(7,7,7,7)
B	(10,10,10,10)	(17,17,17,17)	(0,0,0,0)	(7,7,7,7)
C	(23,23,23,23)	(0,0,0,0)	(0,0,0,0)	(9,9,9,9)
D	(0,0,0,0)	(0,0,0,0)	(7,7,7,7)	(0,0,0,0)

Figure 11.9 Matrix 4.

Minimum cost (time) = sum of cost of cells (1,1), (2,3), (4,4) and (3,2) = (10, 11, 12, 13) + (5, 6, 7, 8) + (20, 21, 22, 23) + (20, 21, 22, 23) = (55, 59, 63, 67).

Problem 3:
Solve the assignment problem where the assignment cost of assigning any operator to any one machine is given below in Figure 11.10.

Performing the row operation as per the previous we get as Figure 11.11.

As per pervious performing the column operation we get as Figure 11.12,

	I	II	III	IV
A	(1,2,3,4)	(4,5,6,7)	(6,7,8,9)	(3,4,5,6)
B	(9,10,11,12)	(7,8,9,10)	(10,11,12,13)	(9,10,11,12)
C	(4,5,6,7)	(5,6,7,8)	(11,12,13,14)	(7,8,9,10)
D	(8,9,10,11)	(7,8,9,10)	(8,9,10,11)	(5,6,7,8)

Figure 11.10 Matrix 1.

	I	II	III	IV
A	(0,0,0,0)	(3,3,3,3)	(5,5,5,5)	(2,2,2,2)
B	(2,2,2,2)	(0,0,0,0)	(3,3,3,3)	(2,2,2,2)
C	(0,0,0,0)	(1,1,1,1)	(7,7,7,7)	(3,3,3,3)
D	(3,3,3,3)	(2,2,2,2)	(3,3,3,3)	(0,0,0,0)

Figure 11.11 Matrix 2.

	I	II	III	IV
A	(0,0,0,0)	(3,3,3,3)	(2,2,2,2)	(2,2,2,2)
B	(2,2,2,2)	(0,0,0,0)	(0,0,0,0)	(2,2,2,2)
C	(0,0,0,0)	(1,1,1,1)	(4,4,4,4)	(3,3,3,3)
D	(3,3,3,3)	(2,2,2,2)	(0,0,0,0)	(0,0,0,0)

Figure 11.12 Matrix 3.

Starting with 1st row □ a single zero and cross all other zeros in its column. Then follow the same process for columns we get as Figure 11.13:

	I	II	III	IV
A	(0,0,0,0)	(3,3,3,3)	(2,2,2,2)	(2,2,2,2)
B	(2,2,2,2)	(0,0,0,0)	(0,0,0,0)	(2,2,2,2)
C	(0,0,0,0)	(1,1,1,1)	(4,4,4,4)	(3,3,3,3)
D	(3,3,3,3)	(2,2,2,2)	(0,0,0,0)	(0,0,0,0)

Figure 11.13 Matrix 4.

The order of cost matrix is 3 and also cross out lines is 3. Select the smallest elements among all uncovered elements by cross out lines. Here the element is (1,1,1,1). Now the element is subtracted from all uncovered elements and add to the elements which are at the point of intersection of horizontal and vertical lines. Thus, we obtained the following new reduced cost matrix:

	I	II	III	IV
A	(0,0,0,0)	(2,2,2,2)	(1,1,1,1)	(1,1,1,1)
B	(3,3,3,3)	(0,0,0,0)	(0,0,0,0)	(2,2,2,2)
C	(0,0,0,0)	(0,0,0,0)	(3,3,3,3)	(2,2,2,2)
D	(4,4,4,4)	(2,2,2,2)	(0,0,0,0)	(0,0,0,0)

Figure 11.14 Matrix 5.

Making new assignment as Figure 11.14 we get as Figure 11.15.

	I	II	III	IV
A	(0,0,0,0)	(2,2,2,2)	(1,1,1,1)	(1,1,1,1)
B	(3,3,3,3)	(0,0,0,0)	(0,0,0,0)	(2,2,2,2)
C	(0,0,0,0)	(0,0,0,0)	(3,3,3,3)	(2,2,2,2)
D	(4,4,4,4)	(2,2,2,2)	(0,0,0,0)	(0,0,0,0)

Figure 11.15 Matrix 6.

The order of cost matrix is 4 and also cross out lines is 4, the optimality has been obtained. The optimal assignment is $A \rightarrow I, B \rightarrow III, C \rightarrow II, D \rightarrow IV$. The minimum cost is, from the original matrix = (1, 2, 3, 4) + (10, 11, 12, 13) + (5, 6, 7, 8) + (5, 6, 7, 8) = (21, 25, 29, 33).

11.5 Conclusion and Further Work

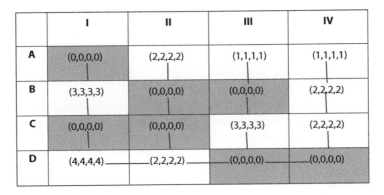

In this paper we mainly described Trapezoidal fuzzy number. To derive the theoretical result the definition of Trapezoidal fuzzy number is useful. Some arithmetic operations also discussed here to use in the experiment. We have also solved an assignment problem using Trapezoidal fuzzy number. Mainly simple examples are used in this paper. To represent uncertain information, we mainly used fuzzy number. The procedure of solving assignment problem using TrFN may help us to solve many optimization problems. The authors will discuss corresponding results for the Trapezoidal Fuzzy number in future studies. The author's future work may consider various reduction strategies in terms of the triangular fuzzy number. Our methods can be effective and easy to involved in a Trapezoidal fuzzy Number Context for all engineering and science fields where imprecision occurs. Further we can use Intuitionistic and Type2 fuzzy number to solve this type of problems.

References

1. Chakraborty, A., Mondal, S.P., Alam, S., Ahmadian, A., Senu, N., De, D., Salahshour, S., Disjunctive Representation of Triangular Bipolar Neutrosophic Numbers, De-Bipolarization Technique and Application in Multi-Criteria Decision-Making Problems. *Symmetry*, 11, 932, 2019.
2. Chakraborty, A., Mondal, S.P., Alam, S., Ahmadian, A., Senu, N., De, D., Salahshour, S., The Pentagonal Fuzzy Number: Its Different Representations, Properties, Ranking, Defuzzification and Application in Game Problems. *Symmetry*, *11*, 2, 248, 2019.
3. Chakraborty, A., Mondal, S.P., Ahmadian, A., Senu, N., Alam, S., Salahshour, S., Different forms of triangular neutrosophic numbers, de-neutrosophication techniques, and their applications. *Symmetry*, *10*, 8, 327, 2018.
4. Chen, S.M., Analyzing fuzzy system reliability using vague set theory. *Int. J. Appl. Sci. Eng.*, *1*, 1, 82–88, 2003.
5. Chen, S.H., Operations on fuzzy numbers with function principal, 1985.
6. Dubois, D. and Prade, H., Operations on fuzzy numbers. *Int. J. Syst. Sci.*, *9*, 6, 613–626, 1978.
7. Hansen, E., Interval arithmetic in matrix computations, Part I. *J. Soc Indust. Appl. Math., Ser. B: Numer. Anal.*, *2*, 2, 308–320, 1965.
8. Hansen, E. and Smith, R., Interval arithmetic in matrix computations, Part II. *SIAM J. Numer. Anal.*, *4*, 1, 1–9, 1967.
9. Hansen, E., On the solution of linear algebraic equations with interval coefficients. *Linear Algebra Appl.*, *2*, 2, 153–165, 1969.
10. Hansen, E., Global optimization using interval analysis, in: *Monographs and Textbooks in Pure and Applied Mathematics*, vol. 165, Marcel Dekker, Inc., New York, 1992.
11. Hussain, S.A.I., Mandal, U.K., Mondal, S.P., Decision maker priority index and degree of vagueness coupled decision making method: A synergistic approach. *Int. J. Fuzzy Syst.*, *20*, 5, 1551–1566, 2018.
12. Kaufmann, A., *Introduction to the theory of fuzzy subsets*, vol. 2, Academic Pr., 1975.

13. Kaufmann, A. and Gupta, M.M., Introduction to fuzzy arithmetic theory and it li ti, in: *VN t dR ih ldC NY k its applications*, Van Nostrand Reinhold Company, New York, 1985.
14. Lodwick, W.A. and Jamison, K.D., Interval methods and fuzzy optimization. *Int. J. Uncertain. Fuzz. Knowl.-Based Syst.*, *5*, 03, 239–249, 1997.
15. Mahapatra, G.S. and Roy, T.K., Reliability evaluation using triangular intuitionistic fuzzy numbers arithmetic operations. *World Acad. Sci. Eng. Technol.*, *50*, 574–581, 2009.
16. Majumder, P., Mondal, S.P., Bera, U.K., Maiti, M., Application of Generalized Hukuhara derivative approach in an economic production quantity model with partial trade credit policy under fuzzy environment. *Oper. Res. Perspect.*, *3*, 77–91, 2016.
17. Moore, R.E., *Methods and applications of interval analysis*, Society for Industrial and Applied Mathematics, 1979.
18. Mon, D.L. and Cheng, C.H., Fuzzy system reliability analysis for components with different membership functions. *Fuzzy Sets Syst.*, *64*, 2, 145–157, 1994.
19. Mondal, S.P., Differential equation with interval valued fuzzy number and its applications. *Int. J. Syst. Assur. Eng. Manage.*, *7*, 3, 370–386, 2016.
20. Kar, R. and Shaw, A.K., Some Arithmetic Operations on Trapezoidal Fuzzy Numbers and its Application in Solving Linear Programming Problem by Simplex Algorithm. *Int. J. Bioinform. Biol. Sci.*, *6*, 2, 77–86, 2018.
21. Kar, R. and Shaw, A.K., Some Arithmetic Operations on Trapezoidal Fuzzy Numbers and its Application in Solving Linear Programming Problem by Simplex Algorithm. *Int. J. Bioinform. Biol. Sci.*, *6*, 2, 77–86, 2018.
22. Mahapatra, G.S., Mahapatra, B.S., Roy, P.K., Fuzzy decision-making on reliability of series system: Fuzzy geometric programming approach. *Ann. Fuzzy Math. Inform.*, *1*, 1, 107–118, 2011.
23. Garg, H., Reliability analysis of repairable systems using Petri nets and Vague Lambda-Tau methodology. *ISA Trans.*, *52*, 1, 6–18, 2013.
24. Shaw, A.K. and Roy, T.K., Trapezoidal Intuitionistic Fuzzy Number with some arithmetic operations and its application on reliability evaluation. *Int. J. Math. Oper. Res.*, *5*, 1, 55–73, 2013.
25. Kar, R. and Shaw, A.K., Some Arithmetic Operations on Triangular Intuitionistic Fuzzy Number and its Application in Solving Linear Programming Problem by Simplex Algorithm. *Int. J. Bioinform. Biol. Sci.*, *7*, 1 and 2, 21–28, 2019.
26. Zadeh, L.A., Fuzzy sets. *Inf. Control*, *8*, 3, 338–353, 1965.

12

The Connectedness of Fuzzy Graph and the Resolving Number of Fuzzy Digraph

Mary Jiny D. and R. Shanmugapriya*

Department of Mathematics, Vel Tech Rangarajan Dr. Sagunthala R&D Institute of Science and Technology, Avadi, Chennai, India

Abstract

The Modified fuzzy graph is a fuzzy graph in which the weight of any edge of the graph is less than or equal to the maximum membership value of the corresponding two nodes. The strength or weight of any path between two nodes is the minimum edge weight on that path. And the strength of connectedness between any two nodes is the maximum of all path strength between the corresponding two nodes. To find the shortest distance between any two nodes of a weighted graph, we have a number of algorithms. However, to find the strength of connectedness between any two nodes of a fuzzy graph, there does not exist a commendable algorithm. We explain an algorithm to find the strength of connectedness between any two nodes of a fuzzy graph in this paper. And the strength of connectedness is applied to find the shortest and safest path of the fighting humanoid robot for rescuing human lives from fire accidents. We also introduce the concept of fuzzy resolving number in fuzzy digraph or fuzzy network. Fuzzy digraph is a directed fuzzy graph with each edge has a tail and head. We define fuzzy left-super resolving set, fuzzy right-super resolving set, left-super resolving number and right-super resolving number of the fuzzy digraphs. We discuss the resolving properties of isomorphic fuzzy digraph and theorems based on resolving sets.

Keywords: Fuzzy graph, modified fuzzy graph, weight of fuzzy path, resolving number of the graph, adjacency matrix, humanoid robot

**Corresponding author*: spriyasathish11@gmail.com

E. Chandrasekaran, R. Anandan, G. Suseendran, S. Balamurugan and Hanaa Hachimi (eds.) Fuzzy Intelligent Systems: Methodologies, Techniques, and Applications, (335–364) © 2021 Scrivener Publishing LLC

12.1 Introduction

In 1965, Zadeh introduced fuzzy mathematics. In 1975 Rosenfield defined fuzzy graphs, which has plenty of applications in real life. Slater, Harry and Melter introduced the concept of resolving number in graph [1]. Harry and Melter named it as metric dimension, while Slater called it locating set and locating number. Wu introduced fuzzy digraph in 1986 [2]. Gani extended the properties of the fuzzy graph in isomorphism fuzzy labeling tree, Regular fuzzy graphs, Antipodal fuzzy graph [4], Irregular Fuzzy Graphs [5], domination and fuzzy labeling. Abdul-Jabbar, Naoom and Ouda defined Fuzzy dual graphs in 2009 [6]. Samanta and Pal defined irregular bipolar fuzzy graphs in 2012 [7]. Akram and Dudek introduced the operations on interval-valued fuzzy graphs in 2012 [17]. Akram and Davvaz introduced Strong Intuitionistic Fuzzy Graphs in 2012 [8]. Mordeson and Mathew published a textbook on fuzzy graph theory in the year 2018 and discussed fuzzy digraph as a fuzzy network. Shanmugapriya and Jiny D. introduced fuzzy super resolving set in 2019 [1]. Floyd-Warshal found the shortest path algorithm in 1902 which is used to find the shortest path between any two vertices of the weighted graph and the running time of warshall algorithm is $O(n^3)$. However, Roy in 1959 published a similar algorithm and Warshall in 1962. In this chapter, we explain an algorithm to find the safest path in fuzzy graph which is different from the shortest path in the weighted graph. We introduce the concept of left-super resolving set, left-super resolving number, right-super resolving set and right-super resolving number of a fuzzy digraph or fuzzy network. We also see some properties of resolving sets in fuzzy network.

12.2 Definitions

Definition 1. Consider a nonempty set X. A **fuzzy subset** A of X is an ordered pair $A = \{(v, \mu_A(v))/v \in X\}$ where $\mu_A{:}X \rightarrow [0,1]$ and $\mu_A(v)$ is interpreted as the membership value of element v in fuzzy set A for each $v \in X$.

Definition 2. The Graph $G(V(G), E(G))$ is an ordered pair, having a set $V(G)$ of vertices and a set $E(G)$ of edges, together with an incidence map $\Psi(G)$ that relates with each edge of G, a pair of vertices of G which is unordered [9].

Definition 3. Fuzzy Graph is an ordered triple $G(V, \sigma, \mu)$, where V is a nonempty set of vertices together with the functions $\sigma: V \rightarrow [0,1]$ and μ: $V \times V \rightarrow [0,1]$ such that $\forall\, x, y \in V, \mu(x, y) \leq \mu(x) \wedge \mu(y)$ [10]. The support of μ and σ are represented as $\mu^* = \{(x, y)/\mu(x, y) > 0\}$ and $\sigma^* = \{u/\sigma(u) > 0\}$. The fuzzy subgraph induced by S is defined as $H = (S, \tau, \nu)$ where $S \subseteq V, \tau(x) \subseteq \sigma(x) \forall x \in S, \nu(x, y) = \mu(x, y) \forall x, y \in S$ and it is denoted as $\langle S \rangle$ [11].

Example 1. The example of a fuzzy graph is given in Figure 12.1.

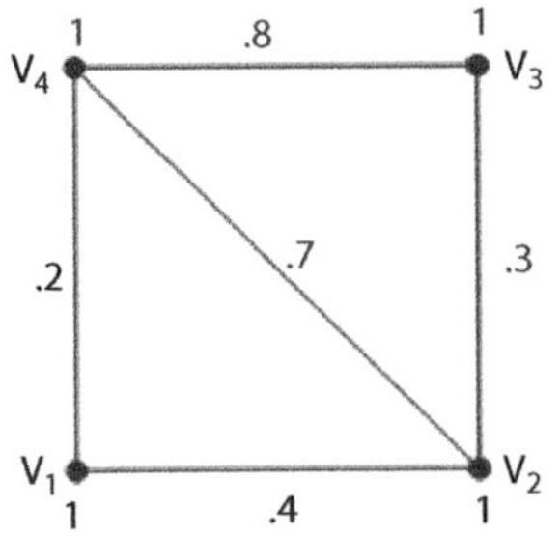

Figure 12.1 Example of a fuzzy graph.

Definition 4. Modified Fuzzy Graph $G(V, \sigma, \mu)$, is an ordered triple, where V is a nonempty set of vertices together with the map σ: $V \rightarrow [0,1]$ and μ: $V \times V \rightarrow [0,1]$ such that $\forall\, u, v \in V, \mu(a, b) \leq \sigma(a) \vee \sigma(b)$.

Definition 5. The Strength of the Fuzzy Path: From a fuzzy graph $G(V, \sigma, \mu)$, the sequence of different vertices $v_1, v_2, \ldots v_n$ with $\mu(v_{i-1}, v_i) > 0$, $i = 1,2,\ldots n$ is said to be a **fuzzy path** $\boldsymbol{P}$ of length 'n' [3]. The consecutive pairs are named us the edges of the path. The length of the longest path between v_1 to v_2 is called the diameter of $v_1 - v_2$ denoted as diam(v_1, v_n). The **strength or weight of the path** P is said to be the weight of the weakest edge in the path. **The weight of connectedness** between v_1 and v_2 is the maximum of the weight of all the paths between v_1 and v_2 and is represented as $\mu^\infty(v_1, v_n)$ [9], for our usage we represent it as $w(v_1, v_n)$. A strongest path joining v_1 and v_n has weight $\mu^\infty(v_1, v_n)$. The fuzzy path P is said to be a fuzzy cycle if $v_1 = v_n$ and $n \geq 3$ [4].

Example 2. Find the strength of connectedness between each pair of vertices of the following fuzzy graph in Figure 12.2.

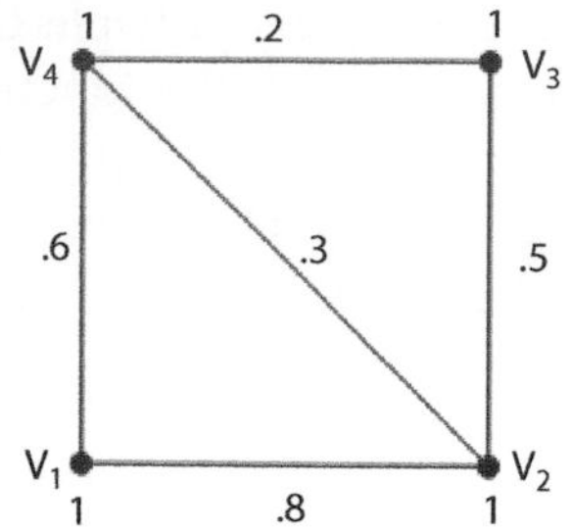

Figure 12.2 Fuzzy Graph *G*.

$w(v_1, v_2) = .8$
$w(v_1, v_2) = .5$
$w(v_1, v_2) = .6$
$w(v_2, v_3) = .5$
$w(v_2, v_4) = .6$
$w(v_3, v_4) = .5$

Definition 6.
Let G be a fuzzy graph, the **adjacency matrix** of G is defined as A_{ij} where $X_{ij} = \mu(v_i, v_j)$ for $i \neq j$ and $X_{ij} = 0$ if $i = j$ [12]. The adjacency matrix of Figure 12.2 is:

$$C_{ij} = \begin{array}{c} \\ v_1 \\ v_2 \\ v_3 \\ v_4 \end{array} \begin{array}{c} \begin{array}{cccc} v_1 & v_2 & v_3 & v_4 \end{array} \\ \begin{bmatrix} 0 & .8 & 0 & .6 \\ .8 & 0 & .5 & .3 \\ 0 & .5 & 0 & .2 \\ .6 & .3 & .2 & 0 \end{bmatrix} \end{array}$$

Definition 7. The **Connectedness matrix** of fuzzy graph G is defined as C_{ij} where $C_{ij} = \mu^{\infty}(v_i, v_j)$ for $i \neq j$ and $C_{ij} = 0$ if $i = j$. The connectedness matrix of Figure 12.2 is:

$$C_{ij} = \begin{array}{c} \\ v_1 \\ v_2 \\ v_3 \\ v_4 \end{array} \begin{array}{c} \begin{array}{cccc} v_1 & v_2 & v_3 & v_4 \end{array} \\ \begin{bmatrix} 0 & .8 & .5 & .6 \\ .8 & 0 & .5 & .6 \\ .5 & .5 & 0 & .5 \\ .6 & .6 & .5 & 0 \end{bmatrix} \end{array}$$

Definition 8. A directed **fuzzy graph or fuzzy digraph** is a triple $\vec{G}(V,\sigma_D,\mu_D)$, σ_D is the fuzzy set or a function σ_D: $V \rightarrow [0,1]$ and μ_D is a function μ_D: $V \times V \rightarrow [0,1]$ which satisfies the condition $\mu_D(x, y) \leq \sigma_D(x) \wedge \sigma_D(y)$. And for any directed arc uv, u is the tail and v is the head. Every arc of the fuzzy di-graph has a tail and head. For $u \in \sigma^*$, $\sum_{v\in\sigma^*} \mu(vu) = d^-(u)$ is the indegree of u and $\sum_{v\in\sigma^*} \mu(uv) = d^+(u)$ is the outdegree of u [13].

Definition 9. Two fuzzy digraphs G_D and $G_{D'}$ are said to be **homomorphic** if there exists a function ϕ: $G_D \rightarrow G_{D'}$, that is, ϕ: $V_1 \rightarrow V_2$ satisfying the condition $\sigma_D(x) \leq \sigma_{D'}(x)$ and $\mu_D(uv) \leq \mu_{D'}(\phi(u), \phi(v))$ for all $u, v \in V$.

Example 3. An example of homomorhic fuzzy graph G and G′ is given in Figure 12.3.

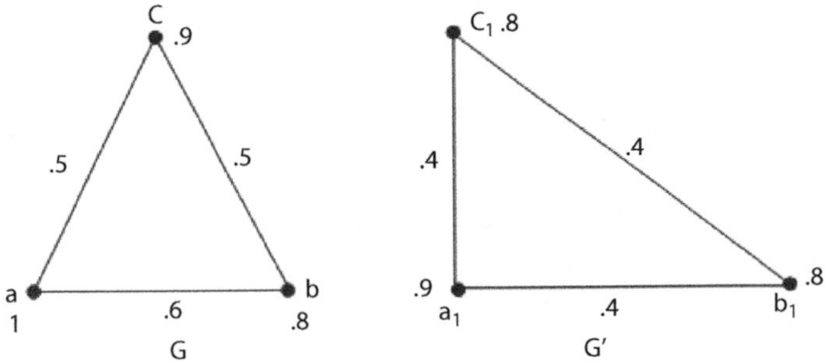

Figure 12.3 Homomorphic fuzzy graphs G and G'.

Definition 10. the fuzzy digraph $\vec{G}$ and $\vec{G}'$ are called **isomorphic**, there exists a bijection ϕ: $V_1 \rightarrow V_2$ that satisfies $\sigma_D(x) = \sigma_{D'}(\phi(x))$ for all $x \in \vec{V_1}$ and $\mu_D(x, y) = \mu_{D'}(\phi(x), \phi(y))$ for all $x, y \in V_1$ and which is denoted as $\vec{G} \cong \vec{G}'$. Two fuzzy digraphs are said to be isomorphic if there exists a one to one correspondence between the vertices and edges having same in degree and out degree [14].

Example 4. An example of isomorhpic fuzzy graph is given in Figure 12.4.

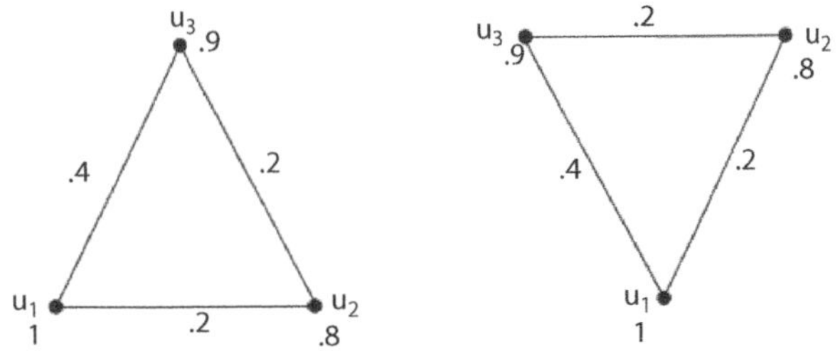

Figure 12.4 Example of an Isomorphic fuzzy graphs G and G′.

Definition 11. An isomorphism of the fuzzy digraph $\vec{G}$ to itself is called an **automorphism.**

Definition 12. $x_1, e_1, x_2, e_2, \ldots x_n$ is called the **directed walk** of fuzzy di-graph, where σ_D and μ_D are alternatively arranged such that e_i has tail x_i and head x_{i+1}. A di-walk is called the **di-path** if $x_i \neq x_j$ in $x_1, e_1, x_2, e_2, \ldots x_n$ except for x_1 and x_n. If $x_1 = x_n$ then the di-path is called **di-cycle.**

The **length** of di-path is said to be the number of directed edges on the path. The strength or **weight of the di-path** $x_0, x_1, x_2, \ldots x_n$ is the strength of the weakest arc in the path, that is $\mu_D(x_0x_1) \wedge \mu_D(x_1x_2) \wedge \ldots \mu_D(x_{n-1}x_n)$. The **strength or weight of the connectedness** between any two element of σ_D say σ_i and σ_j is the maximum of the strength of all possible di-path between x_i and x_j, and is denoted as $w(x_i, x_j)$. The strength of connectedness between each pair of elements of σ_D are arranged in a matrix called the **connectedness matrix**, and is denoted as $C_{ij} = w(x_i, x_j)$ if $i \neq j$. If $i = j$ then $C_{ij} = 0$ and there exist no directed path between v_i and v_j then $C_{ij} = 0$.

Example 5. An example of Fuzzy Digraph is given in Figure 12.5.

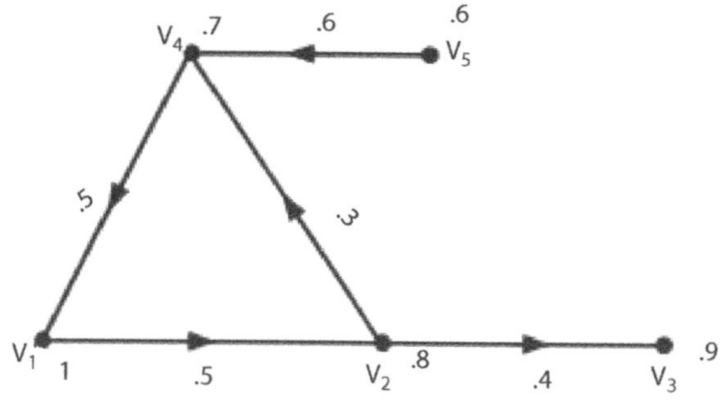

Figure 12.5 Fuzzy digraph.

The connectedness matrix=

	v_1	v_2	v_3	v_4	v_5
v_1	0	.5	.4	.3	0
v_2	.3	0	.4	.3	0
v_3	0	0	0	0	0
v_4	.5	.5	.4	0	0
v_5	.5	.5	.4	.6	0

Definition 13. Let $G(V, \sigma, \mu)$ be a connected fuzzy graph with $|V| \geq 2$. Let $V = \{x_1, x_2, \ldots x_n\}$, a subset $H = \{\sigma_1, \sigma_2, \ldots \sigma_k\}$ of σ with cardinality ≥ 2 is called the **fuzzy resolving set** of G if the representation of $\sigma - H = \{\sigma_{k+1}, \sigma_{k+2}, \ldots \sigma_n\}$ with respect to H, $\sigma_i/H = \{w(x_i, x_1), w(x_i, x_2), \ldots w(x_i, x_k)\}$, $i = k + 1, k + 2, \ldots n$ are distinct $\forall u_i \in (\sigma - H)^*$. Which are arranged as a row of a matrix of order $R_{n-k\times k}$ called **Fuzzy Resolving Matrix** of G with respect to

H, denoted as $R_{n-k \times k}$. The cardinality of the minimum resolving set of G is called the **resolving number** of G denoted as $Fr(G)$. If the representation of σ with respect to H are distinct then H is called the **fuzzy super resolving set** of G. The cardinality of the minimum super resolving set is called the **fuzzy super resolving number** of G, denoted as Sr(G). The representation of elements in with respect to are arranged in a row form a **Fuzzy Super Resolving Matrix** denoted as R_n [15].

Example 6. Find the fuzzy resolving number of the following in Figure 12.6.

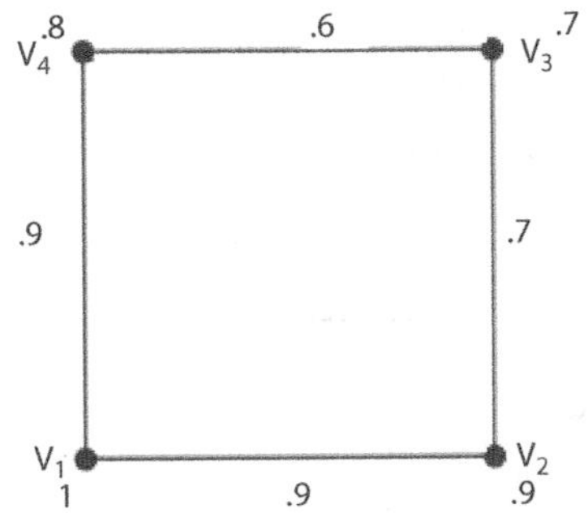

Figure 12.6 Fuzzy graph $G(V, \sigma, \mu)$.

$$V = \{v_1, v_2, v_3, v_4\}\ ; \sigma = \{(v_1, 1), (v_2, .9), (v_3, .7), (v_4, .8)\}$$
$$\mu = \{(v_1v_2,.9), (v_2v_3,.7), (v_3v_4,.6), (v_4v_1,.9)\}$$
$$\text{Let } H_1 = \{\sigma_1, \sigma_2\}; \sigma - H_1 = \{\sigma_3, \sigma_4\} \text{ where } \sigma_1 = (v_1, \sigma(v_1))$$
$$\sigma_3/H_1 = (w(v_3, v_1), w(v_3, v_2)) = (.7,.7)$$
$$\sigma_4/H_1 = (w(v_4, v_1), w(v_4, v_2)) = (.9,.9)$$

The representation of $\sigma - H_1$ with respect to H_1 are all distinct, Hence H_1 is the resolving set of G. We see that, $H_3 = \{\sigma_1, \sigma_4\}$ and $H_5 = \{\sigma_2, \sigma_4\}$ are all fuzzy resolving set of G. $H_2 = \{\sigma_1, \sigma_3\}$, $H_4 = \{\sigma_2, \sigma_3\}$ and $H_6 = \{\sigma_3, \sigma_4\}$ are not fuzzy resolving set of G. Hence, the minimum resolving set has cardinality 2, that is, $Fr(G) = 2$.

12.3 An Algorithm to Find the Super Resolving Matrix

In this section, an algorithm is given to determine the strength or weight of the connectedness between each vertex of the fuzzy graph without loop. Also, an algorithm determines the super resolving matrix of fuzzy graph.

Step 1: The adjacency matrix of $G(V, \sigma, \mu)$ is obtained from $A_{ij} = \mu(v_i, v_j)$ if there is edge from i to j & $A_{ii} = 0$, when $i = j$.
Step 2: Consider there are n vertices of G say $v_1, v_2, \ldots v_n$. Then the sequence of matrices $J_1, J_2 \ldots J_n$ are formed where $J_r = \{J_r(i, j)\}$

Step 3: $J_r(i,j) = \begin{cases} \max[j_{r-1}(i,j), j_{r-1}(i,k) \wedge j_{r-1}(k,j)] \\ \infty \text{ if } i = j \end{cases}$ where $k = 1, 2, \ldots n$

indicate the n iterations.
Step 4: To find J_0, replace the zeros in the diagonal of the adjacency matrix as '∞'.
Step 5: Replace '∞' as '0' in J_n to obtain the connectedness matrix C_{ij}.
Step 6: Replace '∞' in the diagonals as $J_{ii} = \sigma(v_i)$ to find the super resolving matrix R_n.

Example 7. Find the resolving matrix of the following fuzzy graph in Figure 12.7.

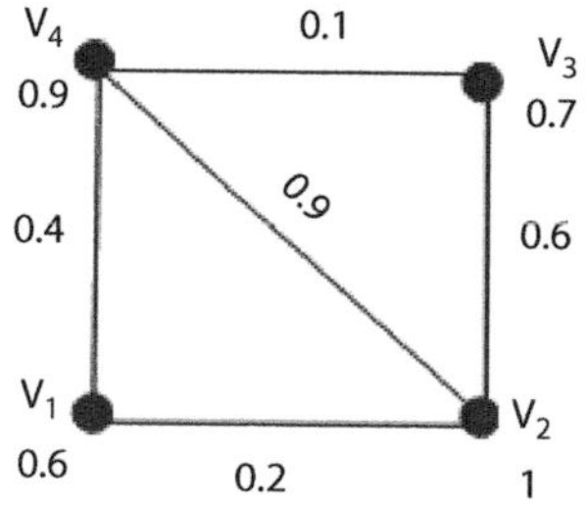

Figure 12.7 $G(V, \sigma, \mu)$.

The adjacency matrix of G, $A_{ij} = \begin{array}{c} \\ v_1 \\ v_2 \\ v_3 \\ v_4 \end{array} \begin{array}{c} \begin{array}{cccc} v_1 & v_2 & v_3 & v_4 \end{array} \\ \begin{bmatrix} 0 & .2 & 0 & .4 \\ .2 & 0 & .6 & .9 \\ 0 & .6 & 0 & .1 \\ .4 & .9 & .1 & 0 \end{bmatrix} \end{array}$

$$J_0 \begin{array}{c} \\ v_1 \\ v_2 \\ v_3 \\ v_4 \end{array} \begin{array}{c} \begin{array}{cccc} v_1 & v_2 & v_3 & v_4 \end{array} \\ \begin{bmatrix} \infty & .2 & 0 & .4 \\ .2 & \infty & .6 & .9 \\ 0 & .6 & \infty & .1 \\ .4 & .9 & .1 & \infty \end{bmatrix} \end{array} J_1(1, 1) = \infty$$

$$\begin{aligned} J_1(1,2) &= \max[j_0(1,2), j_0(1,1) \wedge j_0(1,2)] \\ &= \max[.2, \infty \wedge .2] = .2 \\ J_1(1,3) &= \max[j_0(1,3), j_0(1,1) \wedge j_0(1,3)] \\ &= \max[0, \infty \wedge 0] = 0 \end{aligned}$$

$$J_1(1,4) = \max[j_0(1,4), j_0(1,1) \wedge j_0(1,4)]$$
$$= \max[.4, \infty \wedge .4] = .4$$
$$J_1(2,3) = \max[j_0(2,1), j_0(2,1) \wedge j_0(1,3)]$$
$$= \max[.6,.2 \wedge .0] = .6$$
$$J_1(2,4) = \max[j_0(2,4), j_0(2,1) \wedge j_0(1,4)]$$
$$= \max[.9,.2 \wedge .4] = .9$$
$$J_2(1,2) = \max[j_1(1,2), j_1(1,2) \wedge j_1(2,2)]$$
$$= \max[.2,.2 \wedge \infty] = .2$$
$$J_2(1,3) = \max[j_1(1,3), j_1(1,2) \wedge j_1(2,3)]$$
$$= \max[0,.2 \wedge .6] = .2$$
$$J_2(1,4) = \max[j_1(1,4), j_1(1,2) \wedge j_1(2,4)]$$
$$= \max[0,.2 \wedge .9] = .2$$
$$J_2(2,3) = \max[j_1(2,3), j_1(2,2) \wedge j_1(1,3)]$$
$$= \max[6, \infty \wedge 0] = .6$$
$$J_2(2,4) = \max[j_1(2,4), j_1(2,2) \wedge j_1(1,4)]$$
$$= \max[.6, .2 \wedge 0] = .6$$
$$J_2(3,4) = \max[j_1(3,4), j_1(3,2) \wedge j_1(2,4)]$$
$$= \max[.1, .6 \wedge .9] = .6$$
$$J_1(3,4) = \max[j_0(3,4), j_0(3,1) \wedge j_0(1,4)]$$
$$= \max[.1, .0 \wedge .4] = .1$$

$$J_1 == \begin{matrix} & v_1 & v_2 & v_3 & v_4 \\ v_1 & \infty & .2 & 0 & .4 \\ v_2 & .2 & \infty & .6 & .9 \\ v_3 & 0 & .6 & \infty & .1 \\ v_4 & .4 & .9 & .1 & \infty \end{matrix}$$

$$J_2 = \begin{matrix} & v_1 & v_2 & v_3 & v_4 \\ v_1 & \infty & .2 & .2 & .4 \\ v_2 & .2 & \infty & .6 & .9 \\ v_3 & .2 & .6 & \infty & .6 \\ v_4 & .4 & .9 & .6 & \infty \end{matrix}$$

Similarly we can find $J_3 == \begin{matrix} & v_1 & v_2 & v_3 & v_4 \\ v_1 & \infty & .2 & .2 & .4 \\ v_2 & .2 & \infty & .6 & .9 \\ v_3 & .2 & .6 & \infty & .6 \\ v_4 & .4 & .9 & .6 & \infty \end{matrix}$

$$J_4 = \begin{array}{c} \\ v_1 \\ v_2 \\ v_3 \\ v_4 \end{array} \begin{array}{c} \begin{array}{cccc} v_1 & v_2 & v_3 & v_4 \end{array} \\ \begin{bmatrix} \infty & .4 & .4 & .4 \\ .4 & \infty & .6 & .9 \\ .4 & .6 & \infty & .6 \\ .4 & .9 & .6 & \infty \end{bmatrix} \end{array}$$

$$\text{Connectedness matric } C_{ij} = \begin{array}{c} \\ v_1 \\ v_2 \\ v_3 \\ v_4 \end{array} \begin{array}{c} \begin{array}{cccc} v_1 & v_2 & v_3 & v_4 \end{array} \\ \begin{bmatrix} 0 & .4 & .4 & .4 \\ .4 & 0 & .6 & .9 \\ .4 & .6 & 0 & .6 \\ .4 & .9 & .6 & 0 \end{bmatrix} \end{array}$$

$$\text{Resolving matrix } R_n = \begin{array}{c} \\ v_1 \\ v_2 \\ v_3 \\ v_4 \end{array} \begin{array}{c} \begin{array}{cccc} v_1 & v_2 & v_3 & v_4 \end{array} \\ \begin{bmatrix} .6 & .4 & .4 & .4 \\ .4 & 1 & .6 & .9 \\ .4 & .6 & .7 & .6 \\ .4 & .9 & .6 & .9 \end{bmatrix} \end{array}$$

12.3.1 An Application on Resolving Matrix

The plan of safeguarding VIP/business persons, is becoming tougher because of social media. It is very rare a VIP is traveling in their own name. Those who have life threat will be traveling with high security and they have limited time to enjoy their personal life. It is extremely important that they should have a good travel plane. Especially those who are doing business in the various country need to travel often for their business purpose. Countries like Iceland, Denmark, New Zealand, Australia, Canada etc. are having a good safety index, therefore business persons like to live in these countries. But it is also important for the VIP/Business persons to simultaneously check their air travel safety from place to place they usually travel. Let us consider that a person 'A' is having business in the countries Canada, China, India, Brazil and the US. He needs to travel these countries often through airways. Now he wants to decide that in which country he can build his business headquarters so that he ensures his safe stay and travel to various branches.

We will draw a fuzzy graph with vertices to represent the countries and edges represent the air route between countries. The membership value of the vertices and edges indicate the life risk level of the country and the air travel risk levels between the two countries respectively. The safety index of

Table 12.1 The safety index of each country is given below.

S. no.	Countries	Safety index%	Fuzzy number	Risk level
1	Canada	88.4	.88	0.12
2	China	66.6	.66	0.34
3	India	46.4	.464	0.536
4	Brazil	51.9	.519	0.481
5	Us	68.8	.68	0.32

Table 12.2 Accident per million departure.

S. no.	Countries	Accident/million departure in the year 2018	Accident rate-fuzzy number
1	Canada	1.73	0.00000137
2	China	.43	0.00000043
3	India	.82	0.00000082
4	Brazil	2.32	0.00000232
5	Us	1.28	0.00000128

each country and the accident per million departure are given in the Tables 12.1 and 12.2. Travel risk between countries is calculated by taking an average accident rate of each country departure to the word travel.

v_1 = Canada; v_2 = China; v_3 = India; v_4 = Brazil; v_5 = United States of America

$$\sigma(v_1) = .12;\ \sigma(v_2) = .34;\ \sigma(v_3) = .536;\ \sigma(v_4) = .48;\ \sigma(v_5) = .32$$

$$\mu(v_1, v_2) = \frac{0.00000137 + 0.00000043}{2} = 0.0000009 = .09 \times 10^{-5}$$

$$\mu(v_1, v_3) = \frac{0.00000137 + 0.00000082}{2} = 0.000001095$$

$$\mu(v_1, v_4) = 0.000001845; \mu(v_1, v_5) = 0.00000249; \mu(v_2, v_3) = 0.000000625$$
$$\mu(v_2, v_4) = 0.000001375; \mu(v_2, v_5) = 0.000000855; \mu(v_3, v_4) = 0.00000157$$
$$\mu(v_3, v_5) = 0.00000105; \mu(v_4, v_5) = 0.00000058$$

The adjacency matrix of the fuzzy graph Figure 12.8 is given below.

$A_{ij} =$

	v_1	v_2	v_3	v_4	v_5
v_1	0	.0000009	.000001095	.000001845	.00000249
v_2	.0000009	0	.00000625	.000001375	0.000000855
v_3	.000001095	.00000625	0	.00000157	.00000105
v_4	.000001845	.000001375	.00000157	0	.00000058
v_5	.00000249	0.000000855	.00000105	.00000058	0

Resolving matrix

$R_{ij} =$

	v_1	v_2	v_3	v_4	v_5
v_1	0.12	.000001375	.00000157	.000001845	.00000105
v_2	.000001375	0.34	.000001375	.000001375	.00000105
v_3	.00000157	.000001375	0.536	.00000157	.00000105
v_4	.000001845	.000001375	.00000157	0.48	.00000105
v_5	.00000105	.00000105	.00000105	.00000105	0.32

The connectedness matrix will give the maximum expected risk level in air travel between countries and the Resolving matrix will give the maximum expected risk level in stay and air travel to other country.

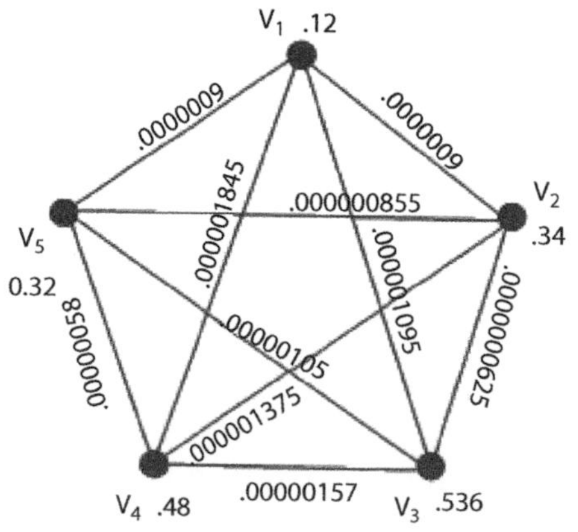

Figure 12.8 Fuzzy graph on life risk rate.

We can see that Canada is having a good safe index than the other countries and China is having the minimum accident rate (china to other countries in the world) in comparison with other countries. But the average of the row/column in the connectedness matrix gives a result that the travel from the US to the remaining four countries, Canada, China, India and brazil having less risk level compared to the all other countries. And the average of the row/column of the Resolving matrix will give the expected stay and travel risk level in all the possible route to other countries, which is less in Canada compared to the other four countries. Therefore it is better to have a headquarters in Canada than anyone the remaining four countries so that the president of the company can have a better stay and travel to the other branches. This model can be applied for roadways if the person is travelling to several places in the same region.

12.3.2 An Algorithm to Find the Fuzzy Connectedness Matrix

In this section, we discuss an algorithm to determine the weight of the connectedness between each pair of vertices of the connected fuzzy graph having no loop and parallel edges.

Step 1: The adjacency matrix of $G(V, \sigma.\mu)$ is obtained from $A_{ij} = \mu(v_i, v_j)$ if there is edge from i to j and $A_{ij} = 0$, when $i = j$.
Step 2: Consider there are n vertices of G say $v_1,v_2,\ldots v_n$. Then the matrix sequences $J_1,J_2,\ldots J_n$ are formed where $J_r = \{J_r(i, j)\}$.
Step 3:

$$J_r(i,j)=\begin{cases} max[j_{r-1}(i,j), j_{r-1}(i,k)\wedge j_{r-1}(k,j)](k=1,2,\ldots n) \\ \infty \quad if \quad i=j. \end{cases} \tag{12.1}$$

Step 4: To find J_0, replace the zeros in the main diagonal of the adjacency matrix as '∞'.
Step 5: Replace '∞' in the main diagonal as '0' in J_n to obtain the connectedness matrix C_ij.

Example 8. Let us see the following fuzzy graph $G(V, \sigma.\mu)$ with four vertices given in Figure 12.9.

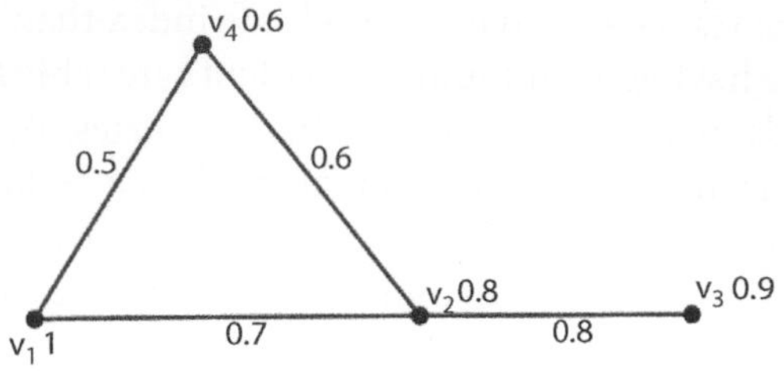

Figure 12.9 $G(V, \sigma, \mu)$.

$$\text{The adjacency matrix of } G,\ A_{ij} = \begin{array}{c} \\ v_1 \\ v_2 \\ v_3 \\ v_4 \end{array} \begin{array}{c} \begin{array}{cccc} v_1 & v_2 & v_3 & v_4 \end{array} \\ \begin{bmatrix} 0 & .7 & 0 & .5 \\ .7 & 0 & .8 & .6 \\ 0 & .8 & 0 & 0 \\ .5 & .6 & 0 & 0 \end{bmatrix} \end{array}$$

$$J_0 = \begin{array}{c} \\ v_1 \\ v_2 \\ v_3 \\ v_4 \end{array} \begin{array}{c} \begin{array}{cccc} v_1 & v_2 & v_3 & v_4 \end{array} \\ \begin{bmatrix} \infty & .7 & 0 & .5 \\ .7 & \infty & .8 & .6 \\ 0 & .8 & \infty & 0 \\ .5 & .6 & 0 & \infty \end{bmatrix} \end{array}$$

$$\begin{aligned} J_1(1,2) &= max[J_0(1,2), j_0(1,1) \wedge j_0(1,2)] \\ &= max[.7, \infty \wedge .7] = .7 \\ J_1(1,3) &= max[J_0(1,3), j_0(1,1) \wedge j_0(1,3)] \\ &= max[0, \infty \wedge 0] = 0 \\ J_1(1,4) &= max[J_0(1,4), j_0(1,1) \wedge j_0(1,4)] \\ &= max[.5, \infty \wedge .5] = .5 \\ J_1(2,3) &= max[J_0(2,3), j_0(2,1) \wedge j_0(1,3)] \\ &= max[.8, .7 \wedge 0] = .8 \\ J_1(2,4) &= max[J_0(2,4), j_0(2,1) \wedge j_0(1,4)] \\ &= max[.6, .7 \wedge .5] = .6 \\ J_1(3,4) &= max[J_0(3,4), j_0(3,1) \wedge j_0(1,4)] \\ &= max[0,0 \wedge .5] = 0 \\ J_1(1,1) &= \infty = J_1(2,2) = J_1(3,3) = J_1(4,4) \end{aligned}$$

$$J_1 = \begin{array}{c} \\ v_1 \\ v_2 \\ v_3 \\ v_4 \end{array} \begin{array}{c} \begin{array}{cccc} v_1 & v_2 & v_3 & v_4 \end{array} \\ \begin{bmatrix} \infty & .7 & 0 & .5 \\ .7 & \infty & .8 & .6 \\ 0 & .8 & \infty & 0 \\ .5 & .6 & 0 & \infty \end{bmatrix} \end{array} \quad J_2 = \begin{array}{c} \\ v_1 \\ v_2 \\ v_3 \\ v_4 \end{array} \begin{array}{c} \begin{array}{cccc} v_1 & v_2 & v_3 & v_4 \end{array} \\ \begin{bmatrix} \infty & .7 & .7 & .6 \\ .7 & \infty & .8 & .6 \\ .7 & .8 & \infty & .6 \\ .6 & .6 & .6 & \infty \end{bmatrix} \end{array}$$

$$J_3 = \begin{array}{c} \\ v_1 \\ v_2 \\ v_3 \\ v_4 \end{array} \begin{array}{c} \begin{array}{cccc} v_1 & v_2 & v_3 & v_4 \end{array} \\ \begin{bmatrix} \infty & .7 & .7 & .6 \\ .7 & \infty & .8 & .6 \\ .7 & .8 & \infty & .6 \\ .6 & .6 & .6 & \infty \end{bmatrix} \end{array} \quad J_4 = \begin{array}{c} \\ v_1 \\ v_2 \\ v_3 \\ v_4 \end{array} \begin{array}{c} \begin{array}{cccc} v_1 & v_2 & v_3 & v_4 \end{array} \\ \begin{bmatrix} \infty & .7 & .7 & .6 \\ .7 & \infty & .8 & .6 \\ .7 & .8 & \infty & .6 \\ .6 & .6 & .6 & \infty \end{bmatrix} \end{array}$$

$$\text{The connectedness matrix } C_{ij} = \begin{array}{c} \\ v_1 \\ v_2 \\ v_3 \\ v_4 \end{array} \begin{array}{c} \begin{array}{cccc} v_1 & v_2 & v_3 & v_4 \end{array} \\ \begin{bmatrix} 0 & .7 & .7 & .6 \\ .7 & 0 & .8 & .6 \\ .7 & .8 & 0 & .6 \\ .6 & .6 & .6 & 0 \end{bmatrix} \end{array}$$

12.4 An Application of the Connectedness of the Modified Fuzzy Graph in Rescuing Human Life From Fire Accident

Today's modern world, buildings are constructed less safety from fire spread. Homes and offices are loaded with plastics, furniture, Cloths, Flour, etc. This can make the fire aggressive and change the result of the fire in case of a fire accident. In emergencies like fire accident and forest fires, it is a high risk to handle it with human resources. From the Statistics of Tamil Nadu Fire Rescue Service (TNFRS) we can see that, due to the three fire calls such as a small fire, medium fire and serious fire, a lot of human lives are lost in the recent years [16]. It is becoming a serious issue in modern society. Fire rescue operators can settle the Small fire faster, but it is difficult to rescue people from medium and large fire in a closed building. In this case, we can use a humanoid robot to detect fire at the initial level and rescue the human lives.

The Robots can detect fire using sensor, fire detection unit in a robot has a temperature sensor, flame sensor and smoke sensor [17]. The commonly used material to make robots are aluminium and steel. Steel melts at 1,370°C and aluminium melts at 660.32°C. The normal human body average temperature is 37°C and it can survive at almost 45°C. Assume that a Humanoid robot is designed to rescue human life from a fire accident in a closed building. The shortest path algorithm in Graph theory is applied to find the shortest path so that the robot can reach the spot within a short span of time, but while coming out it uses obstacle detection modules to identify the obstacle in front and fireman module to analyze the situation and turn the water pipe sprinkler. However, it is also important that the path chooses by the robot is safe for the human and it must be the shortest among all the possible path. That is before it starts moving outside from any part of building to exist, it should analyse the path which is safer for the human so that it can use less water to control the temperature [if it is more than 45°C], this motivates us to see the safest path in Fuzzy Graph rather than the shortest path in Graph Theory.

In real life, always a normal fuzzy graph will not fit to represent the exact situation. Therefore, we use a modified fuzzy graph or anti fuzzy graph to represent the temperature level. Consider that there is a fire accident in a hospital, which is a closed building and a humanoid robot is about to rescue the human lives from fire. The hospital map is given below in Figure 12.10.

In real life, always a normal fuzzy graph will not fit to represent the exact situation. Therefore, we use a modified fuzzy graph or anti fuzzy graph to represent the temperature level. Consider that there is a fire accident in a hospital, which is a closed building and a humanoid robot is about to rescue the human lives from fire. The hospital map is given below in Figure 12.10.

The graphical representation of Figure 12.11 is given below. The vertices represent the blocks and the edges indicate the direct path from one block

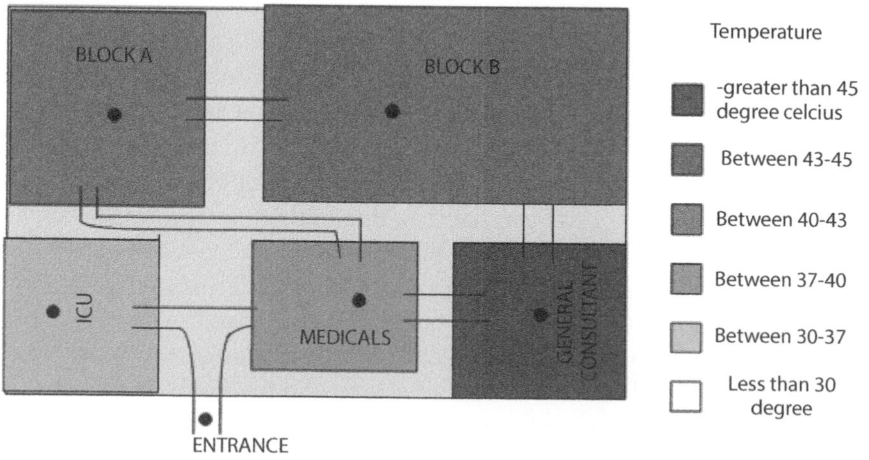

Figure 12.10 Hospital map.

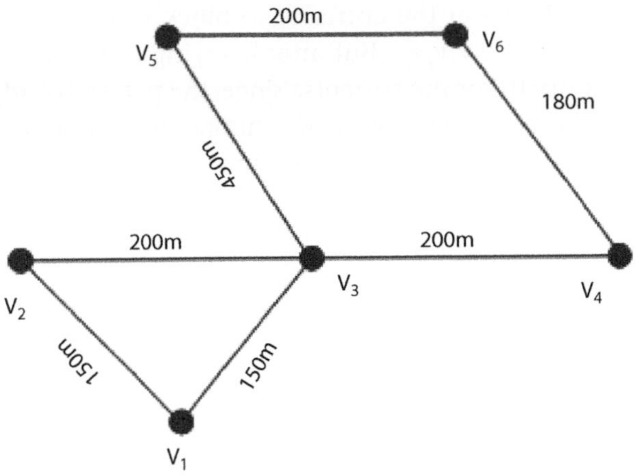

Figure 12.11 Graphical representation of the hospital.

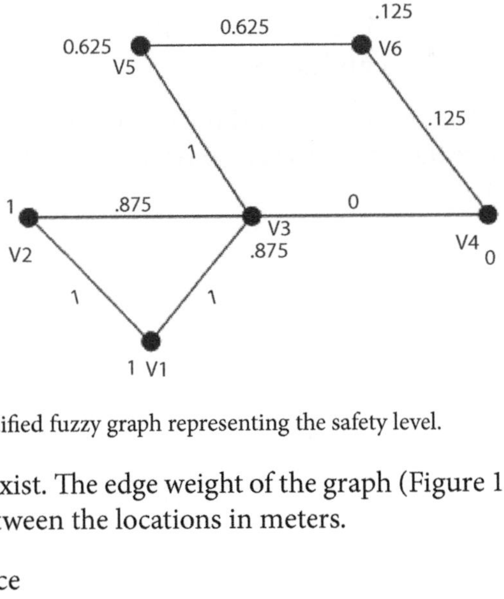

Figure 12.12 Modified fuzzy graph representing the safety level.

to the other, if exist. The edge weight of the graph (Figure 12.12) represents the distance between the locations in meters.

v_1-Entrance
v_2-ICU
v_3-Medicals
v_4-General consultant room
v_5-Block A
v_6-Block B

The Graphical representation of the building with its distance from each vertex is loaded in the robot prior. Assume that the humanoid robot which is there in the entrance [v_1] needs to rescue the patients in block B [v_6].

The shortest path between the entrance to block B, calculated using the Warshall algorithm is '$v_1v_3v_4v_6$'. But after carrying the patients, it should come out in a safe path for the patients. Since, the patient's body condition is weaker than the normal persons. The humanoid robot should choose the path which is safer that is, with less temperature or heat. We consider the safest path between two vertices is the one which has a more safety level in comparison with all other path joining the two vertices v_1 and v_6. Assuming that, there is no obstacle in the path, to find the safest path we will first find the weight of each path between the nodes, then from these weights find out the maximum value and the corresponding path will be considered as the safest path compared to all other paths. That is, we have to find the weight of the connectedness $\mu^{\infty}(x, y)$ between every two vertices x and y, and then choose the paths with weight $\mu^{\infty}(x, y)$. An algorithm to find the safest and shortest path is given in the following subsection.

12.4.1 Algorithm to Find the Safest and Shortest Path Between Two Landmarks

Step 1: The normal temperature of the human body is 37°C and it can bear up to 45°C, therefore the safety level of the vertices and edges are calculated using the formula:

$$\text{Safety level} = \begin{cases} 1 - \dfrac{(x-37)}{8} & \textit{between} \quad 37-45 \\ 0 \quad \textit{if } x > 45 \\ 1 \quad \textit{if } x \leq 37 \end{cases}$$

Step 2: The modified adjacency matrix M_{ij} of $G(V,\sigma.\mu)$ is obtained from $M_{ij} = \mu(v_i, v_j)$ the safety level between v_i and v_j, if there is edge from i to j, and $M_{ii} = \sigma(v_i)$ the safety level of the landmark v_i, zero otherwise.
Step 3: Consider there are n vertices of G say $v_1,v_2,\ldots v_n$. Then the matrix sequences $J_1,J_2,\ldots J_n$ are formed where $J_r = \{J_r(i,j)\}$.
Step 4:

$$J_r(i,j) = \begin{cases} max[j_{r-1}(i,j), min\{j_{r-1}(i,k), j_{r-1}(k,k), j_{r-1}(k,j)\}] \\ \sigma(v_i) \quad if \quad i=j. \end{cases} \tag{12.2}$$

Step 5: J_0 = the modified adjacency matrix M_{ij}.

Step 6: The safety level matrix $S_{ij} = J_n(i,j)$
Step 7: If the safety level between v_i and v_j is s_{ij} and the path having the same weight s_{ij} are $P_1, P_2, \ldots P_k$.
Step 8: Find $\min\{|P_1|, |P_2|, \ldots |P_k|\} = d(say)$, where $|P|$ is the length of the path P.
Step 9: The shortest and safest path from v_i to v_j are the paths P_i's, such that $|P_i| = d$.

In C Programming

```
#define MIN(a,b) ((a) < (b)  ? (a) : (b) )
#define THREE(a,b,c) MIN(MIN(a,b),(c))
#include<stdio.h>
#include<math.h>
#define MAX(a,b) (((a)>(b))?(a):(b))
voidfloyds(float p[10][10],int n)
{
inti,j,k;
for(k=1;k<=n;k++)
for(i=1;i<=n;i++)
for(j=1;j<=n;j++)
if(i==j)
p[i][j]=0;
else
   p[i][j]=MAX(p[i][j],THREE(p[i][k],p[k][k],p[k][j]));
}
void main()
{
float p[10][10],w;
intn,e,u,v,i,j;;
printf("\n Enter the number of vertices:");
scanf("%d",&n);
printf("\n Enter the number of edges:\n");
scanf("%d",&e);
for(i=1;i<=n;i++)
for(i=1;i<=e;i++)
 {
printf("\n Enter the end vertices of edge%d with its weight \n",i);
scanf("%d%d%f",&u,&v,&w);
p[u][v]=w;p[v][u]=w;p[u][u]=0;
 }
printf("\n Matrix of input data:\n");
for(i=1;i<=n;i++)
```

```
 {
for(j=1;j<=n;j++)
printf("%.10f \t",p[i][j]);
printf("\n");
 }
floyds(p,n);
printf("\n Transitive closure:\n");
for(i=1;i<=n;i++)
 {
for(j=1;j<=n;j++)
printf("%.10f \t",p[i][j]);
printf("\n");
 }
printf("\n The shortest paths are:\n");
for(i=1;i<=n;i++)
for(j=1;j<=n;j++)
 {
if(i!=j)
printf("\n <%d,%d>=%.10f",i,j,p[i][j]);
 }
}
printf("\n Enter the vertices %d with its weight \n",i);
scanf("%d%f",&n,&s);
p[u][v]=w;p[v][u]=w;p[n][n]=s;
```

The information about the average temperature detected in each vertex and edges by the temperature sensor is sent to the humanoid robot. The temperature on the vertices v_1, v_2, v_3, v_4, v_5 and v_6 are 29°, 37°, 38°, 60°, 40° and 40°C respectively. And the average temperature(x) of the edges v_1v_2, $v_1v_3, v_2v_3, v_3v_4, v_4v_6, v_6v_5, v_3v_5$ are 32°,37°,38°,50°,44°,40° and 37° respectively. The safety level of the vertices and edges are calculated using Step 1.

$$\sigma(v_1)=1;\sigma(v_2)=1;\sigma(v_3)=1-\frac{38-37}{8}=0.875;\sigma(v_4)=1-\frac{40-37}{8}=0.625;$$

$$\sigma(v_5)=1-\frac{44-37}{8}=0.125;\quad \sigma(v_6)=0.$$

$$\mu(v_1v_2) = 1; \mu(v_1v_3) = 1; \mu(v_2v_3) = 0.875; \mu(v_3v_4) = 0.875; \mu(v_4v_6) = 0.125;$$

$$\mu(v_5v_6) = 0; \mu(v_3v_5) = 0.625$$

The modified fuzzy graph representing the safety level of each land mark is given in Figure 12.12.

The modified adjacency matrix;

$$M_{ij} = J_0\,(i,j) = \begin{array}{c} \\ v_1 \\ v_2 \\ v_3 \\ v_4 \\ v_5 \\ v_6 \end{array} \begin{array}{c} \begin{array}{cccccc} v_1 & v_2 & v_3 & v_4 & v_5 & v_6 \end{array} \\ \begin{bmatrix} 1 & 1 & .875 & 0 & 0 & 0 \\ 1 & 1 & .875 & 0 & 0 & 0 \\ .875 & .875 & .875 & 0 & 1 & 0 \\ 0 & 0 & 0 & 0 & 0 & .125 \\ 0 & 0 & 1 & 0 & .625 & .625 \\ 0 & 0 & 0 & .125 & .625 & .125 \end{bmatrix} \end{array}$$

The safety level matrix $S_{ij} = J_r(i,j)$, will give the minimum safety level of the safest path between each vertices or places. Since the matrix order is 6 × 6 we have used C programming language to obtain the safety level matrix using the algorithm mentioned above.

$$\text{Safety level matrix } S_{ij} = \begin{array}{c} \\ v_1 \\ v_2 \\ v_3 \\ v_4 \\ v_5 \\ v_6 \end{array} \begin{array}{c} \begin{array}{cccccc} v_1 & v_2 & v_3 & v_4 & v_5 & v_6 \end{array} \\ \begin{bmatrix} 1 & 1 & .875 & .125 & .875 & .625 \\ 1 & 1 & .875 & .125 & .875 & .625 \\ .875 & .875 & .875 & .125 & 1 & .625 \\ .125 & .125 & .125 & 0 & .125 & .125 \\ .875 & .875 & 1 & .125 & .625 & .625 \\ .625 & .625 & .625 & .125 & .625 & .125 \end{bmatrix} \end{array}$$

The humanoid robot can move from the vertex v_1 to v_6 [from the entrance to block B] using the shortest path that is $v_1v_3v_4v_6$. And after carrying a person from block B it has to come out in a safest path. From the safety level matrix we can see that the safety level between v_1 and v_6 is 0.625. and the path having this safety levels are $P_1 = v_1v_3v_5v_6$ and $P_2 = v_1v_2v_3v_5v_6$. We can expect a minimum of 40°C in the path but temperature and humidity will affect the patients physical status badly if it sustain for longer time, therefore for this situation, we have to choose not only a safest path but also the shortest path.

$$\min\{|P_1|,|P_2|\} = \min\{800,1{,}000\} = 800$$

Therefore, the safest and shortest path from v_1 to v_6 is P_1.

Similarly, we can calculate the safest and shortest path between every pair of vertices. In case we need to rescue people from General consultant room that is from v_1 to v_4, the safety level is 0.125, in this case, the robot can use the fireman module to turn the water pipe sprinkler and reduce the temperature in the path. The fire man module will be switch on automatically depend on the temperature threshold we set. In this example we have taken the temperature level between 37 and 45 to calculate the safe level. But in case of large fire we can set the temperature level accordingly and can increase the amount of water it sprinkle.

If the Graphical representation of the closed building is a tree then, between any two blocks of the building, there exists only one unique path. In such case we can find the minimum safety level and can take a safety measure in the sense that the amount of water used is measured.

12.5 Resolving Number Fuzzy Graph and Fuzzy Digraph

The subset H_D of $\sigma_D = \{\sigma_1, \sigma_2, \ldots \sigma_n\}$ where $\sigma_1 = (v_1, \sigma(v_1))$, with $2 \leq |H_D| \leq n-1$, $H_D = \{\sigma_1, \sigma_2, \ldots \sigma_m\}$, the **left-representation** of $(y, \sigma(y)) \in \sigma_D - H_D$ with respect to H_D is an ordered m-tuple $(w(y, v_1), w(y, v_2), \ldots w(y, w_m))$ where $w(u, v)$ is the weight of connectedness between u and v. The **right-representation** of $\sigma_D - H_D$ with respect to H_D is $(w(v_1, y), w(v_2, y), \ldots w(w_m, y))$.

Definition 14. Let $\vec{G}(V, \sigma_D, \mu_D)$ is a fuzzy digraph with $|V| \geq 3$, and for any subset $H_D(|H_D| \geq 2)$ of σ_D, the left-representation of $\sigma_D - H_D$ with respect to H_D are all distinct, then H_D is called the **fuzzy left-resolving set** of $\vec{G}$. A fuzzy left-resolving set of minimum cardinality is the **left-resolving number** denoted as $Fr_L\vec{G}$. The left-representation of σ_D with respect to H_D are all distinct, then H_D is called the **fuzzy left-super resolving set** of $\vec{G}$. A fuzzy left-super resolving set of minimum cardinality is the **left-super resolving number** denoted as $Sr_L\vec{G}$.

Definition 15. The right-representation of H_D with respect to $\sigma_D - H_D$ are all distinct, then H_D is called the **fuzzy right-resolving set** of $\vec{G}$. A fuzzy right resolving set of minimum cardinality is the fuzzy right resolving number denoted as $Fr_R\vec{G}$. The right-representation of H_D with respect to σ_D are all distinct, then H_D is called the **fuzzy right-super resolving set** of $\vec{G}$. A fuzzy right-super resolving set of minimum cardinality is the **right-super resolving number** denoted as $Sr_R\vec{G}$. Consider the following fuzzy digraph $\vec{G}$.

Example 9. Consider the fuzzy digraph $\vec{G}$ in Figure 12.13.

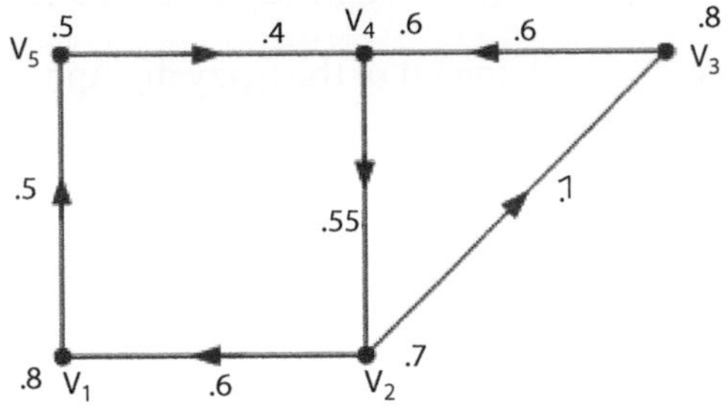

Figure 12.13 Fuzzy digraph.

$$Let\ H_D = \{\sigma_1, \sigma_1\}$$
$$L(\sigma_1/H_D) = w(v_1, v_1), w(v_1, v_2)) = (.8,.4)$$
$$L(\sigma_2/H_D) = w(v_2, v_1), w(v_2, v_2)) = (.6,.7)$$
$$L(\sigma_3/H_D) = w(v_3, v_1), w(v_3, v_2)) = (.55,.55)$$
$$L(\sigma_4/H_D) = w(v_4, v_1), w(v_4, v_2)) = (.55,.55)$$
$$L(\sigma_5/H_D) = w(v_5, v_1), w(v_5, v_2)) = (.4,.4)$$

The left-representation of σ_3 and σ_4 with respect to H_D are not distinct, therefore H_D is not the left-resolving set of $\vec{G}$.

$$R(\sigma_1/H_D) = w(v_1, v_1), w(v_2, v_1)) = (0,.6)$$
$$R(\sigma_2/H_D) = w(v_1, v_2), w(v_2, v_2)) = (.4,0)$$
$$R(\sigma_3/H_D) = w(v_1, v_3), w(v_2, v_3)) = (.4,.7)$$
$$R(\sigma_4/H_D) = w(v_1, v_4), w(v_2, v_4)) = (.4,.6)$$
$$R(\sigma_5/H_D) = w(v_1, v_5), w(v_2, v_5)) = (.5,.5)$$

The right-representation of $\sigma_D - H_D$ with respect to H_D are all distinct therefore H_D is the right-resolving set of $\vec{G}$ and it is also the right-super resolving set of $\vec{G}$.

$$Fr_R(G) = Sr_R(G) = 2$$

Theorem 1. Let H_D is a left-resolving set of the fuzzy digraph $\vec{G}$ and if $\forall u,v \in H_D^*$, $\sigma(u) \neq \sigma(v)$ then H_D is a left-super resolving set of $\vec{G}$.

Proof: Let H_D is a left-resolving set of $\vec{G}$, then the left representation of $\sigma_D - H_D$ with respect to H_D are all distinct. If $\forall u,v \in H_D^*$, $\sigma(u) \neq \sigma(v)$ $[w(u, u) = \sigma(u)]$, then the left representation of H_D with respect to H_D will be distinct. Therefore the left representation of σ_D with respect to H_D are all distinct. Hence H_D is a left-super resolving set of $\vec{G}$.

Corollary 1. Let H_D is a right-resolving set of the fuzzy digraph $\vec{G}$ and if $\forall u,v \in H_D^{*}$, $\sigma(u) \neq \sigma(v)$ then H_D is a right-super resolving set of $\vec{G}$.

Corollary 2. Fuzzy left-resolving set of the fuzzy digraph $\vec{G}$ may not be the fuzzy right-resolving set of $\vec{G}$.

Corollary 3. Let $\vec{G}$ and $\vec{G}'$ are the fuzzy diagraph and ϕ is an isomorphism between $\vec{G}$ and $\vec{G}'$, then $w(u, v) = w'(\phi(u), \phi(v))\ \forall u, v \in V$, where $w(u, v)$ is the weight or strength of connectedness between u and v.

Proof: If the fuzzy digraph $\vec{G}$ and $\vec{G}'$ are isomorphic then, there exist a bijection ϕ: $V_1 \rightarrow V_2$ that satisfy $\sigma_D(x) = \sigma_{D'}(\phi(x))$ for all $x \in V_1$ and $\mu_D(x, y) = \mu_{D'}(\phi(x), \phi(y))$ for all $x, y \in V_1$. And there is one to one correspondence between the vertices and edges having same in degree and out degree. Therefore there exist a equal number of paths between any two vertices of $\vec{G}$ and the corresponding image in $\vec{G}'$. And also the strength of each path in $\vec{G}$ and the corresponding path in $\vec{G}'$ are equal. Which will imply that the strength of connectedness between any two vertices u, v and the strength of connectedness between the corresponding image $\phi(u)$, $\phi(v)$ are equal. That is, $w(u, v) = w_{,}(\phi(u), \phi(v))\ \forall u, v \in V$.

Theorem 2. If the fuzzy digraph $\vec{G}(V, \sigma_D, \mu_D)$ and $\vec{G}'(V', \sigma_{D'}, \mu_{D'})'$ are isomorphic then, $Sr_L(\vec{G}) = Sr_L(\vec{G'})$ and $Sr_R(\vec{G}) = Sr_R(\vec{G'})$.

Proof: Let $V = \{v_1, v_2, \ldots v_n\}$, $Sr_L(\vec{G}) = k$ and let $H_D = \{\sigma_1, \sigma_2, \ldots \sigma_k\}$ is the corresponding left-super resolving set of $\vec{G}$.

Then, $L(\sigma_m/H) = (w(v_m, v_1), w(v_m, v_2), \ldots w(v_m, vk))$ are distinct for all $m = 1,2,\ldots n$ (12.3)

If G and G' are isomorphic, then there is a bijection ϕ: $V \rightarrow V'$ which satisfies $\sigma(v) = \sigma'(\phi(v)) \forall v \in V$ and $\mu(u, v) = \mu'(\phi(u), \phi(v)) \forall u, v \in V$.

Now define, $H' = \{\sigma_1', \sigma_2', \ldots \sigma_k'\}$ $[\sigma(v_1) = v_{1'}]$.

Let,

$$
\begin{aligned}
L(\sigma_m'/H') &= (w'(v_m', v_{1'}), w'(v_m', v_{2'}), \ldots w'(v_m', v_{k'}))[m = 1,2,\ldots n] \\
&= (w'(\phi(v_m), \phi(v_1)), w'(\phi(v_m), \phi(v_2)), \ldots w'(\phi(v_m), \phi(v_k))) \\
&= (w(v_m, v_1), w(v_m, v_2), \ldots w(v_m, v_k))[\text{bycorollary3.3}]
\end{aligned}
$$

these representations are all distinct for $i = 1,2,\ldots n - k$ from Equation (12.3).

H' is the left-super resolving set of $\vec{G}'$ $|H| = |H'| = k$.

To show that H' is the minimum left-super resolving set of $\vec{G}'$.

If there exist a left-super resolving set I' of $\vec{G}'$, $I' = \{\sigma_1', \sigma_2', \ldots \sigma_{k_1}'\} \ni |H'| = k > |I'| = k_1$

$$\text{Then } L(\sigma_m'/I') \text{ are all distinct for } m = 1,2,\ldots n \qquad (12.4)$$

Now let $I' = \{\sigma_1', \sigma_2', \ldots \sigma_{k_1}\}$

$$L(\sigma_m/I) = (w(v_m, v_1), w(v_m, v_2), \ldots w(v_m, v_{k_1}))[m = 1,2,\ldots n]$$
$$= (w'(\phi(v_m), \phi(v_1)), w'(\phi(v_m), \phi(v_2)), \ldots w'(\phi(v_m), \phi(v_{k_1})))[\text{by Corollary3}]$$
$$= (w'(v_m', v_{1'}), w'(v_m', v_{2'}), \ldots w'(v_m', v_{k_1}'))[m = 1,2,\ldots n]$$

which are all distinct for $m = 1,2,\ldots n$ [from Equation (12.4)]

I is the left-super resolving set of $\vec{G}$, that is $Sr_L(\vec{G}) = k_1$.

Which is a contradiction to our assumption that $Sr_L(\vec{G}) = k$.

Therefore, H' is the minimum left-super resolving set of $\vec{G}'$.

Hence, $Sr_L(\vec{G}) = Sr_L(\vec{G'}) = k$.

Sımılarlly, we can prove that $Sr_R(\vec{G}) = Sr_R(\vec{G'})$.

Example 10

From Figure 12.14, we can see that there exist an isomorphism $\phi: V \to V'$, between $\vec{G}$ and $\vec{G'}$ such that $\phi(a) = a1$, $\phi(b) = b1$, $\phi(c) = c1$, $\phi(d) = d1$ and $\phi(e) = e1$. $H_D = \{\sigma_1, \sigma_2\}$ is a fuzzy left-super resolving set of $\vec{G}$ and from Figure 12.14 we can see $H_{D'} = \{\sigma_{1''}, \sigma_{2'}\}$ is the left-super resolving set of $\vec{G}'$.

Definition 16. The fuzzy left resolving set H_D of a fuzzy digraph $\vec{G}$ is called perfect, if $d^-(u) \neq 0 \quad \forall u \in H_D$.

Definition 17. The fuzzy right resolving set H_D of a fuzzy digraph $\vec{G}$ is called perfect, if $d^+(u) \neq 0 \quad \forall u \in H_D$.

Example 11. An example of isomorphic fuzzy digraph is given in the following Figure 12.14.

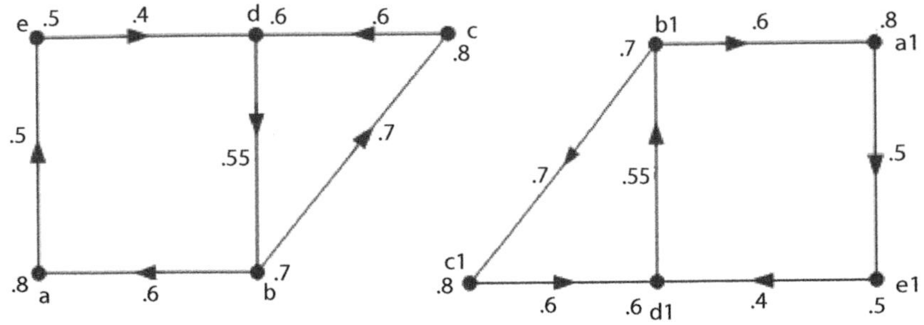

Figure 12.14 The fuzzy digraph $\vec{G}(V, \sigma_D, \mu_D)$ and $\vec{G}'(V, \sigma_D, \mu_D)$ are isomorphic.

Theorem 3. If there exist at least one $v \in V$ of a fuzzy digraph $\vec{G}(V, \sigma_D, \mu_D)$ such that $w(u, v)$ are all distinct for every $u \in V$, then the left super-resolving number of $\vec{G}$ is "2".

Proof: Let $\vec{G}(V, \sigma_D, \mu_D)$ be a fuzzy digraph, $\sigma^* = \{v_1, v_2, \ldots v_n\}$, such that $w(u, v)$ are all distinct for every $u = v_1(say) \in V$.

Now any two element subset of σ_D of the form $H = \{v_1, v_i\}$, $i = 2,3,\ldots n$ is a fuzzy left-super resolving set of $\vec{G}$, since $\sigma_j/H = (w(v_j, v_1), w(v_j, v_i))$ are all distinct for $j = 1,2,\ldots n$.

Hence the left super-resolving number of $\vec{G}$ is "2". If there exists at least one $v \in V$ of a fuzzy digraph $\vec{G}(V, \sigma_D, \mu_D)$ such that $w(v, u)$ are all distinct for every $u \in V$, then the Right super-resolving number of $\vec{G}$ is "2".

Corollary 4. If there exist at least one $v \in V$ of a fuzzy digraph $\vec{G}(V, \sigma_D, \mu_D)$ such that $w(v, u)$ are all distinct for every $u \in V$, then the Right super-resolving number of $\vec{G}$ is "2".

12.5.1 An Algorithm to Find the Resolving Set of a Fuzzy Digraph

After finding the connectedness matrix C_{ij} of the fuzzy digraph $\vec{G}$, one can easily find the left fuzzy resolving set of $\vec{G}$ by inspection if the order of matrix is very small. But for a fuzzy digraph with n vertices (n is large) we use an algorithm to find the right-resolving set of $\vec{G}$.

Now consider a fuzzy digraph $\vec{G}$ with n vertices. Let A_{ij} is the adjacency matrix and C_{ij} is the connectedness matrix of $\vec{G}$. If H is the left-resolving set, then the cardinality of H lies between '2' and '$n - 1$'. Any set of 'n' elements has '2^n' subset and there exist $2^n - (n + 2)$ subset which satisfies the condition $2 \le |H| \le n - 1$. The left-resolving set of $\vec{G}$ is calculated by the following steps:

Step 1. Find the connectedness matrix C_{ij} for $i, j = 1,2,\ldots n \ni$

$$C_{ij} = \begin{cases} w(v_i, v_j) & if \quad i \neq j \\ \sigma(v_i) & if \quad i = j \end{cases} \tag{12.5}$$

Step 2. Find all subset H of $\sigma = \{\sigma_1, \sigma_2, \ldots \sigma_n\}$ such that $2 \le |H| \le n - 1$ namely $H_1, H_2, \ldots H_{2^n-(n+2)}$.

Step 3. Take the subset H_k, $|H_k| = k$ and find the columns for the elements in H_k.

Let $a_1, a_2, \ldots a_k$ are the columns.

Step 4.

for i = 1 to n

for j = I + 1 to n

If the k-tuple $(c_{ia_1}, c_{ia_2}, \ldots c_{ia_k}) = (c_{ja_1}, c_{ja_2}, \ldots c_{ja_k})$ then
H is not a left-resolving set of $\vec{G}$.
else, H is a left-resolving set of $\vec{G}$.

Step 5

for i = 1 to n

for j = I + 1 to n

If the k-tuple $(c_{a_1 i}, c_{a_2 i}, \ldots c_{a_k i}) = (c_{a_1 j}, c_{a_2 j}, \ldots c_{a_k j})$ then
H is not a right-resolving set of $\vec{G}$.
else, H is a right-resolving set of $\vec{G}$.

Example 12

Consider the connectedness matrix C_{ij} in Figure 12.1.
$V = \{v_1, v_2, v_3, v_4, v_5\}$, here we take only the crisp set of the resolving set
The number of subsets with $2 \leq |H| \leq n - 1$ is $= 2n - (n + 2) = 2^5 - (5 + 2) = 25$.

The two-element subsets of V are:

$H_1 = \{c_1, c_2\}$
$H_2 = \{c_1, c_3\}$
$H_3 = \{c_1, c_4\}$
$H_4 = \{c_1, c_5\}$
$H_5 = \{c_2, c_3\}$
$H_6 = \{c_2, c_4\}$
$H_7 = \{c_2, c_5\}$
$H_8 = \{c_3, c_4\}$
$H_9 = \{c_3, c_5\}$
$H_{10} = \{c_4, c_5\}$

The three-element subsets of V are:

$H_{11} = \{c_1, c_2, c_3\}$
$H_{12} = \{c_1, c_2, c_4\}$
$H_{13} = \{c_1, c_2, c_5\}$
$H_{14} = \{c_1, c_3, c_4\}$
$H_{15} = \{c_1, c_3, c_5\}$
$H_{16} = \{c_1, c_4, c_5\}$
$H_{17} = \{c_2, c_3, c_4\}$
$H_{18} = \{c_2, c_3, c_5\}$
$H_{19} = \{c_2, c_4, c_5\}$
$H_{20} = \{c_3, c_4, c_5\}$

The four-element subsets of V are:

$H_{21} = \{c_1, c_2, c_3, c_4\}$
$H_{22} = \{c_1, c_2, c_3, c_5\}$
$H_{23} = \{c_1, c_2, c_4, c_5\}$
$H_{24} = \{c_1, c_3, c_4, c_5\}$
$H_{25} = \{c_2, c_3, c_4, c_5\}$

Out of which $H_3, H_4, H_6, H_{12}, H_{13}, H_{14}, H_{15}, H_{16}, H_{17}, H_{18}, H_{19}, H_{21}, H_{22}, H_{23}, H_{24}$, and H_{25} are the left-super resolving set of $\vec{G}$. And $H_1, H_2, H_3, H_4, H_6,$

$H_7, H_{11}, H_{12}, H_{13}, H_{14}, H_{15}, H_{16}, H_{17}, H_{18}, H_{19}, H_{21}, H_{22}, H_{23}, H_{24}$ and H_{25} are the right-super resolving sets of $\vec{G}$.

12.6 Conclusion

We have suggested an algorithm to find the strength of connectedness between any two vertices of a fuzzy graph and to find the fuzzy super resolving matrix of the fuzzy graph. Their practical application is also discussed. We explained an algorithm to find the connectedness of the modified fuzzy graph from the modified adjacency matrix which can be effectively used in fire fighting humanoid robots to reduce the complications in rescuing human lives from a fire accident. In this paper, the resolving number of a graph is defined for fuzzy digraph. The concepts of fuzzy left-super resolving set, fuzzy right-super resolving set, left-super resolving number $Sr_L(\vec{G})$ and right-super resolving number $Sr_R(\vec{G})$ are discussed. Some properties and theorems based on resolving set are explained. And also suggested an algorithm to find the left-fuzzy resolving set and right-fuzzy resolving set of the fuzzy digraph using the connectedness matrix. The future study can be done in the development of the concept of fuzzy resolving set and its applications.

References

1. Slater, P.J., Leaves of Trees. *Congr. Numer.*, 14, 549–559, 1975.
2. Wu, S.Y., The compositions of fuzzy digraphs. *J. Res. Educ. Sci.*, 31, 603–628, 1986.
3. Nagoor Gani, A. and Subahashini, D. R., Fuzzy labeling tree. *Int. J. Pure Appl. Math.*, 90, 2, 131–141, 2014.
4. Nagoor Gani, A., On Antipodal Fuzzy Graph. *Appl. Math. Sci.*, 4, 43, 2145–2155, 2010.
5. Nagoor Gani, A., On Irregular Fuzzy Graphs. *Appl. Math. Sci.*, 6, 11, 517–523, 2012.
6. Abdul-Jabbar, N., Naoom, J.H., Ouda, E.H., Fuzzy Dual Graph. *J. Al-Nahrain Univ.*, 12, 4, 168–171, 2009.
7. Samanta, S., Irregular Bipolar Fuzzy Graphs. *Int. J. Appl. Fuzzy Sets*, 2, 91–102, 2012, (ISSN 2241-1240).
8. Akram, M. and Davvaz, B., Strong intuitionistic fuzzy graphs. *Filomat*, 26, 1, 177–196, 2012.

9. Bondy, J.A. and Murty, U.S.R., *Graduate Texts in Mathematics series*, pp. 1362, 2008.
10. Rajan, B., Sonia, K.T., Monica Chris, M., Conditional resolvability of Honeycomb and Hexagonal networks. *Math. Comput. Sci.*, 5, 1, 89–90, 2011.
11. Mathew, S., Mordeson, J.N., Malik, D.S., *Fuzzy Graph Theory*, pp. 14–41, Springer International Publishing, 2018.
12. Nagoor Gani, A., Properties of Fuzzy Labeling Graph. *Appl. Math. Sci.*, 6, 3461–3466, 2012.
13. Kumar, K. and Lavanya, S., On Fuzzy Digraph. *Int. J. Pure Appl. Math.*, 115, 3, 599–606, 2017.
14. Nagoor Gani, A. and Malarvizhi, J., Isomorphism properties on strong fuzzy graphs. *IJACM*, 2, 1, 39–47, 2009.
15. Shanmugapriya, R. and Mary Jiny, D., Fuzzy Super Resolving Number of Fuzzy Labeling Graphs. *J. Adv. Res. Dyn. Control Syst.*, 7, 2, 606–611, 2019.
16. Tamilnadu Fire and Rescue Service statistics, http://www.tnfrs.tn.nic.in/.
17. Kadam, K., Bidkar, A., Pimpale, V., Doke, D., Patil, R., Fire Fighting Robot. *Int. J. Eng. Comput. Sci.*, 7, 01, 23383–23485, 2018.

13

A Note on Fuzzy Edge Magic Total Labeling Graphs

R. Shanmugapriya and P.K. Hemalatha*

Vel Tech Rangarajan Dr. Sagunthala R&D Institute of Science and Technology, Avadi, Chennai, India

Abstract
Let graph be a fuzzy simple undirected graph with p nodes and q edges. A fuzzy labeling of a graph G = (V, E) is the existence of two injections on V and E respectively which assigns values in [0, 1] such that the sum of the label on an edge and the labels of its endpoints are uniform. In this paper we show some families of fuzzy graph have edge magic total labeling and are addressed here. An application of finding stronger friendship between two persons using FEMT labeling is explained here.

***Keywords*:** Fuzzy graph, magic labeling, edge magic total (EMT) labeling, fuzzy edge bagic total (FEMT) labeling

13.1 Introduction

Consider a fuzzy graph as a finite simple undirected graph. Fuzzy graphs were defined by Kaufmann in 1973. In 1975, Rosenfield established the property of fuzzy graphs and obtained results of several theoretical ideas. A fuzzy graph has the ability to find solutions in a broad range of fields. Fuzzy Graphs—Basics, Concepts and Applications have been discussed in Ref. [6]. In Ref. [8], Edge-magic labeling of graphs had its foundation in magic valuations of graphs by Kotzig and Rosa. These labelings are said

**Corresponding author*: pkhemalathamsc@gmail.com

E. Chandrasekaran, R. Anandan, G. Suseendran, S. Balamurugan and Hanaa Hachimi (eds.) Fuzzy Intelligent Systems: Methodologies, Techniques, and Applications, (365–386) © 2021 Scrivener Publishing LLC

to be edge-magic total labeling. Fuzzy graph has theoretical application in various areas of mathematics such as linear algebra, group theory and combinatorial number theory. Development of the concept of magic graph with more property that vertices always get smaller labels than edges and named it has super edge magic labeling. Premises on fuzzy edge magic are discussed in Refs. [10, 11].

A fuzzy labeling graph is said to be a fuzzy totally magic graph if and only if there exists a fuzzy labeling f which is both fuzzy edge magic and fuzzy vertex magic. A graph is a FEMT labeling if a fuzzy edge magic total labeling is defined on it. In this paper we give some path related graphs that admits FEMT labeling and proves the admissibility.

13.2 Preliminaries

A fuzzy graph is a pair of functions $\sigma : V \rightarrow [0,1]$ and $\mu : VXV \rightarrow [0,1]$ where for all, $v \in V$, we have $E(u, v) \leq V(u) \Lambda V(v)$ such that the membership values of links and vertices are z, 2z, 3z,..., Nz where N is the total number of vertices and edges and let $z = 0.1$ for $N \leq 6$ & $z = 0.01$ for $N > 6$. A labeling graph is said to be a fuzzy edge-magic labeling if it has a constant $\lambda(v_i) + \lambda(v_j) + \mu(v_i v_j) = k$ for all $v_i, v_j \in V$.

Bistar B(n,m) is the graph obtained by joining the two copies of star graph by an edge. The vertex set of $B(n,m) = \{u, w, v_i', v_i\}$, where u, w are apex vertices and v_i', v_i are pendent vertices. The edge set of B(n, m) is $\{uw, uv_i', vv_i\}$.

The friendship graph F_n is one-point union of n copies of cycle C_3.

An unicyclic graph is a graph containing exactly one cycle Cn, where n ≥3 vertices. A Cn-unicyclic graph is a unicyclic graph where the cycle has n ≥3 vertices. A graph containing exactly one cycle is called as unicyclic graph.

Triangular Snake graph *Tn* is obtained from a path $u_1, u_2, \ldots, u_n$ by joining *ui* and u_{i+1} to a new vertex v_i for $1 \leq i \leq n$. That is, every single edge of a path is replaced by a triangle.

The tadpole graph consisting of a cycle on m ≥3 vertices and a path graph on n vertices, connected with a bridge. Let $u_1, u_2, \ldots, u_m, u_{m+1}$ be the vertices of the path P_m and $u_{m+1}, u_{m+2}, u_{m+3}, \ldots, u_{m+n}$ be the vertices of the cycle C_n incident to a vertex of the cycle` C_n

Jelly Fish *J* (*m*, *n*) is a graph with order of vertices $m + n + 4$ and sizes of edges is $m + n + 5$.*J*(*m*, *n*) is formed from *u*, *v*, *x*, *y* cycle by joining with an edge u and v and (m, n) pendent edges to x and y.

13.3 Theorem

The bi star graph B(m, n) admits FEMT labeling.

Proof:
Let the vertex set $V=\{u,w,v_1,v_2,\ldots,v_m,v_1',v_2',\ldots,v_n'\}$ where u and w are the center vertices of the two stars $K_{1,m}$ *and* $K_{1,n}$ where m, n >1, v_m and v_n' are the vertices of the pendent vertices of two starts $K_{1,m}$ and $K_{1,n}$ and the edge set is E(G) = $\{e_1, e_2,\ldots,e_{n+m+1}\}$. To prove the bistar is FEMT labeling, we consider the below labeling for the edges and vertices.

$$f(u, w) = (m + 1)z; f(w, v_m) = mz \text{ Where m} = 1, 2, 3\ldots.$$

$$f(uv_n')=\mathrm{f(u,w)+z}$$

$$f(uv'_{n-(n-1)})= f(u,v'_{n-1})+\mathrm{z}$$

$$f(v_n')= f(u,w)+ 2nz$$

$$f(w)= f(v_n')+z$$

$$f(u) = f(w) + mz$$

$$f(v_m)= f(v_n')+z$$

$$f(v_{m-(m-1)}) = f(v_{m-(m-2)}) + \mathrm{z}$$

From the above labeling we can say that the graph B (m, n) is FEMT constant λ.

$$f(u) + f(uw) + f(w) = \lambda$$

$$f(u)= f(uv_n')+ f(v_n')=\lambda$$

$$f(w) + f(wv_m) + f(v_m) = \lambda$$

Hence, an individual edge satisfying FEMT labeling that the sum of label on link and label of its two end points is constant λ, independent of the choice of edge. Hence the bi-star B (m,n) graph is FEMT labeling.

13.3.1 Example

Case (1): when m >n, m is even and n is.

The Bi-star B (4, 3) a demonstration of the FEMT labeling is as follows. There are 9 nodes and 8 edges. Here m = 3 and n = 4, we consider the below labeling as given in Figure 13.1 for edges and vertices

We get,

$$f(u) + f(uw) + f(w) = 0.33$$

$$f(u)+f(uv_n')+f(v_n')=0.33$$

$$f(w) + f(wv_m) + f(v_m) = 0.33$$

Hence the FEMT constant is 0.33.

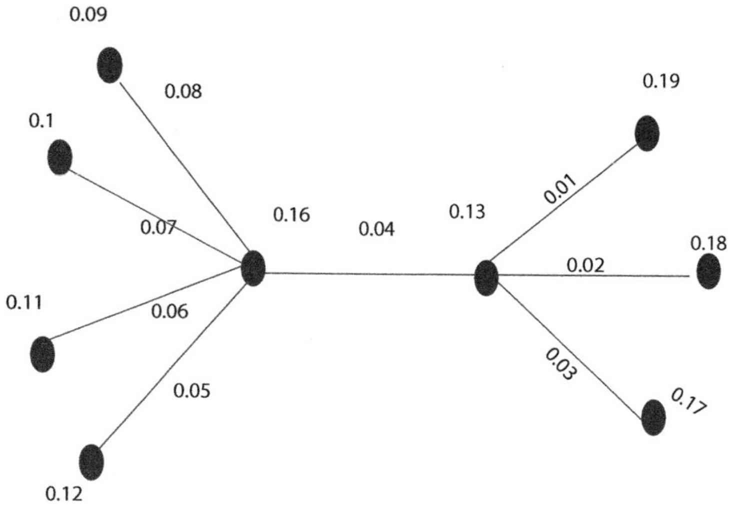

Figure 13.1 Bistar B (4, 3) is FEMT labeling.

Case (2): when m <n, m is odd and n is even, we consider the labeling in Figure 13.2

We get,

$$f(u) + f(uw) + f(w) = 0.33$$

$$f(u)=f(uv_n')+f(v_n')=0.33$$

$$f(w) + f(wv_m) + f(v_m) = 0.33$$

Hence the FEMT constant is 0.33.

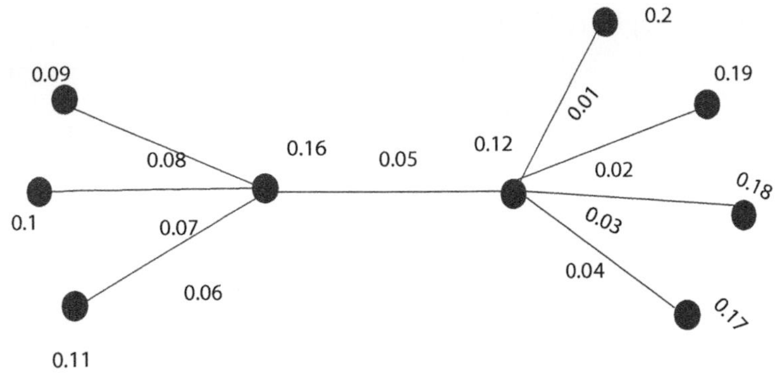

Figure 13.2 Bistar B (3, 4) is FEMT labeling.

Case (3): When m=n consider the below labeling as given in Figure 13.3
We get,

$$f(u) + f(uw) + f(w) = 0.33$$

$$f(u) = f(uv'_n) + f(v'_n) = 0.3$$

$$f(w) + f(wv_m) + f(v_m) = 0.3$$

Hence the FEMT constant is 0.3.

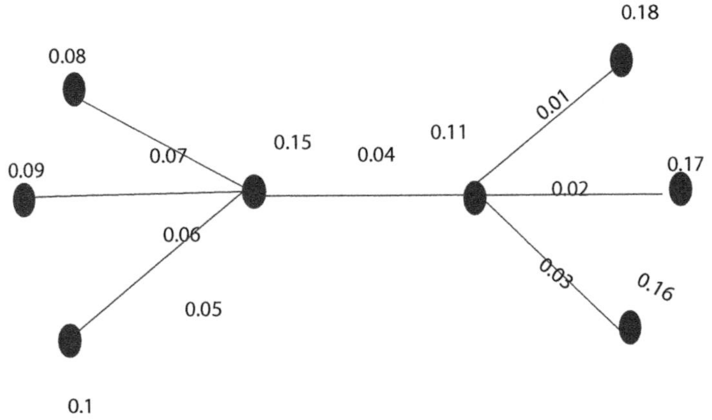

Figure 13.3 Bistar B (3,3) is FEMT labeling.

13.4 Theorem

All unicyclics graph are FEMT labeling.

Proof:

A unicyclic U of order n with v vertices and e edges if and only if f: VUE→[0,1]. Consider the unicyclic graph U(q,m) by fuzzy relation, start assigning the values using membership function, such that the label of the link should be less than the label of two end points and also the values of the nodes and links are distinct.

Let label the vertices of cycle be $\{u_1, u_2, \ldots, u_q\}$ and nodes connected to each vertex on cycle be $\{v_1, v_2, \ldots, v_m\}$.

Define the edges of the cycle

Let $\mu(u_n u_1) = z$

$$\mu(u_n u_{n-1}) = (m+1)z + \mu(u_{n-1}u_{n-2}), \text{ where n} = 1,2,\ldots\text{etc}$$

Consider the edge labeling connected to the vertex on the cycle u_1,

$$\mu(u_1v_1) = \mu(u_nu_1) + z$$

$$\mu(u_1v_m) = \mu(u_1v_{m-1}) + z$$

Edge labeling connected at the vertex u_2,

$$\mu(u_2v_{m+1}) = \mu(u_2u_1) + z$$

$$\mu(u_2v_{2m}) = \mu(u_2v_{2m-1}) + z$$

Similarly we need to find the edge label connected to u_3, u_4 ..... u_n.
Edge labeling connected at the vertex u_n,

$$\mu(u_nv_{nm-(m-1)}) = \mu(u_{n-1}u_n) + z$$

$$\mu(u_nv_{nm-(m-2)}) = \mu(u_nv_{nm-(m-1)}) + z$$

$$\mu(u_nv_{nm}) = \mu(u_nv_{nm-1}) + z$$

Consider the odd vertex on the cycle

$$V(u_1) = (v+e)z$$

$$V(u_{n-(n-3)}) = ((v + e) - (m + 1)) * z$$

$$V(u_n) = (V(u_{n-2}) - (m + 1)) * z$$

Consider the even vertex on the cycle

$$V(u_n) = V(u_{n+m}) - (m + 1) * z$$

$$V(u_n) = V(u_{n-2}) - (m + 1) * z$$

Labeling of the nodes which is connected at the vertex u_n where n = 1, 2,…, (n − 1) and m is same for all the u_n is,

$$V(v_{nm}) = V(u_{n+2}) + z$$

$$V(v_{nm-(m-2)}) = V(v_{nm}) + z$$

$$V(v_{nm-(m-1)}) = V(v_{nm-1}) + z$$

At u_n the label for the node is

$$V(v_{nm}) = \mu(v_{nm}u_n) + z$$

$$V(v_{nm-(m-1)}) = \mu(v_{nm-(m-2)}) + z$$

Thus, an independent edge, satisfies the sum of the label on an edge and the labels of its two end points is constant λ.

13.4.1 Example

Consider the unicyclic U(5,3) graph with 15 vertices and 20 edges. Where q = 5 is the size of the unique cycle and m = 3 represents the number of nodes connected to each vertex on the cycle as shown in Figure 13.4.

Define the following values to the edges

$$E(u_5u_1) = z = 0.01,$$

$$E(u_1u_2) = (m + 1)z = 0.05,$$

$$E(u_2u_3) = (m + 1)z + E(u_1u_2) = 0.09,$$

$$E(u_3u_4) = (m + 1)z + E(u_2u_3) = 0.13,$$

$$E(u_4u_5) = (m + 1)z + E(u_3u_4) = 0.17,$$

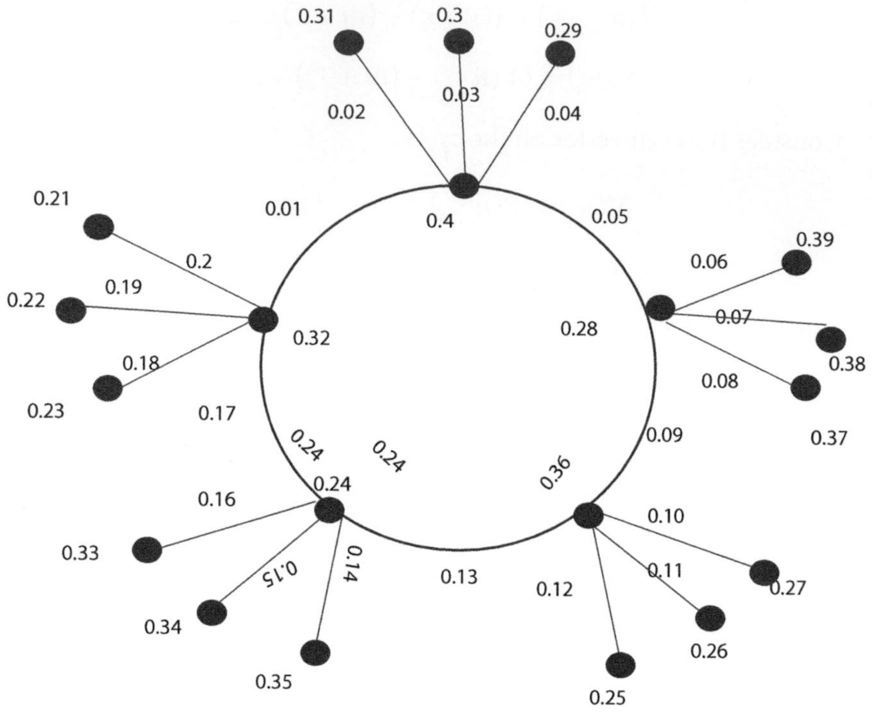

Figure 13.4 Unicyclic U(5,3) is FEMT labeling.

Consider the edge labeling connected to the vertex on the cycle u_1, u_2, u_3, u_4, u_5.

$$E(u_1v_1) = E(u_5u_1) + z = 0.12,$$

$$E(u_1v_2) = E(u_5u_1) + 2z = 0.03,$$

$$E(u_1v_3) = E(u_5u_1) + 3z = 0.04,$$

$$E(u_2v_4) = E(u_1u_2) + z = 0.06,$$

$$E(u_2v_5) = E(u_1u_2) + 2z = 0.07,$$

$$E(u_2v_6) = E(u_1u_2) + 3z = 0.08,$$

$$E(u_3v_7) = E(u_2u_3) + z = 0.1,$$

$$E(u_3v_8) = E(u_2u_3) + 2z = 0.11,$$

$$E(u_3v_9) = E(u_2u_3) + 3z = 0.12,$$

$$E(u_4v_{10}) = E(u_3u_4) + z = 0.14,$$

$$E(u_4v_{11}) = E(u_3u_4) + 2z = 0.15,$$

$$E(u_4v_{12}) = E(u_3u_4) + 3z = 0.16,$$

$$E(u_5v_{13}) = E(u_4u_5) + z = 0.18,$$

$$E(u_5v_{14}) = E(u_4u_5) + 2z = 0.19,$$

$$E(u_5v_{15}) = E(u_4u_5) + 3z = 0.2,$$

Consider the odd and even vertex on the cycle

$$V(u_1) = (v + e)z = 0.4,$$

$$V(u_3) = (v + e)z\text{-}0.4 = 0.36,$$

$$V(u_5) = (v + e)z\text{-}0.08 = 0.32,$$

$$V(u_2) = (v + e)z\text{-}0.12 = 0.28,$$

$$V(u_4) = (v + e)z\text{-}0.16 = 0.24$$

Labeling of the nodes which is connected at the vertex u_1, u_2, u_3, u_4, u_5.

$$V(v_{15}) = \mu(u_5v_{15}) + z = 0.21,$$

$$V(v_{14}) = \mu(u_5v_{15}) + 2z = 0.22,$$

$$V(v_{13}) = \mu(u_5v_{15}) + 3z = 0.23,$$

Similarly the label of the nodes $V(v_{12})$, $V(v_{11})$, ….., $V(v_1)$ can be found. Thus we get,

$$f(u_n) + f(u_nu_{n-1}) + f(u_{n-1}) = 0.73$$

$$f(u_n) + f(u_nv_m) + f(v_m) = 0.73$$

13.4.1.1 Lemma

The graph G(V,σ,μ) be a FEM graph then size of graph is lesser than equal to the order of G (i.e.) S(G) ≤ O(G).

13.4.1.2 Lemma

Every fuzzy edge magic total labeling graph is a fuzzy graph.

13.4.1.3 Lemma

In a fuzzy edge magic total labeling G be an undirected graph, the sum of the degree of the vertices (odd and even) is equal to the twice the degree of membership of all the edges.

13.5 Theorem

Every star graph S(1,n) is FEMT labeling.

Proof:
Consider the star graph S(1,n) with (n – 1) nodes have degree 1 and a single vertex have degree (n – 1) and n edges. Which is constructed as (n – 1) nodes are connected to a single centre vertex. Labeling the edges as $\mu(v, v_i) = z * i$ where $i = 1,2, \ldots, n$.

To the center label, $\sigma(v) = z(n + 1)$. Assigning the values to the nodes which is connected to the center vertex be

$$\sigma(v_n) = \sigma(v) + z$$

$$\sigma(v_{n-(n-1)}) = \sigma(v_{n-(n-2)}) + z$$

Thus star graph satisfies the condition of FEMT labeling.

13.5.1 Example as Shown in Figure 13.5 Star Graph S(1,9) is FEMT Labeling

Consider S(1,9) labeling the edges as follows

$$\mu(v, v_1) = 0.01,$$

$$\mu(v, v_2) = 0.02,$$

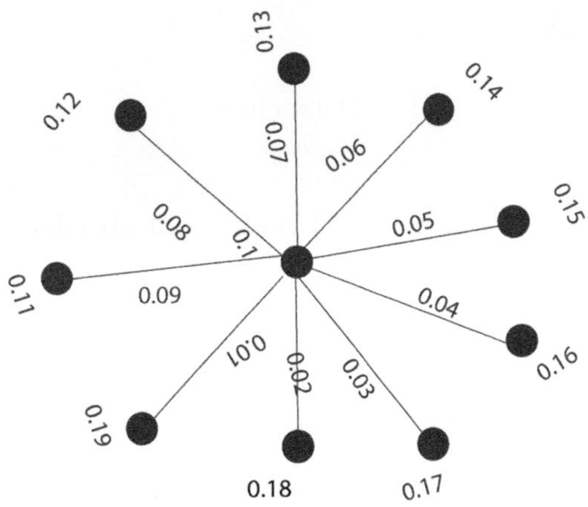

Figure 13.5 Star graph S(1,9) is FEMT labeling.

$$\mu(v, v_3) = 0.03,$$

$$\mu(v, v_4) = 0.04,$$

$$\mu(v, v_5) = 0.05,$$

$$\mu(v, v_6) = 0.06,$$

$$\mu(v, v_7) = 0.07,$$

$$\mu(v, v_8) = 0.08,$$

$$\mu(v, v_9) = 0.09$$

To the center label, $\sigma(v) = 0.1$

Assigning the values to the nodes which is connected to the center vertex be

$$\sigma(v_n) = \sigma(v) + z = 0.11$$

$$\sigma(v_{n-1}) = \sigma(v) + 2z = 0.12$$

$$\sigma(v_{n-2}) = \sigma(v) + 3z = 0.13$$

$$\sigma(v_{n-(n-1)}) = \sigma(v) + nz = 0.19$$

Thus the $\sigma(v) + \mu(v, v_i) + \sigma(v_i) = 0.3$, where i = 2,…,n. which shows FEMT labeling.

13.6 Theorem

Every friendship graph F_n is FEMT labeling.

Proof:
Let friendship graph with (2n + 1) nodes and 3n edges, which is constructed by joining n-copies of cycle graph C_n denoted by $w_1, w_2, \ldots, w_n$ with a common vertex v.

Case (i): when n is odd,

Friendship graph F_3 with 7 vertices and 9 edges shows FEMT using the membership function.

When i is odd,

$$i = 1, E(w_i w_{i+1}) = i * z$$

$$i = 3, E(w_i w_{i+1}) = i * z + 2\,E(w_{i-2} w_{i-1})$$

$$i = n - 1, E(w_{n-1} w_n) = i * z + (n\text{-}2)\,E(w_{(n-1)-(n-2)} w_{(n-1)-(n-3)})$$

For labeling the edges, the nodes that are connected to middle vertex.

$$\text{When } i = 1, E(vw_i) = E(w_i w_{i+1}) + z$$

$$\text{When } i = 2, E(vw_i) = E(w_i w_{i-1}) + z$$

$$\text{When } i = 3, E(vw_i) = E(w_i w_{i+1}) - 2z$$

$$\text{When } i = 4, E(vw_i) = E(w_i w_{i-1}) + 2z$$

$$\text{When } i = 5, E(vw_i) = E(w_i w_{i+1}) + 3z$$

$$\text{When } i = 6, E(vw_i) = E(w_i w_{i-1}) - z$$

For labeling the vertices

$$V(w_{2n}) = E(w_{2n} w_{2n-1}) + z$$

$$V(w_{2n-2}) = V(w_{2n}) + z$$

$$V(w_{2n-1}) = V(w_{2n-2}) + z$$

$$V(v) = V(w_{2n-2}) + z$$

$$V(w_{2n-4}) = V(v)+z$$

$$V(w_{2n-3}) = V(w_{2n-4}) + z$$

$$V(w_{2n-5}) = V(w_{2n-3}) + z$$

As given in Figure 13.6, Friendship graph F_3 admits FEMT labeling

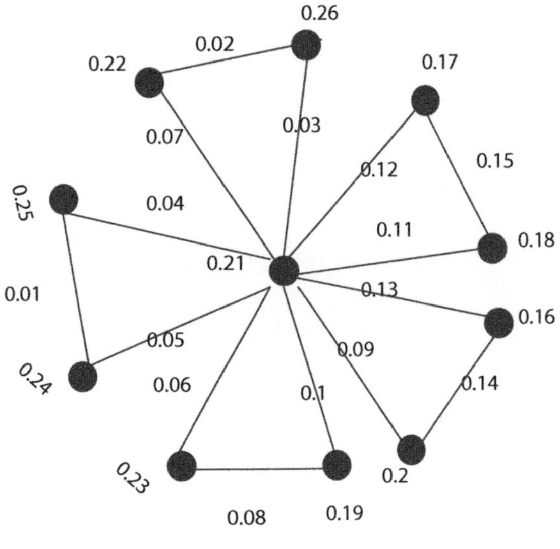

Figure 13.6 Friendship graph F_5 is FEMT labeling.

13.7 Theorem

Every Triangular snake graph T_n is FEMT labeling.

Proof:
Let T_n is a triangular snake graph is formed from the graph P_n by replacing link of the path by a triangle C_3. We obtain triangular snake graph from path $u_1, u_2, \ldots, u_n$ by joining u_i *and* u_{i+1} to a new vertex v_i, $1 \le i \le n$. Hence

we get new vertices $v_1, v_2, \ldots, v_{n-1}$. Labeling the edge connecting the vertex of a path u_n and a new vertex v_{n-1} of T_n n = 2,3,..., etc.

$$E(u_n v_{n-1}) = z * 2(n-1)$$

$$E(u_{n-1} v_{n-1}) = E(u_n v_{n-1}) - z$$

In general, $E(u_{n-(n-1)} v_{n-(n-1)}) = E(u_{n-(n-2)} v_{n-(n-1)}) - z$
Then the induced labeling for edges as follows,

$$E(u_n u_{n-1}) = E(u_n v_{n-1}) + (n * z) + 2z$$

$$E(u_{n-1} u_{n-2}) = E(u_n u_{n-1}) - 2z$$

$$E(u_{n-2} u_{n-3}) = E(u_{n-1} u_{n-2}) - 2z$$

In general, $E(u_{n-(n-1)} u_{n-(n-2)}) = E(u_{n-(n-2)} u_{n-(n-3)}) - 2z$
labeling the vertices of the path

$$V(u_n) = E(u_n u_{n-1}) + (n * z) + 3z$$

$$V(u_{n-1}) = V(u_n) + z$$

In general, $V(u_{n-(n-1)}) = V(u_{n-(n-2)}) + z$
labeling the vertices $v_1, v_2, \ldots, v_{n-1}$

$$V(v_{n-1}) = V(u_{n-(n-1)}) + 4z$$

$$V(v_{n-2}) = V(v_{n-1)}) + z$$

In general, $V(v_{n-(n-1)}) = V(v_{n-(n-2)}) + z$
Hence by fuzzy relation, label of an edge is lesser than the two end points. By taking the label of an edge and the label of two end points is same for all individual edges then we can say Triangular snake graph T_n is FEMT labeling.

13.7.1 Example

Consider the Triangular snake graph T_4 with 7 vertices and 9 edges. As given in the Figure 13.7, the membership value assign to the edges are follows.

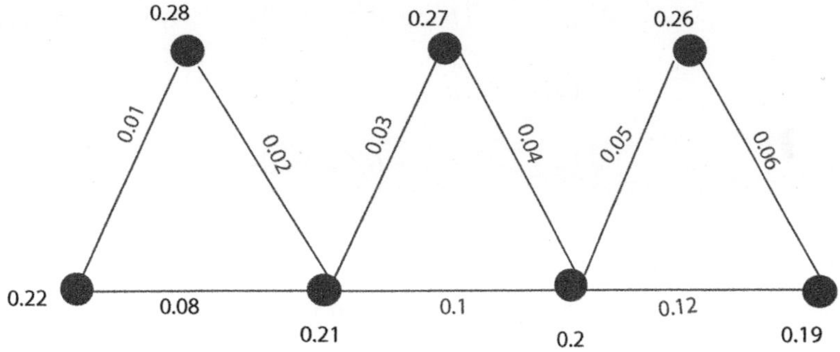

Figure 13.7 Triangular snake graph T_4 is FEMT labeling.

$$E\,(u_1v_1) = z = 0.01,$$

$$E\,(u_2v_1) = 0.02,$$

$$E\,(u_2v_2) = 0.03,$$

$$E\,(u_3v_2) = 0.04,$$

$$E\,(u_3v_3) = 0.05,$$

$$E\,(u_4v_3) = 0.06$$

$$E\,(u_1v_2) = 0.08,$$

$$E\,(u_2u_3) = 0.1,$$

$$E\,(u_3u_4) = 0.12.$$

Path vertices can be labeled as

$$V\,(u_4) = E(u_3u_4) + E(u_3v_2) + 0.03 = 0.19,$$

$$V\,(u_3) = V(u_4) + z = 0.2,$$

$$V\,(u_2) = V(u_3) + z = 0.21,$$

$$V\,(u_1) = V(u_2) + z = 0.22,$$

Labeling the vertices $v_1, v_2, \ldots, v_{n-1}$.

$$V\,(v_3) = V(u_1) + 4Z = 0.26,$$

$$V\,(v_2) = V(u_1) + 5Z = 0.27,$$

$$V\,(v_3) = V(u_1) + 6Z = 0.28,$$

Thus $V\,(u_i) + E\,(u_i u_{i+1}) + V(u_i) = 0.51$

$$V\,(u_i) + E\,(u_i v_i) + V\,(v_i) = 0.51$$

$$V\,(u_{i+1}) + E(u_{i+1} v_i) + V\,(v_i) = 0.51$$

Hence FEMT constant for Triangular snake graph T_4 is 0.51.

13.8 Theorem

The Tadpole graph (m,n) where m ≥3 consisting of a m cycle graph and n vertices of a path graph connected with a bridge is FEMT labeling.

Proof:

The T(m,n) Tadpole graph is obtained by joining a cycle graph C_m where m ≥3 and a path graph P_n on n vertices connected with a bridge. There are (m + n) vertices and edges.

Case (1): Consider T(5, 3) as given in Figure 13.8 when m>n, there are 8 vertices and edges. Fuzzy Tadpole graph is a bijection f:VUE→[0,1]. By fuzzy relation, Labeling graph with distinct vertices and edges, we have $\mu(u_i, u_{i+1}) \leq \sigma\,(u_i) \wedge \sigma\,(u_{i+1})$ A fuzzy T(m,n) graph is said to be a fuzzy edge-magic labeling if it has a constant $\lambda(u_i) + \lambda(u_{i+1}) + \mu(u_i u_{i+1}) = k$. FEM constant for T(5,3) is 0.73.

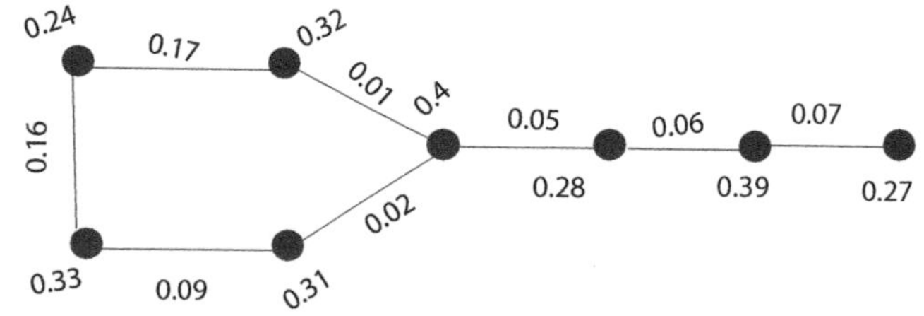

Figure 13.8 Tadpole graph T(5,3) is FEMT labeling.

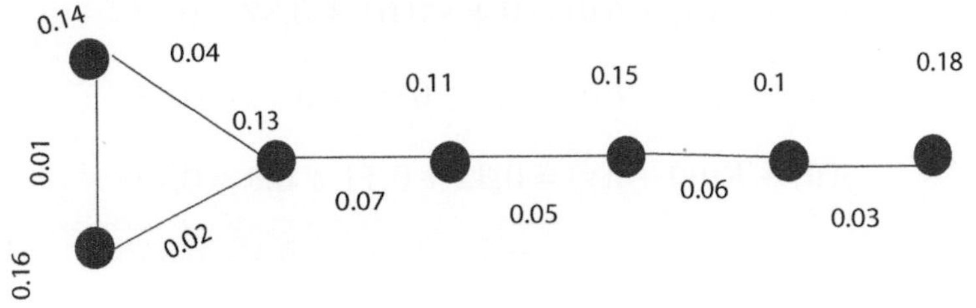

Figure 13.9 Tadpole graph T(3,4) is FEMT labeling.

Case (2): when m <n, Consider T(3,4), there are 7 vertices and edges as given in Figure 13.9. By fuzzy relation edge label is less than the two end points. Applying fuzzy edge magic total labeling, we get

$$\sigma\,(u_1) + \mu(u_1, u_2) + \sigma(u_2) = 0.14 + 0.01 + 0.16 = 0.31,$$

$$\sigma\,(u_2) + \mu(u_2, u_3) + \sigma(u_3) = 0.16 + 0.02 + 0.13 = 0.31,$$

$$\sigma\,(u_2) + \mu(u_1, u_3) + \sigma(u_3) = 0.14 + 0.04 + 0.13 = 0.31,$$

$$\sigma\,(u_3) + \mu(u_3, u_4) + \sigma(u_4) = 0.13 + 0.07 + 0.11 = 0.31,$$

$$\sigma\,(u_4) + \mu(u_4, u_5) + \sigma(u_5) = 0.11 + 0.05 + 0.15 = 0.31,$$

$$\sigma\,(u_5) + \mu(u_5, u_6) + \sigma(u_6) = 0.15 + 0.06 + 0.1 = 0.31,$$

$$\sigma\,(u_6) + \mu(u_6, u_7) + \sigma(u_7) = 0.1 + 0.03 + 0.18 = 0.$$

Thus FEM constant for T(3,4) is 0.31.

13.9 Theorem

The jelly fish J(m,n) graph is a FEMT labeling.

Proof:
Jelly fish graph which have (m,n) pendent edges satisfies FEMT labeling using membership function assigning values to [0,1] to the nodes and edges are all distinct. Thus the label of an edge is lesser than the two end points. J(3,4) is demonstrated below by applying fuzzy edge magic labeling.

$$f(x) + f(xu) + f(u) = 0.4 + 0.01 + 0.32 = 0.73$$

$$f(x) + f(xv) + f(v) = 0.4 + 0.05 + 0.28 = 0.73$$

$$f(u) + f(uy) + f(y) = 0.32 + 0.11 + 0.3 = 0.73$$

$$f(v) + f(vy) + f(y) = 0.28 + 0.15 + 0.3 = 0.73$$

$$f(u) + f(uu_1) + f(u_1) = 0.32 + 0.18 + 0.23 = 0.73$$

$$f(u) + f(uu_2) + f(u_2) = 0.32 + 0.17 + 0.24 = 0.73$$

$$f(u) + f(uu_3) + f(u_3) = 0.32 + 0.2 + 0.21 = 0.73$$

$$f(v) + f(vv_1) + f(v_1) = 0.28 + 0.06 + 0.39 = 0.73$$

$$f(v) + f(vv_2) + f(v_2) = 0.28 + 0.07 + 0.38 = 0.73$$

$$f(v) + f(vv_3) + f(v_3) = 0.28 + 0.08 + 0.37 = 0.73$$

$$f(v) + f(vv_4) + f(v_4) = 0.28 + 0.09 + 0.36 = 0.73$$

$$f(x) + f(xy) + f(y) = 0.4 + 0.03 + 0.3 = 0.73$$

By taking the label of an edge and the label of two end points is same for all individual edges. Hence jelly fish J(m,n) admits FEMT labeling (Figure 13.10).

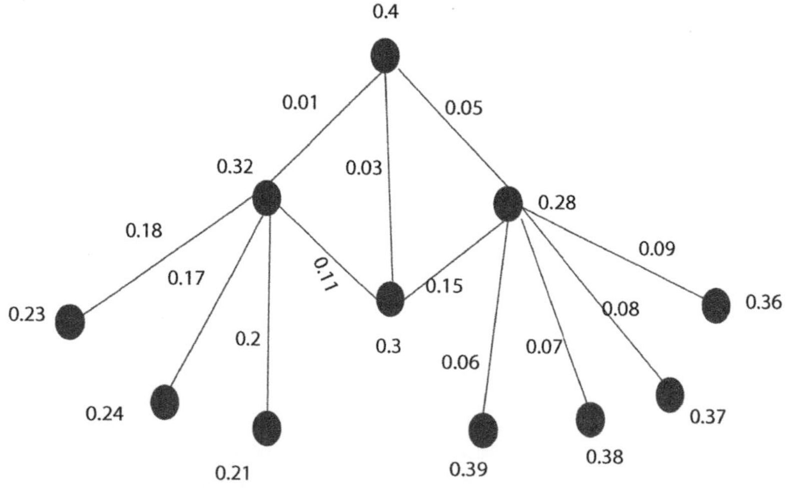

Figure 13.10 Jelly fish J(m,n) is FEMT labeling.

13.10 Application of Fuzzy Edge Magic Total Labeling

We can find the strength of the friendship between two persons using FEMT labeling with uniform edge weight k, the nodes and edges are assigned distinct labels such that the strength of the 2 persons from v_i to v_j is found by $\lambda(v_iv_j) = k - \lambda(v_i) - \lambda(v_j)$.

In the FEMT labeling graphs the vertices could represents the person and the link denotes the strength (friendship) between two persons. Considered the graph $C_n + F_m$, which is obtained from cycle C_n by attaching fan graph F_m at each vertex of the cycle. The graph $C_5 + F_2$ is taken which has 15 nodes and 20 edges. Fuzzy edge magic total labeling is an assignment of membership function [0,1] to all the nodes and edges such that any edge v_iv_j in G, the weight of the edge $\lambda(v_i) + \lambda(v_j) + \lambda(v_iv_j) = k$.

To illustrated strength between the two persons using FEMT of $C_5 + F_2$ as show in Figure13.11, the weight of the edge $\lambda(v_i) + \lambda(v_j) + \lambda(v_iv_j) = k$.

For example to find the strength between two persons.

Start at person v_1 which is connected to 4 persons v_1, v_5, v_6, v_7. The link between the nodes are (v_1v_6), (v_1v_7), (v_1v_5), (v_1v_5), (v_1v_2). The corresponding values for the link is (0.02,0.03,0.01,0.05) are obtained by $k - \lambda(v_i) - \lambda(v_j)$. That is 0.05 is the highest strength of this links. So we say that v_1 having stronger strength with v_5.

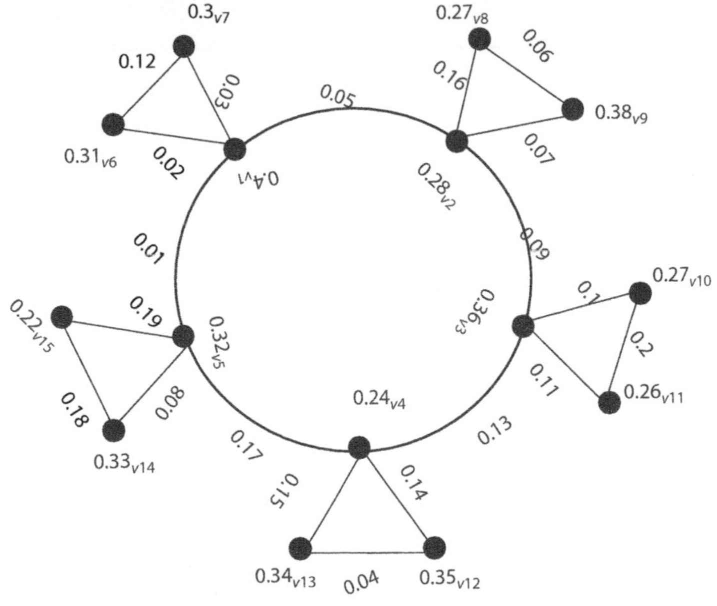

Figure 13.11 The graph $C_5 + F_2$ is FEMT labeling.

Next person v_5 which is connected to 4 persons v_1, v_4, v_{14}, v_{15}. The link between the nodes are (v_5v_4), (v_5v_1), (v_5v_{14}), (v_5v_{15}). The corresponding values for the link is (0.17,0.01,0.08,0.19) are obtained by $k - \lambda(v_i) - \lambda(v_j)$. We get 0.19 is the highest strength of this link. So we say that v_5 having stronger strength with person v_{15}. Like wise we can find the strength between of all persons using fuzzy edge magic total labeling as shown in below Table 13.1.

Therefore, all persons have distinct strength with the other persons.

Table 13.1 Strength between two person using FEMT labeling.

No. of persons	Membership value v_i	Links	Stronger strength between the links	$k - \lambda(v_i) - \lambda(v_j)$
v_1	0.4	(v_1v_6), (v_1v_7), (v_1v_5), (v_1v_2)	(v_1v_5)	0.05
v_2	0.28	(v_2v_1), (v_2v_3), (v_2v_8), (v_2v_9)	(v_2v_8)	0.16
v_3	0.36	(v_3v_2), (v_3v_4), (v_3v_{10}), (v_3v_{11})	(v_3v_4)	0.13
v_4	0.24	(v_4v_3), (v_4v_5), (v_4v_{12}), (v_4v_{13})	(v_4v_5)	0.17
v_5	0.32	(v_5v_4), (v_5v_1), (v_5v_{14}), (v_5v_{15})	(v_5v_{15})	0.19
v_6	0.31	(v_1v_6), (v_6v_7)	(v_6v_7)	0.12
v_7	0.3	(v_7v_6), (v_7v_1)	(v_7v_6)	0.12
v_8	0.29	(v_8v_2), (v_8v_9)	(v_8v_2)	0.16
v_9	0.38	(v_9v_2), (v_9v_8)	(v_9v_2)	0.07
v_{10}	0.27	$(v_{10}v_3)$, $(v_{10}v_{11})$	$(v_{10}v_{11})$	0.2
v_{11}	0.26	$(v_{11}v_3)$, $(v_{11}v_{10})$	$(v_{11}v_{10})$	0.2
v_{12}	0.35	$(v_{12}v_4)$, $(v_{12}v_{13})$	$(v_{12}v_4)$	0.14
v_{13}	0.34	$(v_{13}v_4)$, $(v_{13}v_{12})$	$(v_{13}v_4)$	0.15
v_{14}	0.33	$(v_{14}v_5)$, $(v_{14}v_{15})$	$(v_{14}v_{15})$	0.18
v_{15}	0.22	$(v_{15}v_5)$, $(v_{15}v_{14})$	$(v_{15}v_5)$	0.19

13.11 Conclusion

In this chapter the concept of fuzzy edge magic total labeling has investigated for various families of graphs such as bi-star graph $B(n, m)$, unicyclic graph $U(q, m)$, Jelly fish $J(m, n)$, $C_n + F_m$, Triangular snake graph T_n, Friendship graph F_5, Tadpole graph, Star graph $S(1, n)$ with odd and even number of vertices. An application to find the strength of the two persons using FEMT labeling have been discussed here. In future, the focus would be on fuzzy anti-magic labeling of graphs.

References

1. Gallian, J.A., A dynamic survey of Graph labeling. *Electron. J. Comb.*, 14, DS6, 67–79, 2007.
2. F. Harary, *Graph Theory*, Addison Wesley, Massachusetts,New Delhi, 1972.
3. Pathinathan, T., Arockiaraj, J.J., Jesintha Rosline, J., Hesistancy Fuzzy Graphs. *Indian J. Sci. Technol.*, 8, 35, 1-5, Dec. 2015.
4. Rifayathali, M.A., Prasanna, A., & Mohid, *Hesitancy fuzzy magic labeling graph. The Journal of Analysis*, 27, 1, 39-53, Publisher-Springer, Singapore, 2019.
5. Enomoto, H., Lladó, A.S., Nakamigawa, T., Ringel, G., Super edge-magic graphs. *Sut J. Math.*, 34, 2, 105-109, 1998.
6. Mathew, S. and Sunitha, M.S., *Fuzzy Graphs—Basics, Concepts and Applications*, Lap Lambert Academic Publishing, August 17, 2012.
7. Goguen, J. (1973). L. A. Zadeh. *Fuzzy sets. Information and control*, vol. 8 (1965), pp. 338–353. - L. A. Zadeh. Similarity relations and fuzzy orderings. Information sciences, vol. 3 (1971), pp. 177–200. Journal of Symbolic Logic, 38(4), 656-657.
8. Kotzig, A. and Rosa, A., Magic valuations of finite graphs. *Can. Math. Bull.*, 13, 451–461, 1970.
9. Nagoor Gani, A. and Rajalaxmi, D., (a) Subahashini, Properties of Fuzzy Labeling Graph. *Appl. Math. Sci.*, 6, 70, 3461–3466, 2012.
10. Kaliraja, M. and Sasikala, M., Premises on fuzzy factorizable perfect intrinsic edge-magic graphs. *Malaya J. Mat.*, 7, 4, 767–770, 2019.
11. Kaliraja, M. and Sasikala, M., Fuzzy Pseudo Intrinsic Edge-Magic Graphs. *Adv. Math.: Sci. J.*, 8, 3, 214–220, 2019.
12. Mathew Varkey, T.K. and Sreena, T.D., Fuzzy Fractional Prime Product Labeling, The International journal of analytical and experimental modal analysis. Volume XII, Issue II, February/2020.

13. Shanmugapriya, R., Hemalatha, P.K., Suba, M., Fuzzy Graceful Labeling on the Double Fan Graphs and the Double Wheel Graphs. *Int. J. Innov. Technol. Explor. Eng. (IJITEE)*, 8, 9, 1808–1810, July 2019.
14. Shanmugapriya, R. and Mary Jiny., D., Fuzzy Super Resolving Number of Fuzzy Labelling Graphs. *J. Adv. Res. Dyn. Control Syst.*, 11, 09, 606–611, 2019.

14

The Synchronization of Impulsive Time-Delay Chaotic Systems with Uncertainties in Terms of Takagi–Sugeno Fuzzy System

Balaji Dharmalingam[1], Suresh Rasappan[2*], V. Vijayalakshmi[3] and G. Suseendran[4†]

[1]*Department of Electronics and Communication Engineering, Vel Tech Rangarajan Dr. Sagunthala R&D Institute of Science and Technology, Chennai, India*
[2]*Department of Mathematics, Vel Tech Rangarajan Dr. Sagunthala R&D Institute of Science and Technology, Chennai, India*
[3]*Department of Information Technology, SRM Institute of Science and Technology, Chennai, India*
[4]*Department of Information Technology, Vels Institute of Science, Technology & Advanced Studies, Chennai, India*

Abstract

The control of impulsive chaotic system based on T–S fuzzy model is investigated. The asymptotic mean square stability criterion is designed. A robust supervisory control is proposed. When fuzzy based impulsive chaotic systems are subjected to system uncertainties and external disturbance, the supervisory control can induce the convergence speed of the designed system. The Genesio–Tesi chaotic is utilized and the fuzzy logic tool box in MATLAB is invoked forgetting results.

Keywords: Impulsive, chaotic system, T–S fuzzy system, stable, Genesio–Tesi chaotic system

14.1 Introduction

A non-linear dynamical system that exhibits complex and unpredictable behavior is called chaotic system. The parameter values are varying with

**Corresponding author*: mrpsuresh83@gmail.com
†*Corresponding author*: suseendar_1234@yahoo.co.in

E. Chandrasekaran, R. Anandan, G. Suseendran, S. Balamurugan and Hanaa Hachimi (eds.) Fuzzy Intelligent Systems: Methodologies, Techniques, and Applications, (387–412) © 2021 Scrivener Publishing LLC

range and sensitivity depends on initial conditions are the remarkable properties of chaotic systems [1–5]. Sometimes, the chaotic systems are deterministic and it has long-term unpredictable behaviors.

The controlling of the chaotic systems are significantly classified in three ways: 1. stabilization of unsteady intermittent movement "contained" in the set of chaotic [6, 7]. 2. Repression of chaotic nature by outer forcing like periodic noise, periodic parametric perturbation [8–11] and 3. algorithm of various automatic control like feedback, backstepping, sample feedback, time delay feedback, etc [11–20].

There might be two different ways to apply the controls in chaotic system. In particular a difference in attractor in the system and the subsequent one is change in the situation of the point in the stage space of the system at a steady value of its parameter.

The fuzzy logic and intelligent systems are the key factors for development of artificial neural networks. It induces the theoretical and applications based works in this research area.

Recently, fuzzy-based chaotic control systems are notable research areas in various engineering and science applications. It gives research achievements and insightful ideas on the intrinsic relationships between fuzzy logic and chaos theory.

A variety of schemes for ensuring the control of fuzzy-based systems have been demonstrated based on their potential application in the field of fuzzy-based chaos generator, secure communication, physical and chemical, ecological, delay and information science systems [21–25].

Practically, the impulsive control method is more popular than other because it deals with chaotic systems which cannot endure continuous disturbance. It receives the feedback only at discrete times during the control processes. Additionally this method reduces the amount of feedback processes from the chaotic system, which makes it more efficient and useful in real life applications [26–31].

This chapter deals with fuzzy impulsive control of chaotic systems based on T–S fuzzy model involving with uncertainties. It is a new idea to control the chaotic systems on the basis of fuzzy concept. The rigorous stability criteria of the proposed method are derived. The effectiveness of the fuzzy impulsive control is tested on Genesio–Tesi chaotic system. MATLAB fuzzy tool box is invoked for verifying the derived stability criteria.

14.2 Problem Description and Preliminaries

14.2.1 Impulsive Differential Equations

Let us take a general stochastic impulsive system

$$dx_c(t_c) = [f(t_c, x_c(t_c))]dt_c + [g(t_c, y(t_c))]d\omega(t_c) \tag{14.1}$$

where $f: R_+ \times R^n \rightarrow R^n$ is continuous.

Suppose that a sequence of instants $\{\tau_{ci}\}$ satisfies $0 < \tau_{c1} < \tau_{c2} < \cdots < \tau_{ci} < \tau_{c(i+1)} < \cdots$, $\tau_{ci} \rightarrow \infty$ as $i \rightarrow \infty$

Let

$$\begin{aligned} U(i, x_c(t_c)) &= \Delta x_c(t_c) \\ V(i, y(t_c)) &= \Delta y(t_c) \end{aligned} \tag{14.2}$$

where $t_c = \tau_{ci}$

$$\begin{aligned} U(i, x_c(t_c)) &= x_c(\tau_{ci}^+) - x_c(\tau_{ci}^-) \\ V(i, y(t_c)) &= y(\tau_{ci}^+) - y(\tau_{ci}^-) \end{aligned}$$

are the changes in the state variables at instant τ_{ci}.

The impulsive differential system, associated with Equation (14.1) is given by

$$\begin{array}{rclll} dx_c(t_c) & = & [f(t_c, x_c(t_c))]dt_c + [g(t_c, y(t_c))]d\omega(t_c) & \text{if} & t_c \neq \tau_{ci} \\ \Delta x_c(t_c) + \Delta y(t_c) & = & (U(i, x_c(t_c)))dt_c + (V(i, y(t_c)))d\omega t_c & \text{if} & t_c = \tau_{ci} \\ & & x_c(t_{c0}) = x_{c0}, y(t_{c0}) = y_0 & t_{c0} > 0 & \end{array} \tag{14.3}$$

To study the stability of impulsive differential equation, we use the following definitions.

Definition 1

Let $V: R_+ \times R^n \rightarrow R_+$, then $V \in V_0$ if

i. V is continuous in $[t_{c(i-1)}, \tau_{ci}] \times R^n$ and for all $x_c(t_c) \in R^n$, $i = 1, 2, \cdots$

$$\lim_{(t_c, y(t_c)) \rightarrow (\tau_{ci}^+, x_c(t_c))} V(t_c, y(t_c)) = V(\tau_{ci}^+, x_c(t_c)) \text{ exists} \tag{14.4}$$

ii. V is locally Lipschitzian in $x_c(t_c)$

Definition 2
For $(t_c, x_c(t_c)) \in (\tau_{c(i-1)}, \tau_{ci}] \times R^n$, define

$$D^+V(t_c,x_c(t_c)) = \lim_{h\to 0}\sup \frac{1}{h}[V(t_c+h, x_c(t_c)+hf(i,x_c(t_c))) - V(t_c,x_c(t_c))] \tag{14.5}$$

Definition 3 (Comparison system)
Let $V \in V_0$ and assume that

$$\begin{aligned} D^+(V(t_c,x_c(t_c))) &\le g(t_c, V(t_c,x_c(t_c))),\ t_c \ne \tau_{ci} \\ V(t_c,x_c(t_c)) + u(i,x_c(t_c)) &\le \chi_i(V(t_c,x_c(t_c))),\ t_c = \tau_{ci} \end{aligned} \tag{14.6}$$

where $g : R_+ \times R_+ \to R$ is continuous and

$\chi_i : R_+ \to R_+$ is non-decreasing

Then, the system

$$\begin{aligned} \dot{\omega}(t_c) &= g(t_c, \omega(t_c)), t_c \ne \tau_{ci} \\ \omega(\tau_{ci}^+) &= \chi_i(\omega(t_{ci})) \\ \omega(t_{c0}^+) &= \omega_0 \ge 0 \end{aligned} \tag{14.7}$$

is a comparison system of Equation (14.3).

Now $S_\rho = \{x_c \in R^n / ||x_c(t_c)|| < \rho\}$
where $||\bullet||$ represents Euclidean norm on R^n.

Definition 4
A function α is said to be in class K if $\alpha \in C[R_+, R_+]$, $\alpha(0) = 0$ and $\alpha(x_c(t_c))$ is strictly increasing in $x_c(t_c)$.

In system Equations (14.3) and (14.7), assume that

$$\begin{aligned} f(t_c, 0) &= 0 \\ u(i, 0) &= 0 \\ g(t_c, 0) &= 0 \end{aligned}$$

for all i, then the following theorem gives some sufficient condition in a unified way for various stability criteria.

Theorem 1
Assume that the following three conditions are satisfied:

1. $V: R_+ \times S_p \rightarrow R_+, \rho > 0, V \in V_0, D^+V(t_c, x_c(t_c)) < g(t_c, V(t_c, x_c(t_c))), t_c \neq \tau_{ci}$
2. There exists a $\rho_0 > 0$ such that $x_c(t_c) \in S_{\rho_0}$ implies that $x_c(t_c) + U(i, x_c(t_c)) \in S_{\rho_0}, \forall i \,\&\, V(t_c, x_c(t_c)) + U(i, x_c((t_c))) \leq \chi_i(V(t_c, x_c(t_c))), t_c = \tau_{ci}, x_c(t_c) \in S_{\rho_0}$
3. $\beta(\|x_c(t_c)\|) \leq V(t_c, x_c(t_c)) \leq \alpha(\|x_c(t_c)\|)$ on $R_+ \times S_p$ where $\alpha(\bullet) \times \beta(\bullet) \in K$ then the system Equation (14.7) implies the system Equation (14.3).

Theorem 2
Let $g(t_c, \omega(t_c)) = \lambda(t_c)\omega(t_c)$, $\lambda(t_c) \in C'[R_+, R_+]$. $\chi_i(\omega(t_c)) = d_i\omega(t_c)$, $d_i \geq 0$ for all i, then the origin of system Equation (14.3) is asymptotically stable if the conditions

$$\lambda(\tau_{c(i+1)}) + \eta_n(\gamma d_i) \leq \lambda(\tau_{ci}) \text{ for all } i, \text{ where } \gamma > 1 \text{ and}$$

$$\lambda(t_c) \geq 0$$

are satisfied.

14.3 The T–S Fuzzy Model

The T–S fuzzy model are depicted by fuzzy IF–THEN standards, in which each rule locally speaks to a straight info yield acknowledgment of the system over a specific area of the state space. The general system in then an accumulation of the their neighbourhood linear system model explicitly, an overall T–S fuzzy system is portrayed as follows
Rule i: IF $\mathbb{Z}_1(t_c)$ in M_{i_1} and, …, $\mathbb{Z}_p(t_c)$ in M_{i_p}

$$\text{THEN } dx_c(t_c) = [A_i x_c(t_c) + u(t_c)]dt_c + [C_i y(t_c) + \upsilon(t)]d\omega(t_c), i = 1,2,\ldots$$

where $M_{ij}(j = 1,2,\ldots,p)$ be the fuzzy set, $r$be the number of fuzzy IF-THEN rules, $x_c(t_c) \in R^n$ be the state vector, $u(t_c) \in R^m$ be the input state vector, $A_i \in R^{n\times n}$, $C_i \in R^{n\times n}$ and $\mathbb{Z}_1(t_c) \vee \mathbb{Z}_p(t_c)$ be premise variable.

Each consequent linear equation by $[A_i x_c(t_c)]dt_c + [C_i x_c(t_c)]d\omega(t_c) + u(t_c)$ be the subsystem. The yield of the fuzzy system can be attained by utilizing the singleton, product inference and weighted normal defuzzifier

$$dx_c(t_c) = \frac{\sum_{i=1}^{r} \omega_i(z_c(t_c))\{[A_i x_c(t_c) + u(t_c) + [C_i y(t_c) + v(t_c)]]\}d\omega(t_c)}{\sum_{i=1}^{r} \omega_i(z_c(t_c))} \tag{14.8}$$

where $z_c(t_c) = (z_{c1}(t_c), z_{c2}(t_c), \ldots, z_{cp}(t_c))$ and

$$\omega_i(z_c(t_c)) = \prod_{j=1}^{p} M_{ij}(z_{cj}(t_c))$$

For all t_c, $M_{ij}(z_{cj}(t_c))$ is the grade of membership of $z_{cj}(t_c)$ in M_{ij}; satisfying the following conditions

$$\sum_{i=1}^{r} \omega_i(z_c(t_c)) > 0$$

$$\omega_i(z_c(t_c)) \geq 0, i = 1, 2, \ldots, r.$$

Substituting

$$h_i(z_c(t_c)) = \frac{\omega_i(z_c(t_c))}{\sum_{i=1}^{r} \omega_i(z_c(t_c))}$$

into the Equation (14.8), this gives

$$dx_c(t_c) = \sum_{i=1}^{r} h_i(z_c(t_c))\{[A_i x_c(t_c) + u(t_c) + [C_i y(t_c) + v(t_c)]]\}d\omega(t_c) \tag{14.9}$$

We know that $\sum_{i=1}^{r} h_i(z_c(t_c)) = 1$, then Equation (14.9) becomes

$$dx_c(t_c) = \{[A_i x_c(t_c) + u(t_c) + [C_i y(t_c) + v(t_c)]]\} d\omega(t_c)$$

where $h_i(z_c(t_c))$ be the normalized weight of the IF–THEN rules.

14.4 Designing of Fuzzy Impulsive Controllers

A general T–S fuzzy-based controller $u(t_c)$ and $v(t_c)$ are given as follows
Control rule i: IF $\mathbb{Z}_1(t_c)$ in M_{i_1} and, …, $\mathbb{Z}_p(t_c)$ in M_{i_p}

$$\text{THEN } u(t_c) = \sum_{k=1}^{\infty} \delta(t_c - \tau_{ck}) B_i x_c(t_c)$$

$$v(t) = \sum_{k=1}^{\infty} \gamma(t_c - \tau_{ck}) D_i y(t_c), i = 1, 2, ..., r$$

$\delta(t_c)$ represents Dirac delta function.

The fuzzy impulsive controller $u(t_c)$ and $v(t_c)$ are

$$\begin{aligned} u(t_c) &= \sum_{i=1}^{r} h_i(z_c(t_c)) \left[\sum_{i=1}^{\infty} \delta(t_c - \tau_{ck}) B_i x_c(t_c) \right] \\ v(t_c) &= \sum_{i=1}^{r} h_i(z_c(t_c)) \left[\sum_{i=1}^{\infty} \gamma(t_c - \tau_{ck}) D_i y(t_c) \right] \end{aligned} \tag{14.10}$$

Substituting Equation (14.10) in Equation (14.9), which gives

$$dx_c(t_c)=\sum_{i=1}^{r}h_i(z_c(t_c))\left\{A_ix_c(t_c)+\sum_{i=1}^{r}h_i(z_c(t_c))\left[\sum_{i=1}^{\infty}\delta(t_c-\tau_{ck})B_ix_c(t_c)\right]dt_c\right.$$

$$\left.+\left[C_iy(t_c)+\sum_{i=1}^{r}h_i(z_c(t_c))\left[\sum_{i=1}^{\infty}\gamma(t_c-\tau_{ck})D_iy(t_c)\right]\right]d\omega(t_c)\right\}$$

$$=\sum_{i=1}^{r}h_i(z_c(t_c))\left\{\left[A_i+\sum_{i=1}^{\infty}\delta(t_c-\tau_{ck})B_ix_c(t_c)\right]dt_c\right.$$

$$\left.+\left[C_i+\sum_{i=1}^{\infty}\gamma(t_c-\tau_{ck})D_iy(t_c)\right]\right\}d\omega(t_c) \tag{14.11}$$

$$x_c\left(\tau_{ck}^{+}\right)-x_c\left(\tau_{ck}^{-}\right)=\sum_{i=1}^{r}h_i(z_c(\tau_{ck}))B_ix_c(\tau_{ck})+\sum_{i=1}^{r}h_i(z_c(\tau_{ck}))D_ix_c(\tau_{ck})$$

$$=\sum_{i=1}^{r}h_i(z_c(\tau_{ck}))[B_ix_c(\tau_{ck})+D_ix_c(\tau_{ck})]$$

14.5 Main Result

Therefore, the impulsive form of the system Equation (14.11) is

$$\begin{aligned} dx_c(t_c) &= \sum_{i=1}^{r}h_i(z_c(t_c))\{[A_ix_c(t_c)]dt_c+[C_iy(t_c)]d\omega(t_c)\} \quad \text{if} \quad t_c\neq\tau_{ck} \\ \Delta x_c(t_c) &= \sum_{i=1}^{r}h_i(z_c(t_c))[B_ix_c(t_c)dt_c+C_iy(t_c)d\omega(t_c)] \quad \text{if} \quad t_c=\tau_{ck} \end{aligned} \tag{14.12}$$

Theorem 3

Let λ be the largest latent value of the matrix $A_i + A_i^T$, where A_i^T is the transpose of A_i. Let λ_0' and λ_1' be the largest latent value of the matrix $(I + B_i)^T (I + B_i)$, $(I + D_i)^T (I + D_i)$ respectively, where B_i, D_i are the symmetric matrices and also the spectral of $(I + B_i)$, $(I + D_i)$ are $(I + B_i) \leq 1$ and $(I + D_i) \leq 1$ Then the fuzzy impulsive control system Equation (14.11) is asymptotically mean square stable at the origin, if

$$0 \leq \lambda\,(\tau_{c(k+1)} - \tau_{ck}) \leq -\ln(\xi\lambda')$$

where $\xi > 1$.

Proof

Consider the Lyapunov functions

$$V(x_c(t_c)) = x_c^T(t_c)x_c(t_c)$$

Now by using the Itô's formula

$$D^+V(x_c(t_c)) = L(V(x_c(t_c)))dt_c + 2x_c^T(t_c)g(t_c)d\omega(t_c)$$

where

$$L(V(x_c(t_c))) = V_{t_c}(t_c) + V_{x_c}(t_c)f(t_c) + \frac{1}{2}\text{trace}\left(g^T V_{x_c x_c} g\right)$$

$$\frac{\partial V(x_c(t_c))}{\partial t_c} = 0$$

$$\frac{\partial V(x_c(t_c))}{\partial x_c} = \dot{x}_c^T(t_c)x_c(t_c) + \dot{x}_c(t_c)x_c^T(t_c)$$

$$\frac{\partial^2 V(x_c(t_c))}{\partial x_c^2} = 2$$

$$L(V(x_c(t_c))) = 0 + 2x_c^T(t_c)[A_i x_c(t_c)] + \frac{1}{2}\text{trace}\left(g_2^T g\right)$$
$$= 2x_c^T(t_c)A_i x_c(t_c) + g^T g$$

Now $g^T g \leq x_c^T(t_c)D_0 x_c(t_c)$ where D_0 is small positive matrix

$$= x_c^T(t_c)A_i x_c(t_c) \leq x_c^T(t_c)A_i x_c(t_c) + x_c^T(t_c)A_i^T x_c(t_c)$$
$$\leq \lambda_0 V(x_c(t_c)) + \lambda_1 V(x_c(t_c))$$
$$\leq (\lambda_0 + \lambda_1)V(x_c(t_c))$$
$$L(V(x_c(t_c))) \leq \lambda V(x_c(t_c))$$
$$D^+(V(x_c(t_c))) \leq \lambda V(x_c(t_c))dt_c + 2x_c^T(t_c)g(t_c)d\omega(t_c)$$

Taking Expectation on both sides

$$E[D^+(V(x_c(t_c)))] \leq E[\lambda V(x_c(t_c))dt_c] + E\left[2x_c^T(t_c)g(t_c)d\omega(t_c)\right]$$
$$\leq \lambda V(x_c(t_c)) + 0$$
$$\therefore D^+(V(x_c(t_c))) \leq \lambda V(x_c(t_c))$$

By condition (1) of theorem, $g(t_c,\omega(t_{c1})) = \lambda\omega(t_c)$
Since B_i and $I + B_i$ are symmetric matrices,
By using Euclidean norm,

$$\rho(I + B_i) = ||I + B_i|| \quad \& \quad \rho(I + D_i) = ||I + D_i||$$

Given any $\rho_0 > 0$ and $x_c(t_c) \in S\rho_0$, one obtains

$$\begin{aligned}\|x_c(t_c)+U(k,x_c(t_c))+y(t_c)+V(k,y(t_c))\| &= \left\|x_c(t_c)+\sum_{i=1}^{r}h_i(z_c(t_c))B_ix_c(t_c)\right\| \\ &+\left\|y(t_c)+\sum_{i=1}^{r}h_i(z_c(t_c))D_iy(t_c)\right\| \\ &\le \left\|I+\sum_{i=1}^{r}h_i(z_c(t_c))B_i\right\|\|x_c(t_c)\| \\ &+\left\|I+\sum_{i=1}^{r}h_i(z_c(t_c))D_i\right\|\|y(t_c)\| \\ &\le \sum_{i=1}^{r}h_i(z_c(t_c))\left[\|x_c(t_c)\|+\|y_c(t_c)\|\right] \\ &\le \|x_c(t_c)\|+\|y(t_c)\|\end{aligned}$$

It follows that $x_c(t_c)+U(k,x_c(t_c))+y(t_c)+V(k,y(t_c))\in S\rho_0$ where $t_c=\tau_{ck}$

$$\begin{aligned}&x_c^T(t_c)(I+B_i)^T(I+B_j)x_c(t_c) \\ &+x_c^T(t_c)(I+B_j)^T(I+B_i)x_c(t_c) \\ &+y^T(t_c)(I+D_i)^T(I+D_j)y(t_c) \\ &+y^T(t_c)(I+D_j)^T(I+D_i)y(t_c)=x_c^T(t_c)\left(B_i^T+I\right)(I+B_i)x_c(t_c)+x_c^T(t_c)\left(B_j^T+I\right)(I+B_i)x_c(t_c) \\ &\qquad+y^T(t_c)\left(D_i^T+I\right)(I+D_i)y(t_c)+y^T(t_c)\left(D_j^T+I\right)(I+D_i)y(t_c) \\ &\qquad=x_c^T(t_c)B_i^Tx_c(t_c)+x_c^T(t_c)B_i^TB_jx_c(t_c)+x_c^T(t_c)x_c(t_c) \\ &\qquad+x_c^T(t_c)B_jx_c(t_c)+x_c^T(t_c)B_j^Tx_c(t_c) \\ &\qquad+x_c^T(t_c)B_j^TB_ix_c(t_c)+x_c^T(t_c)x_c(t_c)+x_c^T(t_c)B_ix_c(t_c) \\ &\qquad+y^T(t_c)D_i^Ty(t_c)+y^T(t_c)D_i^TD_jy(t_c)+y^T(t_c)y(t_c) \\ &\qquad+y^T(t_c)D_jy(t_c)+y^T(t_c)D_j^Ty(t_c) \\ &\qquad+y^T(t_c)D_j^TD_iy(t_c)+y^T(t_c)y(t_c)+y^T(t_c)D_iy(t_c)+\end{aligned}$$

Put

$$
\begin{aligned}
B_i^T B_j &= B_i^T B_i + B_j^T B_j - B_j^T B_j - B_i^T B_i + B_i^T B_j \text{ and} \\
D_i^T D_j &= D_i^T D_i + D_j^T D_j - D_j^T D_j - D_i^T D_i + D_i^T D_j \\
&= x_c^T(t_c) B_i^T x_c(t_c) + x_c^T(t_c)\left[B_i^T B_i + B_j^T B_j - B_j^T B_j - B_i^T B_i + B_i^T B_j\right] x_c(t_c) \\
&\quad + x_c^T(t_c) x_c(t_c) + x_c^T(t_c) B_j x_c(t_c) \\
&\quad + x_c^T(t_c) B_j^T x_c(t_c) + x_c^T(t_c) B_j^T B_i x_c(t_c) + x_c^T(t_c) x_c(t_c) + x_c^T(t_c) B_i x_c(t_c) \\
&\quad + y^T(t_c) D_i^T y(t_c) + y^T(t_c)\left[D_i^T D_i + D_j^T D_j - D_j^T D_j - D_i^T D_i + D_i^T D_j\right] y(t_c) \\
&\quad + y^T(t_c) y(t_c) + y^T(t_c) D_j y(t_c) \\
&\quad + y^T(t_c) D_j^T y(t_c) + y^T(t_c) D_j^T D_i y(t_c) + y^T(t_c) y(t_c) + y^T(t_c) D_i y(t_c) \\
&= x_c^T(t_c)(I + B_i)^T (I + B_i) x_c(t_c) + x_c^T(t_c)(I + B_j)^T (I + B_j) x_c(t_c) \\
&\quad + (B_i - B_j) x_c^T(t_c)(B_i - B_j)^T x_c(t_c) \\
&\quad + y^T(t_c)(I + D_i)^T (I + D_i) y(t_c) + y^T(t_c)(I + D_j)^T (I + D_j) y(t_c) \\
&\quad + (D_i - D_j) y^T(t_c)(D_i - D_j)^T y(t_c) \\
&= x_c^T(t_c)(I + B_i)^T (I + B_i) x_c(t_c) + x_c^T(t_c)(I + B_j)^T (I + B_j) x_c(t_c) \\
&\quad + x_c^T(t_c)(B_i - B_j)(B_i - B_j)^T x_c(t_c) \\
&\quad + y^T(t_c)(I + D_i)^T (I + D_i) y(t_c) + y^T(t_c)(I + D_j)^T (I + D_j) y(t_c) \\
&\quad + y^T(t_c)(D_i - D_j)(D_i - D_j)^T y(t_c) \\
&\le x_c^T(t_c)(I + B_i)^T (I + B_i) x_c(t_c) + x_c^T(t_c)(I + B_j)^T (I + B_j) x_c(t_c) \\
&\quad + y^T(t_c)(I + D_i)^T (I + D_i) y(t_c) + y^T(t_c)(I + D_j)^T (I + D_j) y(t_c)
\end{aligned}
$$

when $\tau_c = \tau_{ck}$ i.e., $i = j$

$$V\begin{pmatrix} x_c(t_c) \\ +\sum_{i=1}^{r} h_i(z_c(t_c))B_i x_c(t_c) \\ +y(t_c) \\ +\sum_{i=1}^{r} h_i(z_c(t_c))D_i y(t_c) \end{pmatrix} = V\left(\sum_{i=1}^{r} h_i(z_c(t_c))(I+B_i)x_c(t_c)\right) + V\left(\sum_{i=1}^{r} h_i(z_c(t_c))(I+D_i)y(t_c)\right)$$

$$= x_c^T(t_c)\left(\sum_{i=1}^{r} h_i(z_c(t_c))(I+B_i)^T\right)\left(\sum_{i=1}^{r} h_i(z_c(t_c))(I+B_i)\right)x_c(t_c)$$

$$+ y^T(t_c)\left(\sum_{i=1}^{r} h_i(z_c(t_c))(I+D_i)^T\right)\left(\sum_{i=1}^{r} h_i(z_c(t_c))(I+D_i)\right)y(t_c)$$

$$= x_c^T(t_c)(I+B_i)^T(I+B_i)x_c(t_c) + y^T(t_c)(I+D_i)^T(I+D_i)y(t_c)$$

$$\leq \lambda_0^1 x_c^T(t_c)x_c(t_c) + \lambda_1^1 y^T(t_c)y(t_c)$$

$$\leq \lambda_0^1 V(z_c(t_c)) + \lambda_1^1 V(y(t_c))$$

where $V(y(t_c)) = y^T(t_c)y(t_c)$

On sequence, second condition of the theorem 1 is satisfied with $\chi_k(\omega(t_c)) = \lambda'\omega(t_c)$. As like a second condition, the theorem 1 with the third condition is also satisfied.

Therefore from the theorem (1), the asymptotic mean square stability of the impulsively control system (c) is implied by the comparison system which is given below,

$$\dot{\omega}(t_c) = \lambda\omega(t_c)$$
$$\omega\left(\tau_{ck}^{+}\right) = \lambda'\omega(\tau_{ck})$$
$$\omega\left(\tau_{c0}^{+}\right) = \omega_0 > 0$$

Finally, it follows from the theorem 2, which gives

$$0 \leq \int_{\tau_{ck}}^{\tau_{c(k+1)}} \lambda_0\, dt_c + \int_{\tau_{ck}}^{\tau_{c(k+1)}} \lambda_1\, d\omega(t_c) \leq -\ln\left(\xi\lambda_0'\right) \text{ where } \xi > 1$$

On simplification, we get

$$0 \le \lambda_0(\tau_{c(k+1)} - \tau_{ck}) \le -\ln(\xi\lambda_0'),$$

Then the origin of (c) is asymptotically mean square stable.

14.6 Numerical Example

The Genesio–Tesi chaotic system can be described by the following dynamics

$$\begin{aligned}\dot{x}_1 &= x_2 \\ \dot{x}_2 &= x_3 \\ \dot{x}_3 &= -cx_1 - bx_2 - ax_3 + x_1^2\end{aligned}$$

where x_1, x_2 and x_3 are state variables, a, b, c are the constant parameters.

When $a = 1$, $b = 3.03$ and $c = 5.55$ the Genesio–Tesi system exhibits the chaotic nature as shown in Figure 14.1. Figures 14.2, 14.3, 14.4 shows the chaotic nature between the state variables.

The linear part of the system is defined as

$$A = \begin{bmatrix} 0 & 1 & 0 \\ 0 & 0 & 1 \\ -c & -b & -a \end{bmatrix}$$

and the non-linear part of the system is

$$f(x_c, t_c) = \begin{bmatrix} 0 \\ 0 \\ x_1^2 \end{bmatrix}$$

The impulsive fuzzy control for the system is defined by

Rule i: If $x_{c1}(t_c)$ in M_i then

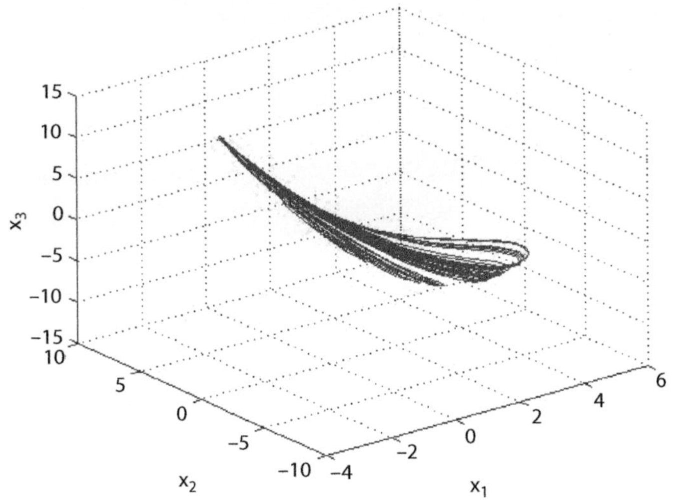

Figure 14.1 Chaotic portait of Genesio–Tesi system.

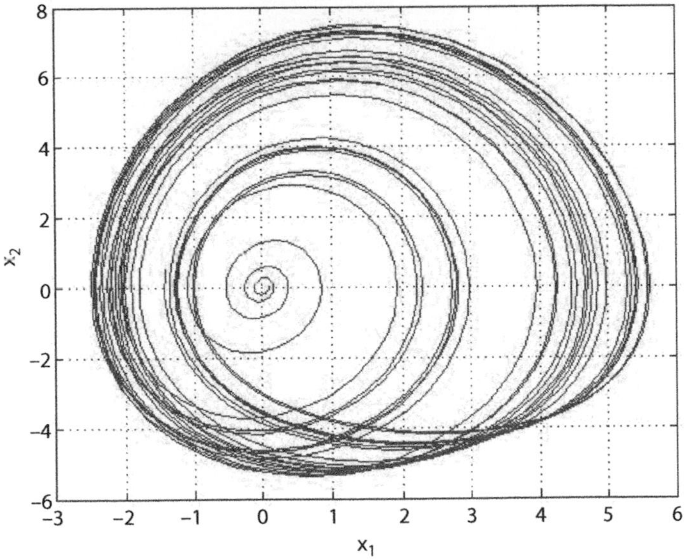

Figure 14.2 Chaotic nature between x_1 and x_2.

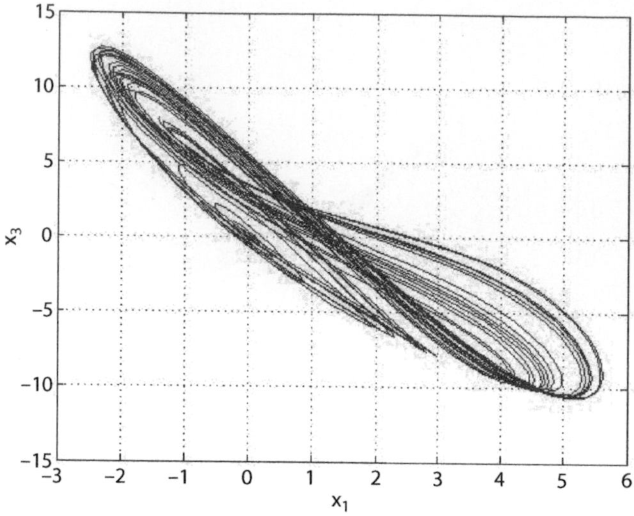

Figure 14.3 Chaotic nature between $\boldsymbol{x}_1$ and $\boldsymbol{x}_3$.

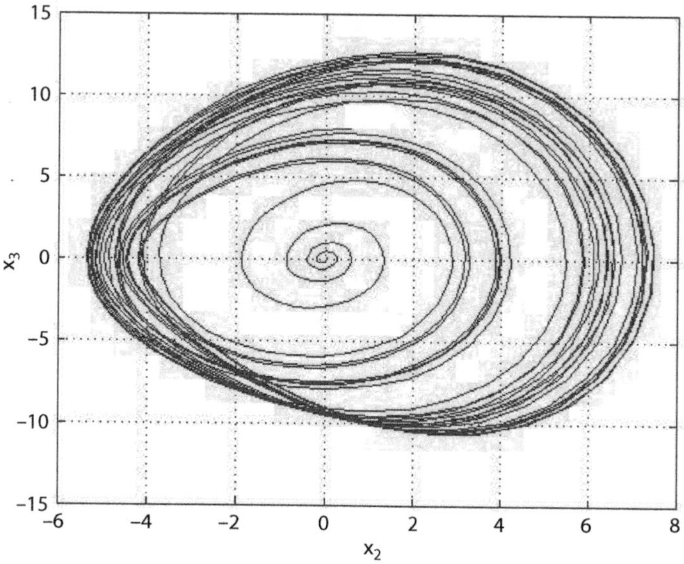

Figure 14.4 Chaotic nature between $\boldsymbol{x}_2$ and $\boldsymbol{x}_3$.

$$\begin{aligned} dx_c(t_c) &= A_i x_c(t_c)dt_c + C_i y(t_c)d\omega(t_c) \quad \text{if} \quad t_c \neq \mathbb{Z}_k \\ \Delta x_c(t_c) &= B_i x_c(t_c)dt_c + C_i y(t_c)d\omega(t_c) \quad \text{if} \quad t_c = \mathbb{Z}_k \end{aligned}$$

$$i = 1, 2 \text{ and } k \in N$$

$$x_c(t_c) = [x_{c1}(t_c) \quad x_{c2}(t_c) \quad x_{c3}(t_c)]^T$$

$$A_1 = \begin{bmatrix} 0 & d-1 & 0 \\ 0 & 0 & 1 \\ -c & -b & -a \end{bmatrix} \text{and } A_2 = \begin{bmatrix} 0 & -d+1 & 0 \\ 0 & 0 & 1 \\ -c & -b & -a \end{bmatrix}$$

Figure 14.5 depicts the control of Genesio–Tesi chaotic system.

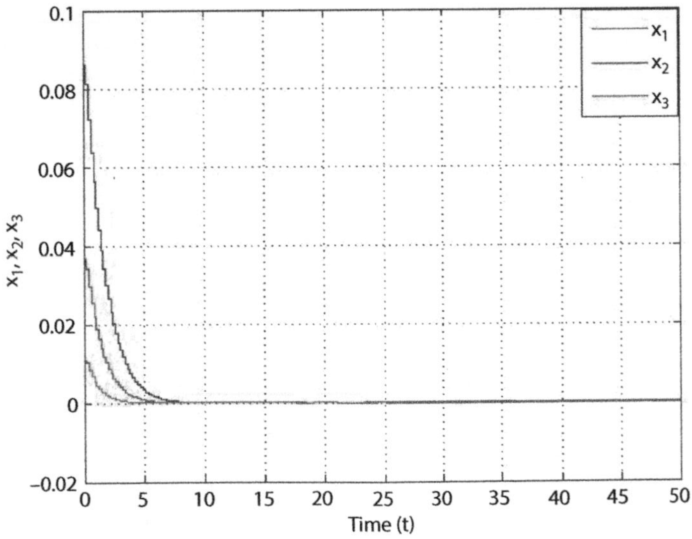

Figure 14.5 Impulsive control of Genesio–Tesi chaotic system.

The output of the Impulsive Genesio–Tesi chaotic system can be split into two groups of data namely training data and checking data.

The training data values are tabulated in Table 14.1.

The checking data values are tabulated in Table 14.2.

From the impulsive control of Genesio–Tesi chaotic system, training data and checking data tables are generated.

Figures 14.6 to 14.8 show the training and checking data from Tables 14.1 and 14.2.

For initiating the fuzzy inference system four membership functions are considered. The generalized bell-shaped membership function computes the fuzzy membership value.

The generalized fuzzy inference system generates a Sugeno type Fuzzy Inference System structure from the training data Table 14.1 and it generates a single-output Sugeno-type fuzzy inference system using a grid partition on the data. It generates the following structured fuzzy inference system.

Table 14.1 Training data for impulsive control genesio–Tesi chaotic system.

t	$x+_1$	x_2	x_3	t	x_1	x_2	x_3
0	0.0912	0.0394	0.0125	4.1768	0.0056	0.0014	0.0002
0.1005	0.0862	0.0368	0.0113	4.6428	0.0039	0.0009	0.0001
0.2010	0.0813	0.0343	0.0102	5.1088	0.0028	0.0006	0.0001
0.6117	0.0638	0.0255	0.0068	5.6088	0.0019	0.0004	0.0000
1.0225	0.0497	0.0188	0.0045	6.1088	0.0013	0.0003	0.0000
1.4147	0.0388	0.0139	0.0030	6.6088	0.0008	0.0002	0.0000
1.8069	0.0300	0.0102	0.0021	7.1088	0.0006	0.0001	0.0000
2.2002	0.0231	0.0074	0.0014	7.6088	0.0004	0.0001	0.0000
2.5934	0.0176	0.0054	0.0009	8.1088	0.0002	0.0000	0.0000
2.9866	0.0134	0.0039	0.0006	8.6088	0.0002	0.0000	0.0000
3.3798	0.0101	0.0028	0.0004	9.1088	0.0001	0.0000	0.0000
3.7783	0.0075	0.0020	0.0003	10.0000	0.0001	0.0000	0.0000

Table 14.2 Checking data for impulsive control Genesio–Tesi chaotic system.

t	x_1	x_2	x_3	t	x_1	x_2	x_3
0.0502	0.0887	0.0381	0.0119	4.4098	0.0047	0.0011	0.0002
0.1507	0.0837	0.0355	0.0108	4.8758	0.0033	0.0008	0.0001
0.4063	0.0721	0.0296	0.0083	5.3588	0.0023	0.0005	0.0001
0.8171	0.0564	0.0219	0.0055	5.8588	0.0015	0.0003	0.0000
1.2186	0.0439	0.0162	0.0037	6.3588	0.0010	0.0002	0.0000
1.6108	0.0341	0.0119	0.0025	6.8588	0.0007	0.0001	0.0000
2.0036	0.0263	0.0087	0.0017	7.3588	0.0005	0.0001	0.0000
2.3968	0.0202	0.0063	0.0011	7.8588	0.0003	0.0001	0.0000
2.7900	0.0153	0.0046	0.0008	8.3588	0.0002	0.0000	0.0000
3.1832	0.0116	0.0033	0.0005	8.8588	0.0001	0.0000	0.0000
3.5790	0.0087	0.0023	0.0003	9.3316	0.0001	0.0000	0.0000
3.9775	0.0065	0.0017	0.0002	9.7772	0.0001	0.0000	0.0000

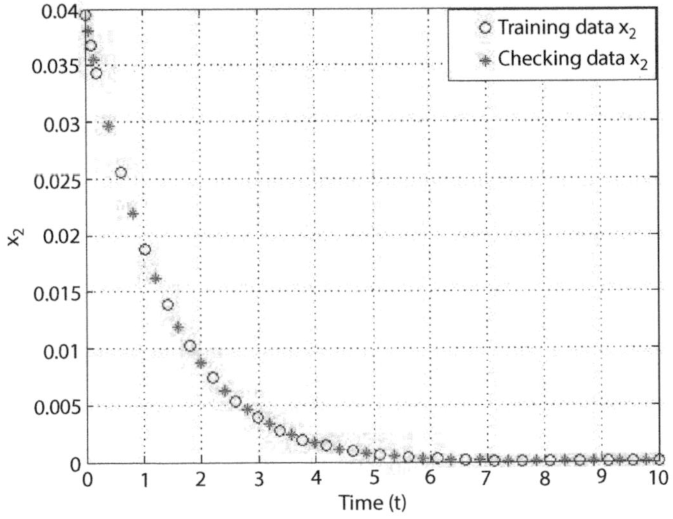

Figure 14.6 Training and checking data of x_1.

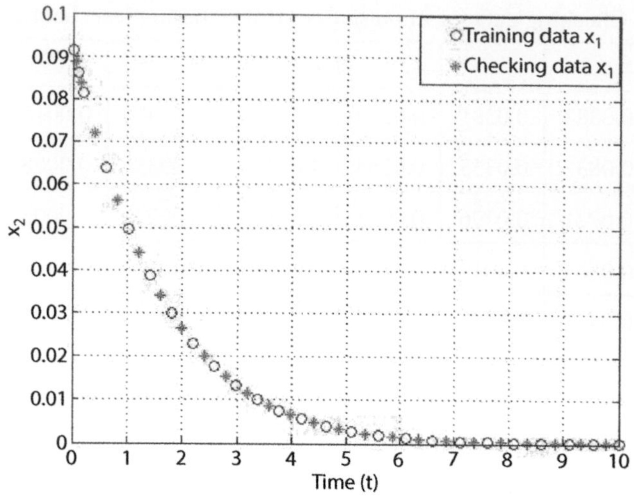

Figure 14.7 Training and checking data of x_2.

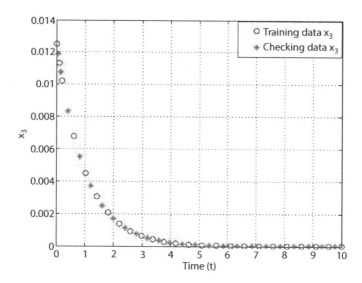

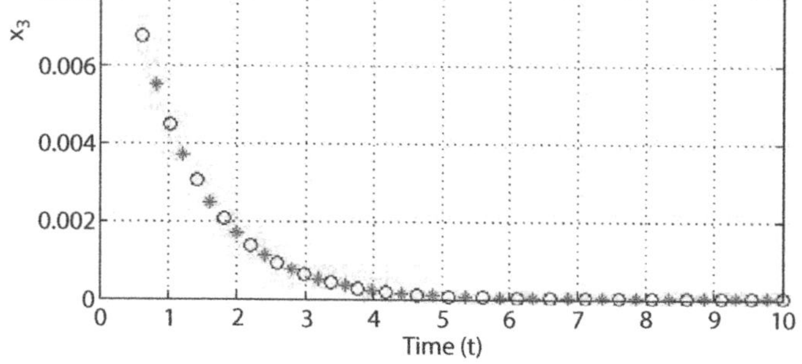

Figure 14.8 Training and checking data of x_3.

```
        name: 'anfis'
        type: 'sugeno'
   andMethod: 'prod'
    orMethod: 'max'
defuzzMethod: 'wtaver'
   impMethod: 'prod'
   aggMethod: 'max'
       input: [1x3 struct]
      output: [1x1 struct]
        rule: [1x64 struct]
```

Figures 14.9 to 14.11 depict the initial membership functions for Adaptive Network Based Fuzzy Inference System (ANFIS).

For getting best FIS, 50 numbers of iterations are considered. It gives the following output.

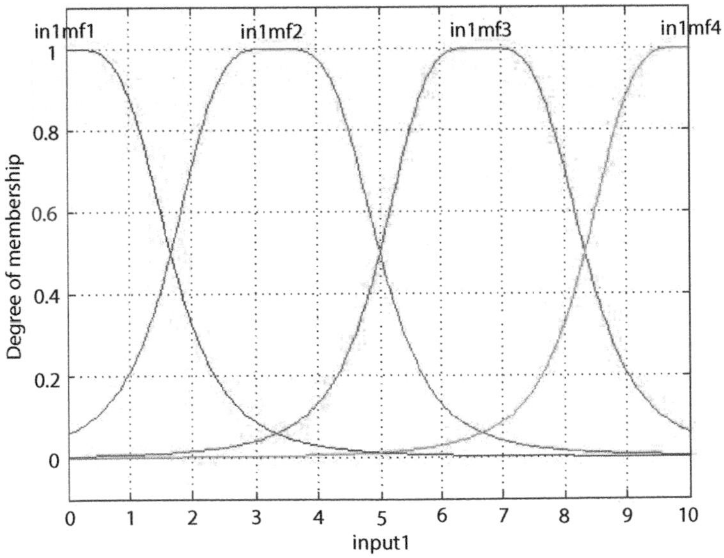

Figure 14.9 Initial fuzzy membership function for ANFIS.

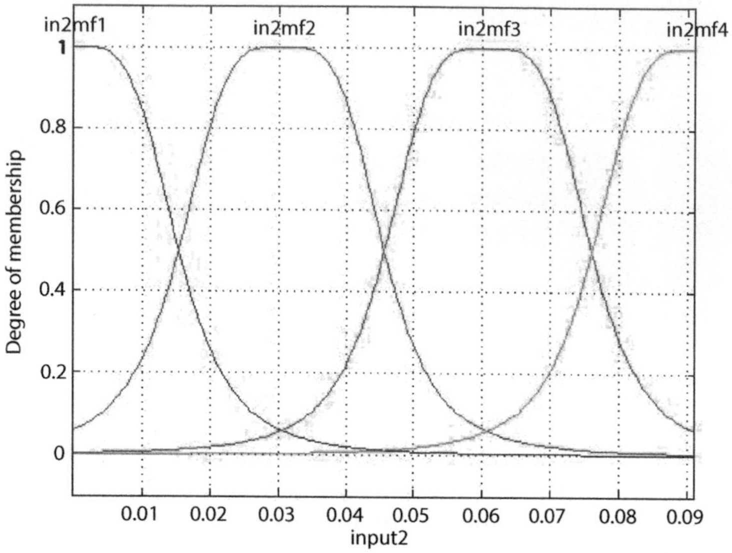

Figure 14.10 Initial fuzzy membership function for ANFIS.

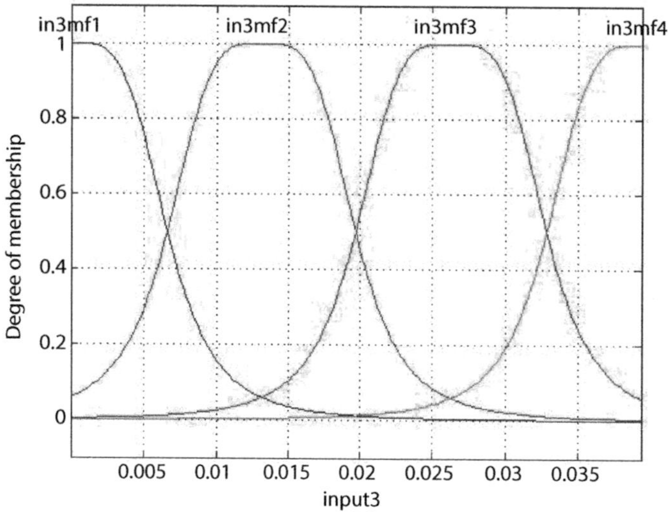

Figure 14.11 Initial fuzzy membership function for ANFIS.

```
ANFIS info:
    Number of nodes: 158
    Number pf linear parameters: 256
    Number of nonlinear parameters: 36
    Total number of parameters: 292
    Number of training data pairs: 25
    Number of checking data pairs: 24
    Number of fuzzy rules: 64

Warning: number of data is smaller than number of modifiable parameters

Start training ANFIS ...

   1        1.67847e-007      8.41349e-005
   2        1.59489e-007      0.000148039
   3        1.56886e-007      0.00025281
   4        2.55938e-007      0.000110276
   5        6.65183e-007      0.000973569
   6        2.47841e-007      7.3924e-005
   7        4.77866e-007      0.000475227
   8        2.82946e-007      2.43206e-005


Step size decreases to 0.009000 after epoch 8.
   9        6.99586e-007   0.000806573
  10        2.61652e-007   4.3078e-005
  11        1.67108e-007   7.94518e-005
  12        2.28139e-007   6.31018e-005
  13        2.6013e-007    0.000123181
  14        2.20639e-007   0.000203789
  15        1.17118e-007   9.98158e-005
  16        1.18158e-007   0.000117943
  17        4.4237e-007    2.72318e-005
  18        2.07621e-007   0.00010719
  19        1.78194e-007   2.04016e-005
  20        7.87094e-008   0.000159833
  21        1.66484e-007   0.00017764
  22        1.08536e-007   6.33289e-005
  23        1.25237e-007   3.37518e-005
  24        1.26919e-007   0.000136784
  25        8.06537e-008   1.29047e-005
  26        1.11494e-007   0.000107775
  27        1.97979e-007   0.000182832
  28        9.48111e-008   7.38481e-005
  29        1.24252e-007   3.35886e-005
  30        1.68424e-007   4.45685e-005
  31        1.09352e-007   2.38117e-005
  32        6.62974e-008   4.14531e-005
  33        1.46569e-007   3.92242e-005
  34        6.49249e-008   0.000140514
  35        2.16081e-007   0.000151733
  36        9.9736e-008    2.93905e-005
```

```
Step size decreases to 0.008100 after epoch 36.
  37       1.81368e-007     0.000126723
  38       1.76736e-007     9.62571e-005
  39       1.87184e-007     4.36286e-005
  40       1.44978e-007     2.40567e-005
Step size decreases to 0.007290 after epoch 40.
  41       7.60449e-008     2.79897e-005
  42       1.06115e-007     6.353e-005
  43       1.99175e-007     0.000100277
  44       1.56653e-007     4.80987e-005
  45       1.703e-007       5.43361e-005
  46       2.34919e-007     9.96205e-005
  47       2.54855e-007     9.0088e-005
  48       1.05353e-007     1.46485e-005
  49       1.84783e-007     9.44886e-005
  50       2.55005e-007     9.36062e-005

Designated epoch number reached --> ANFIS training completed at epoch 50.
```

14.7 Conclusion

In this chapter, fuzzy impulsive control of chaotic system based on T–S fuzzy model with uncertainities is designed. Fuzzy intelligent system is strong research area in Artificial Intelligence. Fuzzy based chaotic is a new branch in Artificial Intelligence. Based on T–S fuzzy model, the stability criterions are designed. The Genesio–Tesi chaotic is involved for verifying the desired result. MATLAB is a key tool for verifying derived result. MATLAB fuzzy tool box is utilized for designed impulsive control. The fuzzy impulsive control is reduce the amount of feedback processes.

References

1. Alligood, K.T., Sauer, T., Yorke, J.A., *Chaos: An introduction to Dynamical Systems*, 1996.
2. Ott, E., Grebogi, C., Yorke, J.A., Controlling chaos. *Phys. Rev. Lett.*, 64, 11, 1196, 1990.
3. Park, J.H., Lee, S.M., Kwon, O.M., Adaptive synchronization of Genesio–Tesi chaotic system via a novel feedback control. *Phys. Lett. A*, 371, 4, 263–270, 2007.

4. Zhang, Q., Impulsive control and synchronization of a critical chaotic system. *Wuhan Univ. J. Nat. Sci.*, 12, 3, 426–430, 2007.
5. Zhang, X., Khadra, A., Li, D., Yang, D., Impulsive stability of chaotic systems represented by TS model. *Chaos Solitons Fractals*, 41, 4, 1863–1869, 2009.
6. Osipov, G.V., Kozlov, A.K., Shalfeev, V.D., Impulse control of chaos in continuous systems. *Phys. Lett. A*, 247, 1–2, 119–128, 1998.
7. Zheng, Y. and Chen, G., Fuzzy impulsive control of chaotic systems based on TS fuzzy model. *Chaos Solitons Fractals*, 39, 4, 2002–2011, 2009.
8. Hua, H., Liu, Y., Lu, J., Zhu, J., A new impulsive synchronization criterion for T–S fuzzy model and its applications. *Appl. Math. Modell.*, 37, 20–21, 8826–8835, 2013.
9. Hu, C., Jiang, H., Teng, Z., General impulsive control of chaotic systems based on a TS fuzzy model. *Fuzzy Sets Syst.*, 174, 1, 66–82, 2011.
10. Hu, C. and Jiang, H., Time-delayed impulsive control of chaotic system based on TS fuzzy model. *Math Probl. Eng.*, 2014, Article ID 910351, 12, 2014.
11. Liu, Y. and Zhao, S., T–S fuzzy model-based impulsive control for chaotic systems and its application. *Math. Comput. Simul.*, 81, 11, 2507–2516, 2011.
12. Hu, C., Jiang, H., Teng, Z., Fuzzy impulsive control and synchronization of general chaotic system. *Acta Appl. Math.*, 109, 2, 463–485, 2010.
13. Sun, C.H. and Wang, W.J., An improved stability criterion for TS fuzzy discrete systems via vertex expression. *IEEE Trans. Syst. Man Cybern. Part B (Cybern.)*, 36, 3, 672–678, 2006.
14. Liu, Y., Zhao, S., Lu, J., A new fuzzy impulsive control of chaotic systems based on T–S fuzzy model. *IEEE Trans. Fuzzy Syst.*, 19, 2, 393–398, 2010.
15. Zhong, Q., Bao, J., Yu, Y., Liao, X., Exponential stabilization for discrete Takagi–Sugeno fuzzy systems via impulsive control. *Chaos Solitons Fractals*, 41, 4, 2123–2127, 2009.
16. Yoneyama, J., Nonlinear control design based on generalized Takagi–Sugeno fuzzy systems. *J. Franklin Inst.*, 351, 7, 3524–3535, 2014.
17. Liu, X. and Zhong, S., T–S fuzzy model-based impulsive control of chaotic systems with exponential decay rate. *Phys. Lett. A*, 370, 3–4, 260–264, 2007.
18. Ding, B.C., Development of stability research on Takagi–Sugeno fuzzy control systems and approximation of the necessary and sufficient conditions. *Fuzzy Inf. Eng.*, 1, 4, 367–383, 2009.
19. Wang, Y.W., Guan, Z.H., Wang, H.O., Impulsive synchronization for Takagi–Sugeno fuzzy model and its application to continuous chaotic system. *Phys. Lett. A*, 339, 3–5, 325–332, 2005.
20. Chen, Z., Cao, J., Huang, J., Impulsive TS fuzzy control for unified chaotic system, in: *2010 8th World Congress on Intelligent Control and Automation*, 2010, July, IEEE, pp. 3882–3886.

21. Zhang, X., Khadra, A., Li, D., Yang, D., Impulsive stability of chaotic systems represented by TS model. *Chaos Solitons Fractals*, 41, 4, 1863–1869, 2009.
22. Zhong, Q., Bao, J., Yu, Y., Liao, X., Impulsive control for T–S fuzzy model-based chaotic systems. *Math. Comput. Simul.*, 79, 3, 409–415, 2008.
23. Ho, D.W. and Sun, J., Stability of Takagi–Sugeno fuzzy delay systems with impulse. *IEEE Trans. Fuzzy Syst.*, 15, 5, 784–790, 2007.
24. Liu, Y. and Zhao, S., T–S fuzzy model-based impulsive control for chaotic systems and its application. *Math. Comput. Simul.*, 81, 11, 2507–2516, 2011.
25. Zhong, Q., Yu, Y., Xu, S., Impulsive control for TS fuzzy model based Chaotic Systems with Adaptive Feedback, in: *2009 International Conference on Communications, Circuits and Systems*, 2009, July, IEEE, pp. 872–875.
26. Kim, J.H., Shin, H., Kim, E., Park, M., Synchronization of Time-Delayed T–S Fuzzy Chaotic Systems via Scalar Output Variable. *Int. J. Bifurcation Chaos*, 15, 08, 2593–2601, 2005.
27. Yang, D., Li, A., Liu, Y., Yang, Y., Impulsive synchronization control of fuzzy chaotic systems based on output feedback, in: *2011 6th IEEE Joint International Information Technology and Artificial Intelligence Conference*, 2011, August, vol. 1, IEEE, pp. 147–151.
28. Kim, J.H., Hyun, C.H., Kim, E., Park, M., Adaptive synchronization of uncertain chaotic systems based on T–S fuzzy model. *IEEE Trans. Fuzzy Syst.*, 15, 3, 359–369, 2007.
29. Shin, H., Kim, E., Park, M., The state feedback control based on fuzzy observer for TS fuzzy systems with unknown time-delay. *IEICE Trans. Fundam. Electron. Commun. Comput. Sci.*, 86, 9, 2333–2339, 2003.
30. Yan-Bin, L.U.O., Yong-Yan, C.A.O., You-Xian, S.U.N., Robust stability of uncertain Takagi–Sugeno fuzzy systems with time-varying input-delay. *Acta Autom. Sin.*, 34, 1, 87–92, 2008.
31. Hou, Y.Y., Liao, T.L., Yan, J.J., Lien, C.H., Guaranteed cost control for uncertain non-linear systems with time-varying delays using T–S fuzzy model. *Int. J. Gen. Syst.*, 38, 5, 485–504, 2009.

15

Theorems on Soft Fuzzy Metric Spaces by Using Control Function

Sneha A. Khandait[1], Chitra Singh[1], Ramakant Bhardwaj[2*] and Amit Kumar Mishra[3]

[1]*Department of Mathematics, Rabindranath Tagore University, Bhopal, India*
[2]*Department of Mathematics, Amity University, Kolkata, India*
[3]*Department of Computer Science & Engineering, Sagar Institute of Science & Technology (SISTEC), Bhopal, India*

Abstract

In this chapter we proved some common invariant points theorem in $\varphi - \psi$ weak contraction on soft fuzzy metric spaces by using control function or altering distance function. Here we define mapping by using some proven results and obtain result on the actuality of fixed points. We were inspired by the concept of soft sets and fuzzy sets. To prove the results the basic concepts of soft sets and fuzzy sets were used. Results for the rational expressions are more difficult than the others, but in this chapter maximum results are proved for rational expressions. These results will generalize the basic result of soft fuzzy metric spaces.

Keywords: Soft sets (SS), soft fuzzy metric (SFM), soft fuzzy metric spaces (SFMS), continuous soft T-Norm, $\varphi - \psi$ weak contraction, fixed point (FT)

15.1 Introduction

For avoiding uncertainties, 2 types of mathematical tools namely FST [19] and SST were introduced that helped to solve the problem in all areas. After that, many authors generalized soft set theory. Roy *et al.* [16, 17] propounded several operations in soft sets and fuzzy soft sets. The notion of

**Corresponding author*: rkbhardwaj100@gmail.com

E. Chandrasekaran, R. Anandan, G. Suseendran, S. Balamurugan and Hanaa Hachimi (eds.) Fuzzy Intelligent Systems: Methodologies, Techniques, and Applications, (413–430) © 2021 Scrivener Publishing LLC

soft metric space was proposed by Das and Samanta [5, 6]. The definition of fuzzy soft metric spaces was defined by Beaula and Gunseli [4]. Erduran *et al.* [9], very recently, introduced SFMS as was given by for this notion where they gave definition of soft t-norm $\tilde{*}$ for the triangle inequality of soft fuzzy metric and gave some properties of soft t-norm.

FPT have been studied in many contexts, one of which is fuzzy setting. Heilpern [11] introduced FPT for the mapping in fuzzy. Kramosil and Michalek [13] propounded new notion of fuzzy metric spaces. Grabiec [10] proved an analogy of Banach contraction theorem in fuzzy metric spaces in 1988. Scientists and researchers are now developing fuzzy metric spaces in various forms. Khan, Swaleh, and Sessa [12] propounded a control function called altering distance function for Banach Fixed point theorem in metric spaces in 1984. In 2012, Shen, Qiu and Chen [18] introduced the notion of fuzzy metric spaces $(X, M, *)$ using control function as follows

$$\varphi(M(Tx, Ty, t)) \geq k(t).\ \varphi(M(x, y, t)),\ \forall x, y \in X,\ t > 0, \quad (15.1)$$

and obtained fixed point result for self-mapping T. Recently many authors use control function and gave their contribution in various metric spaces [4, 16].

In this chapter we established some fixed point theorems on soft fuzzy metric space by using control function which is motivated by references [1, 3, 7, 8, 14, 15, 18].

Now we give some important definitions and results which are used in this chapter.

Here X denotes initial universal set, for the set of all possible parameters we take E and the set of all subset of X be denoted by $P(X)$.

15.2 Preliminaries and Definition

Let $X \neq \varnothing$ & $E \neq \varnothing$ is collection of parameters.

$\tilde{X}$ = Absolute SS

$SP(\tilde{X})$ = collection of all soft points of $\tilde{X}$

$\mathbb{R}(E)^*$ = soft positive real numbers

Definition 1. [6] A SS (F, E) on X is called soft point, $\exists x \in X$, $e \in E$:

$F(e) = \{x\}$

$F(e') = \varnothing$ if some $x \in X$, $\forall\ e' \in E\{e\}$, denoted as $\tilde{x}_e$.

Definition 2. [9] *A SFS, in* $\tilde{X}$ *is defined as:*

$$\{(\tilde{x}_e, \mu_s(\tilde{x}_e)) : \tilde{x}_e \in \tilde{X}, e \in E\} = S,$$

where $\mu_s : \tilde{X} \to [0,1](E)$ = soft membership function

$\mu_s(\tilde{x}_e)$ = *grade of soft membership of* $\tilde{x}_e$ *in S.*

The definition for soft t norm, soft fuzzy metric spaces, and all required terms can be studied in the literature of Refs. [2] and [9].

Definition 3. [2] A soft fuzzy metric space $(\tilde{X}, S, *)$ is called complete, if every Cauchy sequence is convergent.

Definition 4. [2] A sequence $\{\tilde{x}^n_{e_j}\}$ of soft points in $(\tilde{X}, S, \tilde{*})$ is said to be bounded if there exist a positive soft real number $\tilde{M} \tilde{>} \bar{0}$ such that $S(\tilde{x}^n_{e_j}, \tilde{x}^m_{e_j}, \tilde{t}) \tilde{<} \tilde{M}$ for all $\tilde{t} \tilde{>} \bar{0}$.

Theorem 1. [2] Every convergent sequence in $(\tilde{X}, S, \tilde{*})$ is Cauchy sequence.

Basic result 1. Let $(\tilde{X}, S, \tilde{*})$ be a complete SFM space. $\tilde{x}_{e_1}, \tilde{y}_{e_2} \tilde{\in} \tilde{X}, S(\tilde{x}_{e_1}, \tilde{y}_{e_2}, .)$ Non-decreasing

Proof: If $S(\tilde{x}_{e_1}, \tilde{y}_{e_2}, \tilde{t}) \tilde{>} S(\tilde{x}_{e_1}, \tilde{y}_{e_2}, \tilde{s})$ for some $\bar{0} \tilde{<} \tilde{t} \tilde{<} \tilde{s}$.

$$\Rightarrow S(\tilde{x}_{e_1}, \tilde{y}_{e_2}, \tilde{t}) \tilde{*} S(\tilde{y}_{e_2}, \tilde{y}_{e_2}, \tilde{s} - \tilde{t}) \tilde{\leq} S(\tilde{x}_{e_1}, \tilde{y}_{e_2}, \tilde{s}) \tilde{\leq} S(\tilde{x}_{e_1}, \tilde{y}_{e_2}, \tilde{t}),$$

Thus $S(\tilde{x}_{e_1}, \tilde{y}_{e_2}, \tilde{t}) \tilde{<} S(\tilde{x}_{e_1}, \tilde{y}_{e_2}, \tilde{t}) \tilde{<} S(\tilde{x}_{e_1}, \tilde{y}_{e_2}, \tilde{t}), (since\ S(\tilde{y}_{e_2}, \tilde{y}_{e_2}, \tilde{s} - \tilde{t}) = \bar{1})$ which is contradiction.

Definition 7. φ : [0,1] → [0,1] is said to be control function or an altering distance function:

(CF1). φ is strictly decreasing & continuous;

(CF2). $\varphi(\lambda) \geq \bar{0}, \forall \lambda \neq \bar{1}$ if $\varphi(\lambda) = \bar{0}$ iff $\lambda \neq \bar{1}$.

$\Rightarrow \lim_{\lambda \to 1^-} \varphi(\lambda) = \varphi(1) = \bar{0}$, where φ in a class of function Φ.

(CF3). $\varphi(\lambda, \mu) \tilde{\leq} \varphi(\lambda) + \varphi(\mu), \lambda, \mu \tilde{\in} \{S(\tilde{x}_{ej}, T\tilde{x}_{ej}, \tilde{t}) : \tilde{x}_{ej} \tilde{\in} \tilde{X}, \tilde{t} \tilde{>} \bar{0}\}$.

15.3 Main Results

Theorem 2: $\tilde{X}$ be a non-empty set. Let $(\tilde{X}, S, \tilde{*})$ be a complete strong soft fuzzy metric spaces with continuous soft t – norm $\tilde{*}$ and Q self-mapping in $\tilde{X}$ such that

$$\varphi\big(S(Q\tilde{x}_{e_j},Q\tilde{y}_{e_j},\tilde{t})\big)$$
$$\tilde{\le}\varphi(S(\tilde{x}_{e_j},Q\tilde{y}_{e_j},\tilde{t})+S(\tilde{y}_{e_j},Q\tilde{y}_{e_j},\tilde{t})$$
$$+S(Q\tilde{x}_{e_j},\tilde{y}_{e_j},\tilde{t})+S(\tilde{x}_{e_j},Q\tilde{y}_{e_j},\tilde{t})+S(\tilde{x}_{e_j},\tilde{y}_{e_j},\tilde{t})$$
$$+\left[\frac{S(Q\tilde{x}_{e_j},\tilde{y}_{e_j},\tilde{t})+S(\tilde{x}_{e_j},Q\tilde{y}_{e_j},\tilde{t})}{1+S(Q\tilde{x}_{e_j},\tilde{y}_{e_j},\tilde{t}).S(\tilde{x}_{e_j},Q\tilde{y}_{e_j},\tilde{t})}\right]$$
$$+\max\left\{S(\tilde{x}_{e_j},Q\tilde{x}_{e_j},\tilde{t}),S(\tilde{y}_{e_j},Q\tilde{y}_{e_j},\tilde{t}),\frac{[S(Q\tilde{x}_{e_j},\tilde{y}_{e_j},\tilde{t}),S(\tilde{x}_{e_j},Q\tilde{y}_{e_j},\tilde{t})]}{S(\tilde{x}_{e_j},\tilde{y}_{e_j},\tilde{t})}\right\}\Bigg)$$
$$-\psi S(\tilde{x}_{e_j},Q\tilde{x}_{e_j},\tilde{t})+S(\tilde{y}_{e_j},Q\tilde{y}_{e_j},\tilde{t})$$
$$+S(Q\tilde{x}_{e_j},\tilde{y}_{e_j},\tilde{t})+S(\tilde{x}_{e_j},Q\tilde{y}_{e_j},\tilde{t})+S(\tilde{x}_{e_j},\tilde{y}_{e_j},\tilde{t})$$
$$+\left[\frac{S(Q\tilde{x}_{e_j},\tilde{y}_{e_j},\tilde{t})+S(\tilde{x}_{e_j},Q\tilde{y}_{e_j},\tilde{t})}{1+S(Q\tilde{x}_{e_j},\tilde{y}_{e_j},\tilde{t}).S(\tilde{x}_{e_j},Q\tilde{y}_{e_j},\tilde{t})}\right]$$
$$+\max\left\{S(\tilde{x}_{e_j},Q\tilde{x}_{e_j},\tilde{t}),S(\tilde{y}_{e_j},Q\tilde{y}_{e_j},\tilde{t}),\frac{[S(Q\tilde{x}_{e_j},\tilde{y}_{e_j},\tilde{t}),S(\tilde{x}_{e_j},Q\tilde{y}_{e_j},\tilde{t})]}{S(\tilde{x}_{e_j},\tilde{y}_{e_j},\tilde{t})}\right\}\Bigg) \tag{15.2}$$

where φ and ψ are control function and ultra-control function respectively, $\varphi(t+s)\tilde{\le}\varphi(t)+\varphi(s)$. Then Q has a unique fixed point in $\tilde{X}$.

Proof: Suppose arbitrary point $\tilde{x}_{e_j}\tilde{\in}\tilde{X}$ and define a sequence $\{\tilde{x}^n_{e_j}\}\tilde{\in}\tilde{X}$, such that $\tilde{x}^{n+1}_{e_j}=Q\tilde{x}^n_{e_j}$.

Let us assume that $\tilde{x}^{n+1}_{e_j}=Q\tilde{x}^n_{e_j}=\tilde{x}^n_{e_j}$, $n\tilde{\in}\mathbb{N},\Rightarrow\tilde{x}^n_{e_j}$ is a FP of Q.

Consider $\tilde{x}^{n+1}_{e_j}\neq Q\tilde{x}^n_{e_j}$, put $\tilde{x}_{e_j}=\tilde{x}^{n-1}_{e_j}$ and $\tilde{y}_{e_j}=\tilde{x}^n_{e_j}$, we get

$$\varphi\Big(S\big(Q\tilde{x}^{n-1}_{e_j},Q\tilde{x}^n_{e_j},\tilde{t}\big)\Big)\tilde{\le}\varphi\Big(S\big(\tilde{x}^{n-1}_{e_j},Q\tilde{x}^{n-1}_{e_j},\tilde{t}\big)+S\big(\tilde{x}^n_{e_j},Q\tilde{x}^n_{e_j},\tilde{t}\big)$$
$$+S\big(Q\tilde{x}^{n-1}_{e_j},\tilde{x}^n_{e_j},\tilde{t}\big)+S\big(\tilde{x}^{n-1}_{e_j},Q\tilde{x}^n_{e_j},\tilde{t}\big)+S\big(\tilde{x}^{n-1}_{e_j},\tilde{x}^n_{e_j},\tilde{t}\big)$$
$$+\left[\frac{S\big(Q\tilde{x}^{n-1}_{e_j},\tilde{x}^n_{e_j},\tilde{t}\big)+S\big(\tilde{x}^{n-1}_{e_j},Q\tilde{x}^n_{e_j},\tilde{t}\big)}{1+S\big(Q\tilde{x}^{n-1}_{e_j},\tilde{x}^n_{e_j},\tilde{t}\big).S\big(\tilde{x}^{n-1}_{e_j},Q\tilde{x}^n_{e_j},\tilde{t}\big)}\right]$$
$$+\max\left\{S\big(\tilde{x}^{n-1}_{e_j},Q\tilde{x}^{n-1}_{e_j},\tilde{t}\big),S\big(\tilde{x}^n_{e_j},Q\tilde{x}^n_{e_j},\tilde{t}\big),\frac{\Big[S\big(Q\tilde{x}^{n-1}_{e_j},\tilde{x}^n_{e_j},\tilde{t}\big),S\big(\tilde{x}^{n-1}_{e_j},Q\tilde{x}^n_{e_j},\tilde{t}\big)\Big]}{S\big(\tilde{x}^{n-1}_{e_j},\tilde{x}^n_{e_j},\tilde{t}\big)}\right\}\Bigg)$$

$$-\psi\Big(S\big(\tilde{x}_{e_j}^{n-1},Q\tilde{x}_{e_j}^{n-1},\tilde{t}\big)+S\big(\tilde{x}_{e_j}^{n},Q\tilde{x}_{e_j}^{n},\tilde{t}\big)$$
$$+S\big(Q\tilde{x}_{e_j}^{n-1},\tilde{x}_{e_j}^{n},\tilde{t}\big)+S\big(\tilde{x}_{e_j}^{n-1},Q\tilde{x}_{e_j}^{n},\tilde{t}\big)+S\big(\tilde{x}_{e_j}^{n-1},\tilde{x}_{e_j}^{n},\tilde{t}\big)$$
$$+\left[\frac{S\big(Q\tilde{x}_{e_j}^{n-1},\tilde{x}_{e_j}^{n},\tilde{t}\big)+S\big(\tilde{x}_{e_j}^{n-1},Q\tilde{x}_{e_j}^{n},\tilde{t}\big)}{1+S\big(Q\tilde{x}_{e_j}^{n-1},\tilde{x}_{e_j}^{n},\tilde{t}\big).S\big(\tilde{x}_{e_j}^{n-1},Q\tilde{x}_{e_j}^{n},\tilde{t}\big)}\right]$$
$$+\max\left\{S\big(\tilde{x}_{e_j}^{n-1},Q\tilde{x}_{e_j}^{n-1},\tilde{t}\big),S\big(\tilde{x}_{e_j}^{n},Q\tilde{x}_{e_j}^{n},\tilde{t}\big),\frac{\big[S\big(Q\tilde{x}_{e_j}^{n-1},\tilde{x}_{e_j}^{n},\tilde{t}\big),S\big(\tilde{x}_{e_j}^{n-1},Q\tilde{x}_{e_j}^{n},\tilde{t}\big)\big]}{S\big(\tilde{x}_{e_j}^{n-1},\tilde{x}_{e_j}^{n},\tilde{t}\big)}\right\}\Bigg)$$

(15.3)

$$\tilde{\le}\,\varphi\Big(S\big(\tilde{x}_{e_j}^{n-1},\tilde{x}_{e_j}^{n-1},\tilde{t}\big)+S\big(\tilde{x}_{e_j}^{n},\tilde{x}_{e_j}^{n+1},\tilde{t}\big)$$
$$+S\big(\tilde{x}_{e_j}^{n},\tilde{x}_{e_j}^{n},\tilde{t}\big)+S\big(\tilde{x}_{e_j}^{n-1},\tilde{x}_{e_j}^{n+1},\tilde{t}\big)$$
$$+S\big(\tilde{x}_{e_j}^{n-1},\tilde{x}_{e_j}^{n},\tilde{t}\big)+\left[\frac{S\big(\tilde{x}_{e_j}^{n},\tilde{x}_{e_j}^{n},\tilde{t}\big)+S\big(\tilde{x}_{e_j}^{n-1},\tilde{x}_{e_j}^{n+1},\tilde{t}\big)}{1+S\big(\tilde{x}_{e_j}^{n},\tilde{x}_{e_j}^{n},\tilde{t}\big).S\big(\tilde{x}_{e_j}^{n-1},\tilde{x}_{e_j}^{n+1},\tilde{t}\big)}\right]$$
$$+\max\left\{S\big(\tilde{x}_{e_j}^{n-1},\tilde{x}_{e_j}^{n},\tilde{t}\big),S\big(\tilde{x}_{e_j}^{n},\tilde{x}_{e_j}^{n+1},\tilde{t}\big),\frac{\big[S\big(\tilde{x}_{e_j}^{n},\tilde{x}_{e_j}^{n},\tilde{t}\big),S\big(\tilde{x}_{e_j}^{n-1},\tilde{x}_{e_j}^{n+1},\tilde{t}\big)\big]}{S\big(\tilde{x}_{e_j}^{n-1},\tilde{x}_{e_j}^{n},\tilde{t}\big)}\right\}\Bigg)$$
$$-\psi\Big(S\big(\tilde{x}_{e_j}^{n-1},\tilde{x}_{e_j}^{n},\tilde{t}\big)+S\big(\tilde{x}_{e_j}^{n},\tilde{x}_{e_j}^{n+1},\tilde{t}\big)+1$$
$$S\big(\tilde{x}_{e_j}^{n},\tilde{x}_{e_j}^{n},\tilde{t}\big)+S\big(\tilde{x}_{e_j}^{n-1},\tilde{x}_{e_j}^{n+1},\tilde{t}\big)+S\big(\tilde{x}_{e_j}^{n-1},\tilde{x}_{e_j}^{n},\tilde{t}\big)$$
$$+\left[\frac{S\big(\tilde{x}_{e_j}^{n},\tilde{x}_{e_j}^{n},\tilde{t}\big)+S\big(\tilde{x}_{e_j}^{n-1},\tilde{x}_{e_j}^{n+1},\tilde{t}\big)}{1+S\big(\tilde{x}_{e_j}^{n},\tilde{x}_{e_j}^{n},\tilde{t}\big).S\big(\tilde{x}_{e_j}^{n-1},\tilde{x}_{e_j}^{n+1},\tilde{t}\big)}\right]$$
$$+\max\left\{S\big(\tilde{x}_{e_j}^{n-1},\tilde{x}_{e_j}^{n},\tilde{t}\big),S\big(\tilde{x}_{e_j}^{n},\tilde{x}_{e_j}^{n+1},\tilde{t}\big),\frac{\big[\big(\tilde{x}_{e_j}^{n},\tilde{x}_{e_j}^{n},\tilde{t}\big),S\big(\tilde{x}_{e_j}^{n-1},\tilde{x}_{e_j}^{n+1},\tilde{t}\big)\big]}{S\big(\tilde{x}_{e_j}^{n-1},\tilde{x}_{e_j}^{n},\tilde{t}\big)}\right\}\Bigg)$$

$$
\begin{aligned}
&\tilde{\le}\varphi\Big(S\big(\tilde{x}_{e_j}^{n-1},\tilde{x}_{e_j}^{n},\tilde{t}\big)+S\big(\tilde{x}_{e_j}^{n},\tilde{x}_{e_j}^{n+1},\tilde{t}\big)+1+S\big(\tilde{x}_{e_j}^{n-1},\tilde{x}_{e_j}^{n+1},\tilde{t}\big)\\
&+S\big(\tilde{x}_{e_j}^{n-1},\tilde{x}_{e_j}^{n},\tilde{t}\big)+\left[\frac{1+S\big(\tilde{x}_{e_j}^{n-1},\tilde{x}_{e_j}^{n+1},\tilde{t}\big)}{1+1.S\big(\tilde{x}_{e_j}^{n-1},\tilde{x}_{e_j}^{n+1},\tilde{t}\big)}\right]\\
&+\max\left\{S\big(\tilde{x}_{e_j}^{n-1},\tilde{x}_{e_j}^{n},\tilde{t}\big),S\big(\tilde{x}_{e_j}^{n},\tilde{x}_{e_j}^{n+1},\tilde{t}\big),\frac{\big[1,S\big(\tilde{x}_{e_j}^{n-1},\tilde{x}_{e_j}^{n+1},\tilde{t}\big)\big]}{S\big(\tilde{x}_{e_j}^{n-1},\tilde{x}_{e_j}^{n},\tilde{t}\big)}\right\}\Bigg)\\
&+\psi\Big(S\big(\tilde{x}_{e_j}^{n-1},\tilde{x}_{e_j}^{n},\tilde{t}\big)+S\big(\tilde{x}_{e_j}^{n},\tilde{x}_{e_j}^{n+1},\tilde{t}\big)+1+S\big(\tilde{x}_{e_j}^{n-1},\tilde{x}_{e_j}^{n+1},\tilde{t}\big)\\
&+S\big(\tilde{x}_{e_j}^{n-1},\tilde{x}_{e_j}^{n},\tilde{t}\big)+\left[\frac{1+S\big(\tilde{x}_{e_j}^{n-1},\tilde{x}_{e_j}^{n+1},\tilde{t}\big)}{1+1.S\big(\tilde{x}_{e_j}^{n-1},\tilde{x}_{e_j}^{n+1},\tilde{t}\big)}\right]\\
&+\max\left\{S\big(\tilde{x}_{e_j}^{n-1},\tilde{x}_{e_j}^{n},\tilde{t}\big),S\big(\tilde{x}_{e_j}^{n},\tilde{x}_{e_j}^{n+1},\tilde{t}\big),\frac{\big[1,S\big(\tilde{x}_{e_j}^{n-1},\tilde{x}_{e_j}^{n+1},\tilde{t}\big)\big]}{S\big(\tilde{x}_{e_j}^{n-1},\tilde{x}_{e_j}^{n},\tilde{t}\big)}\right\}\Bigg)\\
&\tilde{\le}\varphi\Big(S\big(\tilde{x}_{e_j}^{n-1},\tilde{x}_{e_j}^{n},\tilde{t}\big)+S\big(\tilde{x}_{e_j}^{n},\tilde{x}_{e_j}^{n+1},\tilde{t}\big)+1+S\big(\tilde{x}_{e_j}^{n-1},\tilde{x}_{e_j}^{n+1},\tilde{t}\big)\\
&+S\big(\tilde{x}_{e_j}^{n-1},\tilde{x}_{e_j}^{n},\tilde{t}\big)+1+\max\big\{S\big(\tilde{x}_{e_j}^{n-1},\tilde{x}_{e_j}^{n},\tilde{t}\big),S\big(\tilde{x}_{e_j}^{n},\tilde{x}_{e_j}^{n+1},\tilde{t}\big)\big\}\Big)\\
&-\psi\Big(S\big(\tilde{x}_{e_j}^{n-1},\tilde{x}_{e_j}^{n},\tilde{t}\big)+S\big(\tilde{x}_{e_j}^{n},\tilde{x}_{e_j}^{n+1},\tilde{t}\big)+1+S\big(\tilde{x}_{e_j}^{n-1},\tilde{x}_{e_j}^{n+1},\tilde{t}\big)\\
&+S\big(\tilde{x}_{e_j}^{n-1},\tilde{x}_{e_j}^{n},\tilde{t}\big)+1+\max\big\{S\big(\tilde{x}_{e_j}^{n-1},\tilde{x}_{e_j}^{n},\tilde{t}\big),S\big(\tilde{x}_{e_j}^{n},\tilde{x}_{e_j}^{n+1},\tilde{t}\big)\big\}\Big)
\end{aligned}
$$

$$
\begin{aligned}
&\varphi\Big(S\big(\tilde{x}_{e_j}^{n},\tilde{x}_{e_j}^{n+1},\tilde{t}\big)\Big)\\
&\quad\tilde{\le}\varphi\Big(S\big(\tilde{x}_{e_j}^{n-1},\tilde{x}_{e_j}^{n},\tilde{t}\big)\Big)+\varphi\Big(S\big(\tilde{x}_{e_j}^{n},\tilde{x}_{e_j}^{n+1},\tilde{t}\big)\Big)+\varphi\Big(S\big(\tilde{x}_{e_j}^{n-1},\tilde{x}_{e_j}^{n+1},\tilde{t}\big)\Big)\\
&\quad+\varphi\Big(S\big(\tilde{x}_{e_j}^{n-1},\tilde{x}_{e_j}^{n},\tilde{t}\big)\Big)+\varphi\max\big\{S\big(\tilde{x}_{e_j}^{n-1},\tilde{x}_{e_j}^{n},\tilde{t}\big),S\big(\tilde{x}_{e_j}^{n},\tilde{x}_{e_j}^{n+1},\tilde{t}\big)\big\}\\
&\quad-\Big[\psi\Big(S\big(\tilde{x}_{e_j}^{n-1},\tilde{x}_{e_j}^{n},\tilde{t}\big)\Big)+\psi\Big(S\big(\tilde{x}_{e_j}^{n},\tilde{x}_{e_j}^{n+1},\tilde{t}\big)\Big)+\psi\Big(S\big(\tilde{x}_{e_j}^{n-1},\tilde{x}_{e_j}^{n+1},\tilde{t}\big)\Big)\\
&\quad+\psi\Big(S\big(\tilde{x}_{e_j}^{n-1},\tilde{x}_{e_j}^{n},\tilde{t}\big)\Big)+\psi\max\big\{S\big(\tilde{x}_{e_j}^{n-1},\tilde{x}_{e_j}^{n},\tilde{t}\big),S\big(\tilde{x}_{e_j}^{n},\tilde{x}_{e_j}^{n+1},\tilde{t}\big)\big\}\Big]
\end{aligned}
\tag{15.4}
$$

Here $(\tilde{X}, S, \tilde{*})$ be soft fuzzy metric space, then we have,

$$S\left(\tilde{x}_{e_j}^{n-1}, \tilde{x}_{e_j}^{n+1}, \tilde{t}\right) \tilde{\geq} S\left(\tilde{x}_{e_j}^{n-1}, \tilde{x}_{e_j}^{n}, \tilde{t}\right) \tilde{*} S\left(\tilde{x}_{e_j}^{n}, \tilde{x}_{e_j}^{n+1}, \tilde{t}\right) (\text{by using } FSM\text{-}4)$$

$$\varphi\left(S\left(\tilde{x}_{e_j}^{n-1}, \tilde{x}_{e_j}^{n+1}, \tilde{t}\right)\right) \tilde{\leq} \varphi\left(S\left(\tilde{x}_{e_j}^{n-1}, \tilde{x}_{e_j}^{n}, \tilde{t}\right) \tilde{*} S\left(\tilde{x}_{e_j}^{n}, \tilde{x}_{e_j}^{n+1}, \tilde{t}\right)\right)$$

By using CF3, we can write

$$\varphi\left(S\left(\tilde{x}_{e_j}^{n-1}, \tilde{x}_{e_j}^{n+1}, \tilde{t}\right)\right) \tilde{\leq} \varphi\left(S\left(\tilde{x}_{e_j}^{n-1}, \tilde{x}_{e_j}^{n}, \tilde{t}\right)\right) + \varphi\left(S\left(\tilde{x}_{e_j}^{n}, \tilde{x}_{e_j}^{n+1}, \tilde{t}\right)\right) \quad (15.5)$$

The above inequalities in Equation (15.4), we get

$$\begin{aligned}
&\varphi\left(S\left(\tilde{x}_{e_j}^{n}, \tilde{x}_{e_j}^{n+1}, \tilde{t}\right)\right) \\
&\quad \tilde{\leq} \varphi\Big(S\left(\tilde{x}_{e_j}^{n-1}, \tilde{x}_{e_j}^{n}, \tilde{t}\right) + S\left(\tilde{x}_{e_j}^{n}, \tilde{x}_{e_j}^{n+1}, \tilde{t}\right) + \Big[S\left(\tilde{x}_{e_j}^{n-1}, \tilde{x}_{e_j}^{n}, \tilde{t}\right) \\
&\quad + S\left(\tilde{x}_{e_j}^{n}, \tilde{x}_{e_j}^{n+1}, \tilde{t}\right)\Big] + S\left(\tilde{x}_{e_j}^{n-1}, \tilde{x}_{e_j}^{n}, \tilde{t}\right) + 1 \\
&\quad + \max\left\{S\left(\tilde{x}_{e_j}^{n-1}, \tilde{x}_{e_j}^{n}, \tilde{t}\right), S\left(\tilde{x}_{e_j}^{n}, \tilde{x}_{e_j}^{n+1}, \tilde{t}\right)\right\}\Big) \\
&\quad - \psi\Big(S\left(\tilde{x}_{e_j}^{n-1}, \tilde{x}_{e_j}^{n}, \tilde{t}\right) + S\left(\tilde{x}_{e_j}^{n}, \tilde{x}_{e_j}^{n+1}, \tilde{t}\right) + \Big[S\left(\tilde{x}_{e_j}^{n-1}, \tilde{x}_{e_j}^{n}, \tilde{t}\right) \\
&\quad + S\left(\tilde{x}_{e_j}^{n}, \tilde{x}_{e_j}^{n+1}, \tilde{t}\right)\Big] + S\left(\tilde{x}_{e_j}^{n-1}, \tilde{x}_{e_j}^{n}, \tilde{t}\right) \\
&\quad + \max\left\{S\left(\tilde{x}_{e_j}^{n-1}, \tilde{x}_{e_j}^{n}, \tilde{t}\right), S\left(\tilde{x}_{e_j}^{n}, \tilde{x}_{e_j}^{n+1}, \tilde{t}\right)\right\}\Big)
\end{aligned}$$

$$\begin{aligned}
&\varphi\left(S\left(\tilde{x}_{e_j}^{n}, \tilde{x}_{e_j}^{n+1}, \tilde{t}\right)\right) \\
&\quad \tilde{\leq} \varphi\left(S\left(\tilde{x}_{e_j}^{n-1}, \tilde{x}_{e_j}^{n}, \tilde{t}\right)\right) + \varphi\left(S\left(\tilde{x}_{e_j}^{n}, \tilde{x}_{e_j}^{n+1}, \tilde{t}\right)\right) + \varphi\left(S\left(\tilde{x}_{e_j}^{n-1}, \tilde{x}_{e_j}^{n}, \tilde{t}\right)\right) \\
&\quad + \varphi\left(S\left(\tilde{x}_{e_j}^{n}, \tilde{x}_{e_j}^{n+1}, \tilde{t}\right)\right) + \varphi\left(S\left(\tilde{x}_{e_j}^{n-1}, \tilde{x}_{e_j}^{n}, \tilde{t}\right)\right) \\
&\quad + \varphi \max\left\{S\left(\tilde{x}_{e_j}^{n-1}, \tilde{x}_{e_j}^{n}, \tilde{t}\right), S\left(\tilde{x}_{e_j}^{n}, \tilde{x}_{e_j}^{n+1}, \tilde{t}\right)\right\} \qquad (15.6)
\end{aligned}$$

$$\text{If } \max\left\{S\left(\tilde{x}_{e_j}^{n-1}, \tilde{x}_{e_j}^{n}, \tilde{t}\right), S\left(\tilde{x}_{e_j}^{n}, \tilde{x}_{e_j}^{n+1}, \tilde{t}\right)\right\} = S\left(\tilde{x}_{e_j}^{n-1}, \tilde{x}_{e_j}^{n}, \tilde{t}\right) \quad (15.7)$$

Then using above inequality, Equation (15.6) becomes,

$$\begin{aligned}\varphi\left(S\left(\tilde{x}_{e_j}^{n},\tilde{x}_{e_j}^{n+1},\tilde{t}\right)\right) &\tilde{\leq}\varphi\left(S\left(\tilde{x}_{e_j}^{n-1},\tilde{x}_{e_j}^{n},\tilde{t}\right)\right)+\varphi\left(S\left(\tilde{x}_{e_j}^{n},\tilde{x}_{e_j}^{n+1},\tilde{t}\right)\right)+\varphi\left(S\left(\tilde{x}_{e_j}^{n-1},\tilde{x}_{e_j}^{n},\tilde{t}\right)\right)\\ &+\varphi\left(S\left(\tilde{x}_{e_j}^{n},\tilde{x}_{e_j}^{n+1},\tilde{t}\right)\right)+\varphi\left(S\left(\tilde{x}_{e_j}^{n-1},\tilde{x}_{e_j}^{n},\tilde{t}\right)\right)+\varphi\left(S\left(\tilde{x}_{e_j}^{n-1},\tilde{x}_{e_j}^{n},\tilde{t}\right)\right)\end{aligned}$$

Continuing this process, we obtained,

$$\varphi\left(S\left(\tilde{x}_{e_j}^{n},\tilde{x}_{e_j}^{n+1},\tilde{t}\right)\right)\tilde{\leq}\varphi\left(S\left(\tilde{x}_{e_j}^{n-1},\tilde{x}_{e_j}^{n},\tilde{t}\right)\right)\tilde{\leq}\varphi\left(S\left(\tilde{x}_{e_j}^{n-1},\tilde{x}_{e_j}^{n},\tilde{t}\right)\right) \quad (15.8)$$

Similarly,

$$\text{If } \max\left\{S\left(\tilde{x}_{e_j}^{n-1},\tilde{x}_{e_j}^{n},\tilde{t}\right),S\left(\tilde{x}_{e_j}^{n},\tilde{x}_{e_j}^{n+1},\tilde{t}\right)\right\}=S\left(\tilde{x}_{e_j}^{n-1},\tilde{x}_{e_j}^{n},\tilde{t}\right) \quad (15.9)$$

Then using above inequality, Equation (15.6) becomes

$$\varphi\left(S\left(\tilde{x}_{e_j}^{n},\tilde{x}_{e_j}^{n+1},\tilde{t}\right)\right)\tilde{\leq}\varphi\left(S\left(\tilde{x}_{e_j}^{n-1},\tilde{x}_{e_j}^{n},\tilde{t}\right)\right)\tilde{\leq}\varphi\left(S\left(\tilde{x}_{e_j}^{n-1},\tilde{x}_{e_j}^{n},\tilde{t}\right)\right) \quad (15.10)$$

Therefore $\varphi\left(S\left(\tilde{x}_{e_j}^{n},\tilde{x}_{e_j}^{n+1},\tilde{t}\right)\right)\tilde{\leq}\varphi\left(S\left(\tilde{x}_{e_j}^{n-1},\tilde{x}_{e_j}^{n},\tilde{t}\right)\right)$
This gives $S\left(\tilde{x}_{e_j}^{n},\tilde{x}_{e_j}^{n+1},\tilde{t}\right)\tilde{\leq}S\left(\tilde{x}_{e_j}^{n-1},\tilde{x}_{e_j}^{n},\tilde{t}\right)$
Since the sequence $\left\{S\left(\tilde{x}_{e_j}^{n},\tilde{x}_{e_j}^{n+1},\tilde{t}\right)\right\}$ is non-decreasing sequence.
Taking the limit as $n \to \infty$, we obtained

$$\lim_{n\to\infty} S\left(\tilde{x}_{e_j}^{n},\tilde{x}_{e_j}^{n+1},\tilde{t}\right)=\eta(\tilde{r}),\text{ for } \eta:(0,\infty)\to[0,1] \quad (15.11)$$

Consider that $\eta(\tilde{r})\neq 1$ for some $\tilde{r}\tilde{>}0$ as $n\to\infty$,
Now Equation (15.10) becomes,

$$\varphi(\eta(\tilde{r}))\tilde{\leq}\varphi(\eta(\tilde{r}))\tilde{<}\varphi(\eta(\tilde{r})) \quad (15.12)$$

which is contradiction.

Therefore $\lim_{n\to\infty} S\left(\tilde{x}_{e_j}^{n}, \tilde{x}_{e_j}^{n+1}, \tilde{t}\right) = 1$, $\tilde{t}$ *is positive*

Next we prove the seq. $\left\{\tilde{x}_{e_j}^{n}\right\}$ is a Cauchy's seq.

Let us assume that $\tilde{x}_{e_j}^{n}$ is not a Cauchy's sequence then for any $\bar{0} \tilde{<} \tilde{\varepsilon} \tilde{<} \bar{1}$, $\tilde{t} \tilde{>} \bar{0}$, then $\exists$ sequence $\tilde{x}_{e_j}^{n_k}$ and $\tilde{x}_{e_j}^{m_k}$ where $n_k, m_k \tilde{\geq} n$ and $n_k, m_k \tilde{\in} \mathbb{N}(n_k \tilde{>} m_k)$,

$$\text{such that } S\left(\tilde{x}_{e_j}^{n_k}, \tilde{x}_{e_j}^{m_k}, \tilde{t}\right) \tilde{\leq} 1 - \tilde{\varepsilon} \tag{15.13}$$

Let n_k be least integer exceeding m_k satisfying the above property, therefore

$$S\left(\tilde{x}_{e_j}^{n_k-1}, \tilde{x}_{e_j}^{m_k}, \tilde{t}\right) \tilde{>} 1 - \tilde{\varepsilon}, n_k, m_k \tilde{\in} \mathbb{N} \text{ and } \tilde{t} \tilde{>} \bar{0} \tag{15.14}$$

Put $\tilde{x}_{e_j} = \tilde{x}_{e_j}^{n_k-1}$ and $\tilde{y}_{e_j} = \tilde{y}_{e_j}^{m_k-1}$ in Equation (15.12),

$$\begin{aligned}
&\varphi\left(S\left(Q\tilde{x}_{e_j}^{n_k-1}, Q\tilde{x}_{e_j}^{m_k-1}, \tilde{t}\right)\right) \\
&\quad \tilde{\leq} \varphi\Bigg(S\left(\tilde{x}_{e_j}^{n_k-1}, Q\tilde{x}_{e_j}^{n_k-1}, \tilde{t}\right) + S\left(\tilde{x}_{e_j}^{n_k-1}, \tilde{x}_{e_j}^{m_k-1}, \tilde{t}\right) \\
&\quad S\left(Q\tilde{x}_{e_j}^{n_k-1}, \tilde{x}_{e_j}^{m_k-1}, \tilde{t}\right) \\
&\quad + S\left(\tilde{x}_{e_j}^{n_k-1}, Q\tilde{x}_{e_j}^{m_k-1}, \tilde{t}\right) + S\left(Q\tilde{x}_{e_j}^{n_k-1}, \tilde{x}_{e_j}^{m_k-1}, \tilde{t}\right) \\
&\quad + \left[\frac{S\left(Q\tilde{x}_{e_j}^{n_k-1}, \tilde{x}_{e_j}^{m_k-1}, \tilde{t}\right) + S\left(\tilde{x}_{e_j}^{n_k-1}, Q\tilde{x}_{e_j}^{m_k-1}, \tilde{t}\right)}{1 + S\left(Q\tilde{x}_{e_j}^{n_k-1}, \tilde{x}_{e_j}^{m_k-1}, \tilde{t}\right).S\left(\tilde{x}_{e_j}^{n_k-1}, Q\tilde{x}_{e_j}^{m_k-1}, \tilde{t}\right)}\right] + \\
&\quad max\left\{\begin{array}{c} S\left(\tilde{x}_{e_j}^{n_k-1}, Q\tilde{x}_{e_j}^{n_k-1}, \tilde{t}\right), S\left(\tilde{x}_{e_j}^{m_k-1}, Q\tilde{x}_{e_j}^{m_k-1}, \tilde{t}\right), \\ \dfrac{\left[S\left(Q\tilde{x}_{e_j}^{n_k-1}, \tilde{x}_{e_j}^{m_k-1}, \tilde{t}\right), S\left(\tilde{x}_{e_j}^{n_k-1}, Q\tilde{x}_{e_j}^{m_k-1}, \tilde{t}\right)\right]}{S\left(\tilde{x}_{e_j}^{n_k-1}, \tilde{x}_{e_j}^{m_k-1}, \tilde{t}\right)} \end{array}\right\}\Bigg)
\end{aligned}$$

$$
\begin{aligned}
&-\psi\Bigg(S\left(\tilde{x}_{e_j}^{n_k-1}, Q\tilde{x}_{e_j}^{n_k-1}, \tilde{t}\right)\\
&+S\left(\tilde{x}_{e_j}^{m_k-1}, Q\tilde{x}_{e_j}^{m_k-1}, \tilde{t}\right)\\
&+S\left(Q\tilde{x}_{e_j}^{n_k-1}, \tilde{x}_{e_j}^{m_k-1}, \tilde{t}\right)+S\left(\tilde{x}_{e_j}^{n_k-1}, Q\tilde{x}_{e_j}^{m_k-1}, \tilde{t}\right)+S\left(\tilde{x}_{e_j}^{n_k-1}, \tilde{x}_{e_j}^{m_k-1}, \tilde{t}\right)\\
&+\left[\frac{S\left(Q\tilde{x}_{e_j}^{n_k-1}, \tilde{x}_{e_j}^{m_k-1}, \tilde{t}\right)+S\left(\tilde{x}_{e_j}^{n_k-1}, Q\tilde{x}_{e_j}^{m_k-1}, \tilde{t}\right)}{1+S\left(Q\tilde{x}_{e_j}^{n_k-1}, \tilde{x}_{e_j}^{m_k-1}, \tilde{t}\right).S\left(\tilde{x}_{e_j}^{n_k-1}, Q\tilde{x}_{e_j}^{m_k-1}, \tilde{t}\right)}\right]+\\
&max\left\{\begin{array}{c} S\left(\tilde{x}_{e_j}^{n_k-1}, Q\,\tilde{x}_{e_j}^{n_k-1}, \tilde{t}\right), S\left(\tilde{x}_{e_j}^{m_k-1}, Q\tilde{x}_{e_j}^{m_k-1}, \tilde{t}\right),\\ \dfrac{\left[S\left(Q\tilde{x}_{e_j}^{n_k-1}, \tilde{x}_{e_j}^{m_k-1}, \tilde{t}\right), S\left(\tilde{x}_{e_j}^{n_k-1}, Q\tilde{x}_{e_j}^{m_k-1}, \tilde{t}\right)\right]}{S\left(\tilde{x}_{e_j}^{n_k-1}, \tilde{x}_{e_j}^{m_k-1}, \tilde{t}\right)}\end{array}\right\}\Bigg)
\end{aligned}
$$

$$
\begin{aligned}
&\varphi\left(S\left(\tilde{x}_{e_j}^{n_k}, \tilde{x}_{e_j}^{m_k}, \tilde{t}\right)\right.\\
&\tilde{\leq}\varphi\Bigg(S\left(\tilde{x}_{e_j}^{n_k-1}, \tilde{x}_{e_j}^{n_k}, \tilde{t}\right)+S\left(\tilde{x}_{e_j}^{m_k-1}, \tilde{x}_{e_j}^{m_k}, \tilde{t}\right)+\\
&S\left(\tilde{x}_{e_j}^{n_k}, \tilde{x}_{e_j}^{m_k-1}, \tilde{t}\right)+S\left(\tilde{x}_{e_j}^{n_k-1}, \tilde{x}_{e_j}^{m_k}, \tilde{t}\right)+S\left(\tilde{x}_{e_j}^{n_k-1}, \tilde{x}_{e_j}^{m_k-1}, \tilde{t}\right)\\
&+\left[\frac{S\left(\tilde{x}_{e_j}^{n_k}, \tilde{x}_{e_j}^{m_k-1}, \tilde{t}\right)+S\left(\tilde{x}_{e_j}^{n_k-1}, \tilde{x}_{e_j}^{m_k}, \tilde{t}\right)}{1+S\left(\tilde{x}_{e_j}^{n_k}, \tilde{x}_{e_j}^{m_k-1}, \tilde{t}\right).S\left(\tilde{x}_{e_j}^{n_k-1}, \tilde{x}_{e_j}^{m_k}, \tilde{t}\right)}\right]+\\
&max\left\{\begin{array}{c} S\left(\tilde{x}_{e_j}^{n_k-1}, \tilde{x}_{e_j}^{n_k}, \tilde{t}\right), S\left(\tilde{x}_{e_j}^{m_k-1}, \tilde{x}_{e_j}^{m_k}, \tilde{t}\right),\\ \dfrac{\left[S\left(\tilde{x}_{e_j}^{n_k}, \tilde{x}_{e_j}^{m_k-1}, \tilde{t}\right), S\left(\tilde{x}_{e_j}^{n_k-1}, \tilde{x}_{e_j}^{m_k}, \tilde{t}\right)\right]}{S\left(\tilde{x}_{e_j}^{n_k-1}, \tilde{x}_{e_j}^{m_k-1}, \tilde{t}\right)}\end{array}\right\}\Bigg)\\
&-\psi\Bigg(S\left(\tilde{x}_{e_j}^{n_k-1}, \tilde{x}_{e_j}^{n_k-1}, \tilde{t}\right)+S\left(\tilde{x}_{e_j}^{m_k-1}, \tilde{x}_{e_j}^{m_k}, \tilde{t}\right)+\\
&S\left(\tilde{x}_{e_j}^{n_k}, \tilde{x}_{e_j}^{m_k-1}, \tilde{t}\right)+S\left(\tilde{x}_{e_j}^{n_k-1}, \tilde{x}_{e_j}^{m_k}, \tilde{t}\right)+S\left(\tilde{x}_{e_j}^{n_k-1}, \tilde{x}_{e_j}^{m_k-1}, \tilde{t}\right)\\
&+\left[\frac{S\left(\tilde{x}_{e_j}^{n_k}, \tilde{x}_{e_j}^{m_k-1}, \tilde{t}\right)+S\left(\tilde{x}_{e_j}^{n_k-1}, \tilde{x}_{e_j}^{m_k}, \tilde{t}\right)}{1+S\left(\tilde{x}_{e_j}^{n_k}, \tilde{x}_{e_j}^{m_k-1}, \tilde{t}\right).S\left(\tilde{x}_{e_j}^{n_k-1}, \tilde{x}_{e_j}^{m_k}, \tilde{t}\right)}\right]+
\end{aligned}
$$

$$max\left\{\begin{array}{c} S\left(\tilde{x}_{e_j}^{n_k-1},\tilde{x}_{e_j}^{n_k},\tilde{t}\right),S\left(\tilde{x}_{e_j}^{m_k-1},\tilde{x}_{e_j}^{m_k},\tilde{t}\right), \\ \dfrac{\left[S\left(\tilde{x}_{e_j}^{n_k},\tilde{x}_{e_j}^{m_k-1},\tilde{t}\right),S\left(\tilde{x}_{e_j}^{n_k-1},\tilde{x}_{e_j}^{m_k},\tilde{t}\right)\right]}{S\left(\tilde{x}_{e_j}^{n_k-1},\tilde{x}_{e_j}^{m_k-1},\tilde{t}\right)} \end{array}\right\}\Bigg)\Bigg)$$

$$\tilde{\leq}\varphi\Bigg(S\left(\tilde{x}_{e_j}^{n_k-1},\tilde{x}_{e_j}^{n_k},\tilde{t}\right)+S\left(\tilde{x}_{e_j}^{m_k-1},\tilde{x}_{e_j}^{m_k},\tilde{t}\right)+$$
$$S\left(\tilde{x}_{e_j}^{n_k},\tilde{x}_{e_j}^{m_k-1},\tilde{t}\right)+S\left(\tilde{x}_{e_j}^{n_k-1},\tilde{x}_{e_j}^{m_k},\tilde{t}\right)+S\left(\tilde{x}_{e_j}^{n_k-1},\tilde{x}_{e_j}^{m_k-1},\tilde{t}\right)$$
$$+\left[\frac{S\left(\tilde{x}_{e_j}^{n_k},\tilde{x}_{e_j}^{m_k-1},\tilde{t}\right)+S\left(\tilde{x}_{e_j}^{n_k-1},\tilde{x}_{e_j}^{m_k},\tilde{t}\right)}{1+S\left(\tilde{x}_{e_j}^{n_k},\tilde{x}_{e_j}^{m_k-1},\tilde{t}\right).S\left(\tilde{x}_{e_j}^{n_k-1},\tilde{x}_{e_j}^{m_k},\tilde{t}\right)}\right]+$$
$$max\left\{S\left(\tilde{x}_{e_j}^{n_k-1},\tilde{x}_{e_j}^{n_k},\tilde{t}\right),S\left(\tilde{x}_{e_j}^{m_k-1},\tilde{x}_{e_j}^{m_k},\tilde{t}\right)\right\}\Bigg)$$
$$-\psi\Bigg(S\left(\tilde{x}_{e_j}^{n_k-1},\tilde{x}_{e_j}^{n_k},\tilde{t}\right)+S\left(\tilde{x}_{e_j}^{m_k-1},\tilde{x}_{e_j}^{m_k},\tilde{t}\right)+$$
$$S\left(\tilde{x}_{e_j}^{n_k},\tilde{x}_{e_j}^{m_k-1},\tilde{t}\right)+S\left(\tilde{x}_{e_j}^{n_k-1},\tilde{x}_{e_j}^{m_k},\tilde{t}\right)+S\left(\tilde{x}_{e_j}^{n_k-1},\tilde{x}_{e_j}^{m_k-1},\tilde{t}\right)$$
$$+\left[\frac{S\left(\tilde{x}_{e_j}^{n_k},\tilde{x}_{e_j}^{m_k-1},\tilde{t}\right)+S\left(\tilde{x}_{e_j}^{n_k-1},\tilde{x}_{e_j}^{m_k},\tilde{t}\right)}{1+S\left(\tilde{x}_{e_j}^{n_k},\tilde{x}_{e_j}^{m_k-1},\tilde{t}\right).S\left(\tilde{x}_{e_j}^{n_k-1},\tilde{x}_{e_j}^{m_k},\tilde{t}\right)}\right]+$$
$$max\left\{S\left(\tilde{x}_{e_j}^{n_k-1},\tilde{x}_{e_j}^{n_k},\tilde{t}\right),S\left(\tilde{x}_{e_j}^{m_k-1},\tilde{x}_{e_j}^{m_k},\tilde{t}\right)\right\}\Bigg) \tag{15.15}$$

If $max\left\{S\left(\tilde{x}_{e_j}^{n_k-1},\tilde{x}_{e_j}^{n_k},\tilde{t}\right),S\left(\tilde{x}_{e_j}^{m_k-1},\tilde{x}_{e_j}^{m_k},\tilde{t}\right)\right\}=S\left(\tilde{x}_{e_j}^{n_k-1},\tilde{x}_{e_j}^{n_k},\tilde{t}\right)$, then

$$\varphi\Big(S\left(\tilde{x}_{e_j}^{n_k},\tilde{x}_{e_j}^{m_k},\tilde{t}\right)$$
$$\tilde{\leq}\varphi\Big(S\left(\tilde{x}_{e_j}^{n_k-1},\tilde{x}_{e_j}^{n_k},\tilde{t}\right)+S\left(\tilde{x}_{e_j}^{m_k-1},\tilde{x}_{e_j}^{m_k},\tilde{t}\right)$$

$$+S\left(\tilde{x}_{e_j}^{n_k-1},\tilde{x}_{e_j}^{m_k},\tilde{t}\right)+S\left(\tilde{x}_{e_j}^{n_k-1},\tilde{x}_{e_j}^{m_k},\tilde{t}\right)+S\left(\tilde{x}_{e_j}^{n_k-1},\tilde{x}_{e_j}^{m_k-1},\tilde{t}\right)$$

$$\left.+\left[\frac{S\left(\tilde{x}_{e_j}^{n_k},\tilde{x}_{e_j}^{m_k-1},\tilde{t}\right)+S\left(\tilde{x}_{e_j}^{n_k-1},\tilde{x}_{e_j}^{m_k},\tilde{t}\right)}{1+S\left(\tilde{x}_{e_j}^{n_k},\tilde{x}_{e_j}^{m_k-1},\tilde{t}\right).S\left(\tilde{x}_{e_j}^{n_k-1},\tilde{x}_{e_j}^{m_k},\tilde{t}\right)}\right]+S\left(\tilde{x}_{e_j}^{n_k-1},\tilde{x}_{e_j}^{n_k},\tilde{t}\right)\right)$$

$$-\psi\left(S\left(\tilde{x}_{e_j}^{n_k-1},\tilde{x}_{e_j}^{n_k},\tilde{t}\right)+S\left(\tilde{x}_{e_j}^{m_k-1},\tilde{x}_{e_j}^{m_k},\tilde{t}\right)\right.$$

$$+S\left(\tilde{x}_{e_j}^{n_k},\tilde{x}_{e_j}^{m_k-1},\tilde{t}\right)+S\left(\tilde{x}_{e_j}^{n_k-1},\tilde{x}_{e_j}^{m_k},\tilde{t}\right)+S\left(\tilde{x}_{e_j}^{n_k-1},\tilde{x}_{e_j}^{m_k-1},\tilde{t}\right)$$

$$\left.+\left[\frac{S\left(\tilde{x}_{e_j}^{n_k},\tilde{x}_{e_j}^{m_k-1},\tilde{t}\right)+S\left(\tilde{x}_{e_j}^{n_k-1},\tilde{x}_{e_j}^{m_k},\tilde{t}\right)}{1+S\left(\tilde{x}_{e_j}^{n_k},\tilde{x}_{e_j}^{m_k-1},\tilde{t}\right).S\left(\tilde{x}_{e_j}^{n_k-1},\tilde{x}_{e_j}^{m_k},\tilde{t}\right)}\right]+S\left(\tilde{x}_{e_j}^{n_k-1},\tilde{x}_{e_j}^{n_k},\tilde{t}\right)\right) \quad (15.16)$$

$$\tilde{\leq}\varphi\left(S\left(\tilde{x}_{e_j}^{n_k-1},\tilde{x}_{e_j}^{n_k},\tilde{t}\right)\right)+\varphi\left(S\left(\tilde{x}_{e_j}^{m_k-1},\tilde{x}_{e_j}^{m_k},\tilde{t}\right)\right)+\varphi\left(S\left(\tilde{x}_{e_j}^{n_k},\tilde{x}_{e_j}^{m_k-1},\tilde{t}\right)\right)$$

$$+\varphi\left(S\left(\tilde{x}_{e_j}^{n_k-1},\tilde{x}_{e_j}^{m_k},\tilde{t}\right)\right)+\varphi\left(S\left(\tilde{x}_{e_j}^{n_k-1},\tilde{x}_{e_j}^{m_k-1},\tilde{t}\right)\right)$$

$$+\varphi\left[\frac{S\left(\tilde{x}_{e_j}^{n_k},\tilde{x}_{e_j}^{m_k-1},\tilde{t}\right)+S\left(\tilde{x}_{e_j}^{n_k-1},\tilde{x}_{e_j}^{m_k},\tilde{t}\right)}{1+S\left(\tilde{x}_{e_j}^{n_k},\tilde{x}_{e_j}^{m_k-1},\tilde{t}\right).S\left(\tilde{x}_{e_j}^{n_k-1},\tilde{x}_{e_j}^{m_k},\tilde{t}\right)}\right]+\varphi\left(S\left(\tilde{x}_{e_j}^{n_k-1},\tilde{x}_{e_j}^{n_k},\tilde{t}\right)\right)$$

Then we get,

$$\varphi\left(S\left(\tilde{x}_{e_j}^{n_k},\tilde{x}_{e_j}^{m_k-1},\tilde{t}\right)\right)\tilde{\leq}\varphi\left(S\left(\tilde{x}_{e_j}^{n_k},\tilde{x}_{e_j}^{m_k},\tilde{t}\right)\right)+\varphi\left(S\left(\tilde{x}_{e_j}^{m_k},\tilde{x}_{e_j}^{m_k-1},\tilde{t}\right)\right) \quad (15.17)$$

And

$$\varphi\left(S\left(\tilde{x}_{e_j}^{n_k-1},\tilde{x}_{e_j}^{m_k-1},\tilde{t}\right)\right)\tilde{\leq}\varphi\left(S\left(\tilde{x}_{e_j}^{n_k-1},\tilde{x}_{e_j}^{n_k-1},\tilde{t}\right)\right)+\varphi\left(S\left(\tilde{x}_{e_j}^{n_k},\tilde{x}_{e_j}^{m_k-1},\tilde{t}\right)\right)$$

On applying the previous inequality, we get,

$$\varphi\left(S\left(\tilde{x}_{e_j}^{n_k-1},\tilde{x}_{e_j}^{m_k-1},\tilde{t}\right)\right)\tilde{\leq}\varphi\left(S\left(\tilde{x}_{e_j}^{n_k-1},\tilde{x}_{e_j}^{n_k},\tilde{t}\right)\right)+\varphi\left(S\left(\tilde{x}_{e_j}^{n_k},\tilde{x}_{e_j}^{m_k},\tilde{t}\right)\right)$$
$$+\varphi\left(S\left(\tilde{x}_{e_j}^{m_k},\tilde{x}_{e_j}^{m_k-1},\tilde{t}\right)\right) \tag{15.18}$$

Also using Equation (15.14) and (CF1) we obtained,

$$\varphi\left(S\left(\tilde{x}_{e_j}^{n_k-1},\tilde{x}_{e_j}^{m_k},\tilde{t}\right)\right)\tilde{\leq}\varphi(1-\tilde{\varepsilon}) \tag{15.19}$$

Now substituting Equations (15.17), (15.18) and (15.19) in Equation (15.16), we get,

$$\varphi\left(S\left(\tilde{x}_{e_j}^{n_k},\tilde{x}_{e_j}^{m_k},\tilde{t}\right)\right)$$
$$\tilde{\leq}\varphi\left(S\left(\tilde{x}_{e_j}^{n_k-1},\tilde{x}_{e_j}^{n_k},\tilde{t}\right)+S\left(\tilde{x}_{e_j}^{m_k-1},\tilde{x}_{e_j}^{m_k},\tilde{t}\right)+S\left(\tilde{x}_{e_j}^{n_k},\tilde{x}_{e_j}^{m_k},\tilde{t}\right)\right.$$
$$+S\left(\tilde{x}_{e_j}^{m_k},\tilde{x}_{e_j}^{m_k-1},\tilde{t}\right)+(1-\tilde{\varepsilon})+S\left(\tilde{x}_{e_j}^{n_k-1},\tilde{x}_{e_j}^{n_k},\tilde{t}\right)$$
$$+S\left(\tilde{x}_{e_j}^{n_k},\tilde{x}_{e_j}^{m_k},\tilde{t}\right)+S\left(\tilde{x}_{e_j}^{m_k},\tilde{x}_{e_j}^{m_k-1},\tilde{t}\right)$$
$$+\left[\frac{S\left(\tilde{x}_{e_j}^{n_k},\tilde{x}_{e_j}^{m_k},\tilde{t}\right).S\left(\tilde{x}_{e_j}^{m_k},\tilde{x}_{e_j}^{m_k-1},\tilde{t}\right).(1-\tilde{\varepsilon})}{1+S\left(\tilde{x}_{e_j}^{n_k},\tilde{x}_{e_j}^{m_k},\tilde{t}\right).S\left(\tilde{x}_{e_j}^{m_k},\tilde{x}_{e_j}^{m_k-1},\tilde{t}\right).(1-\tilde{\varepsilon})}\right]$$
$$+S\left(\tilde{x}_{e_j}^{n_k-1},\tilde{x}_{e_j}^{n_k},\tilde{t}\right)$$
$$-\psi\left(S\left(\tilde{x}_{e_j}^{n_k-1},\tilde{x}_{e_j}^{n_k},\tilde{t}\right)+S\left(\tilde{x}_{e_j}^{m_k-1},\tilde{x}_{e_j}^{m_k},\tilde{t}\right)+S\left(\tilde{x}_{e_j}^{n_k},\tilde{x}_{e_j}^{m_k},\tilde{t}\right)\right.$$
$$+S\left(\tilde{x}_{e_j}^{m_k},\tilde{x}_{e_j}^{m_k-1},\tilde{t}\right)+(1-\tilde{\varepsilon})+S\left(\tilde{x}_{e_j}^{n_k-1},\tilde{x}_{e_j}^{n_k},\tilde{t}\right)$$
$$+S\left(\tilde{x}_{e_j}^{n_k},\tilde{x}_{e_j}^{m_k},\tilde{t}\right)+S\left(\tilde{x}_{e_j}^{m_k},\tilde{x}_{e_j}^{m_k-1},\tilde{t}\right)$$
$$+\left[\frac{S\left(\tilde{x}_{e_j}^{n_k},\tilde{x}_{e_j}^{m_k},\tilde{t}\right).S\left(\tilde{x}_{e_j}^{m_k},\tilde{x}_{e_j}^{m_k-1},\tilde{t}\right)+(1-\tilde{\varepsilon})}{1+S\left(\tilde{x}_{e_j}^{n_k},\tilde{x}_{e_j}^{m_k},\tilde{t}\right).S\left(\tilde{x}_{e_j}^{m_k},\tilde{x}_{e_j}^{m_k-1},\tilde{t}\right).(1-\tilde{\varepsilon})}\right]$$
$$\left.+S\left(\tilde{x}_{e_j}^{n_k-1},\tilde{x}_{e_j}^{n_k},\tilde{t}\right)\right),$$

$$\varphi\left(S\left(\tilde{x}_{e_j}^{n_k},\tilde{x}_{e_j}^{m_k},\tilde{t}\right)\right.$$
$$\tilde{\leq}\varphi\left(S\left(\tilde{x}_{e_j}^{n_k-1},\tilde{x}_{e_j}^{n_k},\tilde{t}\right)+S\left(\tilde{x}_{e_j}^{m_k-1},\tilde{x}_{e_j}^{m_k},\tilde{t}\right)+S\left(\tilde{x}_{e_j}^{n_k},\tilde{x}_{e_j}^{m_k},\tilde{t}\right)\right.$$
$$+S\left(\tilde{x}_{e_j}^{m_k-1},\tilde{x}_{e_j}^{m_k-1},\tilde{t}\right)+(1-\tilde{\varepsilon})+S\left(\tilde{x}_{e_j}^{n_k-1},\tilde{x}_{e_j}^{n_k},\tilde{t}\right)$$
$$+S\left(\tilde{x}_{e_j}^{n_k},\tilde{x}_{e_j}^{m_k},\tilde{t}\right)+S\left(\tilde{x}_{e_j}^{m_k},\tilde{x}_{e_j}^{m_k-1},\tilde{t}\right)$$
$$+\left[\frac{S\left(\tilde{x}_{e_j}^{n_k},\tilde{x}_{e_j}^{m_k},\tilde{t}\right).S\left(\tilde{x}_{e_j}^{m_k},\tilde{x}_{e_j}^{m_k-1},\tilde{t}\right)+(1-\tilde{\varepsilon})}{1+S\left(\tilde{x}_{e_j}^{n_k},\tilde{x}_{e_j}^{m_k},\tilde{t}\right).S\left(\tilde{x}_{e_j}^{m_k},\tilde{x}_{e_j}^{m_k-1},\tilde{t}\right).(1-\tilde{\varepsilon})}\right]$$
$$\left.+S\left(\tilde{x}_{e_j}^{n_k-1},\tilde{x}_{e_j}^{n_k},\tilde{t}\right)\right)$$

$$\varphi\left(S\left(\tilde{x}_{e_j}^{n_k},\tilde{x}_{e_j}^{m_k},\tilde{t}\right)\right.$$
$$\tilde{\leq}\varphi\left(S\left(\tilde{x}_{e_j}^{n_k-1},\tilde{x}_{e_j}^{n_k},\tilde{t}\right)\right)+\varphi\left(S\left(\tilde{x}_{e_j}^{m_k},\tilde{x}_{e_j}^{m_k-1},\tilde{t}\right)\right)+\varphi(1-\tilde{\varepsilon})$$
$$+\varphi\left[\frac{S\left(\tilde{x}_{e_j}^{n_k},\tilde{x}_{e_j}^{m_k},\tilde{t}\right).S\left(\tilde{x}_{e_j}^{m_k},\tilde{x}_{e_j}^{m_k-1},\tilde{t}\right)+(1-\tilde{\varepsilon})}{1+S\left(\tilde{x}_{e_j}^{n_k},\tilde{x}_{e_j}^{m_k},\tilde{t}\right).S\left(\tilde{x}_{e_j}^{m_k},\tilde{x}_{e_j}^{m_k-1},\tilde{t}\right).(1-\tilde{\varepsilon})}\right] \tag{15.20}$$

Using Equation (15.13) we get,

$$\varphi\left(S\left(\tilde{x}_{e_j}^{n_k},\tilde{x}_{e_j}^{m_k},\tilde{t}\right)\right)\tilde{>}\varphi(1-\tilde{\varepsilon}) \tag{15.21}$$

So, Equation (15.20) becomes

$$\varphi(1-\tilde{\varepsilon})\tilde{\leq}\varphi\left(S\left(\tilde{x}_{e_j}^{n_k-1},\tilde{x}_{e_j}^{n_k},\tilde{t}\right)\right)+\varphi\left(S\left(\tilde{x}_{e_j}^{m_k},\tilde{x}_{e_j}^{m_k-1},\tilde{t}\right)\right)+\varphi(1-\tilde{\varepsilon})$$
$$+\varphi\left[\frac{(1-\tilde{\varepsilon}).S\left(\tilde{x}_{e_j}^{m_k},\tilde{x}_{e_j}^{m_k-1},\tilde{t}\right)+(1-\tilde{\varepsilon})}{1+(1-\tilde{\varepsilon}).S\left(\tilde{x}_{e_j}^{m_k},\tilde{x}_{e_j}^{m_k-1},\tilde{t}\right)+(1-\tilde{\varepsilon})}\right] \tag{15.22}$$

Taking $k\rightarrow\infty$ in above inequality, we obtain

$$\varphi(1-\tilde{\varepsilon})\tilde{\leq}\varphi(1-\tilde{\varepsilon})+\varphi\left[\frac{1+1}{1/(1-\tilde{\varepsilon})+(1-\tilde{\varepsilon})}\right] \tag{15.23}$$
$$\varphi(1-\tilde{\varepsilon})\tilde{\leq}\varphi(1-\tilde{\varepsilon})$$

that is $\varphi(1-\tilde{\varepsilon})\tilde{\leq}\overline{0}$,
which implies that $\tilde{\varepsilon}=0$ and we get contradiction, $\tilde{\varepsilon}\tilde{>}\overline{0}$.

Therefore $\{\tilde{x}^n_{e_j}\}$ is Cauchy's seq.

$\exists\,\tilde{v}_{e_j}\tilde{\in}\tilde{X}:\lim_{n\to\infty}\tilde{x}^n_{e_j}=\tilde{v}_{e_j}$ because X is taken to be complete

That is at $n\to\infty, S\left(\tilde{x}^n_{e_j},\tilde{v}_{e_j},\tilde{t}\right)=\overline{1}$.

Put $\tilde{x}_{e_j}=\tilde{x}^{n-1}_{e_j}$ and $\tilde{y}_{e_j}=\tilde{v}_{e_j}$ in equation (15.2), we obtain

$$\begin{aligned}
&\varphi\left(S\left(Q\tilde{x}^{n-1}_{e_j},Q\tilde{v}_{e_j},\tilde{t}\right)\right)\\
&\quad\tilde{\leq}\varphi\Bigg(S\left(\tilde{x}^{n-1}_{e_j},Q\tilde{x}^{n-1}_{e_j},\tilde{t}\right)+S\left(\tilde{v}_{e_j},Q\tilde{v}_{e_j},\tilde{t}\right)+1\\
&\quad S\left(Q\tilde{x}^{n-1}_{e_j},\tilde{v}_{e_j},\tilde{t}\right)+S\left(\tilde{x}^{n-1}_{e_j},Q\tilde{v}_{e_j},\tilde{t}\right)+S\left(\tilde{x}^{n-1}_{e_j},\tilde{v}_{e_j},\tilde{t}\right)\\
&\quad+\left[\frac{S\left(Q\tilde{x}^{n-1}_{e_j},\tilde{v}_{e_j},\tilde{t}\right)+S\left(\tilde{x}^{n-1}_{e_j},Q\tilde{v}_{e_j},\tilde{t}\right)}{1+S\left(Q\tilde{x}^{n-1}_{e_j},\tilde{v}_{e_j},\tilde{t}\right).S\left(\tilde{x}^{n-1}_{e_j},Q\tilde{v}_{e_j},\tilde{t}\right)}\right]+\\
&\quad\max\left\{S\left(\tilde{x}^{n-1}_{e_j},Q\tilde{x}^{n-1}_{e_j},\tilde{t}\right),S\left(\tilde{v}_{e_j},Q\tilde{v}_{e_j},\tilde{t}\right),\frac{\left[S\left(Q\tilde{x}^{n-1}_{e_j},\tilde{v}_{e_j},\tilde{t}\right)+S\left(\tilde{x}^{n-1}_{e_j},Q\tilde{v}_{e_j},\tilde{t}\right)\right]}{S\left(\tilde{x}^{n-1}_{e_j},\tilde{v}_{e_j},\tilde{t}\right)}\right\}\Bigg)
\end{aligned}$$

$$\begin{aligned}
&\varphi\left(S\left(\tilde{x}^{n}_{e_j},Q\tilde{v}_{e_j},\tilde{t}\right)\right)\\
&\quad\tilde{\leq}\varphi\Bigg(S\left(\tilde{x}^{n-1}_{e_j},\tilde{x}^{n}_{e_j},\tilde{t}\right)+S\left(\tilde{v}_{e_j},Q\tilde{v}_{e_j},\tilde{t}\right)+\\
&\quad S\left(\tilde{x}^{n}_{e_j},\tilde{v}_{e_j},\tilde{t}\right)+S\left(\tilde{x}^{n-1}_{e_j},Q\tilde{v}_{e_j},\tilde{t}\right)+S\left(\tilde{x}^{n-1}_{e_j},\tilde{v}_{e_j},\tilde{t}\right)\\
&\quad+\left[\frac{S\left(\tilde{x}^{n}_{e_j},\tilde{v}_{e_j},\tilde{t}\right)+S\left(\tilde{x}^{n-1}_{e_j},Q\tilde{v}_{e_j},\tilde{t}\right)}{1+S\left(\tilde{x}^{n}_{e_j},\tilde{v}_{e_j},\tilde{t}\right).S\left(\tilde{x}^{n-1}_{e_j},Q\tilde{v}_{e_j},\tilde{t}\right)}\right]+\\
&\quad\max\left\{S\left(\tilde{x}^{n-1}_{e_j},\tilde{x}^{n}_{e_j},\tilde{t}\right),S\left(\tilde{v}_{e_j},Q\tilde{v}_{e_j},\tilde{t}\right),\frac{\left[S\left(\tilde{x}^{n}_{e_j},\tilde{v}_{e_j},\tilde{t}\right)+S\left(\tilde{x}^{n-1}_{e_j},Q\tilde{v}_{e_j},\tilde{t}\right)\right]}{S\left(\tilde{x}^{n-1}_{e_j},\tilde{v}_{e_j},\tilde{t}\right)}\right\}\Bigg)
\end{aligned}\tag{15.24}$$

On taking limit $n\to\infty$ in Equation (15.24), we have

$$\varphi\left(S\left(\tilde{v}_{e_j},Q\tilde{v}_{e_j},\tilde{t}\right)\right)\tilde{\leq}\overline{0},\tilde{t}\tilde{>}\overline{0}\tag{15.25}$$

Therefore, $S\left(\tilde{v}_{e_j},Q\tilde{v}_{e_j},\tilde{t}\right)=1$ and $\tilde{v}_{e_j}=Q\tilde{v}_{e_j}$.

For **exclusivity,**

If t $\tilde{u}_{e_j}$ is another FP of Q, that is $Q\tilde{u}_{e_j} = \tilde{u}_{ej}$, where $\tilde{u}_{e_j} \neq \tilde{v}_{ej}$

$$\varphi\left(S\left(\tilde{v}_{e_j},\tilde{u}_{e_j},\tilde{t}\right)\right) \tilde{\leq} \overline{0}, \tilde{t} \tilde{>} \overline{0} \tag{15.26}$$

Hence $\tilde{u}_{e_j} = \tilde{v}_{e_j}$ is unique fixed point of Q.

Corollary 2: $\tilde{X}$ be a non-empty set. Let $(\tilde{X}, S, \tilde{*})$ be a complete strong soft fuzzy metric spaces with continuous soft t – norm $\tilde{*}$ and Q self-mapping in $\tilde{X}$. ∃ a control fun. $\varphi(\tilde{t})$:

$$\begin{aligned}\varphi\left(S\left(Q\tilde{x}_{e_j},Q\tilde{y}_{e_j},\tilde{t}\right)\right) &\tilde{\leq} \varphi\Big(S\left(\tilde{x}_{e_j},Q\tilde{x}_{e_j},\tilde{t}\right)+S\left(\tilde{y}_{e_j},Q\tilde{y}_{e_j},\tilde{t}\right)+\\ &S\left(Q\tilde{x}_{e_j},\tilde{y}_{e_j},\tilde{t}\right)+S\left(\tilde{x}_{e_j},Q\tilde{y}_{e_j},\tilde{t}\right)+S\left(\tilde{x}_{e_j},\tilde{y}_{e_j},\tilde{t}\right)\\ &+\left[\frac{S\left(Q\tilde{x}_{e_j},\tilde{y}_{e_j},\tilde{t}\right)+S\left(\tilde{x}_{e_j},Q\tilde{y}_{e_j},\tilde{t}\right)}{1+S\left(Q\tilde{x}_{e_j},\tilde{y}_{e_j},\tilde{t}\right).S\left(\tilde{x}_{e_j},Q\tilde{y}_{e_j},\tilde{t}\right)}\right]\\ &-\psi\Big(S\left(\tilde{x}_{e_j},Q\tilde{x}_{e_j},\tilde{t}\right)+S\left(\tilde{y}_{e_j},Q\tilde{y}_{e_j},\tilde{t}\right)\Big)+\\ &S\left(Q\tilde{x}_{e_j},\tilde{y}_{e_j},\tilde{t}\right)+S\left(\tilde{x}_{e_j},Q\tilde{y}_{e_j},\tilde{t}\right)+S\left(\tilde{x}_{e_j},\tilde{y}_{e_j},\tilde{t}\right)\\ &+\left[\frac{S\left(Q\tilde{x}_{e_j},\tilde{y}_{e_j},\tilde{t}\right)+S\left(\tilde{x}_{e_j},Q\tilde{y}_{e_j},\tilde{t}\right)}{1+S\left(Q\tilde{x}_{e_j},\tilde{y}_{e_j},\tilde{t}\right).S\left(\tilde{x}_{e_j},Q\tilde{y}_{e_j},\tilde{t}\right)}\right]\end{aligned} \tag{15.27}$$

Then Q has a unique fixed point in $\tilde{X}$.

Proof: The proof of the above theorem (15.2) considering soft fuzzy contraction on the soft fuzzy metric space $(\tilde{X}, S, \tilde{*})$,

$$\begin{aligned}\varphi\left(S\left(Q\tilde{x}_{e_j},Q\tilde{y}_{e_j},\tilde{t}\right)\right) &\tilde{\leq} \varphi\Big(S\left(\tilde{x}_{e_j},Q\tilde{x}_{e_j},\tilde{t}\right)+S\left(\tilde{y}_{e_j},Q\tilde{y}_{e_j},\tilde{t}\right)\\ &+S\left(Q\tilde{x}_{e_j},\tilde{y}_{e_j},\tilde{t}\right)+S\left(\tilde{x}_{e_j},Q\tilde{y}_{e_j},\tilde{t}\right)+S\left(\tilde{x}_{e_j},\tilde{y}_{e_j},\tilde{t}\right)\end{aligned}$$

$$+\left[\frac{S\left(Q\tilde{x}_{e_j},\tilde{y}_{e_j},\tilde{t}\right)+S\left(\tilde{x}_{e_j},Q\tilde{y}_{e_j},\tilde{t}\right)}{1+S\left(Q\tilde{x}_{e_j},\tilde{y}_{e_j},\tilde{t}\right).S\left(\tilde{x}_{e_j},Q\tilde{y}_{e_j},\tilde{t}\right)}\right]$$

$$-\psi\left(S\left(\tilde{x}_{e_j},Q\tilde{x}_{e_j},\tilde{t}\right)+S\left(\tilde{y}_{e_j},Q\tilde{y}_{e_j},\tilde{t}\right)\right)$$

$$+S\left(Q\tilde{x}_{e_j},\tilde{y}_{e_j},\tilde{t}\right)+S\left(\tilde{x}_{e_j},Q\tilde{y}_{e_j},\tilde{t}\right)+S\left(\tilde{x}_{e_j},\tilde{y}_{e_j},\tilde{t}\right)$$

$$+\left[\frac{S\left(Q\tilde{x}_{e_j},\tilde{y}_{e_j},\tilde{t}\right)+S\left(\tilde{x}_{e_j},Q\tilde{y}_{e_j},\tilde{t}\right)}{1+S\left(Q\tilde{x}_{e_j},\tilde{y}_{e_j},\tilde{t}\right).S\left(\tilde{x}_{e_j},Q\tilde{y}_{e_j},\tilde{t}\right)}\right].$$

15.4 Conclusion

In this chapter, the investigations concerning the uniqueness theorem for weak contraction type mapping in soft fuzzy metric space by using control function are established. It concluded that the fixed point results can be generalized not only for fuzzy metric spaces but also can be for specified spaces which can be obtained using the concept of soft sets and fuzzy sets both. The obtained results can be generalized for different mapping by taking specified conditions. Obviously, the present investigation enriches our knowledge of fixed point theorems in soft fuzzy metric spaces. There are many scopes for further research on soft fuzzy metric spaces.

References

1. Aage, C.T., Choudhury, B.S., Das, K., Some fixed point results in fuzzy metric spaces using control function. *Surv. Math. Appl.*, 12, 23–34, 2017.
2. Alar, R., Yigit, E., Erduran, F.S., Gezici, A., On Soft Fuzzy Metric spaces and Topological structure. *J. Adv. Stud. Topol.*, 9, 1, 61–70, 2018.
3. Amit, K. and Ramesh, K.V., Common fixed point theorem in fuzzy metric space using control function. *Commun. Korean Math. Soc.*, 28, 517–526, 2013.
4. Bealua, T. and Gunaseeli, C., On fuzzy soft metric spaces. *Malaya J. Math.*, 2, 3, 197–202, 2014.
5. Das, S. and Samanta, S.K., On soft metric spaces. *J. Fuzzy Math.*, 21, 3, 707–734, 2013.

6. Das, S. and Samanta, S.K., Soft metric. *Ann. Fuzzy Math. Inform.*, 6, 1, 77–94, 2013.
7. George, A. and Veeramani, P., On some results in fuzzy metric spaces. *Fuzzy Sets Syst.*, 64, 395–399, 1994.
8. George, A. and Veeramani, P., On some results of analysis for fuzzy metric spaces. *Fuzzy Sets Syst.*, 90, 365–399, 1997.
9. Gezici, A., Alar, R., Erduran, F.S., Yigit, E., Soft fuzzy metric spaces. *Gen. Lett. Math.*, 3, 2, 91–101, 2017.
10. Grabiec, M., Fixed points in fuzzy metric spaces. *Fuzzy Sets Syst.*, 27, 385–389, 1988.
11. Heilpern, S., Fuzzy mapping and Fixed point theorem. *J. Math. Appl.*, 83, 566–569, 1981.
12. Khan, M.S., Swaleh, M., Sessa, S., Fixed point theorems by altering distance between the points. *Bull. Aust. Math. Soc.*, 30, 1–9, 1984.
13. Kramosil, J. and Michalek, J., Fuzzy metric and Statistical metric spaces. *Kybernetica*, 11, 326–334, 1975.
14. Krishnakumar, R., Dinesh, K., Dhamodharan, D., Some Fixed point theorems in φ ψ weak Contraction on Fuzzy Metric Space. *Int. J. Sci. Res. Math. Stat. Sci.*, 5, 146–152, 2018.
15. Molodtsov, D., Soft set theory—first results. *Comput. Math. Appl.*, 37, 4–5, 19–31, 1999.
16. Roy, A., Maji, P.K., Biswas, R., An application of soft sets in a decision making problem. *Comput. Math. Appl.*, 44, 1077–1083, 2002.
17. Roy, A., Maji, P.K., Biswas, R., Soft set theory. *Comput. Math. Appl.*, 45, 4–5, 555–562, 2003.
18. Shen, Y., Qiu, D., Chen, W., Fixed point theorems in fuzzy metric spaces. *Appl. Math. Lett.*, 25, 138–141, 2012.
19. Zadeh, L.A., Fuzzy sets. *Inf. Control*, 8, 338–353, 1965.

16

On Soft $\alpha_{(\gamma,\beta)}$-Continuous Functions in Soft Topological Spaces

N. Kalaivani*, **E. Chandrasekaran**† **and K. Fayaz Ur Rahman**‡

Department of Mathematics, Vel Tech Rangarajan Dr. Sagunthala R&D Institute of Science and Technology, Chennai, Tamil Nadu, India

Abstract

In this paper the concept of soft $\alpha_{(\gamma,\beta)}$-continuous functions in soft topological spaces has been introduced and discussed. Further, the soft $\alpha_{(\gamma,\beta)}$-open functions, soft $\alpha_{(\gamma,\beta)}$-closed functions, and soft $\alpha_{(\gamma,\beta)}$-homeomorphisms have been introduced and analyzed. Also, the idea of soft $\alpha_{(\gamma,\beta)}$-contra continuous functions, soft (α_γ,β_s)-contra continuous functions are introduced and analyzed. Further, the relationship and among soft $\alpha_{(\gamma,\beta)}$-contra continuous functions with other forms of continuous functions, and soft $\alpha_{(\gamma,\beta)}$-open functions, soft $\alpha_{(\gamma,\beta)}$-closed functions with another forms of, open, closed functions, soft $\alpha_{(\gamma,\beta)}$-contra continuous functions with other forms of contra continuous functions has been detailed.

Keywords: Soft α_γ-open set, soft α_γ-closed set, soft $\alpha_{(\gamma,\beta)}$-continuous functions, soft $\alpha_{(\gamma,\beta)}$-open functions, soft $\alpha_{(\gamma,\beta)}$-closed functions, soft $\alpha_{(\gamma,\beta)}$-homeomorphisms, soft $\alpha_{(\gamma,\beta)}$-contra continuous functions, soft (α_γ,β_s)-contra continuous functions

**Corresponding author*: kalaivani.rajam@gmail.com
†*Corresponding author*: e_chandrasekaran@yahoo.com
‡*Corresponding author*: fiyazurrahman@veltech.edu.in

E. Chandrasekaran, R. Anandan, G. Suseendran, S. Balamurugan and Hanaa Hachimi (eds.) Fuzzy Intelligent Systems: Methodologies, Techniques, and Applications, (431–460) © 2021 Scrivener Publishing LLC

16.1 Introduction

Soft set theory, which is a generalization of fuzzy set theory, was created by Molodtsov [10] as a general mathematical tool for dealing with ambiguous fuzzy, not clearly defined objects. Maji *et al.* [8, 9], D. Chen *et al.* [3, 4], Kong *et al.* [7], Xiao *et al.* [15], and Pei and Miao [11] subsidized many thoughts to the soft set theory and applications.

Shabir and Naz [12] familiarized the concept of soft sets over an initial universe with a fixed set of parameters. They also deliberated some of the basic concepts of soft topological spaces. Aygünoğlu *et al.* [1], Zorlutuna *et al.* [16], Sabir Hussain [13], and Ahmad [14] contemplated the properties of soft topological spaces. N. Kalaivani *et al.* [6] launched γ-operations in soft topological spaces and soft α_γ-open sets in soft topological spaces and deliberated their properties. Further, the thought of soft (α_γ, β)-continuous functions in soft topological spaces was presented by N. Kalaivani.

The soft set, null soft set, union, intersection, complement of soft sets, soft open sets, soft closed sets, soft interior, soft closure, and soft topology are discussed by Bin Chen [2], Degang Chen [4], Feng Feng [5], Zhi Kong [8], and P.K. Maji [9] respectively.

16.2 Preliminaries

16.2.1 Outline

In this chapter, the idea of $\tau_{s(\alpha_\gamma)}$, which is the gathering of all soft α_γ-open sets in a soft topological space (X_s, τ_s, E_s), is introduced. Further, the concepts of soft $\tau_{s(\alpha_\gamma)}$ interior and soft $\tau_{s(\alpha_\gamma)}$ closure operators are familiarized and certain properties are deliberated. Also, soft α_γ T_i spaces $\left(i = 0, \frac{1}{2} 1, 2\right)$ are characterized using the thought of soft α_γ-closed sets or soft α_γ-open sets and the relationship between them is investigated.

Throughout this chapter, let X_s denote the topological space (X_s, τ_s, E_s) and $\gamma_s{:}\tau_s \rightarrow P(X_s)$ be an operation on τ_s.

16.2.2 Soft α_γ-Open Set

In this section, the idea of $\tau_{s(\alpha_\gamma)}$-the group of all soft α_γ-open sets in a soft topological space (X_s, τ_s, E_s) is elaborated. Further, we launch the concept of $\tau_{s(\alpha_\gamma)}$-interior and $\tau_{s(\alpha_\gamma)}$-closure operators and review some of their properties.

Definition 2.2.1. A (G, E_s) in a soft topological space (X_s, τ_s, E_s) is assumed to be a soft α_γ-open set if and only if $(G,E_s)\tilde{\subseteq} int_{\tau s\gamma}(cl_{\tau s\gamma}(int_{\tau s\gamma}(G,E_s)))$

Theorem 2.2.1. Every soft γ_s-open set in a soft topological space (X_s, τ_s, E_s) is a soft α_γ-open set. However, the reverse need not be true.

Theorem 2.2.2. Let (X_s, τ_s, E_s) be a soft topological space besides and $\{(A\kappa, E_s):\kappa \in J\}$ be the tribe of soft α_γ-open sets in (X_s, τ_s, E_s). Formerly $\tilde{\cup}_{\kappa\in J}(A\kappa,E_s)$ is also a soft α_γ-open set.

Definition 2.2.2. Let (X_s, τ_s, E_s) be a soft topological space and (P, E_s) be a soft subset of X_s. (P, E_s) is said to be soft α_γ-closed set if and only if $X_s-(P, E_s)$ is a soft α_γ-open set.

Remark 2.2.1. Let (X_s, τ_s, E_s) be a soft topological space and γ_s be an action on τ_s. If (P, E_s), (Q, E_s) are any two soft α_γ -open sets in (X_s, τ_s, E_s), then the following example shows that $(P,E_s)\tilde{\cap}(Q,E_s)$ need not be a soft α_γ-open set.

Remark 2.2.2. Let (X_s, τ_s, E_s) be a soft topological space and also γ_s be an action on τ_s. Then the concepts of soft α-open set and soft α_γ-open sets are independent.

Remark 2.2.3. Let (X_s, τ_s, E_s) be a soft topological space and also γ_s be an action on τ_s. Then the concepts of soft α-open set and soft α_γ-open sets are independent.

Definition 2.2.3. A member (M, E_s) of X_s is forenamed to be a soft α_γ-closed set contingent upon X_s—(M, E_s) is a soft α_γ-open set, which is equivalently explained as: Let (X_s, τ_s, E_s) be a soft topological space and γ_s a labor on τ_s and also (M, E_s) be a member of X_s. Then (M, E_s) is a soft α_γ-closed set in the case that $(M,E_s)\tilde{\subseteq} cl_{\tau s\gamma}(int_{\tau s\gamma}(cl_{\tau s\gamma}(M,E_s)))$.

Definition 2.2.4. Let (X_s, τ_s, E_s) be a soft topological space and (Q, E_s) be a soft subset of (X_s, τ_s, E_s). Then the soft interior of (Q, E_s) is the amalgamation of all soft α_γ-OSs contained in (Q, E_s) and it is denoted by $int_A\tau_{s(\alpha_\gamma)}(Q,E_s)$.

That is $int_A\tau_{s(\alpha_\gamma)}(Q,E_s)=\tilde{\cup}\{(U,E_s):(U,E_s)$ is a soft α_γ-open set and $(U,E_s)\tilde{\subseteq}(Q,E_s)\}$.

Remark 2.2.4. Let (X_s, τ_s, E_s) be a soft topological space. Let (C, E_s),(D, E_s) be a soft subsets of (X_s, τ_s, E_s). Then the subsequent declarations hold good:

(i) $int_A\tau_{s(\alpha_\gamma)}(G,E_s)$ is the prevalent soft α_γ-open subset of (X_s, τ_s, E_s) enclosed in (G, E_s).
(ii) (H, E_s) is a soft α_γ-open set contingent upon $int_A\tau_{s(\alpha_\gamma)}(H,E_s)=(H,E_s)$
(iii) $int_A\tau_{s(\alpha_\gamma)}int_A\tau_{s(\alpha_\gamma)}(G,E_s)=int_A\tau_{s(\alpha_\gamma)}(G,E_s)$
(iv) If $(P,E_s)\tilde{\subseteq}(Q,E_s)$ then $int_A\tau_{s(\alpha_\gamma)}(P,E_s)\tilde{\subseteq} int_A\tau_{s(\alpha_\gamma)}(Q,E_s)$
(v) $int_A\tau_{s(\alpha_\gamma)}(G,E_s)\tilde{\cup} int_A\tau_{s(\alpha_\gamma)}(H,E_s)\tilde{\subseteq} int_A\tau_{s(\alpha_\gamma)}int_A\tau_{s(\alpha_\gamma)}$ $((G,E_s)\tilde{\cup}(H,E_s))$

Definition 2.2.5. Let (X_s, τ_s, E_s) be a soft topological space as well as (M, E_s) be a soft subset of (X_s, τ_s, E_s). Then $\tau_{s(\alpha_\gamma)}$-closure of (M, E_s) is the intersection of the entire soft α_γ-closed sets encompassing (M, E_s). Besides it is designated by $cl_A\tau_{s(\alpha_\gamma)}(M,E_s)$.

That is, $cl_A\tau_{s(\alpha_\gamma)}(M,E_s)=\tilde{\cap}\{(G,E_s): (G,E_s)$ is a soft α_γ-closed set and $(M,E_s)\tilde{\subseteq}(G,E_s)\}$.

Remark 2.2.5. (i) If (M, E_s) is a subset of (X_s, τ_s, E_s), then $cl_A\tau_{s(\alpha_\gamma)}(M,E_s)$ is a soft α_γ- closed set containing (M, E_s)

(ii) (M, E_s) is a soft α_γ-closed set if and only if $cl_A\tau_{s(\alpha_\gamma)}(M,E_s)=(M,E_s)$.

Theorem 2.2.3. Let (M, E_s) and (N, E_s) be soft subsets of (X_s, τ_s, E_s). Then the subsequent statements hold:

(i) $cl_A\tau_{s(\alpha_\gamma)}cl_A\tau_{s(\alpha_\gamma)}(M,E_s))=cl_A\tau_{s(\alpha_\gamma)}(M,E_s)$
(ii) If $(M,E_s)\tilde{\subseteq}(N,E_s)$, then $cl_A\tau_{s(\alpha_\gamma)}(M,E_s)\tilde{\subseteq} cl_A\tau_{s(\alpha_\gamma)}(N,E_s)$
(iii) $cl_A\tau_{s(\alpha_\gamma)}(M,E_s)\tilde{\cup} cl_A\tau_{s(\alpha_\gamma)}(N,E_s)\tilde{\subseteq} cl_A\tau_{s(\alpha_\gamma)}((M,E_s)\tilde{\cup}(N,E_s))$
(iv) $cl_A\tau_{s(\alpha_\gamma)}((M,E_s)\tilde{\cap}(N,E_s))\tilde{\subseteq} cl_A\tau_{s(\alpha_\gamma)}(M,E_s)\tilde{\cap} cl_A\tau_{s(\alpha_\gamma)}(N,E_s)$

Theorem 2.2.4. Let (X_s, τ_s, E_s) be a soft topological space. Then for a point $u\in X_s, u\in cl_A\tau_{s(\alpha_\gamma)}(M,E_s)$ if and only if $(P,E_s)\tilde{\cap}(M,E_s)=\emptyset$ for any $(P,E_s)\in\tau_{s(\alpha_\gamma)}$ such that $u\in(P, E_s)$.

Theorem 2.2.5. Let (X_s, τ_s, E_s) be an STS and $(M,E_s)\tilde{\subseteq} X_s$. Then the following statements hold:

(i) $int_A\tau_{s(\alpha_\gamma)}(X_s-(M,E_s))=X_s-cl_A\tau_{s(\alpha_\gamma)}(M,E_s)$
(ii) $cl_A\tau_{s(\alpha_\gamma)}(X_s-(M,E_s))=X_s-int_A\tau_{s(\alpha_\gamma)}(M,E_s)$

16.2.3 Soft α_γ T_i Spaces

In this chapter, we investigate soft α_γ Ti spaces where i = 0, 1/2, 1, 2.

Definition 2.3.1. A soft topological space (X_s, τ_s, E_s) is entitled a soft α_γ T_0 space if for each different point p, $q \in X_s$ nearby occurs a soft α_γ-open set, (P, E_s) corresponding that p $\in$ (P, E_s) and $q \notin (P, E_s)$ or $q \in (P, E_s)$ and $p \notin (P, E_s)$.

Definition 2.3.2. A soft topological space (X_s, τ_s, E_s) is termed a soft α_γ T_1 space if for each dissimilar point p, $q \in X_s$ nearby exists soft α_γ-open sets, (P, E_s),(Q, E_s) containing p and q, respectively, such that $q \notin (P, E_s)$ and $p \notin (Q, E_s)$.

Definition 2.3.3. A soft topological space (X_s, τ_s, E_s) is described a soft α_γ T_2 space if for each distinctive point p, $q \in X_s$ nearby exists soft α_γ-open sets, (P, E_s),(Q, E_s) such that $p \in (P, E_s)$, $q \in (Q, E_s)$ and $(P,E_s)\tilde{\cap}(Q,E_s)=\varnothing$.

Definition 2.3.4. Let (X_s, τ_s, E_s) be a soft topological space. Then a soft subset (M, E_s) of X_s is said to be soft α_γg-closed set if $cl_A\tau_{s(\alpha_\gamma)}(M,E_s)\tilde{\subseteq}(P,E_s)$ whenever $(M,E_s)\tilde{\subseteq}(P,E_s)$ and (P, E_s) is a soft α_γ-open set in (X_s, τ_s, E_s).

Remark 2.3.1. From Definition 4.4, every soft α_γ-closed set in (X_s, τ_s, E_s) is a soft α_γg-closed set. However, the contrary need not be proper.

Definition 2.3.5. A soft topological space (X_s, τ_s, E_s) is termed as a soft $\alpha_\gamma T_{1/2}$ space if every soft α_γg-closed set in (X_s, τ_s, E_s) is a soft α_γ-closed set.

Theorem 2.3.1. Let (X_s, τ_s, E_s) be a soft topological space. Then a member (M, E_s) of X_s is supposed to be a soft α_γg-closed set if and only if $\tau_{s(\alpha_\gamma)}(\{m\})\tilde{\cap}(M,E_s)=\varnothing$ holds for every $m \in cl_A\tau_{s(\alpha_\gamma)}(M,E_s)$.

Theorem 2.3.2. Let (X_s, τ_s, E_s) be a soft topological space. If a soft subset of (M, E_s) of X_s is assumed to be a soft α_γg-closed set, then $cl_A\tau_{s(\alpha_\gamma)}(M,E_s)-(P,E_s)$ does not contain a non-empty soft α_γ-closed set.

Theorem 2.3.3. Let (X_s, τ_s, E_s) be a soft topological space. Then for each m $\in X_s$, {m} is a soft α_γ-closed set or X_s – {m} is a soft α_γg-closed set in (X_s, τ_s, E_s).

Theorem 2.3.4. A soft topological space (X_s, τ_s, E_s) is a soft $\alpha_\gamma T_2$ space given for every $m \in X_s$, $\{m\}$ is a soft α_γ-closed set or a soft α_γ-open set in (X_s, τ_s, E_s).

Theorem 2.3.5. A soft topological space (X_s, τ_s, E_s) is a soft α_γ T_1 space in the event for every $m \in X_s$, $\{m\}$ is a soft α_γ-closed set.

16.2.4 Soft (α_γ, β_s)-Continuous Functions

Definition 2.4.1. A function $f_M:(X_s, \tau_s, E_s) \to (Y_s, \sigma_s, K_s)$ is supposed to be a soft (α_γ, β_s)-continuous function if the inverse image of every soft β_s-open set in (Y_s, σ_s, K_s) is a soft α_γ-open set in (X_s, τ_s, E_s).

Definition 2.4.2. A function $f_M:(X_s, \tau_s, E_s) \to (Y_s, \sigma_s, K_s)$ is aforesaid to be a soft (γ_s, β_s)-continuous function if the inverse image of every soft β_s-open set in (Y_s, σ_s, K_s) is a soft γ_s-open set in (X_s, τ_s, E_s).

Theorem 2.4.1. For a function $f_M:(X_s, \tau_s, E_s) \to (Y_s, \sigma_s, K_s)$, the following descriptions are commensurate:

(i) f_M is a soft (α_γ, β_s)-continuous function;
(ii) For any point g in X_s and various soft β_s-open set V in Y_s alike that $f_M(g) \in V$, there occurs a soft α_γ-open set W in X_s aforesaid that $g \in W$, $f_M(W) \tilde{\subseteq} V$;
(iii) The inverse image of each soft β_s-closed set in Y_s is a soft α_γ-closed set in X_s.

Theorem 2.4.2. Let $f_M:(X_s, \tau_s, E_s) \to (Y_s, \sigma_s, K_s)$ be a function and $\beta_s : \sigma_s \to P(Y_s)$ be an open maneuver on σ_s. Formerly the consecutive comments are comparable:

(i) f_M is a soft (α_γ, β_s)- continuous function;
(ii) $\tau_{s\gamma}$-cl$(\tau_{s\gamma}$-int$(\tau_{s\gamma}$-cl$(f_M^{-1}(B)))) \tilde{\subseteq} f_M^{-1}\sigma_{s\beta}$-cl$(B))$ for each $B \subseteq Y_s$;
(iii) $f_M(\tau_{s\gamma}$-cl$(\tau_{s\gamma}$-int$(\tau_{s\gamma}$-cl$(A)))) \tilde{\subseteq} \sigma_{s\beta}$-cl$(f_M(A))$ for each $A \subseteq X_s$

Theorem 2.4.3. For a function $f_M:(X_s, \tau_s, E_s) \to (Y_s, \sigma_s, K_s)$, the following affidavits are proportionate:

(i) f_M is a soft (α_γ, β_s)-continuous function;
(ii) For each member P of X_s, $f_M(\tau_{s\alpha_\gamma}$-cl$(P))) \tilde{\subseteq} \sigma_{s\beta}$-cl$(f_M(P))$;
(iii)For each member B of Y_s, $\tau_{s\alpha_\gamma}$-cl$(f_M^{-1}(B)) \tilde{\subseteq} f_M^{-1}(\sigma_{s\beta}$-cl$(B))$;
(iv) For each member C of Y_s, $f_M^{-1}(\sigma_{s\beta}$-int$(C)) \tilde{\subseteq} \tau_{s\alpha_\gamma}$-int$(f_M^{-1}(C))$.

Remark 2.4.1. Every soft (γ_s, β_s)-irresolute function is a soft (α_γ, β_s)-continuous function. Nevertheless, the contrary need not be factual.

Definition 2.4.3. A function f_M:(X_s, τ_s, E_s) → (Y_s, σ_s, K_s) is held to be a soft (γ_s, α_β)-open (closed) function if the image of each soft β_s-open (closed) set in X_s is a soft α_β-open (closed) set in Y_s.

Definition 2.4.4. A function f_M:(X_s, τ_s, E_s) → (Y_s, σ_s, K_s) is held to be a soft (γ_s, β_s)-irresolute function if $f_M^{-1}(P)$ is a soft γ_s-open set in X_s for each β_s-open set P in Y_s.

Definition 2.4.5. A function f_M:(X_s, τ_s, E_s) → (Y_s, σ_s, K_s) is held to be a soft (γ_s, β_s)-contra irresolute function if $f_M^{-1}(P)$ is a soft γ_s-open set in X_s for each β_s-closed set P in Y_s.

Theorem 2.4.4. A function f_M:(X_s, τ_s, E_s) → (Y_s, σ_s, K_s) is a soft (γ_s, α_β)-open function on the condition that to respective $d \in X_s$ and all soft γ_s-neighborhood U of d, there occurs a soft α_β- open set V of Y_s encompassing $f_M(d)$ like that $V \tilde{\subseteq} f_M(U)$.

Theorem 2.4.5. A function f_M:(X_s, τ_s, E_s) → (Y_s, σ_s, K_s) is a soft (γ_s, α_β)-open function in case that for each subset $W \tilde{\subseteq} Y_s$ and each soft γ_s-closed set F of X_s containing $f_M^{-1}(W)$, there exists a soft α_β-closed set H of Y_s containing W such that $f_M^{-1}(H) \tilde{\subseteq} F$.

Theorem 2.4.6. If a function f_M:(X_s, τ_s, E_s) → (Y_s, σ_s, K_s) is a soft (γ_s, α_β)-open function and $\gamma_s : \tau_s \to P(X_s)$ is an open maneuver on τ_s, then the ensuing properties hold:

(i) $f_M^{-1}(\sigma_{s\beta}\text{-cl}(\sigma_{s\beta}\text{-int}(\sigma_{s\beta}\text{-cl}(P)))) \tilde{\subseteq} \tau_{s\gamma}\text{-cl}(f_M^{-1}(P))$ for each set $P \subseteq Y_s$;
(ii) $f_M^{-1}(\sigma_{s\beta}\text{-cl}(Q) \tilde{\subseteq} \tau_{s\gamma}\text{-cl}(f_M^{-1}(Q))$ for each soft α_β-open set Q of Y_s.

Theorem 2.4.7. Suppose f_M:(X_s, τ_s, E_s) → (Y_s, σ_s, K_s) is a soft (γ_s, α_β)-open function and $\gamma_s : \tau_s \to P(X_s)$ is an open maneuver on τ_s. Then the following conditions are comparable:

(i) f_M is a soft (γ_s, α_β)-open function.
(ii) $f_M(\tau_{s\gamma}\text{-int}(A)) \tilde{\subseteq} \sigma_{s\alpha_\beta}\text{-int}(f_M(A))$ for $A \tilde{\subseteq} X_s$;
(iii) $\tau_{s\gamma}\text{-int}(f_M^{-1}(B)) \tilde{\subseteq} f_M^{-1}(\sigma_{s\alpha_\beta}\text{-int}(B))$ for $B \tilde{\subseteq} Y_s$.

Theorem 2.4.8. For any bijective function f_M:(X_s, τ_s, E_s) → (Y_s, σ_s, K_s), the succeeding conditions correspond:

(i) $f_M^{-1}:(Y_s,\sigma_s,K_s)\rightarrow(X_s,\tau_s,E_s)$ is a soft (γ_s, α_β)-continuous function;
(ii) f_M is a soft (γ_s, α_β)-open function;
(iii) f_M is a soft (γ_s, α_β)-closed function.

16.3 Soft $\alpha_{(\gamma,\beta)}$-Continuous Functions in Soft Topological Spaces

16.3.1 Outline

In this episode, the thought of soft $\alpha_{(\gamma,\beta)}$-continuous functions is presented and few of their basic qualities are studied. Further, the idea soft $\alpha_{(\gamma,\beta)}$-open (closed) functions is familiarized and examined.

Further, the perception of soft (α_γ, β_s)-contra continuous functions is presented; in addition, few of their attributes are deliberated. As well soft $\alpha_{(\gamma,\beta)}$- contra continuous functions in soft topological spaces are announced besides evaluating their attributes.

In this section, X_s, Y_s denote the soft topological spaces, (X_s, τ_s, E_s), (Y_s, τ_s, E_s), f_{Ma} denotes a function $f_{Ma}:(X_s, \tau_s, E_s) \rightarrow (Y_s, \tau_s, K_s)$, and $\gamma_s:\tau_s \rightarrow P(X_s)$ and $\beta_s:\sigma_s \rightarrow P(Y_s)$ are operations on τ_s and σ_s, respectively.

16.3.2 Soft $\alpha_{(\gamma,\beta)}$-Continuous Functions

Definition 3.2.1. A function $f_{Ma}:(X_s, \tau_s, E_s) \rightarrow (Y_s, \sigma_s, K_s)$ is said to be a soft $\alpha_{(\gamma,\beta)}$-continuous function given for each soft α_β- open set U of Y_s, the contrary image $f_{Ma}^{-1}(U)$ is a soft α_γ - open set in X_s.

Example 3.2.1. Given $X_s = \{a_1, a_2, a_3\}$, $E_s = \{e_1, e_2\}$, $\tau_s = \{\emptyset, X_s, (F_1, E_s), (F_2, E_s), (F_3, E_s), (F_4, E_s)\}$ where $(F_1, E_s),\ldots(F_4, E_s)$ are soft sets over X_s, which are defined as follows:

$(F_1, E_s) = \{(e_1, a_1), (e_2, a_1)\}$, $(F_2, E_s) = \{(e_1, a_3), (e_2, a_3)\}$, $(F_3, E_s) = \{(e_1, a_1, a_2), (e_2, a_1, a_2)\}$ and $(F_4, E_s) = \{(e_1, a_1, a_3), (e_2, a_1, a_3)\}$

Define γ_s on τ_s such that

$$(M,E_s)\gamma_s=\begin{cases}(M,E_s)\ if\ (M,E_s)=(F_1,E_s)\\(M,E_s)\tilde{\cup}(F_2,E_s)\ if\ (M,E_s)\neq(F_1,E_s)\end{cases}\quad \text{for every}\,(M,E_s)\in\tau_s.$$

Then $\tau_{s\alpha_\gamma}=\{\emptyset,X_s,(F_1,E_s),(F_2,E_s),(F_4,E_s)\}$

Let $Y_s = \{b_1, b_2, b_3\}$, $K_s = \{h_1, h_2\}$, $\sigma_s = \{\emptyset, Y_s, (G_1, K_s), (G_2, K_s), (G_3, K_s), (G_4, K_s))\}$ where $(G_1, K_s),\ldots(G_4, K_s)$ are soft sets over Y_s, defined as follows:

$(G_1, K_s) = \{(h, b_1), (h_2, b_1), (G_2, K_s) = \{(h_1, b_3), (h_2, b_3), (G_3, K_s) = \{(h_1, b_1, b_2), (h_2, b_1, b_2)\}, (G_4, K_s) = \{\{(h_1, b_1, b_3), (h_2, b_1, b_3)\}\}\}$

Define an operation β_s on σ_s such that

$$(P,K_s)\beta_s = \begin{cases} (P,K_s)\, if\ (P,E_s)=(G_1,K_s) \\ (P,K_s)\tilde{\cup}(G_2,K_s)\, if\ (P,E_s)\neq(G_1,K_s) \end{cases} \quad \text{for every } (P,K_s)\in\sigma_s.$$

for every $(P, K_s) \in \sigma_s$. Then $\sigma_{s\alpha\beta} = \{\varnothing, Y_s, (G_1,K_s), (G_2,K_s), (G_4,K_s))\}$.

Define $f_{Ma}: X_s \to Y_s$ as $f_{Ma}(a_1) = b_1, f_{Ma}(a_2) = b_2$ and $f_{Ma}(a_3) = b_3$ and $p_{Ma}: E_s \to K_s$ as $p_{Ma}(e_1) = h_1$, $p_{Ma}(e_2) = h_2$. Then the inverted image of exclusive soft α_β-open set is a soft α_γ- open set underneath f_{Ma}. Hence, f_{Ma} is a soft $\alpha_{(\gamma,\beta)}$-continuous function.

The subsequent Remark 3.2.1 and Remark 3.2.2 display that the thought of soft $\alpha_{(\gamma,\beta)}$-continuous functions and soft (γ_s, β_s)-irresolute functions are autonomous, but when X_s is a soft γ_s-regular space and Y_s is a soft β_s-regular space, both concepts coincide.

Remark 3.2.1. The perceptions of soft $\alpha_{(\gamma,\beta)}$-continuous functions and soft (γ_s, β_s)-irresolute functions are independent.

Let $X_s = \{a_1, a_2, a_3\}$, $E_s = \{e_1, e_2\}$, $\tau_s = \{\varnothing, X_s, (F_1, E_s), (F_2, E_s), (F_3, E_s), (F_4, E_s), (F_5, E_s), (F_6, E_s\}$
where $(F_1, E_s), \ldots (F_6, E_s)$ are soft sets over X_s, defined as follows:

$(F_1, E_s) = \{(e_1, a_1), (e_2, a_1)\}$, $(F_2, E_s) = \{(e_1, a_2), (e_2, a_2)\}$, $(F_3, E_s) = \{(e_1, a_3), (e_2, a_3)\}$, $(F_4, E_s) = \{(e_1, a_1, a_2), (e_2, a_1, a_2)\}$, $(F_5, E_s) = \{(e_1, a_1, a_3), (e_2, a_1, a_3)\}$ and $(F_6, E_s) = \{(e_1, a_2, a_3), (e_2, a_2, a_3)\}$

Define γ_s on τ_s such that

$$(M,E_s)^{\gamma_s} = \begin{cases} (M,E_s)\, if\ (M,E_s)=(F_1,E_s) \\ (M,E_s)\tilde{\cup}(F_3,E_s)\, if\ (M,E_s)\neq(F_1,E_s) \end{cases} \quad \text{for every } (M,E_s)\in\tau_s.$$

Let $Y_s = \{b_1, b_2, b_3\}$, $K_s = \{h_1, h_2\}$, $\sigma_s = \{\varnothing, Y_s, (G_1, K_s), (G_2, K_s), (G_3, K_s), (G_4, K_s))\}$ where $(G_1, K_s), \ldots (G_4, K_s)$ are soft sets over Y_s, defined as follows: $(G_1, K_s) = \{(h, b_1), (h_2, b_1)\}$, $(G_2, K_s) = \{(h_1, b_3)\}, (h_2, b_3)\}$, $(G_3, K_s) = \{(h_1, b_1, b_2), (h_2, b_1, b_2)\}$, $(G_3, K_s) = \{(h_1, b_1, b_2), (h_2, b_1, b_2)\}$ and $(G_4, K_s) = \{\{(h_1, b_1, b_3), (h_2, b_1, b_3)\}\}\}$

Define an operation β_s on σ_s such that

$$(P,K_s)^{\beta_s} = \begin{cases} (P,K_s)\, if\ b_2\in(P,K_s) \\ cl(P,K_s) if\ b_2\notin(P,K_s) \end{cases} \quad \text{for every } (P,K_s)\in\sigma_s.$$

Define f_{Ma}:$X_s \to Y_s$ as $f_{Ma}(a_1) = b_1, f_{Ma}(a_2) = b_2$ and $f_{Ma}(a_3) = b_3$ and p_{Ma}:$E_s \to K_s$ as $p_{Ma}(e_1) = h_1, p_{Ma}(e_2) = h_2$. Then f_{Ma} is a soft (γ_s, β_s) irresolute function. But $f_{Ma}^{-1}(\{b_1, b_2\}) = \{a_1, a_2\}$, is not a soft α_γ-open set under f_{Ma}. Hence, f_{Ma} is not a soft $\alpha_{(\gamma,\beta)}$-continuous function.

Remark 3.2.2. If X_s is a soft γ_s-regular space and Y_s is a soft β_s-regular space, at that time the perception of soft (γ_s, β_s)-irresoluteness and soft $\alpha_{(\gamma,\beta)}$-continuity concur.

Definition 3.2.2. A soft member H of X_s is supposed to be a soft α_γ-neighborhood of a point $t \in X_s$ if there occurs a soft α_γ-open set G like that $t \in G \tilde{\subseteq} H$.

Theorem 3.2.1. A function f_{Ma}:$(X_s, \tau_s, E_s) \to (Y_s, \tau_s, E_s)$ is a soft $\alpha_{(\gamma,\beta)}$-continuous function in the event that for every r of X_s, the contrary of every soft α_β-neighborhood of f_{Ma}(r) is a soft α_γ-neighborhood of r.

Proof. Assume r $\in X_s$ and B to be a soft α_γ-neighborhood of f_{Ma}(r). By the declaration of Definition 3.2.2, there happens a $V \in \sigma_{s\alpha\beta}$ such that $f_{Ma}(\mathrm{r}) \in V \tilde{\subseteq} B$. This infers that $\mathrm{x} \in f_{Ma}^{-1}(V) \subseteq f_{Ma}^{-1}(B)$. Since f_{Ma} is a soft $\alpha_{(\gamma,\beta)}$-continuous function, $f_{Ma}^{-1}(V) \in \tau_{s\alpha_\gamma}$. Henceforward, $f_{Ma}^{-1}(B)$ is a soft α_γ-neighborhood of r.

Conversely, let $B \in \sigma_{s\alpha\beta}$, $A = f_{Ma}^{-1}(B)$ and r $\in A$. Hence, by the statement of Definition 3.2.2, there occurs a set $A_r \in \tau_{s\alpha_\gamma}$ alike that $\mathrm{r} \in A_r \tilde{\subseteq} A$. This infers that $A = \cup_{r\,\alpha\,A} A_r$. Via the declaration of Theorem 2.2.2, A is a soft α_γ-open set in X_s. Therefore f_{Ma} is a soft $\alpha_{(\gamma,\beta)}$-continuous function.

Theorem 3.2.2 A function f_{Ma}:$(X_s, \tau_s, E_s) \to (Y_s, \tau_s, E_s)$ is a soft $\alpha_{(\gamma,\beta)}$-continuous function on the condition that for apiece point m in X_s and each soft α_β-neighborhood B of f_{Ma}(m), there is a soft α_γ-neighborhood A of m such that $f_{Ma}(A) \tilde{\subseteq} B$.

Proof. Let m $\in X_s$ and B be a soft α_β-neighborhood of f_{Ma}(m). Then there exists a set $O_{f(m)} \in \sigma_{s\alpha\beta}$ such that $f_{Ma}(\mathrm{m}) \in O_{f(m)} \tilde{\subseteq} B$. It follows that m $\in f_{Ma}^{-1}(O_{f(m)}) \tilde{\subseteq} f_{Ma}^{-1}(B)$. By hypothesis, $f_{Ma}^{-1}(O_{f(m)}) \tilde{\subseteq} \tau_{s\alpha_\gamma}$. Let $A = f_{Ma}^{-1}(B)$. Then it trails that A is a soft α_γ-neighborhood of m and $f_{Ma}(A) = f_{Ma}(f_{Ma}^{-1}(B)) \tilde{\subseteq} B$.

Conversely, let $U \in \sigma_{s\alpha\beta}$. Take $W = f_{Ma}^{-1}(U)$. Let m $\in W$. Then f_{Ma}(m) $\in U$. Thus, U is a soft α_γ-neighborhood of f_{Ma}(m) and hence there exists a soft α_γ-neighborhood V_m of m such that $f_{Ma}(V_m) \tilde{\subseteq} U$. Thus, it follows that m $\in V_m \tilde{\subseteq} f_{Ma}^{-1}(f_{Ma}(V_m)) \tilde{\subseteq} f_{Ma}^{-1}(U) = W$. Since V_m is a soft α_γ-neighborhood of m, this implies that there exists a $W_m \in \tau_{s\alpha_\gamma}$ such that $m \in W_m \tilde{\subseteq} W$. This implies that $W = \cup_{m} \in_W W_m$. By Theorem 2.2.2, W is a soft α_γ-open set in X_s. Thus, f_{Ma} is a soft $\alpha_{(\gamma,\beta)}$-continuous function.

Theorem 3.2.3. Let $f_{Ma}:(X_s, \tau_s, E_s) \rightarrow (Y_s, \tau_s, E_s)$ be a function. Then the ensuing declarations are comparable:

(i) $f_{Ma}:(X_s, \tau_s, E_s) \rightarrow (Y_s, \tau_s, E_s)$ is a soft $\alpha_{(\gamma,\beta)}$-continuous function;
(ii) $f_{Ma}(\tau_{s\alpha_\gamma}\text{-cl}(D)) \tilde{\subseteq} \sigma_{s\alpha_\beta}\text{-cl}(f_{Ma}(D))$ holds for every member D of X_s;
(iii) For every soft α_β-closed set V of Y_s, $f_{Ma}^{-1}(V)$ is a soft α_γ-closed set in X_s.

Proof. (i) $\Rightarrow$ (ii) Let $t \in f_{Ma}(\tau_{s\alpha_\gamma}\text{-cl}(D))$ and V be any soft α_β-open set comprising t. By means of Theorem 3.2.2, here happens a point $x \in X_s$ and a soft α_γ-open set U analogous that $x \in U$ with $f_{Ma}(x) = t$ and $f_{Ma}(U) \subseteq V$. Since $x \in \tau_{s\alpha_\gamma}\text{-cl}(D)$, $U \tilde{\cap} D \neq \varnothing$ and hence $\varnothing \neq f_{Ma}(U \tilde{\cap} D) \tilde{\subseteq} f_{Ma}(U) \tilde{\cap} f_{Ma}(D) \tilde{\subseteq} V \tilde{\cap} f_{Ma}(D)$. This implies that $t \in \sigma_{s\alpha_\beta}\text{-cl}(f_{Ma}(A))$. Therefore $f_{Ma}(\tau_{s\alpha_\gamma}\text{-cl}(D)) \tilde{\subseteq} \sigma_{s\alpha_\beta}\text{-cl}(f_{Ma}(D))$.

(ii) $\Rightarrow$ (iii) Let V be a soft α_β-closed set in Y_s. Then $\sigma_{s\alpha_\beta}\text{-cl}(V) = V$. Through (ii), $f_{Ma}(\tau_{s\alpha_\gamma}\text{-cl}(f_{Ma}^{-1}(V))) \tilde{\subseteq} \sigma_{s\alpha_\beta}\text{-cl}(f_{Ma}(f_{Ma}^{-1}(V))) \tilde{\subseteq} \sigma_{s\alpha_\beta}\text{-cl}(V) = V$ holds. Therefore $\tau_{s\alpha_\gamma}\text{-cl}(f_{Ma}^{-1}(A)) \tilde{\subseteq} f_{Ma}^{-1}(V)$ and $f_{Ma}^{-1}(V)\tau_{s\alpha_\gamma}\text{-cl}(f_{Ma}^{-1}(V))$. Hence $f_{Ma}^{-1}(V)$ is a soft α_γ-closed set in X_s.
(iii) $\Rightarrow$ (i) Consider B as a soft α_β-open set in Y_s. Deliberate $V = Y_s - B$. Then V is a soft α_β-closed set in Y_s. By (iii) $f_{Ma}^{-1}(V)$ is a soft α_γ-closed set in X_s. Hence, $f_{Ma}^{-1}(B) = X_s - f_{Ma}^{-1}(Y_s - B) = X_s - f_{Ma}^{-1}(V)$, is a soft α_γ-open set in X_s. Henceforth, f_{Ma} is a soft $\alpha_{(\gamma,\beta)}$- continuous function.

Theorem 3.2.4. Let $f_{Ma}:(X_s, \tau_s, E_s) \rightarrow (Y_s, \tau_s, E_s)$ be a soft $\alpha_{(\gamma,\beta)}$-continuous and injective function. If Y_s is a soft $\alpha_\beta T_2$ space (resp. soft $\alpha_\beta T_1$ space), then X_s is a soft $\alpha_\gamma T_2$ space (resp. soft $\alpha_\gamma T_1$ space).

Proof. Suppose Y_s is a soft $\alpha_\beta T_2$ space. Let g and h be two distinct points of X_s. Then, there present two soft α_β-open sets U and V akin that $f_{Ma}(g) \in U$, $f_{Ma}(h) \in V$ and $U \tilde{\cap} V = \varnothing$. Since f_{Ma} is a soft $\alpha_{(\gamma,\beta)}$- continuous function, for U and, there occur two soft α_γ- open sets W and S such that $g \in W$ and $h \in S$, $f_{Ma}(W) \tilde{\subseteq} U$ and $f_{Ma}(S) \tilde{\subseteq} V$, infers that $W \tilde{\cap} S = \varnothing$. Henceforth, X_s is a soft $\alpha_\gamma T_2$ space. In the analogous method, it can be evidenced that X_s is a soft $\alpha_\gamma T_1$ space whenever Y_s is a soft $\alpha_\beta T_1$ space.

Theorem 3.2.5. Let $f_{Ma}:(X_s, \tau_s, E_s) \rightarrow (Y_s, \sigma_s, E_s)$ and $g_{Ma}:(Y_s, \sigma_s, E_s) \rightarrow (Z_s, \delta_s, E_s)$ be two functions. If f_{Ma} is a soft $\alpha_{(\gamma,\beta)}$-continuous function and g_{Ma} is a soft $\alpha_{(\beta,\delta)}$-continuous function, then $g_{Ma}f_{Ma}$:$(X_s, \tau_s, E_s) \rightarrow (Z_s, \delta_s, E_s)$ is a soft $\alpha_{(\gamma,\beta)}$-continuous function.

Proof. Proof trails from Definition 3.2.1

Definition 3.2.3. Let D be a subset of X_s and r be any point in X_s. Then r is called a soft α_γ-limit point of D if $U \tilde{\cap} (D - \{r\}) \neq \emptyset$, for any soft α_γ-open set U containing r. The set of all soft α_γ-limit points of D is demanded a soft α_γ-derived set of A and is signified by $d_{s\alpha_\gamma}(D)$.

Remark 3.2.3. Let L, M be some subsets of X_s. Then,

(i) if $L \tilde{\subseteq} M$, then $d_{s\alpha_\gamma}(L) \tilde{\subseteq} d_{s\alpha_\gamma}(M)$.
(ii) $r \in d_{s\alpha_\gamma}(L)$ if and only if $r \in \tau_{s\alpha_\gamma}(L)$-cl$(L - \{r\})$.

Proof. Verification trails from the statement of Definition 3.2.3.

Theorem 3.2.6. Assume A and B are any two soft subsets of X_s. At that time the subsequent reports hold good.

(i) $A \tilde{\cup} d_{s\alpha_\gamma}(A) \tilde{\subseteq} \tau_{s\alpha_\gamma}$-cl$(A)$;
(ii) $d_{s\alpha_\gamma}(A \tilde{\cup} B) = d_{s\alpha_\gamma}(A) \tilde{\cup} d_{s\alpha_\gamma}(B)$;
(iii) $\tilde{\bigcup}_i d_{s\alpha_\gamma}(A_i) = d_{s\alpha_\gamma}\left(\tilde{\bigcup}_i (A_i)\right)$;
(iv) $d_{s\alpha_\gamma}(d_{s\alpha_\gamma}(A)) \tilde{\subseteq} d_{s\alpha_\gamma}(A)$;
(v) $\tau_{s\alpha_\gamma}$-cl$(d_{s\alpha_\gamma}(A)) = d_{s\alpha_\gamma}(A)$

Proof. (i) In case $x \in A \tilde{\cup} d_{s\alpha_\gamma}(A)$, then to demonstrate that $x \in \tau_{s\alpha_\gamma}$-cl$(A)$. If $x \in A$ then $x \in \tau_{s\alpha_\gamma}$-cl$(A)$. If $x \in A$, then to evidence that $x \in \tau_{s\alpha_\gamma}$-cl$(A)$. If not, then there is a soft α_γ- closed set C comprising A but not encompassing x. Then $x \in X_s - C$, which is a soft α_γ-open set and $U \tilde{\cap} A = \emptyset$. This suggests that $x \notin d_{s\alpha_\gamma}(A)$. This incongruity shows that $x \in \tau_{s\alpha_\gamma}$-cl$(A)$. Hereafter $A \tilde{\cup} d_{s\alpha_\gamma}(A) \tilde{\subseteq} \tau_{s\alpha_\gamma}$-cl$(A)$.

(ii) Let $x \in d_{s\alpha_\gamma}(A \tilde{\cup} B)$. Through Definition 3.2.3, $\emptyset \neq U \tilde{\cap} ((A \tilde{\cup} B) - \{x\}) = U \tilde{\cap} [(A - \{x\}) \tilde{\cup} (B - \{x\})] = [U \tilde{\cap} (A - \{x\})] \tilde{\cup} [U \tilde{\cap} (B - \{x\})]$ and hence either $x \in d_{s\alpha_\gamma}(A)$ or $d_{s\alpha_\gamma}(B)$. Therefore $d_{s\alpha_\gamma}(A \tilde{\cup} B) \tilde{\subseteq} d_{s\alpha_\gamma}(A) \tilde{\cup} d_{s\alpha_\gamma}(B)$. The outcome $d_{s\alpha_\gamma}(A) \tilde{\cup} d_{s\alpha_\gamma}(B) \tilde{\subseteq} d_{s\alpha_\gamma}(A \tilde{\cup} B)$, tracks by the Remark 3.2.3 (i) result.
(iii) Proof follows from the Remark 3.2.3 and (ii) result.
(iv) Assume that $x \notin d_{s\alpha_\gamma}(A)$. Then $x \notin \tau_{s\alpha_\gamma}$-cl$(A - \{x\})$. This point towards that there occurs a soft α_γ- open set U in case that $x \in U$ and

$U\tilde{\cap}(A-\{x\})=\varnothing$. To attest that $x\notin d_{s\alpha_\gamma}(d_{s\alpha_\gamma}(A))$. Supposing on the conflict that $x\in d_{s\alpha_\gamma}(d_{s\alpha_\gamma}(A))$. Then $x\in\tau_{s\alpha_\gamma}\text{-cl}(d_{s\alpha_\gamma}(A)-\{x\})$. Since $x \in U$, $U\tilde{\cap}(d_{s\alpha_\gamma}(A)-\{x\})\neq\varnothing$. Consequently there is a $q \neq x$ so that $q\in U\tilde{\cap}(d_{s\alpha_\gamma}(A))$. This suggests that $q\in(U-\{x\})\tilde{\cap}(d_{s\alpha_\gamma}(A)-\{x\})$. Later $((U-\{x\})\tilde{\cap}(d_{s\alpha_\gamma}(A)-\{x\})\neq\varnothing$, a illogicality to the datum that $U\tilde{\cap}(d_{s\alpha_\gamma}(A)-\{x\})=\varnothing$. This hints that $x\notin d_{s\alpha_\gamma}(A))$ and after this $d_{s\alpha_\gamma}(d_{s\alpha_\gamma}(A))\tilde{\subseteq} d_{s\alpha_\gamma}(A)$.
(v) This tracks after Definition 3.2.3.

Theorem 3.2.7. A function $f_{Ma}:(X_s, \tau_s, E_s)\rightarrow(Y_s, \sigma_s, K_s)$ is a soft $\alpha_{(\gamma,\beta)}$-continuous function contingent upon $f_{Ma}(d_{s\alpha_\gamma}(A))\tilde{\subseteq}\sigma_{s\alpha_\beta}\text{-cl}(f_{Ma}(A))$, for entire $A\tilde{\subseteq}X_s$.

Proof. Let $f_{Ma}:(X_s, \tau_s, E_s)\rightarrow(Y_s, \sigma_s, K_s)$ be a soft $\alpha_{(\gamma,\beta)}$-continuous function. Approve that $A\tilde{\subseteq}X_s$, and $x\in d_{s\alpha_\gamma}(A)$. Undertake that $f_{Ma}(x) \in f_{Ma}(A)$ and let V denote a soft α_β-neighborhood of $f_{Ma}(x)$. Meanwhile f_{Ma} is a soft $\alpha_{(\gamma,\beta)}$-continuous function. By way of Theorem 3.2.2, there arises a soft α_γ- neighborhood U of x like that $f_{Ma}(U)\tilde{\subseteq}V$. From $x\in d_{s\alpha_\gamma}(A)$, it trails that $U\tilde{\cap}A\neq\varnothing$. There occurs at least a component $a\in U\tilde{\cap}A$, which suggests that $f_{Ma}(a) \in f_{Ma}(A)$ and $f_{Ma}(a) \in V$. Meanwhile $f_{Ma}(x) \notin f_{Ma}(A)$ and $f_{Ma}(a) \neq f_{Ma}(x)$. Therefore, each soft α_β- neighborhood of $f_{Ma}(x)$ encompasses a component$f_{Ma}(a) \in f_{Ma}(A)$ unalike from $f_{Ma}(x)$. Henceforward, $f_{Ma}(x)\in d_{s\alpha_\beta}(f_{Ma}(A))$. By means of the declaration of Theorem 3.2.6. (i) $f_{Ma}(d_{s\alpha_\gamma}(A))\tilde{\subseteq}\sigma_{s\alpha_\beta}\text{-cl}(f_{Ma}(A))$.

On the contrary, assume that f_{Ma} is not a soft $\alpha_{(\gamma,\beta)}$-continuous function. Then via Theorem 3.2.2, there occur $x \notin X_s$ and a soft α_β-neighborhood V of $f_{Ma}(x)$ so that every single soft α_γ-neighborhood U of x covers somewhat one member $a\in U$, for which $f_{Ma}(a) \notin V$. Let $A = \{a\in X_s : f_{Ma}(a) \notin V\}$. Since $f_{Ma}(x) \in V$, therefore $x \notin A$ and hence $f_{Ma}(x) \notin f_{Ma}(A)$. Since $f_{Ma}(A) \cap (V - f_{Ma}(x)) = \emptyset$, therefore $f_{Ma}(x)\notin d_{s\alpha_\beta}((f_{Ma}(A))$. It surveys that $f_{Ma}(x)\in f_{Ma}(d_{s\alpha_\beta}((A))-(f_{Ma}(A)\tilde{\cup}d_{s\alpha_\beta}((f_{Ma}(A)))\neq\varnothing$, which is a flaw to the given condition. Hence f_{Ma} is a soft $\alpha_{(\gamma,\beta)}$-continuous function.

Theorem 3.2.8 continuous function on condition that $f_{Ma}(d_{s\alpha_\gamma}(A))$ $\tilde{\subseteq}d_{s\alpha_\beta}(f_{Ma}(A))$, for all that $A\tilde{\subseteq}X_s$.

Proof. Let $A\tilde{\subseteq}X_s$, $x\in d_{s\alpha_\gamma}(A)$ and V is a soft α_β-neighborhood of $f_{Ma}(x)$. By the reason of f_{Ma} is a soft $\alpha_{(\gamma,\beta)}$-continuous function by the statement of Theorem 3.2.2, here occurs a soft α_γ- neighborhood U of x analogous that $f_{Ma}(U)\tilde{\subseteq}V$. But $x\in d_{s\alpha_\gamma}(A)$ stretches and there happens a component a $\in U \tilde{\cap} A$ equivalent that a $\neq$ x, $f_{Ma}(a) \in f_{Ma}(A)$ and by the reason of f_{Ma} is one-to-one, $f_{Ma}(a) \neq f_{Ma}(x)$. Consequently, every soft α_β-neighborhood V of $f_{Ma}(x)$ comprises a component $f_{Ma}(a)$ of $f_{Ma}(A)$ dissimilar from $f_{Ma}(x)$. Accordingly, $f_{Ma}(x) \in d_{s\alpha_\beta}(f_{Ma}(A))$. Thus $f_{Ma}(d_{s\alpha_\gamma}(A)) \tilde{\subseteq} d_{s\alpha_\beta}(f_{Ma}(A))$, for altogether $A \tilde{\subseteq} X_s$.

Contrary portion trails from Theorem 3.2.7.

16.3.3 Soft $\alpha_{(\gamma,\beta)}$-Open Functions

Definition 3.3.1. A function $f_{Ma}:(X_s, \tau_s, E_s) \to (Y_s, \sigma_s, K_s)$ is said to be a soft $\alpha_{(\gamma,\beta)}$-open function in the event that for all soft α_γ-open set $M \in \tau_{s\alpha_\gamma}$, the image $f_{Ma}(M) \in \sigma_{s\alpha_\beta}$.

Example 3.3.1. Let $X_s = \{a_1, a_2, a_3\}$, $E_s = \{e_1, e_2\}$,$\tau_s = \{\emptyset, X_s, (F_1, E_s), (F_3, E_s), (F_4, E_s), (F_5, E_s)\}$

where(F_1, E_s),…(F_5, E_s) are soft sets over X_s,defined as follows:

$(F_1, E_s) = \{(e_1, a_1), (e_2, a_1)\}$, $(F_3, E_s) = \{(e_1, a_3), (e_2, a_3)\}$, $(F_4, E_s) = \{(e_1, a_1, a_2), (e_2, a_1, a_2)\}$ and $(F_4, E_s) = \{(e_1, a_1, a_3), (e_2, a_1, a_3)\}$

Define γ_s on τ_s such that $(M, E_s)^{\gamma_s} = \text{cl}((M, E_s))$ for every $(M, E_s) \in \tau_s$.

Let $Y_s = \{b_1, b_2, b_3\}$, $K_s = \{h_1, h_2\}$, $\sigma_s = \{\emptyset, Y_s, (G_1, K_s\}, (G_2, K_s)\}$ where $(G_1, K_s\}$, (G_2, K_s) are soft sets over Y_s defined as follows: $(G_1, K_s\} = \{(h_1, b_2), (h_2, b_2)\}$, $(G_2, K_s) = \{(h_1, b_1, b_3), (h_2, b_1, b_3)\}$,

Define an operation β_s on σ_s such that $(P, K_s)\beta_s = \text{cl}((P, K_s))$ for every $(P, K_s) \in \sigma_s$

Define $f_{Ma}:X_s \to Y_s$ as $f_{Ma}(a_1) = b_1$, $f_{Ma}(a_2) = b_3$ and $f_{Ma}(a_3) = b_2$ and $p_{Ma}:E_s \to K_s$ as $p_{Ma}(e_1) = h_1$, $p_{Ma}(e_2) = h_2$. Hence f_{Ma} is a soft $\alpha_{(\gamma,\beta)}$-open function.

Theorem 3.3.1. If $f_{Ma}:(X_s, \tau_s, E_s) \to (Y_s, \sigma_s, K_s)$ is a soft $\alpha_{(\gamma,\beta)}$-open function and if $g_{Ma}:(Y_s, \sigma_s, K_s) \to (Z_s, \delta_s, L_s)$ is a soft $\alpha_{(\beta,\delta)}$-open function, then the composition $g_{Ma} \circ f_{Ma}:(X_s, \tau_s, K_s) \to (Z_s, \delta_s, L_s)$ is a soft $\alpha_{(\gamma,\delta)}$-open function.

Proof. Demonstration tracks from Definition 3.3.1.

Theorem 3.3.2. A function $f_{Ma}:(X_s, \tau_s, E_s) \to (Y_s, \sigma_s, K_s)$ is a soft $\alpha_{(\gamma,\beta)}$-open function in case that for all x $\in X_s$, and for every single $A \in \tau_{s\alpha_\gamma}$ alike that x $\in A$, there happens a $B \in \sigma_{s\alpha_\beta}$ like that $f_{Ma}(x) \in B$ and $B \tilde{\subseteq} f_{Ma}(A)$.

Proof. Assume A as a soft α_γ- open set and x $\in X_s$. At that time $f_{Ma}(x) \in f_{Ma}(A)$. Then $f_{Ma}(A)$ is a soft α_β-neighborhood of $f_{Ma}(x)$ in Y_s. Formerly by the declaration of Theorem 3.2.2, there presents a soft α_γ-open neighborhood $B \in \sigma_{s\alpha_\beta}$ akin that $f_{Ma}(x) \in B \tilde{\subseteq} f_{Ma}(A)$.

In reverse, let $A \in \tau_{s\alpha_\gamma}$ like that $x \in A$. At that time by supposition, there is a $B \in \sigma_{s\alpha_\beta}$ alike that $f_{Ma}(x) \in B \tilde{\subseteq} f_{Ma}(A)$. So $f_{Ma}(A)$ is a soft α_β-neighborhood of $f_{Ma}(x)$ in Y_s and this infers that $f_{Ma}(A) = \cup_{f_{Ma}(x) \in f_{Ma}(A)} B$. Formerly through Theorem 2.2.2, $f_{Ma}(A)$ is a soft α_β-open set in Y_s. Henceforward f_{Ma} is a soft $\alpha_{(\gamma,\beta)}$-open function.

Theorem 3.3.3. A function $f_{Ma}:(X_s, \tau_s, E_s) \rightarrow (Y_s, \sigma_s, K_s)$ is a soft $\alpha_{(\gamma,\beta)}$-open function in case that for all $x \in X_s$, and for every single soft α_γ-neighborhood U of $x \in X_s$, there presents a soft α_β–neighborhood V of $f_{Ma}(x)$ alike that $V \tilde{\subseteq} f_{Ma}(U)$.

Proof. Let U be a soft α_γ-neighborhood of $x \in X_s$. At that time via the statement Definition 3.2.1, there occurs a soft α_γ-open set W analogous that $x \in W \subseteq U$. This hints that $f_{Ma}(x) \in f_{Ma}(W) \tilde{\subseteq} f_{Ma}(U)$. Then f_{Ma} is a soft $\alpha_{(\gamma,\beta)}$-open function, $f_{Ma}(W)$ is a soft α_β-open set. Henceforward $V = f_{Ma}(W)$ is a soft α_β-neighborhood of $f_{Ma}(x)$ and $V \tilde{\subseteq} f_{Ma}(U)$.

Conversely, let $U \in \tau_{s\alpha_\gamma}$ and $x \in U$. Then U is a soft α_γ-neighborhood of x and thence, there prevails a soft α_β-neighborhood V of $f_{Ma}(x)$ akin that $f_{Ma}(x) \in V \tilde{\subseteq} f_{Ma}(U)$. That is, $f_{Ma}(U)$ is a soft α_β-neighborhood of $f_{Ma}(x)$. Thus, $f_{Ma}(U)$ is a soft α_β-neighborhood to each of its points. Consequently, $f_{Ma}(U)$ is a soft α_β-open set. Hence, f_{Ma} is a soft $\alpha_{(\gamma,\beta)}$-open function.

Theorem 3.3.4. A function $f_{Ma}:(X_s, \tau_s, E_s) \rightarrow (Y_s, \sigma_s, K_s)$ is a soft $\alpha_{(\gamma,\beta)}$-open function in the event if $f_{Ma}(\tau_{s\alpha_\gamma}\text{-int}(A)) \tilde{\subseteq} \sigma_{s\alpha_\beta}\text{-int}(f_{Ma}(A))$, for each $A \tilde{\subseteq} X_s$.

Proof. Let $x \in \tau_{s\alpha_\gamma}\text{-int}(A)$. Then there occurs a $U \in \tau_{s\alpha_\gamma}$ alike that $x \in U \tilde{\subseteq} A$. So $f_{Ma}(x) \tilde{\subseteq} f_{Ma}(U) \tilde{\subseteq} f_{Ma}(A)$. Meanwhile f_{Ma} is a soft $\alpha_{(\gamma,\beta)}$-open function, $f_{Ma}(U)$ is a soft α_β-open set in Y_s. Later $f_{Ma}(x) \in \sigma_{s\alpha_\beta}\text{-int}(f_{Ma}(A))$. Thus, $f_{Ma}(\tau_{s\alpha_\gamma}\text{-int}(A)) \tilde{\subseteq} \sigma_{s\alpha_\beta}\text{-int}(f_{Ma}(A))$.

Contrariwise, let $U \in \tau_{s\alpha_\gamma}$ and hereafter $f_{Ma}(U) = f_{Ma}(\tau_{s\alpha_\gamma}\text{-int}(U)) \tilde{\subseteq} \sigma_{s\alpha_\beta}\text{-int}((f_{Ma}(U)) \tilde{\subseteq} f_{Ma}(U)$ or $f_{Ma}(U) \tilde{\subseteq} \sigma_{s\alpha_\beta}\text{-int}(f_{Ma}(U)) \tilde{\subseteq} f_{Ma}(U)$. This implies that $f_{Ma}(U)$ is a soft α_β-open set. Thus, f_{Ma} is a soft $\alpha_{(\gamma,\beta)}$-open function.

Theorem 3.3.5. A function $f_{Ma}:(X_s, \tau_s, E_s) \rightarrow (Y_s, \sigma_s, K_s)$ is a soft $\alpha_{(\gamma,\beta)}$-open function on the assumption that $\tau_{s\alpha_\gamma}\text{-int}(f_{Ma}^{-1}(B)) \tilde{\subseteq} f_{Ma}^{-1}(\sigma_{s\alpha_\beta}\text{-int}(B))$, for each $B \tilde{\subseteq} Y_s$.

Proof. Let B be any soft subset of Y_s. Obviously $\tau_{s\alpha_\gamma}\text{-int}(f_{Ma}^{-1}(B))$ is a soft α_γ-open set in X_s. Also $f_{Ma}(\tau_{s\alpha_\gamma}\text{-int}(f_{Ma}^{-1}(B)) \tilde{\subseteq} f_{Ma}(f_{Ma}^{-1}(B)) \tilde{\subseteq} B$.

Since f_{Ma} is a soft $\alpha_{(\gamma,\beta)}$-open function and by Theorem 3.3.4, $f_{Ma}(\tau_{s\alpha_\gamma}\text{-int}(f_{Ma}^{-1}(B)) \tilde{\subseteq} \sigma_{s\alpha_\beta}\text{-int}(B)$. Hence, $\tau_{s\alpha_\gamma}\text{-int}(f_{Ma}^{-1}(B)) \tilde{\subseteq} f_{Ma}^{-1}(f_{Ma}(\tau_{s\alpha_\gamma}\text{-int}(f_{Ma}^{-1}(B))))$. This implies that $\tau_{s\alpha_\gamma}\text{-int}(f_{Ma}^{-1}(B)) \tilde{\subseteq} f_{Ma}^{-1}(\sigma_{s\alpha_\beta}\text{-int}(B))$ for all $B \tilde{\subseteq} Y_s$.

Contrarywise, accredit that $A \tilde{\subseteq} X_s$, at that time $\tau_{s\alpha_\gamma}\text{-int}(A) \tilde{\subseteq} \tau_{s\alpha_\gamma}\text{-int}(f_{Ma}^{-1}(f_{Ma}(A)) \tilde{\subseteq} f_{Ma}^{-1}(\sigma_{s\alpha_\beta}\text{-int}(f_{Ma}(A)))$. This implies that $f_{Ma}(\tau_{s\alpha_\gamma}\text{-int}(A)) \tilde{\subseteq} f_{Ma}(\tau_{s\alpha_\gamma}\text{ int}(f_{Ma}^{-1}(f_{Ma}(A)))) \tilde{\subseteq} f_{Ma}(f_{Ma}^{-1}(\sigma_{s\alpha_\beta}\text{-int}(f_{Ma}(A)))) \tilde{\subseteq} \sigma_{s\alpha_\beta}\text{-int}(f_{Ma}(A))$. Consequently $f_{Ma}(\tau_{s\alpha_\gamma}\text{-int}(A)) \tilde{\subseteq} \sigma_{s\alpha_\beta}\text{-int}(f_{Ma}(A))$, for all $A \tilde{\subseteq} X_s$. By Theorem 3.3.4, f_{Ma} is a soft $\alpha_{(\gamma,\beta)}$-open function.

Theorem 3.3.6. A function $f_{Ma}:(X_s, \tau_s, E_s) \to (Y_s, \sigma_s, K_s)$ is a soft $\alpha_{(\gamma,\beta)}$-open function on the assumption that $f_{Ma}^{-1}(\sigma_{s\alpha_\beta}\text{-cl}(B)) \tilde{\subseteq} \tau_{s\alpha_\gamma}\text{-cl}(f_{Ma}^{-1}(B))$, for all $B \tilde{\subseteq} Y_s$.

Proof. Let B be a soft subset of Y_s. Via Theorem 3.3.5, $\tau_{s\alpha_\gamma}\text{-int}(f_{Ma}^{-1}(Y_s -)) \tilde{\subseteq} f_{Ma}^{-1}(\sigma_{s\alpha_\beta}\text{-int}(Y_s - B))$. Then $\tau_{s\alpha_\gamma}\text{-int}(X_s - f_{Ma}^{-1}(B)) \tilde{\subseteq} f_{Ma}^{-1}(\sigma_{s\alpha_\beta}\text{-int}(Y_s - B))$. As $\sigma_{s\alpha_\beta}\text{-int}(B) = Y_s - \sigma_{s\alpha_\beta}\text{-cl}(Y_s - B))$, therefore $X_s - \tau_{s\alpha_\gamma}\text{-cl}(f_{Ma}^{-1}(B)) \tilde{\subseteq} f_{Ma}^{-1}(Y_s - \sigma_{s\alpha_\beta}\text{-cl} B))$ or $X_s - \tau_{s\alpha_\gamma}\text{-cl}(f_{Ma}^{-1}(B)) \tilde{\subseteq} X_s - f_{Ma}^{-1}(\sigma_{s\alpha_\beta}\text{-cl}(B))$. Hence, $f_{Ma}^{-1}(\sigma_{s\alpha_\beta}\text{-cl}(B)) \tilde{\subseteq} \tau_{s\alpha_\gamma}\text{-cl}(f_{Ma}^{-1}(B))$.

Conversely, let $B \tilde{\subseteq} Y_s$ and hence, $f_{Ma}^{-1}(\sigma_{s\alpha_\beta}\text{-cl}(Y_s - B)) \tilde{\subseteq} \tau_{s\alpha_\gamma}\text{-cl}(f_{Ma}^{-1}(Y_s - B))$. Then $X_s - \tau_{s\alpha_\gamma}\text{-cl}(f_{Ma}^{-1}(Y_s -)) \tilde{\subseteq} X_s - f_{Ma}^{-1}(\sigma_{s\alpha_\beta}\text{-cl}(Y_s - B))$. Hence, $X_s - \tau_{s\alpha_\gamma}\text{-cl}(X_s - f_{Ma}^{-1}(B)) \tilde{\subseteq} f_{Ma}^{-1}(Y_s - \sigma_{s\alpha_\beta}\text{-cl}(Y_s - B))$. This gives that $\tau_{s\alpha_\gamma}\text{-int}(f_{Ma}^{-1}(B)) \tilde{\subseteq} f_{Ma}^{-1}(\sigma_{s\alpha_\beta}\text{-int}(B))$. Using Theorem 3.3.5, it follows that f_{Ma} is a soft $\alpha_{(\gamma,\beta)}$-open function.

Theorem 3.3.7. Let $f_{Ma}:(X_s, \tau_s, E_s) \to (Y_s, \sigma_s, K)$ and $g_{Ma}:(Y_s, \sigma_s, K_s) \to (Z_s, \zeta_s, L_s)$ be two functions such that $g_{Ma} \circ f_{Ma}:(X_s, \tau_s, E_s) \to (Z_s, \zeta_s, L)$ is a soft $\alpha_{(\gamma,\beta)}$-continuous function. Then

(i) If g_{Ma} is a soft $\alpha_{(\gamma,\beta)}$-open injection then f_{Ma} is a soft $\alpha_{(\gamma,\beta)}$-continuous function.
(ii) If f_{Ma} is a soft $\alpha_{(\gamma,\beta)}$-open surjection then g_{Ma} is a soft $\alpha_{(\gamma,\beta)}$-continuous function.

Proof. (i) Let $U \in \sigma_{s\alpha_\beta}$. Since g_{Ma} is a soft $\alpha_{(\gamma,\beta)}$-open function, then $g_{Ma}(U) \in \zeta_{s\alpha_\delta}$. Since g_{Ma} is injective and $g_{ma} \circ f_{Ma}$ is a soft $\alpha_{(\gamma,\beta)}$-continuous function, $(g_{ma} \circ f_{Ma})^{-1}\ (g_{Ma}(U)) = (f_{Ma}{}^{-1} \circ g_{Ma}{}^{-1})((g_{Ma}(U)) = f_{Ma}^{-1}(g_{Ma}^{-1}(g_{Ma}(U)) = f_{Ma}^{-1}(U)$ is a soft α_γ- open function in X_s. This proves that f_{Ma} is a soft $\alpha_{(\beta,\delta)}$-continuous function.

(ii) Let $\in \zeta_{s\alpha\delta}$. Meanwhile $g_{ma} \circ f_{Ma}$ is a soft $\alpha_{(\gamma,\beta)}$-continuous function, then $(g_{Ma} \circ f_{Ma})^{-1}(V) \in \tau_{s\alpha\gamma}$. Also f_{Ma} is a soft $\alpha_{(\gamma,\beta)}$-open function, so $f_{Ma}((g_{ma} \circ f_{Ma})^{-1}(V))$ is a soft α_β-open set in Y_s. Since f_{Ma} is surjective, we obtain $(f_{Ma} \circ (g_{ma} \circ f_{Ma})^{-1})(V) = (f_{Ma} \circ (f_{Ma}^{-1} \circ g_{ma}^{-1}))(V) = ((f_{Ma} \circ f_{Ma}^{-1}) \circ g_{ma}^{-1})(V) = g_{Ma}^{-1}(V)$. It follows that $g_{Ma}^{-1}(V) \in \sigma_{s\alpha\beta}$. This proves that g_{Ma} is a soft $\alpha_{(\beta,\delta)}$-continuous function.

16.3.4 Soft $\alpha_{(\gamma,\beta)}$-Closed Functions

Definition 3.4.1. A function $f_{Ma}:(X_s, \tau_s, E_s) \to (Y_s, \sigma_s, E_s)$ is supposed to be a soft $\alpha_{(\gamma,\beta)}$- closed function on the condition that the image set $f_{Ma}(A)$ is a soft α_β-closed set for all soft α_γ- closed subset A of X_s.

Example 3.4.1. Given $X_s = \{a_1, a_2, a_3\}$, $E_s = \{e_1, e_2\}$, $\tau_s = \{\varnothing, X_s, (F_1, E_s), (F_3, E_s), (F_4, E_s), (F_5, E_s)\}$ where $(F_1, E_s), \ldots (F_5, E_s)$ are soft sets over X_s defined as follows:

$(F_1, E_s) = \{(e_1, a_1), (e_2, a_1)\}$, $(F_3, E_s) = \{(e_1, a_3), (e_2, a_3)\}$,$(F_4, E_s) = \{(e_1, a_1, a_2), (e_2, a_1, a_2)\}$ and $(F_4, E_s) = \{(e_1, a_1, a_3), (e_2, a_1, a_3)\}$

Define γ_s on τ_s such that

$$(M,E_s)^{\gamma_s} = \begin{cases} (M,E_s)\,if\,(M,E_s) = (F_1,E_s) \\ (M,E_s) \cup (F_3,E_s)\,if\,(M,E_s) \neq (F_1,E_s) \end{cases} \quad \text{for every } (M,E_s) \in \tau_s.$$

Let $Y_s = \{b_1, b_2, b_4\}$, $K_s = \{h_1, h_2\}$, $\sigma_s = \{\varnothing, Y_s, (G_1, K_s), (G_2, K_s), (G_3, K_s), (G_4, K_s)\}$ where $(G_1, K_s), (G_2, K_s)$ are soft sets over Y_s defined as follows: $(G_1, K_s) = \{(h_1, b_1), (h_2, b_1)\}$, $(G_2, K_s) = \{(h_1, b_4), (h_2, b_4)\}$, $(G_3, K_s) = \{(h_1, b_1, b_2), (h_2, b_1, b_2)\}$, $(G_4, K_s) = \{(h_1, b_1, b_4), (h_2, b_1, b_4)\}$,

Define an operation β_s on σ_s such $(P,K_s)^{\beta_s} = \begin{cases} cl(P,K_s)\,if\,b_2 \in (P,K_s) \\ (P,K_s)\,if\,b_2 \notin (P,K_s) \end{cases}$

Define $f_{Ma}:X_s \to Y_s$ as $f_{Ma}(a_1) = b_1$, $f_{Ma}(a_2) = b_2$ and $f_{Ma}(a_3) = b_2$ and $p_{Ma}:E_s \to K_s$ as $p_{ma}(e_1) = h_1$, $p_{ma}(e_2) = h_2$. Hence, f_{Ma} is a soft $\alpha_{(\gamma,\beta)}$-closed function.

Theorem 3.4.1. Let $f_{Ma}:(X_s, \tau_s, E_s) \to (Y_s, \sigma_s, E_s)$ be a soft $\alpha_{(\gamma,\beta)}$-closed function; formerly the ensuing announcements hold good.

(i) Given $g_{Ma}:(Y_s, \sigma_s, E_s) \to (Z_s, \delta_s, E_s)$ is a soft $\alpha_{(\gamma,\beta)}$-closed function, then $g_{Ma} \circ f_{Ma}:(X_s, \tau_s, E_s) \to (Z_s, \delta_s, E_s)$ is a soft $\alpha_{(\gamma,\beta)}$-closed function;
(ii) $\sigma_{s\alpha\beta}$-cl$(f_{Ma}(A)) \subseteq f_{Ma}(\tau_{s\alpha\gamma}$-cl$(A))$, for each subset A of X_s;

(iii) $\sigma_{s\alpha_\beta}$-cl($\sigma_{s\alpha_\beta}$-int($\sigma_{s\alpha_\beta}$-cl($f_{Ma}(A)$)))$\subseteq f_{Ma}(\tau_{s\alpha_\gamma}$-cl$(A))$, for all soft subset A of X_s;
(iv) for all soft subset B of Y_s and to every soft α_γ- open set A of X_s encompassing $f_{Ma}^{-1}(B)$, there occurs a soft α_β-open set C in Y_s comprising B alike that $f_{Ma}^{-1}(C)\tilde{\subseteq} A$.

Proof. Verifications are similar to the verifications of Theorems 3.3.1, 3.3.2, 3.3.4, 3.3.5, and 3.3.6.

Theorem 3.4.2. Let f_{Ma}:$(X_s, \tau_s, E_s) \rightarrow (Y_s, \sigma_s, E_s)$ be a soft bijective function. Formerly the subsequent declarations are comparable:

(i) f_{Ma} is a soft $\alpha_{(\gamma,\beta)}$-closed function;
(ii) f_{Ma} is a soft $\alpha_{(\gamma,\beta)}$-open function;
(iii) f_{Ma}^{-1} is a soft $\alpha_{(\gamma,\beta)}$-continuous function.

Proof. (i) $\Rightarrow$ (ii) Verification tracks from the statements of Definition 3.3.1 and Definition 3.4.1.

(ii) $\Rightarrow$ (iii) Given A is a soft α_γ-closed set in X_s. Formerly $\tau_{s\alpha_\gamma}$-cl$(A)=A$. By means of (ii) and through Theorem 3.3.5, $f_{Ma}^{-1}(\sigma_{s\alpha_\beta}$-cl$(f_{Ma}(A)))\tilde{\subseteq}\tau_{s\alpha_\gamma}$-cl$(f_{Ma}^{-1}(f_{Ma}(A)))$ infers that $\sigma_{s\alpha_\beta}$-cl$(f_{Ma}(A))$ $\tilde{\subseteq} f_{Ma}(\tau_{s\alpha_\gamma}$-cl$(A))$. Consequently, $\sigma_{s\alpha_\beta}$-cl$((f_{Ma}^{-1})^{-1}(A))\tilde{\subseteq}(f_{Ma}^{-1})^{-1}(A)$, for every single subset A of X_s, it follows that f_{Ma}^{-1} is a soft $\alpha_{(\gamma,\beta)}$-continuous function.
(iii) $\Rightarrow$ (i) Given A is a soft α_γ-closed set in X_s. Formerly $X_s - A$ is a soft α_γ-open set in X_s. Since f_{Ma}^{-1} is an $\alpha_{(\gamma,\beta)}$-continuous function, $\left(f_{Ma}^{-1}\right)^{-1}(X_s - A)$ is a soft α_β-open set in Y_s. But $\left(f_{Ma}^{-1}\right)^{-1}(X_s - A) = f_{Ma}(X_s - A) = Y_s - f_{Ma}(A)$. Thus, $f_{Ma}(A)$ is a soft α_β-closed set in Y_s. This proves that f_{Ma} is a soft $\alpha_{(\gamma,\beta)}$-closed function.

Definition 3.4.2. Let *id*: $\tau \rightarrow P(X)$ be the identity operation. A function f_{Ma}:$(X_s, \tau_s, E_s) \rightarrow (Y_s, \sigma_s, E_s)$ is held to be a soft $\alpha_{(id,\beta)}$-closed function if aimed at any soft α-closed set F of X_s; $f_{Ma}(F)$ is a soft α_β-closed set in Y_s.

Theorem 3.4.3. If f_{Ma}:$(X_s, \tau_s, E_s) \rightarrow (Y_s, \sigma_s, E_s)$ is a bijective function and $f_{Ma}^{-1}:(Y_s,\sigma_s,E_s)\rightarrow(X_s,\tau_s,E_s)$ is a soft $\alpha_{(id,\beta)}$-continuous function, then f_{Ma} is a soft $\alpha_{(id,\beta)}$-closed function.

Proof. Validation pursues after the descriptions of Definition 3.4.1 and Definition 3.4.2.

Theorem 3.4.4. Supposing that f_{Ma} is a soft $\alpha_{(\gamma,\beta)}$-continuous function. Then

(i) If A is a soft $\alpha_{\gamma}g$-closed set in (X_s, σ_s, E_s), later the image $f_{Ma}(A)$ is a soft $\alpha_{\beta}g$-closed set.
(ii) Given B be a soft $\alpha_{\beta}g$-closed set of (Y_s, τ_s, E_s), later the set $f_{Ma}^{-1}(B)$ is a soft $\alpha_{\gamma}g$-closed set.

Proof. (i) Suppose V be a soft α_{β}-open set in Y_s alike that $f_{Ma}(A)\tilde{\subseteq} V$. By means of Theorem 3.2.3 statement, $f_{Ma}^{-1}(V)$ is a soft α_{γ}-open set encompassing A. By postulation $\tau_{s\alpha_{\gamma}}\text{-cl}(A)\tilde{\subseteq} f_{Ma}^{-1}(V)$, so $f_{Ma}(\tau_{s\alpha_{\gamma}}\text{-cl}(A))\tilde{\subseteq} V$. Since f_{Ma} is a soft $\alpha_{(\gamma,\beta)}$-closed function, $f_{Ma}(\tau_{s\alpha_{\gamma}}\text{-cl}(A))$ is a soft α_{β}-closed set comprising $f_{Ma}(A)$ entails that $\sigma_{s\alpha_{\beta}}\text{-cl}(f_{Ma}(A))\tilde{\subseteq}\sigma_{s\alpha_{\beta}}\text{-cl}(f_{Ma}(\tau_{s\alpha_{\gamma}}\text{-cl}(A)))= f_{Ma}(\tau_{s\alpha_{\gamma}}\text{-cl}(A))\tilde{\subseteq} V$. Hence, $f_{Ma}(A)$ is a soft $\alpha_{\beta}g$-closed set.

(ii) Given U be a soft α_{γ}- open set of X_s akin that $f_{Ma}^{-1}(B)\tilde{\subseteq} U$ for any subset B in Y_s. Put $F=\tau_{s\alpha_{\gamma}}\text{-cl}(f_{Ma}^{-1}(B))\tilde{\cap}(X_s-U)$. It tracks from Remark 2.2.8.(ii) and Theorem 2.2.12 that F is a soft α_{γ}-closed set in X_s. Meanwhile f_{Ma} is a soft $\alpha_{(\gamma,\beta)}$-closed function, $f_{Ma}(F)$ is a soft $\alpha_{(\gamma,\beta)}$-closed set in Y_s. By Theorem 2.3.2 declaration and Theorem 3.2.3. (ii) declaration and the subsequent insertion $f_{Ma}(F)\tilde{\subseteq}\sigma_{s\alpha_{\beta}}\text{-cl}(B)-B$, it is gained that $f_{Ma}(F) = \emptyset$, and henceforth $F=\emptyset$. This implies that $\tau_{s\alpha_{\gamma}}\text{-cl}(f_{Ma}^{-1}(B))\tilde{\subseteq} U$. Therefore $f_{Ma}^{-1}(B)$ is a soft $\alpha_{\gamma}g$-closed set.

Theorem 3.4.5. Let $f_{Ma}:(X_s, \tau_s, E_s) \rightarrow (Y_s, \sigma_s, E_s)$ be a soft $\alpha_{(\gamma,\beta)}$-continuous and soft $\alpha_{(\gamma,\beta)}$-closed function. Then

(i) If f_{Ma} is a soft injective function and in addition Y_s is a soft $\alpha_{\beta}T_{\frac{1}{2}}$ at that time X_s is a soft $\alpha_{\gamma}T_{\frac{1}{2}}$ space.

(ii) If f_{Ma} is a soft surjective function besides X_s is a soft $\alpha_{\gamma}T_{\frac{1}{2}}$ formerly Y_s is a soft $\alpha_{\beta}T_{\frac{1}{2}}$ space.

Proof. (i) Assume A be a soft $\alpha_{\gamma}g$-closed set in X_s. Formerly via Theorem 3.4.4 statement (i), $f_{Ma}(A)$ is a soft $\alpha_{\beta}g$-closed set. Accordingly, by postulation A is a soft α_{γ}-closed set in X_s. So X_s is a soft $\alpha_{\gamma}T_{\frac{1}{2}}$ space.

(ii) Let B be a soft $\alpha_\beta g$-closed set in Y_s. At that moment it surveys from Proposition 3.4.4. (ii) and the supposition that $f_{Ma}^{-1}(B)$ is a soft α_γ-closed set. Hence, f_{Ma} is a soft $\alpha_{(\gamma,\beta)}$-closed function, which implies that $f_{Ma}(f_{Ma}^{-1}(B)) = B$ is a soft α_β-closed set in Y_s. Therefore, Y_s is a soft $\alpha_\beta T_{\frac{1}{2}}$ space.

16.3.5 Soft $\alpha_{(\gamma,\beta)}$-Homeomorphism

Definition 3.5.1. A function $f_{Ma}:(X_s, \tau_s, E_s) \rightarrow (Y_s, \sigma_s, K_s)$ is a soft $\alpha_{(\gamma,\beta)}$-homeomorphism, if f_{Ma} is a bijective, soft $\alpha_{(\gamma,\beta)}$-continuous function and f_{Ma}^{-1} is a soft $\alpha_{(\gamma,\beta)}$-continuous function.

Remark 3.5.1. Each bijective, soft $\alpha_{(\gamma,\beta)}$-continuous and soft $\alpha_{(\gamma,\beta)}$- closed function is a soft $\alpha_{(\gamma,\beta)}$-homeomorphism.

Theorem 3.5.1. Let $f_{Ma}:(X_s, \tau_s, E_s) \rightarrow (Y_s, \sigma_s, K_s)$ be a soft $\alpha_{(\gamma,\beta)}$-homeomorphism. If X_s is a soft $\alpha_\gamma T_{\frac{1}{2}}$ space then Y_s is a soft $\alpha_\beta T_{\frac{1}{2}}$ space.

Proof. Given $\{y\}$ be a singleton set of Y_s. At that time there occurs a point x of X_s akin that $y = f_{Ma}(x)$. Via Theorem 2.3.4. statement, it tracks that the singleton set $\{y\}$ is moreover a soft α_β-open set or a soft α_β-closed set. Thus, Y_s is a soft $\alpha_\beta T_{\frac{1}{2}}$ space.

Remark 3.5.2. Every soft $\alpha_{(\gamma,\beta)}$-open (closed) function is a soft (γ_s, α_β)-open (closed) function. Nevertheless, the contrary need not be accurate. The subsequent remark displays the association between the $\alpha_{(\gamma,\beta)}$-open (closed) functions, (γ_s, α_β)-open (closed) functions and (γ_s, α_β)-open (closed) functions.

Remark 3.5.3. From Definitions 2.4.1, 2.4.4, and 3.2.1, and Remarks 3.2.1 and 2.4.1, the subsequent illustrative inferences Figure 16.3.6.1. is attained.

Remark 3.5.4. As of Definitions 2.4.3, 3.3.1, and 3.4.1 and Remark 3.7.2, the ensuing pictorial inferences Figure 16.3.6.2 is gained.

16.3.6 Soft (α_γ, β_s)-Contra Continuous Functions

Definition 3.6.1. A function f_{Ma}: $(X_s,\tau_s,K_s) \rightarrow (Y_s,\sigma_s,K_s)$ is said to be a soft (α_γ,β_s)-contra continuous function if the inverse image of every soft β_s-open set in Y_s is a soft α_γ-closed set in X_s.

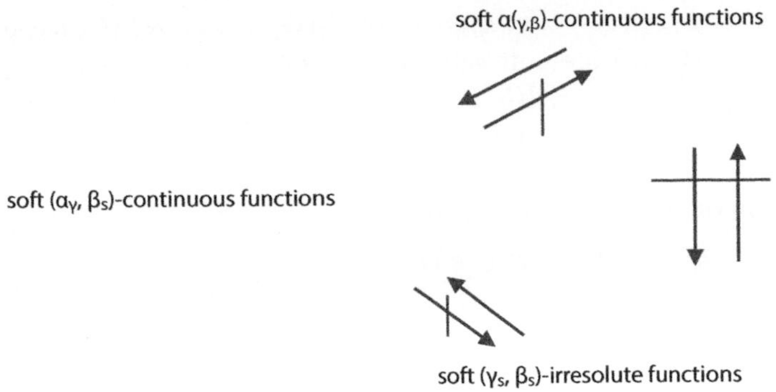

$A \rightarrow B$ represents A infer B, $A \nrightarrow B$ represents A does not infer B.

Figure 16.3.6.1 Relationship between soft continuous functions.

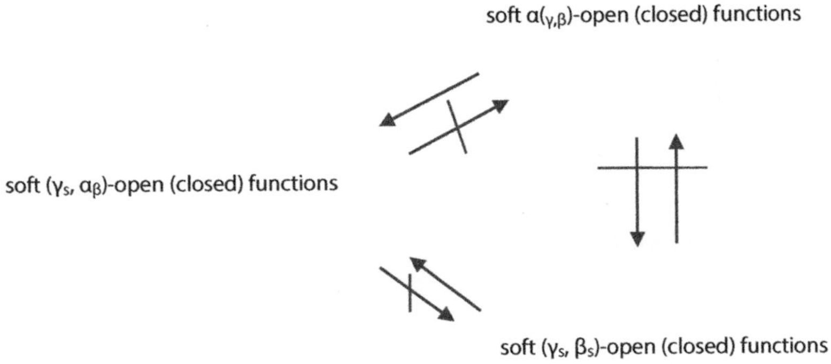

$A \rightarrow B$ denotes A hint at B, $A \nrightarrow B$ signifies A does not hint at B.

Figure 16.3.6.2 Association between soft open (closed) functions.

Example 3.6.1 Let $X_s = \{a_1,a_2,a_3\}$, $E_s = \{e_1,e_2\}$, $\tau_s = \{\varnothing,X_s,(F_1,E_s),(F_2,E_s),(F_4,E_s),(F_5,E_s)\}$

where $(F_1,E_s), \dots (F_5,E_s)$ are soft sets over X_s, defined as follows:

$(F_1,E_s) = \{(e_1,a_1),(e_2,a_1)\}$, $(F_2,E_s) = \{(e_1,a_2),(e_2,a_{32})\}$, $(F_4,E_s) = \{(e_1,a_1,a_2),(e_2,a_1,a_2)\}$ and $(F_4,E_s) = \{(e_1,a_1,a_3),(e_2,a_1,a_3)\}$

Define γ_s on τ_s such that

$$(M,E_s)^{\gamma_s} = \begin{cases} (M,E_s)\, if\ a_2 \in (M,E_s) \\ cl(M,E_s)\, if\ a_2 \notin (M,E_s)) \end{cases} \quad \text{for every } (M,E_s) \in \tau_s.$$

Let $Y_s = \{b_1,b_2,b_4\}$, $K_s = \{h_1,h_2\}$, $\sigma_s = \{\emptyset,Y_s,(G_1,K_s),(G_2,K_s),(G_3,K_s),G_4,K_s))\}$ where $(G_1,K_s),(G_2,K_s)$ are soft sets over Y_s, defined as follows: $(G_1,K_s) = \{(h_1,b_1),(h_2,b_1)\}$, $(G_2,K_s) = \{(h_1,b_4),(h_2,b_4)\}$, $(G_3,K_s) = \{(h_1,b_1,b_2),(h_2,b_1,b_2)\}$ and $(G_4,K_s) = \{(h_1,b_1,b_4),(h_2,b_1,b_4)\}$,

Define an operation β_s on σ_s such

$$(P,K_s)^{\beta_s} = \begin{cases} cl(P,K_s)\, if\ b_2 \notin (P,K_s) \\ (P,K_s)\cup\{b_4\}\, if\ b_2 \in (P,K_s) \end{cases}$$

Define $f_{Ma}: X_s \to Y_s$ as $f_{Ma}(a_1) = b_1$, $f_{Ma}(a_2) = b_4$ and $f_{Ma}(a_3) = b_2$ and $p_{Ma}:E_s \to K_s$ as $p_{Ma}(e_1) = h_1$, $p_{Ma}(e_2) = h_2$. Hence, f_{Ma} is a soft (α_γ,β_s) -contra continuous function.

Definition 3.6.2. Consider L as a soft subset in X_s. Then soft α_γ-kernel of L is defined as the intersection of all soft α_γ-open sets that contains L and is denoted as $\tau_{s\alpha_\gamma}$ -ker(L).

That is $\tau_{s\alpha_\gamma}$ -ker$(L) = \{O : O \in \tau_{s\alpha_\gamma}\ \ and\ L \tilde{\subseteq} O\}$

Theorem 3.6.1. Assume L,M as soft sub members in X_s. Then

(i) $m \in \tau_{s\alpha_\gamma}$ -ker(L) if and only if $L \tilde{\cap} N = \emptyset$ for any soft α_γ-closed set N in X_s that contains m.
(ii) $L \tilde{\subseteq} \tau_{s\alpha_\gamma}$ -ker(L) if L is a soft α_γ-open set of X_s.
(iii) $L \tilde{\subseteq} M$, then $\tau_{s\alpha_\gamma}$ -ker $(L) \tilde{\subseteq} \tau_{s\alpha_\gamma}$ -ker $M()$.

Proof. Demonstration tracks from the Definition 3.6.2 statement.

Theorem 3.6.2. Assume $f_{Ma}:(X_s,\tau_s,E_s) \to (Y_s,\sigma_s,K_s)$ is a function. Then the succeeding declarations are comparable:

(i) f_{Ma} is a soft (α_γ,β_s) - contra continuous function.
(ii) for a particular point x in X_s and exclusive soft β_s-closed set V in Y_s like that $f_{Ma}(x) \in V$, there occurs an open set W in X_s akin that $x \in W$, $f_{Ma}(W) \tilde{\subseteq} V$
(iii) for each soft β_s-closed set F in Y_s, $f_{Ma}^{-1}(F) \in \tau_{s\alpha_\gamma}$
(iv) $f_{Ma}(\tau_{s\alpha_\gamma}$ -cl $(A)) \tilde{\subseteq} \sigma_{s\alpha\beta}$ -ker$(f_{Ma}(A))$ for altogether subsets A of X_s
(v) $\tau_{s\alpha_\gamma}$ -cl $(f_{Ma}^{-1}(B)) \tilde{\subseteq} f_{Ma}^{-1}(\sigma_{s\alpha\beta}$ -ker$(B))$

Proof. (i) ⇒ (ii) Given $x \in X_s$ and W be a soft β_s-closed set of Y_s comprising $f_{Ma}(x)$. Established $W = f_{Ma}^{-1}(V)$ then through Definition 3.8.1, W is a soft α_γ-open set encompassing x and $f_{Ma}(W) = f_{Ma}(f_{Ma}^{-1}(V))) \tilde{\subseteq} V$.

(ii) ⇒ (iii) Let V be any soft β_s-closed set in Y_s. Let $F = Y_s - V$, then F is a soft β_s-open set in Y_s. Let $x \in f_{Ma}^{-1}(V)$, through (ii) there occurs a soft open set set W of X_s like that $f_{Ma}(W) \tilde{\subseteq} V$. Thus $x \in W \tilde{\subseteq} \tau_{s\gamma}\text{-int}(\tau_{s\gamma}\text{-cl}(\tau_{s\gamma}\text{-int}(W))) \tilde{\subseteq} \tau_{s\gamma}\text{-int}(\tau_{s\gamma}\text{-cl}(\tau_{s\gamma}\text{-int}(f_{Ma}^{-1}(W))))$ and hence $f_{Ma}^{-1}(F) \tilde{\subseteq} \tau_{s\gamma}\text{-int}(\tau_{s\gamma}\text{-cl}(\tau_{s\gamma}\text{-int}(f_{Ma}^{-1}(F))))$. Then $f_{Ma}^{-1}(F)$ is a soft α_γ-closed set in X_s. Hence $f_{Ma}^{-1}(V) = X_s - f_{Ma}^{-1}(Y_s - V) = X_s - f_{Ma}^{-1}(F)$ is a soft α_γ-open set in X_s.

(iii) ⇒ (i) Considering B as a soft β_s-open set of Y_s. Later $F = Y_s - B$ is a soft β_s-closed set in Y_s. Using (iii), $f_{Ma}^{-1}(F)$ is a soft α_γ-open set in X_s. Hence, $f_{Ma}^{-1}(B) = X_s - f_{Ma}^{-1}(Y_s - B) = X_s - f_{Ma}^{-1}(F)$ is a soft α_γ-closed set in X_s.

(iii) ⇒ (iv) Considering A as a soft subset of X_s and supposing that $y \notin \sigma_{s\alpha_\beta}\text{-ker}(f_{Ma}(A))$, formerly there is a soft β_s-closed set F in Y_s, alike that $y \in F$ and $f_{Ma}(A) \tilde{\cap} F = \emptyset$, consequently, $f_{Ma}^{-1}(f_{Ma}(A) \tilde{\cap} F) = \tilde{\emptyset}$. This infers that $A \tilde{\cap} f_{Ma}^{-1}(F) = \emptyset$, and therefore $\tau_{s\alpha_\gamma}\text{-cl}(A) \tilde{\subseteq} X_s - f_{Ma}^{-1}(F)$. It tracks that $f_{Ma}(\tau_{s\alpha_\gamma}\text{-cl}(A)) \tilde{\cap} F = \emptyset$, which infers that $y \notin f_{Ma}(\tau_{s\alpha_\gamma}\text{-cl}(A))$. Henceforward, it is demonstrated that $f_{Ma}(\tau_{s\alpha_\gamma}\text{-cl}(A)) \tilde{\subseteq} \sigma_{s\alpha_\beta}\text{-ker}(f_{Ma}(A))$ for each subset A of X_s.

(iv) ⇒ (v) Given B be any soft subset of Y_s. Formerly, $f_{Ma}^{-1}(B) \tilde{\subseteq} X_s$. By hypothesis $f_{Ma}(\tau_{s\alpha_\gamma}\text{-cl}(f_{Ma}^{-1}(B))) \tilde{\subseteq} \sigma_{s\alpha_\beta}\text{-ker}(f_{Ma}(f_{Ma}^{-1}(B))$. It follows that $f_{Ma}(\tau_{s\alpha_\gamma}\text{-cl}(f_{Ma}^{-1}(B))) \tilde{\subseteq} \sigma_{s\alpha_\beta}\text{-ker}(B)$ and $\tau_{s\alpha_\gamma}\text{-cl}(f_{Ma}^{-1}(B)) \tilde{\subseteq} f_{Ma}^{-1}(\sigma_{s\alpha_\beta}\text{-ker}(B)$.

(v) ⇒ (i) Let V be a soft β_s-open set of Y_s. By proposition, $\tau_{s\alpha_\gamma}\text{-cl}(f_{Ma}^{-1}(V)) \tilde{\subseteq} f_{Ma}^{-1}(\sigma_{s\alpha_\beta}\text{-ker}(V))$, since V is a soft β_s-open set then, $\sigma_{s\alpha_\beta}\text{-ker}(V) = V$. Hence $\tau_{s\alpha_\gamma}\text{-cl}(f_{Ma}^{-1}(V)) \tilde{\subseteq} f_{Ma}^{-1}(V)$. It follows that $\tau_{s\alpha_\gamma}\text{-cl}(f_{Ma}^{-1}(V)) = f_{Ma}^{-1}(V)$.

The frontier of any set A in a topological space X_s is defined as $\text{Fr}(A) = \text{cl}(A) \tilde{\cap}\text{-cl}(X_s - A)$.

Definition 3.6.2. Let X_s be a soft topological space and γ_s be a monotone operator. The soft α_γ-frontier of any set M of X_s is demarcated as trails:

$$\tau_{s\alpha_\gamma}\text{-Fr}(M) = \tau_{s\alpha_\gamma}\text{-cl}(M) \tilde{\cap} \tau_{s\alpha_\gamma}\text{-cl}(X_s - M)$$

It is observed that the frontier of any set M of X_s is a soft α_γ-closed set and $\tau_{s\alpha_\gamma}\text{-Fr}(M) = \tau_{s\alpha_\gamma}\text{-cl}(M) - \tau_{s\alpha_\gamma}\text{-int}(M)$.

Using the above notions, the set of points where any function f_{Ma}: $(X_s,\tau_s,E_s) \to (Y_s,\sigma_s,K_s)$ is not a soft (α_γ,β_s)-contra continuous is characterized as follows:

Theorem 3.6.3. Let f_{Ma}: $(X_s,\tau_s,E_s) \rightarrow (Y_s,\sigma_s,K_s)$ be a function and γ_s be a monotone operator. The set of all points x in X_s alike that f_{Ma} is not a soft (α_γ,β_s)-contra continuous function is exactly the union of the soft α_γ- frontier of the inverse image of the soft β_s-closed set in Y_s that contains f_{Ma}(x).

Proof. Suppose that f_{Ma} is not a soft (α_γ,β_s)-contra continuous function at the point x $\in X_s$, then there occurs a soft β_s-closed set F such that f_{Ma}(x) $\in F$ and $f_{Ma}(U)\tilde{\cap}(Y_s - F) \neq \varnothing$ for all soft α_γ-open set U, alike that x $\in U$. It follows that $U \tilde{\cap} f_{Ma}^{-1}((Y_s - F) \neq \varnothing$, but this means that $x \in \tau_{s\alpha_\gamma}$-cl $(f_{Ma}^{-1}(Y_s - F)) = \tau_{s\alpha_\gamma}$-cl $(X_s - (f_{Ma}^{-1}(F)))$. Since $x \in f_{Ma}^{-1}(F)$, then $x \in \tau_{s\alpha_\gamma}$-cl $(f_{Ma}^{-1}(F)) \tilde{\cap} \tau_{s\alpha_\gamma}$-cl$(X_s - f_{Ma}^{-1}(F))$. Therefore {x $\in X_s$: f_{Ma} is not a soft (α_γ,β_s)-contra continuous function at the point x} is contained in $\tau_{s\alpha_\gamma}$-Fr $(f_{Ma}^{-1}(F))$.

Conversely, suppose that $x \in \tau_{s\alpha_\gamma}$-Fr $(f_{Ma}^{-1}(F))$, where F is a soft β_s-closed set in Y_s, f_{Ma}(x) $\in F$ and f_{Ma} is a soft (α_γ,β_s)-contra continuous function. Then there happens a soft α_γ- open set U like that x $\in U$ and $f_{Ma}(U) \tilde{\subseteq} F$; therefore, $x \in U \tilde{\subseteq} f_{Ma}^{-1}(F)$. From this, $x \in \tau_{s\alpha_\gamma}$-int $(f_{Ma}^{-1}(F)) \tilde{\subseteq} \tau_{s\alpha_\gamma}$-Fr $(f_{Ma}^{-1}(F))$. In consequence, $x \notin \tau_{s\alpha_\gamma}$-Fr $(f_{Ma}^{-1}(F))$, contradiction. Therefore, f_{Ma} is not a soft (α_γ,β_s)-contra continuous function.

In the same way, the following theorem is obtained and it can be proved in the similar form as the above theorem.

Theorem 3.6.4. Let f_{Ma}: $(X_s,\tau_s,K_s) \rightarrow (Y_s,\sigma_s,K_s)$ be a function. The set of all points x in X_s such that f_{Ma}: $(X_s,\tau_s,K_s) \rightarrow (Y_s,\sigma_s,K_s)$ is not a soft (α_γ,β_s)-contra continuous function is exactly the union of all soft α_γ-frontier of the inverse image of the soft β_s-closed set in Y_s that contains f_{Ma}(x).

Definition 3.6.3. A soft topological space X_s is supposed to be a soft α_γ-locally indiscrete space if each soft α_γ-open set in Y_s is a soft α_γ-closed set in X_s.

The succeeding lemma privileges that for the functions that are (α_γ,id)-continuous, the reverse image of any soft open set in Y_s is a soft α_γ-open set in X_s.

Lemma 3.6.1. Given f_{Ma}: $(X_s,\tau_s,K_s) \rightarrow (Y_s,\sigma_s,K_s)$ is a soft (α_γ,id)-continuous function, then $f_{Ma}^{-1}(V)$ is a soft α_γ-open set for every $V \in \sigma_s$.

Proof. Let $V \in \sigma_s$ and $x \in f_{Ma}^{-1}(V)$. Then f_{Ma} (x) $\in V$. By means of the proposition, there occurs a set $U_x \in \tau_s$ like that $x \in U_x \tilde{\subseteq} f_{Ma}(U_x) \tilde{\subseteq} V$; therefore $U_x \tilde{\subseteq} f_{Ma}^{-1}(V)$ and the result follows.

Theorem 3.6.5. If f_{Ma}: $(X_s,\tau_s,K_s) \to (Y_s,\sigma_s,K_s)$ is a soft (α_γ,id)-continuous function and X_s is a soft α_γ-locally indiscrete space, then f_{Ma} is a soft (α_γ,β_s)-contra continuous function.

Proof. Demonstration trails after Theorem 3.6.1, Definition 3.6.1, and Definition 3.6.3.

16.3.7 Soft $\alpha_{(\gamma,\beta)}$-Contra Continuous Functions

Definition 3.7.1. A function f_{Ma}: $(X_s,\tau_s,K_s) \to (Y_s,\sigma_s,K_s)$ is said to be a soft $\alpha_{(\gamma,\beta)}$-contra continuous function in the event that for a soft α_β -open set U of Y_s, $f_{Ma}^{-1}(U)$ is a soft α_γ-closed set in X_s.

Example 3.7.1. Consider Let $X_s = \{a_1,a_2,a_3\}$, $E_s = \{e_1,e_2\}$, $\tau_s = \{\varnothing,X_s,(F_1,E_s),(F_3,E_s),(F_4,E_s),(F_5,E_s)\}$ where (F_1,E_s), ... (F_5,E_s) are soft sets over X_s, defined as follows:

$(F_1,E_s) = \{(e_1,a_1),(e_2,a_1)\}$, $(F_3,E_s) = \{(e_1,a_3),(e_2,a_3)\}$, $(F_4,E_s) = \{(e_1,a_1,a_2),(e_2,a_1,a_2)\}$ and $(F_4,E_s) = \{(e_1,a_1,a_3),(e_2,a_1,a_3)\}$

Define γ_s on τ_s such that

$$(M,E_s)^{\gamma_s} = \begin{cases} (M,E_s) \\ (M,E_s)\cup\{a_3\} \end{cases} \quad \text{for every } (M,E_s)\in\tau_s.$$

Let $Y_s = \{b_1,b_2,b_3\}$, $K_s = \{h_1,h_2\}$, $\sigma_s = \{\varnothing,Y_s,(G_1,K_s),(G_2,K_s),(G_3,K_s),(G_4,K_s)\}$, where (G_1,K_s), ... (G_4,K_s) are soft sets over Y_s, defined as follows: $(G_1,K_s) = \{(h_1,b_1),(h_2,b_1)\}$, $(G_2,K_s) = \{(h_1,b_3),(h_2,b_3)\}$, $(G_3,K_s) = \{(h_1,b_1,b_2),(h_2,b_1,b_2)\}$ *and* $(G_4,K_s) = \{(h_1,b_1,b_3),(h_2,b_1,b_3)\}$

Define an operation β_s on σ_s such that

$$(P,K_s)^{\beta_s} = \begin{cases} (P,K_s) \\ (P,K_s)\cup\{b_3\} \end{cases} \quad \text{for every } (P,K_s)\in\sigma_s.$$

Define f_{Ma}:$X_s \to Y_s$ as $f_{Ma}(a_1) = b_2$, $f_{Ma}(a_2) = b_1$ and $f_{Ma}(a_3) = b_3$ and p_{Ma}:$E_s \to K_s$ as $p_{Ma}(e_1) = h_1$, $p_{Ma}(e_2) = h_2$. Formerly the reverse image of a α_β-open set is an α_γ-closed set under f_{Ma}. From now f_{Ma} is a soft $\alpha_{(\gamma,\beta)}$-contra continuous function.

Remark 3.7.1. Every soft $\alpha_{(\gamma,\beta)}$-contra continuous function is a soft (α_γ,β_s)-contra continuous function.

The subsequent example displays that the reverse of the overhead remark need not be accurate.

Example 3.7.2. Let $X_s = \{a_1,a_2,a_3\}$, $E_s = \{e_1,e_2\}$, $\tau_s = \{\varnothing,X_s,(F_1,E_s),(F_3,E_s),(F_4,E_s),(F_5,E_s)\}$
where $(F_1,E_s), \ldots (F_5,E_s)$ are soft sets over X_s, defined as follows:

$(F_1,E_s) = \{(e_1,a_1),(e_2,a_1)\}$, $(F_3,E_s) = \{(e_1,a_3),(e_2,a_3)\}$, $(F_4,E_s) = \{(e_1,a_1,a_2),(e_2,a_1,a_2)\}$ and $(F_4,E_s) = \{(e_1,a_1,a_3),(e_2,a_1,a_3)\}$

Define γ_s on τ_s such that $(M,E_s)^{\gamma_s} = \mathrm{cl}((M,E_s))$ for every $(M,E_s)\in\tau_s$.

Let $Y_s = \{b_1,b_2,b_3\}$, $K_s = \{h_1,h_2\}$, $\sigma_s = \{\varnothing,Y_s,(G_1,K_s),(G_2,K_s)\}$, where (G_1,K_s), (G_2,K_s) are soft sets over Y_s, defined as follows: $(G_1,K_s) = \{(h_1,b_2),(h_2,b_2)\}$, $(G_2,K_s) = \{(h_1,b_1,b_3),(h_2,b_1,b_3)\}$

Define an operation β_s on σ_s such that
$(P,K_s)^{\beta_s} = \mathrm{cl}((P,K_s))$ for every $(P,K_s)\in\sigma_s$.

Define $f_{Ma}:X_s \to Y_s$ as $f_{Ma}(a_1) = b_1$, $f_{Ma}(a_2) = b_3$ and $f_{Ma}(a_3) = b_2$ and $p_{Ma}:E_s \to K_s$ as $p_{Ma}(e_1) = h_1$, $p_{Ma}(e_2) = h_2$. Formerly the reverse image of a β_s-open set is an α_γ-closed set under f_{Ma}. From now f_{Ma} is a soft (α_γ,β_s)-contra continuous function. Here $f_{Ma}^{-1}(\{b_3\})=\{a_2\}$ and $f_{Ma}^{-1}(\{b_1\})=\{a_1\}$ are not α_γ-closed sets. Hence, f_{Ma} is not a soft $\alpha_{(\gamma,\beta)}$-contra continuous function.

Remark 3.7.2. The perception of soft $\alpha_{(\gamma,\beta)}$-contra continuous functions and soft (γ_s,β_s)-contra irresolute functions are autonomous.

The subsequent example displays the outcome.

Let $X_s = \{a_1,a_2,a_3\}$, $E_s = \{a_1,a_2\}$, $\tau_s = \{\varnothing,X_s,(F_1,E_s),(F_2,E_s),(F_3,E_s),(F_4,E_s),(F_5,E_s),(F_6,E_s)\}$
where $(F_1,E_s), \ldots (F_6,E_s)$ are soft sets over X_s, defined as follows:

$(F_1,E_s) = \{(e_1,a_1),(e_2,a_1)\}$, $(F_2,E_s) = \{(e_1,a_2),(e_2,a_2)\}$, $(F_3,E_s) = \{(e_1,a_3),(e_2,a_3)\}$, $(F_4,E_s) = \{(e_1,a_1,a_2),(e_2,a_1,a_2)\}$, $(F_5,E_s) = \{(e_1,a_1,a_3),(e_2,a_1,a_3)\}$ and $(F_6,E_s) = \{(e_1,a_2,a_3),(e_2,a_2,a_3)\}$

Define γ_s on τ_s such that

$$(M,E_s)^{\gamma_s} = \begin{cases} (M,E_s)\, if (M,E_s)=(F_1,E_s) \\ (M,E_s)\cup(F_3,E_s)\, if (M,E_s)\neq(F_1,E_s) \end{cases} \quad \text{for every } (M,E_s)\in\tau_s$$

Let $Y_s = \{b_1,b_2,b_3\}$, $K_s = \{h_1,h_2\}$, $\sigma_s = \{\varnothing,Y_s,(G_1,K_s),(G_2,K_s),(G_3,K_s),(G_4,K_s))\}$ where $(G_1,K_s), \ldots (G_4,K_s)$ are soft sets over Y_s, defined as follows: $(G_1,K_s) = \{(h,b_1),(h_2,b_1)\}$, $(G_2,K_s) = \{(h_1,b_3),(h_2,b_3)\}$, $(G_3,K_s) = \{(h_1,b_1,b_2),(h_2,b_1,b_2)\}$ and $(G_4,K_s) = \{(h_1,b_1,b_3),(h_2,b_1,b_3)\}$

Define an operation β_s on σ_s such that

$$(P,K_s)^{\beta_s} = \begin{cases} (P,K_s)\, if (P,K_s)=\{b_1\} \\ cl(P,K_s)\, if (P,K_s)\neq\{b_1\} \end{cases} \quad \text{for every } (P,K_s)\in\sigma_s.$$

Define $f_{Ma}: X_s \to Y_s$ as $f_{Ma}(a_1) = b_1, f_{Ma}(a_2) = b_2$ and $f_{Ma}(a_3) = b_3$ and $p_{Ma}:E_s \to K_s$ as $p_{Ma}(e_1) = h_1, p_{Ma}(e_2) = h_2$. Then f_{Ma} is a soft (γ_s,β_s)- irresolute function. But $f_{Ma}^{-1}(\{b_1,b_3\})=\{a_1,a_3\}$, is not a soft α_γ-closed set under f_{Ma}. Hence f_{Ma} is not a soft $\alpha_{(\gamma,\beta)}$- contra continuous function.

As of Example 3.7.2, f_{Ma} is a soft $\alpha_{(\gamma,\beta)}$-contra continuous function but not a soft (γ_s,β_s)- contra irresolute function.

Remark 3.7.3. On or after Definitions 2.4.5, 3.6.1, and 3.7.1, and Remarks 3.7.1 and 3.7.2, the ensuing illustrative insinuations Figure 16.3.7.1 is attained.

$A \to B$ signifies A refer B, $A \nrightarrow B$ signifies A does not refer B.

Remark 3.7.4. Consider X_s is a soft γ_s-regular space and Y_s is a soft β_s-regular space, at that time the thought of soft (γ_s,β_s)-contra irresolute and soft $\alpha_{(\gamma,\beta)}$-contra continuity accord.

Theorem 3.7.1. Given $f_{Ma}:(X_s,\tau_s,E_s) \to (Y_s,\sigma_s,K_s)$ is afunction. Formerly the succeeding declarations are comparable:

(i) f_{Ma} is a soft $\alpha_{(\gamma,\beta)}$-contra continuous function.
(ii) for each point x in X_s and each soft α_β - closed set V in Y_s such that $f_{Ma}(x) \in V$, there exists a soft α_γ- open set W in X_s such that $x \in W$, $f_{Ma}(W) \tilde{\subseteq} V$.
(iii) for all soft α_β- closed set F in Y_s, $f_{Ma}^{-1}(F) \in \tau_{s\alpha_\gamma}$
(iv) $f_{Ma}(\tau_{s\alpha_\gamma}\text{-cl}(A)) \tilde{\subseteq} \sigma_{s\alpha_\beta}\text{-ker}(f_{Ma}(A))$ for all subsets A of X_s
(v) $\tau_{s\alpha_\gamma}\text{-cl}(f_{Ma}^{-1}(B)) \tilde{\subseteq} f_{Ma}^{-1}(\sigma_{s\alpha_\beta}\text{-ker}(B))$

Proof. (i) $\Rightarrow$ (ii) Assume $x \in X_s$ and V be any soft β_s-closed set of Y_s encompassing $f_{Ma}(x)$. Established $W = f_{Ma}^{-1}(V)$ at that time via Theorem 3.8.2, W is a soft α_γ-open set comprising x besides $f_{Ma}(W) = f_{Ma}(f_{Ma}^{-1}(V)) \tilde{\subseteq} V$.

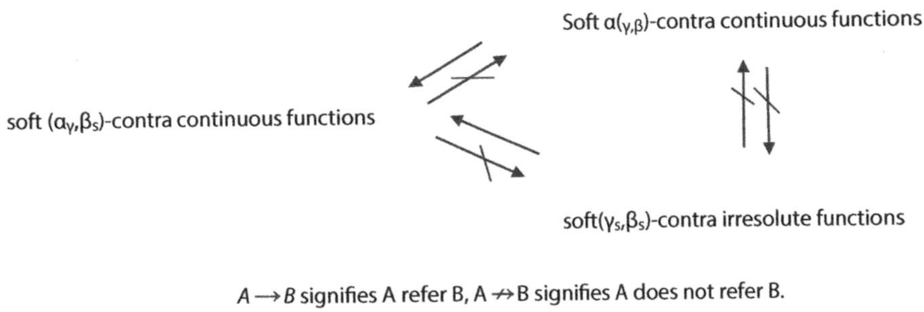

Figure 16.3.7.1 Association between soft contra-continuous functions.

(ii) ⇒ (iii) Consider V as a soft β_s-closed set in Y_s. Let $F = Y_s - V$, then F is a soft β_s-open set in Y_s. Assume $x \in f_{Ma}^{-1}(V)$, by (ii) there occurs a soft open set W of X_s so that $f_{Ma}(W) \tilde{\subseteq} V$. Accordingly $x \in W \subseteq \tau_{s\gamma}\text{-int}(\tau_{s\gamma}\text{ - cl }(\tau_{s\gamma}\text{ -int}(W))) \tilde{\subseteq} \tau_{s\gamma}\text{ -int}(\tau_{s\gamma}\text{ - cl }(\tau_{s\gamma}\text{ -int }(f_{Ma}^{-1}(F))))$ and hence $f_{Ma}^{-1}(F) \tilde{\subseteq} \tau_{s\gamma}\text{ -int}(\tau_{s\gamma}\text{-cl}(\tau_{s\gamma}\text{-int}(f_{Ma}^{-1}(F))))$. Then $f_{Ma}^{-1}(F)$ is a soft α_γ - closed set in X_s. Hence $f_{Ma}^{-1}(V) = X_s - f_{Ma}^{-1}(Y_s - V) = X_s - f_{Ma}^{-1}(F)$ is a soft α_γ - open set in X_s.

(iii) ⇒ (i) Consider B be a soft β_s-open set in Y_s. Formerly $F = Y_s - B$ is a soft β_s-closed set in Y_s. By (iii), $f_{Ma}^{-1}(F)$ is a soft α_γ-open set in X_s. Hence $f_{Ma}^{-1}(B) = X_s - f_{Ma}^{-1}(Y_s - B) = X_s - f_{Ma}^{-1}((F)$ is a soft α_γ-closed set in X_s.

(iii) ⇒ (iv) Given A be a soft subset of X_s and assume that $y \notin \sigma_{s\alpha_\beta}\text{-ker }(f_{Ma}(A))$, then there occurs a soft β_s-closed set F in Y_s, like that $y \in F$ and $f_{Ma}(A) \tilde{\cap} F = \varnothing$, therefore $f_{Ma}^{-1}(f_{Ma}(A) \tilde{\cap} F) = \varnothing$. This infers that $A \tilde{\cap} F = \varnothing$, and so $\tau_{s\alpha_\gamma}\text{-cl }(A)) \tilde{\subseteq} X_s - f_{Ma}^{-1}(F)$. It follows that $f_{Ma}(\tau_{s\alpha_\gamma}\text{-cl }(A)) \tilde{\cap} F = \varnothing$, which indicates that $y \notin f_{Ma}(\tau_{s\alpha_\gamma}\text{-cl }(A))$. Henceforth, it is showed that $f_{Ma}(\tau_{s\alpha_\gamma}\text{-cl }(A)) \tilde{\subseteq} \sigma_{s\alpha_\beta}\text{-ker }(f_{Ma}(A))$ for all soft subset A of X_s.

(iv) ⇒ (v) Given B be any soft subset of Y_s. Then $f_{Ma}^{-1}(B) \subseteq X_s$. By supposition $f_{Ma}(\tau_{s\alpha_\gamma}\text{-cl }(f_{Ma}^{-1}(B))) \tilde{\subseteq} \sigma_{s\alpha_\beta}\text{-ker}(f_{Ma}(\tau_{s\alpha_\gamma}(f_{Ma}^{-1}(B)))$. It follows that $f_{Ma}(\tau_{s\alpha_\gamma}\text{-cl }(f_{Ma}^{-1}(B))) \tilde{\subseteq} \sigma_{s\alpha_\beta}\text{-ker}(B)$, consequently, $f_{Ma}(\tau_{s\alpha_\gamma}\text{-cl }(f_{Ma}^{-1}(B))) \tilde{\subseteq} \sigma_{s\alpha_\beta}\text{-ker}(B))$.

(v) ⇒ (i) Let V be any soft β_s-open set in Y_s. By proposition $\tau_{s\alpha_\gamma}\text{-cl}(V) \tilde{\subseteq} f_{Ma}^{-1}(\sigma_{s\alpha_\beta}\text{-ker }(V))$, since V is a soft β_s-open set then, $\sigma_{s\alpha_\beta}\text{-ker }(V) = V$. In consequence $\tau_{s\alpha_\gamma}\text{-cl }(f_{Ma}^{-1}(V)) \tilde{\subseteq} f_{Ma}^{-1}(V)$. It follows that $\tau_{s\alpha_\gamma}\text{-cl }(f_{Ma}^{-1}(V)) = f_{Ma}^{-1}(V)$.

Theorem 3.7.2. Let $f_{Ma}: (X_s,\tau_s,E_s) \to (Y_s,\sigma_s,K_s)$ be a function and γ_s be a monotone operator. The set of all points x in X_s so that f_{Ma} is not a soft (α_γ,β_s) - contra continuous function is exactly the union of the soft α_γ - frontier of the reverse image of the soft β_s-closed set in Y_s that contains $f_{Ma}(x)$.

Proof. Assume that f_{Ma} is not a soft $\alpha_{(\gamma,\beta)}$- contra continuous function at the point $x \in X_s$, then there exists a soft α_β - closed set F alike that $f_{Ma}(x) \in F$ and $f_{Ma}(U) \tilde{\cap} (Y_s - F) \neq \varnothing$ for a soft α_γ - open set U, such that $x \in U$. It follows that $U \tilde{\cap} f_{Ma}^{-1}((Y_s - F) \neq \varnothing$, but this means that $x \in \tau_{s\alpha_\gamma}\text{-cl }(f_{Ma}^{-1}(Y_s - F)) = \tau_{s\alpha_\gamma}\text{-cl }(X_s - (f_{Ma}^{-1}(F)))$. Since $x \in f_{Ma}^{-1}(F)$, then $x \in \tau_{s\alpha_\gamma}\text{-cl }(f_{Ma}^{-1}(F)) \tilde{\cap} \tau_{s\alpha_\gamma}\text{-cl}(X_s - f_{Ma}^{-1}(F))$. Therefore $\{x \in X_s$: f_{Ma} is not a soft $\alpha_{(\gamma,\beta)}$-contra continuous function at the point x} is contained in $\tau_{s\alpha_\gamma}$-Fr $(f_{Ma}^{-1}(F))$.

Conversely, suppose that $x \in \tau_{s\alpha_\gamma}$-Fr $(f_{Ma}^{-1}(F))$, where F is a soft α_β-closed set in Y_s, $f_{Ma}(x) \in F$ and f_{Ma} is a soft $\alpha_{(\gamma,\beta)}$- contra continuous function. At that time there occurs a soft α_γ-open set U so that $x \in U$ and $f_{Ma}(U) \tilde{\subseteq} F$, therefore $x \in U \tilde{\subseteq} f_{Ma}^{-1}(F)$. From this, $x \in \tau_{s\alpha_\gamma}$-int $(f_{Ma}^{-1}(F)) \tilde{\subseteq} \tau_{s\alpha_\gamma}$-Fr $(f_{Ma}^{-1}(F))$ is obtained. Hence, $x \notin \tau_{s\alpha_\gamma}$-Fr $(f_{Ma}^{-1}(F))$, which is a contradiction. Therefore f_{Ma} is not a soft $\alpha_{(\gamma,\beta)}$-contra continuous function.

In the same way, the following theorem is obtained.

Theorem 3.7.3. Let f_{Ma}: $(X_s,\tau_s,E_s) \rightarrow (Y_s,\sigma_s,K_s)$ be a function. The set of all points x in X_s such that f_{Ma}: $(X_s,\tau_s,E_s) \rightarrow (Y_s,\sigma_s,K_s)$ is not a soft $\alpha_{(\gamma,\beta)}$-contra continuous function is exactly the union of all soft α_γ-frontier of the reverse image of the soft α_β-closed set in Y_s that contains $f_{Ma}(x)$.

Proof. Demonstration can be done in the analogous procedure of the above-mentioned Theorem 3.7.2.

16.4 Conclusion

In this document, the perception of soft $\alpha_{(\gamma,\beta)}$-continuous functions that are generated through soft α_γ-open sets are deliberated and few of their basic properties are explored. Further, the soft $\alpha_{(\gamma,\beta)}$-open (closed) functions, soft $\alpha_{(\gamma,\beta)}$-contra continuous functions, and soft (α_γ,β_s)-contra continuous functions are announced and examined their basic properties. The soft α_γ-derived set, soft α_γ-frontier, and soft α_γ-kernel are demarcated and practiced to establish the notions of various soft continuous functions, soft open (closed) functions, and soft contra continuous functions. The connections among these soft continuous functions, soft open, soft closed functions, and soft contra continuous functions are epitomized through diagrams and evaluated their behaviour.

References

1. Aygünoğlu, A. and Aygün, H., Some notes on soft topological spaces. *Neural Comput. Appl.*, *21*, 1, 113–119, 2012.
2. Chen, B., Soft semi-open sets and related properties in soft topological spaces. *Appl. Math. Inf. Sci.*, *7*, 1, 287–294, 2013.
3. Chen, D.G., Tsang, E.C.C., Yeung, D.S., Some notes on the parameterization reduction of soft sets, in: *Proceedings of the 2003 International Conference*

on Machine Learning and Cybernetics (IEEE Cat.No. 03EX693), vol. 3, pp. 1442–1445, IEEE, November, 2003.
4. Chen, D., Tsang, E.C.C., Yeung, D.S., Wang, X., The parameterization reduction of soft sets and its applications. *Comput. Math. Appl., 49*, 5-6, 757–763, 2005.
5. Feng, F., Jun, Y.B., Zhao, X., Soft semirings. *Comput. Math. Appl.*, 56, 2621–2628, 2008.
6. Kalaivani, N., Anitha, K., Saravanakumar, D., Sai Sundara Krishnan, G., On γ-Operations in Soft Topological Spaces. *Far East J. Math. Sci.*, 101, 9, 2067–2077, 2017.
7. Kong, Z., Gao, L., Wang, L., Li, S., The normal parameter reduction of soft sets and its algorithm. *Comput. Math. Appl., 56*, 12, 3029–3037, 2008.
8. Maji, P.K., Biswas, R., Roy, A.R., Soft set theory. *Comput. Math. Appl.*, 45, 555–562, 2003.
9. Maji, P.K., Roy, A.R., Biswas, R., An application of soft sets in a decision making problem. *Comput. Math. Appl., 44*, 8-9, 1077–1083, 2002.
10. Molodtsov, D., Soft set theory—first results. *Comput. Math. Appl., 37*, 4-5, 19–31, 1999.
11. Pei, D. and Miao, From soft sets to information systems, in: *Proceedings of Granular Computing*, X. Hu, Q. Liu, Skowron, T.Y. Lin, R.R. Yager, B. Zhang (Eds.), vol. 2, pp. 617–621, IEEE, Beijing, China, 2005.
12. Shabir, M. and Naz, M., On soft topological spaces. *Comput. Math. Appl., 61*, 7, 1786–1799, 2011.
13. Hussain, S. and Ahmad, B., Some properties of soft topological spaces. *Comput. Math. Appl.*, 62, pp 4058–4067, 2011.
14. Ahmad, B. and Hussain, S., On some structures of soft topology. *Math. Sci.*, *6*, 1, 64, 2012.
15. Xiao, Z., Chen, L., Zhong, B., Ye, S., Recognition for soft information based on the theory of soft sets, in: *Proceedings of ICSSSM'05.2005 International Conference on Services Systems and Services Management, 2005*, 2005, June, vol. 2, IEEE, pp. 1104–1106.
16. Zorlutuna, İ., Akdag, M., Min, W.K., Atmaca, S., Remarks on soft topological spaces. *Ann. Fuzzy Math. Inform., 3*, 2, 171–185, 2012.

Index